KNIVES
2018

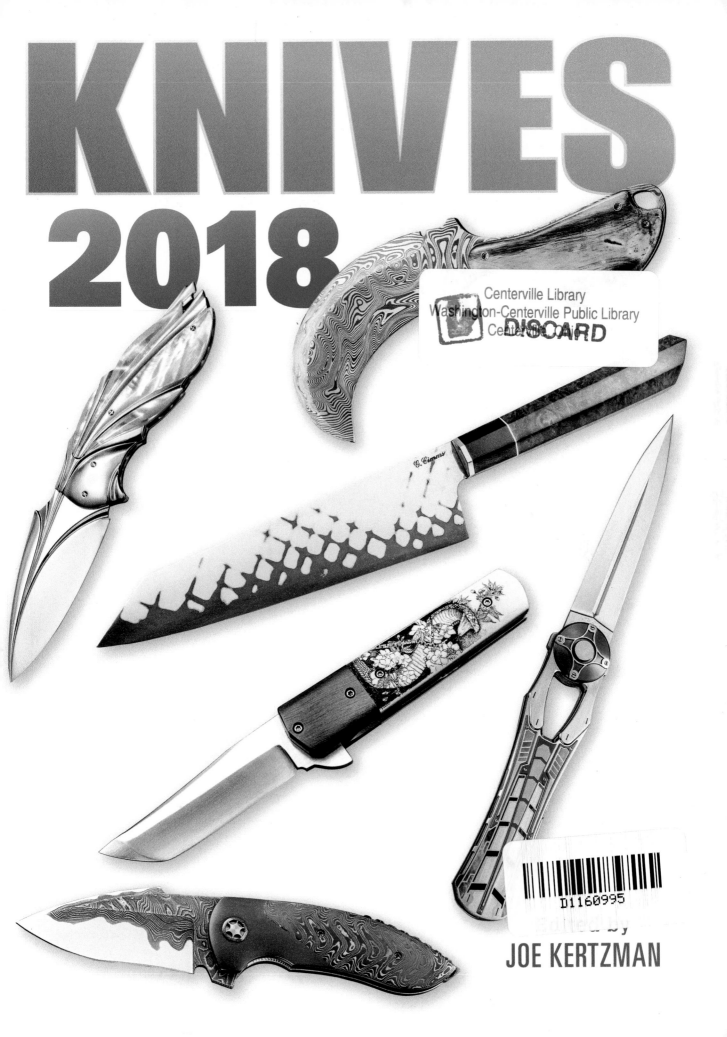

Edited by
JOE KERTZMAN

Published by

Krause Publications a division of F+W Media, Inc.
700 East State Street • Iola, WI 54990-0001
715-445-2214 • 888-457-2873
www.krausebooks.com

To order books or other products call toll-free 1-800-258-0929
or visit us online at www.shopblade.com

Cover photography by Kris Kandler

ISSN: 0277-0725
ISBN-13: 978-1-4402-4819-1
ISBN-10: 1-4402-4819-2

Designed by Dane Royer
Edited by Chris Berens

Printed in the United States of America

10 9 8 7 6 5 4 3 2 1

Dedication and Acknowledgments

"We stand on the shoulders of giants"—whether it was Sir Isaac Newton who first coined the phrase with, "If I have seen a little further, it is by standing on the shoulders of giants," or 12th century theologian and author John Salisbury, who remarked, "We are like dwarfs sitting on the shoulders of giants." What the phrase has come to mean is that great men and women (giants) in history blazed trails, making it possible for us to further their visionary quests. Or at least that's what it means to me. In other words, my successes are only made possible because of the enlightened people who came before me.

With that in mind, how on earth did custom knives ever evolve to the point where they are today? And make no mistake about it—knives have reached unpredictable levels of craftsmanship, material makeup and beauty. A solid argument could be made that today's custom blade builders stand on the shoulders of giants. Robert Waldorf Loveless was one such giant who designed and popularized the dropped (drop-point) hunter, brought ATS-34 stainless steel to the American masses, fashioned tapered tangs and built chute knives, fighters and so much more.

Buster Warenski had artistic flair and his edged masterpieces exhibited impeccable fit and finish. He incorporated gold, precious metals and engraving into knives like his reproductions of King Tut's dagger and the Gem of the Orient. Gil Hibben designed the first line of Browning hunting knives in 1968, the Rambo knife for the films *Rambo* and *Rambo II*, and he was the "Klingon Armorer" for the *Star Trek* franchise. Michael Price was a San Francisco gold rush-era maker of fine, highly embellished knives, particularly daggers and other fixed blades, with precious metal- and stone-inlaid handles and silver frames.

Remember William F. "Bill" Moran? He was a pioneering American knifemaker who reintroduced damascus, or pattern-welded steel, to the American market at an early Knifemakers' Guild Show. Often called the father of modern knifemaking, Moran fashioned such knives as the ST-24 fighter that will live in infamy. Ron Lake changed the folding knife industry forever with his inter-frame-style folders, patented locks and world-class quality. D.E. Henry strove for near perfection in his knives, and really helped put bowies back on the map. The crispness of his work spurred other knifemakers into going the extra mile. W.W. "Bud" Cronk was decades ahead of his time and executed some of the most challenging designs ever produced, such as the Camelot model, among many others. Jimmy Lile, along with John Nelson Cooper and Jody Samson, put knives on the silver screen in the 1960s through the '80s. His Rambo knife had a great impact on the buying public following the release of the movie *First Blood*.

George Herron's slick, functional hunters were only part of the story. It was the man behind the knives, a true gentleman, who encouraged so many to become knifemakers. Ted Dowell made integral California knives and opened up a whole new facet to the art knife genre. His integral-hilt construction caught on with knifemakers worldwide. Jim Schmidt was the epitome of sole authorship in art knives and folders. His early work with damascus helped create techniques that are still used today. H.H. Frank's engraved folders were far ahead of their time in the 1970s. Form followed function with Jess Horn's knives, and collectors took notice. He was the first maker to be so popular that he had to have a lottery for his knives at the Guild Show.

And how about Phill Hartsfield, William Scagel, Michael Walker, Rudy Ruana, Jack Busfield, Ron Appleton, Frank Centofante, Al Dippold, Frank Potter, Steve Hoel, D' Holder, Bob Lum, Herman Schneider, Lloyd Hale, Harvey McBurnette, Don Fogg, Fred Carter, Rod Chappel, Don Hastings, Billy Mace Imel, Mel Pardue, Barry Wood or Sid Birt?

There are 2,200 custom knifemakers listed in the back of this, the 38th Edition of the *KNIVES* annual book, and some of them could be added to this list of giants. Yes, we stand on the shoulders of giants, we acknowledge their foresight, talent, ingenuity and greatness, and I dedicate the *KNIVES 2018* book to all of them. I apologize for those who I omitted. ☐

Joe Kertzman

Contents

On The Cover

The trio of knives gracing the front cover of *KNIVES 2018* would be the envy of any knife collector, with the question being only which one to purchase first. At left is a pretty little piece fashioned by Gaetan Beauchamp for the front pants pocket or display case, whichever the case may be. The fine LinerLock folder showcases a mammoth ivory handle and color scrimshaw in a floral motif with hummingbirds in flight, a Mike Norris stainless damascus blade and 416 stainless steel bolsters. At the center of attention is a Curt Erickson art dagger parading a plum-agate-rock handle, a hot-gun-blued guard and pommel that are gold- and silver-inlaid and engraved by Julie Warenski-Erickson, including gold dot English borders, yellow sapphire inlays, yellow citrines in the pommel, and more silver and gold inlays within the confines of the hollow-ground 440C blade. To its right is a Jumbo Gent's dress folder in a lock-back configuration from the hands of Rick Genovese, complete with a CPM 154 blade, black jade handle inlays with white jade in the middle oval, and engraving in a gold-inlay leaf pattern by Mitch Moschetti. Hopefully one or all three of the cover knives will whet your appetite for what's inside the book. (cover photo by Kris Kandler) ☐

Introduction

What makes a guy—after toiling for days on end, weeks and months on a knife, forging the steel, shaping the blade, sanding it endlessly, fashioning a handle and guard, gluing, pinning, polishing, fitting and finishing—decide, when it appears that the edged tool couldn't be more perfect, to sculpt a handle charm for the piece out of precious metal? What would possess a person to embellish pinheads, create piqué work, make a chain and fob, engrave imagery and scrimshaw scenes on edged tools and weapons that are already impeccable precision cutting instruments? Is it sadistic or just plain insane? Is that person an incurable perfectionist or a true artist, a half-cocked workaholic or a handcrafting genius?

From what I know of the makers I've met, they can't decide either. They have no answers, or maybe I should say they don't readily reveal the methods behind their madness. Most just feign ignorance, give slight hints of smiles, shake their heads, stare blankly and say that they just wanted to give the knives a little extra touch or two in the shop ... at 3 o'clock in the morning, with their wives sleeping in the house next to the shop, and knowing full well they have another full day of work ahead of them. They just had to finish the custom knife and make it better than the one that came before it.

I was recently at a community event, and while I enjoyed myself, spending time with family and friends, listening to music and indulging in fried food and liquid refreshments, a few of my neighbors were behind the scenes, volunteering to haul garbage, secure tent flaps, stock bathrooms and arrange tables and chairs. I thanked one of them and asked if he'd eventually be able to take a break and partake in the festivities. He shook his head back and forth, almost too quickly, as if to dismiss the question as ridiculous or irrelevant, and replied that he was alright, would rather keep busy. Then, in an attempt to explain his abruptness, he said, "You see the same guys doing the work at most functions. It's nearly always the same crew. There are doers and then there are those who don't volunteer. I'm a doer. I have to keep busy."

I would have been offended had it not been so true, and the fact that I don't take offense easily.

Knifemakers are doers. They not only make the knives, but also the sheaths. In fact, some make their own tools, tooling and machines. They even make the parts for the knives. I'm talking about the screws, springs, pins and pivots. Yes, they make those. While some of us buy the kitchen knife block set at Target or Walmart, blade builders make their own "Chef, Sushi, Steak & Veggie Knives," craft "Close-Shave Straight Razors" and "Full-Tilt Tacticals," build "Burled Barehanders," "Cultural Curiosities," "Desert Warriors" and "Foxy Flippers," and fashion "Top-Tier Tantos," "Little Utility Knives," "No Drag Dags" and "Rings, Split Rings and D-Guards."

In the "State of the Art" section of the *KNIVES 2018* book, you'll find mindboggling examples of forged mosaic damascus and feather damascus, as well as the aforementioned "Charming Handle Charms," "Classic Carving, Checkering and Fluting," "Gold-i-Lops," "Gripping, Palpable Art," "No Flaw Scrimshaw," "Sculpted Scalpels," "Sheath Delights" and touches of mokumé.

Feature articles in "The World's Greatest Knife Book" cover Washington D.C. tourist knives, heavenly blades with designs inspired by the starry skies and celestial bodies, "Knifemakers of the North Country," the magic and mystery of the bowie knife, "Plunging into Dive Knives," tactical folder collaborations between custom knifemakers and manufacturers, tactical knives with wharncliffe blade shapes, modern tomahawks and "Traveling with Knives in Europe."

Why do they do it? Ask 10 knifemakers that question and you'll get 10 different, vague, noncommittal answers. But don't let their indirectness take you aback. It's a labor of love, time well spent and a way to keep their minds and hands busy, their creativity sparked and their senses aware. It gives them a sense of purpose and accomplishment, and honestly, there's a lot to be said for that. But knifemakers won't admit it. They'll just give you a shrug, a half-apologetic look and say they wanted to make this blade a little better than the last one. Thank goodness for that. □

Joe Kertzman

2018 WOODEN SWORD AWARD

opened the package and pulled out a CD with images and information about the knives pictured. After staring gape-mouthed at the images, I read the detailed specifications of each art folder depicted in the images. The descriptions of the folders were simply labeled Knife 1, Knife 2 … Knife 5, with corresponding numbers written on the prints provided by the knifemaker, Anders Hedlund, of Sweden. But each knife has a name, and in order shown here, they are the "Love Me Twice," "Golden Dream," "Fortune Dagger," "Classic Moment" and "Split Vision" art folders. All are LinerLocks with engraved RWL-34 blades and handle frames. Two, however—the aptly named Love Me Twice and Split Vision—are "two-bladed LinerLock folding daggers." As depicted in the two-blade LinerLock images here, one blade of each folder folds closed into one side of the handle, and the second blade tucks

neatly into the other side of the handle. When both blades are opened, or swung open from their opposite handle halves, they form one double-edged dagger blade that is seemingly, if you didn't know it was two blades, "split" down the middle. The five folders also showcase black-lip-pearl and gold inlays, gold pins, gold-anodized titanium liners, and one (Classic Moment) even parades 24 white sapphires set in a round circle on each side of the handle. By the way, no screw heads show on the outside of any of the handles, and all work, including the engraving and gold and precious stone inlays are by the maker. For no other reason than those mentioned—what more reason could there be?!—I give Anders Hedlund the 2018 Wooden Sword Award. □

Joe Kertzman

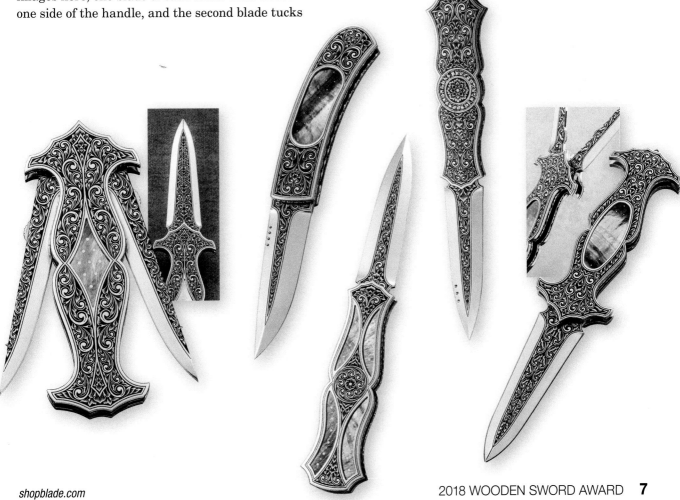

Magic & Mystery of the Bowie Knife

*The man behind the blade was the true legend,
yet the knife's fate was forever sealed*

By Steve E. Hill

The midday sun bore down on Samuel Wells and Thomas Maddox as they faced each other only eight paces apart. Each had in attendance a surgeon and their seconds who loaded the two pistols of the duelists in view of the aforementioned principals. At the signal, both pistols spat lead, and after the smoke cleared, both men stood untouched.

The Code Duello required that another shot be exchanged before honors could be restored to the gentlemen involved. The shots again had no effect on either man. Relieved that they had each been spared being killed or wounded, Wells and Maddox were satisfied that their honor was intact. The duelists now wished to celebrate the positive outcome and partake of refreshments in the shade where they had friends observing the duel in separate groups. This warm September 1827 day was about to get much hotter for all present.

Animosities between some of those men watching had been simmering for over a year. Robert Crain, the second to Maddox in this duel, had been previously ambushed and shot in the arm by the hotheaded Sam Cuny of the Wells group of friends, which included James Bowie. Another key figure was Norris Wright, in the Maddox camp. He was the former sheriff of Rapides Parish who had been recently defeated when Samuel Wells was elected the new sheriff.

During his term, Wright had made disparaging allegations concerning Bowie's land grants. He wasn't alone in his thinking about Bowie's dealings, but Wright was more outspoken, perhaps due to his lawman status. When James heard about Wright talking smack behind his back, he confronted him and demanded he say it to his face. Wright instead pulled his pistol on Bowie, who grabbed a chair for cover and then swiftly raised it over his head to strike. Wright shot, the pistol ball struck a coin or watch in Bowie's coat pocket, and the enraged Bowie leapt on Wright, pinning him to the floor.

With one hand around Wright's throat, Bowie tried to open his clasp knife in his other hand with his teeth. Friends began to pull Bowie off the pinned man, but before they did, Bowie sunk his teeth into Wright's hand, which had been clawing at Bowie's face. Seeing a trail of blood as James was carried to a room, it was assumed that he had been mortally wounded by Wright's shot, but the blood was from a tooth lost when Bowie bit Wright's hand. The shot only produced a painful bruise to his ribcage.

After the altercation, Bowie's older brother, Rezin, gave James a large hunting knife that the plantation blacksmith had forged from a big rasp. Both brothers opined that Wright might make another attempt on James' life and a large knife would be a good defense in a close-quarters fight. That was to become a self-fulfilling prophesy on the sandbar just above Natchez, Mississippi.

Crain felt uneasy to see Cuny and Bowie emerge from the trees because he had stated that he would shoot Cuny on sight. The two blocked the way to Crain's people several more yards distant, which included Wright and Alfred Blanchard. Cuny told Crain that this was a good time to settle their score, and he and Bowie drew their pistols. Crain still carried the two pistols he had loaded in case of a third exchange between Maddox and Wells. Dr. Richard Cuny, acting as Wells' surgeon, tried talking his quick-tempered brother, Sam, from starting trouble. Crain suddenly fired one pistol at Bowie and the other at Sam, severing Cuny's femoral artery and causing him to bleed to death within minutes.

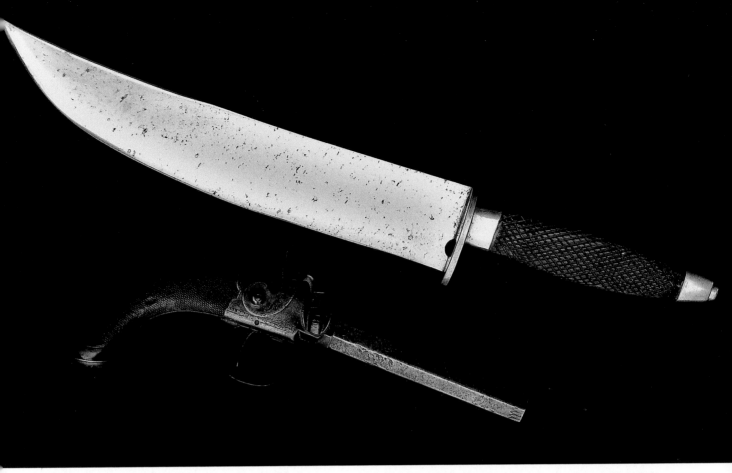

The early Bowie knife sports a Daniel Searles-style handle without silver pin pique decoration and a flat-ground, instead of beveled, blade. This is close to Rezin Bowie's description of a knife he gave James after the first altercation with Norris Wright. Eyewitnesses called it a big butcher knife.

STILL STANDING

Amazingly, Bowie had once again been shot and was still on his feet, but his unsteady return shot missed Crain. The frightening countenance of Bowie's face chilled Crain's blood as Bowie drew the big knife from its scabbard under his coat and advanced saying he would kill Crain for shooting him. Terrified, Crain threw the empty pistol at Bowie and ran. Bowie received a severe head gash from the tossed weapon and stumbled to the ground as blood obstructed his sight.

His enemy, Wright, saw his chance to get rid of Bowie and advanced toward the stricken man with a pistol and sword cane. Painfully, Bowie made his way to a thin snag sticking out of the sandbar. It afforded little protection and he called out to Wright that he was now unarmed but if Norris was a man, then shoot and be damned. Another man handed Bowie a pistol to protect himself and then Dr. Denny, the surgeon for Maddox, grabbed Bowie from behind and implored him to stop this madness.

Wright fired, and the ball entered Bowie's breast and exited out his back, taking a piece of Dr. Denny's finger with it. Bowie returned fire and hit Wright in his side. Now both wounded men advanced, driven by their mutual hatred of each other. One held a sword cane and the other a large knife. Wright's thrust inflicted another wound to Bowie's left arm in his blocking of the sword blade as he stabbed Wright in the shoulder with his knife.

Blanchard shot Bowie in the thigh and James was again on the ground. Blanchard and Wright began to stab at the fallen Bowie with their sword canes. Bowie slashed Blanchard across the abdomen, taking the fight out of Alfie. Wright stabbed Bowie again, and the sword blade became lodged in Bowie's chest, pinning his left hand to his breast in the process. Bowie tore his hand free of the sword cane, grabbed the coat of Wright, who recoiled, pulling Bowie to a near standing position. With his last bit of strength, he plunged his knife into Wright's heart, instantly killing him. Both fell to the ground, Wright's body atop Bowie's with the sword blade still in James' chest.

A pair of Mexican Bowies includes, at right, a Hill Pearce south-of-the-border-inspired knife, and on the left, an antique Mexican Bowie with etched blade and an unusual grind to the clip point and the ricasso, as well as a bone handle with coin-silver dog-head pommel.

Thus ended this affair of honor, which had deteriorated into a brawl, leaving two dead and two wounded, and nobody expected the severely wounded Bowie to survive. However, this had been a most unusual day and Bowie was a most unusual man.

It seems as though the laws of physics were reversed that day, whereon ripples that usually wash up to shore instead emanated from the sandbar's scenario of mortal desperation, and rippled up the Mississippi to the Ohio River and onward to the port towns upon the Ohio's banks. That ripple traveled downstream to New Orleans and flowed upon the Gulf Stream to the Eastern Seaboard ports and eventually across the Atlantic to England and Europe. The Sandbar Fight, as it had become known, was on the lips of all from landed gentry to rough river boatmen. All who heard of it were fascinated

that a man could bring a knife to a gun fight and prevail over multiple assailants even while suffering many severe wounds.

Newspapers throughout the country carried the story. A November 21, 1827, edition of *The New Hampshire Statesman of Concord* that covered the Sandbar Fight mentioned a terribly wounded Mr. James Bowie with a large knife killing his assailant. Folks' imaginations ran wild! What kind of knife could perform such feats? What did it look like? Nobody outside of Bowie's close circle knew that answer, but it must have been fearsome looking, they deduced. "I want a knife like Bowie's!"

MAKE MINE A BOWIE

The sentiment eventually became, "Make me a Bowie knife," and it was off to the local blacksmith. Or, for a well-heeled gentleman from the city, a visit to the local surgical instrument maker or cutler was in order. The general populace bestowed magical and mystical qualities to the knife, when, in actuality, the outcome of the Sandbar incident had more to do with Bowie's iron will to survive. The knife Bowie used on the sandbar was a rather ordinary implement. However, once it became the people's knife, it morphed into a plethora of profiles and diverse degrees of ornamentation or straightforward lack thereof.

The first wave of Bowie knives would appear in the Southwest, which at that time consisted of Mississippi, Louisiana and the Arkansas Territory. On the vanguard of skilled cutlers were Daniel Searles, who made a few knives commissioned by Rezin as presentations to friends. It has been thought that these highly refined examples bore the basic pattern of the knife Rezin gave James to defend his life.

Rees Fitzpatrick from Mississippi was known for his long clip-point blades with dog bone-shaped hilts. High-end knifemaker Samuel Bell appeared in the 1830's in Knoxville, Tennessee, and later in San Antonio, Texas. At the other end of the spectrum were the small-town and frontier blacksmiths. From Louisiana, Jesse Clifft also made knives for Rezin. It may have been Clifft's knife in Bowie's hand as he faced his sandbar adversaries.

In Washington, Arkansas, was the aptly named smithy, James Black. Many who passed through on their way to the Mexican state of Texas required his services shoeing horses, repairing wagon wheels and making Bowie knives. It's believed that he made knives for James and Rezin. His were guard-less, coffin-handle knives with slightly clipped-point blades

Old Southwest Bowies, at top is a swayback blade with sharpened false edge ground on one side, a walnut hilt and iron mounts. Below it is a rough frontier-style Bowie forged with a deep clip-point blade, a hand-carved ironwood handle and a forge-brazed iron ferrule.

and sharpened false edges, fashioned in utilitarian to ornate styles, depending on the patron's finances. Cincinnati, Ohio, cutlers Marks & Rees made similar Black-style knives.

James himself journeyed to Texas in 1828 and found that he was already a known figure among the American colonists and native Tejanos. Noah Smithwick and other blacksmiths filled the bill for those needing a good fighting knife on the wild frontier. These Bowie knives tended to have swayed backs with deep clip-point, wide blades and sharpened secondary edges. This partial double-edge feature was common on 1830-1840 Bowies, be they American, English or Continental, and was quite handy for a quick defensive backstroke.

Knives from 1850 and later generally lacked fully sharpened secondary edges, although they were ground to appear so and became known as "false edges." This may have been due to the advent of the revolver pistol, thus relegating the knife as a secondary weapon.

On the East Coast, Philadelphia played host to James and Rezin in 1832. While consulting the famous Dr. Pepper about Rezin's failing sight, the brothers discovered the cutler Henry Huber's shop just two blocks away. Huber made knives to their fancy, and it's been said that James ordered his clip-point blades with pistol-grip stag hilts to outfit a company of rangers in San Antonio.

DR. PEPPER & MR. PIBB

Rezin wrote an account of their San Saba, Texas, Indian battle for a Philadelphia publication while on that visit. The Bowie boys concluded that traveling so far north to see Dr. Pepper had to stop, so they moved Dr. Pepper to Texas, which irritated

From the Mexican War/Gold Rush Era are, from right to left, a John Walters & Co. Globe Works double-edge blade etched "California Knife" with a stag hilt; a George Wostenholm spear-point blade with multiple stampings; and an S.C.Wragg model circa 1840-1845 displaying a sharpened secondary edge, and a stamped two-piece German silver hilt with 45 stars that may denote the Republic of Texas's admission into the Union as 45th state, which was instrumental in starting the Mexican War.

Early Sheffield Bowies (1830s-1840s); at right is a Frederic Barnes blade featuring a sharpened secondary edge, wood hilt, and pewter and pearl inlays. At center is a George Wostenholm bowie showcasing a sharp secondary edge, a ricasso stamped "Celebrated Cast Steel Bowie Knife," iron mounts and a stag hilt. This knife looks to be a copy of the Philadelphia Henry Huber knives made for the Bowie brothers in profile and size. At left is a Thomas Barnes knife with a 7-inch blade etched "Made For Use," a German silver anvil guard, rosewood scales and pearl disc inlays.

a certain Mr. Pibb. Another Philadelphia cutler of note is Henry Schively, whom Rezin patronized, and David Crockett was presented one of his knives by citizens of that city.

New York's Peter Rose, Alfred Hunter and John Chevalier made fine Bowie knives. Massachusetts had a clan of Bowie knifemakers in John Russell, Hassam, Ames, Roby and the Buck Brothers. Others were interspersed throughout New England.

The demand for Bowie knives couldn't be met in America, and Sheffield, England, the world leader in cutlery, saw the opportunity to fill this void. In

the early 1830s, George Wostenholm made several trips to ascertain American cutlery needs. No doubt he heard of the Bowie knife's growing popularity. Soon he had offices in America, and one of his firm's earliest knives, stamped Celebrated Cast Steel Bowie knife, was surely inspired by the aforementioned Huber knife. His IXL trademark became the gold standard of knives worldwide.

Other early Sheffield makers of note are W & S Butcher, Woodhead, S.C. Wragg and James Rodgers. These early knives were very idiosyncratic in blade and handle shape, as well as ornamentation.

Civil War Sheffield Bowies include, from top, an Alexander blade stamped "For Self Defense" and boasting stag handle scales and an anvil guard; a Tillotson Columbia Place, Sheffield, handsome spear-point blade with false edge along the spine, German silver guard and ferrule, and a stag hilt; and a Corsan Denton & Burdekin blade etched "The Volunteer," complemented by a fancy stamped German silver hilt and a felt veneer sheath.

The 1840's Mexican War, the California Gold Rush and The Civil War brought new Sheffield names to American markets, such as Westa, Tillotson, Barnes, Burnand, Joseph Rogers and many others.

Cutlers in Birmingham, London and Manchester also got on the Bowie bandwagon. Some Bowie knives were made in British colonies such as India. Across the channel, the French and Germans offered their stylish and well-made contributions too. Perusing the antique section of the BLADE Show and joining the Antique Bowie Knife Association are great ways to learn more about these knives.

The need for large Bowie knives dwindled as reliable cartridge firearms came to the forefront in the post-Civil War years as the frontier became settled.

Knives shrank in size to become called "Bowie hunters" from the 1880s to the early 20th century. A renaissance of sorts began after World War II when Florida's Bo Randall offered big Bowie knives and television shows focused on Western lore in the 1950s. Solingen knives stamped "Original Bowie Knife" flooded the market, and custom knifemakers were on the rise in the '60s and '70s.

Nearly 200 years has passed since Bowie carved his name into history on that sandbar, as well as in Texas at San Saba, Mission Concepcion and upon his death defending the Alamo. His story of fearlessly facing overwhelming odds inspires today's makers and collectors to ensure his knife's popularity for ages to come. □

The Wharncliffe Goes Tactical

Largely regarded as a gent's folder blade design, the Wharncliffe shows versatility

By Michael Janich

A Wharncliffe is a distinctive style of knife blade characterized by a perfectly straight cutting edge and a spine that tapers to meet that edge at an acute point. Often associated with gentlemen's folders intended for fine utilitarian cutting, its history can actually be traced back to a specific gentleman of the 19th century—Colonel James Archibald Stuart-Wortley-Mackenzie—the first Lord Wharncliffe of England.

According to the book *British Manufacturing Industries*, around 1820 the first Lord Wharncliffe and his relative Archdeacon Corbett were sipping wine after dinner and lamenting the relative lack of creativity of the British cutlery industry. To address the problem, they put their heads together and designed a new blade pattern that they presented to the Joseph Rodgers & Sons cutlery company in Sheffield. Rodgers adopted the pattern and soon introduced the world to the first "Wharncliffe" blades.

Original Wharncliffe blades sported full flat-ground edges and had rounded spines that tapered to the points. The pattern has since evolved to include many other variations, but as long as the cutting edge is straight and the spine tapers to meet it at an acute point, it's a Wharncliffe.

From a utilitarian perspective, the biggest

The author's second-generation Wharncliffe folder design for Spyderco is the Yojimbo 2 (bottom), which also inspired a second-generation fixed blade called the Ronin 2 (top).

advantage of a Wharncliffe blade is that it cuts with full power all the way to the point. No matter where the cutting edge makes contact, it transfers its energy directly into the material being cut and consistently increases that pressure as the cut goes deeper. Even if you're cutting with the extreme tip of the cutting edge, a Wharncliffe's straight profile ensures that you'll do it with maximum power and leverage. That's why razor knives, box cutters and similar utility cutting tools are typically Wharncliffe patterns.

In contrast, swept edges actually curve away from the material, paralleling the arc of motion of the hand and purposely limiting the depth of the cut. This is best for skinning knives used for chores where cutting too deeply could nick an animal's intestines or cut through the hide.

The Wharncliffe's acute point also makes it a great tool for detailed work and, interestingly, enables it to penetrate with less resistance than most other blade styles. Although the tip is admittedly not as strong as some other profiles, it does its job exceptionally well.

Interestingly, all of the things that make the Wharncliffe an outstanding utilitarian blade style also allow it to excel as a personal-defense tool. Until recently, however, Wharncliffe tactical knives (at least the pocket-size kind) were relatively uncommon. At the risk of being immodest, I'd like to think I had a hand in changing all that.

DESIGN EPIPHANY

I've been a knife enthusiast since I was a kid and an avid student of knife combat since my early teens. I also had the great privilege of working closely with the late Col. Rex Applegate during his later years and learning the conventional wisdom of knife fighting and combat knife design directly from one of the topic's most respected sources.

When I had the opportunity to design my first production knife—the Masters of Defense Tempest— back in 1997, it reflected what I believed worked based on what I'd been taught. It had a classic bowie-style blade, plenty of blade curve, or belly, to slash better and a swedge (false edge along the spine) that created an acute, well-centered point. Essentially, it was a very traditional approach to a fighting blade, scaled down to fit into a folder.

A few years later, Sal Glesser of Spyderco took an interest in my Martial Blade Concepts (then, Martial Blade Craft) curriculum and offered me the opportunity to teach knife tactics under the Spyderco banner. He also asked me to design a signature knife that fit my approach to personal defense.

By that time, I had begun incorporating live-blade cutting demonstrations into all of my courses. With the help of "Pork Man"—a pork roast tied around a wooden dowel and wrapped with multiple layers of plastic—I showed students exactly how to quantify the cutting power of their actual carry knives. In the process, I began to realize that the performance of different blade designs in this simple test varied considerably. In fact, many highly regarded

fighting knife patterns actually cut pretty poorly.

Since my system focused on small, legal-to-carry knives and cutting tactics geared toward disabling an attacker, I wanted to make sure that whatever I designed for Spyderco would cut as effectively as possible. To do that, I invested a small fortune in pork roasts and crafted an army of Pork Men. I then pulled out all the knives in my collection and went to work.

The side-by-side cutting experiment was extremely revealing. After several hundred cuts with all conceivable blade styles, grinds and edge configurations, the hands-down winners were a pair of Frank Centofante-designed gentlemen's folders from Spyderco with classic Wharncliffe-style blades and beautifully executed full, flat grinds.

Their perfectly straight edges invariably cut the meat targets deeper and cleaner than other blade profiles and did not snag on clothing or the target's wooden "bone." They also penetrated almost effortlessly during thrusts. Despite their elegant demeanor, they were tactical cutting machines and a clear direction for my knife design efforts.

THE JANICH/SNODY RONIN™

Around the same time that I was sketching and modeling my folder design for Spyderco, I wrote an article about the work of a then-new custom knifemaker named Mike Snody. Snody was very pleased with my analysis of his knives in the article and even more thrilled when the orders that resulted from that piece launched his career as a full-time knifemaker.

The original inspiration for the author's focus on Wharncliffe-style tactical blades was the work of the late Frank Centofante, whose gentlemen's folders cut with extreme authority.

The author's first tactical Wharncliffe design was the Ronin neck knife, which began as a custom project with knifemaker Mike Snody. Here are several Snody custom Ronins, including an extremely rare (one of two) Ronin trainer (top).

To thank me for my part in making that possible, he invited me to design a knife for him—specifically the "ultimate neck knife." I was already convinced of the merits of the Wharncliffe, so I took him up on his offer and designed a small fixed blade I named the Ronin. Unfortunately, Snody wasn't as convinced as I was … at least at first.

After Snody's underwhelming initial response, I thanked him for his offer and suggested that he abandon the project to move on with his new career. He politely agreed, only to call me back several days later. His first words when I answered were, "You evil _____ [expletive deleted]! I've never cut with anything like this before!" It was then I realized that he actually made my design and, more importantly, did some cutting with it.

Snody embraced the Ronin design and began turning out a variety of custom expressions of it. Although I had already submitted a folding knife design to Spyderco, they were still apprehensive about the concept of a tactical Wharncliffe. To test the waters, they decided to do a production version of the Ronin, since product development and production of fixed blades is more economical than folders.

The Spyderco Ronin was a reasonably faithful expression of Snody's custom version produced in

Japan. The Kydex sheaths for it, however, were made at Spyderco's factory in the United States. Unfortunately, the hand-finishing of the G-10 handles done by the Japanese factory created some dimensional variances in the finished knives that made it necessary to have a one-to-one match of sheaths to individual knives. This made mass-production methods challenging and ultimately contributed to the demise of the design, which only lasted one production run.

Despite its limited commercial success, the Ronin did manage to change some minds with regard to tactical knife design. Following the live-blade Pork Man demonstrations I did in my seminars, I had students lined up to buy Ronins. However, I also had a deluge of requests for a folding version of the design. Unfortunately, Spyderco still wasn't ready to make that investment, so I decided to tip the scales a bit.

I contacted Snody again, who was now firmly established as a full-time maker and had expanded his skills to folder making, and asked him if I could commission a special one-off folding knife. I sent him the drawings of my folder design, which I had dubbed the Yojimbo™ (Japanese for "bodyguard") and asked him

Spyderco put the Janich/Snody Ronin design into production. The knife was sold with three different sheath patterns, all shown here. Also shown is the author's well-carried Ronin in a Mike Sastre custom Kydex sheath with a J-clip.

The first-generation Yojimbo folder from Spyderco was the first dedicated tactical Wharncliffe. Available in blue or black G-10 handles, it is shown here with a one-of-a-kind Mike Snody Yojimbo prototype that the author commissioned to validate the design and tip the scales.

to make one for me, post photos of it on the Internet, and mention that Spyderco might be working on a production version of it. He eagerly agreed and honored all three of my wishes, generating enough interest in the design to get Spyderco to commit to producing it.

THE YOJIMBO™

Spyderco's expression of the Yojimbo was released in 2003. Manufactured in their Golden, Colorado, factory, it featured a fully flat-ground CPM S30V Wharncliffe blade, nested stainless steel liners, blue or black textured G-10 scales and an early version of their patented Compression Lock™ mechanism.

Its 3-inch blade was purposely shorter than its tapered handle because I had designed it before the 9/11 attacks to be legal to carry on airplanes even during heightened security alerts. Although that point was moot after 9/11, it still made the knife a viable choice for carry in jurisdictions with restrictive blade-length limits.

Although it received wider acceptance than the Ronin, the Yojimbo was still greeted with skepticism by most tactical knife fans. Many dismissed it as a "box cutter on steroids" and couldn't get past the imbalance of its blade-to-handle ratio. The brave few that bought one and cut with it, however, quickly understood its advantages and joined the ranks of the converts.

Interestingly, during this same period, Snody was recruited as a designer for Benchmade Knives. Shortly after receiving the good news, he approached me at the BLADE Show and said he wanted to ask me a favor. He then reached into his pocket and produced a prototype of his Gravitator design—a Wharncliffe folder that he unabashedly admitted was directly inspired by the Yojimbo.

Grateful for his help in creating a tipping point for the Yojimbo, I gave him my blessing to move forward with the design. Deep down, I also took pride in the fact that the tactical Wharncliffe was gaining ground.

In 2004, I accepted a position with BlackHawk Products Group to design for the Masters Of Defense brand, which they had just acquired. Since it was inappropriate for me to work for one company while endorsing a design produced by another, I asked Spyderco if we could part ways as friends. They agreed, and shortly thereafter discontinued the Yojimbo design, just as it was beginning to attract a following.

BE-WHARNED™

During my tenure at BlackHawk, I ultimately took over management of Masters Of Defense and a second knife brand, BlackHawk Blades. In the process, I designed and brought to market a number of designs, but my hands-down favorite was a folder

While managing BlackHawk's knife brands, the author designed the Be-Wharned—an economical tactical Wharncliffe that packed lots of cutting edge into a compact package.

called the Be-Wharned. Based on lessons learned from the Yojimbo, I designed it so, closed, it was no larger than the ubiquitous Spyderco Delica (my favorite back-pocket knife), yet offered a very capable 3.5-inch Wharncliffe blade.

Its handle consisted of coarse-textured G-10 scales that housed a nested LinerLock mechanism and supported a four-position pocket clip. Made in Taiwan by that country's premier manufacturer, the Be-Wharned retailed for less than $100 and represented another significant step in spreading the word of the tactical Wharncliffe.

In addition to my full-time job in the knife industry, I also pursued my personal passion for Wharncliffes with a number of other custom knifemakers, most notably Mickey Yurco and Fred Perrin. Their deep understanding of blade design and cutting performance allowed them to share my appreciation for Wharncliffe dynamics and has resulted in a variety of both custom and, more recently, factory designs, including the Perrin/Janich Fusion neck knife made by the French company Max Knives.

In 2009, BlackHawk abandoned its focus on knife production. Fortunately, Spyderco was still interested in my skills and offered me a full-time position with the company. Although my primary focus is technical writing and product education, they also wanted me to have a signature design in their current product line.

Since the first-generation Yojimbo never achieved its full potential, I set my sights on designing a revised version, taking full advantage of my lessons learned since the first one. The result was the Yojimbo 2, which was released in late 2011.

Like the original, the Yojimbo 2 features a CPM S30V blade, a Compression Lock and textured G-10 handle scales with nested liners. However, its ergonomics are greatly refined and its blade-to-handle ratio provides much greater blade length. Its blade is also hollow ground with a full-thickness spine for increased strength and mass, and it includes a four-position pocket clip that supports all carry positions.

By the time the Yojimbo 2 was released, my proselytizing efforts and the gradual introduction of tactical Wharncliffes by other companies allowed it to be much better received. In a reversal of the sequence of the first-generation models, the Yojimbo 2 inspired a second-generation fixed-blade version—the Ronin 2.

In fact, the very first Ronin 2, a custom blade made by Yurco, was based on his hand-traced outline of a Yojimbo 2. When it was shown in Spyderco's prototype case at the BLADE Show, customer response was immediate and a Spyderco factory version followed quickly thereafter.

As an instructor of knife tactics, I owe it to my students to recommend only the best personal-defense knives. That commitment and the extensive cutting tests it inspired led me to not only believe in the tactical Wharncliffe, but to make it a central focus of my efforts as a knife educator. If you're looking for a knife you can trust your life to, get a Wharncliffe. □

⌄ French custom knifemaker Fred Perrin is also a big proponent of Wharncliffe blade patterns for personal defense. After the author confessed his love for Perrin's Neck Bowie (second from bottom), the maker tweaked the design to include a Wharncliffe blade. The result was a Janich-Perrin collaboration called the "Fusion" and produced by Max Knives.

⌃ Custom knifemaker and retired law-enforcement officer Mickey Yurco is one of the author's favorite makers of Wharncliffe blades. Shown here are several examples of Mickey's take on the Ronin.

My Move into Mid-Tech Knifemaking

One of the world's most renowned bladesmiths starts Porterfield Knife and Tool

By Steve Schwarzer

I have spent most of my adult life making hand-crafted, forged knives. I love the creativity and science involved in producing these one-of-a-kind, usable works of art. I started my knife journey in this art form in the late 1960s, grinding a few very rough knife-shaped objects. There wasn't much information that I was aware of at that time.

In the early part of 1972, I started working with a construction company that employed boilermakers. The associated union represented not only boiler-makers, but also blacksmiths and iron shipfitters. Back when schools had shop classes, I had forged a chisel as a project in junior high, so I was interested in forging. Yet, after a little research, I found out there were no blacksmiths left in the local union. I finally found a blacksmithing book with a chapter on forging blades. At that point, the fire was lit. I acquired all of the tools—an anvil, forge and ham-mer—and a large passion for shaping steel.

I followed the same path as many who studied the art of forging steel, through reading and experiment-ing, and by sheer luck I used steels that worked to make an efficient knife—crosscut saw blades and car springs. They were cheap and readily available.

As my interest grew, I found other like-minded people interested in the blacksmithing end of knife-making. At that time there was only a handful of people forging blades in the country. I ran into a man who was making pocketknives and folding knives, and lived in Jacksonville, Florida, at the time. Bobby Tison made the mistake of inviting me to his shop, and that one trip changed the course of my life.

He had the few books published at the time containing information on making knives, and they opened a door to a new world for me. Mr. Tison was using steels I had never heard of before—D2 and

Renowned bladesmith Steve Schwarzer recently took the step from solely being a custom knifemaker specializing in hand-forged blades, to making semi-production "mid-tech" knives. Here Steve is shown at a forging demonstration in Ocala, Florida.

A2—and he very patiently taught me to make folding knives. The first few were one-offs and usually re-quired a pair of pliers to open them. I had customers complain about the stiffness of the springs, and my reply was that they were manly knives. After some tutoring, my knives began to function ... properly.

Mr. Tison said that if I made a pattern of the ones that worked I could save time and have some repeatability. This was my first step toward mid-tech (or semi-production) knifemaking. As I met more aspiring knifemakers, we began to exchange ideas and form groups to promote the craft. I ran into several skilled craftsmen who came primarily from the tool-and-die industry, and they built knives like Henry Ford built cars. I was not sharp enough at the time to see the benefit of making knives in small batches, probably a little arrogance on my part.

I visited other people's shops as the opportunities presented themselves, and I would study the methods used by those makers and adapt the practices I liked best into my own scheme of things. One guy in particular made dozens of pocketknives using a half-dozen cheap drill presses so he would not have to change tools—another early mid-tech method. I was bitten with the forged blade and damascus diseases, and the production end of knife construction fell to the wayside. Forged blades do not lend themselves to mass production without very expensive and heavy equipment.

AN INDUSTRY DIVIDED

Over the years, a big competition between the forged blade crowd and the high-tech machining crowd basically divided the knife industry at the individual level. The great argument of what makes a handmade knife began, and the forged blade bunch, myself included, used the phrase that, "We make our own steel." The machinist crowd would beat back with, "Our knives are like precision watches." If you farmed out any part of your knife, it was considered factory made or less than pure by the forge crowd. The interaction was even bitter. The machinist crowd even began to fight amongst themselves over technique. If you had parts laser or water-jet cut, that was somehow unfair to the guy who was scribing templates onto bars of steel and band-sawing and grinding them to fit.

To me, laser and water-jet cutting made good sense, and I figured Ford would have approved. The end product was a great knife at a price that a larger number of customers could afford. Even the hard-headed damascus bunch began to see the benefit of using standard parts married to high-tech steel. At that period of time, I was caught up in what I call the "pattern steel wars," and that competition is actually still on to this day, with some of the most creative new makers leading the pack.

I was very early in seeing that you could use high-tech machines to produce shapes and designs that would have taken years to make by hand. With the help of a very bright and interested machinist, I began to incorporate material shaping processes into my blade patterns, and of course, using high-tech machines to achieve art in steel is now common practice. It made sense to fashion more than one knife using CNC (Computer Numerically Controlled) machine patterns combined with forged or pattern-welded (damascus) steel to make one-of-a-kind art knives.

There is only so much work you can produce in a lifetime, no matter the skill. I have a few friends who took time to provide guidance and great advice when I finally made the decision to go into semi-production/mid-tech knifemaking. I have watched the "small batch" tactical crowd steadily grow over the last few years, and some of the most successful in this group started out as bladesmiths. They used hard-earned knowledge gained from years of learning to move hot iron and understand the properties of a chosen steel to get the most performance from it.

I set goals for myself and I feel I've done a lot in helping develop the pattern-welded-steel industry. I also shared my learned techniques freely, and in return, developed friendships that have lasted many years. I called on a few of these friends when I de-

Porterfield Knife and Tool assembly and finishing manager, Eric Morton, grinds a skinner blade.

cided to embark on my new mid-tech adventure. The road to success is never easy, and I made up my mind a few years ago to not only make a few standard models of knives, but also to produce enough of them to sell in a price range that the average guy could afford.

I have several hobbies, and one of them is air boating. I love these boats that will literally go anywhere, with my first boat having been built By Norman Clifton in Ocala, Florida. He is a bright young guy that has developed several companies, two being GTO (Good Time Outdoors) and Core Rifle Systems. If it has to do with hunting and fishing, or just having fun outside, he is the man, and we have been friends for many years. I was making small batches of skinning knives, and Norman bought a few to put in his gun and airboat shop. Last spring, Norman approached me about designing a line of knives for his shop. The discussion went back and forth over a month or two before we agreed that I would build a series of very high-quality knives.

The author called in some old friends to give him guidance and avoid production pitfalls when he made the move to mid-tech knifemaking. One of them, Ryan Johnson, makes these "Combat Africa" fixed blades in his own semi-production knife shop.

FROM ONE MAN TO A TEAM

Going from a one-man shop to a full production facility is not an easy task. I have always worked at my own pace and met my own standards, but Norman and I have fully incorporated my quality standards and performance into these first few knives, and I have a core group of very dedicated and bright individuals working with me. My assembly and finishing manager, for instance, is an ex-military man and accomplished knifemaker named Eric Morton. My high-tech guru and design engineer is Henry Gallops, who has a long history in tool and design machining and was the powerhouse behind two of the major bow companies in the United States. I have a great team.

As a company, Core Rifle Systems is hugely successful, and with Norman's input, we as a team feel that our newly incorporated Porterfield Knife and Tool, a Division of Good Time Outdoors, Inc., will do equally well. Each of the knives and axes is made to the same exacting standards as my one-off handcrafted tools.

Once Norman and I decided to pull the trigger on this project, I called in some old friends to give me guidance and avoid production pitfalls. I wanted to talk with successful bladesmiths who had already made the transition to mid-tech knifemaking. One of my oldest friends is Ryan Johnson, who I met when he was about 14 years old at a hammer-in. He is a gentle giant of a young man and very bright. Ryan became serious about mid-tech knifemaking around the year 2000. He had started forging with his grandfather when he was about 12 years old, and his parents were history buffs. Ryan fell in love with swords and axes. His real love is forging tomahawks, and he is one of the best in the business.

A few years ago, he was approached by a Special Operations soldier who wanted a unique tomahawk. That was the event that really pushed Ryan into production on an industrial scale. As far as I know, he was the first modern independent bladesmith to set up a production forging line, with Spec Ops use as the primary design factor. Ryan bought a used CNC milling machine and taught himself how to use it. That is no easy task. I promise you that I have been in that learning curve for many years, but it could be that I am just slow.

Ryan does nearly everything in-house, from

Steve Schwarzer (shown at left with Daniel Winkler) consulted several knifemakers, Winkler included, who had successfully transitioned from solely fashioning custom knives to mid-tech operations. Pictured are two of Winkler's belt knives.

design to heat-treating to leatherwork. His laid-back management style and increasing talent show in the quality of the knives and axes that come out of his studio. They are a mixture of forging and CNC machining rarely seen. Ryan was a great help to me getting my project off the ground.

I have researched everything and taken all of the technical advice that I can from those who have been successful. Danny Winkler, a forged-blade traditionalist, and I have been friends since 1982. I first met Danny at a blackpowder rifle event in northern Georgia, and he and Karen Shook have forged a friendship and a business that have always been successful. Danny is one of the very few knifemakers that I know who has always run his craft like a well-oiled machine. While my interest lies only with producing a quality product, Danny wants to know how every cent is spent and how to make the product as useful as possible. His work speaks for itself, and he and Karen have spent years developing their business, and going to trade shows and blackpowder events to promote it.

In 1993, Danny was approached by a Navy Spec Ops operator about building an axe for breaching. Danny made it, and the SEAL carried it all during Desert Storm. In 2006, the same man returned and placed an order for his unit. By 2007, Danny had two

employees plus Karen and himself, and he is now up to 12 full-time employees. Most of his knives and axes go to military and law enforcement, though he still makes the occasional custom knife. Danny runs his business like a military officer manages his unit. I checked in with him before Norman and I began the process of developing Porterfield Knife and Tool. He was very helpful on many of the technical aspects of my project and saved me hours and dollars on the problems of production that he spent years working out. Friendships do count.

I was on the road for weeks gathering information with my sidekick and design engineer Henry Gallops. On returning to Florida, we decided that the only excuse we could come up with for going out of our way and stopping at a good seafood restaurant Norman had discovered on another road trip, was to drive to Spartan Blades. I had met Mark Carey and Curtis Iovito, owners of Spartan Blades, at a sniper shoot at Fort Bragg. Well, we were only 300 miles from Boone, North Carolina, home of Spartan Blades, so I made a phone call, and Mark and Curtis welcomed us with open arms. The two business partners do not come from bladesmithing backgrounds, but rather from Special Operations, and we were treated to a great tour of their facility and exposed to the exceptional knife work they are doing.

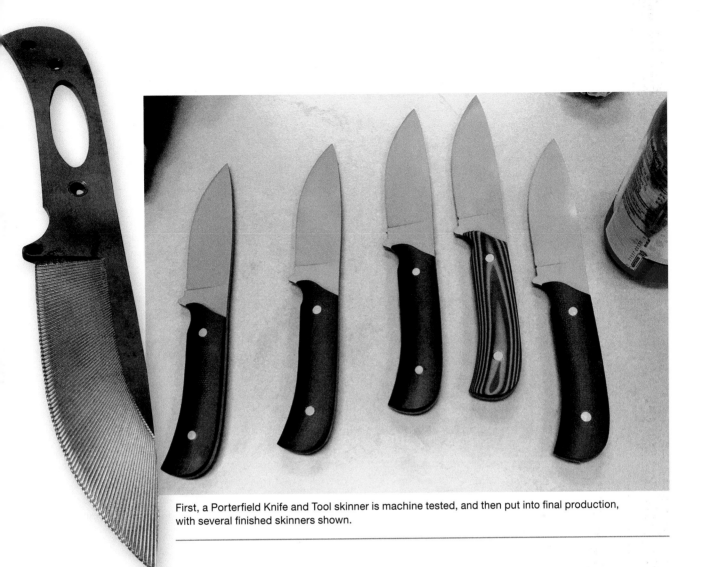

First, a Porterfield Knife and Tool skinner is machine tested, and then put into final production, with several finished skinners shown.

SOME MORE EQUAL THAN OTHERS

Speaking of exceptional, bladesmith Rick Hinderer is one of those "God made all men equal, but some more equal than others" guys. Like most independent craftsmen, Rick marches to the beat of his own drum. He started forging under the instruction of Hugh Bartrug in 1989, and he also runs with John Richter, another longtime friend of mine. Rick, like most of us old-timers, was banging out one blade at a time. He started making folders, but the problem with making folding knives is that all of the parts have to fit perfectly – or the knives won't function properly.

In 1995, he bought his first CNC milling machine and then had to learn how to use it. Learning how to program a CNC mill, or any CNC machine, is a tall order. Once he managed to get the beast working, though, he began producing folders in batches of 25 or so—a very moderate production, but better than a year of "ones" and "twos." Today, Rick has a bunch of

machines and is a very fine success story. His work is in high demand worldwide, and he has been a great help to me and many others, sharing hard-earned knowledge.

Mid-tech knifemaking is not any easy place to start, even if you have a running business producing other products. The learning curve is steep. As my friend Joe once told me, a CNC machine never complains—it is just as happy making junk as it is making good parts. Making knives of high quality in quantity is a daunting task. The more people you get involved, the more chance for error. Finding a group of people with the same passion for quality is also difficult. But that is the challenge. There are many makers and small companies producing limited-edition knives. You can recognize who is or will be successful by the quality of their work.

The new team at Porterfield Knife and Tool, myself included, are dedicated to making real hard-use tools for people who expect the best. □

A True History of the Tomahawk

Embodied within a tomahawk's spirit are the frontiersman, woodsman and warrior

By Ryan M. Johnson

My love affair with tomahawks began when I was 9 years old. My father bought me the book *Swords and Blades of the American Revolution* by George Neumann. In it was a chapter on tomahawks—pipe tomahawks, spike tomahawks and trade hawks that were used by the frontiersmen fighting in the Revolutionary War. There was a rough romance about the shapes and materials that to this day intrigues me.

The parallels between the use of the tomahawk in the 18th century and that of the modern battlefield are numerous and worth our consideration. It turns out the reasons behind the tomahawk's popularity in the woods of Colonial America are often the same reasons they are popular with U.S. troops fighting terrorism around the world.

The word tomahawk is a variation of the Algonquian word tomahac, which means "to strike." It was a term that was used originally for any striking weapon, from wooden clubs to axes made of stone. In 1608, Capt. John Smith of Jamestown, Virginia, author of many texts, was the first person to record the word, mentioning it was used to describe the hatchets carried by his men.

Axes and clubs were symbols of power and status for native cultures as far back as the mound builders. This, combined with the numerous advantages held by the metal tomahawk over its stone predecessors, made the European-fashioned metal tomahawks popular trade items with Native Americans. As trade increased, new forms evolved to meet the demands of the market, and tomahawks with pipes, spikes and hammers were traded by the thousands. Carl

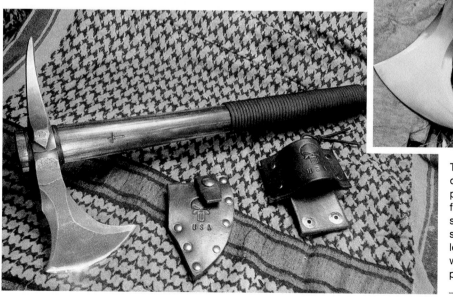

The Virginia father-and-son team of Mark and Dylan McCoun is very popular with the military community, forging 4140 chrome-molybdenum steel tomahawks, such as the one shown, with hickory handles and often leather carrying systems. Note the wicked-sharp beard on the hammer poll tomahawk in the inset image.

D.J. Urbanovsky of American Kami crafts high-tech, high-end tomahawks such as the Maniaxe (bottom) and Chickenhawk (top). Inset is an American Kami tomahawk being tested on Range 37 at Fort Bragg, North Carolina.

Russell, author of *Firearms, Traps & Tools of the Mountain Men*, speculates that, as the classic trade 'hawk became the norm with Native Americans, newer, less pragmatic forms evolved to fill the warrior status niche.

The tomahawk was a true multi-purpose tool. With it one could dress game, chop wood and clear brush. Choking up on the handle, the user could use it much like a knife. The length of the handle gave the blade tremendous velocity and force as well, making it a formidable weapon. These attributes were not lost on the frontiersmen of the time who often adopted the tools and lifestyles of the Native Americans.

This adoption became even more apparent as the frontiersmen went to war. They employed the same guerrilla warfare tactics used by the Native tribes, and they carried the tomahawks so prized by them. One equipment list for volunteers into the American militias mentions "a sword or tomahawk" as a required item right along with a rifle, powder and lead.

LEWIS & CLARK 'HAWKS

The Corps of Discovery carried hundreds of tomahawks on their expedition. While most of these were items for trade, Capt. Meriwether Lewis and 2nd Lt. William Clark issued every one of their men a pipe tomahawk. On the return trip, Clark's pipe tomahawk was stolen by a native and the men spent an entire day tracking him down to get it back. While wintering with the Mandan tribe, explorer Pvt. John Shields forged tomahawks in trade for corn, keeping the group from starving during the harsh winter months. As they made their way to the Pacific Coast, they were surprised to find that the tomahawks forged for the Mandan had beaten them there through the extensive trade routes.

This rich history would be enough to secure the tomahawk's place among the tools and weapons of American history, but the story does not stop there. After a long hiatus, the tomahawk made a comeback. My uncle related to me that during the Korean War, some soldiers were known to modify the issued hatchets into tomahawk-like shapes and sizes, grinding crude spikes out of the polls to be carried as weapons. There was also a tomahawk commercially available that was privately bought and carried by some U.S. troops during that time.

Peter LaGana, founder of the American Tomahawk Company, was famous for his tomahawk made popular during the Vietnam War. Also privately purchased by soldiers, it proved a valuable tool and weapon in the jungles of Southeast Asia.

The true rebirth of the tomahawk, however, would be brought about by the Global War on Terrorism after the attacks on 9/11. Some members of the Special Operations community began carrying tomahawks as part of Col. John Mulholland's Joint Special Operations Task Force, also known as Task Force Dagger, when only 300 Americans were in Afghanistan on the hunt for Bin Laden.

The number of soldiers carrying tomahawks increased throughout the next decade of war, but why? There are several reasons. The wars in Afghanistan and Iraq were anything but conventional

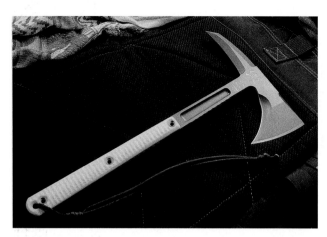

The RMJ Tactical "Kestrel" is based on an 18th-century design.

natural resistance to penetration: historically speaking, it takes a tremendous amount of training to overcome the tendency to slash with a blade instead of stabbing. For many people there is an inherent resistance to stabbing. The spike of a tomahawk takes this slashing tendency and translates it into deep penetrating wounds.

PSYCHOLOGICAL EFFECT

Ask any veteran of the wars of Iraq and Afghanistan, and they'll tell you that the cultures involved are blade cultures. These are often people that do no respect many modern weapons, guns included, but take notice of a blade being carried. Blades carry a certain machismo effect in most Third World countries. As one soldier put it, "When you carry something like a 'hawk, it sends the message 'I'm willing to take it to this level. I'm not just hiding behind a gun.'" Many tomahawks are pretty scary to look at, and in the right hands, are downright terrifying.

MODERN TOMAHAWK DESIGN

Traditional tomahawks were forged from iron, had steel cutting edges and wooden handles. While some modern tactical tomahawks are made this way, most use solid steel construction with slab handles. This style lends itself to a wide variety of designs and materials, and makes for an incredibly strong platform.

Some modern considerations for tactical tomahawks are strength and ability to pry, ability to cut through common vehicle materials such as safety glass and sheet steel, nonconductive handles for those who may possibly breach live electrical wires and the ability to carry conveniently using dedicated carry systems. As retired Senior Master Sgt. John Blair at Air Force Special Operations Command once told me, "If you can't carry it, you can't use it." Carry options usually include belt carry, MOLLE/PALS webbing attachments and weapon sling options.

MODERN MAKERS

There are so many excellent makers of tactical tomahawks that it would be difficult to list them all here. I will, however, list a few who represent what's out there. The Virginia father-and-son team of Mark and Dylan McCoun is very popular with the military community, forging well-made and reasonably priced spike and hammer poll tomahawks. Each hawk is forged in their shop and hand finished. Their hawks feature 4140 chrome-molybdenum steel and hickory handles.

Jack Stottlemire worked in the Special Operations

wars. Instead, they were asymmetric wars that had more in common with the guerrilla fighting of frontier America. The tomahawk once again served as a valuable tool and weapon in this environment.

BREACHING

The most common use of the modern tomahawk is breaching doors, walls, locks and windows. In the past, breaching was a specialized job for a handful of soldiers. As urban warfare increased, there weren't enough soldiers specialized in breaching to go around, and the job fell to whoever was moving forward. While the tomahawk is no replacement for a hooligan bar or explosive breaching charges, it is very good at light breaching: breaking and raking windows, breaking locks and chains, cutting hinges, etc., while being lightweight and taking up relatively little space. The tomahawk helped a shooter "move to target."

WEAPON

As mentioned, the physics of the tomahawk make it a formidable weapon. But in the era of laser-guided missiles, FLIR (Forward Looking Infrared) and night vision, where could it possibly fit in? Usually the answer is in close-quarters combat. Often when I hear of a tomahawk used in combat, it goes something like this: "So we were clearing a room when this bad guy gets into a struggle with my buddy for his gun. I couldn't shoot the guy off of my buddy for fear of hitting him, too, so I pulled out my tomahawk and … it was over pretty quickly."

Tomahawks have greater reach than a knife, strike with greater force, and combine blunt force trauma with cutting and deep penetration. In particular, the spike of a tomahawk overcomes a

The "Winkler II Combat Axe" comes in a choice of a recycled rubber or curly maple haft. The spike geometry of the Combat Axe shows serious attention to detail.

(SharpByCoop images)

for making the blades carried by SEAL Team Six. Of special interest is the Sayoc Fighting Tomahawk.

The author of this feature article, I am the RMJ (Ryan M. Johnson) of RMJ Tactical, but the company itself is made up of a team of talented artists and craftsmen in Chattanooga, Tennessee, that makes a wide variety of both forged and machined tactical tomahawks. From the Eagle Talon tomahawk popular in the early days of the Afghan war to the Shrike and Jenny Wren carried today by soldiers around the world, RMJ Tactical hawks are standards in the field. You can also find RMJ designs in the CRKT production knife line.

James Helm of Helm Forge in Texas crafts no-nonsense tactical tomahawks in both spike and hammer poll configurations. Of special note is his wrecker series of tomahawks.

American Kami's D.J. Urbanovsky is a knife-maker and designer from Omaha, Nebraska. A one-man shop that crafts high-tech, high-end knives and tomahawks, American Kami is known for its Maniaxe and Chickenhawk. You can also find D.J.'s designs in the Boker USA production knife line.

SPIRIT OF THE TOMAHAWK

What is the difference between a tomahawk and a hatchet or axe? I get this question quite often. My standard answer is "the same difference between a fiddle and a violin. It has a lot to do with who is holding it and how it is used."

Many hatchets of the 18th and 19th centuries were called tomahawks because of how they were used and carried. To me, hatchets and axes are tools only, with very specialized purposes. Tomahawks, on the other hand, are tools that serve a multitude of purposes, including that of being weapons. The spirit of a tomahawk's use, whether the year was 1776 or 2017, is that of the frontiersman, woodsman and warrior. □

community during the Global War on Terrorism and uses that experience for forging and grinding some of the best tactical knives and tomahawks available. Working out of Fayetteville, North Carolina, Jack forges traditional, historically based tomahawks and makes a spike tomahawk popular with many of the "high-speed, low-drag, door-kick" types.

Then there's Daniel Winkler. The team at Winkler II Knives in North Carolina crafts a unique blend of modern designs with Old World feels. Using input from Tier One teams and their combat trainers, the Winkler team uses both manmade and natural materials to create its own distinctive look and style. Daniel is mentioned extensively in popular culture

---

SUGGESTED READING

Firearms Traps and Tools of the Mountain Men, Carl P. Russell
Swords and Blades of the American Revolution, George C. Neumann
Undaunted Courage, Stephen Ambrose

SUGGESTED WEBSITES

www.rmjtactical.com
www.winklerknives.com
www.helmgrind.com
www.americankami.com
www.rustickknives.com

Knifemakers of the North Country

Canada's custom blade builders share their artistry and vision with the rest of the world

By Mike Haskew

Art, tactical, fantasy, fighting, bowie or folding, the breadth of Canadian knifemaking is worthy of much more than a passing nod. Canadians set trends, push the creative envelope, take home loads of awards and pass along their experience, trade savvy and vision to a new generation.

"Canada is a large, diverse country, and so are the knifemakers from coast to coast," observed native son Brian Tighe, who was born in Brantford, Ontario, and has lived just west of Niagara Falls most of his life. "In Canada there are some great knifemakers, and many of us have become friends over the years. Wolfe Loerchner and Jose de Braga continue to produce amazing art pieces year after year."

Kirby Lambert lives in Regina, Saskatchewan, and loves the legacy that Canadian knifemakers have established and continue to build. "Each maker has a unique and different personality," he commented. "A number of years ago—when the Canadian Guild was at its peak—that was such a great and memorable time for me. Having my best friends and makers such as Brian Lyttle, Brian Tighe, Greg Lightfoot, Sean O'Hare, Peter Rassenti, Wolfe Loerchner, Thomas Haslinger and so many more all gathered in a room was so much fun."

"One of the main reasons I do as many shows as I do now is to travel to see many of these people," Lambert continued. "They live too far away from me to just visit for the day or the weekend."

True enough, the names of so many makers, familiar and even lesser known, conjure up expectations and images of the best in the craft. Rod Olson,

With a full-tang ATS 34 stainless steel blade and a handle composed of six layers of anodized titanium, Jose de Braga's Predator was inspired for use in feature films. It also includes a 14k-gold mask inset between the three prongs of the guard. Overall length is 19 inches.

(SharpByCoop image)

Gaetan Beauchamp, Christoph Derringer, Chantal Gilbert, Stephanie Lemelin, Brent Beshara and Elizabeth Loerchner are just a few more. Their styles may vary, but they share that common Canadian thread.

The son of immigrants from the Azores, de Braga remembers picking up Sid Latham's book *Knives and Knifemakers*, in 1973, and reading about the great Bob Dozier. He also remembers seeing an automatic knife while in a barber's chair as a little boy. Both events influenced his decision to begin making knives years ago and to use his experience as a jeweler to turn it into a full-time occupation in the 1980s.

A veteran of the Canadian army, de Braga captured back-to-back awards for Most Unique Design at the 1989 and 1990 BLADE Shows, and the 1992 award for Best Fantasy Knife.

NO CREATIVE TIMELINE

"My specialty," he paused, "I would say it is design, the conception of new shapes and mechanisms in the folding knife area. Then the toughest part is determining a date to complete a project. You see, as an artist, I have never been able to fully master this aspect. Too many variables come up during the creation, but the artwork always gets completed."

De Braga likes working in ivory and hardwoods such as ebony, along with gold, silver, titanium, Timascus, bronze, stainless steel and nickel silver.

Beshara, who lives in Holyrood, Newfoundland, spent 24 years in the Canadian military working with light infantry, Special Forces and bomb disposal units. His keen eye for design led to some outstanding custom knives, but these days he concentrates solely in the design arena. Well known for the success of his BESH Wedge, a geometrically innovative dagger blade that combines two diagonally opposed bevels converging to form a third cutting edge at the tip, Brent's genius has caught the attention of knife manufacturers. He landed deals with KA-BAR, Blackhawk, TOPS, Buck, SOG, Boker, and most recently, Case, which has introduced the BESH Wedge blade style on its famed V-42 stiletto.

Wally Hayes started making knives in 1987 and admits he had "absolutely nothing" to get his enterprise going. "I was grinding knives out with a 1x30-inch belt grinder," he grinned. "Next I started forging with a laundry tub and a hair dryer for a forge. I had one of the first KNIVES annual books, written by Ken Warner, and a knife book by Tim McCrate. I made a lot of calls to Don Fogg and to Mick Langley when I started. They helped me out over the phone."

Wally served as president of the Canadian Knifemakers Guild for four years and owned a dog kennel for 15 years while he established his knife business on firm ground. He went full time in 2001. A member of the American Bladesmith Society (ABS), he earned his master smith stamp in 1995. Making his own damascus steel and doing some engraving, he

W.R. Case & Sons Cutlery Co. unveiled the Besh Wedge last autumn to pay homage to the company's legendary V-42 combat knife. The knife features Brent Beshara's innovative geometric blade design.

A Wally Hayes wakizashi features a 16-inch hand-forged blade of W-2 tool steel, copper and steel fittings, a stingray skin handle wrapped in brown silk and a wooden saya, or sheath. (SharpByCoop image)

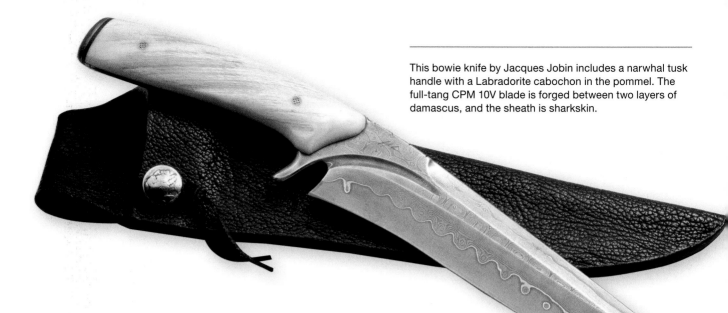

This bowie knife by Jacques Jobin includes a narwhal tusk handle with a Labradorite cabochon in the pommel. The full-tang CPM 10V blade is forged between two layers of damascus, and the sheath is sharkskin.

devoted plenty of time to making Japanese swords before moving largely into high-end folders with a few camp knives, neck knives and swords in the mix. He believes mother-of-pearl and damascus make a dynamite package.

"I have made so many friends through the years, whether they are collectors or makers," Hayes said. "I had a blast making knives for Axl Rose and hanging out with him." Other luminaries who own Wally's work include Ted Nugent, Chris Stein of the rock group Blondie, Richard Fortus of Guns N' Roses and actor Joey "Pants" Pantoliano, probably best known for his role in the HBO series *The Sopranos*.

FUTURISTIC ARTWORKS

Shaping blades and fashioning futuristic works of art are challenging in their own right, but for Jacques Jobin they simply cannot compare to having to fight for his own life. A knifemaker for more than 30 years, Jacques beat cancer six years ago and returned to the vocation that he loves.

"I did have an encounter with cancer," he reflected, "and it kept me relatively quiet for a year. But I now feel as if nothing ever happened, and I am not ruined."

From 1975 to 1991, Jacques worked as a bodyguard for ministers of the government of Quebec. The firstborn of nine children, he still lives in the town of Levis on the Saint Lawrence River near Quebec City. His shop is part of the 200-year-old house where he and Louise, his wife of 46 years, take care of two dogs and two cats.

"I'm 65, and I consider myself semi-retired," he said. "I still make knives but at a much slower pace. I still have a lot of fun in making them, and I have a few pieces in the works that will come out in the next few months. On the design side, I like to think that I have my own style, and each knife I make is unique. I have designed and made a wide range of knives from miniatures to swords, as well as folders, some with unique and original mechanisms."

"They are designed and made according to a general idea or concept," he continued. "A lot of improvisation takes place on the way to completion. I use titanium, one of my favorite materials, on all my folders, and incorporate it in futuristic pieces also. Most of my knives have a classic look, and I try to keep simple, flowing lines. But sometimes I like to fly! What I particularly like to do is futuristic knives that look like they can fly as much as they can cut."

Lambert acknowledges that many of his fellow knifemakers trace their skills to machining backgrounds; however, his beginnings were in fine arts along with an appreciation of edged tools and weaponry. A knifemaker for 25 years, he went full time in 2003.

A MENTOR AND FRIEND

"When I was 17, I took a course on how to make a fixed-blade skinning knife from a maker named Bill Schiller," commented Kirby. "At this point I really just wanted to know what kinds of equipment knifemakers used. This was long before the Internet—YouTube, Facebook, Instagram and such—so finding any information was difficult! A few years later I moved to Calgary, Alberta, where I enrolled in a fine arts/education program. At that time I met

△ Kirby Lambert's Augustus includes an XHP 3V Chad Nichols damascus blade, matte finished zirconium bolsters, a Nichols Mokuti handle, dual-colored anodized titanium hardware and a sculpted zirconium pocket clip. *(SharpByCoop image)*

⧨ The compound-ground tanto blades of the Brian Tighe automatic fighters are laminated steel with zirconium and Beta "C" titanium cores, while the knives also feature black Timascus handle scales subjected to high- and low-temperature burns. *(Point Seven image)*

one of the most talented makers I have known, Brian Lyttle. Brian became my mentor and best friend."

"He was an incredible maker and teacher who taught me many things about forging damascus, fit and finish, and metallurgy, among other things ... even cooking! Sadly, Brian passed away this year. I can never thank him enough for all he did for me," Lambert concluded.

Kirby specializes in tactical/dress tactical utility folding knives. Early work included Japanese-inspired fixed blades. "I still love Japanese swords more than anything in the blade world," he said, "and play around with making the odd one here and there. There was a time when I did a lot of forging and damascus making, but I don't do a lot of that anymore. I do stock removal for the most part and buy my damascus from people who specialize in it, like Chad Nichols."

Like many of today's best-known knifemakers, Lambert is trying to catch up on a backlog of orders. He is also working on new designs along with a few collaborations with other makers and with Boker knives.

Years ago, when his son Grayson was a child, Tighe was enjoying a springtime walk with the boy alongside a stream near their home. Grayson spotted a deer antler that had been shed the previous year. Brian thought it would make a great handle for his fishing knife.

"That started it all," said the winner of the Most Innovative Design award at the 2010 BLADE Show for his "NIRK Tighe" model, landing the award again in 2012 for the "Buy Tighe." "I enjoyed fitting the blade to the antler handle, and finishing it, so much that I found the book *How to Make Knives* by David Boye and made a few fixed blades, and was soon making folding knives. With my experience in metal cutting and tool design, it was a natural progression. Thirty years later, I still have that first knife."

LINE OF CRAFTSMEN

Brian's lineage includes craftsmen. His father was a tool and die maker and his grandfather a blacksmith. Grayson is now a world renowned pen

This large folding dagger by Wolfgang Loerchner showcases a carved 440C stainless steel blade and a sculpted 416 stainless handle with gold and damascus inlays.

(Francesco Pachi image)

maker. Along with his background in the tool and die trade, Brian has four college courses in metallurgy on his resumé. He manages to work a few fixed blades into his schedule, and his favorite blade material is Damasteel. He likes black Timascus for handles, appreciating the stunning effects of the black shades of zirconium and the colors of anodized titanium.

Two days after returning from the 2014 BLADE Show, Brian discovered a disaster. A pump had failed, and his shop was flooded with five feet of muddy water. It was a total loss, but Brian came back even stronger. He recently started working on both single- and double-action automatics with "improved" mechanisms. He is also on the cutting edge of technology.

"There have been many changes through the years," Brian reasoned. "Most notably the computer has changed designing and machining, and with 3-D printing you can have a feel of the finished product in your hand before you start to cut valuable material."

Forty years ago, Wolfgang Loerchner built the house that he still lives in on the shore of Lake Huron in Bayfield, Ontario. Similar to that foray into homebuilding, he also struck out on his own to make knives.

"My first knives were filed by hand since I had no machines," Wolfe noted. "I have since added a drill press and band saw, but still continue making knives the same way. I soon discovered that I could not compete with makers producing hunting and using knives with machines, so I decided very early to put my efforts into art and collectors knives. Working in isolation from other makers allowed me to develop my own style, and I have been full time for the past 10 years."

For 20 years Wolfe made knives on a part-time basis while working as an engineer at a nearby nuclear plant. During those years he specialized in large daggers and highly sculpted integrals. From there he gravitated to stock-removal folders with sculpted frames and intricate inlays. Through the years he has captured numerous accolades but is most proud of the three W.W. Cronk Memorial awards presented by the Knifemakers' Guild.

"These are special," he said, "because other winners include some of the greatest, like Buster Warenski."

ACCLAIMED CAREER

Another significant aspect of Wolfe's acclaimed career is sharing the art of making knives with his daughter, Elizabeth. "She works out of her own shop now and is certainly developing her own style," he assessed. "She did move back into our home for one full year to apprentice with me. We spent the year working three feet apart, seven days a week, 15 hours a day. It has certainly led to a much closer father-daughter bond in spite of the occasional tears and stressful moments. We have collaborated on three or four special projects, but normally work completely separate from each other."

Wolfe uses 416 stainless steel, gold, mother-of-pearl and damascus most often. He appreciates their permanence—no tendencies to move or crack—and the ability to sculpt them with files and sandpaper.

Elizabeth took some cues from her father, but she has become her own knifemaker, body and soul. Her home and shop are in the town of Auburn, Ontario, about an hour away from her parents.

"In the early years of this millennium, I attempt-

Elizabeth Loerchner fashioned the Noctis lock-back folder with a file-worked blade of 440C stainless steel and 416 stainless handle scales. Gold wire highlights the cloisonné inlays. Overall length is 7.75 inches. *(SharpByCoop image)*

ed to make knives for a short period," she remarked candidly. "I learned quickly that it was not the right time for me. In 2010, I revisited the prospect, and it became apparent that making knives was something I seriously wanted to pursue. My father was eager to teach me and dedicated a great deal of time to me."

Elizabeth finds 416 stainless steel ideal for filing and finishing as a handle material, and likes inlays of various pearls. Her favorite blade steel is 440C, which lends itself well to heat-treating and file work. "It's often apparent in my work that I have a strong influence, naturally so, from my father," she offered. "I have been working at obtaining my own style to

set me apart. Something that is constantly on my mind is attempting to do something that is unique and different all around. One prospect I have is learning to make large daggers. I find it important to keep learning new things to expand your horizons and alter the way you see what can be accomplished."

Although she is among the youngest of Canada's knifemaking cadre, Elizabeth has already shown the kind of talent of which a father can be proud. Undoubtedly, she will continue to add to the prestige of the knifemakers of the North Country.

Have a glimpse at their spectacular amount of work. As said in the national anthem, "O Canada!" □

Heavenly Blades

Knifemakers look skyward and take design and materials inspiration from celestial bodies

By Leslie Clary

Space – that vast universe of effervescent lights, shooting meteorites, colorful gases and luminous moons. From the dawn of time, it has served as muse to poets, artists, dreamers, lovers – and knifemakers.

But the influence of space reaches beyond mystical inspiration. Take a look around your home. Do you have a microwave, cell phone, smoke detector? They all contain material or technology developed by NASA.

Space touches just about every area of our modern lives. We can thank NASA for Nike air shoes, improved ski boots and high-tech golf clubs. Space technology has brought artificial limbs to a nearly lifelike level, giving many men and women the chance for fuller, more functional existences. It has given us better medical and dental care. Because of NASA we have sunglasses that cut the glare, pill transmitters, handheld vacuum cleaners and improved highways. While it might seem contradictory, the space program has also contributed to a greener planet with solar-power technologies now used widely by solar manufacturing companies.

And it's brought new innovations to contemporary knives.

MATERIALS FROM NASA

It could be argued that the elements making their way into blades and handles are not really "space-age" materials. Titanium, for instance, now used frequently in many knives because of its strength and durability, was discovered in 1791 by the British chemist, Rev. William Gregor, and then

The name of the innovative Ron Appleton folding art knife alone—Cosmos 2—speaks volumes for the inspiration behind the design. Among many amenities, the blade locks in the fully open position and in the half-stop position, the latter for use as a quasi-push dagger. *(David Bloch image)*

in 1793, independently discovered by German chemist M.H. Klaproth who named it titanium after the super-humanly strong Titans of Greek mythology. The element, however, was not successfully isolated until 1910 when it became the 22nd element on the periodic table.

Its superior strength-to-weight ratio, resistance to corrosion and its ability to perform well at high temperatures has made titanium the metal of choice in military aircraft, and for decades it was used exclusively in aerospace applications.

Eventually, those outside of the aerospace industry caught on that titanium's unique qualities make it a superior choice for many items previously fashioned from steel, and titanium began making its way into many of our everyday appliances, as well as finding new, creative outlets in the world of art and sculpture.

In the knife industry, nearly all of the titanium comes from the aerospace industry as scrap metal. As knifemaker Les George puts it, "We're eating the scraps of the aerospace and defense industries. A lot of what we take for granted exists because of NASA technology and space research."

Niobium is also becoming increasingly common in jewelry and blades. This shiny, white transition metal will begin to oxidize in air at 200 degrees Celsius, and will take on a soft bluish hue when exposed to air for an extended period. Thousands of pounds of niobium have been used in the Gemini space program's air frame systems.

Tantalum ores often contain niobium as well, so both metals are extracted for use. The two are similar in other ways, as well, and are sometimes confused with each other. With a silvery sheen, tantalum is highly resistant to corrosion. Its oxide layer, which forms on the surface, acts as an insulating sheet and can be used to coat other materials with a very thin layer, making it a great choice for portable electronics like mobile phones. Tantalum alloys have also been used for turbine blades, rocket nozzles and nose caps for supersonic aircraft.

DENSE MALLEABLE METAL

Since it is a dense and malleable metal, tantalum has also been used for surgical instruments and in weaponry for armor-piercing projectiles. Its rarity makes it an expensive metal and, therefore, not commonly used for knives, although some bladesmiths are experimenting with it. Both niobium and tantalum are difficult to work with, and like titanium, anodize nicely with brilliant colors, but

Titanium can also be carved to take on an exotic look and feel, as evidenced by Les George's "Harpy" damascus flipper folder.

they are not strong enough for structural purposes.

One knifemaker who experiments with many of these metals is Ron Appleton. You might say Appleton was born with space in his genes. He grew up learning from his father, Ray, who employed Electrical Discharge Machining (EDM) to cut deep, narrow cavities in parts commissioned for President Ronald Reagan's "Star Wars," or missile defense program.

Following in his father's footsteps, Ron became a proficient machinist and said, "A number of the materi-

The colorful Les George dagger is 100 percent Mokuti, a mixture of multiple titanium alloys, including Chad Nichols Mokume.

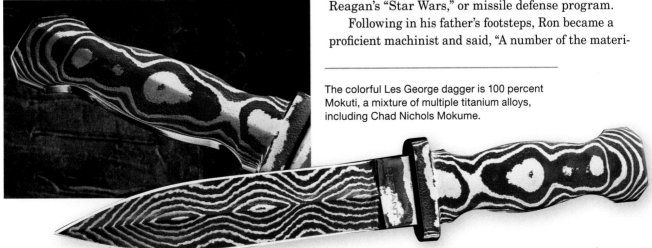

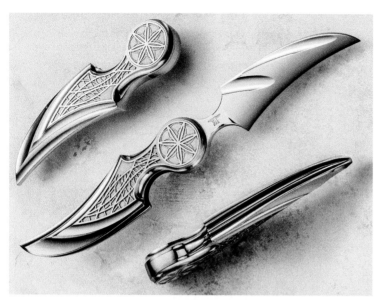

The stars and planets are a big influence for Ron Appleton, as evidenced by this sculpted metal knife called "Venus Rising." *(SharpByCoop image)*

als I use were perfected by the aviation and space industry, such as Kovar [a nickel-cobalt ferrous alloy] for its expansion qualities, titanium alloys for strength-to-weight ratios, and beryllium alloys for structural strength and electrical qualities."

All of these materials also have good resistance to corrosion. Tool steels such as A2, S7 and 01 also have exceptional edge-holding qualities and are primary steels for blades. Appleton learned to make single-point threads on a lathe and made hundreds of screws from these materials and others like Invar (a nickel-iron alloy) and Kovar, which have expansion coefficients similar to glass.

He says, "I found out that many of these fasteners were bound for deep space, as they had been made for Martin Marietta, JPL [NASA's Jet Propulsion Laboratory] and the Mars Mariner and Voyager spacecrafts."

NASA technology has drastically evolved as well. CNC (Computer Numerically Controlled) machines have made it possible for knifemakers to build stronger, more precise edged implements than ever before. Innovative designs that were not possible in the past are now a reality. Some craftsmen embrace this new technology. Others shudder. Most have found a way to adapt, combining their organic, creative vision with the precision that technology offers.

CELESTIAL INSPIRATIONS

While a quick glance at the innovative knives being produced today will show the influence of

NASA and technology, knifemakers are also dreamers, romantics and visionaries. Technology has improved the functionality of blades, but it's still the mystical heavens that inspire these artists to keep creating.

Appleton says, "I have always turned to the stars for balance. I live in Texas and the horizons are clear in all directions. To place myself in space, I look to the stars, which are the same ones I watched when I was young. I loved watching the TV shows with Carl Sagan and Jack Horkheimer. I had a small refractor telescope when I was a child and I built my own reflector telescope about 18 years ago. I still occasionally find time to observe enough of the sky to make me feel insignificant."

Another knifemaker who finds inspiration in the skies is Glenn Waters, whose work has gained an excellent reputation in the world of art knives. His training as a jeweler transfers to his blades, which are as beautiful as they are functional. He says, "I want my knives to survive in their full glory, so I decorate them so as to protect them from use. They are all sharp and designed with the intention of being practically useful as defense weapons, but the kind of weapons you would only use if really necessary."

It's not surprising that the universe has influenced many of Waters' creations. He says, "I have a love of the universe and our earth, and I believe that our world was in some way helped by the intervention of aliens, or people from another dimension, or from a hidden place on our earth, maybe from the far side of the South Pole—a place that is off limits for all people today.

"Things like the pyramids scattered around our world, and strange, unexplainable structures that are not even possible for us today to recreate with all our high-tech machinery—it seems that the technology of the long, previous civilizations on this earth was far superior than our present technology," Waters hypothesizes. "I want to convey this message in my knives whenever I can."

The heavens represent more than just beauty for Waters, and many of his knives hold secret messages for the people of the future to discover. He says, "As a Japanese sword collector, I can anticipate the reaction of someone in the future discovering one of the messages hidden on my knife. They will either say, 'Wow, he was so right,' or maybe, 'How misguided

Many of Glenn Waters' knives are engraved with secret messages for people of the future to discover. The symbols in the inset image, from left to right, represent: God or life force, a UFO, Sirius star system, the sun and moon, a pyramid, the Egyptian hieroglyphics for "eternal life" and human DNA.

the people of his time were.' In any case, for better or worse, I leave my messages."

Space and art are both emotional. As George says, "The esoteric nature has driven the grounded nature. There is no logical reason to leave the earth. To send a man to the moon was emotionally driven."

This combination of emotion and passion with technical expertise and rational judgment has elevated modern knives to a new level.

METEORITE

Natural minerals, elements and alloys that we clearly associate with outer space, particularly meteorite, are also used as knifemaking materials.

Meteorites, with their concentrated amounts of iron, have been found in Egypt dating back to approximately 3,300 B.C. During the Bronze Age, meteorite's rarity made it more valuable than gold, and it was used for both ornamentation and ceremonial objects. One of the prized items found in King Tut's tomb was a decorated meteorite dagger.

Primitive meteorite blades have also been uncovered from Ohio to Greenland.

Meteorites are still being used for blades today. Technology and advanced tools have helped bring knives to aesthetically new levels, while meteorite, often combined with other natural materials like wood, bone or gemstones, adds to the look and personality of the knife.

Appleton, who sometimes uses meteorite in his work, says, "I consider these rough materials for looks mostly, as they do not have comparable intrinsic structural strength or homogeneity as other pure metals or alloys that are usually used in the machine shop. Etching meteorite and damascus can give many effects, from slight visual reflections to deep finger-catching cavities that are stunning in appearance and feel."

THE FUTURE OF KNIVES

With innovations in technology happening at light speed, what does this mean for the future of knives? George says he'd love to find a blade material that is strong, has cutting ability and is non-magnetic and non-conducive to electricity. Since all metals, including titanium, conduct electricity, "that's one area where, whoever figures it out, he or she will get rich," he projects.

In many ways, knifemakers have simply been building on 5,000-year-old technology. The basic techniques primitive people used are still intact, only with more refined tools and advanced materials. Most blade builders find that they employ a combination of the old and new.

Waters believes there is a bright future for knifemakers, users and collectors. He says, "New and innovative materials are always making their way into the craft. Better, stronger, cleaner and rust-resistant metals for blades and superior materials suitable for handles are always appearing. I love these new materials, but at the same time I love natural materials like gold, silver, gems, meteorite and mammoth ivory. I feel it is very compatible to mix the best of the ancient materials with the best of the modern high-tech materials to create an object of superior quality and beauty. I don't expect this to change anytime soon."

To separate earth from space may be a little egocentric, and a small shift in perception can put a new twist on our role in the greater scheme of things. Rather than looking at ourselves as earthlings and space as a mysterious vastness that's somewhere "out there," when we look at the big picture—the entire universe—we're all space creatures, and earth is just one tiny microcosm, a fairly inconspicuous speck floating in all of that vastness. □

Plunge in with Dive Knives

The water is not yet murky or overfished, but clean and fresh for exploration

By Evan F. Nappen, Esquire

Dive knives present an opportunity for collectors to get in on the "ocean floor" of an industry segment. Having been a knife collector for more than 40 years, my interest in different collecting areas of knives grew with consideration of certain factors. The most important factor was whether the subset of collecting held my interest, and the other consideration always had to do with the size of my bank account.

It was never my goal as a collector to spend big money to get knives that I found of interest. Anyone with money can do that. The real joy was in collecting knives at bargain prices and being ahead of the curve when it came to what I was focused on gathering.

As a young collector, I was exposed to the book *A Collection of U.S. Military Knives, Book Two* by M.H. Cole. I was fortunate because not that many folks had seen the first edition. A deep appreciation for U.S. military knives was not yet widespread in the marketplace.

I could purchase U.S. military knives at gun shows and flea markets reasonably, and I acquired some absolutely awesome pieces at prices that made them more affordable than buying a standard hunting knife from the local department store.

Since I was ahead of the curve, I was able to build a substantial collection at low prices. These knives have increased dramatically in value over the years since then. From collecting U.S. military knives, I branched off into a subset known as "theater-made" knives, which were often handmade or military blades that were modified by armed forces personnel during the theater of war.

Prior to a book coming out on theater-made knives, they were usually some of the cheapest knives you could buy at a gun show or a flea market.

Shown here are the author's piles of dive knives purchased for bargain prices at gun shows and flea markets.

Nowadays, theater-made knives are some of the most expensive U.S. military blades because the appreciation for their individuality has grown by leaps and bounds, particularly due to scholarly research and publication about such pieces.

I believe that dive knives present a similar collector's opportunity today. Other than modern,

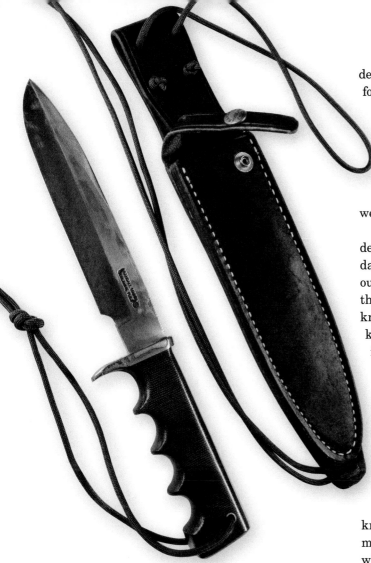

Among other features, the high-quality Randall Model 16 dive knife came with a wax-impregnated leather sheath.

designs and materials make them desirable knives for outdoor adventurists.

Most dive knives were made between the late 1950s and today. There are earlier "hard-hat" deep diver knives often accompanied by brass scabbards that can be quite pricey. However, a typical dive knife with a rubber, plastic or synthetic handle and sheath is usually priced well within the average person's means.

Anytime I find reasonably priced examples in decent condition, I buy them. I am confident that one day a book on dive knives will be published that thoroughly explores the subject. Much like the impact that Cole's books had on U.S. military knives, dive knives will gain appreciation and the prices for these knives will reflect the market's demand for collecting the aquatic pieces of sharpened steel. You, dear reader, now have a chance to get in "on the ocean floor" of dive knife collecting.

Dive knives are currently the "sleepers" of the knife world, and investment opportunities abound for the collector who has an interest in such pieces. Before we look at inexpensive dive knives, one should be aware of the pricey ones available today.

There are some expensive, desirable dive knives out there now, many coming from high-end makers. The expensive pieces are often associated with military and sporting uses, and include, but aren't limited to, Randall, Gerber, Puma, Benchmade and Mission Knives & Tools, or those made specifically for the military.

Becoming familiar with expensive dive knives may help one find a bargain and to recognize certain qualities that make a dive knife valuable. Additionally, the expensive dive knives lay the foundation for price appreciation of the vintage sleepers waiting out there for savvy collectors to scoop them up.

The Randall Model 16 comes with a wax-impregnated leather sheath that resists water damage. Randall describes the Model 16 as having a sharpened top cutting edge, a 4.5-inch black Micarta handle similar to the company's Models 14 and 15, a single or double brass hilt, brass ferrule and a wrist thong. The blade spine nearest the hilt is notched for thumb placement.

A green Micarta handle is available upon request, and customers' names can be etched on the nameplates. Other extra features include saw teeth and a nickel silver hilt. Designed specifically for heavy-duty saltwater use, the knife is nearly indestructible.

imported low-end knives, vintage dive knives are often the lowest priced blades at a gun show or flea market. The overwhelming majority of dive knives are easily acquired for between $5 and $40 apiece, similar to how U.S. military knives and theater-made knives were priced years ago, before folks woke up and recognized their true value.

There are exceptions, of course. A Randall dive knife is still a Randall. It's highly unlikely that you're going to find a Randall for $25, but there are plenty of quality models out there that can be acquired reasonably.

DESIGNED TO TAKE ABUSE

Dive knives are often well made and designed to take a certain amount of abuse in exploring the underwater world. The blades are usually stainless steel and rarely rusted to destruction. Their robust

A NEW STYLE OF RANDALL

On pages 162-163 of the book *Randall Made Knives: the History of the Man and the Blades* by Robert L. Gaddis, the author discusses the development the Model 16. The year 1958 ushered in another new style of Randall knife, the number 16 Diver's Knife. The first of these was made for a man as well known in writing circles as Bo Randall was with knife aficionados, James Jones, the author of such best-seller action novels as *From Here to Eternity, Some Came Running* and *The Thin Red Line.*

The Diver's Knife first appeared in the twelfth printing of the Randall catalog. It was illustrated by a heavily retouched photo and described as having a 7-inch blade of 1/4-inch stainless steel, a sharpened top cutting edge and a 3⅞-inch green Tenite handle, similar to that on Models 14 and 15. Designed for heavy-duty saltwater use, it featured a nickel silver hilt, wrist thong and a special oil-tanned leather sheath with a keeper thong and arm and leg thongs. The overall package weighed 14 ounces.

Micarta handles were advertised as an option starting in March 1965, and by early 1967, the Micarta handle and wax-impregnated sheath had become standard features, with saw teeth on the blade spine a continued option.

Gerber made a variation of the company's famous Mark II survival knife specifically for diving. In late 1970 and early '71, Gerber produced Mark II dive knives with yellow Armorhide handles. The military never officially used them, but they were sold to the general public, and many military divers privately purchased and employed Mark II dive knives. They also came with oil-impregnated leather sheaths, complete with two leg straps, made to withstand saltwater. The knife and sheath packages came in brown cardboard boxes.

Unlike gray-handle Gerber Mark II survival knives, yellow-handle dive knives did not have serial numbers. Gerber Mark II dive knives sported 6.5- to 7-inch wasp-shaped blades and overall lengths of 11.5 to 12 inches.

Gerber also offered the Neptune dive knife at about the same time period. It boasted a clip-point, perch-belly blade and a more traditional handle. There were two models—one with an orange Armorhide handle and rubber sheath, and a second piece sporting a yellow Armorhide handle and oil-impregnated leather sheath. The knives have already proven to be valuable collectibles.

THE FROGMAN & SEA HUNTER

Puma of Germany made high-quality dive knives, including the "Frogman," "Sea Hunter" and "Capri." The Frogman showcased a 7-inch, double-edge, drop-forged stainless steel blade, stainless bow knuckle guard and a red handle. The Sea Hunter had a 6.5-inch, drop-forged stainless steel blade, a broad, grooved thumb rest and a red rubber handle. It was designed for deep-sea fishing and diving.

The Frogman and Sea Hunter were made in the 1960s, with the Capri ushering in the '80s and featured a black plastic handle and a 6.5-inch blade similar to the well-known Puma White Hunter, yet the Capri was specifically marketed as a dive knife.

In the early '60s, the U.S. government paid just under an unheard of $100 per knife for the Imperial nonmagnetic dive knife. The nonmagnetic blade was vitally important for mine probing and other uses by Frogmen when destroying ships and underwater targets. The knives were periodically tested to

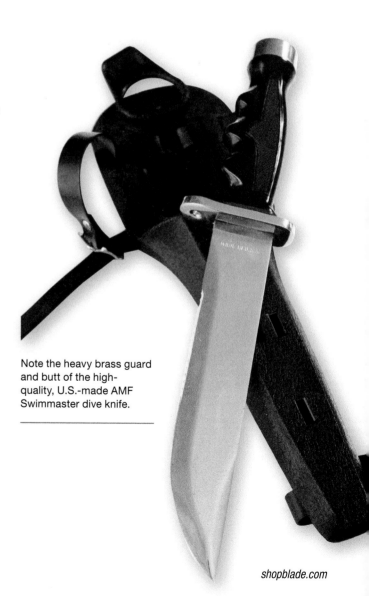

Note the heavy brass guard and butt of the high-quality, U.S.-made AMF Swimmaster dive knife.

ensure their nonmagnetic quality, and have stamps indicating those test dates.

Modern nonmagnetic dive knives sport titanium blades, and Mission Knives is a manufacturer of some of the best in the business. Titanium has other advantages, including corrosion resistance. Company literature touts Mission's titanium as being corrosion proof in all naturally occurring environments. The MPK12-Ti knife was soaked in seawater for more than four years without a hint of corrosion, and the blades are cleaned in concentrated hydrochloric acid.

Titanium is also 40 to 50 percent lighter than steel and thermally stable up to 800 degrees Fahrenheit higher than steel. Its thermal range is from minus 100 to more than 700 degrees Fahrenheit. It will not break in subzero weather, whereas steel can shatter at minus 65 degrees and ceramics are brittle at room temperatures.

As far as wear and abrasion resistance, Mission's titanium is reportedly a self-healing metal that forms a titanium oxide ceramic skin over itself when scratched and has five times the abrasion resistance of steel. This gives it the ability to retain an edge and resist damage due to contact with dirt, sand, ice, mud, nylon webbing and rope.

Mission defines superior ductility, or "percent elongation," as the deformation that results from the application of a tensile force, which is calculated as the change in length divided by original length. This is usually measured over a 5-centimeter gauge length, and the higher the number, the better the ductility. The Navy SEALS have been unable to break the titanium MPK12-Ti in almost 20 years of service. This is due to 12 percent elongation, coupled with toughness and flexibility under load. It is also the alloy of choice for jet aircraft landing gear.

OPPOSITE OF BRITTLE

Mission's titanium is tough at both high and low temperatures, with toughness being the relative resistance of the metal to breaking, cracking or chipping under impact or stress. Think of it as the opposite of brittleness. It should be noted that toughness and wear resistance are inversely proportional.

Titanium can be flexed or bowed repeatedly without undergoing rupture. It has half of the modulus of steel, and therefore will bend at least twice as far

The nickel-plated P.I.C. dive knife boasts a 1918 trench knife-style handle that protects the user's knuckles underwater.

before breaking. It is nonpoisonous and biologically inert, and often used as human replacement joints.

Benchmade makes the H2O series of fixed-blade and folding diving knives. "Born from water, the H2O fixed blade was originally developed for an elite military program," according to company literature. "The knife features a blunt tip, opposing bevel for torsion strength and an integrated hook for cutting through straps, webbing and other pliable materials."

The H2O folder is explained as being the same model as the Benchmade Griptilian, but with stainless steel hardware and blade steel designed specifically for saltwater applications. Of course, Benchmade is recognized as a high-end knife brand.

There have also been expensive, commemorative

models, such as those made in the 1980s by Wenoka to commemorate the company's years of dive-knife production. Wenoka had planned to offer 10 commemorative knives, but only produced six in the series. They all came in wood presentation boxes, and to this day would likely hold higher-than-normal value for knife dealers or purveyors of collectible knives.

The odds of finding low-priced Randall, Gerber, Mission or Benchmade, and likewise special military dive knives, are slim – but not impossible. Knowledge is the key. Best of all, there are many bargain dive knives just waiting to be purchased by the knowledgeable collector.

BARGAIN KNIVES ABOUND

When it comes to bargain dive knives, one sees names such as U.S. Divers, Healthways, Wenoka, AMF Swim Master, AMF Voit, Sportways, Dacor, Scubapro, Scubaskin, P.I.C., Eternal, etc. The general pattern of the knife is a stainless steel blade with a plastic or rubber handle and sheath. There are models that can be picked up for incredibly low prices, and for what one is paying, "it's worth it just as a knife." It's those kinds of investments that seem to be can't-lose propositions, although nothing is ever guaranteed in life.

Considering the potential collector value and strong possibility for growth, dive knives present an incredible bargain for the knife world. Let's look a little more closely at some dive knife brands one is likely to encounter today at bargain prices.

Wenoka knives are some of my favorites. They were very well made in Japan. There is a wide variety of models. The larger Wenoka dive knives have a great, sturdy feel and are nicely designed for the task at hand. The AMF Swimmaster is a beautiful well-made knife, very high quality, serial numbered, with a heavy brass butt and guard, and made in the U.S.A.

Healthways offered the "Skin Diver," a double-edged blade made in Solingen, Germany, with a large, red cork handle. The P.I.C. Model 728 "Sea Hunter," made in Japan, is also of high quality. It is easily recognized by its handle, which is a nickel-plated replica of the 1918 World War I trench knuckle knife. Many such dive knives were made in

The sturdy Wenoka dive knife was designed by Blackie Collins.

Japan, and even a dive hatchet, which was a hatchet, pry bar and hammer combination set that came in a vinyl sheath was available.

There are so many variations of dive knives, and they appear to be limited only by the imaginations of various makers. Most scuba companies sold some sort of dive knife at one time. They say the sea, not space, is the last true final frontier. Dive knives have been the personal tools of undersea explorers for as long as there have been divers. What the bowie knife was to the West, the dive knife is to the sea. The collector now has a chance to reasonably acquire these fascinating knives that were once strapped to divers exploring the underworld of the earth. □

Traveling with Knives in Europe

Avoiding scrutiny while traveling with knives often involves common sense and blade choice

By James Morgan Ayres

All images by ©MLAyres

I might go on a trip to Europe. Can I take my knife with me?"

Since I write about travel, and about knives, I receive many emails from readers asking this question. I understand. You always have a knife handy. It's your basic tool. How do you open packages, or cut anything? How can you get through your day without a knife? What if you need your knife to punch out the window of an overturned bus, or escape from a burning building?

What about that picnic next to the Canal du Midi, or on the train? You don't want to be reduced to ripping and tearing at salami, cheese and baguettes with teeth and nails. You need your knife. But you don't know laws and regulations in Europe and you're a law-abiding person. So can you take your knife with you?

Yes, you can. But there are some things you need to know. In the United States, laws and regulations concerning knives are a confusing patchwork that varies from state to state, town to town, and which sometimes make no sense whatsoever. It is not possible to travel from California to New York with any kind of knife without violating a law or regulation in some place along the way.

Few of those laws and regulations are actually enforced. Enforcement is up to decisions made by an individual police officer. Those decisions will vary from officer to officer, and most importantly, according to his perception of you and the situation.

It is similar in Europe. The European Union is made up of almost 30 countries, each with its own laws, customs and regulations, which like in the United States, can seem confusing and senseless. As in the Unites States, enforcement of those laws and

When traveling in Europe, the author and his wife often use small folding knives—from right to left, a Victorinox EVOGrip, Spyderco Dragonfly and Spyderco Cricket—for everyday tasks, sometimes including food preparation.

regulations is dependent upon the decisions of the individual police officer or security person.

I've worked and traveled in Europe for decades, and lived there for the past 10 years. I've written for *BLADE Magazine* and for the *KNIVES* annual book for almost 20 years, and have written two books on knives: *The Tactical Knife* and *Survival Knives*. As a result, I've met many folks in the European knife community—knifemakers, bushcraft enthusiasts, and so on.

Nonlocking folders such as the Spyderco C94PBK3 "UK Penknife" (left) and C154PPN "Squeak" (right) are acceptable to carry in most European locales.

CONSULTING THE LAW

I know many people who work in the security services and police departments in many European countries, and have talked with them about travelers carrying knives. What follows are my personal experiences and opinions based on traveling and living in almost every country in the European Union, and some that are not members of the Union. I am not a lawyer. I offer no legal advice.

Some examples of regulations concerning knives in Europe: In Germany a person may not carry on his person any folding knife with a locking blade. He can, however, carry a fixed blade up to 3½ inches long. In France a person may not carry on his person any object that can be, or is, used as a weapon. That includes France's famous Opinel or Laguiole knives, which are national icons and are in the pockets of every third Frenchman.

Spain has considerable history as a knife culture and has knives of all kinds available for purchase pretty much everywhere – including village bars, and a confusing morass of regulations that my friends, who are Spanish police officers, cannot understand or explain. In the United Kingdom, there was a recent attempt to prohibit chef's knives from having a point. That regulation did not pass.

My understanding of the current U.K. laws is that you must have a reason to have a knife, such as being a carpenter. Locking folders are not allowed. Bushcrafters carrying fixed blades while on the way to do some bushcraft seem to get a pass. In Denmark a person may not have any folding knife with a blade lock, or that opens with one hand. Wait! That regulation was just changed. Locking folders are OK now, for today.

Attitudes about knives also vary by region. Eastern Europe, the Balkans and Turkey are much more liberal about knives than in Western Europe. I'll delve more into that later.

What's a European traveler to do? How could anyone know or conform to all of the different laws and regulations while traveling through four or five countries? You cannot. So, you have two choices: 1. Choose not to carry a knife. 2. Use some common sense. You can stop reading now if you select choice number one.

⩔ In France, a person may not carry any object that can be used as a weapon. That includes France's famous Opinel (shown here amidst a picnic lunch) or Laguiole knives, which are national icons and are in the pockets of every third Frenchman.

⩓ The author uses a CRKT M-16 to deconstruct part of an abandoned house in Huescar, Spain.

U.K. laws dictate that a person must have a reason to have a knife, such as being a carpenter. Locking folders are not allowed. Bushcrafters carrying fixed blades while on the way to do some bushcraft seem to get a pass. From top to bottom are the Spyderco Bushcraft, Condor Tool & Knife Bushcraft, Morakniv Garberg, Fällkniven F1, a Bud Nealy Cave Bear and an ESEE DPX H.E.S.T. knife.

ML (my wife and companion of many adventures) and I always travel in Europe (and everyplace else) with knives, carrying at least two each, and often more. We frequently rent holiday apartments and live for a month or so in various places where we shop, cook and settle in to experience local life. The kitchens in those apartments never have usable knives.

A NEED FOR KNIVES

We also teach survival and bushcraft classes during which we make shelters, primitive tools and so on. During the past year I've been attacked twice by feral dog packs in the Balkans. On one occasion I had no stick and my knife was my only defense. Often I'm toting a half-dozen or so knives that I'm reviewing for various publications. We need our knives.

Many Americans we meet traveling in Europe also need their knives, the ones who have knives. In addition to the practical everyday uses of a knife and its indispensable use in disasters, a blade can provide steely comfort in a dark and lonely place, and not only from dog packs.

A young American woman, a solo world traveler I wrote about in my recent book, *Essential Survival*

Gear, used her J.A. Henckels paring knife for daily camp chores while hiking in coastal mountains in Turkey, and was glad to have her little blade one night when a crowd of drunken men made her very uncomfortable.

A retired American who I met in Romania used his Benchmade 710 to cut the fuel line on his BMW motorcycle while doing some repairs, and for frequent picnics, and one dark night to confront two muggers, who then decided to find easier prey. Potentially violent incidents like this are rare. Europe in general is safe for travelers, arguably more so than in the Unites States. But hey, you never know.

So how do I and other folks travel in and through European countries with knives and not run afoul of the law? We do so by using common sense and being sensible in our selection of knives, and by not doing stupid things such as going to a sketchy bar, getting drunk, hitting on a local girl, and when her boyfriend, also drunk, forcefully objects, waving a knife around and threatening him.

In Spain I saw three guys passing a bottle of wine and a folding knife around, cutting bread and cheese while picnicking at the beach. It was all good, except they were talking loudly, arguing with each other and annoying the folks around them. When one fellow politely objected to their behavior, one of the idiots grabbed the knife, shook it at the follow and yelled, "Allahu Akbar!" Then he collapsed laughing, as did his friends.

This incident didn't end well. Personal demeanor, behavior and appearance affect how a person is perceived and treated by security people, and everyone else.

As to knife selection, attitudes in Western Europe regarding knives and security have changed considerably in recent years due to many terrorist attacks, some of which have been carried out with knives. As a consequence, although not yet common, there are security checks in some Western European train and bus stations, and of course in all airports.

ZOMBIE KILLER IS OVERKILL

We've never encountered a security check at an Eastern European train or bus station. If you encounter one of these security checks and have a black, 10-inch blade with "Zombie Killer" etched in steel and stuffed into your waistband, it will not endear you to the security people.

When ML and I travel, in Western Europe or elsewhere, we each always have a tiny folder with a locking blade of about 2 inches on our persons and

Ideal travel knife attributes include minimum size and maximum strength, like these bulldogs, from left to right: the Zero Tolerance Les George 0900, DPX H.E.A.T and Spyderco Li'l Lion.

a small fixed blade in our bags. These knives look inoffensive and have caused no alarms with security people, or anyone else. Probably folders with blades a bit larger, single blade or multi-bladed, such as small Swiss Army Knives, would also be seen as inoffensive.

Most regulations address carrying a knife on the person, with knives in bags being considered differently. Security people also seem to see a difference between carrying on your person and in a bag. Maybe not in all instances, but this has been our experience. I've never seen a knife in a day bag with bread and cheese and other picnic things, whether my knife or someone else's, cause scrutiny.

Our tiny folders are for everyday tasks, sometimes including food preparation when we don't care

The author's picnic basket was filled with goodies, including a plastic fork and spoon banded to the sheath of a Fred Perrin Street Beat, the latter for cutting cheese and sausage.

to get out our fixed blades. ML can girdle a baguette and reduce it to slices in less than a minute with her Spyderco Cricket. My Spyderco Dragonfly will slice salami, cheese, tomatoes and so on about as well as my fixed blade. They will also serve in an emergency, if you know what you're doing.

These little folders and others in the same size range or a bit larger are convenient everyday carry knives. We use the fixed blades in our kitchens, for field work and in emergency situations. I also carry a small red-handle Swiss Army Knife (SAK) with a locking main blade and the all-important corkscrew. We add to this selection if needed, say, a machete in the tropics.

Our day bags are also our ready bags, or bug-out bags, and are always with us. Our fixed blades have much daily utility and will serve in an emergency, such as having to cut through a locked steel fire door to escape a high-rise fire, serve as a climbing aid to escape freezing water, or fend off a pack of feral dogs. I've done all of these things and know that, if needed, our fixed blades will provide us with a measure of protection.

We've only ever been questioned about our knives during a few security checks. Before boarding a high-speed train in Barcelona, we put our bags through the X-ray machine and walked through the metal detector. One of the security officers asked if I had a knife. I said I did. He asked to see it. I first took out my Spyderco Dragonfly, intending to next get my Fallkniven F1 out of my bag. The security guy looked at the little Dragonfly, smiled, and said, "Oh never mind. It's so little. Just put it back in your pocket." He waved us through and said nothing about my F1, or ML's Sypderco Cricket and Fred Perrin Street Beat.

Clearly, he made his evaluation based on our appearance and behavior, as well as our choice of knives. On another occasion, while disembarking from a bus in Lyon, France, we encountered an intensive security check due to an alert that a terrorist suspect might be on our bus. Results were the same as in Barcelona, as they have been on other occasions. European police, like American police, evaluate the person and the situation when making a decision. We do not appear to be a threat, nor do our knives. When asked, we give a straightforward explanation of why we have knives, and have had no problems.

LAX EASTERN ATTITUDES

In Eastern Europe, the Balkans and Turkey,

attitudes concerning knives are very different. Full-size tactical folders are popular for everyday carry, and no one seems alarmed by them. Fixed blades that are 6 to 10 inches long are preferred for field activities, hunting, backpacking and so on, and for use in villages to do everyday village things, such as killing pigs and goats.

I asked a friend, who is a Bulgarian undercover cop, what the laws were governing carrying knives in Bulgaria, and what the police attitude was. I also explained the regulations in Western Europe. He said, "We don't concern ourselves with such silly things as that. We don't care what kind of knife you have. But, if someone attacks and harms another person with a knife, or any weapon, then we do care." A former Czech special forces officer now in a civilian security service said much the same thing.

We've only been questioned about knives in the East once, at Ataturk Airport in Istanbul. Going through first layer security at the entrance to the airport, I tossed a bag on the counter containing a kindjal, a yatagan, a 10-inch bowie, and a half-dozen or so tactical folders and fixed-blade survival knives, all for field work and photography for articles and books.

The security guy said, "You have quite a few knives in your bag."

"Yes," I replied, "I do."

"You're going to check them, not carry them on, right?"

"Of course."

"Have a nice day."

Obviously we check all knives before boarding a commercial aircraft.

When dealing with police or security people, be polite. Your attitude will have a great deal to do with how you are treated. Select knives that are not likely to alarm people, such as those in this article. Avoid black blades – even if the black coating is only meant to protect it from corrosion. Black blades just look like weapons to some people, rather than tools.

If you like to drink and hang out in sketchy

Some full-size tactical folders often seen in Eastern Europe include, from top to bottom, the Spyderco Military model, Benchmade 710 and ZT Knives 350.

bars and clubs, leave your knife in your room. Don't try to use your knife as a weapon, except in extreme circumstances when your own life is actually at stake. Doing so is considered lethal force everywhere, and you will have to defend your actions.

Again, use common sense. You have an internal compass that points in the right direction. Pay attention to it. This approach has worked for us. Your results may vary. No guarantee is offered or implied.

Before your trip, use the Internet to locate knife shows. There are many all over Europe. Attend one. Perhaps visit one of the famous knife-producing towns: Thiers, France; Solingen, Germany; and Maniago, Italy. You'll meet friendly people with a common interest.

Do go. You'll have a great time. Bon voyage. □

In Eastern Europe, the Balkans and Turkey, full-size tactical folders such as the ZT Knives 0452CF Sinkevich are popular for everyday carry and no one seems alarmed by them.

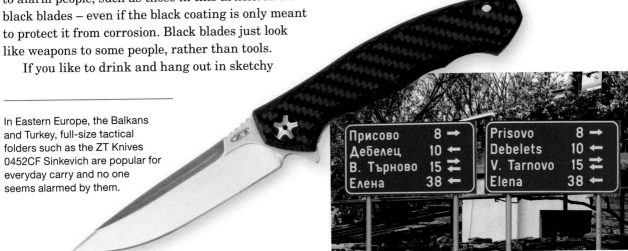

Eye-Popping Edges

New alloys open the door to an explosion of color

By Pat Covert

Heat coloring knives has been popular for decades, especially with the advent of anodizing titanium and aluminum handles. Damascus and mokume gane together make for a pleasing package as well. Nothing to date, however, compares to the eye-shattering brilliance of new alloys in knives.

In the knife world, titanium has been at the forefront of space-age metals for well over two decades, due in great part to the boom in the tactical knife genre borne out of the first Gulf War in the early 1990s. Titanium was originally used in the U.S. space program for its weight savings and toughness, and from there bled into military programs for the very same characteristics.

Titanium is also nonmagnetic, proving useful in certain applications. While tough, titanium is softer than steel, and although some knifemakers have used it as blade material, it never quite caught fire like the new exotic stainless steels that dominate the upper end of the market today. Aluminum is also nonmagnetic and anodizes quite well, but it gets little respect in the knife industry because as an extremely soft metal it's considered an inexpensive alternative to titanium.

Titanium is a reactive metal—its characteristics can be changed by outside influences. Heat-treating knife handles or dipping them into an electrolyte solution that has been both positively and negatively charged color enhances the metallic surface. The amount of heat or electric charging can be varied by the amount of direct heat or voltage applied, and this determines the color hue that the metal takes.

Titanium is the common bond of two more metallurgical advances that have raised the bar on the color equation. Forging titanium with zirconium—itself an extremely tough metal that is finding popularity in custom knives today—results in a patterned alloy known as Zircu-Ti. Titanium can also be blended with nickel (TiNi) to achieve an alloy much harder than any form of steel. A side benefit is

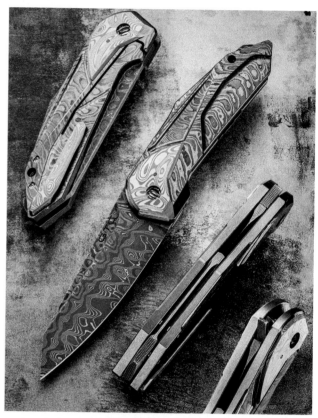

Gus Cecchini celebrated 10 years of knifemaking with this exquisite folder. His Stampede model integral-lock folder features the maker's SLT spring-loaded flipper mechanism integrated into a Chad Nichols Zircu-Ti handle with Damasteel inlays. The blade is Nichols' "blackout" pattern stainless damascus. *(SharpByCoop image)*

the eye-popping colors of TiNi and Zurcu-Ti.

Avid knife enthusiasts have become familiar with Timascus (titanium damascus) and Moku-Ti (titanium mokume, achieved by fusing two titanium alloys). More recently, Zircu-Ti has gained exposure because it is tough, and thus more expensive, appealing to those who want the absolute best. Colored via electric currents just like titanium, a hard black coating can also be achieved using zirconium, which, by itself, is so hard that it does not have the spring necessary for folding knife leaf locks that titanium does. Some knifemakers get around this by adding separate titanium leaf locks to the frames of folding knives.

COLOR CREDIT WHERE DUE

Most credit knifemaker Tom Ferry and Alpha Knife Supply's Jon Walker for blending two metals to create Timascus more than 15 years ago, and marketing it under the trademarked name "Black Timascus." Today Timascus sales are better than ever, and Alpha Knife Supply also remains a popular source for zirconium.

One of the top suppliers of damascus to the U.S. market, Chad Nichols trademarked the name "Zircu-Ti," which he details as a pattern-welded blend of zirconium with 6AL-4V and CP titanium alloys. Acknowledging the expense of the material, Nichols says the process of making Zircu-Ti is more complicated and error-ridden than that of forging pattern-welded, or damascus, steel. At $100 a pound, zirconium costs considerably more than titanium.

Custom knifemaker Darrel Ralph, who employs quite a bit of zirconium and Zircu-Ti on his high-end knives, suggests the use of either adds approximately 30 percent to the overall price of a knife. Working the incredibly tough zirconium and Zircu-Ti is intensive in nature, increasing the time it takes to make a knife.

Unlike zirconium, Zircu-Ti exhibits enough spring memory for use as locking-leaf material, so building true Zircu-Ti integral-lock folders is not a problem. And is it ever being used! Many of the hottest knifemakers on the planet fashion Zircu-Ti and Moku-Ti folders parading a rainbow of brilliant, unadulterated colors.

Blades incorporating zirconium and titanium are a rare breed, but according to custom knifemaker Brian Tighe, Alpha Knife Supply has made strides in this area. Walker has come up with a laminated san mai-style material with a center core of Beta C titanium and outer layers of zirconium. Brian, who refers to it as "composite layered Beta C titanium," has successfully used the laminate for folding knife blades. Building the knives with Timascus handle frames, he uses heat coloring to

⌃ Knifemaker Ron Best makes some exquisite eye-burners, like his Phaze integral-lock folder with an Alpha Knife Supply Timascus frame in a "Moire" pattern, and beautiful mother-of-pearl inlays. *(SharpByCoop image)*

⌄ The business half of R.J. Martin's Transfusion integral-lock folder is a Chad Nichols damascus blade, while a Nichols "crosswalk"-pattern Moku-Ti handle frame and pocket clip do the second-half honors. *(SharpByCoop image)*

⌃ The Dominator integral-lock folder is one of knifemaker Darrel Ralph's most popular models. Here we see it in blazing blues with reds and oranges thrown in for contrast. Darrel recommends direct flame for the best effect. *(Jim Skelton image)*

⌄ This custom Duane Dwyer Strider SMF model encapsulates the trend in eye-popping color. The blade is brightly heat colored SM-100 (HIPTiNite) and the frame is made up of Moku-Ti in blues and purples with toned-down steps in a deep gray. *(Brady Miller image)*

match the blades and grips with striking results. Brian further notes that the hybrid zirconium and titanium blade laminate is nonmagnetic but doesn't work well with locking liners or integral locks. It does, however, work well with his button lock, flipper and auto folders.

All of the high-tech patterned metals can be colored using either direct flame or the positive/negative electrolyte process. I asked custom knife guru par excellence Darrel Ralph if one method was better than the other, and he intimated that, while both processes work, he gets the best results using direct flame. So there you have it ... flame on!

Steel, in both high carbon and stainless forms, has been the overwhelming choice for knife blades for centuries. By its very nature steel is a rather dull material unless highly polished or given a satin finish. For pure aesthetics, damascus adds a tremendous amount of eye appeal to a knife, and some custom knifemakers have goosed it up to another level by bluing and heat-treating the pattern-welded steel. The techniques, however, can only take the color process so far.

ENTER SM-100

Enter SM-100, a titanium and nickel alloy that is not only harder than any steel known to man, it has the ability to be heat treated to produce brilliant colors. Nitinol, also referred to as "Ni-Ti-Nol," was first discovered back in 1959 by scientists William Buehler and Frederic Wang at the Naval Ordnance Laboratory. The Ni-Ti-Nol acronym stands for "Nickel-Titanium-Naval Ordnance Laboratory."

Beuhler and Wang were searching for a super-elastic alloy for missile nose cones that would be pliable at extreme heat, yet return to its original shape after cooling. Their efforts were a success, but because the incredibly tough alloy was so difficult to process and machine, it wasn't used until much later.

Custom knifemaker Duane Dwyer of Strider Knives became interested in Nitinol back in 2005 while searching for a super hard metal alloy that would not rust. He approached metallurgist and friend Scott Devanna, vice president of technology at SB Specialty Metals, and inquired about the possibility of producing Nitinol using the particle metallurgy process, which had never been done. Shortly afterwards Devanna introduced Dwyer to Eric Bono, a metallurgist and knifemaker who also had an interest in the alloy, and the three men began to explore the possibilities of incorporating the alloy into knives.

With his metallurgical knowledge and experience, Bono developed a working, powdered metal version of the alloy in 2006, which the partners dubbed "SM-100." It took several more years to refine the alloy and processes, and in 2009, Bono and business partner Fred Yolton formed a company, Summit Metals LLC, to produce SM-100. Since that time, SM-100

⌄ An Eric Bono SM-100 fixed blade is heavily heat treated to bring out the wild colors lurking within. Eric covers the SM-100 in foil and pokes holes in it to allow different areas to oxidize at different rates under heat.

⌃ Duane Dwyer of Strider Knives was the main force behind SM-100 (HIPTiNite), and his signed custom Strider MT2 showcases a brilliantly heat-treated SM-100 blade mated to machined carbon fiber handle scales.
(Brady Miller image)

(60 percent nickel and 40 percent titanium), which the company markets under the name "HIPTiNite," has garnered interest not only in the knife industry, but by NASA and the Formula 1 racing industry.

The SM-100 brand of Nitinol, like its forerunner, is extremely tough. While a typical sanding belt can be used to grind several typical, mono-steel knife blades, it requires several belts, in many cases six or more, for the same process using the SM-100 alloy. Made and sold in small quantities, the cost of SM-100 isn't cheap. Add to that the cost of belts and additional time to shape and grind the material, and the cost per knife skyrockets. On the positive side, SM-100 is noncorrosive, and while stainless steel will rust, Devanna says you can throw an SM-100 knife into saltwater for 50 years without the steel corroding.

Bono discovered during his development of SM-100 that it can be heat colored into an exquisite rainbow of colors. Due to the titanium content, SM-100 oxidizes into a blaze of bright hues just like other alloys incorporating titanium, but the process of achieving the color effects is quite different.

MAKING MAGIC

Bono confides that the magic happens during the heat-treating process, in which he allows small pockets of air to leak onto the surface of the knife. Prior to heat treating, the blades are wrapped in foil and small holes are punched into the wrapping. When heat treated, different colors occur depending on the oxygen content of certain areas of the blade steel as the surface oxidizes. The end result is the explosion of color on the SM-100 blades.

The price for bright, eye-popping colors doesn't come cheap, but then new innovations rarely do. The cobalt-alloy Talonite and Stellite blades that Ralph, David Boye and Rob Simonich offered in the early 2000s came with higher prices as well, typically adding anywhere from $75-$100 per knife. Today, the exotic alloys still command premium price points. Damascus was much more expensive before knifemakers had so many choices of pattern-welded steel. Damascus remains expensive, and highly intricate patterns with figurative elements go for a pretty penny.

On the other hand, the high prices of particle metallurgical and powdered stainless steels drop

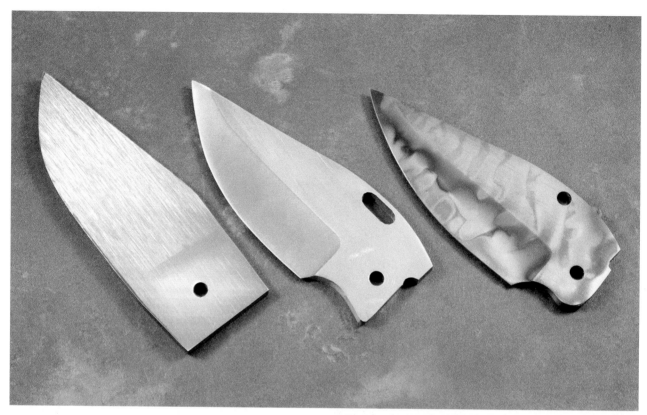

The three basic stages of making an SM-100 folder blade include, from left to right: a blade blank cut out of SM-100 stock, a blade ground and finished, and a blade after heat treating it in foil.

appreciably as output due to demand increases, and as they are replaced by the "latest, greatest steels." Though Crucible Industries blades commanded much higher prices in their infancy, it's not uncommon to see factory knives with high-tech CPM S30V blades today. Even titanium, once considered the créme de la créme of handle materials, is now common and somewhat passé on factory knives.

As long as zirconium commands a high price per pound, the Zircu-Ti patterned alloys will most likely add greatly to the cost of knives. And until the demand for SM-100 (or a like alloy) becomes high enough to increase production levels, it will remain expensive, particularly when the cost and time of working the alloy is added. With that said, there will always be a market for high-end knives, so look for more eye-popping knives like the ones pictured here. Sit back and enjoy the fireworks! □

Ron Best's Model P-51 drop-point TNT-pattern Damasteel wonder is a tour de force of color. The integral frame is sculpted from Alpha Knife Supply's "kaleidoscope" Timascus and parades mother-of-pearl inlays. *(SharpByCoop image)*

Tactical Folder Collaborations Keep Rolling

The tactical train chugs down the track, picking up steam and putting out smoke

By Dexter Ewing

The continuous influx of tactical folders onto the knife market is 20 years running now and still going strong. This sector of the industry is fueled by the designs of custom knifemakers and their subsequent collaborations with manufacturers, both pushing to use the latest in materials, mechanisms, locks and openers.

Every year it seems that new, innovative tactical designs hit the knife circuit running. Companies are constantly on the lookout for fresh talent to add to their design teams, and the knives of a few select makers stand out in a sea of folding blades. Manufacturers want to capture the essence of high-tech, innovative folders and introduce them for mass production.

A Ken Onion design, the CRKT Homefront can be completely disassembled, without tools, in the field for ease of cleaning and maintenance.

FIELD STRIP FOLDER

CRKT has a longstanding tradition of working with a variety of custom knifemakers and designers to bring forth a diverse product line that includes something for everyone. Ken Onion is a known entity in the industry—a prolific knifemaker and designer—and now CRKT and Onion have teamed up to bring forth the Homefront tactical folder.

The Homefront can be completely disassembled, without tools, in the field for ease of cleaning and maintenance. "For a long time Ken has been kicking around the concept of a folder that could be easily disassembled, cleaned and assembled in the field," says Robin Leong, vice president of engineering and new product development for CRKT.

Thus, the patent-pending Field Strip technology was born. Leong says the parameters in place since the beginning were that there should be no small, loose components that could be easily lost, and no tools needed to break the folder down or put it back together.

"There are only three major components [two handle halves and a blade] that are easily separated and cleaned," Leong notes.

How is the Homefront taken apart completely,

without tools, anywhere in the field? A locking lever is conveniently located by the large, black stone-washed pivot bolt, and a notched tightening wheel at the butt of the handle near the spacer. By releasing the locking lever and turning the notched wheel, the entire knife breaks apart easily, and the folder is reassembled by reversing the procedure.

"Field Strip is an out-of-the-box innovation in the knife industry and will define a category for folders," declares Leong.

The Homefront features a 3.5-inch, modified spear-point AUS-8 stainless steel blade and a flipper mechanism for quick and easy deployment. Fullers on both sides of the blade and a green, hard-coat-anodized T6-6061 aircraft-grade aluminum handle give it a military look and feel. The folder also sports a sturdy, deep-seating pocket clip for tip-up carry.

"CRKT is known for design and innovation, and Ken's Field Strip concept fits in well," Leong concludes. "Working with an amazing custom knife designer like Ken is in an honor for me and CRKT."

RAZOR SHARP EDGE

Danish knifemaker Jens Anso is gaining recognition in production knife circles, having current collaborations with Spyderco and Boker. And now Zero Tolerance can be added to that list, as Anso and ZT have brought forth the ZT 0220.

"Jens realized a longtime dream when he joined the ZT team. He has been working toward that end for a number of years," says Thomas Welk, director of sales and marketing for ZT Knives and Kai USA. "And we are excited to have him on board."

Welk says Jens is a thinker. "He never just goes off on a design without thoroughly thinking through all of the various aspects of the project before sending it to us," he states.

Another of the maker's strengths is his profi-ciency with design software and the ability to create the proper files required for ZT's production setting.

Such forethought in design and proficiency with software has yielded the sleek and practical Model ZT 0220 tactical folder. Starting with a CPM S35V modified drop-point blade, Anso gave it a slightly re-curved edge and a reinforced tip for durability.

"The high-quality powdered metallurgical steel is tough, wear resistant and resists chipping," interjects Welk. "Additional niobium and vanadium carbides enable us to sharpen the 0220 to a razor-sharp edge with enhanced edge retention."

A stonewashed finish seals all of the pores in the steel and does a great job at masking scratches that occur from regular use. The frame-lock folder showcases a titanium handle with a hardened steel insert to bolster the strength of the lock bar.

"Opening the blade is easy with our KVT ball bearing opening system," Welk says. The blade literally glides out of the handle quickly and effortlessly.

Known for highly functional and aesthetically pleasing designs, Anso's visual flair includes a ZT medallion inlaid in the nonlock side of the blade near the butt, as well as an orange anodized aluminum spacer that adds just the right pop of color to the otherwise gray-looking knife.

"All of it fits handsomely within the straightforward profile of the knife," Welk remarks. He also hints at the fact that there will definitely be more Anso-designed ZT knives to come in the future. Anso set the bar very high with the ZT 0220, and enthusiasts can't wait to see what the dynamic duo of Jens and ZT Knives will come up with next!

HIGHLY CHARGED POSITRON

"Brad Southard and Spyderco met when he began to visit our retail store regularly," says Joyce Laituri, public and media relations manager for Spyderco.

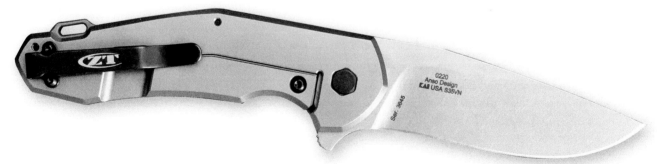

The ZT 0220 is Zero Tolerance's first collaboration with Danish knifemaker Jens Anso. It has all of the hallmarks of a modern tactical flipper folder, including a CPM S35VN blade, titanium handle, frame lock, deep-carry pocket clip and a contrasting orange-anodized aluminum handle spacer.

"He would come into the store and talk knives with our crew. He is an industrial designer, and at the time, was just a budding custom knifemaker."

It was from these modest beginnings that Spyderco began to collaborate with the young knifemaker, resulting in the company's first flipper folder, the Southard.

"Southard's second collaboration with Spyderco is a design based on his custom Ion model. We call it the Positron," explains Laituri. The Positron is more sleek and compact than the Southard Folder, featuring a flipper-only opening feature.

"This is the first folder in Spyderco's product line that relies solely on a flipper mechanism for opening," says Laituri. As with any Spyderco folder, a blade hole is present, but in the Positron's case, the hole is there solely for cosmetic purposes and is too small to function as a blade opening device, as many of the blade holes do in Spyderco's other folders.

The Positron's modified drop point blade measures a bit over 3 inches in length and is flat ground from CPM S30V stainless steel for the ultimate in edge holding and corrosion resistance. It is given a nice tumbled finish to help seal the pores of the steel.

"The handle scales are solid carbon fiber that have been machined, radiused and polished for a comfortable grip and an elegant appearance," Laituri explains. A stylish wire pocket clip, another of Spyderco's innovations, promotes ambidextrous (mounted on the left or right side of the handle) tip-up carry. Under the carbon fiber handle scales are skeletonized steel liners that add rigidity to the frame and form a LinerLock to secure the blade in the open position.

"To ensure smooth opening action, the Positron's blade rides on a ball bearing pivot system," begins Laituri. "Rather than conventional flat washers, the blade pivots between special washers that contain nested ball bearings. This construction reduces friction on the blade, maximizes the efficiency of the flipper mechanism and lays the groundwork for a long service life."

The Shane Sibert-designed Arvensis is a formidable tactical fixed blade.

What all of this translates into is the Positron being one of the smoothest Spyderco folders out of the box. The blade deploys quickly and effortlessly with a tug on the exposed flipper. "Spyderco credits the development of the flipper to knifemaker Kit Carson. Brad includes this feature on many of his custom pieces and it was part of our product version as well," explains Laituri.

STOUT AND OVERBUILT

While Benchmade is best known for its Axis Lock folders, the company makes equally stout fixed blades, like the Shane Sibert-designed model 119 Arvensis, definitely among the largest fixed blades in the Benchmade line.

"In typical fashion with any Shane Sibert collaboration, the 119 Arvensis is stout and overbuilt, similar to the 162 Bushcrafter or the Adamas family of knives that were previous collaborations with Sibert," says Derrick Lau, public relations and communications manager for Benchmade Knife Co.

A hair shy of 12 inches long, the Arvensis strikes an imposing profile with its clip-point blade, pronounced swedge along the spine, and ergonomic G-10 handle – including three titanium handle and thong tubes, a hallmark of Sibert's custom fixed blades.

"The Arvensis features a .193-inch-thick 154CM blade that combines durability and ease of sharpening in the field," Lau points out. The titanium tubes pressed into the handle not only affix the G-10 scales to the tang, but also allow for lashing the knife to a tree branch for use as a survival spear.

"The Arvensis comes with a black Boltaron® sheath with two points of retention that include a pressure-fit point and a retention strap," Lau explains. Similar in composition to Kydex, Boltaron® is thermally stable when exposed to extreme temperatures and is a highly durable material, making it a great choice for sheath material.

"Of all the designers Benchmade collaborates with, Shane Sibert happens to be the only Oregon-based designer," Lau mentions. "Being geographically close to Benchmade headquarters, Sibert can easily visit and meet with Benchmade's engineer team, as well as keep abreast of manufacturing enhancements in the factory."

Furthermore, Lau summarizes, "Sibert's dedication to practicality in design complements Benchmade's Black Class products." The 119 Arvensis is classified as a Black Class (law enforcement/military) product in the Benchmade line and comes in plain edge and partially serrated edge formats, as well as tumbled or black coated blade finishes.

SEXY DESIGN

Hogue Knives is a relative newcomer to the knife industry, but the company has already made a big mark and gained a following with folders designed by Allen Elishewitz. Having several models already in production, this dynamic duo's latest, the X5, is really starting to turn some heads with its sexy design, high-end materials and size and blade shape options.

Modeled after Elishewitz's custom Black Swan (the Wharncliffe blade shape option) and White Dolphin (spear point) custom folders, it's interesting to note that the names actually are derived from two of Russia's toughest prisons!

"Depending on blade selection, the knife can look sweepingly elegant or radically crafted," says Jim Bruhns, president of Hogue Knives. "The ergonomic shape blends nicely into a tight grip where the shape [of the handle] tells the hand where to purchase with complete consistency." It is a very ergonomic handle with all of the curves in the right places, indexing one's grip perfectly each and every time.

"Allen always starts with a set of features that must be honored throughout all aspects of the final product," states Bruhns. "We do our best to guarantee that vision in our production version."

The X5 is as strong as it looks, including a hardened ¼-inch stainless steel pivot bolt and 5/16-inch-diameter button lock mechanism that ensure rock-solid lockup and smooth action every time. The flipper folder boasts a special, patent pending detent system that holds the blade securely in the closed position, but also aids in fast one-hand opening through load pressure on the pivot that, when pressing the flipper mechanism to overcome the detent, causes the blade to rotate out and lock open smoothly and quickly.

"The X5 has a new patent pending design that combines a special springboard and traditional ball detent," Bruhns explains. "The design also includes a ball detent relief channel [in the tang of the blade] so that the springboard is quickly neutralized as a drag element on the blade during deployment."

The ball detent doesn't make contact when opening the blade, but rather drops into a recessed channel, greatly reducing resistance and allowing for fast and smooth opening. The X5 is offered in 3½-inch and 4-inch CPM 154 stainless steel Wharncliffe and spear-point blades, and T6-6061 aluminum handle scales with textured "G-Mascus" inlays for increased hand purchase.

"Allen has done most everything that the rest of the knife community is still working on," comments Bruhns. "His guidance has kept us on track and enlightened our thinking along the way." And considering the cost of Elishewitz's custom knives, the X5, available from select retailers, is a great deal! □

The Hogue X5 is a unique Allen Elishewitz design—a button-lock flipper folder that comes in an aluminum handle, and a choice of two sizes and shapes of CPM 154 blades.

TRENDS

From big, beefy tactical folders with black coatings, gray handles, double-ground blades and Herculean locks to "Little Utility Knives & Folders." That's what's trending now, the utilitarian aspect of knives. "Chef, Sushi, Steak & Veggie Knives" are hot commodities, as are "Foxy Flippers," "Flawless Fossil Walrus" ivory, bowies, "No Drag Dags," "Burled Barehanders," "Top-Tier Tantos" and "Desert Warriors."

What's new is what's back again—how about ring-guard bowies and daggers, split-ring daggers and D-guard bowies making a comeback, as did fantasy knives? I mean, did you ever think fantasy knives would be back with a vengeance? Me either, but I was glad to see several of their kind popping up after asking makers and photographers for images for this *KNIVES 2018* book.

And a Trend that's been trending for the last several years is "Close-Shave Straight Razors." Those came about when people were going back to the basics, around the same time bushcraft blades became popular. By the way, I don't see many of those, and that's a shame, as they're cool knives. I guess that's why they call them Trends, though I'm sure bushcraft knives will be around for a long time to come. □

Folder Refinement

The refined gentleman retires for the evening, slipping into calfskin slippers and silken robe before reclining in his under-stuffed leather chair and unfolding the newspaper. He sips Scotch whiskey and takes stock of the day's events, his accomplishments and unfinished business. It's only then that he allows himself the pleasure of scanning the headlines before landing on an article that holds his attention long enough to delve deeper into the story.

Something stirs him from his reading stupor. It occurred as he shifted his weight in the chair. What was it … something poking gently into his thigh … the folding custom pocketknife? Yes, that's it. What a weekend that turned out to be … a knife show, so many characters, artists, businessmen and blue collar workers alike, all under one roof. It was there he spotted the unremarkable maker of incredibly remarkable pearl-handle locking-liner folders. He wanted one with a gold thumb stud, possibly file worked and inlaid with a diamond, yet there were no such knives on the maker's table.

A gentleman's agreement was reached—he ordered one, paid money down and waited six months. The maker said he could match the titanium liners to the thumb stud, but no mention had been made of a gold chain fob and pearl decoration that trailed off it when he opened the case, an extra touch.

The gentleman sinks deeper into his chair, hand in his pocket fondling the knife. There's no reason to extract the piece. He knows exactly what it looks like, but it's nice to rub the pearl with the forefinger nonetheless. A satisfied sensation envelops him as he drifts off into a Sunday night slumber. □

⌄ TONY MILLER
Mammoth ivory and Devin Thomas twist damascus are assembled just so for a refined locking-liner folder.
(Caleb Royer Studios image)

» DON HANSON III
The gold thumb stud and heat-colored screws help bring out the colors of the antique tortoise shell handle on a folding damascus stiletto.
(Caleb Royer Studios image)

« WILLIAM TUCH
Thank goodness there's blue carbon fiber to match the Devin Thomas damascus, so a gentleman can rest assured it looks as good as it works.
(PointSeven image)

ALAIN and DORIS CHOMILIER

Square sapphires set in carved bronze usually describe a ring, not a knife, but the feather damascus blade lets us know it's more than jewelry.

RAPHAEL DURAND

One might bask in the amber stag and Samuel Lurquin damascus, or simply sever something with the sharp edge.
(SharpByCoop image)

T.R. OVEREYNDER

Her name was black jade and her steely glare laid most gentlemen out.
(PointSeven image)

TOM HEARD

Koi fish and lotus blossoms comingle among the bone handle scales of a 154CM folder done up in damascus bolsters.

GORDON CHARD

The double-action folder is fiercer than the California buckeye burl, blue titanium and mother-of-pearl suggest.

» STEVE MILLER

One wouldn't think jigged bone and Mike Norris stainless damascus, the bolsters blued, could go together so beautifully, but Steve saw it for what it was.

» MEL FASSIO

Gold-lip-pearl handle scales ingratiate themselves to the engraved blade and bolsters, becoming one with them to form a refined pocketknife.

» MICHAEL WALKER

Other makers use Damasteel blades and blued damascus bolsters, but the style reveals it as a Michael Walker LinerLock.

(SharpByCoop image)

» AARON FREDERICK

Copper, Timascus, titanium and damascus, we'd tell him how much we love it if he'd only stop to ask us.

(SharpByCoop image)

» RICK GENOVESE

Nearly every kid dreams of finding a dinosaur bone, an adult fantasy, too, manifesting itself via a lock-back folder in a dinosaur bone grip, Mitch Moschetti engraving and a CPM 154 blade.

《 JOHN GRIFFIN
Mammoth tooth has to be one of the most stunning handle materials, here serving double duty as the button that pops open the damascus blade of a hot little auto folding knife.

《 JEFF CLAIBORNE
The 3⅝-inch Copperhead folder flaunts its mother-of-pearl handle and hand-rubbed 52100 blades like the respectable refined folder that it is.

⩔ ROGER HATT
A Persian-style locking-liner folder makes its presence known in a damascus blade, Chad Nichols bolsters and mammoth ivory handle scales.

⩔ ROSS K. MITSUYUKI
Colorfully engraved bolsters complement the giraffe bone handle scales and lay the groundwork for a Devin Thomas damascus blade.

⩔ CHARLES GEDRAITIS
Start off the day with some Chad Nichols "scrambled eggs damascus" and coffee, awakening your senses to the pearl-inlaid bolsters and Timascus thumb disc. *(SharpByCoop image)*

» LUKE SWENSON

The three blade stag-handle pocketknife is the bomb with or without the shield.
(PointSeven image)

» LARRY NEWTON

The very definition of folder refinement is 10 chocolate diamonds, 14k-gold inlays, blue mammoth ivory, Rob Thomas damascus, and engraving inside and out.
(PointSeven image)

⌃ MILOS KISLINGER

The maker matched up mammoth ivory handle scales and an inlaid pivot screw with Chad Nichols Mokuti bolsters as only an artist could.
(SharpByCoop image)

⌄ SEAN O'HARE

The size of the small Damasteel and mother-of-pearl pocket folder (3 5/8 inches open with a 2 ¾-inch blade) doesn't diminish its stature.

⌄ TIM BRITTON

It takes more than polymer and metal, but also being on one's mettle, to achieve a knife handle such as this, complemented by a BG-42 blade with a delightfully long nail nick. *(PointSeven image)*

MICHAEL RAYMOND

If "drizzle Timascus" doesn't whet your appetite, maybe the curvaceous frame and pointed Crucible 20CV blade will do the trick.

(SharpByCoop image)

LARAMIE JACKSON

"Basketweave damascus" and mother-of-pearl bespeak a certain class of knife.

PETER MARTIN

You've gotta love "lava lamp" san mai damascus, if only for the images it conjures up, here matched with carbon fiber handle scales and jeweled zirconium bolsters.

(Cory Martin Imaging)

MILAN POKORNY

Mokuti makes for a handsome handle and pocket clip on the otherwise damascus folder with cleverly clawed blade.

(Cory Martin Imaging)

» **CONNY PERSSON**
I'm sorry you're feeling blue. Feel this blue and you might fare better. There's a steel mosaic, an explosion along the edge and mammoth within the handle frame.

» **STEVE HILL**
The "Sweethearts" folder is named for the hearts and arrows file work along the back spacer, and not necessarily for the sweet black-lip-pearl handle or damascus blade. *(Chuck Ward image)*

» **RICHARD ROGERS**
A blue suit, one Zircuti necktie and some "Vinland Damasteel," and the tailor can call it a day.
(SharpByCoop image)

⌃ **ANDRE THORBURN**
Gaze at the engraving, and you'll see an owl, lizard, dove and snail, all before feeling the carbon fiber and cutting with the Damasteel blade. *(SharpByCoop image)*

⌃ **BILL DUFF**
Pearl and steel shine bright on a one-hand LinerLock folder.
(Chuck Ward image)

That's a Buncha Bowie!

‹‹ STEVE HILL

Inspiration for the bowie, with fossil walrus ivory handle and 9.25-inch blade, came from the 1837 Rezin Bowie presentation knife made by Daniel Searles and displayed in The Alamo.

‹‹ TIMOTHY POTIER

Touches like a W2 blade with temper line, select Sambar stag handle and nickel silver pommel filed like a sun emitting rays elevate the bowie to new heights. *(Caleb Royer Studios image)*

⌄ MIKE DEIBERT

With a 12.5-inch, clay-hardened 1095 steel blade, it took a length of lumber to handle the piece—screaming hot Oregon maple burl matched up against a damascus guard and pommel. *(Caleb Royer Studios image)*

⌄ DON HANSON III

Bang! Now that's a bowie, belted out in a wavy damascus blade, ancient ivory handle and tapered tang. *(Caleb Royer Studios image)*

⩔ RODRIGO SFREDDO

Gambler bowies come with hearts pierced through their damascus blades, and coffin handles in case one's caught cheating red handed. *(Caleb Royer Studios image)*

» WESS BARNHILL

The wide, clip-point 1084 blade of the Southwest bowie would be menacing if not for the neat-as-a-pin execution and handsome desert ironwood handle. *(SharpByCoop image)*

⩔ GARTH HINDMARCH

Nine inches of slim 440C blade, with swedge along the spine and Spanish notch, jut out from the mesquite burl handle beautifully.

⩕ JOE ZEMITIS

He wrought an iron guard, hammered a high-carbon-damascus blade and cut an Australian burl handle for the Spanish notch bowie.

《 SHAWN ELLIS
The shapely bowie boasts a 1084-and-15N20-damascus blade and an amber stag grip. *(PointSeven image)*

《 LARRY COX
White damascus flames lick the edge of the 16-inch ironwood-handle bowie. *(Ward image)*

⌃ CODY HOFSOMMER
The "laddered W's" damascus blade shows as much character as the Turkish walnut handle, and together they dance in the moonlight. *(Cory Martin Imaging)*

《 STEVE RANDALL
Clean execution and perfect fit and finish define the ironwood handle bowie with lively blade. *(PointSeven image)*

» BILL GREULICH

A foot-long bowie in a coffin-style ebony handle and a 1084 blade cuts the mustard and more.

(SharpByCoop image)

» J. NEILSON

Damascus extends from the 10-inch blade to the S-guard and clear across the stag handle onto the pommel of the piece. *(Ward image)*

» SAMUEL LURQUIN

Voted 2015 Best Bowie by BladeForums readers, the temper line is as wispy as the blade is straight, the clip pronounced and the grip good.

(SharpByCoop image)

» ED BRANDSEY

Turquoise dots the ironwood handle, steel guard, spacers and damascus blade, all complemented by a fringed rawhide sheath adorned with an Indianhead nickel, arrowhead and beads. *(Cory Martin Imaging)*

⌃ CALEB WHITE

With bog oak and leather grip, and hammer marks adorning the face of the forged and copper washed 5150 blade, the bowie looks as tough as it is.

» **JIM POLING**

A frame-handle bowie is done up in rosewood, copper and a well-executed ladder-pattern damascus blade. *(Caleb Royer Studios image)*

« **JEREMY SPAKE**

He smelted something, and it turned out to be a wootz/crucible steel bowie blade, later clay quenched to achieve a hamon, or temper line, to which he added a stellar sea cow rib handle.

« **TOSHIAKI MICHINAKA**

The stag-handle bowie is historically rendered and executed in exacting detail. *(PointSeven image)*

« **KEVIN CASHEN**

Fossil walrus ivory is the clean counterpart to the 9.125-inch 1095 bowie blade.

« **J.W. RANDALL**

"Texas wind damascus" blows across the fighter blade, the edge interrupted only by a Spanish notch, and breezes over an ancient ivory coffin-style grip. *(Tammy Randall image)*

» CHUN-WEI CHANG

The stabilized wood handle is made to grip, the stainless shell guard to embellish and protect, and the differentially heat-treated 1084 blade to cut with abandon.
(SharpByCoop image)

» MIKE CRADDOCK

Mammoth ivory handle scales cover the black Micarta frame of a fine damascus bowie.
(SharpByCoop image)

» CAS/CLAUDIO SOBRAL

The clamshell bowie and auto folder matching set is highlighted by tightly patterned, clip-point damascus blades and red deer stag grips. *(SharpByCoop image)*

⋙ RICK "BEAR BONE" SMITH

The perfect size to wear discreetly on the belt or in a boot, the scaled-down coffin-style bowie enlists a faux-ivory-Micarta handle, nickel silver guard and ATS-34 stainless steel blade.

» SPENCER CLARK
The temper line on the W2 blade dips down live lava flowing from a crater, and the ironwood handle dips right in, too. *(Ward image)*

⩔ RAYMON HUNT
Feel free to point the 1075 and buckeye burl bowie in any direction. *(Ward image)*

⩔ TOM WARD
The 1095-and-15N20 damascus bowie, with fists-like guard, will pump you up, especially considering the curvy stabilized maple grip. She's a looker. *(SharpByCoop image)*

⩔ LIN RHEA
Bowies in blackwood and damascus appeal to the masses. *(Ward image)*

⩔ DAVE SKINNER
Domed 303 stainless steel pins secure the African blackwood and Rhodesian teak handle to the aluminum Formica liners and 1070 high carbon steel blade. *(Dirk Loots Photography)*

Flawless Fossil Walrus

The no-flaw clause is actually in workmanship more than written within the fossil walrus ivory itself. Flawless fossil walrus wouldn't be any fun at all. Such pristine ivory of ancient walruses (or is it walri?) would have little character, color or texture. There would be nothing to catch the eye, just a solid material, albeit creamy, milky or buttery in appearance, but plain and uninterrupted.

Like a person with plenty of character in the face, unique, individual traits are the ones that stand out, the quirky imperfections and unusual features. Expressiveness is a gift. And character flaws are often misjudged as weaknesses when, in reality, they can often be strengths. Being interesting is a nice icebreaker at parties, one that finds inquisitive folk gathered around asking questions and running for refreshments.

The fossil walrus ivory knife handles herein have been known to draw a crowd. They're pleasers, whether because of their outer beauty or timeless imperfections, the worm holes, surface blemishes, age lines or external oxidation.

No, the walrus is not a pretty face, but a distinctive, ugly mug with enough wrinkles and whiskers to elicit curious onlookers and interested parties. The execution of the fossil walrus ivory, adapting it to knife handles, is the flawless part. The rest is just inbred character flaws worn like bulging badges of honor. □

« BRUCE BARNETT
A little san mai steel and some walrus ivory, and you're smitten, aren't you?
(PointSeven image)

⌃ BRUCE FULLER
A gentleman's bird knife flaunts its fossil walrus ivory tail and radial ribbon damascus beak.
(PointSeven image)

⌄ JOHN COHEA
A copper nugget hides in the cavity of a walrus ivory artifact handle, complemented by a patterned copper band and defended by a Chad Nichols "lizard skin damascus" blade.
(Caleb Royer Studios image)

DAVID LISCH

"Feather River damascus" and fossil walrus ivory converge on a damascus split-ring bowie and make a big splash. *(PointSeven image)*

« DON HANSON III

A choice slab of fossil walrus ivory is well suited to the grip of a pattern-welded folder with mosaic damascus bolsters and selectively heat-colored titanium liners.

(Cory Martin Imaging)

« BRION TOMBERLIN

The "Nagabowie" is a mega bowie, with curves that never stop, from the tip of the 1075 blade, complete with smoky temper line, to the butt of the fossil walrus ivory grip.

(Caleb Royer Studios image)

J.P. Miller

The cracks, divot and jagged butt end of the fossil walrus ivory make it palpable and real, enough to hold its own against the sweeping 1095 blade and elongated S-guard. *(PointSeven image)*

BILL BURKE

Walrus ivory was an inspired choice for the harpoon-point damascus bowie, given its color, character and curves.

(PointSeven image)

Little Utility Knives

» ANDY ROY

The maker "spalted" the A2 blade as one would burl, giving the tapered-tang fixed blade natural canvas Micarta bolsters, pins and liners, and a blackwood handle overlay, and calling it the "Monarch" because it's a flitting, layered butterfly that's fit for a king.

» BRIAN GOODE

For his "Luck On Your Side" pattern, the maker infuses koa wood with a blackened blade, which can only bring good luck.

» JORDAN LAMOTHE

Look closely at the utility knife, and you'll see not only walnut handle scales, but a hard maple spacer, a maple frame, file work and freshness.

(SharpByCoop image)

⩘ RICHARD ORTON

Exemplifying that the beauty of a knife can be as much in its utility as its aesthetics is this brown-jigged-bone-handle Wharncliffe-style fixed blade with mosaic pins.

« CHUCK WARD

Why mess up a sleek, beautiful, clean spear-point A2 utility knife when you can just give it Corian handle scales, mosaic pins, and call it exquisitely executed. *(Ward image)*

» MASON RENFER

As to have a choice of utility knife for the day, one CPM 154 fixed blade sports ivory paper Micarta handle scales with black G-10 liners, and the other a red G-10 handle with blue G-10 liners.

(SharpByCoop image)

ZANE BLACKWELL

A dress everyday carry knife, amber stag sings a sweet tune on the CPM 154 fixed blade with file work not only along the spine and spacer, but also on the pommel.

(Ward image)

PETER PRUYN

The number one rule of the "Fight Club All Purpose" knife is that you do not talk about the Fight Club All Purpose, not its "Tyler Durden" composite handle, copper guard nor its raindrop-damascus blade.

(SharpByCoop image)

« LIN RHEA

The stag is sanded to give it an ancient ivory look, but the damascus EDC is all modern utility cutter. *(Ward image)*

Cultural Curiosities

When you visit a foreign country, you are the foreigner. Upon seeing a man dressed in his traditional Scottish kilt carrying a claymore, your blue jeans and drop-point hunting knife appear exotic, even out of place, and possibly laughable, as in, "Look what that guy's wearing and carrying."

Now, mind you, most Scotsmen aren't running around in kilts carrying dirks, but you get the picture. Similarly, not many modern Middle Eastern or Arab businessmen sport kirpans and Sikh daggers in the folds of their turbans, yet fewer still are likely to wear cowboy hats and belt buckles with bowie knives swinging from their hips. There are, however, more than a few Americans who fit that description, good guys, most of them. And they'd look downright silly in Punjab.

Rarely in Japan does one run across a Samurai swinging a wakizashi. And even less plausible would be a frontiersman in Tokyo with a primitive belt knife tucked into his buckskins.

The norm in each country is its own culture, be it dress, dance, art, architecture, language, tools, weapons, traditions or ways. Anything other than the social norm is foreign or exotic. It's whether the foreign is met with curiosity or disdain that determines how much common ground is found. Modern knifemakers tend to be the curious types, researchers in a way, historians, carrying on their own and foreign traditions by building what fascinates them, the alluring and exotic, the cultural curiosities and all the secrets that they hold. □

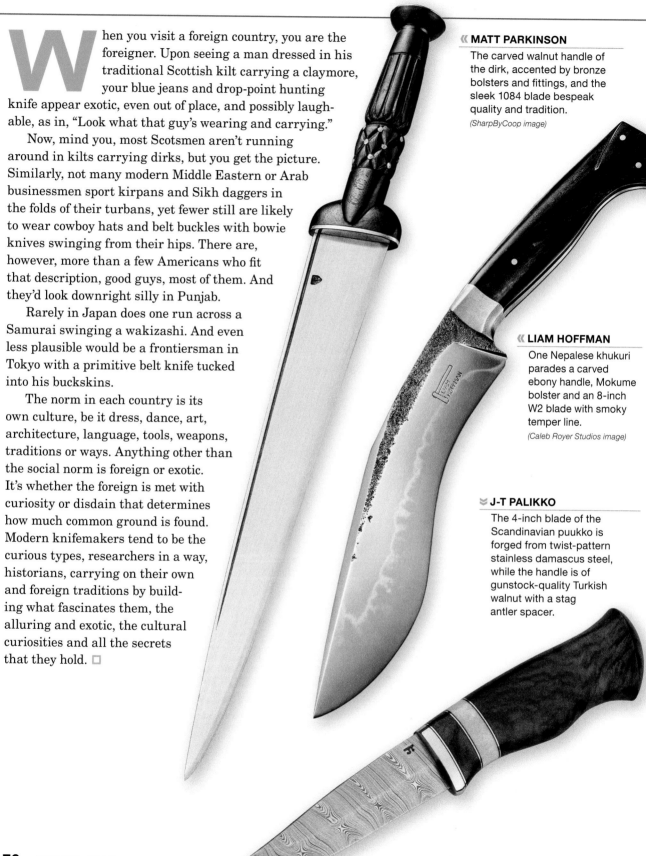

《 MATT PARKINSON

The carved walnut handle of the dirk, accented by bronze bolsters and fittings, and the sleek 1084 blade bespeak quality and tradition.
(SharpByCoop image)

《 LIAM HOFFMAN

One Nepalese khukuri parades a carved ebony handle, Mokume bolster and an 8-inch W2 blade with smoky temper line.
(Caleb Royer Studios image)

《 J-T PALIKKO

The 4-inch blade of the Scandinavian puukko is forged from twist-pattern stainless damascus steel, while the handle is of gunstock-quality Turkish walnut with a stag antler spacer.

» RAYMOND RYBAR

The spectacular blade is traditional Japanese Tamahagane steel complemented by a hilt of silk-wrapped stingray skin as well as carved shakudo and shiboichi decorations. *(PointSeven image)*

» ALLEN NEWBERRY

When blacksmiths of old forged bastard swords, this one in a walnut hilt and 30.25-inch 5160 blade, they meant business. *(Ward image)*

» JOHN COHEA

The Native American dagger is done up in random-pattern damascus, mammoth ivory, wrought iron, rawhide and copper, and the sheath has a few tricks of its own. *(Caleb Royer Studios image)*

» JAMIE LUNDELL

At least one version of a Roman pugio showcases a 15N20- and-1095 "radial explosion pattern" damascus blade, bronze fittings and a maple burl and moose antler handle. *(SharpByCoop image)*

» ANDREW MEERS

A traditional dagger, such as this version of a khanjar in a damascus blade, carved ebony grip and sterling silver fittings, was worn by men originating in Oman for ceremonial occasions.
(Caleb Royer Studios image)

« FACUNDO MONTENEGRO

Red stag is an apt choice for the hilt of a European damascus hunting sword, this of the sculpted shell guard and pommel ilk.
(SharpByCoop image)

» MATT VENIER

A Roman gladius in style with a Japanese braided wrap over a blackwood handle and a W2 blade with distinct hamon (temper line), this one exudes exoticism. *(PointSeven image)*

« DAVE DARPINIAN

Ah, the Persians, so curvaceous, from damascus blade to curly koa handle.
(Caleb Royer Studio image)

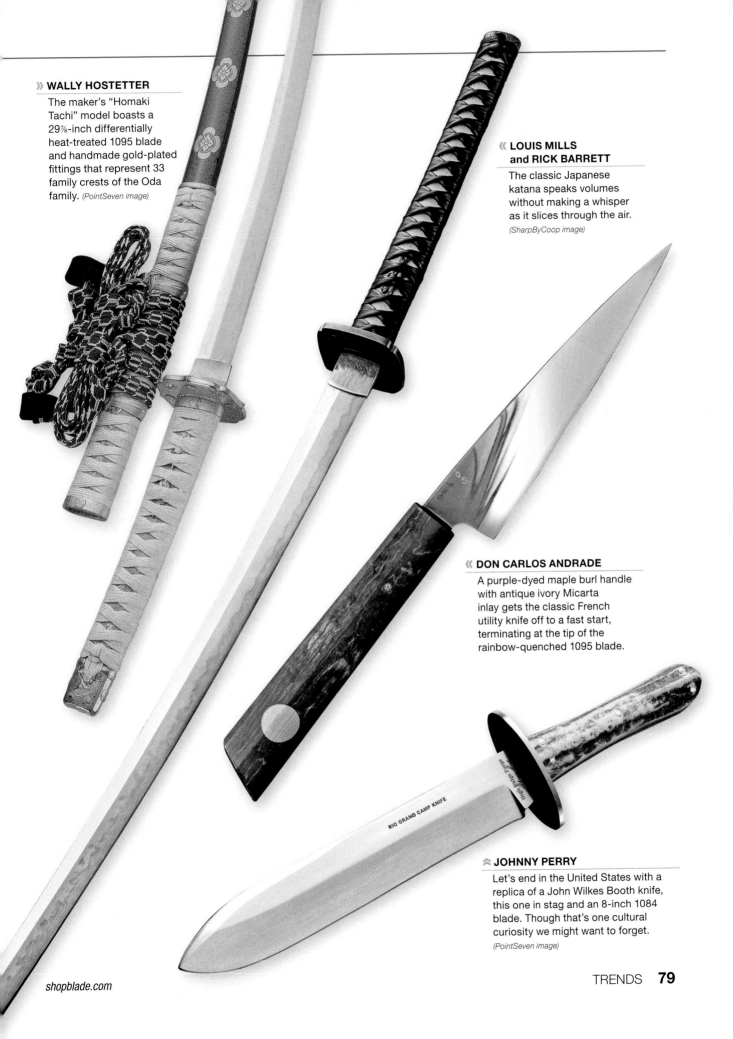

» WALLY HOSTETTER

The maker's "Homaki Tachi" model boasts a 29⅞-inch differentially heat-treated 1095 blade and handmade gold-plated fittings that represent 33 family crests of the Oda family. *(PointSeven image)*

« LOUIS MILLS and RICK BARRETT

The classic Japanese katana speaks volumes without making a whisper as it slices through the air. *(SharpByCoop image)*

« DON CARLOS ANDRADE

A purple-dyed maple burl handle with antique ivory Micarta inlay gets the classic French utility knife off to a fast start, terminating at the tip of the rainbow-quenched 1095 blade.

⌃ JOHNNY PERRY

Let's end in the United States with a replica of a John Wilkes Booth knife, this one in stag and an 8-inch 1084 blade. Though that's one cultural curiosity we might want to forget. *(PointSeven image)*

Foxy Flippers

» FRANK FISCHER

Frank's frame-lock flipper flaunts a sheepsfoot-style CPM S90 blade, a titanium frame, and a MokuTi pocket clip and pivot collars.

(Cory Martin Imaging)

« ALISTAIR BASTIAN

The "Praying Mantis" flipper folder has a pearl stinger, a rockin' Timascus body and a full head of sharp mosaic damascus.

(Cory Martin Imaging)

» BRUCE BINGENHEIMER

The smooth grip is musk ox horn, the sharp blade of Chad Nichols damascus and the rounded bolsters are the zirconium kind.

(Caleb Royer Studios image)

» HERUCUS BLOMERUS

Having Julien Marchal engrave the flipper folder was a stroke of genius, adding to the clean, classy look of the carbon fiber-handle piece.

(SharpByCoop image)

» BUTCH BALL

A double stanza of poetic verse reads: Chad Nichols stainless damascus, Timascus and pearl.

(PointSeven image)

» **CHAD NELL**
Polished zirconium, CTS-XHP steel, Timascus and gold anodized titanium hardware make for a swanky flipper folder.
(Cory Martin Imaging)

⍦ **BUDDY GAINES**
Resin handle scales in a honeycomb pattern add sticky sweetness to a CPM 154 flipper folder with zirconium bolsters.

⍦ **DAN BROWN**
The "Hellion v2" model raises all kinds of heck with its san mai damascus blade, MokuTi handle and zirconium bolsters. It's the good looking ones you have to watch out for. *(Cory Martin Imaging)*

⍦ **JENS ANSO**
This one's about the lines—of the "Takefu VG-10 san mai" damascus blade and Timascus handle of the unnamed prototype. Let's call it the "Linear Curve Flipper Folder."

⍦ **RICHARD ROGERS**
A clean flipper folder exhibits a sharp and sleek Damasteel blade, Chad Nichols MokuTi bolsters, marbled carbon fiber handle and blue anodized titanium hardware.
(SharpByCoop image)

﹤ WILLIAM TUCH

"Marble carbon fiber" is a newer handle material making waves, and Rob Thomas "fireball" damascus burns a trail of its own, and likewise Timascus bolsters and foxy flippers. *(PointSeven image)*

﹤ KIRBY LAMBERT

Not all that's gold glitters, but this one shines in a MokuTi handle, zirconium bolsters and a Chad Nichols CPM 3V-and-CTS-XHP-damascus blade. *(SharpByCoop image)*

﹤ CHARLES GEDRAITIS

Take time to soak in the wood-grain-pattern copper bolsters, two-tone CPM 154 blade and bronze-wired "lightning strike carbon fiber" handle scales of the Yakuza flipper folder.

(SharpByCoop image)

﹥ NATI AMOR

The big-bellied D2 blade keeps good company with zirconium and titanium.

(Cory Martin Imaging)

﹀ LES VOORHIES

Purple Timascus tops off a Chad Nichols stainless damascus flipper folder featuring a zirconium frame and titanium liners.

(Cory Martin Imaging)

» CORY MARTIN

The flipper mechanism resembles the bottom fin of a shark as it cuts through the water, in this case using its CPM S35 steel snout.

(Cory Martin Imaging)

» CRAIG CAMERER

Damascus and MokuTi point the flipper folder in the right direction.

(PointSeven image)

⩔ JEFF PARK

As part of a trio of "Dum Bones," "Bones" and "Mini Bones" flipper folders, the slim, trim, textured-titanium-handle flippers outflank many of their counterparts.

(PointSeven image)

» TONY KARLSSON

Westinghouse rag Micarta invigorates a Damasteel flipper folder sporting space-age meteorite bolsters. *(Cory Martin Imaging)*

« LUCAS BURNLEY

The curvaceous Chad Nichols "boomerang"-pattern damascus beak of the "Pelican" breaks down more than its "marbled carbon fiber" belly can. *(PointSeven image)*

▽ PAUL MARKOW

Old "green eyes" is immortalized via Raluca Markow scrimshaw on a mammoth ivory inlay within the blue titanium handle frame of a damascus flipper folder.

(Ward image)

» ERIC OCHS

A frame-lock Persian flipper folder showcases a Chad Nichols "wave pool" damascus blade in a Bob Lum-style tanto tip, a stippled MokuTi handle and heat colored screws with zirconium collars.

(Ernesto Urdaneta image)

» MICHAEL VAGNINO

The lurking "Jaguar" flipper folder is a big damascus and mammoth ivory cat.

(PointSeven image)

« DAVID S. KULIS

Damascus by Mike Norris makes its presence known on a "marbled carbon fiber"-handle flipper folder highlighted by Timascus bolsters and pocket clip.

(Cory Martin Imaging)

⌃ RON BEST

If the cut matches the curves and the flip equals the aesthetics, then this foxy flipper is worth its price in pearl, Timascus and damascus.

(SharpByCoop image)

Indulge Your Fantasies

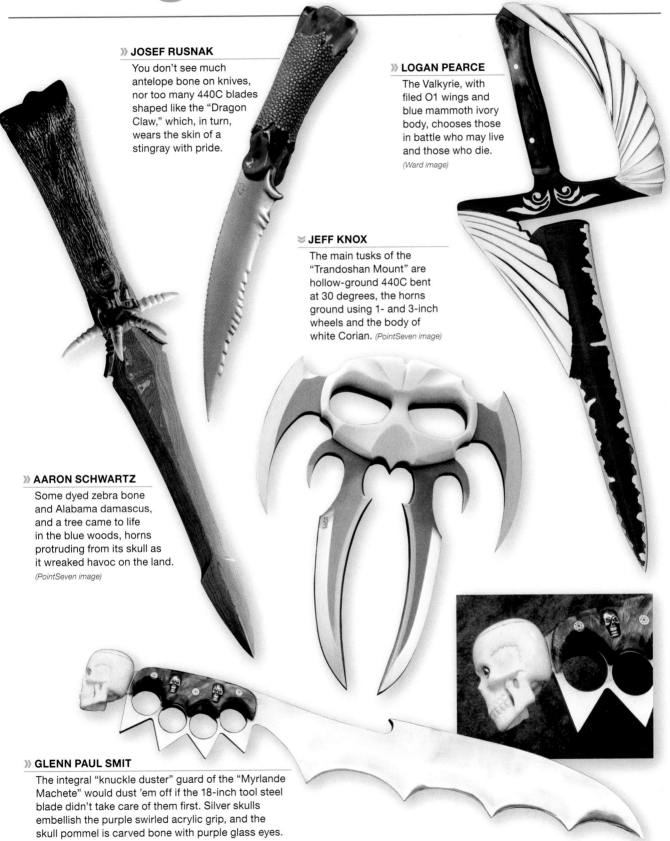

» JOSEF RUSNAK

You don't see much antelope bone on knives, nor too many 440C blades shaped like the "Dragon Claw," which, in turn, wears the skin of a stingray with pride.

» LOGAN PEARCE

The Valkyrie, with filed O1 wings and blue mammoth ivory body, chooses those in battle who may live and those who die. *(Ward image)*

» JEFF KNOX

The main tusks of the "Trandoshan Mount" are hollow-ground 440C bent at 30 degrees, the horns ground using 1- and 3-inch wheels and the body of white Corian. *(PointSeven image)*

» AARON SCHWARTZ

Some dyed zebra bone and Alabama damascus, and a tree came to life in the blue woods, horns protruding from its skull as it wreaked havoc on the land.
(PointSeven image)

» GLENN PAUL SMIT

The integral "knuckle duster" guard of the "Myrlande Machete" would dust 'em off if the 18-inch tool steel blade didn't take care of them first. Silver skulls embellish the purple swirled acrylic grip, and the skull pommel is carved bone with purple glass eyes.

No Drag Dags

» VLADIMIR KOLENKO

When you heft the "Great Helm" dagger, you hold Gabon ebony with sterling silver inlaid crosses, 14k-gold engraved crosses, and a laminated blade made up of a high-carbon-steel core between two layers of Zladinox Turkish-twist mosaic damascus.

» MIKE QUESENBERRY

A coffin handle dagger, this one in exhibition-grade fossil walrus ivory, the real money's in the 300-layer damascus blade, the 24k-gold bolster inlays, gold-plated German silver liners and 18k-gold domed pins. *(Caleb Royer Studios image)*

» REINHARD TSCHAGER

Touches of class include sea cow bone, a perforated gold inlay, gold pins and a Doug Ponzio damascus blade that resembles the galaxy. *(Francesco Pachi image)*

≫ PAUL LEBATARD

The HRF dagger, forged from a half-round file with some file marks still showing for effect, measures a foot long and is hafted in India stag. *(PointSeven image)*

« DAVE SKINNER

The stabilized, dyed curly maple handle is as round as the twist-damascus blade is sharp and pointy, while the guard, spacer and pommel are all hot-blued pattern-welded steel. *(Dirk Loots image)*

« DAVID BROADWELL

A "Night-Day Dagger Set," the sculpted guards and damascus blades are handled in equally appealing carved blackwood and mammoth ivory. *(Ward image)*

⌃ TIM LAMBKIN

Musk ox horn anchors the Alabama Damascus "Scorpion" dagger, which can sting from several ends.

(PointSeven image)

⌃ STEVE VANDERKOLFF

Of frame-handle construction with African blackwood handle scales, the maker file worked the titanium liners and employed a sharp ladder-pattern Delbert Ealy damascus blade. *(Caleb Royer Studios image)*

Chef, Sushi, Steak & Veggie Knives

Some people would say that kitchen knives have been around for as long as there have been stoves and refrigerators, or longer, maybe since caves and fire were discovered, so how could they be more popular today than ever? A legitimate question, but one that ignores the fact that there are more choices, styles, materials, steels and, frankly, creative patterns today than there've ever been.

Combine that with the fact that knifemakers today study historic Japanese, Chinese, Scandinavian, French, American and Latin American designs, blending patterns and styles to fashion new models, exotic-looking pieces, many with damascus or san mai blades.

It's a tired term, but this might just be the Golden Age of cutlery. Cooking shows and competitions are hot, sushi has made major inroads in the U.S. culinary market, home kitchens are the new entertainment centers of the social set, and there's a gigantic trend toward eating fresh, green and healthy. Add to the mix the fact that buying local and making your own food are current trends, and it's a sweet recipe for some of the hottest chef, sushi, steak and veggie knives to ever hit the cutting board. □

« HALEY DESROSIERS
You pull out this chef's knife with a six-bar Merovingian (Frankish dynasty)-damascus blade, and all conversation stops in the kitchen.
(Caleb Royer Studios image)

» GAETAN BEAUCHAMP
Scrimshaw on water buffalo horn depicts famous Native American chiefs and warriors that embellish a set of eight (not all shown) steak knives in 440C stainless steel and sculpted silver.

« GABRIEL BELL
The blade of the gyuto (Japanese style chef's knife) is forged in a "wood grain" pattern, maybe to match the rosewood handle, from a billet of four bundles of forge-welded high-carbon cable steel.

≫ LIAM HOFFMAN

Here's a new one—an aged Tecoma (trumpet vine) handle on an 11-inch damascus chef's knife with integral bolster, and thank goodness for it. *(Caleb Royer Studios image)*

≫ DOUG CAMPBELL

Who says you can't combine stripes with spots? If this 8-inch damascus chef's knife in a curly koa handle is any indication, it's a dang fashion statement. *(Ward image)*

≫ TOM BUCKNER

Stabilized spalted maple and a spalted maple saya highlight the clean 8-inch chef's knife in an AEB-L stainless steel blade. *(SharpByCoop image)*

≫ GREG CIMMS

The 8-inch Kiritsuki blends Japanese yanagi (fish slicer) and usuba (vegetable knife) styles, presented here in a highly patterned san mai blade and purple-dyed burl grip. *(SharpByCoop image)*

≫ KEN HALL

I'd have to give this one a few "likes" on Facebook—I like the octagonal African blackwood and green box elder burl handle, the "laddered W's"-damascus blade and the damascus bolster.

HARVEY DEAN

I've really got to make it to the Art Knife Invitational if this is the kind of knives that are shown there, and it is, including this particularly handsome chef's knife in damascus, wood and gold wire inlay. *(Francesco Pachi image)*

IAN ROGERS

This Kiritsuki comes with a cocobolo saya (sheath), but it's better out where one can admire the 616-layer feather damascus blade, mokume-gane bolster and butt cap, and rosewood burl grip.

(Caleb Royer Studios image)

ISAIAH SCHROEDER

Yanagi-ba-bocho knives, such as this splendid model in an O1 blade and Ziricote, maple burl and nickel silver handle, are "willow blades" used in Japanese kitchens for Sashimi and sushi.

(Cory Martin Imaging)

DON CARLOS ANDRADE

The clay-heat-treated 1095 blades of the utility paring knives go well with the rare tan-and-black Westinghouse Micarta handles, and bronze and mosaic pins.

LARAMIE JACKSON

Arctic blue Kirinite wasn't too shabby a handle choice for an AEB-L stainless steel chef's knife, not shabby at all.

《 KEVIN CROSS

Orange G-10 liners bring even more attention to the already gorgeous stabilized koa handle of a flat-ground chef's knife with a Rob Thomas damascus blade. *(SharpByCoop image)*

》 MATT PARKINSON

Not your average 8-inch French chef's knife, the Peter Swarz-Burt damascus bolster is a nice touch, matched with a mesmerizing damascus blade on one end and a stabilized maple burl grip on the other. *(SharpByCoop image)*

》 ERIK FRITZ

Even the layered steel of Erik's chef's knife is Japanese—Takefu—and complemented by an ebony handle with buffalo horn spacer. *(PointSeven image)*

《 MICHAEL ZIEBA

It's not just the stabilized maple (though that's stunning), the san mai steel and brass, but the clever shape of the knife, where the handle lies in the palm, and the pointy-ness of it all. *(SharpByCoop image)*

⋀ BILL BURKE

The York gum burl handle of the chef's knife is smooth as silk, and the aptly named "Twin river" damascus blade washes over you like a tidal wave. *(PointSeven image)*

Burled Barehanders

ANDERS HOGSTROM
Evidently the superb quality stabilized Masur birch handle gives the "Starburst" fighter its name, and the sterling silver guard and 1050 blade are name worthy, too.
(SharpByCoop image)

DAVID BROADWELL
Now if you go by "Feather Crotch Koa," you have to be tough, and the carved and dimpled koa handle is just that, surrounding itself with textured bronze, titanium and differentially heat treated steel.

ROBERT KOVACIK
The bugling elk lives in a world of Swedish damascus and stabilized maple burl.

DAVE DARPINIAN
Snakewood sandwiches the full tang of an Alabama Damascus hunter with a 3.75-inch blade, integral guard and thumb notches on the spine. *(Ward image)*

ANDREW ROY

The "Bush Hermit" hides out in a Baltic birch handle and wickedly cool damascus blade.

(PointSeven image)

JESS HOFFMAN

Dyed curly white oak is to die for, and the Bohler N690 blade isn't bad, either.

W*(Cory Martin Imaging)*

TONY MILLER

Nine and a half inches of hand forged 5160 are counterbalanced by a dropped curly koa handle with reconstituted malachite and black fiber spacers.

(Caleb Royer Studios image)

TOM BUCKNER

The wood doesn't stop at the black-and-white ebony and stabilized spalted maple handles of the 8-inch chef's knives, but extends to the ebony and maple sheaths.

(SharpByCoop image)

» GREG CIMMS

The chef's knife in burl and damascus will make mincemeat out of a Sunday roast in no time. *(SharpByCoop image)*

» LUDWIG JANSEN VAN VUUREN

A handsome hunter and caping knife set exhibits dark-colored and striated partridge wood handles and Sandvik 12C27 blades.

⌄ ANDY ROY

When foraging for food, it's good to take "The Forager" in dyed maple burl over natural liners, looking much like yellow pinstripes, and a "spalted" A2 blade.

⌄ MICHAEL DEIBERT

The line down the center of the buckeye burl handle leads to the line on the mild steel guard, which leads to the lines of the damascus blade.
(SharpByCoop image)

RAMON MORALES

Love the lines of the spalted maple, of the knife, of the temper line that stretches across the 1095 blade. Love is in the air. *(Caleb Royer Studios image)*

STEVEN NUCKELS

A coffin-style curly maple handle with silver wire inlay is partnered with an L6 blade fashioned from an antique saw blade.

(SharpByCoop image)

E. SCOTT MCGHEE

This one's about the patterns—a hunter, mosaic damascus and Claro walnut— with the only static feature being the bronze guard.

JOHN DOYLE

Like it's been carved on a lathe, the round desert ironwood burl handle has more than a few lines to follow, complemented by a double shell S-guard, a coined collar and accents, and a length of differentially heat treated 1075 blade.

(SharpByCoop image)

KEN HALL

You could do worse than curling fingers around the stabilized curly walnut grip of the CPM 154 fixed blade.

» ISAIAH SCHROEDER

Gorgeous is the purple-dyed maple burl handle and dyed cascara spacers of a Gyuto (Japanese-style chef's knife) in 1095 steel.
(Cory Martin Imaging)

» TOM R. LEWIS

A turquoise star marks the sweet spot of a palm-able stabilized buckeye burl handle, while a smoky temper line shows where hard steel meets less hard steel on the clay-tempered W2 blade.

» LOGAN PEARCE

Turkish twist damascus has its own thing going on the business end of the knife, while dyed box elder burl shows off at the other end.
(SharpByCoop image)

⌃ SEAN O'HARE

The "Finback" model is named for the raised clip of the Mike Norris damascus blade, but the koa wood body of the trophy fish deserves mention.

SCOTT GALLAGHER

Black veins running through an ironwood handle give the 80CrV2 hunter movement that the finely fit and finished knife wouldn't otherwise have.

(PointSeven image)

CODY HOFSOMMER

Buckeye burl is another one of those instantly recognizable woods, here matched with a stainless steel guard, W2 blade and smoky temper line.

(Cory Martin Imaging)

JOSH FISHER

The lines of the black palm handle and 1084-and-15N20-damascus blade might run counter to each other, but they're copacetic counterparts.

(Caleb Royer Studios image)

TRAVIS PAYNE

One lucky hunter is the benefactor of a Damasteel blade, dyed California buckeye burl handle and Matt Litz bolster engraving.

(PointSeven image)

JERRY HOSSOM

The colors emitting from the dyed and stabilized California buckeye handle are as vibrant as the blade is shapely and sharp.

(PointSeven image)

⌄ J-T PALIKKO

The semi-integral hunter emits a high sheen and showcases a linden burl (basswood) handle. The cutting edge is 4 inches long.

⌄ JEREMY SPAKE

It took three burls—African blackwood, stabilized golden amboyna and rosewood—to hold their own against the Mareko Mumasi damascus blade. *(SharpByCoop image)*

» BEN BREDA

While the temper line statically stretches across a W2 blade, sculpted ironwood rests easily in the palm of the hand.

(Caleb Royer Studios image)

⌃ TIM STEINGASS

Wood and carbon fiber combine for the palpable handle of a drop-point hunter.

(SharpByCoop image)

DON HANSON III

The giant dress locking folder features a 5-inch W2 blade with wavy temper line, damascus bolsters and a 5,460-year-old bog oak handle. *(SharpByCoop image)*

JORDAN LAMOTHE

It might be an everyday carry knife, but the twist-damascus dazzler with rope file work along the spine and a maple and blackwood handle is showcase material. *(SharpByCoop image)*

MATT PARKINSON

The swirly patterns of damascus and spalted maple burl on an 8-inch chef's knife are perfect matches.

(SharpByCoop image)

CHUN-WEI CHANG

You know ironwood when you see it, with its dark browns and blacks, but seldom carved and sculpted like this, and matched with a W2 blade. *(SharpByCoop image)*

Rings, Split Rings & D-Guards

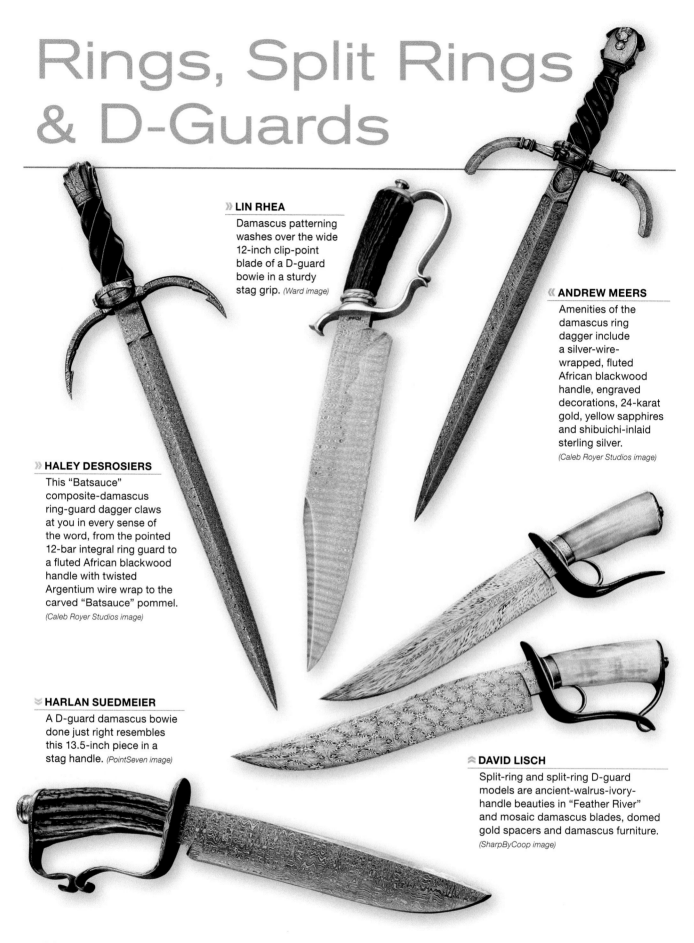

» LIN RHEA
Damascus patterning washes over the wide 12-inch clip-point blade of a D-guard bowie in a sturdy stag grip. *(Ward image)*

« ANDREW MEERS
Amenities of the damascus ring dagger include a silver-wire-wrapped, fluted African blackwood handle, engraved decorations, 24-karat gold, yellow sapphires and shibuichi-inlaid sterling silver.
(Caleb Royer Studios image)

» HALEY DESROSIERS
This "Batsauce" composite-damascus ring-guard dagger claws at you in every sense of the word, from the pointed 12-bar integral ring guard to a fluted African blackwood handle with twisted Argentium wire wrap to the carved "Batsauce" pommel.
(Caleb Royer Studios image)

« HARLAN SUEDMEIER
A D-guard damascus bowie done just right resembles this 13.5-inch piece in a stag handle. *(PointSeven image)*

« DAVID LISCH
Split-ring and split-ring D-guard models are ancient-walrus-ivory-handle beauties in "Feather River" and mosaic damascus blades, domed gold spacers and damascus furniture.
(SharpByCoop image)

Desert Warriors

For the sake of our fighting men and women in uniform, I wish there were no current wars. But if there have to be wars, then for the good of our soldiers, I hope they're not all in deserts in days to come. I mean, talk about the worst of conditions, landscapes and elements!

It's a good thing there are incredibly talented and driven custom knifemakers across the globe providing the best cutting tools to ever reach our fighting men's and women's hands. High tech has met combat knife in a combination that is not only deadly but extremely useful for a slew of chores, not the least of which is opening ammo boxes, crates, MRE's and canvas bags. They cut, chop, puncture, peel, dice, slice and tear. The handles are impervious to the elements, the blades stout and sharp, and the designs utilitarian and comfortable.

Our desert warriors deserve no less! ☐

» DAVE WENGER
With an 80CrV2 head, canvas Micarta haft and two-tone Cerakote finish, the "Beohawk W.C." would make Beowulf cower in a corner. *(Cory Martin Imaging)*

» WILLIAM WELLING
Check out the tiger stripes on the flats of the AEB-L stainless steel blade with satin-finished bevels, and the indentations along the natural tan Micarta grip sporting several thong tubes.

» SCOTT HALL
A fighter in every sense of the word, it wears an olive G-10 handle, a CPM S30V blade with a secondary top edge and partial serrations, and a stainless steel thong tube. *(Cory Martin Imaging)*

» JERRY HOSSOM

The shape, palpable indentations and indexing points of the black and green Micarta handle are nearly upstaged by the curves and point of the CTS 40 blade. *(PointSeven image)*

» THOMAS RICE

One tanto for the desert during the day, one for special operations at night, and no one's the wiser. *(Ward image)*

⌃ SEAN MCWILLIAMS

For the boys in arid climates, the Desert Ranger-7 comes with a 7.5-inch CPM 440V blade, a stainless guard and pommel—the latter with a thong hole for lashing—and a natural canvas Micarta handle.

⌃ GUY STAINTHORP

The "Shadow" boot knife takes stealth in the direction of an RWL-34 blade and a black canvas Micarta handle.

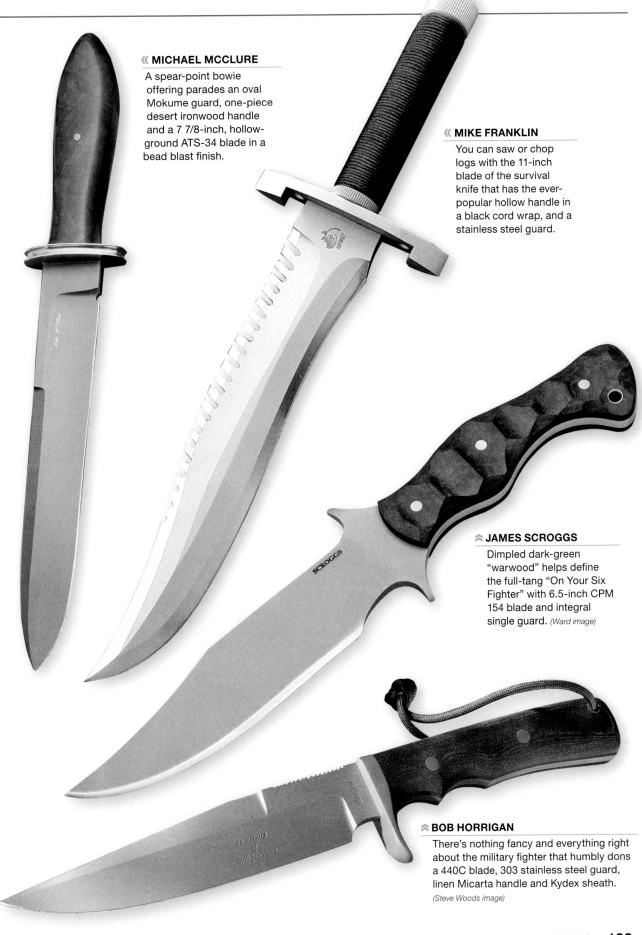

« **MICHAEL MCCLURE**
A spear-point bowie offering parades an oval Mokume guard, one-piece desert ironwood handle and a 7 7/8-inch, hollow-ground ATS-34 blade in a bead blast finish.

« **MIKE FRANKLIN**
You can saw or chop logs with the 11-inch blade of the survival knife that has the ever-popular hollow handle in a black cord wrap, and a stainless steel guard.

» **JAMES SCROGGS**
Dimpled dark-green "warwood" helps define the full-tang "On Your Six Fighter" with 6.5-inch CPM 154 blade and integral single guard. *(Ward image)*

» **BOB HORRIGAN**
There's nothing fancy and everything right about the military fighter that humbly dons a 440C blade, 303 stainless steel guard, linen Micarta handle and Kydex sheath.
(Steve Woods image)

The Fighter Class

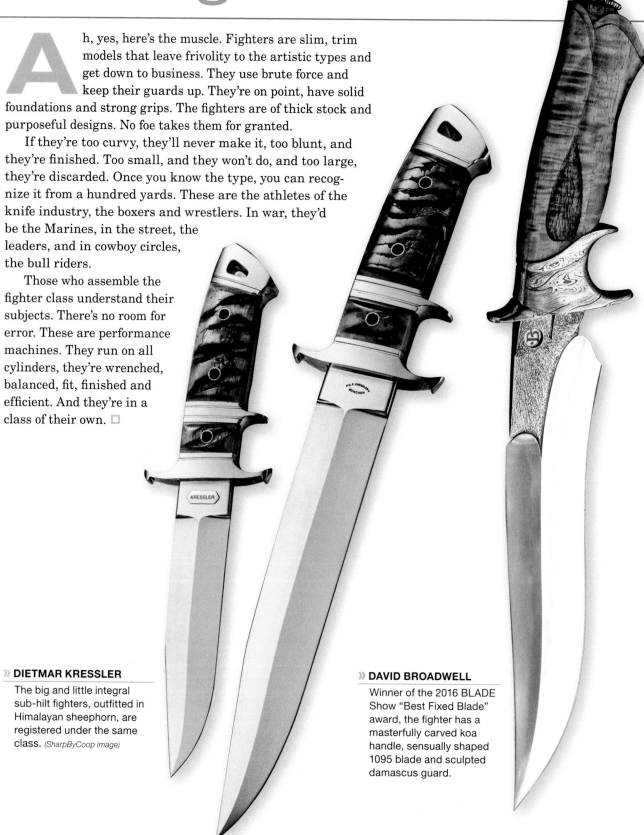

Ah, yes, here's the muscle. Fighters are slim, trim models that leave frivolity to the artistic types and get down to business. They use brute force and keep their guards up. They're on point, have solid foundations and strong grips. The fighters are of thick stock and purposeful designs. No foe takes them for granted.

If they're too curvy, they'll never make it, too blunt, and they're finished. Too small, and they won't do, and too large, they're discarded. Once you know the type, you can recognize it from a hundred yards. These are the athletes of the knife industry, the boxers and wrestlers. In war, they'd be the Marines, in the street, the leaders, and in cowboy circles, the bull riders.

Those who assemble the fighter class understand their subjects. There's no room for error. These are performance machines. They run on all cylinders, they're wrenched, balanced, fit, finished and efficient. And they're in a class of their own. □

» DIETMAR KRESSLER

The big and little integral sub-hilt fighters, outfitted in Himalayan sheephorn, are registered under the same class. *(SharpByCoop image)*

» DAVID BROADWELL

Winner of the 2016 BLADE Show "Best Fixed Blade" award, the fighter has a masterfully carved koa handle, sensually shaped 1095 blade and sculpted damascus guard.

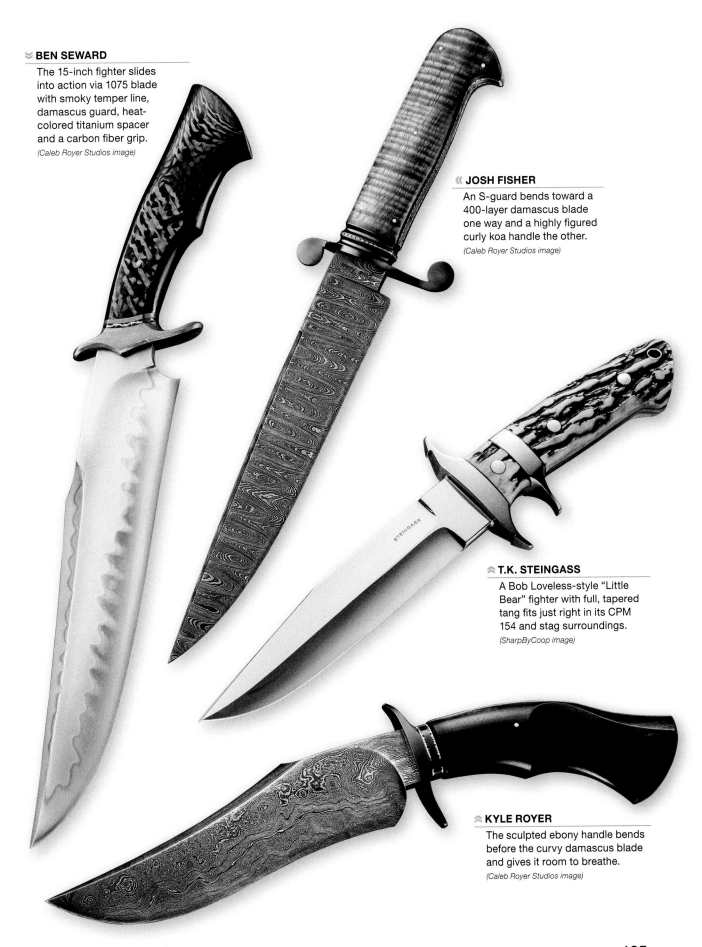

BEN SEWARD

The 15-inch fighter slides into action via 1075 blade with smoky temper line, damascus guard, heat-colored titanium spacer and a carbon fiber grip.

(Caleb Royer Studios image)

JOSH FISHER

An S-guard bends toward a 400-layer damascus blade one way and a highly figured curly koa handle the other.

(Caleb Royer Studios image)

T.K. STEINGASS

A Bob Loveless-style "Little Bear" fighter with full, tapered tang fits just right in its CPM 154 and stag surroundings.

(SharpByCoop image)

KYLE ROYER

The sculpted ebony handle bends before the curvy damascus blade and gives it room to breathe.

(Caleb Royer Studios image)

» CALVIN RICHARDSON

Oil-finished curly koa is a bright spot on a 14.75-inch, clay-tempered and differentially hardened 1084 fighter with visible hamon (temper line). *(Caleb Royer Studios image)*

˅ ANDERS HOGSTROM

The natural Baltic amber handle of the 1050 tanto fighter is as hot as the knife is cool.
(SharpByCoop image)

⌃ SAMUEL LURQUIN

"Explosion" damascus makes up the blade, hilt and sub-hilt of the "Tsavo" bowie/fighter in an oak hilt for a solid base.
(SharpByCoop image)

⌃ DON HANSON III

One looks at the temper line along the long, lanky blade, then at the fossil walrus ivory, then back to the temper line.
(SharpByCoop image)

《 MARK COOKE

Hold onto the carbon
fiber handle tight,
that W2 blade is
about to get away.

(Caleb Royer Studios image)

《 SCOTT GALLAGHER

The maker breaks a clean
example out in 80CrV2
steel and a stabilized
maple burl handle.

(Caleb Royer Studios image)

≫ JON P. MOORE

"Splatter" damascus
sticks it, and orange
curly maple gives it grip.

≫ PAUL LEBATARD

The "PTK-1" (Practical Tactical
Knife) is a sheephorn and
stainless steel model with a
double guard and red thong.

(PointSeven image)

» CLAUDE BOUCHONVILLE

The damascus hilt and sub-hilt nearly form a ring for the forefinger to slide into, the palm resting on the ironwood grip and clasping the winsome weapon.
(SharpByCoop image)

» MIKE QUESENBERRY

Are the timber lines or smoky temper lines more to your liking? That's one sharp fighter.
(SharpByCoop image)

« JEFFREY D. CONTI

The flame-finished D2 spear-point blade is bad to the spine, while the olive-colored Micarta handle will last the duration.

» MAMORU SHIGENO

Crown stag caps both of the ATS-34 fighters, one with a sub-hilt and one without.
(SharpByCoop image)

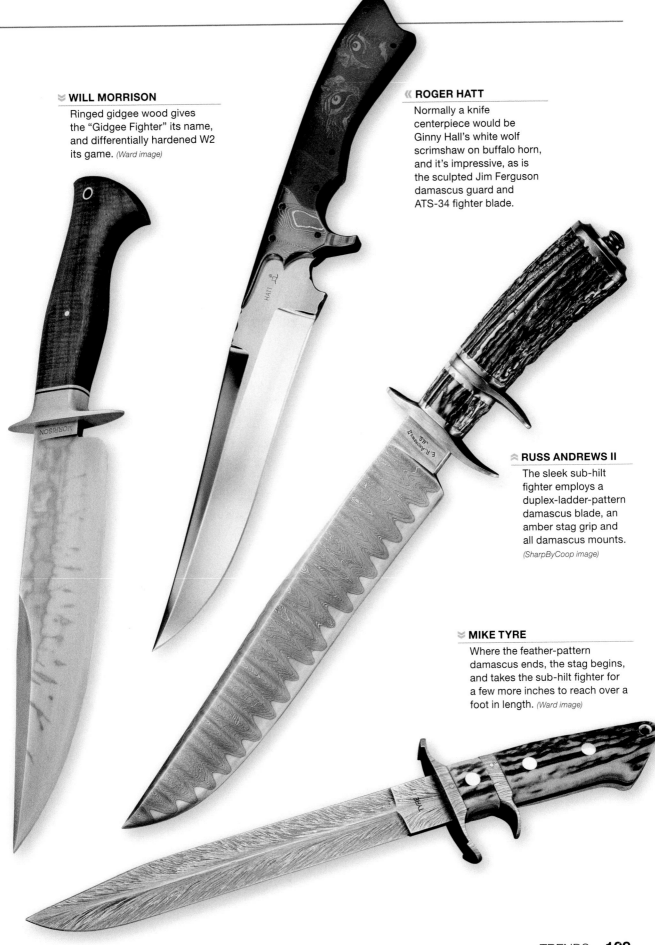

≫ WILL MORRISON

Ringed gidgee wood gives the "Gidgee Fighter" its name, and differentially hardened W2 its game. *(Ward image)*

≪ ROGER HATT

Normally a knife centerpiece would be Ginny Hall's white wolf scrimshaw on buffalo horn, and it's impressive, as is the sculpted Jim Ferguson damascus guard and ATS-34 fighter blade.

≫ RUSS ANDREWS II

The sleek sub-hilt fighter employs a duplex-ladder-pattern damascus blade, an amber stag grip and all damascus mounts.

(SharpByCoop image)

≫ MIKE TYRE

Where the feather-pattern damascus ends, the stag begins, and takes the sub-hilt fighter for a few more inches to reach over a foot in length. *(Ward image)*

» J.R. REEVES

He's got buckshot in his blade, blackwood for a body and stainless steel running through his veins.

» W. ALLEN SURLS

In ironwood, a double guard and re-curved blade we trust.

» MIKE CRADDOCK

Maroon Micarta makes an appearance on a foot-long 5160 fighter featuring a stainless steel guard and a black Micarta frame. *(SharpByCoop image)*

» TIM WITHERS

A reproduction of a Bob Loveless Big Bear fighter, the ATS-34 tapered-tang model puts blue G-10 to good use. *(SharpByCoop image)*

» CHUN-WEI CHANG

The length and physique of the 1084 blade is impressive, while the blackwood grip and gold spacer add depth and aesthetic quality to the piece. *(SharpByCoop image)*

Close-Shave Straight Razors

» HARVEY DEAN

The "Touch of Gold" straight razor does indeed showcase touches of gold on the mammoth ivory handle and spine of the damascus blade.

(Johnny Stout image)

⌄ CALEB WHITE

The "Griffin" does have the nose—a beak-like W2 blade with temper line—and wing—the extended tang—of a griffin, here with a "bone linen Micarta" body.

« JANUSZ BLADOWSKI

The integral, laminated, high-carbon-steel straight razor has a large choil and utilitarian handle shape to choke up on the blade while whisking away whiskers.

(SharpByCoop image)

« TRAVIS PAYNE

I'd even trust my face to the pierced damascus straight razor with hand-filling, wing-like carbon fiber handle and curled extended-tang opener, well, maybe.

(PointSeven image)

« JOE EDSON

The star of any toiletry bag, the "Odin's Edge" folding O1 straight razor dons a musk ox horn handle, mammoth ivory spacer, and nickel, stacked stainless steel, brass and rose-gold-plated hardware, as well as "dragon scale" file work on the spine and tail. *(Caleb Royer Studios image)*

Top-Tier Tantos

In this case, being top tier starts with tradition—a traditional Japanese knife, one that incorporates a distinct blade shape, often a cord-, leather- or silk-wrapped handle over stingray skin, perhaps a small guard or no guard at all, and a sheath that slides silently over the blade, becoming one with the knife.

Top-tier means clean lines, absolutely flawless, evenly ground edges and finely finished blades coming to final, sweeping angles and ending in piercingly sharp tips. It means attention to the smallest of details, handle charms, pinned grips, ricassos that blend seamlessly with the blades, and as much focus on the tsubas (guards) and sayas (sheaths) as on the rest of the tantos.

Top-tier tantos are those worn in sashes, retrieved with the quickness, agility and prowess of cats, used with respect, handled with kid gloves and maintained with patience and care. Someday we'll all own top-tier tantos, sip sake, slowly shovel rice into our mouths using chopsticks and draw Kanji and Hiragan letters on parchment paper with pens dipped in ink. □

» ROBERT OHLEMANN

The only folding tanto in the mix, it's a fine example in Damasteel, zirconium and "thunderstorm" Kevlar.
(PointSeven image)

» RICK POIRIER

The damascus blade is distinctively tanto, the nylon cord wrap over black stingray skin is a work of skill, and the handle charm coy, or is that koi?
(PointSeven image)

« KEVIN CASHEN

An impressive rendering of a Japanese tanto combines a green silk-wrapped handle over stingray skin, a dimpled/carved spacer, copper blade collar and an 11-inch 1080 blade.

» KEITH FLUDDER

This top-tier tanto has it all—a wispy temper line along the blade edge, copper habaki, Mokume guard, handle wrap, stingray skin and a menuki handle charm. *(PointSeven image)*

» KEN HALL

A differentially heat-treated W2 tanto blade is married with a copper habaki (blade collar), an African blackwood hilt, wrought iron tsuba (guard) and copper fittings.

» GEOFF KEYES

Here's a takedown model in a she oak and blackwood handle, sterling silver habaki and an exotic-looking 1080-and-15N20-damascus blade.

(PointSeven image)

» BEN TENDICK

A carbon fiber-wrapped Tero Tuf handle might not be traditional tanto fare, but it sure is sporty on a CPM 3V tanto with copper seppa (spacer) and titanium mekugi (takedown pin).

« MATTHEW GREGORY

It might have a Crucible CPM 154 blade, a Hawaiian koa handle and a holly menuki (handle charm), but it's all Japanese, including the tsuka-ito (handle wrap).

(SharpByCoop image)

Pocketknife Perfection

It's so personal. When you have something that you put in your pocket every day and carry with you, pull out to use, put back in the pocket, and when the evening comes set it on a dresser or nightstand for the next day, it becomes a part of you, something you possess and rely upon.

My dad used to use a mnemonic device when he'd get ready for work in the morning. It was a saying he'd recite out loud or in his head that would help him remember everything he needed to take to the office that day. It went something like, "Cathy [my mom] got weak knees climbing up big ladders." The first letter of each word in his saying stood for "coat, glasses, wallet, keys, coffee, umbrella, briefcase, lunch."

You don't have to remind many guys to carry their pocketknife every day, and most probably don't need a mnemonic device to remember to slide it into their slacks or jeans pocket. But like my memory of my father, it's still something familiar and personal. It would be fun to become familiar with any of the examples of pocketknife perfection on this or the facing page. They are clean, fine examples of the cutler's art, of edged tools for the everyday man, and many are familiar patterns or gorgeous interpretations thereof. □

《 TIM BRITTON
Sometimes the simplest designs and materials—a one-blade pocketknife with a long nail nick and a tan-Micarta handle—pack the most powerful punches. *(SharpByCoop image)*

》 LUKE SWENSON
The highly figured stag handle makes for a fine grip so one can get down to business using whichever CPM 154 blade he or she chooses. *(PointSeven image)*

《 JEFF CLAIBORNE
It takes a long, milled 52100 blade to test a melon, and an equally lengthy walrus ivory handle (with integral liners and bolsters) to fold the edge into when closed. *(Terrill Hoffman image)*

« T.R. OVEREYNDER

A saddle-horn-pattern pocketknife is properly executed in Carpenter CTS-XHP steel, stag horn and 18-karat rose gold. *(PointSeven image)*

» JAVIER VOGT

The "Hidden Bartender's Knife," with Damasteel implements and mother-of-pearl handle scales, features a corkscrew hidden under a pivoting back spacer. *(SharpByCoop image)*

» BILL RUPLE

A long, sleek CPM 154 lock-back whittler, the mother-of-pearl alone is worth its weight in the pocket. *(PointSeven image)*

⌃ TANNER COUCH

Showcasing CPM 154 blades, fluted bolsters, relieved and file-worked liners and a custom arrowhead shield, one has to wonder if the southwestern sun baked the "sunset died jigged bone" handle scales of the South Texas Trapper. *(SharpByCoop image)*

» TONY BOSE

Slide the swing-guard Coke bottle pattern folding knife into your britches pocket, and pull it out once in a while to admire the old bone handle. *(Caleb Royer Studios image)*

We Get Game Blades

» JOHN COHEA

The maker's frontier hunter is handled in mammoth ivory with stag fittings, and bladed in 3.5 inches of damascus steel.

(Ward image)

» LIAM HOFFMAN

He fashioned a bird-and-trout knife from old-stock O1 blade steel and an East Indian rosewood handle.

(Caleb Royer Studios image)

» JOHN WHITE

The drop-point hunter is finely fit and finished, and adorned in some fancy file work and an ancient ivory grip.

(Caleb Royer Studios image)

⌄ STANLEY BUZEK

Folding hunters such as the CPM 154 model in an amber jigged bone handle still find favor, and for good reason.

(Ward image)

» DAVID CRAWFORD

The 4.5-inch CPM 154 steel blade would perform admirably on game, and the amber jigged bone handle is a classic choice, here highlighted by red liners.

(Caleb Royer Studios image)

» RICCARDO MAINOLFI

Floral-style Luca Braschi engraving embellishes the guard and pins of a CPM 154 drop-point hunter handled in Himalayan ram's horn. *(PointSeven image)*

« ADAM DES ROSIERS

Going integral with the multi-bar composite twist damascus hunter was inspired, and the damascus pommel that matches the stag handle was a nice finishing touch.
(SharpByCoop image)

« MARC ALDRICH

The skinner makes a guy want to go out and shoot something just so he can hold the stabilized amboyna burl handle and use that wide, sweeping W2 blade.

» JOSH FISHER

The maker offers this model in a 1084 high-carbon-steel blade and a choice of an ebony, G-10 or black palm handle. You can't go wrong.
(Caleb Royer Studios image)

» CODY HOFSOMMER

The blade parades a tight CruForge V and 15N20 damascus pattern, and the hunter is hafted in some classy koa wood.
(Cory Martin Imaging)

» GUY STAINTHORP

The 67-layer "Suminagashi" laminated blade of the hunter has as many lines as the ironwood handle, and maybe more.

⌄ ZANE BLACKWELL

Get yourself a waistband sheath and the blue jigged bone handle of the CPM 154 drop-point hunter would match up with your jeans real nice. *(Ward image)*

» ED CAFFREY

The maker differentially heat treated the 1084 blade to achieve a telling temper line, and gave the "Beeswing" maple handle a Tru-Oil finish for a high sheen.

» TOM BUCKNER

Nailing a Bob Loveless drop-point hunter pattern, Tom fashioned it from CPM 154 blade steel, a stainless steel guard, stag handle scales and red liners. *(Bob Glassman image)*

⌃ ERIK NYLUND

Exuding tradition is a "Hakkapella" Damasteel hunter embellished with scrimshaw of a Pointer on a reindeer antler and ebony handle.

» RON ROSENBAUGH

The 4.5-inch blade of the ATS-34 drop-point hunter has flinted flats for some aesthetic texturing, and an elk antler handle and red Micarta spacer for more looks and feel.

« DAN LEEPER

Made from a file with marks left over to prove it, the "Elk Hunter" will field dress and skin elk via the 6-inch blade, and also has an elk antler handle, complete with maple burl spacer.

« J.R. REEVES

"Buckshot" damascus is an appropriate pattern for the drop-point blade of a stag-handle hunter with a damascus pommel.

« LANDON ROBBINS

The damascus fixed blade with burl handle is as cool as a keyhole hunter.

(Ward image)

« JEREMY SPAKE

It doesn't get much more Finnish than a puukko with a stabilized Masur birch and reindeer antler handle.

GARY GROVES

Red spacers frame the solid stag handle of an upswept 154CM hunter/skinner with some file work on the thumb ramp.
(PointSeven image)

W. ALLEN SURLES

A fine Bob Loveless-style drop-point hunter in a mammoth ivory handle and a guard engraved by Phillip Fontaine will call in the other hunters if not the wild game.

LIN RHEA

Here's an old-school stacked hunter in damascus steel, and blackwood, Micarta and aluminum handle spacers.
(Ward image)

PEKKA TUOMINEN

There isn't a job you couldn't do in the field using the three Nordic hunters in birch bark handles and leather sheaths. *(SharpByCoop image)*

» J.W. RANDALL
Your calluses will cradle the crevices of the Himalayan ram horn handle on a "Texas wind"-damascus hunter with file-worked spacer.

⌄ JESS HOFFMAN
The knife is just smooth— the desert ironwood burl and the face and lines of the Bohler N690 blade. *(Cory Martin Imaging)*

« DAN DUGDALE
An antique Canadian silver coin ring is fitted to the antler handle of the D2 hunter behind the guard, and a smaller ring coin of the same pattern is mounted on the pommel. *(SharpByCoop image)*

« GREG WARDMAN
So many choices—the two CPM 154 drop-point hunters at left have tulipwood and stag handles, while the CPM S35VN skinner comes in a spalted oak burl grip. *(Cory Martin Imaging)*

» TERRY SCHREINER

The stag was sectioned but used selectively well for a 9.5-inch O1 drop-point hunter, which also happens to have a Mexican centavo shaped to match the pommel.

(Ward image)

« CALVIN ROBINSON

Giraffe bone gives the small trapper some legs to stand on. *(Ward image)*

« JAMES SCROGGS

On occasion you need a "Super Semi Hunter" in a 4.25-inch CPM 154 blade and an English walnut handle to get the job done. *(Ward image)*

« TIMOTHY STEINGASS

Sometimes a guy's in the mood for an amber-stag-handle hunter with a W2 blade and wavy temper line, and at other times a CPM 154 hunting knife in English walnut.

(SharpByCoop image)

Mighty Mammoth & Mastodon

Mighty might be an understatement. In every sense of their being, mammoths and mastodons were behemoths. They tread softly nowhere, shook the earth and rattled the trees, trampled forests and laid down tall grasses. Theirs was a life of largess, munching machines with tusks to fend off fellow foragers and enemy eaters. Layers of fur and feet of flab defended the flanks like coats of armor.

How such beauty arose from gargantuan beasts is the ultimate irony, but one that spans millennia to bring forth aged ivory with so much character, the crusts of the earth could have only created it. From the earth it arose, poking through top layers of ice sheets and glaciers where Inuit Indians harvested the mammoth and mastodon manna for the sale and splendor of all fortunate enough to bow before it.

Mammoth and mastodon ivory are beauties to behold, ancient, once-living artifacts with the power to transport takers-on thousands of years back in time, to an era when behemoth beasts brushed tree canopies with their massive behinds and bellowed out cacophony calls, sending chills through the spines of all other living creatures. □

《 GENE BASKETT
Crosscut mastodon ivory is nature's masterpiece hung on the liners of an art folder featuring a Mike Norris damascus blade and file work throughout. *(PointSeven image)*

》 BRUCE BARNETT
You can't help but imagine earth's molten inner core creating the "River of Fire" damascus and mighty mammoth ivory of the fine folding duo.
(PointSeven image)

》 STEPHEN MACKRILL
Green, white and blue were the Alaskan state colors in 13,000 B.C., but damascus and gold-anodized titanium weren't in vogue yet. *(PointSeven image)*

» ROBERT OHLEMANN

Bespeaking class and fine workmanship is a fine folder in Mike Norris ladder-pattern damascus, mammoth tooth, zirconium, and jeweled and file-worked titanium.

(PointSeven image)

» ALAN DAVIS

Maybe the Rob Thomas "typhoon"-pattern damascus blade represents the seas of time that swept across the tundra to create the mammoth bark handle of the dress locking folder, in Timascus bolsters, blue diamond accents and file work, no less.

(SharpByCoop image)

» DON HANSON III

The multi-ground W2 blade with wavy temper line proved a worthy partner for the green fossil mammoth ivory grip.

(SharpByCoop image)

» JERRY MOEN

Blue mammoth tooth boasts yellow, gold, white, purple and green striations, and there's a mirror-polished CTS XHP blade for bite.

» JIM PROVOST

He harvested the mammoth tooth, pinned it to the tang of razor-sharp CPM 154 steel and let it hang from his neck as a badge of bladed armor.

(Cory Martin Imaging)

» DAVID TABER

A CPM 154 "Lanny's Clip" folder wears a Technicolor dream coat of crosscut mammoth ivory.

(Cory Martin Imaging)

JOHN GRIFFIN

If mammoth tooth (here on the handle and push button of a damascus auto) doesn't make you marvel at the historic markings of Mother Nature, nothing will.

BOB MERZ

Mammoth ivory is framed by Bruce Christensen engraving to better appreciate the inner beauty, and pulls double duty as the handle of a CTS-XHP mid-lock folder.

(PointSeven image)

RON ROSENBAUGH

Before there was Micarta, carbon fiber or G-10 for the handles of drop-point hunting knives, there was "cracked ice" mammoth ivory, though they probably didn't call it that back then.

TIM LAMBKIN

Dimpled bolsters play bookends to the mighty mammoth tooth handle of a tanto-style fixed blade.

(PointSeven image)

W.D. PEASE

Bolster engraving and gold inlay work by Mark Waldrop accessorize the golden hues of mammoth ivory on a stainless damascus folding art knife.

(PointSeven image)

Full-Tilt Tacticals

Full bore, full on, no-holds-barred, overbuilt, hardcore, heavy metal and heavy duty—knifemakers eat this stuff up. They pound steel out, profile it, belt-sand blades, sand the grit out of them and add hardware. They make parts, cut pins, set springs, tighten locks and shape handles. These are the steel workers, the smiths, builders and forgers.

And they dig tactical knives, those mean little blades that flip open, spring into action and eat up sandpaper like Dobermans through chew toys. It shouldn't be surprising that full-tilt tactical fixed blades and folders took the knife market by storm. Why it didn't happen sooner is the amazing part. I mean, why didn't knife-carrying, gun-totin' free Americans make freaky fast and formidable folders with sandblasted blades and Micarta handles years ago?

Full-tilt tactical folders and fixed blades speak to the warrior in all of us. They exude utility and purpose. They are easy to carry, conceal and retrieve. They clip to pockets, and flip open with a flick of a finger or thumb, a push of a button or a nudge of a front bolster. They have tanto, spear-point, multi-ground and recurved blades. The points penetrate and the edges sever cord and webbing alike. These are full-tilt tacticals, and they're built to last, made to work and honed to perfection. □

⌄ KIRBY LAMBERT
The plunge grind at the modified tanto tip defines the flipper folder, which is executed cleanly in XHP steel, Damasteel bolsters, titanium hardware, carbon fiber scales and a zirconium pocket clip.
(PointSeven image)

» RICHARD S. WRIGHT
The ambidextrous tactical auto is defined by a CPM 154 blade with a modified tanto/dagger point, all-titanium construction and textured G-10 and Micarta handle scales and bolsters.

⌃ LARAMIE JACKSON
"Starfire" stainless steel, forged by Chad Nichols, shoots across the blade of the flipper folder, otherwise dressed in titanium and "pearl carbon fiber."

» LES VOORHIES

Designed by Faisal Yamin, the "Claymore" flipper folder is all there in black and gray—the CTS-XHP blade, "pearl carbon fiber" handle and zirconium and titanium parts.
(Cory Martin Imaging)

« JERRY MOEN

Multi-ground push button folders with carbon-fiber handles and blued-titanium hardware, the "Blue Max" and "Blue Max 2" blow maximum smoke. *(PointSeven image)*

» JENS ANSO

When going with the "Monaco" RWL 34 flipper folder, it's good to visit upscale casinos and the yacht-lined harbors of the French Riviera.

« LUCAS BURNLEY

The acid-washed CPM 154 blade with sharp curved edge and plain titanium handle give the frame-lock folder a tactical yet utilitarian look and feel. *(PointSeven image)*

» DAVE WENGER

The "Raptor Hawk" and "Tac-5 LoPro" spike tomahawk and tactical knife combo wears its black canvas Micarta and matte-finished steel like badges of honor. *(Cory Martin Imaging)*

MICHAEL RAYMOND
The Bohler M390 blade and titanium handle blend seamlessly for a far out "Galaxis" frame-lock flipper folder. *(SharpByCoop image)*

MICHAEL ZIEBA
"United We Stand" and divided the cutting media falls after the M390 blade gets done cutting, and then there's the red-hot quivering arrow pocket clip.
(SharpByCoop image)

TYLER TURNER
Blued titanium hardware, zirconium pivot collars and a Mokuti pocket clip jump off the otherwise gray CPM D2 steel and titanium dress tactical folder.
(SharpByCoop image)

SEAN MCWILLIAMS
The maker's "Panama" LinerLock is as full-tilt tactical as it gets, but would also look nice clipped to the khakis of a man wearing a white fedora.

SEAN O'HARE
Milled titanium and other stylish features leave their marks on the "Raider" CTS XHP stainless steel flipper folder.

After all these years of wondering, you'd think I would have just asked a bladesmith who forges "feather damascus" how he or she gets such an incredibly intricate pattern, with tight lines like barbs of feathers stretching out from a shaft to form vanes, barbules and barbicels. And what I really want to know is how blade-smiths then forge that pattern so the shaft and quill of the feather extend lengthwise up the side of a blade, directly to the point, while the barbs, barbules and barbicels stretch out to the sides and towards the edge and the spine of the blade, their very tips ending precisely at the top and bottom of the bade, as if the blade itself were the outline of feather, and the damascus lines the side of the feather.

And how do knifemakers sculpt steel into the forms of ladies using little hand chisels, Dremel tools, abrasives and emery cloth? Are they all trained artists who carve, stipple, texture, chase, jig, scrimshaw and engrave? Who taught them how to create bezels and inlay precious jewels into them? Or how do they automatically know how to machine screws, pins and locks, or fashion spring-assisted openers, bolster releases, flipper mechanisms, locking liners and frame locks?

Were they all born understanding ball bearings, bushings, friction fitting and tight tolerances? I guess I have a lot of questions to ask blademiths and knifemakers. Meantime, enjoy the "State of the Art" in modern handmade knives. I'm sure you'll have questions of your own after turning the next 45 or 50 pages. Jot them down so you don't forget to ask. □

Blades of a Feather

They stick together alright, these blades of a feather—in fine knife collections, on show tables, at exhibitions and in display cases and cabinets. The feather damascus patterning is a knifemaker's dream—how the shaft of the feather extends the length of the blade, the outer vanes flaring out toward the edge in downy fashion, tickling the blade bevel with their barbs, barbules and barbicels.

The feather-damascus pattern is tight, neat and consistent, yet lively and moving, almost fluid, as a feather floating in the air, drifting downward, blowing back and forth in the breeze and landing gently on the workbench. Feather damascus tickles the fancy, it gives a knife lift and lets it soar.

How the bladesmiths achieve such perfect patterning is over my head, aloft, the soaring abilities of the highfalutin class of smithies who stack steel, pound, fold, flatten and fold, cross-cut and hammer until a feather pattern emerges as if plucked from a partridge and planted on the face of a steel billet. □

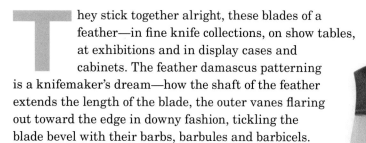

» RICHARD S. WRIGHT
A classic Italian stiletto, the bolster-release switchblade features a feather damascus blade, carved pink pau shell handle scales that continue the feather pattern, fileworked and carved titanium liners and spacers, and bronze cross-guards.

⌃ CODY HOFSOMMER
The rosewood-handle hunter has a feather damascus blade that's to die for. *(Cory Martin Imaging)*

« TERRY VANDEVENTER
Wooly mammoth ivory handle scales are nearly as figured and patterned as the feather damascus blade on the fancy bowie knife with silicon bronze liners, spacers and pins.
(Caleb Royer Studios image)

ALAIN and JORIS CHOMILIER
A sapphire marks the spot where the carved bronze handle points forward to the C. Penot feather-damascus blade.

« BRUCE BARNETT
The feather pattern of the damascus blade is almost as static and electric as the walrus ivory is ancient and fossilized, yet it's a match made in knife heaven.
(PointSeven image)

« HARVEY DEAN
Feather damascus patterning follows the fighter blade straight to the point, flaring out to the edge and spine, and defining the fixed blade in a stag handle and gold-inlaid guard.
(PointSeven image)

« TONY KARLSSON
Feather damascus forged by Randy Haas covers the blade and bolsters of the gent's tactical, all but the North Sea fossil mammoth ivory grip. *(SharpByCoop image)*

⌃ CAL GANSHORN
Feather damascus and ironwood prove a powerfully pretty combination.

Classic Carving, Checkering & Fluting

» JOSEF RUSNAK

A collaborative effort with Buddy Weston, kids carved from bone peer over a wall to the other side on this otherworldly knife parading more carved media—copper, gold, stainless steel and silver—in an urban motif, and a heat-blued mosaic damascus blade.

(Jakub Sebek photo)

» BEN SEWARD

The "Death Angel" parades a "flaming twist"-damascus blade and fittings and a colossally carved blackwood handle.

(Caleb Royer Studios image)

» ED CAFFREY

Carved chevrons highlight the African blackwood handle of a bowie knife sporting a laminated 1080-15N20-and-nickel blade and a mild steel oval guard.

» SHANE TAYLOR

Equally dazzling are the gold-colored damascus blade and bolsters, and the Celtic knot work-style carved African blackwood handle.

(PointSeven image)

» KARL ANDERSEN

A takedown dagger with a ladder-pattern, hot-blued damascus blade, the knife features a wrought iron guard and a fluted and stabilized Bubinga wood handle with twisted silver wire accents.

(Caleb Royer Studios image)

⌄ RICK DUNKERLEY

The frame of this masterpiece is scroll-engraved and case-colored mild steel bookending a carved walrus ivory handle and coming before a six-bar damascus blade.

(PointSeven image)

« BEN BREDA and BEN SEWARD

It took two to tango—Ben and Ben—with Seward classically carving the black walnut handle of the W2 fixed blade, complete with smoky temper line, and Breda forging all the steel, including the damascus guard. *(Caleb Royer Studios image)*

» PAVEL SEVECEK

This work of knife art integrates a carved ivory frog pommel, a "frog" mosaic damascus blade, and spacers fashioned from silver and Serpentinite stone.

« ALISTAIR BASTIAN

A hand carved and fitted carbon fiber handle acts as the winged tail of the "Praying Mantis" flipper folder with a san mai damascus blade and Timascus bolsters.

(Cory Martin Imaging)

STATE OF THE ART   **133**

RICHARD TESARIK

Ah yes, the "Pearl Magnolia," what a beautiful flower she is, sashaying carved mother-of-pearl, stainless steel and German silver.

JULIE WARENSKI-ERICKSON

The renowned engraver carves marble into a basket-weave pattern for the handle of an art dagger that also features a Devin Thomas damascus blade and gold-inlaid highlights.
(SharpByCoop image)

WILLIAM LLOYD

It's all impressive—the carved battle scene, carved dragonhead pommel, tightly patterned, multi-bar damascus blade and overall shape and execution of the knife.
(PointSeven image)

LARRY FUEGEN

The handle, silver frame, gold-inlaid guard and pommel nut are carved to perfection and outfitted properly with a damascus bowie/fighter blade.
(SharpByCoop image)

RUSSELL ROOSEVELT

A damascus dagger is given the fluted-African-blackwood handle treatment, complete with twisted silver wire wrap, and topped off with a sculpted damascus double guard, pommel cap and nut.
(SharpByCoop image)

JOHN HORRIGAN

It's hard to choose a crowning achievement on the "King's Crown Dagger," whether it's the 24k-gold-inlaid "explosion"-pattern damascus blade, hot-blued steel guard and crown-shaped pommel set with rubies, diamonds, sapphires and amethysts, or the fluted pre-ban elephant ivory handle wrapped in gold wire. *(PointSeven image)*

JOSH FISHER

The time it must have taken to hand carve all the checkers in the handle is as mind blowing as that tightly patterned damascus blade.

JOHN DOYLE

The maker's version of a Persian kard does the pattern justice, showcasing a carved African blackwood handle, differentially heat treated W2 blade, thorn and vine file worked spacers, a stippled bronze ferrule and damascus collar. *(SharpByCoop image)*

DANIEL STEPHAN

Everything's carved on the fantasy fighter—the "feather"-damascus blade, O1 guard, gold bail and ivory handle, with more gold planted between the blade and guard.
(SharpByCoop image)

YASUTAKA WADA

Whale tooth carved in a basket weave pattern makes for a powerfully pretty handle on a stainless steel fixed blade.

Pin-Prickling the Ivories

» TOM HEARD

Two-sided scrimshaw in bone is orchestrated in a Japanese theme depicting koi fish, lotus blossoms, masks and waves, all for the handle of a Damasteel automatic folder donning Robert Eggerling mosaic damascus bolsters.

» GAETAN BEAUCHAMP

Part of a set of seven knives, depicted in water buffalo horn and mammoth ivory handles are the seven most dangerous game animals to hunt in Africa—rhino, lion, hippo, leopard, elephant, cape buffalo and crocodile. Each knife sports a Mike Norris damascus blade.

» LINDA KARST STONE

A pair of J.P. Miller mild steel and mammoth ivory fighters depict Johnny Depp as Tonto and William Fichtner as Butch Cavendish from the movie *The Lone Ranger*.
(Cory Martin Imaging)

» DAN HAWKINS

Only a Viking rides a sled pulled by polar bears, at least in the realm of a D'Holder CPM 154V fixed blade with a nickel silver guard engraved by Bruce Christensen.
(SharpByCoop image)

SANDRA BRADY

A Jim Downs Persian bowie is the benefactor of a Persian warrior motif scrimshawed in ivory and butted against heat colored damascus bolsters and an Alabama Damascus blade.

(SharpByCoop image)

BOB HERGERT

A snake lashes out from a bed of flowery vines, captured within the confines of ivory handle slabs on a Chuck Gedraitis flipper folder.

(Cory Martin Imaging)

GINNY HALL

Mountain goats are shown against a backdrop of snowy peaks on the elephant ivory handle of a Roger Hatt RWL-34 clip-point hunter featuring a guard engraved by Gordon Alcorn.

GARY WILLIAMS

A leopard lies in wait on the fossil ivory handle of a Dennis Friedly CPM 154 art knife further enhanced by Ray Cover Jr. gold inlay and engraving.

(SharpByCoop image)

SANDRA BRADY

As the whalers did, a nautical theme is scrimshawed in elephant ivory on a Michael O'Machearley knife with a Jim Coffee damascus blade.

(PointSeven image)

Palpable & Gripping Art

《 RAYMOND RYBAR

This isn't your average cinquedea (Italian civilian short sword), considering a five-bar damascus blade with no less than six fullers on each side, an ebony handle, golden gears, and a carved Brazilian gold guard accented with rubies.

》 KOJI HARA

Stippling and carving steel to resemble bamboo and inlaying abalone are signs of a true craftsman, along with little details like the leaf-like carvings on the Cowry blade.

(SharpByCoop image)

》 ANDERS HEDLUND

It's not just the engraving and gold and black-lip-pearl inlays that make the "Fortune" folding dagger great, but the way it's all executed that elevates the piece.

(SharpByCoop image)

⌃ KEVIN CASEY

Enlisting the services of Russia's Konstantin Pushkarev for the mother-of-pearl, silver-wire and opal handle art, all in a buffalo motif, proved a stroke of creative genius.

(PointSeven image)

》 ANTONIO FOGARIZZU

Geometric pearl inlays and an anodized-titanium frame greatly enhance the carbon fiber handle of an M390 flipper folder of the most fashionable kind. *(SharpByCoop image)*

TOMONARI HAMADA

Not all gold and carved mother-of-pearl girls are this good looking, but some models, like the folder with slide-out blade guard, are a cut above the rest. *(SharpByCoop image)*

JOHNNY STOUT

A mammoth ivory inlay stands out against the Julie Warenski-Erickson gold inlay and engraving covering the rest of the handle of the "Sirocco" double-action automatic folder, complete with Joe Burke "River of Fire"-damascus blade.

(Caleb Royer Studios image)

DAVID BROADWELL

Designed with strong Art Deco elements, the mosaic-damascus folder features a titanium handle with engraved sun rays around a Moku-Ti (mokumé and titanium) pivot.

E. JAY HENDRICKSON

Carved maple even exhibits the correct colors of the autumn leaves, acting as the gripping, palpable handle of a damascus bowie with file-worked oval guard.

(SharpByCoop image)

SHANE TAYLOR

The maker's gears were grinding—for the mosaic-damascus blade and carved and sculpted handle of the folding steam punk masterpiece. *(PointSeven image)*

VLADIMIR KOLENKO

Beautiful and booty-full, the pierced and engraved guard and pommel parade opals, garnets and a London blue topaz, while the fluted mammoth ivory handle with twisted silver wire wrap attempts to get a grip on the Turkish-twist-damascus dagger.

ELIZABETH LOERCHNER

Black-lip pearl is the budding centerpiece of the sculpted stainless steel lock-back folding art dagger.

(SharpByCoop image)

CORRADO MORO

The "Desmo Blue Arrow" makes a bold statement in black-lip pearl, titanium, carbon fiber and RWL-34 steel.

(SharpByCoop image)

JODY MULLER

Death is all around the black-lip pearl inlays of a damascus flipper folder, and death never looked so good.

(SharpByCoop image)

LEONARDO FRIZZI

Sculpted and anodized titanium skulls leer and mock the knife user who dares grab the locking-liner art folder featuring a Simone Raimondi damascus blade.

» PETER PRUYN

The "sunflower" composite handle by Matt Peterson with honeycomb-like cells is as sticky sweet as the ball-peen-hammered copper guard and mosaic damascus blade.

(SharpByCoop image)

« HARUMI HIRAYAMA

Shell, wood, gold and silver inlays makeup the orchid motif of the ironwood handle on a 440C folder with silver liner and bolsters.

▽ W.D. PEASE

Appearing to be pearl, the groovy handle inlays of the stainless damascus folder are actually mammoth ivory enveloped by Mark Waldrop gold inlay and engraving.

(PointSeven image)

» THEO "ROCK" NAZZ

The pig-themed san mai kitchen knife enlists a stacked and twisted mosaic wood handle fashioned from a combination of purpleheart and reclaimed walnut and teak, and a 3D-printed, cast copper pig's head pommel with squiggly tail on the front bolster.

(SharpByCoop image)

« RICHARD TESARIK

The tri-colored "magnolia" handle is carved ebony, ironwood and mammoth ivory, all leading up to a sculpted bolster and leaf-shaped RWL-34 blade.

(SharpByCoop image)

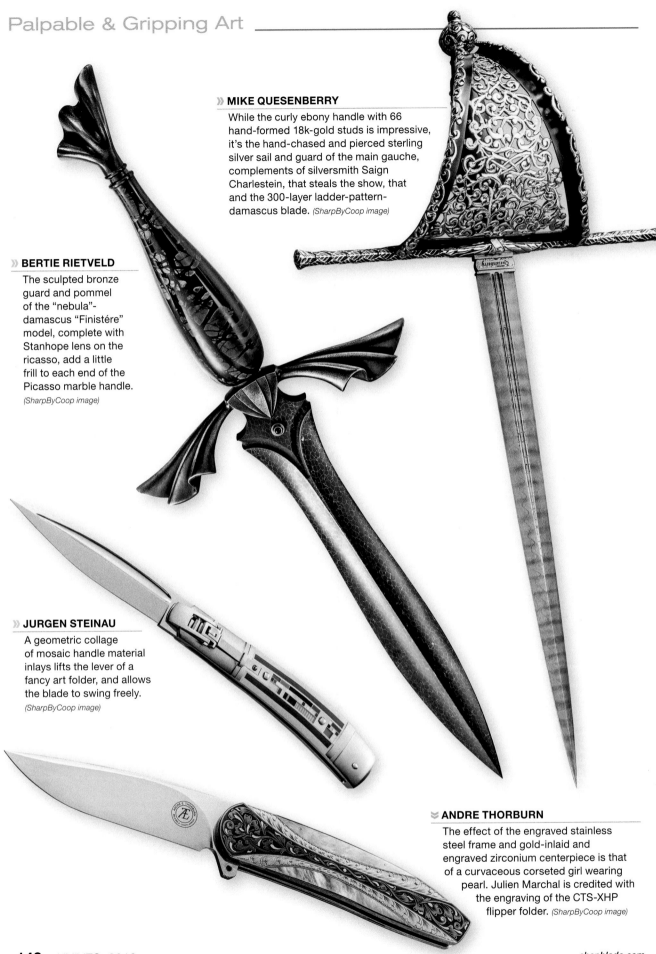

» MIKE QUESENBERRY

While the curly ebony handle with 66 hand-formed 18k-gold studs is impressive, it's the hand-chased and pierced sterling silver sail and guard of the main gauche, complements of silversmith Saign Charlestein, that steals the show, that and the 300-layer ladder-pattern-damascus blade. *(SharpByCoop image)*

» BERTIE RIETVELD

The sculpted bronze guard and pommel of the "nebula"-damascus "Finistére" model, complete with Stanhope lens on the ricasso, add a little frill to each end of the Picasso marble handle.

(SharpByCoop image)

» JURGEN STEINAU

A geometric collage of mosaic handle material inlays lifts the lever of a fancy art folder, and allows the blade to swing freely.

(SharpByCoop image)

≫ ANDRE THORBURN

The effect of the engraved stainless steel frame and gold-inlaid and engraved zirconium centerpiece is that of a curvaceous corseted girl wearing pearl. Julien Marchal is credited with the engraving of the CTS-XHP flipper folder. *(SharpByCoop image)*

Sculpted Scalpels

You don't have to go to a park to see sculptures, or a museum, gallery or studio—no they're all around you if you take the time to look. There are snow sculptures, sculpted architectural elements inside and outside of buildings, at airports, and in offices, theaters and concert halls. Natural sculptures exist in caves and on cliffs, along lakes and rivers, in the desert, atop mountains, in the valleys, growing on trees, under the sea where coral reefs abound and skyward in the form of celestial bodies.

Then there are knives and the sculptors who specialize in steel, copper, titanium, ivory, pearl, bronze and brass. Bronze sculptures are common in public places, but how about knife handles and bolsters? Yes, knifemakers enjoy shaping their cutting media, smoothing the surfaces, molding the knife models until they take on artistic forms. Their masterpieces double as utilitarian edged tools and weapons, eating utensils and pocketknives.

Usable art is an uncommon form of expression, one that takes a creative yet mechanical hand, an eye for form meeting function. They're not just artworks, but sculpted scalpels, and they cut an aesthetic swath. □

STEFAN ALBERT

Mythical beings, some winged, others helmeted and headdress adorned, are armed and ready for battle within the confines of a folding damascus dagger.

(SharpByCoop image)

WOLFGANG LOERCHNER

It wasn't enough to sculpt steel, but the maker required gold and Bertie Rietveld damascus for a folding art knife with a claw-shaped blade.

(SharpByCoop image)

JODY MULLER

The golden tiger stalks the jungle canopy, ready to pounce from the handle of a damascus flipper folder.

(SharpByCoop image)

» WILLIAM TUCH
Where the Rob Thomas stainless damascus ends, the sculpted steel begins, terminating in a winged handle apparatus with Art Deco influences.
(PointSeven image)

» RICHARD TESARIK
The sculpted "Tricolor Magnolia" folder features an ebony, mammoth tusk and ironwood handle, silver pins and a leaf-shaped RWL-34 stainless steel blade.
(SharpByCoop image)

« SPENCER APLIN
Not much isn't sculpted, but perhaps the Randy Haas "lightning" damascus blade of the integral art dagger.
(SharpByCoop image)

» JOSEF RUSNAK
The sculpted bronze nude parades gold dots inlaid and draping from one arm and a gold-inlaid and engraved band on the other arm, all on the handle end of a "Lalique Folding Dagger" in an RWL-34 blade and blued mosaic-damascus bolsters.
(SharpByCoop image)

OWEN WOOD

The visionary Amayak Stapanyan sculpted the handle of the art folder that also showcases a dotted, striped and pattern-welded blade.

(SharpByCoop image)

« T.R. OVEREYNDER

A CTS-XHP split-tail folding dagger is adorned with black-lip-pearl inlays and some creative carving and sculpting by Amayak Stepanyan. *(PointSeven image)*

« RON BEST

The maker plied his trade in damascus, gold, black-lip pearl and steel, among other materials, sculpting all into an Art Deco lock-back folding knife. *(Cory Martin Imaging)*

⌃ SHANE TAYLOR

Sculpted bronze skulls stare out from the "Wall of Souls," in this case the bolsters of a Turkish-twist-damascus folder featuring mammoth ivory handle scales.

(PointSeven image)

⌃ CHARLES BENNICA

The "Piranha" is a sharp little monster, in part because of the meteorite blade with a handcrafted and assembled RWL-34 cutting edge, and partly because of the sculpted 416 stainless steel handle. *(SharpByCoop image)*

Glorious Engraving
(Grabado Glorioso)

Sometimes flowery adjectives like glorious, excellent, incredible, amazing and fabulous are overused to the point of no longer having the desired effect of conveying something special. If the word very is used in front of hot, is that object hotter than regular hot, and what exactly does that mean? If something is incredibly original, how much more original is it than regular original? And when an object is fascinatingly beautiful, what makes it more fascinating than normal beautiful?

None of this applies to gloriously engraved knives, because if anything deserves the adjective glorious put in front of it, it's the engraved pieces on this and the following pages. They truly are glorious in every sense of the word. That would include being illustrious, delightful, wonderful, magnificent, remarkable, bright, dazzling, grand, gorgeous, and marked by beauty and splendor.

So if I use too many flowery adjectives in the descriptions of the knives within the photo captions, forgive me. I'm solely trying to convey their unique qualities, what sets them apart and makes them singularly spectacular. There I go again. The engraving herein is so glorious that I went with Spanish in addition to English to emphasize the glorious engraving, or grabado glorioso. □

« VALERIO PELI

A Reinhard Tschager dagger and drop-point hunter set is dressed in antique tortoise shell, gold, diamonds, engraving, and gold chains and pendants.
(Francesco Pachi image)

⩔ PAUL MARKOW

The long, sleek Bill Kennedy Jr. two-blade trapper in BG-42 steel is highlighted by a musk ox horn handle with some scroll engraving on both ends.
(PointSeven image)

⩗ ANTONIO MONTEJANO

An elaborate Riccardo Mainolfi integral knife is gold inlaid and engraved with imagery depicting Theseus and the Minotaur.
(PointSeven image)

JULIE WARENSKI-ERICKSON

The combination of gold piqué work, platinum insets, engraving, "River of Steel" damascus and walrus ivory make for a remarkable Johnny Stout art folder.

(PointSeven image)

DAN RAFN

Engraved copper koi fish swim toward the RWL-34 sheepsfoot blade of a Jens Anso "Monte Carlo" folder.

AL FRISILLO

Classic engraving ties together the damascus blade of the Jon Finley knife with the Pietersite and black jade handle, as well as the lapis lazuli inlay in the rear bolster.

(PointSeven image)

KYLE ROYER

The 5160 fighter is coined "Black Beauty" for its eloquent, black flowing lines, sculpted African blackwood handle, bronze accents and French greyed "running wheat" engraving.

(Caleb Royer Studios image)

JULIE WARENSKI-ERICKSON

Gold engraving and diamond piqué work surround the stone handle of a damascus Warren Osborne folding dagger.

(Cory Martin Imaging)

BRIAN HOCHSTRAT

If you're going to build a double-action credit card auto such as this Matthew Lerch model, you could do much worse than to have the handle embellished with the well-endowed and armed warrior, or the blade and fantail-style pommel fashioned from Mike Norris damascus. *(SharpByCoop image)*

BRIAN BRIDGES

A lady with golden flowers in her hair beautifies the bolsters of a Steve Hoel pearl-handle folder.
(SharpByCoop image)

RUSS ZIMA

Scroll engraving acts as a centerpiece of a Harvey King drop-point hunter in an Alabama Damascus blade, mammoth ivory handle and red liners. *(SharpByCoop image)*

CURT ERICKSON

Blued steel, blue marble, gold inlay, topaz, engraving and carving—and that's just the handle end of the hand-rubbed 440C fixed blade.
(SharpByCoop image)

DAVID RICCARDO

Look closely for the hidden faces within the engraved and gold inlaid handle of the Rick Genovese folding dagger sporting a Jerry Rados Turkish twist damascus blade.

» RICK EATON

A knight and martyred saint get golden treatment (of the 18-karat rose gold and glorious engraving kind) on a mosaic damascus automatic art folder. *(PointSeven image)*

⌃ RAY COVER

Bank heists are rarely as beautiful as depicted in golden engraving on a damascus Scott Sawby tab-lock folder. *(Cory Martin Imaging)*

« JOE MASON

Gold inlay and engraving highlight a Tom Ploppert hunting set with nice lines and clean elephant ivory handles. *(PointSeven image)*

⌃ ROBERT KOVACIK

An engraved and 24k-gold-inlaid cactus flower blooms on the guard of a damascus fixed blade with maple wood handle.

⌃ DAVID RICCARDO

Usually it's the amber that has waves, but in the case of the Bill Behnke dagger, it's the damascus and engraving. *(Cory Martin Imaging)*

» MICHAEL VAGNINO

A dragon lashes out from the bolster of the "Shadow Hawk" CTS-XHP flipper folder with carbon fiber handle scales.

(Hiro Soga image)

» ELENA BOSIO

The skeletons with golden helmets and horns have lost their lives but apparently not their fight within the gripping confines of a Sergio Consoli flipper folder.

(Cory Martin Imaging)

» JODY MULLER

Though you might not want to ask the ladies on the bolsters to dance, the damascus folder with ancient ivory handle scales will cut a rug.

(SharpByCoop image)

⯆ FRANCINE LARSTEIN

A lifelike etched ostrich scene stretches across the blade of a Don Norris file-worked D2 bowie with a mammoth ivory handle. The knife was assembled and completed by David Ammons from pieces that Don had prepared before his passing. *(SharpByCoop image)*

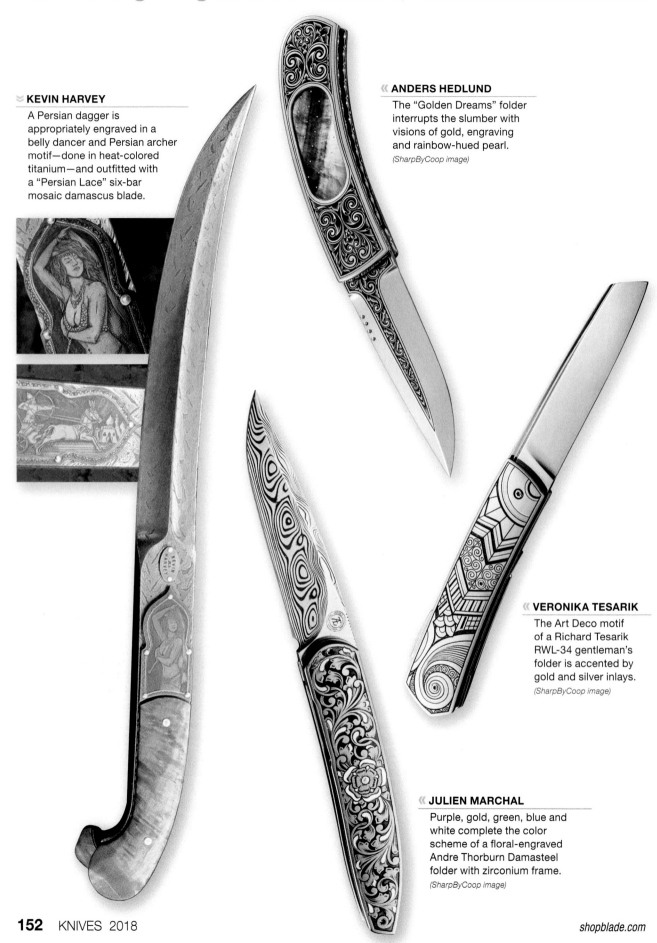

☰ KEVIN HARVEY

A Persian dagger is appropriately engraved in a belly dancer and Persian archer motif—done in heat-colored titanium—and outfitted with a "Persian Lace" six-bar mosaic damascus blade.

❮❮ ANDERS HEDLUND

The "Golden Dreams" folder interrupts the slumber with visions of gold, engraving and rainbow-hued pearl.
(SharpByCoop image)

❮❮ VERONIKA TESARIK

The Art Deco motif of a Richard Tesarik RWL-34 gentleman's folder is accented by gold and silver inlays.
(SharpByCoop image)

❮❮ JULIEN MARCHAL

Purple, gold, green, blue and white complete the color scheme of a floral-engraved Andre Thorburn Damasteel folder with zirconium frame.
(SharpByCoop image)

Gold-i-Lops

RICK GENOVESE
It's hard to upstage an apple-green jade handle inlay, but the Joe Mason engraved gold embellishments do their best on a sleek folding dagger.

« KEN STEIGERWALT
The Art Deco "Astrum X" Damasteel folder features a black-lip pearl handle inlay with 14k-gold accents.
(SharpByCoop image)

« BRUCE BUMP
The "Ming Dagger" is ready to enter the dynasty dressed in a mosaic damascus blade, a gold-wire-wrapped, fluted mammoth tusk handle, a lathe-turned and gold-covered mosaic damascus cross-guard and pommel, and a gold crown adorning the pommel.
(Caleb Royer Studios image)

« MICHAEL HENNINGSSON
There's nothing like scrolled gold and engraving for dressing up an RWL-34 folder, complete with gold thumb stud.

BARRY HAIMS
There's a definite art form to embellishing Victorinox keychain knives with carved gold and inlaid jewels, and Haims is a fine hand at that.
(PointSeven image)

» SHAUN and SHARLA HANSEN

A bolster-release damascus dress automatic folder, gold adorns the blade and guard, and serves as a backdrop for the sculpted 416 stainless steel handle overlays. *(SharpByCoop image)*

⌄ RODRIGO SFREDDO

The integral Turkish-twist-damascus "Moondance" model is a stunner, handled in ironwood and embellished with relief-carved copper and gold. *(SharpByCoop image)*

» JOHNNY STOUT

The gold-inlaid and engraved bolster is the centerpiece of a pearl-handle damascus art folder. *(Ward image)*

» WOLFGANG LOERCHNER

An all-time favorite folder name, the "Squidette," is a sculpted stainless steel masterpiece garnished with gold inlays. *(SharpByCoop image)*

» HARVEY DEAN

Twenty-four-karat gold highlights the shapely guard of an 18.25-inch damascus fighter, also featuring a fossil walrus ivory handle. *(PointSeven image)*

» VLADIMIR KOLENKO

The 14k-gold, sterling silver and garnet embellishments are tastefully executed on a Turkish-twist-damascus (supplied by Zladinox) fighter with a mammoth ivory grip.

« JODY MULLER

Both handle scales of the damascus Persian folder are heavily engraved in a Middle Eastern dancer motif, including inlays of copper, gold, diamonds and garnets. *(SharpByCoop image)*

« STEVE HOEL

Golden vines engraved and inlaid by Barry Lee Hands span the pearl handle and weave around the diamond bolster settings, with the precious stones also cut by Barry.

(SharpByCoop image)

« JOHN HORRIGAN

Gold vines wend their way up the six-bar "twisted W's"-pattern damascus blade of a powerfully pretty pearl-handle bowie.

(PointSeven image)

⌃ ANDERS HEDLUND

He gets a whole bunch of gold stars for his "Persian Star" Damasteel art folder with an RWL-34 frame, black-pearl handle inlays and engraved bolsters.

(SharpByCoop image)

A Metallic Mosaic

» **RICK DUNKERLEY**

Combining heat-colored mosaic damascus, mild steel, engraving and a citrine in the thumb stud was a stroke of artistic knifemaking genius.
(PointSeven image)

» **ANDREA PULISOVA**

Both the lion that's scrimshawed on the hippo tooth handle and the mosaic damascus patterning of the blade belt out some good roars.

» **CONNY PERSSON**

The mosaic damascus pattern explodes out toward the double edges of the art dagger, complete with reindeer antler handle, blackwood spacers and more mosaic damascus for the bolsters.

⌄ **ALAIN and JORIS CHOMILIER**

The pattern of the C. Avakian mosaic damascus dips down toward the edge like seashells lined up along the seashore, an oosic handle acting as the anchor of this cutting vessel.

⌃ **BRUCE BINGENHEIMER**

The 9⅝-inch blade is a four-way mosaic "W's" pattern that's more difficult to forge than to describe, here matched with an ancient walrus ivory handle.
(Caleb Royer Studios image)

« KEVIN HARVEY
A theme knife, the "Golden Garden Bowie" marries a gold-hued "four leaf clover" mosaic damascus blade with an engraved gold hummingbird and a gold-lip-pearl handle.

» J.W. RANDALL
The Fleur-de-lis damascus blade is a stylized flower alright, sprouting out from a walrus ivory handle of the big bowie.

⩔ TONY KARLSSON
If the Conny Persson mosaic damascus of the dress locking-liner folder doesn't make the mouth water, maybe the vintage Westinghouse rag Micarta grip will do the trick. (SharpByCoop image)

« GREG CIMMS
Tightly packed grain structures result in the strongest blades, and here the bladesmith shows you the cells of the steel through mosaic damascus making and etching.
(SharpByCoop image)

⩓ PAVEL SEVECEK
Sometimes the key to successful mosaic damascus is the ability to recognize the subjects—maple leaves—as on the ivory-handle folder with Serpentinite stone spacer.

Charming Handle Charms

I n Japanese sword culture, menuki are handle charms, often tucked under the silk wrappings of stingray skin grips. Like all aspects of Japanese swords, the charms are handmade—fashioned one at a time, sculpted, carved and engraved. They are for decorative purposes only, though one could argue that, if appropriately shaped, they'd add palpability, and perhaps, if lucky charms, good omens for sword wielders.

Knifemakers being knifemakers, whether American, German, Nordic, Australian, Indian or South African, these little handle charms have not gone unnoticed. They've been adopted by knifemakers wanting to add more elements of intrigue to their knives.

A knife's ability to perform the cutting chores for which it was designed is the first priority, but ask any knifemaker, and he or she will tell you that form follows function. And sometimes it's the aesthetics of a knife that catches the eye of a potential buyer. So knifemakers pay attention to the details. They add amenities, embellish the pieces and fashion handle charms. And knife collectors are charmed, I'm sure. □

》 R.J. MARTIN

Shaped like a dragon, bat and lion, menuki (handle charms) are tucked under the cord-wrapped stingray skin handles of a trio of tanto knives.

(SharpByCoop image)

》 GLENN WATERS

Along with "Agyo" and "Ungyo," two Japanese temple guardians, engraved on the VG-10 blade of the "Yari" spear, the knife also sports an ebony handle and a silver dragon handle charm.

⌃ STEVE HILL

Turns out unicorns, the elusive creatures of the Greek and European wilds, do exist, one captured here on the curly maple handle of a damascus folder with a garnet thumb stud.

PETER PRUYN

Pure silver coins engraved by Mike Martyn add charm to each side of the cocobolo handle of a damascus "Recovered Treasure Knife" that also features a ball-peen-hammered nickel silver guard and domed pins.

(SharpByCoop image)

ALAN MITCHELL

The silver and mother-of-pearl dragonfly, fashioned by Tiaan Burger, was hammer-fitted into the dyed and stabilized maple burl handle of the foot-long 1070 fixed blade.

(Dirk Loots image)

SAM EDDLEMAN

A cast silver lion menuki is ensnared in the epoxy-soaked cord of the maker's "Shihan" N690 tanto that also includes a "Cognac" stingray skin handle.

(Cory Martin Imaging)

ANDREW MEERS

The "Ball of Yarn" is named as much for the pivot head as it is the charming kitty adorning the steel handle of the damascus locking-liner folder. *(Ward image)*

RAYMOND RYBAR

A takedown fighter, the polished piece showcases a feathery damascus blade, 24k-gold vine-and-leaf inlay and engraving, and engraved silver hardware, including an escutcheon plate on a buffalo horn handle.

Sheath Delights

BOB WRIGHT

The double sheath can be separated, and therefore worn together or apart. Holding two wood-handle fixed blades, the unit is made from vegetable-tanned leather, and lined and hand tooled by Jim Pickens, complete with silver concho on the outer strap. *(Caleb Royer Studios image)*

VLADIMIR PULIS

Seldom does a sheath integrate leather, silver, ebony, walnut and bear bone into its design, but the home of "The Bear" knife does, and what a knife pommel—sculpted by Andrea Pulisova—that sticks out of the end of the leather pouch.

DENNIS BRADLEY

Three cowhide belt sheaths showcase beavertail, rattlesnake and crocodile skin inlays.

JAY FISHER

The frog-skin-inlaid leather sheath is as fascinating as the cloud-jasper-handled CPM 154 "Arctica" fixed blade itself.

GABRIEL BELL

The black and red "tiger stripe" lacquered saya (sheath) integrates buffalo horn fittings. The handle of the wakizashi sword, by the way, is black-silk-wrapped stingray skin.

PAUL LONG

Row on row, material upon material, checkering near checkering, stitch by stitch and strap over strap, every detail of the leather sheath is exacting. *(SharpByCoop image)*

CLAUDE SCOTT

The tooled and stitched leather sheath that houses a John Doyle bowie knife is as cleanly executed, including a keeper strap, as the knife inside. *(SharpByCoop image)*

STEVEN RAMOS

A Larvikite stone handle with feldspar crystals extends from the end of the dyed, stitched and tooled leather sheath featuring a stingray skin inlay. *(SharpByCoop image)*

STEVE MILLER

A carved oak leaf graces the tooled and stitched leather pouch sheath fashioned to house an Alabama Damascus fixed blade with African blackwood bolsters and a white Micarta grip.

The Damascus Dance

» KARL ANDERSON
Armed with a hot-blued, 324-layer, single-twist-damascus blade and a desert ironwood handle, the cowboy bowie is ready for the wide-open range.
(Caleb Royer Studios image)

» MIKE QUESENBERRY
If the "stacked-W's"-pattern damascus blade and guard of the integral fighter don't dazzle you, the sculpted koa handle and domed Argentium silver pins just might do the trick.
(Caleb Royer Studios image)

» EDUARDO BERARDO
All we know for sure is that "West Texas Wind" damascus blew across the fighter blade and left its mark where it touched down.
(Caleb Royer Studios image)

⌃ SAM LURQUIN
The "BadasSam" damascus blade is actually pretty bad ass, and accompanied by a fine fossil ivory handle.
(Caleb Royer Studios image)

KYLE ROYER

It's cool to see a wharncliffe blade in a tight "W's-twist" damascus pattern, and a curly koa handle of this caliber. Kyle also engraved the spacer for good measure.

(Caleb Royer Studios image)

GAETAN BEAUCHAMP

Ovals of damascus dot the face of the blade, while a scrimshawed hummingbird makes a mark of its own, extracting nectar from a flower on the ivory handle.

BILL BURKE

"River of Fire" damascus wends its way along, highlighted by 24-karat gold and a little blackwood up on the riverbank.

(PointSeven image)

RON NEWTON

Gold-colored feather damascus is a game changer, accented by gold inlays within the guard and matched up with a dyed and stabilized maple burl handle.

(Ward image)

RODRIGO SFREDDO

The gold, silver and copper relief-inlaid guard gives the "Moonlight" full-integral fighter its name, while the Turkish-pattern damascus blade gives the knife game.

(Caleb Royer Studios image)

» **JOHN HORRIGAN**

The upswept "twisted W's"-pattern damascus blade is balanced by a keyhole-style pre-ban elephant ivory handle and 24k-gold-inlaid accents.

(Caleb Royer Studios image)

» **JIM POLING**

Brazilian rosewood and 288-layer ladder-pattern damascus bring the big old fighter to the next level.

(Caleb Royer Studios image)

» **MIKE CRADDOCK**

It's not that it is a 1095-and-15N20 damascus blade, but rather the pattern the bladesmith achieved for the mammoth-ivory-handle bowie that wows the onlookers.

(SharpByCoop image)

⌃ **LARAMIE JACKSON**

Complete with paper ivory Micarta handle, the Chad Nichols "bacon"-pattern damascus blade of the folding Kwaiken model sizzles.

⌃ **JERRY FISK**

The sun rises above the bowie, sending rays of light toward the edge of a damascus blade forged from Twin Towers steel.

(Ward image)

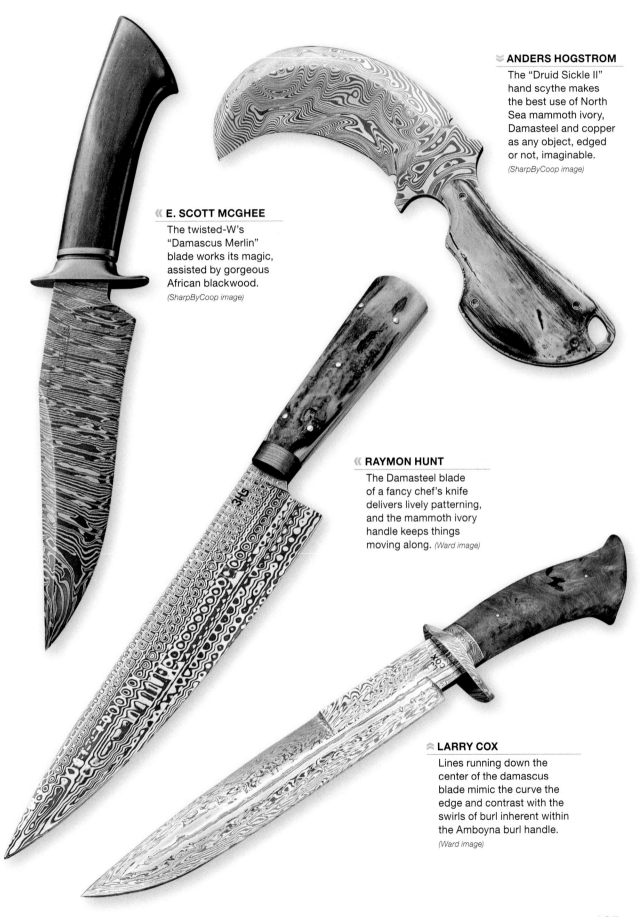

ANDERS HOGSTROM
The "Druid Sickle II" hand scythe makes the best use of North Sea mammoth ivory, Damasteel and copper as any object, edged or not, imaginable.
(SharpByCoop image)

E. SCOTT MCGHEE
The twisted-W's "Damascus Merlin" blade works its magic, assisted by gorgeous African blackwood.
(SharpByCoop image)

RAYMON HUNT
The Damasteel blade of a fancy chef's knife delivers lively patterning, and the mammoth ivory handle keeps things moving along. *(Ward image)*

LARRY COX
Lines running down the center of the damascus blade mimic the curve the edge and contrast with the swirls of burl inherent within the Amboyna burl handle.
(Ward image)

» LEONARDO FRIZZI

Gold-lip pearl handle inlays are like the scales of the beast that breathes fire through its Bertie Rietveld "dragonskin" damascus blade.

» MATTHEW PARKINSON

The 18-inch multi-bar composite damascus blade of the falchion extends out from the S-guard and walnut handle like the crooked finger of an evil witch.

(SharpByCoop image)

≫ EDMUND DAVIDSON

The one-piece, all-integral Alabama Damascus knife is as pleasing to the palm as it is to the eye.

(PointSeven image)

» THEO "ROCK" NAZZ

The "steam punk-mascus" blade of the bowie was forge welded in a canister from nuts, bolts, chopped up gear stock, 1095 high-carbon steel and nickel powder, and then outfitted with a san mai random-pattern 1080-and-1095-damascus cutting edge. The guard is 3D-printed cast bronze, and the ebony handle showcases 3D-printed cast bronze medallions.

(SharpByCoop image)

» OLAMIC TACTICAL

The "Ubari" damascus dagger has an exotic feel, as if it could be carried in the Sahara, with a good grip on the desert ironwood handle, of course.

(SharpByCoop image)

KEITH FLUDDER

Pattern-welded steel does "The Damascus Dance" along the edge of a big bowie that also parades a highly figured slab of Sambar stag.

(PointSeven image)

RAYMOND RYBAR

If it's "Templar Knight" damascus, you outfit it with an ivory handle, fleur-de-lis guard and a wood neck sheath, and call it quits for the day in the kingdom.

(PointSeven image)

RAPHAEL DURAND

The "Suminagashi" blade, made by Takefu Steel, gives the lock-back folder with carbon fiber handle scales more lines than a nightclub comedian.

(SharpByCoop image)

MASON RENFER

Though the "Moneycarta" handle with carbon fiber pins is a colorful delight, the money shot of the utility knife might actually be the "Odin's Eye" Damasteel blade.

(SharpByCoop image)

TIM LAMBKIN

There are diamonds in the rough of a Doug Ponzio damascus blade, some artistic texturing to the guard and colossal coloring on the mammoth tooth handle.

(PointSeven image)

TIMOTHY POTIER

A damascus blade awash with currents and pools of patterning is complemented by a blued S-guard, Sambar stag handle and carved steel pommel.

(PointSeven image)

ROBERT BURNS

The bowie/fighter in a stabilized Claro walnut handle and carved shibuichi (copper and silver) guard boasts multiple damascus blade patterns—standard twist and "twisted jelly roll."

(Caleb Royer Studios image)

DAVID LISCH

A split-ring D-guard bowie benefits from "feather river" damascus, ancient walrus tusk and 14-karat gold.

(Caleb Royer Studios image)

JEREMY KRAMMES

Sculpted "dragonskin" damascus by Bertie Rietveld (handle) meets Mike Norris "Fireclone" damascus (blade) in a battle of the pattern welds.

(SharpByCoop image)

« JAMIE LUNDELL

More than 28 inches of damascus spans the length of the Saxon sword blade, anchored by a moose antler and leather hilt, and a mild steel and silicon bronze guard and pommel. *(SharpByCoop image)*

« ROBERT APPLEBY JR.

The entire knife is one billet of damascus steel, a feat that's reserved for the most skilled knife artisans, particularly those who work up such features as double blade fullers and Spanish notches. *(SharpByCoop image)*

« TERRY VENDEVENTER

The squiggly lines of Turkish Twist damascus contrast nicely with the mammoth ivory patterning of the 14-inch bowie. *(Ward image)*

« STEFAN NEIL PALMER

This one's got brass, damascus, flash and panache. *(Ward image)*

San Mai, My... My!

t just wasn't enough. First there were wispy, smoky, bouncing, distinct and telltale temper lines. Taking their cues from traditional Japanese swordsmiths, modern knifemakers differentially hardened blades, giving them soft backs, or spines, and hard edges. Achieved by coating the blades with clay where the smiths didn't want the steel to be hard or brittle, and then heating and tempering the blades so only the non-coated areas—the last third of the blades, generally, toward and including the edge—would reach full hardness, and then etching and finishing the blades, the temper lines indicated where soft backs met the hard edges.

Meanwhile, bladesmiths were also forging damascus—layering different alloys of steel and nickel onto each other, heating, cutting, folding, hammering, forging, folding, hammering, forging, folding, cutting and repeating until hammered into a blade-shaped billet, then grinding, etching and finishing until damascus patterns emerged from the blade steel.

It just wasn't enough. The bladesmiths hadn't gotten their fill, turning to san mai blades, where two or more steels are forged and fused together with the harder steel in the core, and thus, along the edge once the outer, softer layers of steel are ground down, tapering toward the edge where they are eventually ground off, leaving only the hard core steel. And then, you guessed it, the blades are etched and finished, and voilá! san mai steel! My, my ... san mai! □

« PETER SWARZ-BURT
Few fighters combine crown stag handles with bronze guards and 15N20-and-1095 san mai damascus blades, but perhaps more should.
(SharpByCoop image)

« ED CAFFREY
The feather-pattern damascus blade is laminated with 410 stainless steel and butted up against a fluted nickel silver guard and carved and textured desert ironwood handle.
(Cory Martin Imaging)

⌃ PETER MARTIN
Designed by Faisal Yamin, the "Nebula" model gets groovy with a "lava lamp" san mai damascus blade, zirconium bolsters and a "Thunder-Strike" Kevlar handle. *(Cory Martin Imaging)*

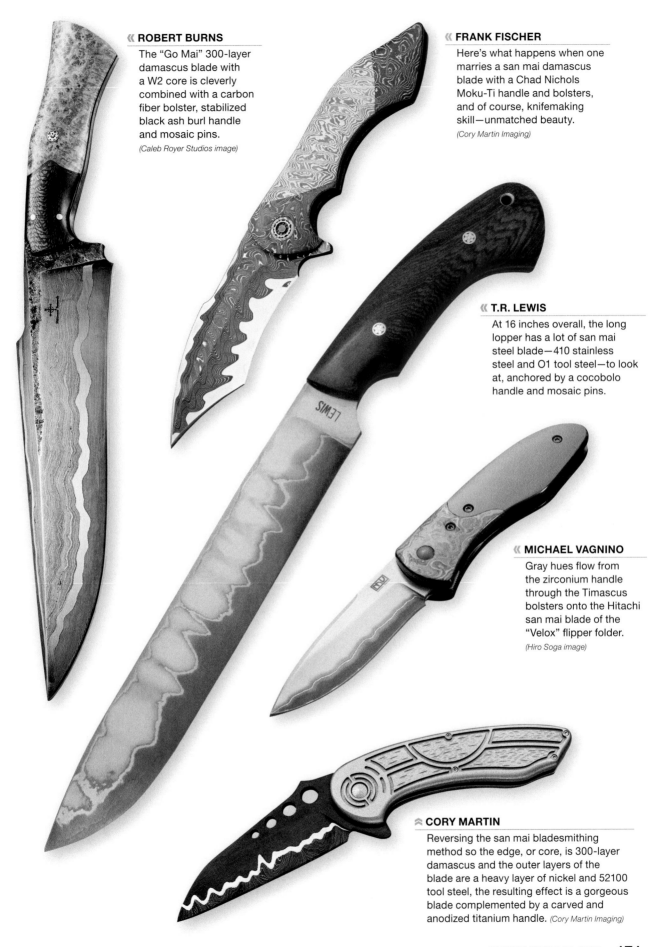

« ROBERT BURNS

The "Go Mai" 300-layer damascus blade with a W2 core is cleverly combined with a carbon fiber bolster, stabilized black ash burl handle and mosaic pins.

(Caleb Royer Studios image)

« FRANK FISCHER

Here's what happens when one marries a san mai damascus blade with a Chad Nichols Moku-Ti handle and bolsters, and of course, knifemaking skill—unmatched beauty.

(Cory Martin Imaging)

« T.R. LEWIS

At 16 inches overall, the long lopper has a lot of san mai steel blade—410 stainless steel and O1 tool steel—to look at, anchored by a cocobolo handle and mosaic pins.

« MICHAEL VAGNINO

Gray hues flow from the zirconium handle through the Timascus bolsters onto the Hitachi san mai blade of the "Velox" flipper folder.

(Hiro Soga image)

⌃ CORY MARTIN

Reversing the san mai bladesmithing method so the edge, or core, is 300-layer damascus and the outer layers of the blade are a heavy layer of nickel and 52100 tool steel, the resulting effect is a gorgeous blade complemented by a carved and anodized titanium handle. *(Cory Martin Imaging)*

Touché Mokumé

⌄ TRAVIS PAYNE

Mammoth ivory matches up nicely with the dovetailed mokumé bolsters of a Damasteel folder that has a small little nail nick in the blade. *(PointSeven image)*

« ALAN MITCHELL

The maker says it was his first time working with M3—the handle of the 1070 art knife being an M3 composite mokumé—but he was happy with the results, as are we. The bolsters are equally likeable Bertie Rietveld "dragon skin" damascus. *(Dirk Loots image)*

» DOUG BOYD

The mokumé guard isn't the only chocolaty goodness on the knife—the 7,000-year-old bog oak handle is pretty sweet, too, and the 1095 blade with wispy temper line is tempting. *(PointSeven image)*

» KEVIN KLEIN

The "Purple Prince" has a lot going for him, including a damascus blade with integral bolster, an African blackwood, mammoth ivory, copper and silver handle and a sheath made up of purpleheart wood with a copper frame on one side and mokumé on the other.
(SharpByCoop image)

FACTORY TRENDS

Even though there's been an ongoing movement for decades involving custom knifemakers and designers collaborating with factories on knife models, there always has been and continues to remain a distinct difference between handmade and production knives. It's not that factory knives aren't quality pieces. In fact, custom knifemakers have helped bring more quality to an industry that was already built on high, exacting standards. It's not that factory knives aren't innovative, because the opposite is true, or that they don't incorporate high-tech materials, mechanisms, parts and steels. They absolutely do.

The difference is only partly in what can and cannot be done in a production setting. Increasingly, factories have been able to adapt their machining and tooling to produce the most complicated custom knife designs. And the production setting has seen a dramatic increase in the types of steel, materials, locks and mechanisms knife manufacturers are able to produce.

In fact, the distinct difference between handmade and production knives doesn't necessarily coincide with the limitations of a factory setting, but instead perhaps the dissimilarities of what people view as factory versus handmade knives. For instance, you don't see a lot of (or any) folding saws or multi-tools coming out of the handmade side of the market. There are a select few, incredibly talented makers fashioning multi-blade folding knives, but not Leatherman-type multi-tools, or folding saws, and only a small, limited amount of custom hatchets, gut-hook skinners, knives with flashlights or things like sickles or tree trimming blades.

It's good that there remains a distinct difference between factory knives and handmade pieces. The knife industry needs as many facets of the business as possible. Trends in factory knives are more diverse and interesting than ever, and that's a good thing. There's no stale end of the business, only technology, innovation, change and advancement. ☐

Greetings from Washington

D. Peres tourist knives depicted famous monuments of the nation's capital

By Richard D. White

My fascination with pocketknives has resulted in a collection of many blades with historical connections, whether knives featuring an early invention, merchant or attraction. A slow but steady accumulation of finely crafted pocketknives dealing with our nation's capital led me to do some research into the historic significance of the edged implements.

They almost always showcase ornate handle scrollwork stamped with the words "Greetings from Washington." They are tourist knives designed to be worn on watch fob chains or inside vest pockets. And they celebrate the most popular attractions in our nation's capital.

Even before opening the blades to read the tang stamps, savvy knife collectors recognize that the intricately stamped aluminum handles and scrollwork are the work of German knife company D. (Daniel) Peres. The D. Peres Cutlery Company was one of the major knife manufacturers located in Solingen, Germany, at the time, and specialized in what has been called "coined knives." The knives flourished in the late 1880's when aluminum was first being used instead of nickel silver for pocketknife handles.

To expand his marketplace, Daniel Peres filed a patent application with the Canadian Patent Office Register of Patents in May of 1903. The German company also filed an American patent for "certain cutlery" on September of 1908, according to the Official Gazette of the United States Patent Office, Volume 138.

The watch fob knives made by the D. Peres Cutlery Company proudly display the slogan "Greetings from Washington."

The U.S. distributor was Magnetic Cutlery of Philadelphia, which marketed itself as "the sole agent for Daniel Peres Barrel Brand Cutlery."

Although historical buildings were the mainstay of D. Peres stamped aluminum knife handles, the company also produced knives bearing bridges, arches, famous personalities, Art Nouveau figures, National Parks and other tourist destinations.

LAW AND ORDER

Historically, Washington, D.C. was designed to be the governmental center of the United States, and its layout, architectural buildings and monuments were built to emphasize the importance of the city's role as

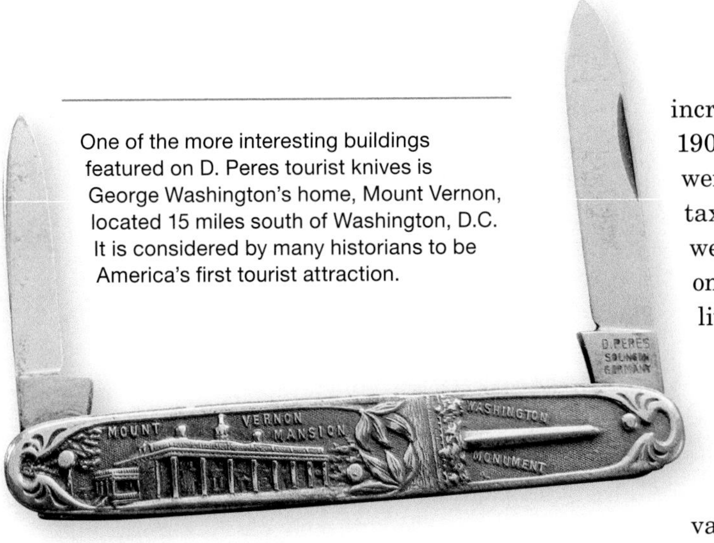

One of the more interesting buildings featured on D. Peres tourist knives is George Washington's home, Mount Vernon, located 15 miles south of Washington, D.C. It is considered by many historians to be America's first tourist attraction.

the focal point of law and order. During the War of 1812, however, many of the Washington's most important buildings, including the White House, U.S. Capitol, the House of Representatives building and the Library of Congress were burned to the ground by British invaders, and most of the important documents and books housed in the Library of Congress were destroyed in the fire.

The catastrophe forced city officials to redesign and restore edifices lost during the British invasion of the city. By the turn of the century, all of the buildings had been successfully reconstructed, although improvements continued into the 1920s and '30s. The 1920s ushered in a new sense of freedom for Americans. With automobiles rolling off the assembly lines by the thousands, American workers were able to take their families on "outings" to explore the scenery and historical places located beyond their own towns and city limits.

It was not only newly constructed buildings that brought tourists to Washington, D.C., but also a huge

increase in the number of paved highways. Before 1900, only four percent of roads in the United States were paved, but by 1923, 33 states had passed a gas tax that provided money for paving roads. There were 369,000 miles of paved roads in 1920, and only nine years later, that number had stretched, literally, to 852,000 miles of roadways.

In fact, Washington, D.C. boasted more paved roads than any other city in the United States. Some historians feel that the automobile and the paved roads they traveled provided a certain "freedom of choice," encouraging families to take vacations to places previously impossible, including the nation's capital.

The increased tourism also made way for D. Peres Cutlery souvenir knives with stamped aluminum handles featuring the capital's most architecturally significant buildings. By examining the depictions and comparing them to the architectural wonders they commemorate, there are some interesting conclusions to be drawn. Notably absent is one of the capital's most frequented monuments—the Lincoln Memorial. Modeled after an ancient Greek Doric temple and located at the western end of the National Mall, it is not featured on any of the D. Peres tourist knives.

Likewise, the Thomas Jefferson Memorial, fashioned after the Pantheon in Rome, is not depicted. Surely, these are two of the most famous monuments to grace the skyline of Washington, D.C. The Lincoln Memorial, however, was not completed until 1922, shortly after the last D. Peres knife was produced, and the Thomas Jefferson Memorial, which resides almost directly south of the Washington Memorial at the edge of the Tidal Basin, was not completed until 1943, long after D. Peres stopped making tourist knives.

MOUNT VERNON

George Washington's home, Mount Vernon, appears on several D. Peres knives even though, located 15 miles south of the capital, it is not traditionally associated with Washington, D.C., and does not appear to fall into

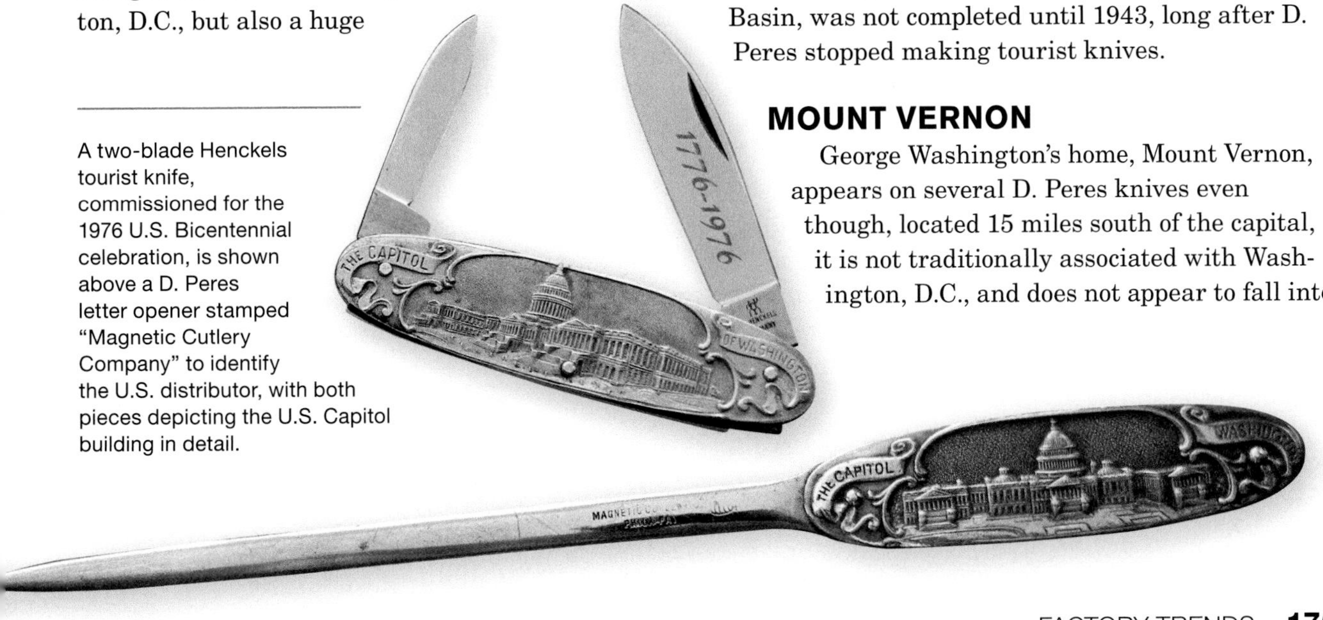

A two-blade Henckels tourist knife, commissioned for the 1976 U.S. Bicentennial celebration, is shown above a D. Peres letter opener stamped "Magnetic Cutlery Company" to identify the U.S. distributor, with both pieces depicting the U.S. Capitol building in detail.

FACTORY TRENDS **175**

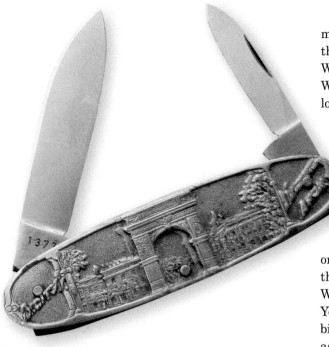

The back panel of the J.A. Henckels knife made for the U.S. Bicentennial Celebration in 1976 showcases an intricate etching of the Washington Square Arch, which is actually in lower Manhattan, New York, not in Washington, D.C.

the category of a "monument." Although originally built between 1758 and 1778, Mount Vernon was opened to paying guests in 1860, and has undergone a series of improvements over the past 156 years.

An interesting puzzle awaits the person who closely examines a stamped tourist knife commemorating the 1976 U.S. Bicentennial celebration. The well-known German knife company, J.A. Henckels, offered a stamped replica of an earlier D. Peres tourist knife featuring the U.S. Capitol building and the words "The Capital, Washington D.C." in ornate scrollwork.

The Henckels knife was designed to not only duplicate the scenes on an earlier D. Peres Washington, D. C. knife, but had the same oval design and blade configuration. However, it is the reverse side of the knife that provides some interesting and striking contrasts. The ornately stamped handle of the original D. Peres model depicts The Library of Congress, but the newer J.A. Henckels knife has an intricate etching of the Washington Square Arch.

I assumed, having only been to Washington, D.C. once in my life and not having seen all of the monu-

ments located in the historic city, that both sides of the Henckels tourist knife also depicted scenes from Washington, D.C. In researching more about the Washington Square Arch, however, I realized it's in lower Manhattan in New York City.

The Washington Square Arch in New York does commemorate George Washington, both as Commander in Chief and as President of the United States, but its inclusion on a knife that depicts monuments from Washington, D.C. is puzzling. Either the designers of the unique Bicentennial knife wanted to highlight monuments in both Washington and New York City, or the German knife company mistakenly thought that the Washington Square Arch was located in Washington, D.C., not in Greenwich Village in New York City, a neighborhood better known as the birthplace of the 1960's counterculture movement, or as a Bohemian artist haven.

D. Peres produced the tourist/souvenir knives from the late 1880s to the 1920s. The term "coined knives" refers to the aluminum handles being made much like coins. An intricate, hardened metal die is used to stamp the likenesses of buildings or statues on sheets of aluminum that are then cut out to be used as knife handles. The subject matter for D. Peres knives ranged from World's Fairs to architectural wonders in major cities, historic events and portraits of famous leaders, the latter of which are rare, but can be found by the diligent collector.

ALE BARREL TRADEMARK

The master blades almost always carry the tang stamp "D. PERES, SOLINGEN, GERMANY". Another key to determining whether a particular aluminum-handle knife is a genuine D. Peres model is to look for the company's ale

In addition to the intricate stamping of the U.S. Capitol building on a D. Peres knife, notice the ale barrel trademark deeply etched on the master blade and the decorative scrollwork surrounding the image of the U.S. Capitol building.

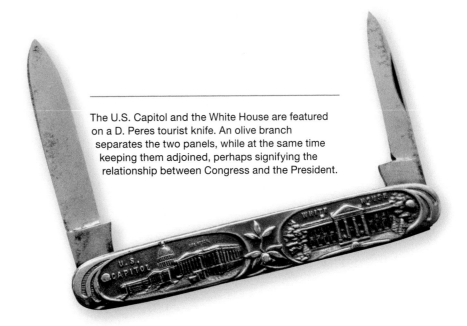

The U.S. Capitol and the White House are featured on a D. Peres tourist knife. An olive branch separates the two panels, while at the same time keeping them adjoined, perhaps signifying the relationship between Congress and the President.

barrel trademark stamped into the master blade. Another tang stamp often used on secondary blades of D. Peres knives refers to the U.S. distributor and reads "MAGNETIC CUTLERY COMPANY, PHILADELPHIA, PA".

Magnetic Cutlery was a little-known knife company owned by Otto Maussner and located at 1013 Arch Street in Philadelphia. According to the Official Gazette of the United States Patent Office, Volume 138, the Magnetic Cutlery mark used on D. Peres knives was "Sole agent for Daniel Peres Barrel Brand Cutlery."

In general, the knives are extremely well made, and since the back springs and blades are fashioned from quality German steel, many examples have lasted for years. D. Peres not only produced traditional penknives, with two opposing blades within the folding knife confines, but also letter openers with Washington, D.C. themes, and perhaps most well known, very small pocket watch chain knives.

These very small watch chain knives showcased the same intricate scenes as their larger counterparts, but one of the two implements was actually a nail file. These knives are identified by a small bail on the end of the handle for attaching it to a pocket watch chain. The knives could be used dangling from the watch chains that were often fastened to vest pocket buttons.

D. Peres Cutlery Company knives have always had a following among collectors, and in addition to tourist knives, Peres made a wide variety of figural models depicting touring cars, alligators, dirigibles, airplanes and other readily identifiable objects. For the specialty collector, the knives afford the opportunity to put together an outstanding regional collection that celebrates the uniqueness of, for example, all of the major tourist sites in a particular state or region.

Since D. Peres knives were made from high-quality Solingen, Germany, steel, and had extremely intricate stampings, they distance themselves from everyday tourist and souvenir knives as outstanding pocketknives with superior images. Available on the Internet through diligent Google searches, putting together a specific series of tourist knives like those that highlight the monuments of Washington, D.C. takes some effort, but great collections are generally assembled one knife at a time. □

The two-blade D. Peres folder parades a stamped image of the Library of Congress. Notice the Magnetic Cutlery (U.S. distributor of the knives) tang stamp on the main blade.

Factory Folding Saws

⌃ The 7-inch blade of the Flip n' Saw is 65Mn high carbon steel with a chrome finish, and the handle is 6061-T6 aluminum coated in rubber. Weight: 5.8 ounces. Approximate closed length: 8 inches. MSRP: $29.95.

⌃ The first thing you notice about KutMaster's Air Frame High Performance Saw is the skeleton Zytel handle. According to the company's Mike Mathews, "The Air Frame 'bridge' design is time tested, having been used by many bridge designers for over a century. The design actually adds strength to the handle and takes away weight."

⌃ The SOG model has two interchangeable 8.25-inch blades of a high carbon steel, one for sawing wood and the other—a fine-toothed saw with a satin finish—designed to cut bone. MSRP for the wood-cutting blade only is $26; for both the wood- and bone-cutting blades is $40.

⌃ Buck's Folding saw has a 6.25-inch blade of S45C carbon steel. Weight: 4.3 ounces. Closed length: 8.5 inches.

Thin Is In!

≫ The SOG Cash Card is an ultra-slim linerlock folder with a stainless steel handle ideal for wallet or pocket carry. Weight: 2 ounces. Approximate closed length: 3.45 inches. MSRP: $45.

≫ With its slim profile and removable pocket clip, the Boker Plus Credit Card Knife fits in the credit card compartment of your wallet and can be carried via the clip in a shirt pocket. Weight: 1.1 ounces. Closed length: 2.75 inches. MSRP: $39.95.

≫ Knives do not get much flatter than the Victorinox SwissCard Lite. The total count of tools includes scissors, blade, magnifying glass, straight pin, writing pen, tweezers, LED flashlight, ruler and four-sided screwdriver.

≫ The carbon fiber/G-10 laminate material is new for the one-piece handle of the Spyderco Dog Tag folder, a Serge Panchenko design. The single-bevel, modified sheepfoot blade is CPM S30V stainless in a no-glare black titanium carbonitride coating. An inlaid stainless steel spring in the handle provides tension for the detent, which keeps the blade fully opened or closed but does not lock it. MSRP: $84.95. *(Spyderco images)*

Economical Assisted-Opening Folders

⌃ The triple-action assisted-opening mechanism of the Kutmaster Greased Lightning folder was designed by the brother tandem of Michael and the late BLADE Magazine Cutlery Hall-Of-Fame© member, Blackie Collins. It is the only folder in the line of Kutmaster knives designed in collaboration with the Sportsman Channel's Brian "Pigman" Quaca. MSRP: $34.95.

⌃ A flipper tab helps actuate the SpeedSafe® assisted-opening mechanism of Kershaw's Intellect. Weight: 3.7 ounces. Closed length: 3.75 inches. MSRP: $49.99.

» Employing SOG Assisted Technology, the SlimJim XL from SOG Specialty Knives & Tools includes a built-in blade-locking safety. Weight: 2.7 ounces. Approximate closed length: 5.18 inches. Though its MSRP is above $50, the SlimJim XL can be found on the Internet for under that amount.

⌃ A textured G-10 grip with an integral guard and an angled blade fuller help distinguish the Remington R11516 assisted-opening tactical folder. MSRP: $39.99.

Piggyback Sheaths

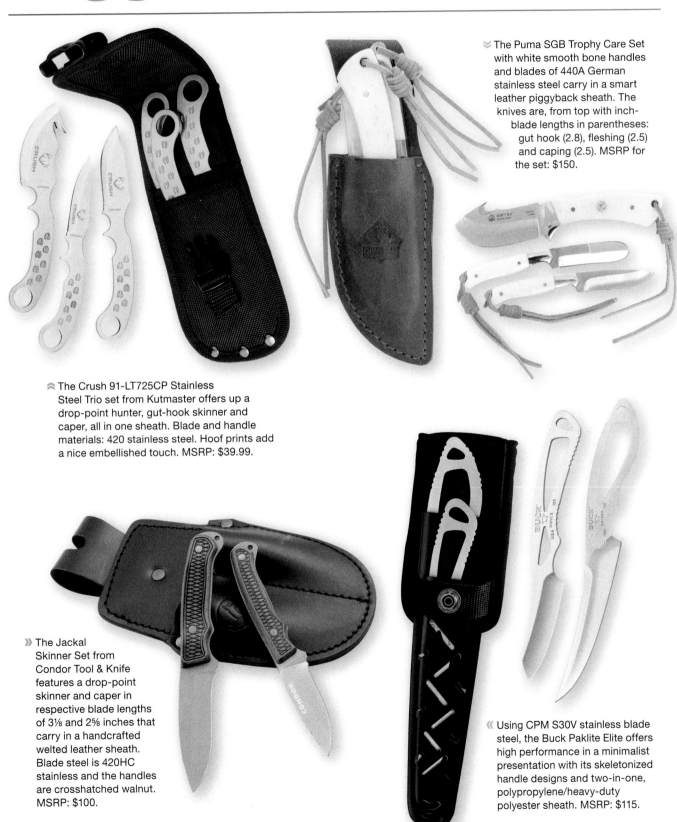

The Puma SGB Trophy Care Set with white smooth bone handles and blades of 440A German stainless steel carry in a smart leather piggyback sheath. The knives are, from top with inch-blade lengths in parentheses: gut hook (2.8), fleshing (2.5) and caping (2.5). MSRP for the set: $150.

The Crush 91-LT725CP Stainless Steel Trio set from Kutmaster offers up a drop-point hunter, gut-hook skinner and caper, all in one sheath. Blade and handle materials: 420 stainless steel. Hoof prints add a nice embellished touch. MSRP: $39.99.

The Jackal Skinner Set from Condor Tool & Knife features a drop-point skinner and caper in respective blade lengths of 3⅛ and 2⅝ inches that carry in a handcrafted welted leather sheath. Blade steel is 420HC stainless and the handles are crosshatched walnut. MSRP: $100.

Using CPM S30V stainless blade steel, the Buck Paklite Elite offers high performance in a minimalist presentation with its skeletonized handle designs and two-in-one, polypropylene/heavy-duty polyester sheath. MSRP: $115.

Knives Marketplace

INTERESTING PRODUCT NEWS FOR BOTH THE CUTLER AND THE KNIFE ENTHUSIAST

The companies and individuals represented on the following pages will be happy to provide additional information — feel free to contact them.

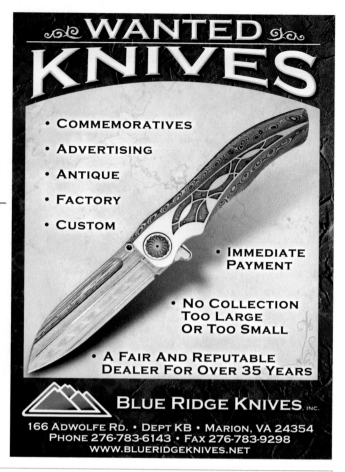

SOCOM ELITE™

www.MicrotechKnives.com

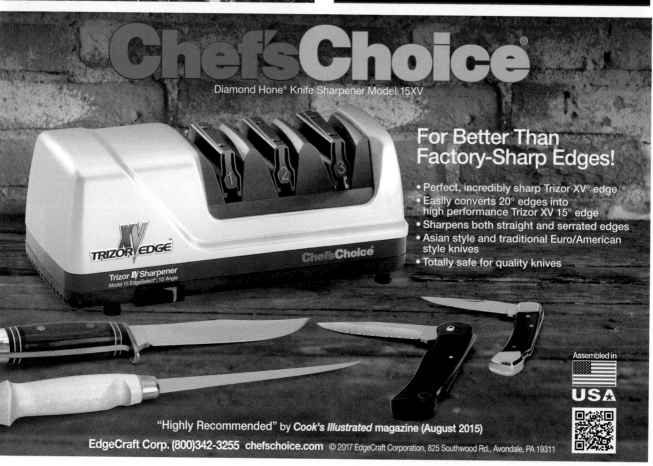

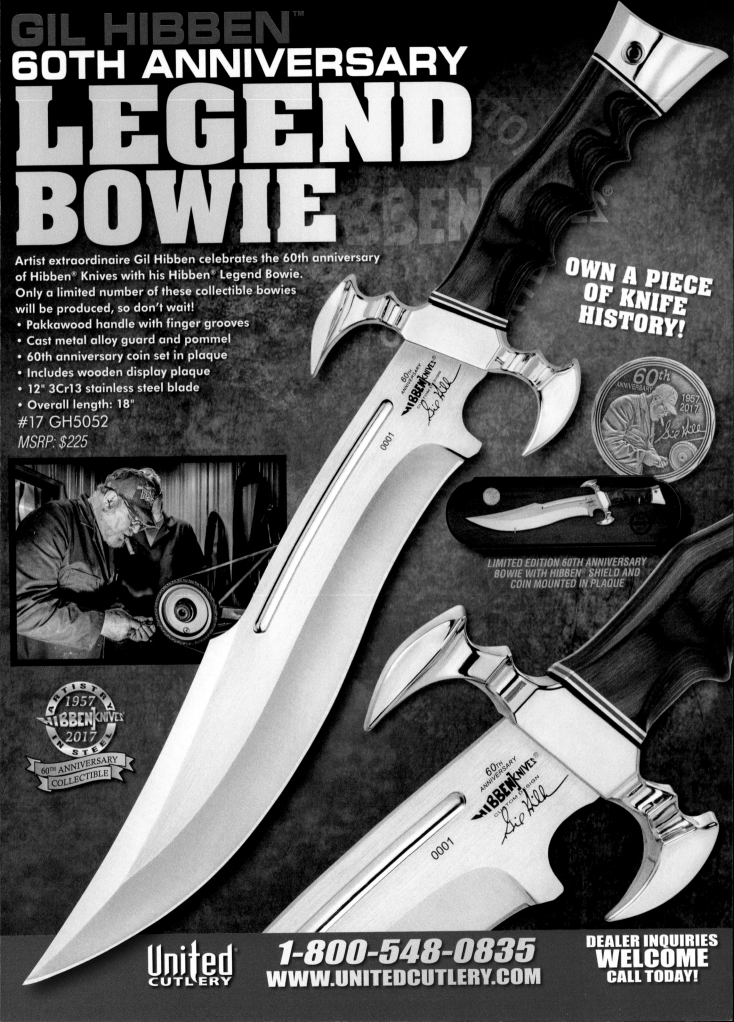

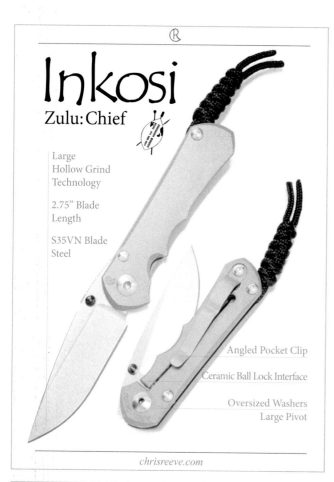

CRAFTSMANSHIP
THAT'S A CUT ABOVE.

Tony Bose

58190
TRIBAL LOCK
(TB612010L SS)
Smooth Antique
Bone Handle

4 1/8 in (10.5 cm) closed,
3.3 oz (92.1 g)

12011
TRIBAL LOCK
(TB812010L SS)
Smooth Abalone Handle

11213
TRIBAL LOCK
(TB1012010L SS)
Smooth Patriot Kirinite™ Handle

Introducing the new Case® Bose Tribal Lock – an exceptional mid-locking folder designed exclusively for Case by esteemed custom maker Tony Bose. Each model pairs Case quality with Bose's flair for design, featuring a Tru-Sharp™ surgical steel spear blade, a skillful swedge and high polished nickel-silver bolsters. With a wide variety of distinctive handle choices, you're sure to find a standout that suits your style.

CASE, Case, ⬭, CASE XX, TESTED XX, XX are registered trademarks of CaseMark, Inc. and used under license to W.R. Case & Sons Cutlery Company in the USA.
Kirinite is a trademark of Eagle Grips, Inc.

Find a Case Authorized Dealer nearest you
» WRCASE.COM

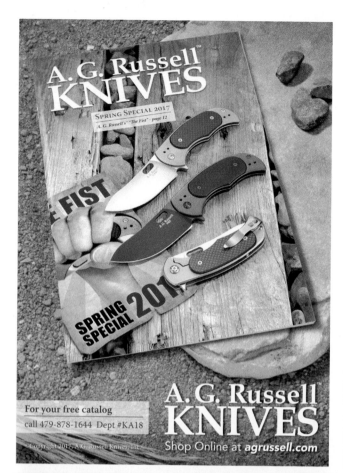
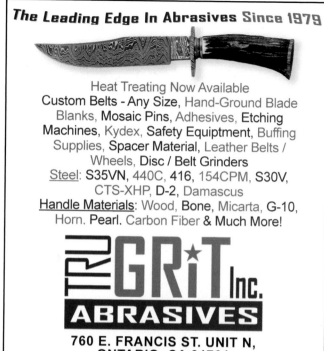
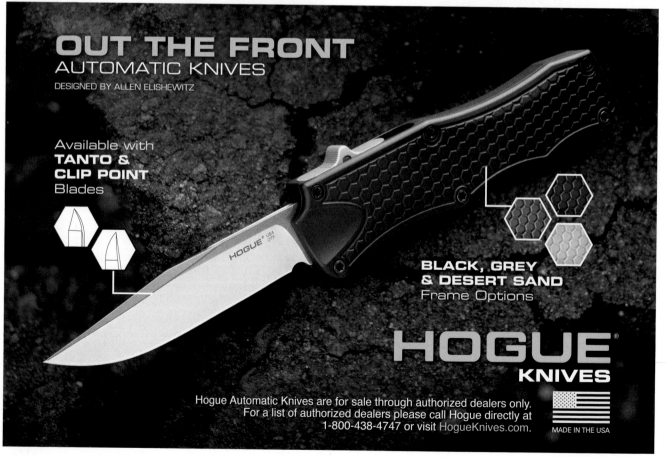

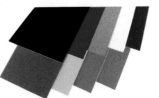

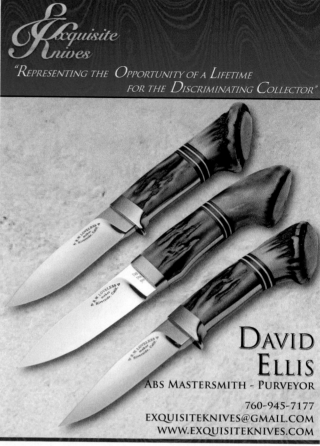
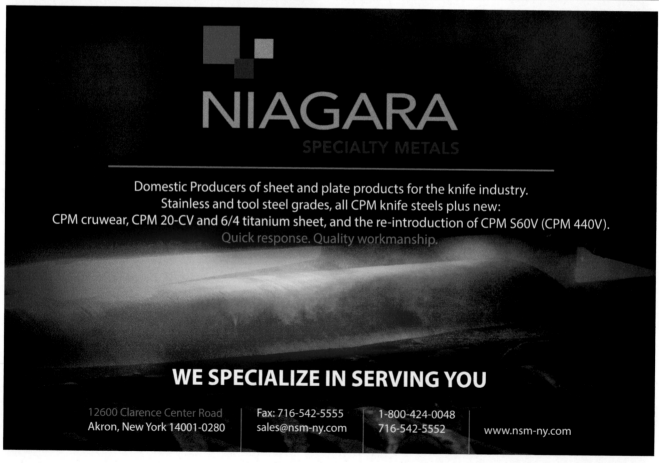

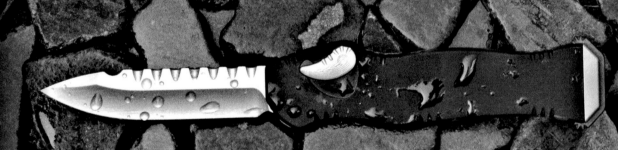

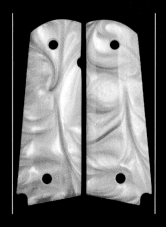

THANK YOU

FOR MAKING THIS YEAR'S SHOW THE BEST YET

PRESENTED BY

THE WORLD'S #1 KNIFE PUBLICATION

THANK YOU TO OUR 2017 SPONSORS!

CRKT.   HOGUE KNIVES  RUIKE   ALONE   BURR KING ZAC BROWN'S Southern GRIND FORGED IN FIRE

  SMKW   CASE xx   A.G. Russell KNIVES   knifenewsroom   WE KNIFE   BladeGallery.com Fine Knives Takefu Steel USA

SAVE THE DATE

JUNE 1-3, 2018
Cobb Galleria | Atlanta

BLADEShow.com

30°
25°
20°
17°

17°
20°
25°
30°

DELUXE
Sharpening System

*Original Controlled-Angle
sharpening for perfect edges
on every knife!*

Lansky's original and legendary Controlled-Angle Sharpening System ensures that your knives get sharpened to the exact bevel you specify for their tasks in the field, at home or workshop. Everything you need comes in a portable case for use at home or in the field. Kit includes knife clamp, honing oil, five hones — Extra Coarse, Coarse, Medium, Fine and Ultra Fine, plus accessory screws and multi-lingual instructions. Choose the knife care system preferred around the world.

LANSKY
SHARPENERS

Learn more at lansky.com
Call 800-825-2675 for FREE catalog

Keeping Knives in American Lives since 1998.

AKTI
AMERICAN
KNIFE & TOOL
INSTITUTE
EDUCATE · PROMOTE · INFORM

Our Valued Knifemaker Members Can't Imagine Their Lives . . . Without Knives!

AKTI's commitment to reasonable, responsible knife laws in the U.S. and educating the public about safe knife use means we work for the benefit of all knife owners, knifemakers and the entire knife community.

Learn more at www.AKTI.org or contact us at (307) 587-8926 or akti@AKTI.org

DIRECTORY

custom knifemakers

A

ABEGG, ARNIE

5992 Kenwick Cr, Huntington Beach, CA 92648, Phone: 714-848-5697

ABERNATHY, LANCE

Sniper Bladeworks, 1924 Linn Ave., North Kansas City, MO 64116, Phone: 816-585-1595, lanceabernathy@sbcglobal.net; Web: www.sniperbladeworks.com

Specialties: Tactical frame-lock and locking-liner folding knives.

ACCAWI, FUAD

130 Timbercrest Dr., Oak Ridge, TN 37830, Phone: 865-414-4836, gaccawi@comcast.net; Web: www.acremetalworks.com

Specialties: I create one of a kind pieces from small working knives to performance blades and swords. **Patterns:** Styles include, and not limited to hunters, Bowies, daggers, swords, folders and camp knives. **Technical:** I forge primarily 5160, produces own Damascus and does own heat treating. **Prices:** $150 to $3000. **Remarks:** I am a full-time bladesmith. I enjoy producing Persian and historically influenced work. **Mark:** My mark is an eight sided Middle Eastern star with initials in the center.

ACKERSON, ROBIN E

119 W Smith St, Buchanan, MI 49107, Phone: 616-695-2911

ADAMS, JIM

1648 Camille Way, Cordova, TN 38016, Phone: 901-326-0441, jim@JimAdamsKnives.com Web: www.jimadamsknives.com

Specialties: Fixed blades in classic design. **Patterns:** Hunters, fighters, and Bowies. **Technical:** Grinds Damascus, O1, others as requested. **Prices:** Starting at $150. **Remarks:** Full-time maker. **Mark:** J. Adams, Cordova, TN.

ADAMS, LES

3516 S.W. 2nd St., Cape Coral, FL 33991, Phone: 786-999-3060

Specialties: Working straight knives of his design. **Patterns:** Fighters, tactical folders, law enforcing autos. **Technical:** Grinds ATS-34, 440C and D2. **Prices:** $100 to $500. **Remarks:** Part-time maker; first knife sold in 1989. **Mark:** First initial, last name, Custom Knives.

ADDISON, KYLE A

588 Atkins Trail, Hazel, KY 42049-8629, Phone: 270-492-8120, kylest2@yahoo.com

Specialties: Hand forged blades including Bowies, fighters and hunters. **Patterns:** Custom leather sheaths. **Technical:** Forges 5160, 1084, and his own Damascus. **Prices:** $175 to $1500. **Remarks:** Part-time maker, first knife sold in 1996. ABS member. **Mark:** First and middle initial, last name under "Trident" with knife and hammer.

ADKINS, RICHARD L

138 California Ct, Mission Viejo, CA 92692-4079

AIDA, YOSHIHITO

26-7 Narimasu 2-chome, Itabashi-ku, Tokyo, JAPAN 175-0094, Phone: 81-3-3939-0052, Fax: 81-3-3939-0058, Web: http://riverside-land.com/

Specialties: High-tech working straight knives and folders of his design. **Patterns:** Bowies, lockbacks, hunters, fighters, fishing knives, boots. **Technical:** Grinds CV-134, ATS-34; buys Damascus; works in traditional Japanese fashion for some handles and sheaths. **Prices:** $700 to $1200; some higher. **Remarks:** Full-time maker; first knife sold in 1978. **Mark:** Initial logo and Riverside West.

ALBERT, STEFAN

U Lucenecka 434/4, Filakovo 98604, SLOVAKIA, albert@albertknives.com Web: www.albertknives.com

Specialties: Art Knives, Miniatures, Scrimshaw, Bulino. **Prices:** From USD $500 to USD $25000. **Mark:** Albert

ALCORN, DOUGLAS A.

14687 Fordney Rd., Chesaning, MI 48616, Phone: 989-845-6712, daalcornknives@gmail.com

Specialties: Gentleman style military, tactical and presentation knives. **Patterns:** Hunters, miniatures, and military type fixed blade knives and axes. **Technical:** Blades are stock removal and forged using best quality stainless, carbon, and damascus steels. Handle materials are burls, ivory, pearl, leather and other exotics. **Prices:** $200 and up. **Motto:** Simple, Rugged, Elegant, Handcrafted **Remarks:** Knife maker since 1989 and full time since 1999, Knife Makers Guild (voting member), member of the Bladesmith Society. **Mark:** D.A. Alcorn, Maker, Chesaning, MI.

ALDERMAN, ROBERT

2655 Jewel Lake Rd., Sagle, ID 83860, Phone: 208-263-5996

Specialties: Classic and traditional working straight knives in standard patterns or to customer specs and his design; period pieces. **Patterns:** Bowies, fighters, hunters and utility/camp knives. **Technical:** Casts, forges and grinds 1084; forges and grinds L6 and O1. Prefers an old appearance. **Prices:** $100 to $350; some to $700. **Remarks:** Full-time maker; first knife sold in 1975. Doing business as Trackers Forge. Knife-making school. Two-week course for beginners; covers forging, stock removal, hardening, tempering, case making. All materials supplied; $1250. **Mark:** Deer track.

ALEXANDER, EUGENE

Box 540, Ganado, TX 77962-0540, Phone: 512-771-3727

Alexander,, Oleg, and Cossack Blades

15460 Stapleton Way, Wellington, FL 33414, Phone: 443-676-6111, Web: www.cossackblades.com

Technical: All knives are made from hand-forged Damascus (3-4 types of steel are used to create the Damascus) and have a HRC of 60-62. Handle materials are all natural, including various types of wood, horn, bone and leather. Embellishments include the use of precious metals and stones, including gold, silver, diamonds, rubies, sapphires and other unique materials. All knives include hand-made leather sheaths, and some models include wooden presentation boxes and display stands. **Prices:** $395 to over $10,000, depending on design and materials used. **Remarks:** Full-time maker, first knife sold in 1993. **Mark:** Rectangle enclosing a stylized Cyrillic letter "O" overlapping a stylized Cyrillic "K."

ALLAN, TODD

TODD ALLAN KNIVES, 6525 W. Kings Ave., Glendale, AZ 85306, Phone: 623-210-3766, todd@toddallanknives.com; www.toddallanknives.com

Patterns: Fixed-blade hunters and camp knives. **Technical:** Stock-removal method of blade making using 154CM, high-carbon damascus, stainless damascus, 5160 and 1095 blade steels. Handle materials include various Micartas, stabilized woods and mammoth ivory. **Prices:** $175 to $1,000. **Remarks:** Full-time maker.

ALLEN, JIM

Three Sisters Forge, LLC, 18830 Macalpine Loop, Bend, OR 97702, knives@threesistersforge.com; Web: www.threesistersforge.com

Specialties: Folders with titanium frames, and stainless steel blades and fixtures. **Technical:** Stock-removal method of blade making using CPM S35VN steel for now, but always evaluating latest steels. **Prices:** $200 to $300. **Remarks:** Ninety percent of knives go to police and military. Special features such as anodizing and Cerakote coated blades available. **Mark:** The sun setting over the Three Sisters Mountains (the view from the maker's shop).

ALLRED, BRUCE F

1764 N. Alder, Layton, UT 84041, Phone: 801-825-4612, allredbf@msn.com

Specialties: Custom hunting and utility knives. **Patterns:** Custom designs that include a unique grind line, thumb and mosaic pins. **Technical:** ATS-34, 154CM and 440C. **Remarks:** The handle material includes but not limited to Micarta (in various colors), natural woods and reconstituted stone.

ALLRED, ELVAN

31 Spring Terrace Court, St. Charles, MO 63303, Phone: 636-936-8871, allredknives@yahoo.com; Web: www.allredcustomknives.com

Specialties: Innovative sculpted folding knives designed by Elvan's son Scott that are mostly one of a kind. **Patterns:** Mostly folders but some high-end straight knives. **Technical:** ATS-34 SS, 440C SS, stainless Damascus, S30V, 154cm; inlays are mostly natural materials such as pearl, coral, ivory, jade, lapis, and other precious stone. **Prices:** $500 to $4000, some higher. **Remarks:** Started making knives in the shop of Dr. Fred Carter in the early 1990s. Full-time maker since 2006, first knife sold in 1993. Take some orders but work mainly on one-of-a-kind art knives. **Mark:** Small oval with signature Eallred in the center and handmade above.

ALVERSON, TIM (R.V.)

209 Spring Rd. SE, Arab, AL 35016, Phone: 256-224-9620, alvie35@yahoo.com Web: cwknives.blogspot.com

Specialties: Fancy working knives to customer specs; other types on request. **Patterns:** Bowies, daggers, folders and miniatures. **Technical:** Grinds 440C, ATS-34; buys some Damascus. **Prices:** Start at $100. **Remarks:** Full-time maker; first knife sold in 1981. **Mark:** R.V.A. around rosebud.

AMERI, MAURO

Via Riaello No. 20, Trensasco St Olcese, Genova, ITALY 16010, Phone: 010-8357077, mauro.ameri@gmail.com

Specialties: Working and using knives of his design. **Patterns:** Hunters, Bowies and utility/camp knives. **Technical:** Grinds 440C, ATS-34 and 154CM. Handles in wood or Micarta; offers sheaths. **Prices:** $200 to $1200. **Remarks:** Spare-time maker; first knife sold in 1982. **Mark:** Last name, city.

AMMONS, DAVID C

6225 N. Tucson Mtn. Dr, Tucson, AZ 85743, Phone: 520-471-4433, dcammons@msn.com

Specialties: Will build to suit. **Patterns:** Yours or his. **Prices:** $250 to $2000. **Mark:** AMMONS.

AMOS, CHRIS

PO Box 1519, Riverton, WY 82501, Phone: 520-271-9752, caknives@yahoo.com

Specialties: HEPK (High Endurance Performance Knives). **Patterns:** Hunters, fighters, bowies, kitchen knives and camp knives. **Technical:** Hand-forged, high rate of reduction 52100 and 5160 steel. **Prices:** $150 to $1,500. **Remarks:** Part-time maker since 1997, full time since 2012. Coach/instructor at Ed Fowler's Knifemaking School. HEPK mastersmith rating, 2013. **Mark:** Early **mark:** CAK stamped; current **mark:** Amos on right side.

AMOUREUX, A W

PO Box 776, Northport, WA 99157, Phone: 509-732-6292

Specialties: Heavy-duty working straight knives. **Patterns:** Bowies, fighters, camp knives and hunters for world-wide use. **Technical:** Grinds 440C, ATS-34 and 154CM. **Prices:** $80 to $2000. **Remarks:** Full-time maker; first knife sold in 1974. **Mark:** ALSTAR.

ANDERS, DAVID

157 Barnes Dr, Center Ridge, AR 72027, Phone: 501-893-2294

Specialties: Working straight knives of his design. **Patterns:** Bowies, fighters and hunters. **Technical:** Forges 5160, 1080 and Damascus. **Prices:** $225 to $3200. **Remarks:** Part-time maker; first knife sold in 1988. Doing business as Anders Knives. **Mark:** Last name/MS.

ANDERS, JEROME

14560 SW 37th St, Miramar, FL 33027, Phone: 305-613-2990, web:www.andersknives.com

Specialties: Case handles and pin work. **Patterns:** Layered and mosiac steel. **Prices:** $275 and up. **Remarks:** All his knives are truly one-of-a-kind. **Mark:** J. Anders in half moon.

ANDERSEN, HENRIK LEFOLII

Jagtvej 8, Groenholt, Fredensborg, DENMARK 3480, Phone: 0011-45-48483026

Specialties: Hunters and matched pairs for the serious hunter. **Technical:** Grinds A2; uses materials native to Scandinavia. **Prices:** Start at $250. **Remarks:** Part-time maker; first knife sold in 1985. **Mark:** Initials with arrow.

ANDERSEN, KARL B.

20200 TimberLodge Rd., Warba, MN 55793, Phone: 218-398-4270, Karl@andersenforge.com Web: www.andersenforge.com

Specialties: Hunters, bowies, fighters and camp knives forged from high carbon tool steels and Andersen Forge Damascus. **Technical:** All types of materials used. Styles include hidden-tang and full-tang fixed blades, Brut de Forge, integrals and frame-handle construction. **Prices:** Starting at $450 and up. **Remarks:** Full-time maker. ABS journeyman smith. All knives sole authorship. Andersen Forge was instrumental in paving the way for take-down knife construction to be more recognized and broadly accepted in knifemaking today. **Mark:** Andersen in script on obverse. J.S. on either side, depending on knife.

ANDERSON, GARY D

2816 Reservoir Rd, Spring Grove, PA 17362-9802, Phone: 717-229-2665

Specialties: From working knives to collectors quality blades, some folders. **Patterns:** Traditional and classic designs; customer patterns welcome. **Technical:** Forges Damascus carbon and stainless steels. Offers silver inlay, mokume, filework, checkering. **Prices:** $250 and up. **Remarks:** Part-time maker; first knife sold in 1985. Some engraving, scrimshaw and stone work. **Mark:** GAND, MS.

ANDERSON, MEL

29505 P 50 Rd, Hotchkiss, CO 81419-8203, Phone: 970-872-4882, Fax: 970-872-4882, artnedge@tds.net, melsscratchyhand@aol.com; Web: www.scratchyhand.com

Specialties: Full-size, miniature and one-of-a-kind straight knives and folders of his design. **Patterns:** Tantos, Bowies, daggers, fighters, hunters and pressure folders. **Technical:** Grinds 440C, 5160, D2, 1095. **Prices:** Start at $175. **Remarks:** Knifemaker and sculptor, full-time maker; first knife sold in 1987. **Mark:** Scratchy Hand.

ANDERSON, TOM

955 Canal Rd. Extd., Manchester, PA 17345, Phone: 717-266-6475, andersontech1@comcast.net Web: artistryintitanium.com

Specialties: Battle maces and war hammers.

ANDRADE, DON CARLOS

CALIFORNIA CUSTOM KNIVES, 1824 Sunny Hill Ave., Los Osos, CA 93402, Phone: 805-528-8837 or 805-550-2324, andradeartworks@gmail.com; www.californiacustomknives.com

Specialties: Chef knife specialist, also integrally forged personal knives and camp knives. **Technical:** Forges to shape, and a small number of stain-resistant, stock-removal blades. All heat-treating in house. Uses 1095, W2, W1, 1084, 52100, 1065, 1070 and 13C26 blade steels. **Prices:** $250 to $1,650. **Remarks:** Full-time maker; first knife made in 2006 under tutorship of mentor Tai Goo. **Mark:** Initials "DCA" and two circles with a strike running through them (maker's version of infinity/continuity.)

ANDREWS, ERIC

132 Halbert Street, Grand Ledge, MI 48837, Phone: 517-627-7304

Specialties: Traditional working and using straight knives of his design. **Patterns:** Full-tang hunters, skinners and utility knives. **Technical:** Forges carbon steel; heat-treats. All knives come with sheath; most handles are of wood. **Prices:** $80 to $160. **Remarks:** Part-time maker; first knife sold in 1990. Doing business as The Tinkers Bench.

ANDREWS, RUSS

PO Box 7732, Sugar Creek, MO 64054, Phone: 816-252-3344, russandrews@sbcglobal.net; Web:wwwrussandrewsknives.com

Specialties: Hand forged bowies & hunters. **Mark:** E. R. Andrews II. ERAII.

ANGELL, JON

22516 East C R1474, Hawthorne, FL 32640, Phone: 352-475-5380, syrjon@aol.com

ANKROM, W.E.

14 Marquette Dr, Cody, WY 82414, Phone: 307-587-3017, weankrom@hotmail.com

Specialties: Best quality folding knives of his design. Bowies, fighters, chute knives, boots and hunters. **Patterns:** Tacticals, flipper folders, lock backs, LinerLocks and single high art. **Technical:** All high-tech steels, including ATS-34, commercial damascus, CPM 154 steel. **Prices:** $500 and up. **Remarks:** Full-time maker; first knife sold in 1975. **Mark:** Name or name, city, state.

ANSO, JENS

GL. Skanderborgvej 116, Sporup, DENMARK 8472, Phone: 45 86968826, info@ansoknives.com; Web: www.ansoknives.com

Specialties: Working knives of his own design. **Patterns:** Balisongs, swords, folders, drop-points, sheepsfoots, hawkbill, tanto, recurve. **Technical:** Grinds RWL-34 Damasteel S30V, CPM 154CM. Handrubbed or beadblasted finish. **Prices:** $400 to $1200, some up to $3500. **Remarks:** Full-time maker since January 2002. First knife sold 1997. Doing business as ANSOKNIVES. **Mark:** ANSO and/or ANSO with logo.

APELT, STACY E

8076 Moose Ave, Norfolk, VA 23518, Phone: 757-583-5872, sapelt@cox.net

Specialties: Exotic wood and burls, ivories, Bowies, custom made knives to order. **Patterns:** Bowies, hunters, fillet, professional cutlery and Japanese style blades and swords. **Technical:** Hand forging, stock removal, scrimshaw, carbon, stainless and Damascus steels. **Prices:** $65 to $5000. **Remarks:** Professional Goldsmith. **Mark:** Stacy E. Apelt - Norfolk VA.

APLIN, SPENCER

5151 County Rd. 469, Brazoria, TX 77422, Phone: 979-964-4448, spenceraplin@aol.com; Web: www.stacustomknives.com

Specialties: Custom skinners, fillets, bowies and kitchen knives. **Technical:** Stainless steel powder metals, stainless damascus. Handles include stabilized woods, various ivory and Micarta. Guard and butt-cap materials are brass, copper, nickel silver and Mokume. **Prices:** $250 and up. **Remarks:** First knife sold in 1989. Knives made to order only, nothing is pre-made. All blades are hand drawn, then cut from sheet stock. No two are exactly the same. **Mark:** Signature and date completed.

APPLEBY, ROBERT

746 Municipal Rd, Shickshinny, PA 18655, Phone: 570-864-0879, applebyknives@yahoo.com; Web: www.applebyknives.com

Specialties: Working using straight knives and folders of his own and popular and historical designs. **Patterns:** Variety of straight knives and folders. **Technical:** Hand forged or grinds O1, 1084, 5160, 440C, ATS-34, commercial Damascus, makes own sheaths. **Prices:** Starting at $75. **Remarks:** Part-time maker, first knife sold in 1995. **Mark:** APPLEBY over SHICKSHINNY, PA.

APPLETON, RON

315 Glenn St, Bluff Dale, TX 76433, Phone: 254-707-2922; cell: 254-396-9328, ronappleton@hotmail.com; Web: www.appletonknives.com

Specialties: One-of-a-kind folding knives. **Patterns:** Unique folding multi-locks and high-tech patterns. **Technical:** All parts machined, D2, S7, 416, 440C, 6A14V et.al. **Prices:** Start at $27,000 U.S.. **Remarks:** Full-time maker; first knife sold in 1996. **Mark:** Initials in anvil or initials in arrowhead. Usually only shows at the Art Knife Invitational every 2 years in San Diego, CA.

ARBUCKLE, JAMES M

114 Jonathan Jct, Yorktown, VA 23693, Phone: 757-867-9578, a_r_buckle@hotmail.com

Specialties: One-of-a-kind of his design; working knives. **Patterns:** Mostly chef's knives and hunters. **Technical:** Forged and stock removal blades using exotic hardwoods, natural materials, Micarta and stabilized woods. Forge 5160 and 1084; stock removal D2, ATS-34, 440C and 154CM. Makes own pattern welded steel. **Prices:** $195 to $700. **Remarks:** Forge, grind, heat-treat, finish and embellish all knives himself. Does own leatherwork. Part-time maker. ABS Journeyman smith 2007; ASM member. **Mark:** J. Arbuckle or J. ARBUCKLE MAKER.

ARCHER, RAY AND TERRI

4207 South 28 St., Omaha, NE 68107, Phone: 402-505-3084, archerrt@cox.net

Specialties: Basic high-finish working knives. **Patterns:** Hunters, skinners camp knives. **Technical:** Flat grinds various steels like 440C, ATS-34 and CPM-S30V. **Prices:** $75 to $500. **Remarks:** Makes own sheaths; first knife sold 1994. **Mark:** Last name over knives.

ARDWIN, COREY

2117 Cedar Dr., Bryant, AR 72019, Phone: 501-413-1184, ardwinca@gmail.com

ARM-KO KNIVES

PO Box 76280, Marble Ray , KZN , SOUTH AFRICA 4035, Phone: 27 31 5771451, arm-koknives.co.za; Web: www.arm-koknives.co.za

Specialties: They will make what your fastidious taste desires. Be it cool collector or tenacious tactical with handles of mother-of-pearl, fossil & local ivories. Exotic dye/stabilized burls, giraffe bone, horns, carbon fiber, g10, and titanium etc. **Technical:** Via stock removal, grinding Damasteel, carbon & mosaic. Damascus, ATS-34, N690, 440A, 440B, 12C27, RWL34 and high carbon EN 8, 5160 all heat treated in house. **Prices:** From $200 and up. **Remarks:** Father a part-time maker for well over 10 years and member of Knifemakers Guild in SA. Son full-time maker over 3 years. **Mark:** Logo of initials A R M and H A R M "Edged Tools."

ARMOUR, DAVE

61 Sugar Creek Hills, Auburn, IL 62615, Phone: 217-741-0246, dave@armourcutlery.com; Web: www.armourcutlery.com

Specialties: Hunters, utilities and occasional camp and bowie knives. **Technical:** Forges blades from 1084 and 80CrV2, with occasional san mai and damascus steels. **Prices:** $100 to $160 for most knives, up to $250 for dressier pieces. **Remarks:** Part-time maker; knives described as "deliberately casual" with a focus on working knives, performance, individuality and affordability. Field-grade knives usually using copper, stainless or bronze with horn (deer, elk or water buffalo), stabilized wood, Micarta or G-10 handles. Dressier knives often use wrought iron or Mokume with stag or oosic. **Mark:** Armour.

ARMS, ERIC

11153 7 Mile Road, Tustin, MI 49688, Phone: 231-829-3726, ericarms@netonecom.net

Specialties: Working hunters, high performance straight knives. **Patterns:** Variety of hunters, scagel style, Ed Fowler design and drop point. **Technical:** Forge 52100, 5160, 1084 hand grind, heat treat, natural handle, stag horn, elk, big horn, flat grind, convex, all leather sheath work. **Prices:** Starting at $150 **Remarks:** Part-time maker **Mark:** Eric Arms

ARNOLD, JOE

47 Patience Cres, London, ON, CANADA N6E 2K7, Phone: 519-686-2623, arnoldknivesandforge@bell.net

Specialties: Traditional working and using straight knives of his design and to customer specs. **Patterns:** Fighters, hunters and Bowies. **Technical:** Grinds 440C, ATS-34, 5160, and Forges 1084-1085 **Prices:** $75 to $500; some to $2500. **Remarks:** Full-time maker; first knife sold in 1988. **Mark:** Last name, country.

ARROWOOD, DALE
556 Lassetter Rd, Sharpsburg, GA 30277, Phone: 404-253-9672
Specialties: Fancy and traditional straight knives of his design and to customer specs. **Patterns:** Bowies, fighters and hunters. **Technical:** Grinds ATS-34 and 440C; forges high-carbon steel. Engraves and scrimshaws. **Prices:** $125 to $200; some to $245. **Remarks:** Part-time maker; first knife sold in 1989. **Mark:** Anvil with an arrow through it; Old English "Arrowood Knives."

ASHBY, DOUGLAS
10123 Deermont Trail, Dallas, TX 75243, Phone: 214-929-7531, doug@ashbycustomknives.com Web: ashbycustomknives.com
Specialties: Traditional and fancy straight knives and folders of his design or to customer specs. **Patterns:** Skinners, hunters, utility/camp knives, locking liner folders. **Technical:** Grinds ATS-34, commercial Damascus, and other steels on request. **Prices:** $125 to $1000. **Remarks:** Part-time maker; first knife sold in 1990. **Mark:** Name, city.

ASHWORTH, BOYD
1510 Bullard Place, Powder Springs, GA 30127, Phone: 404-583-5652, boydashworthknives@comcast.net; Web: www.boydashworthknives.com
Specialties: Gentlemen's and figurative folders. **Patterns:** Fighters, hunters and gents. **Technical:** Forges own Damascus; offers filework; uses exotic handle materials. **Prices:** $500 to $5,000. **Remarks:** Part-time maker; first knife sold in 1993. **Mark:** Last name.

ATHEY, STEVE
3153 Danube Way, Riverside, CA 92503, Phone: 951-850-8612, stevelonnie@yahoo.com
Specialties: Stock removal. **Patterns:** Hunters & Bowies. **Prices:** $100 to $500. **Remarks:** Part-time maker. **Mark:** Last name with number on blade.

ATKINSON, DICK
General Delivery, Wausau, FL 32463, Phone: 850-638-8524
Specialties: Working straight knives and folders of his design; some fancy. **Patterns:** Hunters, fighters, boots; locking folders in interframes. **Technical:** Grinds A2, 440C and 154CM. Likes filework. **Prices:** $85 to $300; some exceptional knives. **Remarks:** Full-time maker; first knife sold in 1977. **Mark:** Name, city, state.

AYARRAGARAY, CRISTIAN L.
Buenos Aires 250, Parana, Entre Rios, ARGENTINA 3100, Phone: 043-231753
Specialties: Traditional working straight knives of his design. **Patterns:** Fishing and hunting knives. **Technical:** Grinds and forges carbon steel. Uses native Argentine woods and deer antler. **Prices:** $150 to $250; some to $400. **Remarks:** Full-time maker; first knife sold in 1980. **Mark:** Last name, signature.

AYLOR, ERIN LUTZER
10519 Highland School Rd., Myersville, MD 21773, Phone: 240-818-2959, hawkwoodfarm@gmail.com; Web: www.hawkwoodmountainfarm.com
Specialties: Custom knives with an Old World feel using mostly pattern-welded (damascus) steel in ladder, twist and random patterns made from 1084, 1075, 15N20 and 1095 with a core of 5100 or 1095. **Patterns:** Many styles of knives, including hunters, fighters, bowies, Japanese and standard kitchen cutlery, folding knives and woodworking chisels. **Technical:** All blades are coal forged. **Prices:** $300 to $3,500. **Remarks:** Full-time artisan working mostly in metal, wood and silver. Studied at The Appalachian Center for Crafts in Cookeville, Tennessee, where he made his first chisel and knife in 1992. **Mark:** Last name, "AYLOR," with earlier work stamped "ELA."

B

BAARTMAN, GEORGE
PO Box 1116, Bela-Bela, LP, SOUTH AFRICA 0480, Phone: 27 14 736 4036, Fax: 086 636 3408, thabathipa@gmail.com
Specialties: Fancy and working LinerLock® folders of own design and to customers specs. **Specialize:** in pattern filework on liners. **Patterns:** LinerLock® folders. **Technical:** Grinds 12C27, ATS-34, and Damascus, prefer working with stainless damasteel. Hollow grinds to hand-rubbed and polished satin finish. Enjoys working with mammoth, warthog tusk and pearls. **Prices:** Folders from $380 to $1000. **Remarks:** Part-time maker. Member of the Knifemakers Guild of South Africa since 1993. **Mark:** BAARTMAN.

BACHE-WIIG, TOM
N-5966, Eivindvik, NORWAY, Phone: 475-778-4290, Fax: 475-778-1099, tom.bache-wiig@enivest.net; Web: www.tombachewiig.com
Specialties: High-art and working knives of his design. **Patterns:** Hunters, utility knives, hatchets, axes and art knives. **Technical:** Grinds Uddeholm Elmax, powder metallurgy tool stainless steel. Handles made of rear burls of Nordic woods stabilized with vacuum/high-pressure technique. **Prices:** $430 to $900; some to $2300. **Remarks:** Part-time maker; first knife sold 1988. **Mark:** Etched name and eagle head.

BAGLEY, R. KEITH
OLD PINE FORGE, 4415 Hope Acres Dr, White Plains, MD 20695, Phone: 301-932-0990, keithbagley14@verizon.net; Web: www.oldpineforge.com
Specialties: Folders. **Technical:** Use ATS-34, 5160, O1, 1085 and 1095. **Patterns:** Ladder-wave lightning bolt. **Prices:** $275 to $750. **Remarks:** Farrier for 37 years, blacksmith for 37 years, knifemaker for 25 years. **Mark:** KB inside horseshoe and anvil.

BAILEY, I.R.
Lamorna Cottage, Common End, Colkirk, ENGLAND NR 21 7JD, Phone: 01-328-856-

183, admin@grommitbaileyknives.com; Web: www.grommitbaileyknives.com
Specialties: Hunters, utilities, Bowies, camp knives, fighters. Mainly influenced by Moran, Loveless and Lile. **Technical:** Primarily stock removal using flat ground 1095, 1075, and 80CrV2. Occasionally forges including own basic Damascus. Uses both native and exotic hardwoods, stag, Leather, Micarta and other synthetic handle materials, with brass or 301 stainless fittings. Does some filework and leather tooling. Does own heat treating. **Remarks:** Part-time maker since 2005. All knives and sheaths are sole authorship. **Mark:** Last name stamped.

BAILEY, JOSEPH D.
3213 Jonesboro Dr, Nashville, TN 37214, Phone: 615-889-3172, jbknfemkr@aol.com
Specialties: Working and using straight knives; collector pieces. **Patterns:** Bowies, hunters, tactical, folders. **Technical:** 440C, ATS-34, Damascus and wire Damascus. Offers scrimshaw. **Prices:** $85 to $1200. **Remarks:** Part-time maker; first knife sold in 1988. **Mark:** Joseph D Bailey Nashville Tennessee.

BAIR, MARK
415 E. 700N, Firth, ID 83236, Phone: 208-681-7534, markbair@gmail.com
Specialties: Fixed blades. Hunters, bowies, kitchen, utility, custom orders. **Technical:** High-end damascus, San Mai steel, stainless steel and 52100. Also mammoth ivory and other exotic handles, custom hand filework, and works with high-end custom engravers. **Prices:** $300 to $7,500. **Remarks:** Part-time maker; first knife made in 1988. **Mark:** MB Custom Knives.

BAKER, HERB
14104 NC 87 N, Eden, NC 27288, Phone: 336-627-0338

BAKER, RAY
PO Box 303, Sapulpa, OK 74067, Phone: 918-224-8013
Specialties: High-tech working straight knives. **Patterns:** Hunters, fighters, Bowies, skinners and boots of his design and to customer specs. **Technical:** Grinds 440C, 1095 spring steel or customer request; heat-treats. Custom-made scabbards for any knife. **Prices:** $125 to $500; some to $1000. **Remarks:** Full-time maker; first knife sold in 1981. **Mark:** First initial, last name.

BAKER, TONY
707 Lake Highlands Dr, Allen, TX 75002, Phone: 214-543-1001, tonybakerknives@yahoo.com
Specialties: Hunting knives, integral made **Technical:** 154cm, S30V, and S90V**Prices:** Starting at $500. **Prices:** $200-$1200 **Remarks:** First knife made in 2001

BAKER, WILD BILL
Box 361, Boiceville, NY 12412, Phone: 914-657-8646
Specialties: Primitive knives, buckskinners. **Patterns:** Skinners, camp knives and Bowies. **Technical:** Works with L6, files and rasps. **Prices:** $100 to $350. **Remarks:** Part-time maker; first knife sold in 1989. **Mark:** Wild Bill Baker, Oak Leaf Forge, or both.

BALL, BUTCH
2161 Reedsville Rd., Floyd, VA 24091, Phone: 540-392-3485, ballknives@yahoo.com
Specialties: Fancy and Tactical Folders and Automatics. **Patterns:** Fixed and folders. **Technical:** Use various Damascus and ATS34, 154cm. **Prices:** $300 - $1500. **Remarks:** Part-time maker. Sold first knife in 1990. **Mark:** Ball or BCK with crossed knives.

BALL, KEN
127 Sundown Manor, Mooresville, IN 46158, Phone: 317-834-4803
Specialties: Classic working/using straight knives of his design and to customer specs. **Patterns:** Hunters and utility/camp knives. **Technical:** Flat-grinds ATS-34. Offers filework. **Prices:** $150 to $400. **Remarks:** Part-time maker; first knife sold in 1994. Doing business as Ball Custom Knives. **Mark:** Last name.

BALLESTRA, SANTINO
via D. Tempesta 11/17, Ventimiglia, ITALY 18039, Phone: 0184-215228, ladasin@libero.it
Specialties: Using and collecting straight knives. **Patterns:** Hunting, fighting, skinners, Bowies, medieval daggers and knives. **Technical:** Forges ATS-34, D2, O2, 1060 and his own Damascus. Uses ivory and silver. **Prices:** $500 to $2000; some higher. **Remarks:** Full-time maker; first knife sold in 1979. **Mark:** First initial, last name.

BALLEW, DALE
PO Box 1277, Bowling Green, VA 22427, Phone: 804-633-5701
Specialties: Miniatures only to customer specs. **Patterns:** Bowies, daggers and fighters. **Technical:** Files 440C stainless; uses ivory, abalone, exotic woods and some precious stones. **Prices:** $100 to $800. **Remarks:** Part-time maker; first knife sold in 1988. **Mark:** Initials and last name.

BANAITIS, ROMAS
84 Winthrop St., Medway, MA 02053, Phone: 774-248-5851, rbanaitis@verizon.net
Specialties: Designing art and fantasy knives. **Patterns:** Folders, daggers and fixed blades. **Technical:** Hand-carved blades, handles and fittings in stainless steel, sterling silver and titanium. **Prices:** Moderate to upscale. **Remarks:** First knife sold in 1996. **Mark:** Romas Banaitis.

BANKS, DAVID L.
99 Blackfoot Ave, Riverton, WY 82501, Phone: 307-856-3154/Cell: 307-851-5599, blackfootforge@bresnan.net
Specialties: Heavy-duty working straight knives. **Patterns:** Hunters, Bowies and camp knives. **Technical:** Forges Damascus 1084-15N20, L6-W1 pure nickel, 5160, 52100 and his own Damascus; differential heat treat and tempers. Handles made of horn, antlers and exotic wood. Hand-stitched harness leather sheaths. **Prices:** $300 to $4,000. **Remarks:** Part-time maker. **Mark:** Banks, Blackfoot Forge, Dave Banks.

BAREFOOT, JOE W.
1654 Honey Hill, Wilmington, NC 28442, Phone: 910-641-1143
Specialties: Working straight knives of his design. **Patterns:** Hunters, fighters and boots; tantos and survival knives. **Technical:** Grinds D2, 440C and ATS-34. Mirror finishes. Uses ivory and stag on customer request only. **Prices:** $50 to $160; some to $500. **Remarks:** Part-time maker; first knife sold in 1980. **Mark:** Bare footprint.

BARKER, JOHN
5725 Boulder Bluff Dr., Cumming, GA 30040, Phone: 678-357-8586, barkerknives@bellsouth.net Web: www.barkerknives.com
Specialties: Tactical fixed blades and folders. **Technical:** Stock removal method and CPM and Carpenter powdered technology steels. **Prices:** $150 and up. **Remarks:** First knife made 2006. **Mark:** Snarling dog with "Barker" over the top of its head and "Knives" below.

BARKER, REGGIE
40 Columbia Rd. 254, Taylor, AR 71861, Phone: 318-539-2958, rbarker014@gmail.com; Web: www.reggiebarkerknives.com
Specialties: Hunters. **Patterns:** Pocketknives, fighters, camp knives and bowies. **Technical:** Forges carbon steel, stainless steel for pocketknives and uses own damascus. **Prices:** $300 and up. **Remarks:** Full-time maker. Three-time World Cutting Champion with over 15 wins. Winner of Best Value of Show 2001; Arkansas Knife Show and Journeyman Smith. Border Guard Forge. **Mark:** Barker JS.

BARKER, ROBERT G.
2311 Branch Rd, Bishop, GA 30621, Phone: 706-769-7827
Specialties: Traditional working/using straight knives of his design. **Patterns:** Bowies, hunters and utility knives, ABS Journeyman Smith. **Technical:** Hand forged carbon and Damascus. Forges to shape high-carbon 5160, cable and chain. Differentially heat-treats. **Prices:** $200 to $500; some to $1000. **Remarks:** Spare-time maker; first knife sold in 1987. **Mark:** BARKER/J.S.

BARKER, STUART
51 Thorpe Dr., Wigston, Leicester, ENGLAND LE18 1LE, Phone: +447887585411, sc_barker@hotmail.com Web: www.barkerknives.co.uk
Specialties: Fixed blade working knives of his design. **Patterns:** Kitchen, hunter, utility/camp knives. **Technical:** Grinds O1, Rw134 & Damasteel, hand rubbed or shot blast finishes. **Prices:** $150 - $1,000. **Remarks:** Part-time maker; first knife sold 2006. **Mark:** Last initial or last name.

BARKES, TERRY
14844 N. Bluff Rd., Edinburgh, IN 46124, Phone: 812-526-6390, terrybarkes@outlook.comt; Web:http:// my.hsonline.net/wizard/TerryBarkesKnives.htm
Specialties: Traditional working straight knives of his designs. **Patterns:** Drop point hunters, boot knives, skinning, fighter, utility, all purpose, camp, and grill knives. **Technical:** Grinds 1095 - 1084 - 52100 - 01, Hollow grinds and flat grinds. Hand rubbed finish from 400 to 2000 grit or High polish buff. Hard edge and soft back, heat treat by maker. Likes File work, natural handle material, bone, stag, water buffalo horn, wildbeast bone, ironwood. **Prices:** $200 and up **Remarks:** Full-time maker, first knifge sold in 2005. Doing business as Barkes Knife Shop. **Marks:** Barkes - USA, Barkes Double Arrow - USA

BARLOW, JANA POIRIER
3820 Borland Cir, Anchorage, AK 99517, Phone: 907-243-4581

BARNES, AUBREY G.
11341 Rock Hill Rd, Hagerstown, MD 21740, Phone: 301-223-4587, a.barnes@myactv.net
Specialties: Classic Moran style reproductions and using knives of his own design. **Patterns:** Bowies, hunters, fighters, daggers and utility/camping knives. **Technical:** Forges 5160, 1085, L6 and Damascus, Silver wire inlays. **Prices:** $500 to $5000. **Remarks:** Full-time maker; first knife sold in 1992. Doing business as Falling Waters Forge. **Mark:** First and middle initials, last name, M.S.

BARNES, GARY L.
112 Brandy Ln., Defuniak Springs, FL 32435, Phone: 410-635-6243, Fax: 410-635-6243, glbarnes@glbarnes.com; Web: www.glbarnes.com
Specialties: Ornate button lock Damascus folders. **Patterns:** Barnes original. **Technical:** Forges own Damascus. **Prices:** Average $2500. **Remarks:** ABS Master Smith since 1983. **Mark:** Hand engraved logo of letter B pierced by dagger.

BARNES, GREGORY
266 W Calaveras St, Altadena, CA 91001, Phone: 626-398-0053, snake@annex.com

BARNES, JACK
PO Box 1315, Whitefish, MT 59937-1315, Phone: 406-862-6078

BARNES, MARLEN R.
904 Crestview Dr S, Atlanta, TX 75551-1854, Phone: 903-796-3668, MRBlives@worldnet.att.net
Specialties: Hammer forges random and mosaic Damascus. **Patterns:** Hatchets, straight and folding knives. **Technical:** Hammer forges carbon steel using 5160, 1084 and 52100 with 15N20 and 203E nickel. **Prices:** $150 and up. **Remarks:** Part-time maker; first knife sold 1999. **Mark:** Script M.R.B., other side J.S.

BARNES, ROGER
BC Cutlery Co., 314 Rosemarie Pl., Bay Point, CA 94565, Phone: 925-483-6982 or 925-231-4367, bccutlerycompany@gmail.com; Facebook.com/bc cutlery co.
Mark: BC usa.

BARNES, ROGER
BC Cutlery Co., 314 Rosemarie Pl., Bay Point, CA 94565, bccutlerycompany@gmail.com
Specialties: Various styles of fixed-blade knives with an emphasis on quality in performance and simple aesthetics. **Patterns:** Karambits, Bob Loveless-inspired drop-point hunters and choppers. **Technical:** Uses 52100, 1095, 5160, AEB-L and CPM-3V blade steels, and Micartas, carbon fiber and G-10 handle scales, all USA-made materials. **Prices:** $75 to $500. **Remarks:** Wait time two weeks to one month.

BARNES, WENDELL
PO Box 272, Clinton, MT 59825, Phone: 406-825-0908
Specialties: Working straight knives. **Patterns:** Hunters, folders, neck knives. **Technical:** Grinds 440C, ATS-34, D2 and Damascus. **Prices:** Start at $75. **Remarks:** Spare-time maker; first knife sold in 1996. **Mark:** First initial, split heart, last name.

BARNES JR., CECIL C.
141 Barnes Dr, Center Ridge, AR 72027, Phone: 501-893-2267

BARNETT, BRUCE
PO Box 447, Mundaring, WA, AUSTRALIA 6073, Phone: 61-4-19243855, bruce@barnettcustomknives.com; web: www.barnettcustomknives.com
Specialties: Most types of fixed blades, folders, carving sets. **Patterns:** Hunters, Bowies, Camp Knives, Fighters, Lockback and Slipjoint Folders. **Prices:** $200 up **Remarks:** Part time maker. Member Australian Knifemakers Guild and ABS journeyman smith. **Mark:** Barnett + J.S.

BARNETT, VAN
BARNETT INT'L INC, 1135 Terminal Way Ste #209, Reno, NV 89502, Phone: 304-727-5512; 775-513-6969; 775-686-9084, ImATimeMachine@gmail.com & illusionknives@gmail.com; Web: www.VanBarnett.com
Specialties: Collector grade one-of-a-kind / embellished high art daggers and art folders. **Patterns:** Art daggers and folders. **Technical:** Forges and grinds own Damascus. **Prices:** Upscale. **Remarks:** Designs and makes one-of-a-kind highly embellished art knives using high karat gold, diamonds and other gemstones, pearls, stone and fossil ivories, carved steel guards and blades, all knives are carved and or engraved, does own engraving, carving and other embellishments, sole authorship; full-time maker since 1981. Does one high art collaboration a year with Dellana. Member of ABS. Member Art Knife Invitational Group (AKI) **Mark:** VBARNETT

BARNHILL, WESS
5846 Meadows Run, Spotsylvania, VA 22551, Phone: 540-582-8758, wess.barnhill@gmail.com; Web: www.wessbarnhillknives.com
Specialties: High-art, collectible and functional straight knives. **Patterns:** Bowies, hunters, camp knives and others. **Technical:** Hand forges high-carbon and damascus steel. Applied art in the forms of engraving, carving and filework. Offers functional leather sheaths in exotic leather. **Prices:** Start at $250. **Remarks:** Sole authorship on all knives, ABS journeyman smith. **Mark:** Last name followed by J.S..

BARR, JUDSON C.
1905 Pickwick Circle, Irving, TX 75060, Phone: 214-724-0564, judsonbarrknives@yahoo.com
Specialties: Bowies. **Patterns:** Sheffield and Early American. **Technical:** Forged carbon steel and Damascus. Also stock removal. **Remarks:** Journeyman member of ABS. **Mark:** Barr.

BARRETT, RICK L. (TOSHI HISA)
18943 CR 18, Goshen, IN 46528, Phone: 574-533-4297, barrettrick@hotmail.com
Specialties: Japanese-style blades from sushi knives to katana and fantasy pieces. **Patterns:** Swords, axes, spears/lances, hunter and utility knives. **Technical:** Forges and grinds Damascus and carbon steels, occasionally uses stainless. **Prices:** $250 to $4000+. **Remarks:** Full-time bladesmith, jeweler. **Mark:** Japanese mei on Japanese pieces and stylized initials.

BARRON, BRIAN
123 12th Ave, San Mateo, CA 94402, Phone: 650-341-2683
Specialties: Traditional straight knives. **Patterns:** Daggers, hunters and swords. **Technical:** Grinds 440C, ATS-34 and 1095. Sculpts bolsters using an S-curve. **Prices:** $130 to $270; some to $1500. **Remarks:** Part-time maker; first knife sold in 1993. **Mark:** Diamond Drag "Barron."

BARRY, SCOTT
Box 354, Laramie, WY 82073, Phone: 307-399-2646, scottyb@uwyo.edu
Specialties: Currently producing mostly folders, also make fixed blade hunters & fillet knives. **Technical:** Steels used are ATS 34, 154CM, CPM 154, D2, CPM S30V, Damasteel and Devin Thomas stainless damascus. **Prices:** Range from $300 $1000. **Remarks:** Part-time maker. First knife sold in 1972. **Mark:** DSBarry, etched on blade.

BARRY III, JAMES J.
115 Flagler Promenade No., West Palm Beach, FL 33405, Phone: 561-832-4197
Specialties: High-art working straight knives of his design also high art tomahawks. **Patterns:** Hunters, daggers and fishing knives. **Technical:** Grinds 440C only. Prefers exotic materials for handles. Most knives embellished with filework, carving and scrimshaw. Many pieces designed to stand unassisted. **Prices:** $500 to $10,000. **Remarks:** Part-time maker; first knife sold in 1975. Guild member (Knifemakers) since 1991. **Mark:** Branded initials as a J and B together.

BARTH, J.D.
101 4th St, PO Box 186, Alberton, MT 59820, Phone: 406-722-4557, mtdeerhunter@blackfoot.net; Web: www.jdbarthcustomknives.com
Specialties: Working and fancy straight knives of his design. LinerLock® folders, stainless and Damascus, fully file worked, nitre bluing. **Technical:** Grinds ATS-34, 440-C, stainless and carbon Damascus. Uses variety of natural handle materials and Micarta. Likes dovetailed bolsters. Filework on most knives, full and tapered tangs. Makes custom fit sheaths for each knife. **Mark:** Name over maker, city and state.

custom knifemakers

BARTLETT, MARK
102 Finn Cir., Lawrenceburg, TN 38464, Phone: 931-477-5444, moosetrax@live.com
Specialties: Mostly hunters and small bowies, but moving into larger bowies. **Technical:** Forges for the most part, with some stock removal, primarily using 1095, 1084 and 52100 blade steels. Has started damascus recently. Uses hardwoods and Micarta mostly for handles. **Prices:** $200 to $500, with some recent orders booked at $900-$1,000. **Remarks:** Part-time maker; first knife made in September 2013. **Mark:** Last name with a dagger through the middle "T."

BARTLOW, JOHN
14 Red Fox Dr., Sheridan, WY 82801, Phone: 307-673-4941, 2jbartlow@gmail.com
Specialties: Skinner/caper sets, classic working patterns, and known for bird-and-trout classics. **Technical:** ATS-34, CPM-154, damascus available on all LinerLocks. **Prices:** $400 to $2,500. **Remarks:** Full-time maker, Guild member from 1988. **Mark:** Bartlow Sheridan, Wyo.

BASKETT, BARBARA
427 Sutzer Ck Rd, Eastview, KY 42732, Phone: 270-862-5019, bgbaskett@yahoo.com; Web: www.baskettknives.com
Specialties: Hunters and LinerLocks. **Technical:** 440-C, CPM 154, S30V. **Prices:** $250 and up. **Mark:** B. Baskett.

BASKETT, LEE GENE
427 Sutzer Ck. Rd., Eastview, KY 42732, Phone: 270-862-5019, Fax: Cell: 270-766-8724, baskettknives@hotmail.com Web: www.baskettknives.com
Specialties: Fancy working knives and fancy art pieces, often set up in fancy desk stands. **Patterns:** Fighters, Bowies, and Surival Knives; lockback folders and liner locks along with traditional styles. Cutting competition knives. **Technical:** Grinds O1, 440-c, S30V, power CPM154, CPM 4, D2, buys Damascus. Filework provided on most knives. **Prices:** $250 and up. **Remarks:** Part-time maker, first knife sold in 1980. **Mark:** Baskett

BASSETT, DAVID J.
P.O. Box 69-102, Glendene, Auckland, NEW ZEALAND 0645, Phone: 64 9 818 9083, Fax: 64 9 818 9013, david@customknifemaking.co.nz; Web:www.customknifemaking.co.nz
Specialties: Working/using knives. **Patterns:** Hunters, fighters, boot, skinners, tanto. **Technical:** Grinds 440C, 12C27, D2 and some Damascus via stock removal method. **Prices:** $150 to $500. **Remarks:** Part-time maker, first knife sold in 2006. Also carries range of natural and synthetic handle material, pin stock etc. for sale. **Mark:** Name over country in semi-circular design.

BATSON, JAMES
1316 McClung Ave., Huntsville, AL 35801, Phone: 256-971-6860, james.1.batson@gmail.com
Specialties: Forged Damascus blades and fittings in collectible period pieces. **Patterns:** Integral art knives, Bowies, folders, American-styled blades and miniatures. **Technical:** Forges carbon steel and his Damascus. **Prices:** $150 to $1800; some to $4500. **Remarks:** Semi retired full-time maker; first knife sold in 1978. **Mark:** Name, bladesmith with horse's head.

BATSON, RICHARD G.
6591 Waterford Rd, Rixeyville, VA 22737, Phone: 540-937-2318, mbatson6591@comcast.net
Specialties: Military, utility and fighting knives in working and presentation grade. **Patterns:** Daggers, combat and utility knives. **Technical:** Grinds O1, 1095 and 440C. Etches and scrimshaws; offers polished, Parkerized finishes. **Prices:** From $400. **Remarks:** Very limited production to active-dute military and vets only. First knife sold in 1958. **Mark:** Bat in circle, hand-signed and serial numbered.

BATTS, KEITH
500 Manning Rd, Hooks, TX 75561, Phone: 903-277-8466, kbatts@cableone.net
Specialties: Working straight knives of his design or to customer specs. **Patterns:** Bowies, hunters, skinners, camp knives and others. **Technical:** Forges 5160 and his Damascus; offers filework. **Prices:** $245 to $895. **Remarks:** Part-time maker; first knife sold in 1988. **Mark:** Last name.

BAUCHOP, ROBERT
PO Box 330, Munster, KN, SOUTH AFRICA 4278, Phone: +27 39 3192449
Specialties: Fantasy knives; working and using knives of his design and to customer specs. **Patterns:** Hunters, swords, utility/camp knives, diver's knives and large swords. **Technical:** Grinds Sandvick 12C27, D2, 440C. Uses South African hardwoods red ivory, wild olive, African blackwood, etc. on handles. **Prices:** $200 to $800; some to $2000. **Remarks:** Full-time maker; first knife sold in 1986. Doing business as Bauchop Custom Knives and Swords. **Mark:** Viking helmet with Bauchop (bow and chopper) crest.

BAXTER, DALE
291 County Rd 547, Trinity, AL 35673, Phone: 256-355-3626, dale@baxterknives.com
Specialties: Bowies, fighters, and hunters. **Patterns:** No patterns: all unique true customs. **Technical:** Hand forge and hand finish. Steels: 1095 and L6 for carbon blades, 1095/L6 for Damascus. **Remarks:** Full-time bladesmith and sold first knife in 1998. **Mark:** Dale Baxter (script) and J.S. on reverse.

BEAM, JOHN R.
1310 Foothills Rd, Kalispell, MT 59901, Phone: 406-755-2593
Specialties: Classic, high-art and working straight knives of his design. **Patterns:** Bowies and hunters. **Technical:** Grinds 440C, Damascus and scrap. **Prices:** $175 to $600; some to $3000. **Remarks:** Part-time maker; first knife sold in 1950. Doing business as Beam's Knives. **Mark:** Beam's Knives.

BEATTY, GORDON H.
121 Petty Rd, Seneca, SC 29672, Phone: 867-723-2966
Specialties: Working straight knives, some fancy. **Patterns:** Traditional patterns, mini-skinners and letter openers. **Technical:** Grinds ATS-34; makes knives one-at-a-time. **Prices:** $185 and up. **Remarks:** Part-time maker; first knife sold in 1982. **Mark:** Name.

BEATY, ROBERT B.
CUTLER, 1995 Big Flat Rd, Missoula, MT 59804, Phone: 406-549-1818
Specialties: Plain and fancy working knives and collector pieces; will accept custom orders. **Patterns:** Hunters, Bowies, utility, kitchen and camp knives; locking folders. **Technical:** Grinds D-2, ATS-34, Dendritie D-2, makes all tool steel Damascus, forges 1095, 5160, 52100. **Prices:** $150 to $600, some to $1100. **Remarks:** Full-time maker; first knife sold 1995. **Mark:** Stainless: First name, middle initial, last name, city and state. Carbon: Last name stamped on Ricasso.

BEAUCHAMP, GAETAN
125 de la Rivire, Stoneham, QC, CANADA G3C 0P6, Phone: 418-848-1914, Fax: 418-848-6859, knives@gbeauchamp.ca; Web: www.gbeauchamp.ca
Specialties: Working knives and folders of his design and to customer specs. **Patterns:** Hunters, fighters, fantasy knives. **Technical:** Grinds ATS-34, 440C, Damascus. Scrimshaws on ivory; specializes in buffalo horn and black backgrounds. Offers a variety of handle materials. **Prices:** Start at $250. **Remarks:** Full-time maker; first knife sold in 1992. **Mark:** Signature etched on blade.

BEAVER, DIRK
BEAVER CUSTOM BLADES, Ellijay, GA, Phone: 706-633-7884, dirk@beavercustomblades.com; Web: www.beavercustomblades.com
Specialties: Enjoys doing custom orders and working with his customers, making skinners, tactical fighters, neck knives and folders, anything a customer wants. **Technical:** Uses stock removal and forging methods of blade making, depending on style of knife, and works with high-carbon steel and damascus. **Remarks:** Full-time maker; first knife made in 2009.

BEERS, RAY
2501 Lakefront Dr, Lake Wales, FL 33898, Phone: 443-841-4143, rbknives@copper.net

BEETS, MARTY
390 N 5th Ave, Williams Lake, BC, CANADA V2G 2G4, Phone: 250-392-7199
Specialties: Working and collectable straight knives of his own design. **Patterns:** Hunter, skinners, Bowies and utility knives. **Technical:** Grinds various steels-does all his own work including heat treating. Uses a variety of handle material specializing in exotic hardwoods, antler and horn. **Prices:** $125 to $400. **Remarks:** Wife, Sandy does handmade/hand stitched sheaths. First knife sold in 1988. Business name Beets Handmade Knives.

BEGG, TODD M.
1341 N. McDowell Blvd., Ste. D, Petaluma, CA 94954, Phone: 707-242-1790, info@beggknives.com; Web: http://beggknives.net
Specialties: High-grade tactical folders and fixed blades. **Patterns:** Folders, integrals, fighters. **Technical:** Specializes in flipper folders using "IKBS" (Ikoma Korth Bearing System). **Prices:** $400 - $15,000. **Remarks:** Uses modern designs and materials.

BEHNKE, WILLIAM
8478 Dell Rd, Kingsley, MI 49649, Phone: 231-263-7447, bill@billbehnkeknives.com Web: www.billbehnkeknives.com
Specialties: Fabricates carbide file/grinding guides, LinerLock folders. **Patterns:** Traditional styling in moderate-sized straight and folding knives. **Technical:** Forges own damascus, prefers W-2. **Prices:** $150 to $2,000. **Remarks:** Full-time maker. **Mark:** "Behnke".

BEHRING, JAMES
Behring Made Knives, POB 17317, Missoula, MT 59808, Phone: 406-926-1193, behringmadeknives@gmail.com; Web: www.behringmade.com
Specialties: Custom handmade fixed blades for users and collectors alike. **Patterns:** Include, but are not limited to, hunters, skinners, bird & trout knives, fighters, kitchen cutlery, pocketknives, hatchets, etc. **Technical:** High-carbon steels (O1, 5160, 1095), CPM S30V, D2 and 440C stainless steel. Copper, nickel silver and brass fittings. Stag, Micarta, wide variety of wood, various horn (buffalo, musk ox, kudu), fossil and artifact walrus, etc. Open to new mediums upon request. **Prices:** $250 to $1,500. **Mark:** "B" logo with crossed hammer and knife, J. Behring Jr. Montana.

BELL, DON
Box 98, Lincoln, MT 59639, Phone: 406-362-3208, dlb@linctel.net
Patterns: Folders, hunters and custom orders. **Technical:** Carbon steel 52100, 5160, 1095, 1084. Making own Damascus. Flat grinds. Natural handle material including fossil. ivory, pearl, and ironwork. **Remarks:** Full-time maker. First knife sold in 1999. **Mark:** Last name.

BELL, DONALD
2 Division St, Bedford, NS, CANADA B4A 1Y8, Phone: 902-835-2623, donbell@accesswave.ca; Web: www.bellknives.com
Specialties: Fancy knives: carved and pierced folders of his own design. **Patterns:** Locking folders, pendant knives, jewelry knives. **Technical:** Grinds Damascus, pierces and carves blades. **Prices:** $500 to $2000, some to $3000. **Remarks:** Spare-time maker; first knife sold in 1993. **Mark:** Bell symbol with first initial inside.

BELL, GABRIEL
88321 North Bank Lane, Coquille, OR 97423, Phone: 541-396-3605, gabriel@dragonflyforge.com; Web: www.dragonflyforge.com & tomboyama.com
Specialties: Full line of combat quality Japanese swords. **Patterns:** Traditional tanto to

katana. **Technical:** Handmade steel and welded cable. **Prices:** Swords from bare blades to complete high art $1500 to $28,000. **Remarks:** Studied with father Michael Bell. Instruction in sword crafts. Working in partnership with Michael Bell.**Mark:** Dragonfly in shield or kunitoshi.

BELL, MICHAEL
88321 N Bank Lane, Coquille, OR 97423, Phone: 541-396-3605, michael@ dragonflyforge.com; Web: www. Dragonflyforge.com & tomboyama.com
Specialties: Full line of combat quality Japanese swords. **Patterns:** Traditional tanto to katana. **Technical:** Handmade steel and welded cable. **Prices:** Swords from bare blades to complete high art $1500 to $28,000. **Remarks:** Studied with Japanese master Nakajima Muneyoshi. Instruction in sword crafts. Working in partnership with son, Gabriel.**Mark:** Dragonfly in shield or tombo kunimitsu.

BELL, TONY
PO Box 24, Woodland, AL 36280, Phone: 256-449-2655, tbell905@aol.com
Specialties: Hand forged period knives and tomahawks. Art knives and knives made for everyday use.**Technical:** Makes own Damascus. Forges 1095, 5160,1080,L6 steels. Does own heat treating. **Prices:** $75-$1200. **Remarks:** Full time maker. **Mark:** Bell symbol with initial T in the middle.

BENJAMIN JR., GEORGE
3001 Foxy Ln, Kissimmee, FL 34746, Phone: 407-846-7259
Specialties: Fighters in various styles to include Persian, Moro and military. **Patterns:** Daggers, skinners and one-of-a-kind grinds. **Technical:** Forges O1, D2, A2, 5160 and Damascus. Favors Pakkawood, Micarta, and mirror or Parkerized finishes. Makes unique para-military leather sheaths. **Prices:** $150 to $600; some to $1200. **Remarks:** Doing business as The Leather Box. **Mark:** Southern Pride Knives.

BENNETT, BRETT C
420 Adamstown Rd., Reinholds, PA 17569, Phone: 307-220-3919, brett@ bennettknives.com; Web: www.bennettknives.com
Specialties: Hand-rubbed satin finish on all blades. **Patterns:** Mostly fixed-blade patterns. **Technical:** ATS-34, D-2, 1084/15N20 damascus, 1084 forged. **Mark:** "B.C. Bennett" in script or "Bennett" stamped in script.

BENNETT, GLEN C
5821 S Stewart Blvd, Tucson, AZ 85706

BENNETT, PETER
PO Box 143, Engadine, NSW, AUSTRALIA 2233, Phone: 02-520-4975 (home), Fax: 02-528-8219 (work)
Specialties: Fancy and embellished working and using straight knives to customer specs and in standard patterns. **Patterns:** Fighters, hunters, bird/trout and fillet knives. **Technical:** Grinds 440C, ATS-34 and Damascus. Uses rare Australian desert timbers for handles. **Prices:** $90 to $500; some to $1500. **Remarks:** Full-time maker; first knife sold in 1985. **Mark:** First and middle initials, last name; country.

BENNICA, CHARLES
11 Chemin du Salet, Moules et Baucels, FRANCE 34190, Phone: +33 4 67 73 42 40, cbennica@bennica-knives.com; Web: www.bennica-knives.com
Specialties: Fixed blades and folding knives; the latter with slick closing mechanisms with push buttons to unlock blade. Unique handle shapes, signature to the maker. **Technical:** 416 stainless steel frames for folders and ATS-34 blades. Also specializes in Damascus.

BENSINGER, J. W.
583 Jug Brook Rd., Marshfield, VT 05658, Phone: 802-917-1789, jwbensinger@ gmail.com Web: www.vermontbladesmith.com
Specialties: Working hunters, bowies for work and defense, and Finnish patterns. Occasional folders. **Technical:** High performance handforged knives in 5160, 52100, 1080, and in-house damascus. **Prices:** Range from $130 for simple bushcraft knives to $500 for larger knives. Damascus prices on request. **Remarks:** First knife made in 1980 or so. Full-time maker. Customer designs welcome. **Mark:** "JWB" and year in cursive.

BENSON, DON
2505 Jackson St #112, Escalon, CA 95320, Phone: 209-838-7921
Specialties: Working straight knives of his design. **Patterns:** Axes, Bowies, tantos and hunters. **Technical:** Grinds 440C. **Prices:** $100 to $150; some to $400. **Remarks:** Spare-time maker; first knife sold in 1980. **Mark:** Name.

BENTLEY, C L
2405 Hilltop Dr, Albany, GA 31707, Phone: 912-432-6656

BER, DAVE
656 Miller Rd, San Juan Island, WA 98250, Phone: 206-378-7230
Specialties: Working straight and folding knives for the sportsman; welcomes customer designs. **Patterns:** Hunters, skinners, Bowies, kitchen and fishing knives. **Technical:** Forges and grinds saw blade steel, wire Damascus, O1, L6, 5160 and 440C. **Prices:** $100 to $300; some to $500. **Remarks:** Full-time maker; first knife sold in 1985. **Mark:** Last name.

BERG, LEE
PO Box 458, Roseburg, OR 97470, leeandlanny@gmail.com
Specialties: One-of-a-kind and investment-quality straight knives of his own design, incorporating traditional, period, Near East and Asian influence. **Patterns:** Daggers, fighters, hunters, bowies, short swords, full size and miniature. **Technical:** Stock removal with file, damascus, meteorite, O1, D2 and ATS-34. **Prices:** $200 and up. **Remarks:** Part-time maker; first knife sold in 1972. **Mark:** Full name.

BERG, LOTHAR
37 Hillcrest Ln, Kitchener ON, CANADA NZK 1S9, Phone: 519-745-3260; 519-745-3260

BERGER, MAX A.
5716 John Richard Ct, Carmichael, CA 95608, Phone: 916-972-9229, bergerknives@ aol.com
Specialties: Fantasy and working/using straight knives of his design. **Patterns:** Fighters, hunters and utility/camp knives. **Technical:** Grinds ATS-34 and 440C. Offers fileworks and combinations of mirror polish and satin finish blades. **Prices:** $200 to $600; some to $2500. **Remarks:** Part-time maker; first knife sold in 1992. **Mark:** Last name.

BERGH, ROGER
Dalkarlsa 291, Bygdea, SWEDEN 91598, Phone: 469-343-0061, knivroger@hotmail. com; Web: www.rogerbergh.com
Specialties: Collectible all-purpose straight-blade knives. Damascus steel blades, carving and artistic design knives are heavily influenced by nature and have an organic hand crafted feel.

BERGLIN, BRUCE
17441 Lake Terrace Place, Mount Vernon, WA 98274, Phone: 360-333-1217, bruce@ berglins.com
Specialties: Working fixed blades and folders of his own design. **Patterns:** Hunters, boots, bowies, utility, liner locks and slip joints some with vintage finish. **Technical:** Forges carbon steel, grinds carbon steel. Prefers natural handle material. **Prices:** Start at $300. **Remarks:** Part-time maker since 1998. **Mark:** (2 marks) 1. Last name; or 2. First initial, second initial & last name, surrounded with an oval.

BERTOLAMI, JUAN CARLOS
Av San Juan 575, Neuquen, ARGENTINA 8300, fliabertolami@infovia.com.ar
Specialties: Hunting and country labor knives. All of them unique high quality pieces and supplies collectors too. **Technical:** Austrian stainless steel and elephant, hippopotamus and orca ivory, as well as ebony and other fine woods for the handles.

BERTUZZI, ETTORE
Via Partigiani 3, Seriate, Bergamo, ITALY 24068, Phone: 035-294262, Fax: 035-294262
Specialties: Classic straight knives and folders of his design, to customer specs and in standard patterns. **Patterns:** Bowies, hunters and locking folders. **Technical:** Grinds ATS-34, D3, D2 and various Damascus. **Prices:** $300 to $500. **Remarks:** Part-time maker; first knife sold in 1993. **Mark:** Name etched on ricasso.

BESEDICK, FRANK E
1257 Country Club Road, Monongahela, PA 15063-1057, Phone: 724-292-8016, bez32@comcast.net
Specialties: Traditional working and using straight knives of his design. **Patterns:** Hunters, utility/camp knives and miniatures; buckskinner blades and tomahawks. **Technical:** Forges and grinds 5160, O1 and Damascus. Offers filework and scrimshaw. **Prices:** $75 to $300; some to $750. **Remarks:** Part-time maker; first knife sold in 1990. **Mark:** Name or initials.

BESHARA, BRENT (BESH)
PO BOX 557, Holyrood, NL, CANADA A0A 2R0, BESH@beshknives.com Web: www. beshknives.com
Specialties: Fixed blade tools and knives. **Patterns:** BESH Wedge tools and knives. **Technical:** Custom design work, grinds 0-1, D-2, 440C, 154cm. Offers kydex sheathing **Prices:** Start at $250. **Remarks:** Inventor of BESH Wedge geometry, custom maker and designer since 2000. Retired (24yrs) Special Forces, Special Operations Navy bomb disposal diver. Lifelong martial artist. **Mark:** "BESH" stamped.

BEST, RON
1489 Adams Lane, Stokes, NC 27884, Phone: 252-714-1264, ronbestknives@msn. com; Web: www.ronbestknives.com
Specialties: Folders and automatics. **Patterns:** Everything including butterfly knives. **Technical:** Grinds 440C, D-2 and ATS-34. **Prices:** $600 to $8000.

BETANCOURT, ANTONIO L.
5718 Beefwood Ct., St. Louis, MO 63129, Phone: 314-306-1869, bet2001@charter.net
Specialties: One-of-a-kind fixed blades and art knives. **Patterns:** Hunters and Bowies with embellished handles. **Technical:** Uses cast sterling silver and lapidary with fine gemstones, fossil ivory, and scrimshaw. Grinds Damascus and 440C. **Prices:** $100 to $800. **Remarks:** Part-time maker, first knife sold in 1974. **Mark:** Initials in cursive.

BEUKES, TINUS
83 Henry St, Risiville, Vereeniging, GT, SOUTH AFRICA 1939, Phone: 27 16 423 2053
Specialties: Working straight knives. **Patterns:** Hunters, skinners and kitchen knives. **Technical:** Grinds D2, 440C and chain, cable and stainless Damascus. **Prices:** $80 to $180. **Remarks:** Part-time maker; first knife sold in 1993. **Mark:** Full name, city, logo.

BEVERLY II, LARRY H
PO Box 741, Spotsylvania, VA 22553, Phone: 540-846-5426, beverlyknives@aol.com
Specialties: Working straight knives, slip-joints and liner locks. Welcomes customer designs. **Patterns:** Bowies, hunters, guard less fighters and miniatures. **Technical:** Grinds 440C, A2 and O1. **Prices:** $125 to $1000. **Remarks:** Part-time maker; first knife sold in 1986. **Mark:** Initials or last name in script.

BEZUIDENHOUT, BUZZ
PO BOX 28284, Malvern, KZN, SOUTH AFRICA 4055, Phone: 031-4632827, Fax: 031-4632827, buzzbee@mweb.co.za
Specialties: Working and Fancy Folders, my or customer design.**Patterns:** Boots,

hunters, kitchen knives and utility/camp knives. **Technical:** Use 12-C-27 + stainless damascus, some carbon damascus. Uses local hardwoods, horn: kudu, impala, buffalo, giraffe bone and ivory for handles.
Prices: $250 to upscale. **Remarks:** Part-time maker; first knife sold in 1985. Member S.A. Knife Makers Guild**Mark:** First name with a bee emblem.

BINGENHEIMER, BRUCE
553 Tiffany Dr., Spring Creek, NV 89815, Phone: 775-934-6295, mbing@citlink.net
Specialties: Forging fixed blade hunters, bowies, fighters. **Technical:** Forges own Damascus. Steel choices 5160, 1084. Damascus steels 15N20, 1080. **Prices:** $300 and up. **Remarks:** ABS Journeyman Smith 2010. Member of Montana Knife Makers Association and Oregon Knife Collector's Association. **Mark:** Bingenheimer (arched over) M B.

BIRDWELL, IRA LEE
PO Box 1448, Congress, AZ 85332, Phone: 928-925-3258, heli.ira@gmail.com
Specialties: Special orders. **Mark:** Engraved signature.

BISH, HAL
9347 Sweetbriar Trace, Jonesboro, GA 30236, Phone: 770-477-2422, hal-bish@hp.com

BISHER, WILLIAM (BILL)
1015 Beck Road, Denton, NC 27239, Phone: 336-859-4686, blackturtleforge@wildblue.net;Web: www.blackturtleforge.com
Specialties: Period pieces, also contemporary belt knives, friction folders. **Patterns:** Own design, hunters, camp/utility, Bowies, belt axes, neck knives, carving sets. **Technical:** Forges straight high carbon steels, and own Damascus, grinds ATS34 and 154CM. Uses natural handle materials (wood, bone, stag horn), micarta and stabilized wood.**Prices:** Starting at $75 - $2500. **Remarks:** Past president of North Carolina Custom Knifemakers Guild, member ABS, Full-time maker as of 2007, first knife made 1989, all work in house, blades and sheaths **Mark:** Last name under crown and turtle

BIZZELL, ROBERT
145 Missoula Ave, Butte, MT 59701, Phone: 406-782-4403, patternweld@yahoo.com
Specialties: Damascus Bowies. **Patterns:** Composite, mosaic and traditional. **Technical:** Fixed blades & LinerLock® folders. **Prices:** Fixed blades start at $275. Folders start at $500. **Remarks:** Currently not taking orders. **Mark:** Hand signed.

BLACK, EARL
3466 South, 700 East, Salt Lake City, UT 84106, Phone: 801-466-8395
Specialties: High-art straight knives and folders; period pieces. **Patterns:** Boots, Bowies and daggers; lockers and gents. **Technical:** Grinds 440C and 154CM. Buys some Damascus. Scrimshaws and engraves. **Prices:** $200 to $1800; some to $2500 and higher. **Remarks:** Full-time maker; first knife sold in 1980. **Mark:** Name, city, state.

BLACK, SCOTT
27100 Leetown Rd, Picayune, MS 39466, Phone: 601-799-5939, copperheadforge@telepak.net
Specialties: Friction folders; fighters. **Patterns:** Bowies, fighters, hunters, smoke hawks, friction folders, daggers. **Technical:** All forged, all work done by him, own hand-stitched leather work; own heat-treating. **Prices:** $100 to $2200. **Remarks:** ABS Journeyman Smith. Cabel / Damascus/ High Carbone. **Mark:** Hot Mark - Copperhead Snake.

BLACK, TOM
921 Grecian NW, Albuquerque, NM 87107, Phone: 505-344-2549, blackknives@comcast.net
Specialties: Working knives to fancy straight knives of his design. **Patterns:** Drop-point skinners, folders, using knives, Bowies and daggers. **Technical:** Grinds 440C, 154CM, ATS-34, A2, D2, CPM-154 and damascus. Offers engraving and scrimshaw. **Prices:** $250 and up; some over $8500. **Remarks:** Full-time maker; first knife sold in 1970. **Mark:** Name, city.

BLACKWELL, ZANE
PO BOX 234, Eden, TX 76837, Phone: 325-869-8821, blackwellknives@hotmail.com; Web: www.blackwellknives.com
Specialties: Hunters, slip-joint folders and kitchen knives. **Patterns:** Drop-point and clip-point hunters, and classic slip-joint patterns like single-blade trappers. **Technical:** CPM 154, ATS-34, 440C and D2 blade steels, and natural handle materials. **Prices:** Single-blade folders start at $400. **Remarks:** Six-month back log. **Mark:** Zane Blackwell Eden Texas.

BLANCHARD, G R (GARY)
PO BOX 292, Dandridge, TN 37725, Phone: 865-397-9515, blanchardcustomknives@yahoo.com; Web: www.blanchardcustomknives.com
Specialties: Fancy folders with patented button blade release and high-art straight knives of his design. **Patterns:** Boots, daggers and locking folders. **Technical:** Grinds 440C and ATS-34 and Damascus. Engraves his knives. **Prices:** $1000 to $15,000 or more. **Remarks:** Full-time maker; first knife sold in 1989. **Mark:** First and middle initials, last name or last name only.

BLAUM, ROY
ROY'S KNIFE & ARCHERY SHOP, 319 N Columbia St, Covington, LA 70433, Phone: 985-893-1060
Specialties: Working straight knives and folders of his design; lightweight easy-open folders. **Patterns:** Hunters, boots, fishing and woodcarving/whittling knives. **Technical:** Grinds A2, D2, O1, 154CM and ATS-34. Offers leatherwork. **Prices:** $40 to $800; some higher. **Remarks:** Full-time maker; first knife sold in 1976. **Mark:** Engraved signature or etched logo.

Bloodworth Custom Knives
3502 W. Angelica Dr., Meridian, ID 83646, Phone: 208-888-7778
Patterns: Working straight knives, hunters, skinners, bowies, utility knives of his designs or customer specs. Scagel knives. Period knives and traditional frontier knives and sheaths. **Technical:** Grinds D2, ATS34, 154CM, 5160, 01, Damascus, Heat treats, natural and composite handle materials. **Prices:** $185.00 to $1,500. **Remarks:** Roger Smith knife maker. Full-time maker; first knife sold in 1978 **Mark:** Sword over BLOODWORTH.

BLOOMER, ALAN T
PO Box 154, 116 E 6th St, Maquon, IL 61458, Phone: Cell: 309-371-8520, alant.bloomer@winco.net
Specialties: Folders & straight knives & custom pen maker. **Patterns:** All kinds. **Technical:** Does own heat treating. **Prices:** $400 to $1000. **Remarks:** Part-time maker. No orders. **Mark:** Stamp Bloomer.

BLUM, KENNETH
1729 Burleson, Brenham, TX 77833, Phone: 979-836-9577
Specialties: Traditional working straight knives of his design. **Patterns:** Camp knives, hunters and Bowies. **Technical:** Forges 5160; grinds 440C and D2. Uses exotic woods and Micarta for handles. **Prices:** $150 to $300. **Remarks:** Part-time maker; first knife sold in 1978. **Mark:** Last name on ricasso.

BLYSTONE, RONALD L.
231 Bailey Road, Creekside, PA 15732, Phone: 724-397-2671, taxibly@hotmail.com
Specialties: Traditional forged working knives. **Patterns:** Hunting utility and skinners of his own design. **Technical:** Forges his own pattern welded Damascus using carbon steel. **Prices:** Starting at $150. **Remarks:** Spare-time maker.**Mark:** Initials - upside-down R against the B, inside a circle, over the word FORGE

BOARDMAN, GUY
39 Mountain Ridge R, New Germany, KZN, SOUTH AFRICA 3619, Phone: 031-726-921
Specialties: American and South African-styles. **Patterns:** Bowies, American and South African hunters, plus more. **Technical:** Grinds Bohler steels, some ATS-34. **Prices:** $100 to $600. **Remarks:** Part-time maker; first knife sold in 1986. **Mark:** Name, city, country.

BOCHMAN, BRUCE
183 Howard Place, Grants Pass, OR 97526, Phone: 541-471-1985, 183bab@gmail.com
Specialties: Hunting, fishing, bird and tactical knives. **Patterns:** Hunters, fishing and bird knives. **Technical:** ATS34, 154CM, mirror or satin finish. Damascus. **Prices:** $250 to $350; some to $750. **Remarks:** Part-time maker; first knife sold in 1977. **Mark:** Custom Knives by B. Bochman

BODEN, HARRY
Via Gellia Mill, Bonsall Matlock, Derbyshire, ENGLAND DE4 2AJ, Phone: 0629-825176
Specialties: Traditional working straight knives and folders of his design. **Patterns:** Hunters, locking folders and utility/camp knives. **Technical:** Grinds Sandvik 12C27, D2 and O1. **Prices:** £70 to £150; some to £300. **Remarks:** Full-time maker; first knife sold in 1986. **Mark:** Full name.

BODOLAY, ANTAL
Rua Wilson Soares Fernandes #31, Planalto, Belo Horizonte, MG, BRAZIL MG-31730-700, Phone: 031-494-1885
Specialties: Working folders and fixed blades of his design or to customer specs; some art daggers and period pieces. **Patterns:** Daggers, hunters, locking folders, utility knives and Khukris. **Technical:** Grinds D6, high-carbon steels and 420 stainless. Forges files on request. **Prices:** $30 to $350. **Remarks:** Full-time maker; first knife sold in 1965. **Mark:** Last name in script.

BOECK, SANDRO EDUARDO
St. Eduardo Macedo de Oliveira, 300, Cachoeira do Sul - RS, BRAZIL CEP - 96 505 - 610, Phone: 55-51-99559106, sandroboeck@gmail.com; Web: www.sandroboeck.com.br
Specialties: Fixed blades, integrals, gaucho style, bowies, hunters, dirks and swords. **Technical:** Forges his own damascus, mosaic damascus and high-carbon steel. Constructs integral knives. **Prices:** $500 to $2,000. **Remarks:** Part-time maker, IBO founding member, ABS journeyman smith, SBC lawyer consultant. **Mark:** S.Boeck JS.

BOEHLKE, GUENTER
Parkstrasse 2, 56412 Grobholbach, GERMANY, Phone: (49) 2602-5440, Fax: (49) 2602-5491, Boehlke-Messer@t-online.de; Web: www.boehlke-messer.de
Specialties: Classic working/using straight knives of his design. **Patterns:** Hunters, utility/camp knives and ancient remakes. **Technical:** Grinds Damascus, CPM-T-440V and 440C. Inlays gemstones and ivory. **Prices:** $220 to $700; some to $2000. **Remarks:** Spare-time maker; first knife sold in 1985. **Mark:** Name, address and bow and arrow.

BOHRMANN, BRUCE
61 Portland St, Yarmouth, ME 04096, Phone: 207-846-3385, bbohr@maine.rr.com; Web: Bohrmannknives.com
Specialties: Fixed-blade sporting, camp and hunting knives. **Technical:** Stock-removal maker using 13C26 Sandvik stainless steel hardened to 58-60 Rockwell. **Prices:** $499 for each model. Also, special "Heritage" production using historic certified woods (from Washington's, Jefferson's, Madison's and Henry's Plantations) - $1,250. **Remarks:** Full-time maker; first knife made in 1955. Always developing new models and concepts, such as steak knives, fixed blades and miniatures with special pocket sheaths. All knives serial #'d and can be personalized by etching initials into blades. **Mark:** The letter "B" connected to and lying beneath deer antlers.

BOJTOS, ARPAD
Dobsinskeho 10, 98403 Lucenec, SLOVAKIA, Phone: 00421-47 4333512; Cell: 00421-91 5875066, bojtos@stonline.sk; Web: www.arpadbojtos.sk

Specialties: Art knives, including over 100 folders. **Patterns:** Daggers, fighters and hunters. **Technical:** Grinds ATS-34 and stainless damascus. Carves on steel, handle materials and sheaths. **Prices:** $5000 to $10,000; some over. **Remarks:** Full-time maker; first knife sold in 1990. **Mark:** AB.

BOLDUC, GARY
1419 Tanglewood Dr., Corona, CA 92882, Phone: 951-739-0137, gary@stillwaterwoods.com; Web: www.bolduckknives.com
Specialties: Fish fillet knives (larger sizes), medium 8" to large 10"-plus. Replica making of primitive Native Alaskan hunting and cutting tools, kitchen cutlery. **Patterns:** Hunters, skinners, fillet, boning, spear points and kitchen cutlery. **Technical:** High-quality stainless steel, mainly CTS-XHP, CPM-154 and CPM-S35VN for improved edge design. **Prices:** $200-$400 and up. **Remarks:** Full-time maker; first knife sold in 2007. **Mark:** First initial, last name with USA under, or grizzly bear with Bolduc Knives underneath.

BOLEWARE, DAVID
PO Box 96, Carson, MS 39427, Phone: 601-943-5372
Specialties: Traditional and working/using straight knives of his design, to customer specs and in standard patterns. **Patterns:** Bowies, hunters and utility/camp knives. **Technical:** Grinds ATS-34, 440C and Damascus. **Prices:** $85 to $350; some to $600. **Remarks:** Part-time maker; first knife sold in 1989. **Mark:** First and last name, city, state.

BOLEY, JAMIE
PO Box 477, Parker, SD 57053, Phone: 605-297-0014, jamie@polarbearforge.com
Specialties: Working knives and historical influenced reproductions. **Patterns:** Hunters, skinners, scramasaxes, and others.**Technical:** Forges 5160, O1, L6, 52100, W1, W2 makes own Damascus. **Prices:** Starts at $125. **Remarks:** Part-time maker. **Mark:** Polar bear paw print with name on the left side and Polar Bear Forge on the right.

BONASSI, FRANCO
Via Nicoletta 4, Pordenone, ITALY 33170, Phone: 0434-550821, frank.bonassi@alice.it
Specialties: Fancy and working one-of-a-kind folder knives of his design. **Patterns:** Folders, linerlocks and back locks. **Technical:** Grinds CPM, ATS-34, 154CM and commercial Damascus. Uses only titanium foreguards and pommels. **Prices:** Start at $350. **Remarks:** Spare-time maker; first knife sold in 1988. Has made cutlery for several celebrities; Gen. Schwarzkopf, Fuzzy Zoeller, etc. **Mark:** FRANK.

BOOCO, GORDON
175 Ash St, PO Box 174, Hayden, CO 81639, Phone: 970-276-3195
Specialties: Fancy working straight knives of his design and to customer specs. **Patterns:** Hunters and Bowies. **Technical:** Grinds 440C, D2 and A2. Heat-treats. **Prices:** $150 to $350; some $600 and higher. **Remarks:** Part-time maker; first knife sold in 1984. **Mark:** Last name with push dagger artwork.

BOOS, RALPH
6018-37A Avenue NW, Edmonton, AB, CANADA T6L 1H4, Phone: 780-463-7094
Specialties: Classic, fancy and fantasy miniature knives and swords of his design or to customer specs. **Patterns:** Bowies, daggers and swords. **Technical:** Hand files O1, stainless and Damascus. Engraves and carves. Does heat bluing and acid etching. **Prices:** $125 to $350; some to $1000. **Remarks:** Part-time maker; first knife sold in 1982. **Mark:** First initials back to back.

BOOTH, PHILIP W
301 S Jeffery Ave, Ithaca, MI 48847, Phone: 989-875-2844, pbooth@charter.net; Web: www.philipbooth.com
Specialties: Folding knives of his design using various mechanisms. **Patterns:** New "Twerp" ball-bearing flipper knife. "Minnow" folding knives, a series of small folding knives started in 1996 and changing yearly. One of a kind hot-rod car themed folding knives. **Technical:** Grinds ATS-34, CPM-154 and commercial damascus. Offers gun blue finishes and file work. **Prices:** $200 and up. **Remarks:** Part-time maker, first knife sold in 1991. **Mark:** Last name or name with city and map logo.

BORGER, WOLF
Benzstrasse 8, Graben-Neudorf, GERMANY 76676, Phone: 07255-72303, Fax: 07255-72304, wolf@messerschmied.de; Web: www.messerschmied.de
Specialties: High-tech working and using straight knives and folders, many with corkscrews or other tools, of his design. **Patterns:** Hunters, Bowies and folders with various locking systems. **Technical:** Grinds 440C, ATS-34 and CPM. Uses stainless Damascus. **Prices:** $250 to $900; some to $1500. **Remarks:** Full-time maker; first knife sold in 1975. **Mark:** Howling wolf and name; first name on Damascus blades.

BOSE, REESE
8810 N. County Rd. 375 E, Shelburn, IN 47879, Phone: 812-397-5114
Specialties: Traditional working and using knives in standard patterns and multi-blade folders. **Patterns:** Multi-blade slip-joints. **Technical:** ATS-34, D2, 154CM and CPM 440V. **Prices:** $600 to $3,000. **Remarks:** Full-time maker; first knife sold in 1992. Photos by Jack Busfield. **Mark:** R. Bose.

BOSE, TONY
7252 N. County Rd, 300 E., Shelburn, IN 47879-9778, Phone: 812-397-5114
Specialties: Traditional working and using knives in standard patterns; multi-blade folders. **Patterns:** Multi-blade slip-joints. **Technical:** Grinds commercial Damascus, ATS-34 and D2. **Prices:** $400 to $1200. **Remarks:** Full-time maker; first knife sold in 1972. **Mark:** First initial, last name, city, state.

BOSSAERTS, CARL
Rua Albert Einstein 906, Ribeirao Preto, SP, BRAZIL 14051-110, Phone: 016 633 7063
Specialties: Working and using straight knives of his design, to customer specs and in standard patterns. **Patterns:** Hunters, fighters and utility/camp knives. **Technical:** Grinds

ATS-34, 440V and 440C; does filework. **Prices:** 60 to $400. **Remarks:** Part-time maker; first knife sold in 1992. **Mark:** Initials joined together.

BOST, ROGER E
30511 Cartier Dr, Palos Verdes, CA 90275-5629, Phone: 310- 541-6833, rogerbost@cox.net
Specialties: Hunters, fighters, boot, utility. **Patterns:** Loveless-style. **Technical:** ATS-34, BG-42, 440C, 59-61RC, stock removal and forge. **Prices:** $300 and up. **Remarks:** First knife sold in 1990. Cal. Knifemakers Assn., ABS. **Mark:** Diamond with initials inside and Palos Verdes California around outside.

BOSWORTH, DEAN
329 Mahogany Dr, Key Largo, FL 33037, Phone: 305-451-1564, DLBOZ@bellsouth.net
Specialties: Free hand hollow ground working knives with hand rubbed satin finish, filework and inlays. **Patterns:** Bird and Trout, hunters, skinners, fillet, Bowies, miniatures. **Technical:** Using 440C, ATS-34, D2, Meier Damascus, custom wet formed sheaths. **Prices:** $250 and up. **Remarks:** Part-time maker; first knife made in 1985. Member Florida Knifemakers Assoc. **Mark:** BOZ stamped in block letters.

BOURBEAU, JEAN YVES
15 Rue Remillard, Notre Dame, Ile Perrot, QC, CANADA J7V 8M9, Phone: 514-453-1069
Specialties: Fancy/embellished and fantasy folders of his design. **Patterns:** Bowies, fighters and locking folders. **Technical:** Grinds 440C, ATS-34 and Damascus. Carves precious wood for handles. **Prices:** $150 to $1000. **Remarks:** Part-time maker; first knife sold in 1994. **Mark:** Interlaced initials.

BOYD, FRANCIS
1811 Prince St, Berkeley, CA 94703, Phone: 510-841-7210
Specialties: Folders and kitchen knives, Japanese swords. **Patterns:** Push-button sturdy locking folders; San Francisco-style chef's knives. **Technical:** Forges and grinds; mostly uses high-carbon steels. **Prices:** Moderate to heavy. **Remarks:** Designer. **Mark:** Name.

BOYE, DAVID
PO Box 1238, Dolan Springs, AZ 86441, Phone: 800-853-1617, Fax: 928-767-4273, boye@cltlink.net; Web: www.boyeknives.com
Specialties: Folders and Boye Basics. Forerunner in the use of dendritic steel and dendritic cobalt for blades. **Patterns:** Lockback folders and fixed blade sheath knives in cobalt. **Technical:** Casts blades in cobalt. **Prices:** From $129 to $360. **Remarks:** Part-time maker; author of Step-by-Step Knifemaking. **Mark:** Name.

BOYES, TOM
2505 Wallace Lake Rd., West Bend, WI 53090, Phone: 262-391-2172
Specialties: Hunters, skinners and fillets. **Technical:** Grinds ATS-34, 440C, O1 tool steel and Damascus. **Prices:** $60 to $1000. **Remarks:** First knife sold in 1998. Doing business as R. Boyes Knives.

BOYSEN, RAYMOND A
125 E St Patrick, Rapid Ciy, SD 57701, Phone: 605-341-7752
Specialties: Hunters and Bowies. **Technical:** High performance blades forged from 52100 and 5160. **Prices:** $200 and up. **Remarks:** American Bladesmith Society Journeyman Smith. Part-time bladesmith. **Mark:** BOYSEN.

BRACH, PAUL
4870 Widgeon Way, Cumming, GA 30028, Phone: 770-595-8952, Web: www.brachknives.com
Specialties: Standard and one-of-a-kind straight knives and locking folders. Nickel silver sheath fittings and gemstone settings used on high-end pieces. **Patterns:** Hunters, bowies, daggers, antique bowies and titanium-frame folders. **Technical:** Grinds CPM-154 and forges high-carbon steel. Usually flat or full convex grinds. **Prices:** $150 to $1,000+. **Remarks:** Part-time maker; first knife sold in 1984. **Mark:** Etched "Paul Brach maker Cumming, GA" or "Brach" stamped.

BRACKETT, JAMIN
PO Box 387, Fallston, NC 28042, Phone: 704-718-3304, jaminbrackett@bellsouth.net; Web: brackettknives.com
Specialties: Hunting, camp, fishing, tactical, and general outdoor use. Handmade of my own design or to customer specs. **Patterns:** Drop point, tanto, fillet, and small EDC the "Tadpole", as well as large camp and tactical knives. **Technical:** Stock removal method, ATS-34 steel cryogenically treated to HRC 59-61. Mirror polish and bead blasted finishes. Handle materials include exotic woods, stag, buffalo horn, colored laminates, Micarta, and G-10. Come hand stitched 8-9 OZ leather sheaths treated in beeswax saddle oil mixture. Tactical models include reinforced tactical nylon sheaths Mollie system compatible. **Prices:** Standard models $150-$325. Personalized engraving available, for gifts and special occasions. **Remarks:** Part-time maker. First knife made in 2009. Member of NC Custom Knifemakers Guild.**Mark:** "Brackett", in bold. Each knife and sheath numbered.

BRADBURN, GARY
BRADBURN CUSTOM CUTLERY, 1714 Park Place, Wichita, KS 67203, Phone: 316-640-5684, gary@bradburnknives.com; Web:www.bradburnknives.com
Specialties: Specialize in clay-tempered Japanese-style knives and swords. **Patterns:** Also Bowies and fighters. **Technical:** Forge and/or grind carbon steel only. **Prices:** $150 to $1200. **Mark:** Initials GB stylized to look like Japanese character.

BRADFORD, GARRICK
582 Guelph St, Kitchener, ON, CANADA N2H-5Y4, Phone: 519-576-9863

BRADLEY, DENNIS
178 Bradley Acres Rd, Blairsville, GA 30512, Phone: 706-745-4364, dbbrad@windstream.net; Web: www.dennisbradleyknives.com
Specialties: Working straight knives and folders, some high-art. **Patterns:** Hunters, boots

custom knifemakers

and daggers; slip-joints and two-blades. **Technical:** Grinds CPM 154, CPM S35VN, ATS-34, D2, 440C and commercial damascus. **Prices:** $100 to $500; some to $2000. **Remarks:** Part-time maker; first knife sold in 1973. **Mark:** BRADLEY KNIVES in double heart logo.

BRADLEY, GAYLE
1383 Old Garner Rd., Weatherford, TX 76088-8720, Phone: 817-504-2262, bradleysblades@aol.com; Web: www.bradleysblades.com
Specialties: High-end folders with wedge locks of maker's own design or lock backs, and work/utility knives. Uses high-end materials, including lapidary work and black-lip-pearl handle inlays. **Technical:** Grinds blades from bar stock, performs own heat treating. **Remarks:** Full-time maker; first knife made in 1988.

BRADLEY, JOHN
PO Box 33, Pomona Park, FL 32181, Phone: 386-649-4739, johnbradleyknives@yahoo.com
Specialties: Fixed-blade using and art knives; primitive folders. **Patterns:** Skinners, Bowies, camp knives and primitive knives. **Technical:** Forged and ground 52100, 1095, O1 and Damascus. **Prices:** $250 to $2000. **Remarks:** Full-time maker; first knife sold in 1988. **Mark:** Last name.

BRANDSEY, EDWARD P
4441 Hawkridge Ct, Janesville, WI 53546, Phone: 608-868-9010, ebrandsey@centurytel.net
Patterns: Large bowies, hunters, neck knives and buckskinner-styles. Native American influence on some. An occasional tanto, art piece. Does own scrimshaw. See Egnath's second book. Now making locking liner folders. **Technical:** ATS-34, CPM154, 440-C, 0-1 and some damascus. Paul Bos heat treating past 20 years. **Prices:** $350 to $800; some to $4,000. **Remarks:** Full-time maker; first knife sold in 1973. **Mark:** Initials connected.

BRANDT, MARTIN W
833 Kelly Blvd, Springfield, OR 97477, Phone: 541-747-5422, oubob747@aol.com

BRANTON, ROBERT
PO BOX 807, Awendaw, SC 29429, Phone: 843-928-3624, www.brantonknives.com
Specialties: Working straight knives of his design or to customer specs; throwing knives. **Patterns:** Hunters, fighters and some miniatures. **Technical:** Grinds ATS-34, A2 and 1050; forges 5160, O1. Offers hollow- or convex-grinds. **Prices:** $25 to $400. **Remarks:** Part-time maker; first knife sold in 1985. Doing business as Pro-Flyte, Inc. **Mark:** Last name; or first and last name, city, state.

BRASCHLER, CRAIG W.
HC2 Box 498, Zalma, MO 63787, Phone: 573-495-2203
Specialties: Art knives, Bowies, utility hunters, slip joints, miniatures, engraving. **Technical:** Flat grinds. Does own selective heat treating. Does own engraving. **Prices:** Starting at $200. **Remarks:** Full-time maker since 2003. **Mark:** Braschler over Martin Oval stamped.

BRATCHER, BRETT
11816 County Rd 302, Plantersville, TX 77363, Phone: 936-894-3788, Fax: (936) 894-3790, brett_bratcher@msn.com
Specialties: Hunting and skinning knives. **Patterns:** Clip and drop point. Hand forged. **Technical:** Material 5160, D2, 1095 and Damascus. **Prices:** $200 to $500. **Mark:** Bratcher.

BRAY JR., W LOWELL
6931 Manor Beach Rd, New Port Richey, FL 34652, Phone: 727-846-0830, brayknives@aol.com Web: www.brayknives.com
Specialties: Traditional working and using straight knives and collector pieces. **Patterns:** One of a kind pieces, hunters, fighters and utility knives. **Technical:** Grinds 440C and ATS-34; forges 52100 and Damascus. **Prices:** $125 to $800. **Remarks:** Spare-time maker; first knife sold in 1992. **Mark:** Lowell Bray Knives in shield or Bray Primative in shield.

BREDA, BEN
56 Blueberry Hill Rd., Hope, ME 04847, Phone: 207-701-7777, bredaknives@gmail.com
Specialties: High-carbon-steel bowies, fighters, hunters chef's knives and LinerLock folders. **Technical:** Forges W2, W1 and 10xx series steels for blades, using natural and stabilized handle materials. **Prices:** Start at $300. **Remarks:** Part-time maker; ABS journeyman smith.

BREED, KIM
733 Jace Dr, Clarksville, TN 37040, Phone: 931-980-4956, sfbreed@yahoo.com
Specialties: High end through working folders and straight knives. **Patterns:** Hunters, fighters, daggers, Bowies. His design or customers. Likes one-of-a-kind designs. **Technical:** Makes own Mosiac and regular Damascus, but will use stainless steels. Offers filework and sculpted material. **Prices:** $150 to $2000. **Remarks:** Full-time maker. First knife sold in 1990. **Mark:** Last name.

BREND, WALTER
415 County Rd. 782, Etowah, TN 37331, Phone: 256-736-3520, Fax: 256-736-3474, walterbrend@outlook.com or walter@brendknives.com; Web: www.brendknives.com
Specialties: Tactical-style knives, fighters, automatics. **Technical:** Grinds D-2 and 440C blade steels, 154CM steel. **Prices:** Micarta and titanium handles.

BRENNAN, JUDSON
PO Box 1165, Delta Junction, AK 99737, Phone: 907-895-5153, Fax: 907-895-5404
Specialties: Period pieces. **Patterns:** All kinds of Bowies, rifle knives, daggers. **Technical:** Forges miscellaneous steels. **Prices:** Upscale, good value. **Remarks:** Muzzle-loading gunsmith; first knife sold in 1978. **Mark:** Name.

BRESHEARS, CLINT
1261 Keats, Manhattan Beach, CA 90266, Phone: 310-372-0739, Fax: 310-372-0739,

breshears1@verizon.net; Web: www.clintknives.com
Specialties: Working straight knives and folders. **Patterns:** Hunters, Bowies and survival knives. Folders are mostly hunters. **Technical:** Grinds 440C, 154CM and ATS-34; prefers mirror finishes. **Prices:** $125 to $750; some to $1800. **Remarks:** Part-time maker; first knife sold in 1978. **Mark:** First name.

BREUER, LONNIE
PO Box 877384, Wasilla, AK 99687-7384
Specialties: Fancy working straight knives. **Patterns:** Hunters, camp knives and axes, folders and Bowies. **Technical:** Grinds 440C, AEB-L and D2; likes wire inlay, scrimshaw, decorative filing. **Prices:** $60 to $150; some to $300. **Remarks:** Part-time maker; first knife sold in 1977. **Mark:** Signature.

BREWER, CRAIG
425 White Cedar, Killeen, TX 76542, Phone: 254-634-6934, craig6@embarqmail.com
Specialties: Folders; slip joints, some lock backs and an occasional liner lock. **Patterns:** I like the old traditional patterns. **Technical:** Grinds CPM steels most being CPM-154, 1095 for carbon and some Damascus. **Prices:** $500 and up. **Remarks:** Full-time maker, first knife sold in 2005.**Mark:** BREWER.

BRITTON, TIM
5645 Murray Rd., Winston-Salem, NC 27106, Phone: 336-923-2062, tim@timbritton.com; Web: www.timbritton.com
Specialties: Small and simple working knives, sgian dubhs, slip joint folders and special tactical designs. **Technical:** Forges and grinds stainless steel. **Prices:** $165 to ???. **Remarks:** Veteran knifemaker. **Mark:** Etched signature.

BROADWELL, DAVID
PO Box 3373, Wichita Falls, TX 76301, Phone: 940-782-4442, david@broadwellstudios.com; Web: www.broadwellstudios.com
Specialties: Sculpted high-art straight and folding knives. **Patterns:** Daggers, sub-hilted fighters, folders, sculpted art knives and some Bowies. **Technical:** Grinds mostly Damascus; carves; prefers natural handle materials, including stone. Some embellishment. **Prices:** $500 to $4000; some higher. **Remarks:** Full-time maker since 1989; first knife sold in 1981. **Mark:** Stylized emblem bisecting "B"/with last name below.

BROCK, KENNETH L
PO Box 375, 207 N Skinner Rd, Allenspark, CO 80510, Phone: 303-747-2547, brockknives@nedernet.net
Specialties: Custom designs, full-tang working knives and button lock folders of his design. **Patterns:** Hunters, miniatures and minis. **Technical:** Flat-grinds D2 and 440C; makes own sheaths; heat-treats. **Prices:** $75 to $800. **Remarks:** Full-time maker; first knife sold in 1978. **Mark:** Last name, city, state and serial number.

BRODZIAK, DAVID
27 Stewart St, PO Box 1130, Albany, WA, AUSTRALIA 6331, Phone: 61 8 9841 3314, brodziak3@bigpond.com; Web: www.brodziakcustomknives.com

BROMLEY, PETER
BROMLEY KNIVES, 1408 S Bettman, Spokane, WA 99212, Phone: 509-534-4235 or 509-710-8365, Fax: 509-536-2666, bromleyknives@q.com
Specialties: Period Bowies, folder, hunting knives; all sizes and shapes. **Patterns:** Bowies, boot knives, hunters, utility, folder, working knives. **Technical:** High-carbon steel (1084, 1095 and 5160). Stock removal and forge. **Prices:** $85 to $750. **Remarks:** Almost full-time, first knife sold in 1987. A.B.S. Journeyman Smith. **Mark:** Bromley, Spokane, WA.

BROOKER, DENNIS
55858 260th Ave., Chariton, IA 50049, Phone: 641-862-3263, dbrooker@dbrooker.com Web: www.dbrooker.com
Specialties: Fancy straight knives and folders of his design. Obsidian and glass knives. **Patterns:** Hunters, folders and boots. **Technical:** Forges and grinds. Full-time engraver and designer; instruction available. **Prices:** Moderate to upscale. **Remarks:** Part-time maker. Takes no orders; sells only completed work. **Mark:** Name.

BROOKS, BUZZ
2345 Yosemite Dr, Los Angles, CA 90041, Phone: 323-256-2892

BROOKS, MICHAEL
2811 64th St, Lubbock, TX 79413, Phone: 806-438-3862, chiang@clearwire.net
Specialties: Working straight knives of his design or to customer specs. **Patterns:** Martial art, Bowies, hunters, and fighters. **Technical:** Grinds 440C, D2 and ATS-34; offers wide variety of handle materials. **Prices:** $75 & up. **Remarks:** Part-time maker; first knife sold in 1985. **Mark:** Initials.

BROOKS, STEVE R
1610 Dunn Ave, Walkerville, MT 59701, Phone: 406-782-5114, Fax: 406-782-5114, steve@brooksmoulds.com; Web: brooksmoulds.com
Specialties: Working straight knives and folders; period pieces. **Patterns:** Hunters, Bowies and camp knives; folding lockers; axes, tomahawks and buckskinner knives; swords and stilettos. **Technical:** Damascus and mosaic Damascus. Some knives come embellished. **Prices:** $400 to $2000. **Remarks:** Full-time maker; first knife sold in 1982. **Mark:** Lazy initials.

BROOME, THOMAS A
1212 E. Aliak Ave, Kenai, AK 99611-8205, Phone: 907-283-9128, tomlei@ptialaska.ent; Web: www.alaskanknives.com
Specialties: Working hunters and folders **Patterns:** Traditional and custom orders. **Technical:** Grinds ATS-34, BG-42, CPM-S30V. **Prices:** $175 to $350. **Remarks:** Full-time maker; first knife sold in 1979. Doing business as Thom's Custom Knives, Alaskan Man O; Steel Knives. **Mark:** Full name, city, state.

BROTHERS, DENNIS L.
2007 Kent Rd., Oneonta, AL 35121, Phone: 205-466-3276, blademan@
brothersblades.com Web: www.brothersblades.com
Specialties: Fixed blade hunting/working knives of maker's deigns. Works with customer designed specifications. **Patterns:** Hunters, camp knives, kitchen/utility, bird, and trout. Standard patterns and customer designed. **Technical:** Stock removal. Works with stainless and tool steels. SS cryo-treatment. Hollow and flat grinds. **Prices:** $200 - $400. **Remarks:** Sole authorship knives and customer leather sheaths. Part-time maker. Find on facebook "Brothers Blades by D.L. Brothers" **Mark:** "D.L. Brothers, 4B, Oneonta, AL" on obverse side of blade.

BROTHERS, ROBERT L
989 Philpott Rd, Colville, WA 99114, Phone: 509-684-8922
Specialties: Traditional working and using straight knives and folders of his design and to customer specs. **Patterns:** Bowies, fighters and hunters. **Technical:** Grinds D2; forges Damascus. Makes own Damascus from saw steel wire rope and chain; part-time goldsmith and stone-setter. **Prices:** $100 to $400; some higher. **Remarks:** Part-time maker; first knife sold in 1986. **Mark:** Initials and year made.

BROUS, JASON
POB 550, Buellton, CA 93427, Phone: 805-717-7192, jbrous@live.com or brousblades@outlook.com; Web: www.brousblades.com
Patterns: Tactical mid-tech folders, production and customized. **Technical:** Stock removal method using D2 steel. **Prices:** $99 - $700. **Remarks:** Started May 2010.

BROUWER, JERRY
Vennewaard 151, 1824 KD, Alkmaar, NETHERLANDS, Phone: 00-31-618-774146, brouwern1@hotmail.nl; Web: www.brouwerknives.com
Specialties: Tactical fixed blades with epoxy-soaked Japanese wrapped handles, tactical and outdoor knives with Micarta or G-10 handles, tactical frame-lock folders. Fine, embellished knives for the demanding VIP. **Patterns:** Fixed-blade tantos, drop points, either V-ground or chisel ground, hunting knives, outdoor knives, folders, desk knives, pocket tools. **Technical:** Stock removal, only premium powder metallurgy steels and fine stainless damascus. **Prices:** $100 to $1,000. **Remarks:** Part-time maker; first knife sold in 2010. **Mark:** Laser etched "Brouwer" with a jack-o-lantern logo.

BROWER, MAX
2016 Story St, Boone, IA 50036, Phone: 515-432-2938, jmbrower@mchsi.com
Specialties: Hunters. Working/using straight knives. **Patterns:** Hunters. **Technical:** Grinds ATS-34. **Prices:** $300 and up. **Remarks:** Spare-time maker; first knife sold in 1981. **Mark:** Last name.

BROWN, DOUGLAS
1500 Lincolnshire Way, Fort Worth, TX 76134, www.debrownphotography.com

BROWN, HAROLD E
3654 NW Hwy 72, Arcadia, FL 34266, Phone: 863-494-7514, brknives@strato.net
Specialties: Fancy and exotic working knives. **Patterns:** Folders, slip-lock, locking several kinds. **Technical:** Grinds D2 and ATS-34. Embellishment available. **Prices:** $175 to $1000. **Remarks:** Part-time maker; first knife sold in 1976. **Mark:** Name and city with logo.

BROWN, JIM
1097 Fernleigh Cove, Little Rock, AR 72210

BROWN, ROB E
PO Box 15107, Emerald Hill, Port Elizabeth, EC, SOUTH AFRICA 6011, Phone: 27-41-3661086, Fax: 27-41-4511731, rbknives@global.co.za
Specialties: Contemporary-designed straight knives and period pieces. **Patterns:** Utility knives, hunters, boots, fighters and daggers. **Technical:** Grinds 440C, D2, ATS-34 and commercial Damascus. Knives mostly mirror finished; African handle materials. **Prices:** $100 to $1500. **Remarks:** Full-time maker; first knife sold in 1985. **Mark:** Name and country.

BROWNE, RICK
980 West 13th St, Upland, CA 91786, Phone: 909-985-1728
Specialties: Sheffield pattern pocket knives. **Patterns:** Hunters, fighters and daggers. No heavy-duty knives. **Technical:** Grinds ATS-34. **Prices:** Start at $450. **Remarks:** Part-time maker; first knife sold in 1975. **Mark:** R.E. Browne, Upland, CA.

BROWNING, STEVEN W
3400 Harrison Rd, Benton, AR 72015, Phone: 501-316-2450

BRUCE, RICHARD L.
13174 Surcease Mine Road, Yankee Hill, CA 95965, Phone: 530-532-0880, richardkarenbruce@yahoo.com
Specialties: Working straight knives. Prefers natural handle material; stag bone and woods. Admires the classic straight knife look. **Patterns:** Hunters, Fighters, Fishing Knives. **Technical:** Uses 01, 1095, L6, W2 steel. Stock removal method, flat grind, heat treats and tempers own knives. Builds own sheaths; simple but sturdy. **Prices:** $150-$400. **Remarks:** Sold first knife in 2006; part-time maker. **Mark:** RL Bruce.

BRUNCKHORST, LYLE
COUNTRY VILLAGE, 23706 7th Ave SE Ste B, Bothell, WA 98021, Phone: 425-402-3484, bronks@bronksknifeworks.com; Web: www.bronksknifeworks.com
Specialties: Forges own Damascus with 1084 and 15N20, forges 5160, 52100. Grinds CPM 154 CM, ATS-34, S30V. Hosts Biannual Northwest School of Knifemaking and Northwest Hammer In. Offers online and in-house sharpening services and knife sharpeners. Maker of the Double L Hoofknife. Traditional working and using knives, the new patent pending Xross-Bar Lock folders, tomahawks and irridescent RR spike knives. **Patterns:** Damascus Bowies, hunters, locking folders and featuring the ultra strong locking tactical folding knives. **Prices:** $185 to $1500; some to $3750. **Remarks:** Full-time maker; first knife made in 1976. **Mark:** Bucking horse or bronk.

BRUNER, FRED JR.
BRUNER BLADES, E10910W Hilldale Dr, Fall Creek, WI 54742, Phone: 715-225-8017, fredbruner200@gmail.com
Specialties: Tomahawks, pipe tomahawks and period pieces. **Patterns:** Drop point hunters, long knives, French and working knives. **Technical:** Steels used include 1095, 52100, CPM 154 and 5160. **Prices:** $120 to $1,500. **Remarks:** Voting member of the Knifemakers Guild. Made knives for Herters into the 1980s. **Mark:** F.C. Bruner Jr.

BUCHANAN, THAD
THAD BUCHANAN CUSTOM KNIVES, 16401 S.W. Ranchview Rd., Powell Butte, OR 97753, buchananblades@gmail.com; Web: www.buchananblades.com
Specialties: Fixed blades. **Patterns:** Various hunters, trout, bird, utility, boots & fighters, including most Loveless patterns. **Technical:** Stock removal, high polish, variety handle materials. **Prices:** $450 to $2000. **Remarks:** 2005 and 2008 Blade Magazine handmade award for hunter/utility. 2006 Blade West best fixed blade award; 2008 Blade West best hunter/utility. 2010 and 2011 Best Fixed Blade at Plaza Cutlery Show. **Mark:** Thad Buchanan - maker

BUCHANAN, ZAC
168 Chapel Dr., Eugene, OR 97404, Phone: 541-815-6706, zacbuchananknives@gmail.com; Web: www.zacbuchananknives.com
Specialties: R.W. Loveless-style fixed blades. **Technical:** Stock-removal knifemaker using CPM-154 blade steel, 416 stainless steel fittings and pre-ban elephant ivory, mammoth ivory, buffalo horn, stag and Micarta handles. **Prices:** $500 to $2,000. **Remarks:** Full-time maker; first knife sold in 2009. **Mark:** Zac Buchanan Eugene, Oregon.

BUCHARSKY, EMIL
23 Linkside Pl., Spruce Grove, Alberta, CANADA T7X 3C5, Phone: 587-341-5066, ebuch@telus.net; Web: www.ebuchknives.com
Specialties: Fancy working utility hunters and art folders, usually carved with overlays or inlays of damascus, hidden frames and screws. **Patterns:** Folders, hunters, bowies of maker's own design. **Technical:** Forges own damascus using 1095, 1084, 15N20 and nickel, stock-removal steels from Crucible, CPM alloys and UHB Elmax, natural handle materials of pearl, ancient ivory, bone, stabilized woods and others such as carbon fiber, titanium, stainless steel, mokume gane and gemstones. **Prices:** $400 to $1,000; art knives $1,500 and up. **Remarks:** Full-time maker; first knife made in 1989. **Mark:** Name, city and province in oval on fixed blades. Hand-engraved first name, initial and last name with year, in lower case, on folders.

BUCHNER, BILL
PO Box 73, Idleyld Park, OR 97447, Phone: 541-498-2247, blazinhammer@earthlink.net; Web: www.home.earthlin.net/~blazinghammer
Specialties: Working straight knives, kitchen knives and high-art knives of his design. **Technical:** Uses W1, L6 and his own Damascus. Invented "spectrum metal" for letter openers, folder handles and jewelry. Likes sculpturing and carving in Damascus. **Prices:** $40 to $3000; some higher. **Remarks:** Full-time maker; first knife sold in 1978. **Mark:** Signature.

BUCKNER, JIMMIE H
PO Box 162, Putney, GA 31782, Phone: 229-436-4182
Specialties: Camp knives, Bowies (one-of-a-kind), liner-lock folders, tomahawks, camp axes, neck knives for law enforcement and hide-out knives for body guards and professional people. **Patterns:** Hunters, camp knives, Bowies. **Technical:** Forges 1084, 5160 and Damascus (own), own heat treats. **Prices:** $195 to $795 and up. **Remarks:** Full-time maker; first knife sold in 1980, ABS Master Smith. **Mark:** Name over spade.

BUCKNER, TOM
1842 Overhulse Rd. NW, Olympia, WA 98502, Phone: 360-970-1668, tbuckner1967@gmail.com; Web: www.bucknerknives.com
Specialties: Kitchen knives with custom wooden sayas (sheaths) and folding knives. **Patterns:** Chef's, Santoku, boning, paring and folding knives fashioned using various types of material, all with titanium liners. **Technical:** Blade steels include CPM 154, CPM S30V, CPM S35VN, AEB-L, stainless damascus and high-carbon damascus. Maker heat treats and cryogenically heats and quenches all the listed steels. **Prices:** $200 to $2,000. **Mark:** Tom Buckner Maker Olympia, WA.

BUDELL, MICHAEL
3733 Wieghat Ln., Brenham, TX 77833, Phone: 979-836-3148, mbbudell@att.net
Specialties: Slip Joint Folders. **Technical:** Grinds 01, 440C. File work springs, blades and liners. Natural material scales giraffe, mastadon ivory, elephant ivory, and jigged bone. **Prices:** $175 - $350. **Remarks:** Part-time maker; first knife sold 2006. **Mark:** XA

BUEBENDORF, ROBERT E
108 Lazybrooke Rd, Monroe, CT 06468, Phone: 203-452-1769
Specialties: Traditional and fancy straight knives of his design. **Patterns:** Hand-makes and embellishes belt buckle knives. **Technical:** Forges and grinds 440C, 01, W2, 1095, his own Damascus and 154CM. **Prices:** $200 to $500. **Remarks:** Full-time maker; first knife sold in 1978. **Mark:** First and middle initials, last name and MAKER.

BULLARD, BENONI
4416 Jackson 4, Bradford, AR 72020, Phone: 501-344-2672, benandbren@earthlink.net
Specialties: Bowies and hunters. **Patterns:** Camp knives, bowies, hunters, slip joints, folders, lock blades, miniatures, Hawks Tech. **Technical:** Makes own Damascus. Forges 5160, 1085, 15 N 20. Favorite is 5160. **Prices:** $150 - $1500. **Remarks:** Part-time maker. Sold first knife in 2006. **Mark:** Benoni with a star over the letter i.

BULLARD, RANDALL

7 Mesa Dr., Canyon, TX 79015, Phone: 806-655-0590

Specialties: Working/using straight knives and folders of his design or to customer specs. **Patterns:** Hunters, locking folders and slip-joint folders. **Technical:** Grinds O1, ATS-34 and 440C. Does file work. **Prices:** $125 to $300; some to $500. **Remarks:** Part-time maker; first knife sold in 1993. Doing business as Bullard Custom Knives. **Mark:** First and middle initials, last name, maker, city and state.

BULLARD, TOM

117 MC 8068, Flippin, AR 72634, Phone: 870-656-3428, tbullard8@live.com

Specialties: Traditional folders and hunters. **Patterns:** Bowies, hunters, single and 2-blade trappers, lockback folders. **Technical:** Grinds 440C, A2, D2, ATS-34 and O1. **Prices:** $175 and up. **Remarks:** Offers filework and engraving by Norvell Foster and Terry Thies. Does not make screw-together knives. **Mark:** T Bullard.

BUMP, BRUCE D.

1103 Rex Ln, Walla Walla, WA 99362, Phone: 509-386-8879, brucebump1@gmail.com; Web: www.brucebumpknives.com

Specialties: Slip joints, bowies and muzzle-loading pistol-knife combinations. **Patterns:** Maker's own damascus patterns including double mosaics. **Technical:** One-of-a-kind pieces. **Prices:** Please email for prices. **Remarks:** Full-time maker, ABS master smith since 2003. **Mark:** Bruce D. Bump "Custom", Bruce D. Bump "MS".

BURDEN, JAMES

405 Kelly St, Burkburnett, TX 76354

BURGER, FRED

Box 436, Munster, KZN, SOUTH AFRICA 4278, Phone: 27 39 3192316, info@swordcane.com; Web: www.swordcane.com

Specialties: Sword canes, folders, and fixed blades. **Patterns:** 440C and carbon steel blades. **Technical:** Double hollow ground and Poniard-style blades. **Prices:** $300 to $3000. **Remarks:** Full-time maker with son, Barry, since 1987. Member South African Guild. **Mark:** Last name in oval pierced by a dagger.

BURGER, PON

12 Glenwood Ave, Woodlands, Bulawayo, ZIMBABWE 75514

Specialties: Collector's items. **Patterns:** Fighters, locking folders of traditional styles, buckles. **Technical:** Scrimshaws 440C blade. Uses polished buffalo horn with brass fittings. Cased in buffalo hide book. **Prices:** $450 to $1100. **Remarks:** Full-time maker; first knife sold in 1973. Doing business as Burger Products. **Mark:** Spirit of Africa.

BURGER, TIAAN

69 Annie Botha Ave, Riviera,, Pretoria, GT, SOUTH AFRICA, tiaan_burger@hotmail.com

Specialties: Sliplock and multi-blade folder. **Technical:** High carbon or stainless with African handle materials **Remarks:** Occasional fixed blade knives.

BURKE, BILL

20 Adams Ranch Rd., Boise, ID 83716, Phone: 208-336-3792, billburke@bladegallery.com

Specialties: Hand-forged working knives. **Patterns:** Fowler pronghorn, clip point and drop point hunters. **Technical:** Forges 52100 and 5160. Makes own Damascus from 15N20 and 1084. **Prices:** $450 and up. **Remarks:** Dedicated to fixed-blade high-performance knives. ABS Journeyman. Also makes "Ed Fowler" miniatures. **Mark:** Initials connected.

BURNLEY, LUCAS

1005 La Font Rd. SW, Albuquerque, NM 87105, Phone: 505-814-9964, burnleyknives@comcast.net; www.burnleyknives.com

Specialties: Contemporary tactical fixed blade, and folder designs, some art knives. **Patterns:** Hybrids, neo Japanese, defensive, utility and field knives. **Technical:** Grinds CPM154, A2, D2, BG42, Stainless Damascus as well as titanium and aerospace composites. **Prices:** Most models $225 to $1,500. Some specialty pieces higher. **Remarks:** Full-time maker, first knife sold in 2003. **Mark:** Last name or BRNLY.

BURNS, ROBERT

104 W. 6th St., Carver, MN 55315, Phone: 412-477-4677, wildernessironworks@gmail.com; www.wildernessironworks.org

Specialties: Utility knives, fighters, axes, pattern-welded axes and Viking swords. **Technical:** Trained as a blacksmith in Colonial style, forges 1095, 1090, 1084, 15N20, 5160, W1, W2, D2, 440C and wrought iron. **Prices:** $135 to $3,000-plus. **Remarks:** Full-time maker; first knife made in 2005. **Mark:** A compass rose with all of the cardinal directions, and underneath, in cursive, "Wilderness Ironworks."

BURRIS, PATRICK R

1263 Cty. Rd. 750, Athens, TN 37303, Phone: 423-336-5715, burrispr@gmail.com

Specialties: Traditional straight knives and locking-liner folders. **Patterns:** Hunters, bowies, locking-liner folders. **Technical:** Flat grinds high-grade stainless and damascus. **Remarks:** Offers filework, embellishment, exotic materials and damascus **Mark:** Last name in script.

BURROWS, CHUCK

WILD ROSE TRADING CO, 289 La Posta Canyon Rd, Durango, CO 81303, Phone: 970-259-8396, chuck@wrtcleather.com; Web: www.wrtcleather.com

Specialties: Presentation knives, hawks, and sheaths based on the styles of the American frontier incorporating carving, beadwork, rawhide, braintan, and other period correct materials. Also makes other period style knives such as Scottish Dirks and Moorish jambiyahs. **Patterns:** Bowies, Dags, tomahawks, war clubs, and all other 18th and 19th century frontier style edged weapons and tools. **Technical:** Carbon steel only: 5160, 1080/1084, 1095, O1, Damascus-Our Frontier Shear Steel, plus other styles available on request. Forged knives, hawks, etc. are made in collaborations with bladesmiths

Gib Guignard (under the name of Cactus Rose) and Mark Williams (under the name UB Forged). Blades are usually forge finished and all items are given an aged period look. **Prices:** $500 plus. **Remarks:** Full-time maker, first knife sold in 1973. 40+ years experience working leather. **Mark:** A lazy eight or lazy eight with a capital T at the center. On leather either the lazy eight with T or a WRTC makers stamp.

BURROWS, STEPHEN R

1020 Osage St, Humboldt, KS 66748, Phone: 816-921-1573

Specialties: Fantasy straight knives of his design, to customer specs and in standard patterns; period pieces. **Patterns:** Fantasy, bird and trout knives, daggers, fighters and hunters. **Technical:** Forges 5160 and 1095 high-carbon steel, O1 and his Damascus. Offers lost wax casting in bronze or silver of cross guards and pommels. **Prices:** $65 to $600; some to $2000. **Remarks:** Full-time maker; first knife sold in 1983. Doing business as Gypsy Silk. **Mark:** Etched name.

BUSBIE, JEFF

John 316 Knife Works, 170 Towles Rd., Bloomingdale, GA 31302, Phone: 912-656-8238, jbusbie@comcast.net; Web: www.john316knifeworks.com

Specialties: Working full-tang and hidden-tang fixed blades, locking-liner folders and hard-use knives. **Patterns:** Bowies, skinners, fighters, neck knives, work knives, bird knives, swords, art knives and other creations. **Technical:** Stock-removal maker using Alabama Damascus, CPM stainless steels and D2. Handles from hardwoods, G-10, ivory, bone and exotic materials. **Prices:** $100 to $800 and up. **Remarks:** Part-time maker building 150 to 200 knives a year; first knife sold in 2008. **Mark:** john 316 knife works with a cross in the middle.

BUSCH, STEVE

1989 Old Town Loop, Oakland, OR 97462, Phone: 541-459-2833, steve@buschcustomknives.com; Web: wwwbuschcustomknives.blademakers.com

Specialties: D/A automatic right and left handed, folders, fixed blade working mainly in Damascus file work, functional art knives, nitrate bluing, heat bluing most all scale materials. **Prices:** $150 to $2000. **Remarks:** Trained under Vallotton family 3 1/2 years on own since 2002. **Mark:** Signature and date of completion on all knives.

BUSFIELD, JOHN

153 Devonshire Circle, Roanoke Rapids, NC 27870, Phone: 252-537-3949, Fax: 252-537-8704, busfield@charter.net

Specialties: Investor-grade folders; high-grade working straight knives. **Patterns:** Original price-style and trailing-point interframe and sculpted-frame folders, drop-point hunters and semi-skinners. **Technical:** Grinds 154CM and ATS-34. Offers interframes, gold frames and inlays; uses jade, agate and lapis. **Prices:** $275 to $2000. **Remarks:** Full-time maker; first knife sold in 1979. **Mark:** Last name and address.

BUSSE, JERRY

11651 Co Rd 12, Wauseon, OH 43567, Phone: 419-923-6471

Specialties: Working straight knives. **Patterns:** Heavy combat knives and camp knives. **Technical:** Grinds D2, A2, INFI. **Prices:** $1100 to $3500. **Remarks:** Full-time maker; first knife sold in 1983. **Mark:** Last name in logo.

BUTLER, BART

822 Seventh St, Ramona, CA 92065, Phone: 760-789-6431

BUTLER, JOHN

777 Tyre Rd, Havana, FL 32333, Phone: 850-539-5742

Specialties: Hunters, Bowies, period. **Technical:** Damascus, 52100, 5160, L6 steels. **Prices:** $80 and up. **Remarks:** Making knives since 1986. Journeyman (ABS). **Mark:** JB.

BUTLER, JOHN R

20162 6th Ave N E, Shoreline, WA 98155, Phone: 206-362-3847, rjjjrb@sprynet.com

BUXTON, BILL

155 Oak Bend Rd, Kaiser, MO 65047, Phone: 573-348-3577, camper@yhti.net; Web: www.billbuxtonknives.com

Specialties: Forged fancy and working straight knives and folders. Mostly one-of-a-kind pieces. **Patterns:** Fighters, daggers, Bowies, hunters, linerlock folders, axes and tomahawks. **Technical:** Forges 52100, 0-1, 1080. Makes own Damascus (mosaic and random patterns) from 1080, 1095, 15n20, and powdered metals 1084 and 4800a. Offers sterling silver inlay, n/s pin patterning and pewter pouring on axe and hawk handles. **Prices:** $300 to $2,500. **Remarks:** Full-time maker, sold first knife in 1998. **Mark:** First initial and last name.

BUZEK, STANLEY

PO Box 731, Waller, TX 77484, Phone: 936-372-1933, stan@sbuzekknives.com; Web: www.sbuzekknives.com

Specialties: Traditional slip-joint pocketknives, LinerLocks and frame-lock folders, and fixed-blade hunters and skinners. **Technical:** Grinds, heat treats and Rockwell tests CPM-154, and some traditional folders in O1 tool steel. Hand-rubbed finishes. Dyed jigged bone, mammoth ivory and fine stabilized woods. **Prices:** $250 and up. **Remarks:** Serious part-time maker; first knife sold in 2006. **Mark:** S. Buzek on riccasso.

BYBEE, BARRY J

795 Lock Rd. E, Cadiz, KY 42211-8615

Specialties: Working straight knives of his design. **Patterns:** Hunters, fighters, boot knives, tantos and Bowies. **Technical:** Grinds ATS-34, 440C. Likes stag and Micarta for handle materials. **Prices:** $125 to $200; some to $1000. **Remarks:** Part-time maker; first knife sold in 1968. **Mark:** Arrowhead logo with name, city and state.

BYRD, WESLEY L

189 Countryside Dr, Evensville, TN 37332, Phone: 423-775-3826, w.l.byrd@worldnet.att.net

Specialties: Hunters, fighters, Bowies, dirks, sgian dubh, utility, and camp knives. **Patterns:** Wire rope, random patterns. Twists, W's, Ladder, Kite Tail. **Technical:** Uses 52100, 1084, 5160, L6, and 15n20. **Prices:** Starting at $180. **Remarks:** Prefer to work with customer for their design preferences. ABS Journeyman Smith. **Mark:** BYRD, WB <X.

C

CABRERA, SERGIO B
24500 Broad Ave, Wilmington, CA 90744

CAFFREY, EDWARD J
2608 Central Ave West, Great Falls, MT 59404, Phone: 406-727-9102, caffreyknives@gmail.com; Web: www.caffreyknives.net
Specialties: One-of-a-kind using and collector quality pieces. Will accept some customer designs. **Patterns:** Bowies, folders, hunters, fighters, camp/utility, tomahawks and hatchets. **Technical:** Forges all types of Damascus, specializing in Mosaic Damascus, 52100, 5160, 1080/1084 and most other commonly forged steels. **Prices:** Starting at $185; typical hunters start at $400; collector pieces can range into the thousands. **Remarks:** Offers one-on-one basic and advanced bladesmithing classes. ABS Mastersmith. Full-time maker. **Mark:** Stamped last name and MS on straight knives. Etched last name with MS on folders.

CALDWELL, BILL
255 Rebecca, West Monroe, LA 71292, Phone: 318-323-3025
Specialties: Straight knives and folders with machined bolsters and liners. **Patterns:** Fighters, Bowies, survival knives, tomahawks, razors and push knives. **Technical:** Owns and operates a very large, well-equipped blacksmith and bladesmith shop with six large forges and eight power hammers. **Prices:** $400 to $3500; some to $10,000. **Remarks:** Full-time maker and self-styled blacksmith; first knife sold in 1962. **Mark:** Wild Bill and Sons.

CALLAHAN, F TERRY
PO Box 880, Boerne, TX 78006, Phone: 210-260-2378, ftclaw@gvtc.com
Specialties: Custom hand-forged edged knives, collectible and functional. **Patterns:** Bowies, folders, daggers, hunters & camp knives . **Technical:** Forges damascus and 5160. Offers filework, silver inlay and handmade sheaths. **Prices:** $150 to $500. **Remarks:** First knife sold in 1990. ABS/Journeyman Bladesmith. **Mark:** Initial "F" inside a keystone.

CALVERT JR., ROBERT W (BOB)
911 Julia, Rayville, LA 71269, Phone: 318-348-4490, rcalvert1@gmail.com
Specialties: Using and hunting knives; your design or his. Since 1990. **Patterns:** Forges own Damascus; all patterns. **Technical:** 5160, D2, 52100, 1084. Prefers natural handle material. **Prices:** $250 and up. **Remarks:** TOMB Member, ABS. Journeyman Smith. ABS Board of directors **Mark:** Calvert (Block) J S.

CAMBRON, HENRY
169 Severn Way, Dallas, GA 30132-0317, Phone: 770-598-5721, worldclassknives@bellsouth.net; Web: www.worldclassknives.com
Specialties: Everyday carry, working and small neck knives. **Patterns:** Hunters, bowies, camp, utility and combat. **Technical:** Forge, stock removal, filework. Differential quench. Tuff-etched finish. Hand-sewn and Kydex sheaths. **Prices:** $65 to $650. **Remarks:** Full-time maker. **Mark:** First and last name over USA on blades. HC on sheaths.

CAMERER, CRAIG
3766 Rockbridge Rd, Chesterfield, IL 62630, Phone: 618-753-2147, craig@camererknives.com; Web: www.camererknives.com
Specialties: Everyday carry knives, hunters and Bowies. **Patterns:** D-guard, historical recreations and fighters. **Technical:** Most of his knives are forged to shape. **Prices:** $100 and up. **Remarks:** Member of the ABS and PKA. Journeymen Smith ABS.

CAMERON, RON G
PO Box 183, Logandale, NV 89021, Phone: 702-398-3356, rntcameron@mvdsl.com
Specialties: Fancy and embellished working/using straight knives and folders of his design. **Patterns:** Bowies, hunters and utility/camp knives. **Technical:** Grinds ATS-34, AEB-L and Devin Thomas Damascus or own Damascus from 1084 and 15N20. Does filework, fancy pins, mokume fittings. Uses exotic hardwoods, stag and Micarta for handles. Pearl & mammoth ivory. **Prices:** $175 to $850 some to $1000. **Remarks:** Part-time maker; first knife sold in 1994. Doing business as Cameron Handmade Knives. **Mark:** Last name, town, state or last name.

CAMPBELL, DICK
196 Graham Rd, Colville, WA 99114, Phone: 509-684-6080, dicksknives@aol.com
Specialties: Working straight knives, folders and period pieces. **Patterns:** Hunters, fighters, boots and 19th century bowies. **Technical:** Grinds 440C and 154CM. **Prices:** $350 to $4,500. **Remarks:** Full-time maker. First knife sold in 1975. **Mark:** Name.

CAMPBELL, DOUG
46 W Boulder Rd., McLeod, MT 59052, Phone: 406-222-8153, dkcampbl@yahoo.com
Specialties: Sole authorship of fixed blades and folding knives. **Patterns:** Fixed blades, LinerLocks and frame-cock folders. **Technical:** Forged high-carbon, pattern-welded damascus, Elmax and CPM 154 steels. **Prices:** $300-$1,300. **Remarks:** ABS journeyman smith. **Mark:** Grizzly track surrounded by a "C," or "Campbell" etched on spine.

CAMPOS, IVAN
R.XI de Agosto 107, Tatui, SP, BRAZIL 18270-000, Phone: 00-55-15-997120993, Fax: 00-55-15-2594368, ivan@ivancampos.net; Web: www.ivancampos.net
Specialties: Brazilian handmade and antique knives.

CANDRELLA, JOE
1219 Barness Dr, Warminster, PA 18974, Phone: 215-675-0143

Specialties: Working straight knives, some fancy. **Patterns:** Daggers, boots, Bowies. **Technical:** Grinds 440C and 154CM. **Prices:** $100 to $200; some to $1000. **Remarks:** Part-time maker; first knife sold in 1985. Does business as Franjo. **Mark:** FRANJO with knife as J.

CANTER, RONALD E
96 Bon Air Circle, Jackson, TN 38305, Phone: 731-668-1780, canterr@charter.net
Specialties: Traditional working knives to customer specs. **Patterns:** Beavertail skinners, Bowies, hand axes and folding lockers. **Technical:** Grinds 440C, Micarta & deer antler. **Prices:** $75 and up. **Remarks:** Spare-time maker; first knife sold in 1973. **Mark:** Three last initials intertwined.

CANTRELL, KITTY D
19720 Hwy 78, Ramona, CA 92076, Phone: 760-788-8304

CAPDEPON, RANDY
553 Joli Rd, Carencro, LA 70520, Phone: 318-896-4113, Fax: 318-896-8753
Specialties: Straight knives and folders. **Patterns:** Hunters and locking folders. **Technical:** Grinds ATS-34, 440C and D2. **Prices:** $200 to $600. **Remarks:** Part-time maker; first knife made in 1992. Doing business as Capdepon Knives. **Mark:** Last name.

CAPDEPON, ROBERT
829 Vatican Rd, Carencro, LA 70520, Phone: 337-896-8753, Fax: 318-896-8753
Specialties: Traditional straight knives and folders of his design. **Patterns:** Boots, hunters and locking folders. **Technical:** Grinds ATS-34, 440C and D2. Hand-rubbed finish on blades. Likes natural horn materials for handles, including ivory. Offers engraving. **Prices:** $250 to $750. **Remarks:** Full-time maker; first knife made in 1992. **Mark:** Last name.

CAREY, PETER
P.O. Box 4712, Lago Vista, TX 78645, Phone: 512-358-4839, Web: www.careyblade.com
Specialties: Tactical folders, Every Day Carry to presentation grade. Working straight knives, hunters, and tactical. **Patterns:** High-tech patterns of his own design, Linerlocks, Framelocks, Flippers. **Technical:** Hollow grinds CPM154, CPM S35VN, stainless Damascus, Stellite. Uses titanium, zirconium, carbon fiber, G10, and select natural handle materials. **Prices:** Starting at $450. **Remarks:** Full-time maker, first knife sold in 2002. **Mark:** Last name in diamond.

CARLISLE, JEFF
PO Box 282 12753 Hwy 200, Simms, MT 59477, Phone: 406-264-5693

CARPENTER, RONALD W
Rt. 4 Box 323, Jasper, TX 75951, Phone: 409-384-4087

CARR, JOSEPH E.
W183 N8974 Maryhill Drive, Menomonee Falls, WI 53051, Phone: 920-625-3607, carsmith1@SBCGlobal.net; Web: Hembrook3607@charter.net
Specialties: JC knives. **Patterns:** Hunters, Bowies, fighting knives, every day carries. **Technical:** Grinds ATS-34 and Damascus. **Prices:** $200 to $750. **Remarks:** Full-time maker for 2 years, being taught by Ron Hembrook.

CARR, TIM
3660 Pillon Rd, Muskegon, MI 49445, Phone: 231-766-3582, tim@blackbearforgemi.com Web:www.blackbearforgemi.com
Specialties: Hunters, camp knives. **Patterns:** His or yours. **Technical:** Hand forges 5160, 52100 and Damascus. **Prices:** $125 to $700. **Remarks:** Part-time maker. **Mark:** The letter combined from maker's initials TRC.

CARRILLO, DWAINE
C/O AIRKAT KNIVES, Phone: 405-503-5879, tripwire7@cox.net; Web: www.airkatknives.com

CARROLL, CHAD
12182 McClelland, Grant, MI 49327, Phone: 231-834-9183, CHAD724@msn.com
Specialties: Hunters, Bowies, folders, swords, tomahawks. **Patterns:** Fixed blades, folders. **Prices:** $100 to $2000. **Remarks:** ABS Journeyman May 2002. **Mark:** A backwards C next to a forward C, maker's initials.

CARTER, FRED
5219 Deer Creek Rd, Wichita Falls, TX 76302, Phone: 904-723-4020, fcarter40@live.com
Specialties: High-art investor-class straight knives; some working hunters and fighters. **Patterns:** Classic daggers, Bowies; interframe, stainless and blued steel folders with gold inlay. **Technical:** Grinds a variety of steels. Uses no glue or solder. Engraves and inlays. **Prices:** Generally upscale. **Remarks:** Full-time maker. **Mark:** Signature in oval logo.

CARTER, MIKE
2522 Frankfort Ave, Louisville, KY 40206, Phone: 502-387-4844, mike@cartercrafts.com Web: www.cartercrafts.com
Remarks: Voting Member Knifemakers Guild.

CARTER, MURRAY M
2038 N.W. Aloclek Dr. #225, Hillsboro, OR 97124, Phone: 503-466-1331, murray@cartercutlery.com; Web: www.cartercutlery.com
Specialties: Traditional Japanese kitchen knives, utilizing San soh ko (three layer) or Kata-ha (two layer) blade construction. Laminated neck knives, traditional Japanese etc. **Patterns:** Works from over 200 standard Japanese and North American designs. **Technical:** Hot forges and cold forges Hitachi white steel #1, Hitachi blue super steel exclusively. **Prices:** $400 to $4,000. **Remarks:** Owns and operates North America's most exclusive traditional Japanese bladesmithing school and Apprentice Program; web site available at which viewers can subscribe to 10 free knife sharpening and maintenance reports. **Mark:** Name in cursive, often appearing with Japanese characters. **Other:** Offers the world's finest video instruction on sharpening.

CARTER, SHAYNE

5302 Rosewood Cir., Payson, UT 84651, Phone: 801-913-0181, shaynemcarter@hotmail.com

Specialties: Fixed blades. **Patterns:** Hunters, bowies and fighters. **Technical:** Flat grinds, hand finishes, forges blade steel, including own damascus, some 1084, 52100 and 5160. **Remarks:** Part-time maker; first damascus made in 1984.

CASEY, KEVIN

4 Broken Arrow Rd., Lander, WY 82520, Phone: 269-719-7412, kevinvecasey@gmail.com; Web: www.kevincaseycustomknives.com

Specialties: Fixed blades and folders. **Patterns:** Liner lock folders and feather Damascus pattern, mammoth ivory. **Technical:** Forges Damascus and carbon steels. **Prices:** Starting at $500 - $2500. **Remarks:** Member ABS, Knifemakers Guild, Custom Knifemakers Collectors Association.

CASHEN, KEVIN R

Matherton Forge, 5615 Tyler St., Hubbardston, MI 48845, Phone: 989-981-6780, kevin@cashenblades.com; Web: www.cashenblades.com

Specialties: User-oriented straight knives and medieval and renaissance period European swords and daggers. **Patterns:** Hunters and skinners, bowies and camp knives, swords and daggers. **Technical:** Hand forged blades of O1, L6 and maker's own O1-L6-and-O2 damascus, occasionally W2 or 1095, all heat-treated to exacting metallurgical standards. **Prices:** $200 for small hunters to $9,000+ for museum-quality swords, with an average range of $400-$2,000. **Remarks:** Full-time maker, instructor/speaker/consultant; first knife sold in 1985. **Mark:** Gothic "K.C." with master smith stamp. On period pieces, a crowned castle encircled with "Cashen."

CASTEEL, DIANNA

PO Box 63, Monteagle, TN 37356, Phone: 931-212-4341, ddcasteel@charter.net; Web: www.casteelcustomknives.com

Specialties: Small, delicate daggers and miniatures; most knives one-of-a-kind. **Patterns:** Daggers, boot knives, fighters and miniatures. **Technical:** Grinds 440C. Offers stainless Damascus. **Prices:** Start at $350; miniatures start at $250. **Remarks:** Full-time maker. **Mark:** Di in script.

CASTEEL, DOUGLAS

PO Box 63, Monteagle, TN 37356, Phone: 931-212-4341, Fax: 931-723-1856, ddcasteel@charter.net; Web: www.casteelcustomknives.com

Specialties: One-of-a-kind collector-class period pieces. **Patterns:** Daggers, Bowies, swords and folders. **Technical:** Grinds 440C. Offers gold and silver castings.Offers stainless Damascus **Prices:** Upscale. **Remarks:** Full-time maker; first knife sold in 1982. **Mark:** Last name.

CASTELLUCIO, RICH

220 Stairs Rd, Amsterdam, NY 12010, Phone: 518-843-5540, rcastelluccio@nycap.rr.com

Patterns: Bowies, push daggers, and fantasy knives. **Technical:** Uses ATS-34, 440C, 154CM. I use stabilized wood, bone for the handles. Guards are made of copper, brass, stainless, nickle, and mosaic.

CASTON, DARRIEL

125 Ashcat Way, Folsom, CA 95630, Phone: 916-539-0744, darrielc@gmail.com

CASWELL, JOE

173 S Ventu Park Rd, Newbury, CA 91320, Phone: 805-499-0707, Web:www.caswellknives.com

Specialties: Historic pattern welded knives and swords, hand forged. Also high precision folding and fixed blade "gentleman" and "tactical" knives of his design, period firearms. Inventor of the "In-Line" retractable pocket clip for folding knives. **Patterns:** Hunters, tactical/utility, fighters, bowies, daggers, pattern welded medieval swords, precision folders. **Technical:** Forges own Damascus especially historic forms. Sometimes uses modern stainless steels and Damascus of other makers. Makes some knives entirely by hand, others using the latest CNC techniques and by hand. Makes sheaths too.**Prices:** $100-$5,500. **Remarks:** Full time makers since 1995. Making mostly historic recreations for exclusive clientele. Recently moving into folding knives and 'modern' designs. **Mark:** CASWELL or CASWELL USA Accompanied by a mounted knight logo.

CATOE, DAVID R

4024 Heutte Dr, Norfolk, VA 23518, Phone: 757-480-3191

Technical: Does own forging, Damascus and heat treatments. **Prices:** $200 to $500; some higher. **Remarks:** Part-time maker; trained by Dan Maragni 1985-1988; first knife sold 1989. **Mark:** Leaf of a camellia.

CECCHINI, GUSTAVO T.

2841 XV Novembro, Sao Jose Rio Preto SP, BRAZIL 15015110, Phone: +55 (17)3222-4267, tomaki@terra.com.br; Web: www.gtcknives.com

Specialties: Tactical and HiTech folders. **Technical:** Stock removal. Stainless steel fixed blades. S30V, S35Vn, S90V, CowryX, Damasteel, Chad Nichols SS damascus, RWL 34, CPM 154 CM, BG 42. **Prices:** $500 - $1500. **Remarks:** Full-time since 2004. **Mark:** Tang Stamp "GTC"

CEPRANO, PETER J.

213 Townsend Brooke Rd., Auburn, ME 04210, Phone: 207-786-5322, bpknives@gmail.com

Specialties: Traditional working/using straight knives; tactical/defense straight knives. Own designs or to a customer's specs. **Patterns:** Hunters, skinners, utility, Bowies, fighters, camp and survival, neck knives. **Technical:** Forges 1095, 5160, W2, 52100 and old files; grinds CPM154cm, ATS-34, 440C, D2, CPMs30v, Damascus from other makes and other tool steels. Hand-sewn and tooled leather and Kydex sheaths. **Prices:** Starting at $125. **Remarks:** Full-time maker, first knife sold in 2001. Doing business as Big Pete Knives. **Mark:** Bold BPK over small BigPeteKnivesUSA.

CHAFFEE, JEFF L

14314 N. Washington St, PO Box 1, Morris, IN 47033, Phone: 812-212-6188

Specialties: Fancy working and utility folders and straight knives. **Patterns:** Fighters, dagger, hunter and locking folders. **Technical:** Grinds commercial Damascus, 440C, ATS-34, D2 and O1. Prefers natural handle materials. **Prices:** $350 to $2000. **Remarks:** Part-time maker; first knife sold in 1988. **Mark:** Last name.

CHAMBERLAIN, JON A

15 S. Lombard, E. Wenatchee, WA 98802, Phone: 509-884-6591

Specialties: Working and kitchen knives to customer specs; exotics on special order. **Patterns:** Over 100 patterns in stock. **Technical:** Prefers ATS-34, D2, L6 and Damascus. **Prices:** Start at $50. **Remarks:** First knife sold in 1986. Doing business as Johnny Custom Knifemakers. **Mark:** Name in oval with city and state enclosing.

CHAMBERLIN, JOHN A

11535 Our Rd., Anchorage, AK 99516, Phone: 907-346-1524, Fax: 907-562-4583

Specialties: Art and working knives. **Patterns:** Daggers and hunters; some folders;. **Technical:** Grinds ATS-34, 440C, A2, D2 and Damascus. Uses Alaskan handle materials such as oosic, jade, whale jawbone, fossil ivory. **Prices:** Start at $200. **Remarks:** Favorite knives to make are double-edged. Does own heat treating and cryogenic deep freeze. Full-time maker; first knife sold in 1984. **Mark:** Name over English shield and dagger.

CHAMBERS, RONNY

1900 W. Mississippi St., Beebe, AR 72012, Phone: 501-288-1476, chambersronny@yahoo.com; Web: www.chamberscustomknives.net

CHAMBLIN, JOEL

960 New Hebron Church Rd, Concord, GA 30206, Phone: 678-588-6769, chamblinknives@yahoo.com Web: chamblinknives.com

Specialties: Fancy and working folders. **Patterns:** Fancy locking folders, traditional, multi-blades and utility. **Technical:** Uses ATS-34, CPM 154, and commercial Damascus. Offers filework. **Prices:** Start at $400. **Remarks:** Full-time maker; first knife sold in 1989. **Mark:** Last name.

CHAMPION, ROBERT

7001 Red Rock Rd., Amarillo, TX 79118, Phone: 806-622-3970, rchampknives@gmail.com; www.rchampknives.com

Specialties: Traditional working straight knives. **Patterns:** Hunters, skinners, camp knives, bowies and daggers. **Technical:** Grinds 440C, ATS-34, D2 and stainless damascus. **Prices:** $100 to $1,800. **Remarks:** Part-time maker; first knife sold in 1979. Stream-lined hunters. **Mark:** Last name with dagger logo, city and state.

CHAPO, WILLIAM G

45 Wildridge Rd, Wilton, CT 06897, Phone: 203-544-9424

Specialties: Classic straight knives and folders of his design and to customer specs; period pieces. **Patterns:** Boots, Bowies and locking folders. **Technical:** Forges stainless Damascus. Offers filework. **Prices:** $750 and up. **Remarks:** Full-time maker; first knife sold in 1989. **Mark:** First and middle initials, last name, city, state.

CHARD, GORDON R

104 S. Holiday Lane, Iola, KS 66749, Phone: 620-365-2311, Fax: 620-365-2311, gchard@cox.net

Specialties: High tech folding knives in one-of-a-kind styles. **Patterns:** Liner locking folders of own design. Also fixed blade Art Knives. **Technical:** Clean work with attention to fit and finish. Blade steel mostly ATS-34 and 154CM, some CPM440V Vaso Wear and Damascus. **Prices:** $150 to $2500. **Remarks:** First knife sold in 1983. **Mark:** Name, city and state surrounded by wheat on each side.

CHASE, JOHN E

217 Walnut, Aledo, TX 76008, Phone: 817-441-8331, jchaseknives@sbcglobal.net

Specialties: Straight working knives in standard patterns or to customer specs. **Patterns:** Hunters, fighters, daggers and Bowies. **Technical:** Grinds D2 and O1; offers mostly satin finishes. **Prices:** Start at $325. **Remarks:** Part-time maker; first knife sold in 1974. **Mark:** Last name in logo.

CHAUVIN, JOHN

200 Anna St, Scott, LA 70583, Phone: 337-237-6138, Fax: 337-230-7980

Specialties: Traditional working and using straight knives of his design, to customer specs and in standard patterns. **Patterns:** Bowies, fighters, and hunters. **Technical:** Grinds ATS-34, 440C and O1 high-carbon. Paul Bos heat treating. Uses ivory, stag, oosic and stabilized Louisiana swamp maple for handle materials. Makes sheaths using alligator and ostrich. **Prices:** $200 and up. Bowies start at $500. **Remarks:** Part-time maker; first knife sold in 1995. **Mark:** Full name, city, state.

CHAVEZ, RAMON

314 N. 5th St., Belen, NM 87002, Phone: 505-453-6008, ramon@chavezknives.com; Web: www.chaveskhives.com

Specialties: Frame-lock folding knives and fixed blades. **Patterns:** Hunters, skinners, bushcraft, tactical, neck knives and utility. **Technical:** Grind/stock removal of CPM D2, D2 and CPM 3V. Handles are mostly titanium and Micarta. Thermal molding plastic for sheaths. **Prices:** Start at $225. **Remarks:** Full-time maker; first knife made in 1993, first knife sold in 2010. **Mark:** CHAVES USA with skeleton key.

CHEATHAM, BILL

PO Box 636, Laveen, AZ 85339, Phone: 602-237-2786, blademan76@aol.com

Specialties: Working straight knives and folders. **Patterns:** Hunters, fighters, boots and axes; locking folders. **Technical:** Grinds 440C. **Prices:** $150 to $350; exceptional knives to $600. **Remarks:** Full-time maker; first knife sold in 1976. **Mark:** Name, city, state.

CHERRY, FRANK J

3412 Tiley N.E., Albuquerque, NM 87110, Phone: 505-883-8643

CHEW, LARRY

3025 De leon Dr., Weatherford, TX 76087, Phone: 817-573-8035, chewman@swbell.net; Web: www.voodooinside.com

Specialties: High-tech folding knives. **Patterns:** Double action automatic and manual folding patterns of his design. **Technical:** CAD designed folders utilizing roller bearing pivot design known as "VooDoo." Double action automatic folders with a variety of obvious and disguised release mechanisms, some with lock-outs. **Prices:** Manual folders start at $475, double action autos start at $750. **Remarks:** Made and sold first knife in 1988, first folder in 1989. Full-time maker since 1997. **Mark:** Name and location etched in blade, Damascus autos marked on spring inside frame. Earliest knives stamped LC.

CHILDERS, DAVID

15575 Marina Dr., Unit 227, Montgomery, TX 77356, childersdavid@att.net; Web: www.davidchildersknives.com

CHINNOCK, DANIEL T.

380 River Ridge Dr., Union, MO 63084, Phone: 314-276-6936, Web: www.DanChinnock.com; email: Sueanddanc@cs.com

Specialties: One of a kind folders in Damascus and Mammoth Ivory. Performs intricate pearl inlays in snake wood and giraffe bone. Makes matchingt ivory pistol grips for colt 1911's and Colt SAA. **Patterns:** New folder designs each year, thin ground and delicate gentleman's folders, large "hunting" folders in stainless Damascus and CPM154. Several standard models carried by Internet dealers. **Prices:** $500-$1500 **Remarks:** Full-time maker in 2005 and a voting member of the Knifemakers Guild. Performs intricate file work on all areas of knife. **Mark:** Signature on inside of backbar, starting in 2009 blades are stamped with a large "C" and "Dan" buried inside the "C".

CHOMILIER, ALAIN AND JORIS

20 rue des Hauts de Chanturgue, Clermont-Ferrand, FRANCE 63100, Phone: + 33 4 73 25 64 47, jo_chomilier@yahoo.fr

Specialties: One-of-a-kind knives; exclusive designs; art knives in carved patinated bronze, mainly folders, some straight knives and art daggers. **Patterns:** Liner-lock, side-lock, button-lock, lockback folders. **Technical:** Grind carbon and stainless damascus; also carve and patinate bronze. **Prices:** $400 to $3000, some to $4000. **Remarks:** Spare-time makers; first knife sold in 1995; Use fossil stone and ivory, mother-of-pearl, (fossil) coral, meteorite, bronze, gemstones, high karat gold. **Mark:** A. J. Chomilier in italics.

CHRISTENSEN, JON P

516 Blue Grouse, Stevensville, MT 59870, Phone: 406-697-8377, jpcknives@gmail.com; Web: www.jonchristensenknives.com

Specialties: Hunting/utility knives, folders, art knives. **Patterns:** Mosaic damascus**Technical:** Sole authorship, forges 01, 1084, 52100, 5160, Damascus from 1084/15N20. **Prices:** $220 and up. **Remarks:** ABS Mastersmith, first knife sold in 1999. **Mark:** First and middle initial surrounded by last initial.

CHURCHMAN, T W (TIM)

475 Saddle Horn Drive, Bandera, TX 78003, Phone: 210-240-0317, tim.churchman@nustarenergy.com

Specialties: Fancy and traditional straight knives. Bird/trout knives of his design and to customer specs. **Patterns:** Bird/trout knives, Bowies, daggers, fighters, boot knives, some miniatures. **Technical:** Grinds 440C, D2 and 154CM. Offers stainless fittings, fancy filework, exotic and stabilized woods, elk and other antler, and hand sewed lined sheaths. Also flower pins as a style. **Prices:** $350 to $450; some to $2,250. **Remarks:** Part-time maker; first knife made in 1981 after reading "KNIVES '81." Doing business as "Custom Knives Churchman Made." **Mark:** "Churchman" over Texas outline, "Bandera" under.

CIMMS, GREG

Kayne Custom Knife Works, 2297 Rt. 44, Ste. B, Pleasant Valley, NY 12569, Phone: 845-475-7220, cimms1@aol.com

Patterns: Kitchen knives, hunters, bowies, fighters, small swords, bird-and-trout knives, tactical pieces, tomahawks, axes and bushcraft blades. **Technical:** Damascus and straight-carbon-steel cutlery, with some mosaic-damascus and powder-metal pieces. **Prices:** $300 to $4,000. **Remarks:** Full-time maker since 2014; first knife made in 2013. **Mark:** A compass with a "K" in the middle.

CLAIBORNE, JEFF

1470 Roberts Rd, Franklin, IN 46131, Phone: 317-736-7443, jeff@claiborneknives.com; Web: www.claiborneknives.com

Specialties: Multi blade slip joint folders. All one-of-a-kind by hand, no jigs or fixtures, swords, straight knives, period pieces, camp knives, hunters, fighters, ethnic swords all periods. Handle: uses stag, pearl, oosic, bone ivory, mastadon-mammoth, elephant or exotic woods. **Technical:** Forges high-carbon steel, makes Damascus, forges cable grinds, 01, 1095, 5160, 52100, L6. **Prices:** $250 and up. **Remarks:** Full-time maker; first knife sold in 1989. **Mark:** Stylized initials in an oval.

CLAIBORNE, RON

2918 Ellistown Rd, Knox, TN 37924, Phone: 615-524-2054, Bowie@icy.net

Specialties: Multi-blade slip joints, swords, straight knives. **Patterns:** Hunters, daggers, folders. **Technical:** Forges Damascus: mosaic, powder mosaic. Prefers bone and natural handle materials; some exotic woods. **Prices:** $125 to $2500. **Remarks:** Part-time maker; first knife sold in 1979. Doing business as Thunder Mountain Forge Claiborne Knives. **Mark:** Claiborne.

CLARK, D E (LUCKY)

413 Lyman Lane, Johnstown, PA 15909-1409

Specialties: Working straight knives and folders to customer specs. **Patterns:** Customer designs. **Technical:** Grinds D2, 440C, 154CM. **Prices:** $100 to $200; some higher. **Remarks:** Part-time maker; first knife sold in 1975. **Mark:** Name on one side; "Lucky" on other.

CLARK, HOWARD F

115 35th Pl, Runnells, IA 50237, Phone: 515-966-2126, howard@mvforge.com; Web: mvforge.com

Specialties: Currently Japanese-style swords. **Patterns:** Katana. **Technical:** Forges L6 and 1086. **Prices:** $1200 to 5000. **Remarks:** Full-time maker; first knife sold in 1979. Doing business as Morgan Valley Forge. Prior **Mark:** Block letters and serial number on folders; anvil/initials logo on straight knives. Current **Mark:** Two character kanji "Big Ear."

CLARK, JASON

24896 77th Rd., O'Brien, FL 32071, Phone: 386-935-2922, jclark@clarkcustomknives.com; Web: www.clarkcustomknives.com

Specialties: Frame-lock and LinerLock folders. **Patterns:** Drop points, tantos, Persians, clip points, razors and wharncliffes. **Technical:** Sole authorship of knives, constructing 100 percent in house, including designing, cutting, shaping, grinding, heat treating, fitting and finishing. Top quality materials and components, as well as hand-rubbed finishes, media blasting, stonewashing, anodizing and polishing. Licensed to use IKBS (Ikoma Korth Bearing System). **Remarks:** Part-time maker. **Mark:** Cross with initials incorporated.

CLEVELAND, MIKE

Half Life Knives, 329 W. Strasburg Way, Mustang, OK 73064, Phone: 405-627-6097, lawdawg3006@yahoo.com

Specialties: Stock removal fixed-blade knives, multi-ground tactical, hunting, chef's knives and tactical 'hawks. **Patterns:** Multi-ground tactical, hunting, kitchen knives and 'hawks. **Technical:** Stock-removal method of blade making, including 80CrV2, 1095, 1084, 1075, 5160, 52100, CPM M4 REX and damascus steels. **Remarks:** Full-time maker, 'hawk maker. **Mark:** Half skull with half Life Knives circling it.

CLINCO, MARCUS

821 Appelby Street, Venice, CA 90291, Phone: 818-610-9640, marcus@clincoknives.com; Web: www.clincoknives.com

Specialties: I make mostly fixed blade knives with an emphasis on everyday working and tactical models. Most of my knives are stock removal with the exception of my sole authored damascus blades. I have several integral models including a one piece tactical model named the viper. **Technical:** Most working knife models in ATS 34. Integrals in O-1, D-2 and 440 C. Damascus in 1080 and 15 N 20. Large camp and Bowie models in 5160 and D-2. Handle materials used include micarta, stabilized wood, G-10 and occasionally stag and ivory. **Prices:** $200 - $600.

COATS, KEN

317 5th Ave, Stevens Point, WI 54481, Phone: 715-544-0115

Specialties: Does own jigged bone scales **Patterns:** Traditional slip joints - shadow patterns **Technical:** ATS-34 Blades and springs. Milled frames. Grinds ATS-34, 440C. Stainless blades and backsprings. Does all own heat treating and freeze cycle. Blades are drawn to 60RC. Nickel silver or brass bolsters on folders are soldered, neutralized and pinned. Handles are jigged bone, hardwoods antler, and Micarta. Cuts and jigs own bone, usually shades of brown or green. **Prices:** $300 and up

COCKERHAM, LLOYD

1717 Carolyn Ave, Denham Springs, IA 70726, Phone: 225-665-1565

COFFEE, JIM

2785 Rush Rd., Norton, OH 44203, Phone: 330-631-3355, jcoffee735@aol.com

Specialties: Stock Removal, hunters, skinners, fighters. **Technical:** Bowie handle material - stabilized wood, micarta, mammoth ivory, stag. Full tang and hidden tang. Steels - 0-1, d-2, 5160, damascus **Prices:** $150 to $500 and up. **Remarks:** Part-time maker since 2008.**Mark:** full name in a football etch.

COFFEY, BILL

68 Joshua Ave, Clovis, CA 93611, Phone: 559-299-4259, williamccoffey@comcast.net

Specialties: Working and fancy straight knives and folders of his design. **Patterns:** Hunters, fighters, utility, LinerLock® folders and fantasy knives. **Technical:** Grinds 440C, ATS-34, A-Z and commercial Damascus. **Prices:** $250 to $1000; some to $2500. **Remarks:** Full-time maker. First knife sold in 1993. **Mark:** First and last name, city, state.

COFFMAN, DANNY

541 Angel Dr S, Jacksonville, AL 36265-5787, Phone: 256-435-1619

Specialties: Straight knives and folders of his design. Now making liner locks for $650 to $1200 with natural handles and contrasting Damascus blades and bolsters. **Patterns:** Hunters, locking and slip-joint folders. **Technical:** Grinds Damascus, 440C and D2. Offers filework and engraving. **Prices:** $100 to $400; some to $800. **Remarks:** Spare-time maker; first knife sold in 1992. Doing business as Customs by Coffman. **Mark:** Last name stamped or engraved.

COHEA, JOHN M

114 Rogers Dr., Nettleton, MS 38855, Phone: 662-322-5916, jhncohea@hotmail.com Web: http://jmcknives.blademakers.com

Specialties: Frontier style knives, hawks, and leather. **Patterns:** Bowies, hunters, patch/neck knives, tomahawks, and friction folders. **Technical:** Makes both forged and stock removal knives using high carbon steels and damascus. Uses natural handle materials that include antler, bone, ivory, horn, and figured hardwoods. Also makes rawhide covered sheaths that include fringe, tacks, antique trade beads, and other period correct materials. **Prices:** $100 - $1500, some higher. **Remarks:** Part-time maker, first knife sold in 1999. **Mark:** COHEA stamped on riccasso.

custom knifemakers

COHEN, N J (NORM)
2408 Sugarcone Rd, Baltimore, MD 21209, Phone: 410-484-3841, inquiry@ njcknives.com; Web: www.njcknives.com
Specialties: Working class knives. **Patterns:** Hunters, skinners, bird knives, push daggers, boots, kitchen and practical customer designs. **Technical:** Stock removal 440C, ATS-34, CPM 154 and D2. Handles of Micarta, Corian and stabilized woods. **Prices:** $50 to $250. **Remarks:** Part-time maker; first knife sold in 1982. **Mark:** NJC engraved.

COLE, JAMES M
505 Stonewood Blvd, Bartonville, TX 76226, Phone: 817-430-0302, dogcole@swbell.net

COLEMAN, JOHN A
7325 Bonita Way, Citrus Heights, CA 95610-3003, Phone: 916-335-1568, slimsknifes@yahoo.com
Specialties: Minis, hunters, bowies of his design or yours. **Patterns:** Plain to fancy file back working knives. **Technical:** Grinds 440C, ATS-34, 145CM, D2, 1095, 5160. Some hand-forged blades. Exotic woods bone, antler and some ivory. **Prices:** $100 to $500. **Remarks:** Does some carving in handles. Part-time maker. First knife sold in 1989. OKCA 2010 Award winner for best mini of show. **Mark:** Cowboy setting on log whittling Slim's Custom Knives above cowboy and name and state under cowboy.

COLLINS, LYNN M
138 Berkley Dr, Elyria, OH 44035, Phone: 440-366-7101
Specialties: Working straight knives. **Patterns:** Field knives, boots and fighters. **Technical:** Grinds D2, 154CM and 440C. **Prices:** Start at $200. **Remarks:** Spare-time maker; first knife sold in 1980. **Mark:** Initials, asterisks.

COLTER, WADE
PO Box 2340, Colstrip, MT 59323, Phone: Shop: 406-748-2010, Fax: Cell: 406-740-1554
Specialties: Fancy and embellished straight knives, folders and swords of his design; historical and period pieces. **Patterns:** Bowies, swords and folders. **Technical:** Hand forges 52100 ball bearing steel and L6, 1090, cable and chain Damascus from 5N20 and 1084. Carves and makes sheaths. **Prices:** $250 to $3500. **Remarks:** SemiRetired; first knife sold in 1990. Doing business as "Colter's Hell" Forge. **Mark:** Initials on left side ricasso.

COLWELL, KEVIN
Professor's Forge, 15 Stony Hill Rd., Cheshire, CA 06410, Phone: 203-439-2223, colwellk2@southernct.edu
Specialties: Swords (Dao, jian, seax, messer, baurnwehr, etc.) and knives (puukko, Viking-style, hunters, skinners, bowies, fighters and chef's knives). **Technical:** Forges blades, vivid pattern welding or subtle pattern welding with beautiful hamon and grain structure. **Prices:** $175 to $500, swords $900 and up, depending upon what customer wants in adornment. **Remarks:** Associate professor of psychology.

CONKLIN, GEORGE L
Box 902, Ft. Benton, MT 59442, Phone: 406-622-3268, Fax: 406-622-3410, 7bbgrus@3rivers.net
Specialties: Designer and manufacturer of the "Brisket Breaker." **Patterns:** Hunters, utility/camp knives and hatchets. **Technical:** Grinds 440C, ATS-34, D2, 1095, 154CM and 5160. Offers some forging and heat-treats for others. Offers some jewelling. **Prices:** $65 to $200; some to $1000. **Remarks:** Full-time maker. Doing business as Rocky Mountain Knives. **Mark:** Last name in script.

CONLEY, BOB
1013 Creasy Rd, Jonesboro, TN 37659, Phone: 423-753-3302
Specialties: Working straight knives and folders. **Patterns:** Lockers, two-blades, gents, hunters, traditional-styles, straight hunters. **Technical:** Grinds 440C, 154CM and ATS-34. Engraves. **Prices:** $250 to $450; some to $600. **Remarks:** Full-time maker; first knife sold in 1979. **Mark:** Full name, city, state.

CONN JR., C T
206 Highland Ave, Attalla, AL 35954, Phone: 205-538-7688
Specialties: Working folders, some fancy. **Patterns:** Full range of folding knives. **Technical:** Grinds O2, 440C and 154CM. **Prices:** $125 to $300; some to $600. **Remarks:** Part-time maker; first knife sold in 1982. **Mark:** Name.

CONNOLLY, JAMES
2486 Oro-Quincy Hwy, Oroville, CA 95966, Phone: 530-534-5363, rjconnolly@ sbcglobal.net
Specialties: Classic working and using knives of his design. **Patterns:** Boots, Bowies, daggers and swords. **Technical:** Grinds ATS-34, BG42, A2, O1. **Prices:** $100 to $500; some to $1500. **Remarks:** Part-time maker; first knife sold in 1980. Doing business as Gold Rush Designs. **Mark:** First initial, last name, Handmade.

CONNOR, JOHN W
PO Box 12981, Odessa, TX 79768-2981, Phone: 915-362-6901

CONNOR, MICHAEL
Box 502, Winters, TX 79567, Phone: 915-754-5602
Specialties: Straight knives, period pieces, some folders. **Patterns:** Hunters to camp knives to traditional locking folders to Bowies. **Technical:** Forges 5160, O1, 1084 steels and his own Damascus. **Prices:** Moderate to upscale. **Remarks:** Spare-time maker; first knife sold in 1974. ABS Master Smith 1983. **Mark:** Last name, M.S.

CONTI, JEFFREY D
POB 16, Judith Gap, MT 59453, Phone: 253-569-6303, Web: FaceBook at JL Knives
Specialties: Working straight knives. **Patterns:** Tactical, survival, hunting, campting, fishing and kitchen knives. **Technical:** Grinds D2, 154CM, 440C and O1. Engraves.

Prices: Start at $150. **Remarks:** Part-time maker; first knife sold in 1980. Does own heat treating. **Mark:** Electrical etch: "JG Knives."

CONWAY, JOHN
13301 100th Place NE, Kirkland, WA 98034, Phone: 425-823-2821, jcknives@ Frontier.com
Specialties: Folders; working and Damascus. Straight knives, camp, utility and fighting knives. **Patterns:** LinerLock® folders of own design. Hidden tang straight knives of own design. **Technical:** Flat grinds forged carbon steels and own Damascus steel, including mosaic. **Prices:** $300 to $850. **Remarks:** Part-time maker since 1999. **Mark:** Oval with stylized initials J C inset.

COOGAN, ROBERT
1560 Craft Center Dr, Smithville, TN 37166, Phone: 615-597-6801, http://iweb.tntech. edu/rcoogan/
Specialties: One-of-a-kind knives. **Patterns:** Unique items like ulu-style Appalachian herb knives. **Technical:** Forges; his Damascus is made from nickel steel and W1. **Prices:** Start at $100. **Remarks:** Part-time maker; first knife sold in 1979. **Mark:** Initials or last name in script.

COOK, JAMES R
455 Anderson Rd, Nashville, AR 71852, Phone: 870 845 5173, jr@jrcookknives.com; Web: www.jrcookknives.com
Specialties: Working straight knives and folders of his design or to customer specs. **Patterns:** Bowies, hunters and camp knives. **Technical:** Forges 1084 and high-carbon Damascus. **Prices:** $800 to $20,000. **Remarks:** Full-time maker; first knife sold in 1986. **Mark:** First and middle initials, last name.

COOK, LOUISE
475 Robinson Ln, Ozark, IL 62972, Phone: 618-777-2932
Specialties: Working and using straight knives of her design and to customer specs; period pieces. **Patterns:** Bowies, hunters and utility/camp knives. **Technical:** Forges 5160. Filework; pin work; silver wire inlay. **Prices:** Start at $50/inch. **Remarks:** Part-time maker; first knife sold in 1990. Doing business as Panther Creek Forge. **Mark:** First name and Journeyman stamp on one side; panther head on the other.

COOK, MIKE
475 Robinson Ln, Ozark, IL 62972, Phone: 618-777-2932
Specialties: Traditional working and using straight knives of his design and to customer specs. **Patterns:** Bowies, hunters and utility/camp knives. **Technical:** Forges 5160. Filework; pin work. **Prices:** Start at $50/inch. **Remarks:** Spare-time maker; first knife sold in 1991. **Mark:** First initial, last name and Journeyman stamp on one side; panther head on the other.

COOK, MIKE A
10927 Shilton Rd, Portland, MI 48875, Phone: 517-242-1352, macook@hughes.net Web: www.artofishi.com
Specialties: Fancy/embellished and period pieces of his design. **Patterns:** Daggers, fighters and hunters. **Technical:** Stone bladed knives in agate, obsidian and jasper. Scrimshaws; opal inlays. **Prices:** $60 to $300; some to $800. **Remarks:** Part-time maker; first knife sold in 1988. Doing business as Art of Ishi. **Mark:** Initials and year.

COOKE, MARK
LongDog Forge, 21619 Slippery Creek Ln., Spring, TX 77388, markcooke5@gmail.com; Web: www.longdogforge.com
Specialties: One-off handforged blades featuring bold design, technical processes, sole authorship and an emphasis on a clean, complete package. **Technical:** Presently working with mono steel blades via W2, 1084, 80CrV2, as well as others upon request. **Remarks:** Enjoys challenging commissions that push the boundaries of the maker's skill set. All work done under the same roof, from initial forging of the blade to stitching of the sheath to ensure quality and adherence to the original design. Combines Old World techniques with modern design elements to achieve balance between form and function. **Mark:** Dachshund (LongDog) mark typically located on the spine of the blade.

COOMBS JR., LAMONT
546 State Rt 46, Bucksport, ME 04416, Phone: 207-469-3057, Fax: 207-469-3057, theknifemaker@hotmail.com; Web: www.knivesby.com/coombs-knives.html
Specialties: Classic fancy and embellished straight knives; traditional working and using straight knives. Knives of his design and to customer specs. **Patterns:** Hunters, folders and utility/camp knives. **Technical:** Hollow- and flat-grinds ATS-34, 440C, D2 and O1; grinds Damascus from other makers. **Prices:** $100 to $500; some to $3500. **Remarks:** Full-time maker; first knife sold in 1988. **Mark:** Last name on banner, handmade underneath.

COON, RAYMOND C
21135 S.E. Tillstrom Rd, Damascus, OR 97089, Phone: 503-658-2252, Raymond@ damascusknife.com; Web: Damascusknife.com
Specialties: Working straight knives in standard patterns. **Patterns:** Hunters, Bowies, daggers, boots and axes. **Technical:** Forges high-carbon steel and Damascus or 97089. **Prices:** Start at $235. **Remarks:** Full-time maker; does own leatherwork, makes own Damascus, daggers; first knife sold in 1995. **Mark:** First initial, last name.

COOPER, PAUL
9 Woods St., Woburn, MA 01801, Phone: 781-938-0519, byksm@yahoo.com
Specialties: Forged, embellished, hand finished fixed-blade knives. **Patterns:** One of a kind designs, often inspired by traditional and historic pieces. **Technical:** Works in tool steel, damascus and natural materials. **Prices:** $500 - $2000. **Remarks:** Part-time maker, formally apprenticed under J.D. Smith. Sold first piece in 2006. **Mark:** Letter C inside bleeding heart.

COPELAND, THOM
136 Blue Bayou Ests., Nashville, AR 71852, tcope@cswnet.com
Specialties: Hand forged fixed blades; hunters, Bowies and camp knives. **Remarks:** Member of ABS and AKA (Arkansas Knifemakers Association). **Mark:** Copeland.

COPPINS, DANIEL
700 S. 9th St., Cambridge, OH 43725, Phone: 740-995-9009, info@battlehorseknives.com; Web: www.battlehorseknives.com
Specialties: Bushcraft knives, tacticals, hunting. **Technical:** Grinds 440C, D2. Antler handles. **Patterns:** Many. **Prices:** $40 to $600. **Remarks:** Sold first knife in 2002; formerly Blind Horse Knives. **Mark:** Horse-Kicking Donkey.

CORBY, HAROLD
218 Brandonwood Dr, Johnson City, TN 37604, Phone: 423-926-9781
Specialties: Large fighters and Bowies; self-protection knives; art knives. Along with art knives and combat knives, Corby now has a all new automatic MO.PB1, also side lock MO LL-1 with titanium liners G-10 handles. **Patterns:** Sub-hilt fighters and hunters. **Technical:** Grinds 154CM, ATS-34 and 440C. **Prices:** $200 to $6000. **Remarks:** Full-time maker; first knife sold in 1969. Doing business as Knives by Corby. **Mark:** Last name.

CORDOVA, JOEY
1594 S. Hill Rd., Bernalillo, NM 87004, Phone: 505-410-3809, joeyscordova@gmail.com; www.joelouiknives.com
Patterns: High-carbon full-tang knives and hidden-tang bowies, as well as small neck knives. **Technical:** Differentially heat-treats blades producing hamons (temper lines). **Prices:** $120 and up. **Remarks:** Full-time knifemaker and part-time ring maker.

CORDOVA, JOSEPH G
1450 Lillie Dr, Bosque Farms, NM 87068, Phone: 505-869-3912, kcordova@rt66.com
Specialties: One-of-a-kind designs, some to customer specs. **Patterns:** Fighter called the 'Gladiator', hunters, boots and cutlery. **Technical:** Forges 1095, 5160; grinds ATS-34, 440C and 154CM. **Prices:** Moderate to upscale. **Remarks:** Full-time maker; first knife sold in 1953. Past chairman of American Bladesmith Society. **Mark:** Cordova made.

CORICH, VANCE
POB 97, Morrison, CO 80465, Phone: 303-999-1553, vancecorichcutlery@gmail.com; https://sites.google.com/site/vancesproject/
Specialties: Fixed blades, usually 2 - 7 inches, recurved blades, locking-liner folders and friction folders. **Technical:** Differential heat treating on high-carbon steels. **Prices:** $150 to $1,000. **Remarks:** Part-time maker working on going full time. **Mark:** Stamped "VCC" or VANCE.

CORKUM, STEVE
34 Basehoar School Rd, Littlestown, PA 17340, Phone: 717-359-9563, sco7129849@aol.com; Web: www.hawknives.com

CORNETT, BRIAN
1511 N. College St., McKinney, TX 75069, Phone: 972-310-7289, devildogdesign@tx.rr.com; www.d3devildogdesigns.com
Patterns: Tactical, hunting, neck knives and personal-defense tools. **Technical:** Stock removal of 1095, O1 tool steel, 52100, D2, CPM 154 and damascus. **Prices:** $50 to $300. **Remarks:** Full-time maker; first knife made in 2011. **Mark:** D3.

CORNWELL, JEFFREY
Treasure Art Blades, PO Box 244014, Anchorage, AK 99524, Phone: 907-887-1661, cornwellsjej@alaska.net
Specialties: Organic, sculptural shapes of original design from damascus steel and mokume gane. **Technical:** Blade creations from Robert Eggerling damascus and Mike Sakmar mokume. **Remarks:** Free-time maker. **Mark:** Stylized J inside a circle.

COSTA, SCOTT
409 Coventry Rd, Spicewood, TX 78669, Phone: 830-693-3431
Specialties: Working straight knives. **Patterns:** Hunters, skinners, axes, trophy sets, custom boxed steak sets, carving sets and bar sets. **Technical:** Grinds D2, ATS-34, 440 and Damascus. Heat-treats. **Prices:** $225 to $2000. **Remarks:** Full-time maker; first knife sold in 1985. **Mark:** Initials connected.

COTTRILL, JAMES I
1776 Ransburg Ave, Columbus, OH 43223, Phone: 614-274-0020
Specialties: Working straight knives of his design. **Patterns:** Caters to the boating and hunting crowd; cutlery. **Technical:** Grinds O1, D2 and 440C. Likes filework. **Prices:** $95 to $250; some to $500. **Remarks:** Full-time maker; first knife sold in 1977. **Mark:** Name, city, state, in oval logo.

COUSINO, GEORGE
7818 Norfolk, Onsted, MI 49265, Phone: 517-467-4911, cousinoknives@yahoo.com; Web: www.cousinoknives.com
Specialties: Hunters, Bowies using knives. **Patterns:** Hunters, Bowies, buckskinners, folders and daggers. **Technical:** Grinds 440C. **Prices:** $95 to $300. **Remarks:** Part-time maker; first knife sold in 1981. **Mark:** Last name.

COVER, JEFF
11355 Allen Rd, Potosi, MO 63664, Phone: 573-749-0008, jeffcovercustomknives@hotmail.com
Specialties: Folders and straight knives. **Patterns: Technical:** Various knife steels and handle materials. **Prices:** $70 to $500. **Mark:** Jeff Cover J.C. Custom Knives.

COVER, RAYMOND A
16235 State Hwy. U, Mineral Point, MO 63660, Phone: 573-749-3783
Specialties: High-tech working straight knives and folders in working patterns. **Patterns:** Slip joints, lockbacks, multi-blade folders. **Technical:** Various knife steels and handle materials. **Prices:** Swords from bare blades to complete high art $200 to $600. **Mark:** "R Cover"

COWLES, DON
1026 Lawndale Dr, Royal Oak, MI 48067, Phone: 248-541-4619, don@cowlesknives.com; Web: www.cowlesknives.com
Specialties: Straight, non-folding pocket knives of his design. **Patterns:** Gentlemen's pocket knives. **Technical:** Grinds CPM154, S30V, Damascus, Talonite. Engraves; pearl inlays in some handles. **Prices:** Start at $300. **Remarks:** Full-time maker; first knife sold in 1994. **Mark:** Full name with oak leaf.

COX, LARRY
701 W. 13th St, Murfreesboro, AR 71958, Phone: 870-258-2429, Fax: Cell: 870-557-8062, cox870@windstream.net
Specialties: Forges his own "ghost flame" damascus. **Patterns:** Skinners, hunters, camp knives and bowies. **Technical:** Forges 5160, 1084, and L6 with 1084 and 5160 for damascus, as well as doing own heat treating. **Prices:** $300 and up. **Remarks:** Sole ownership of knives. Part-time maker; first knife sold in 2007. Member ABS and Arkansas Knifemakers Association. **Mark:** "L U" over "COX."

COX, SAM
1756 Love Springs Rd, Gaffney, SC 29341, Phone: 864-489-1892, Web: www.coxworks.com
Remarks: Started making knives in 1981 for another maker. 1st knife sold under own name in 1983. Full-time maker 1985-2009. Retired in 2010. Now part time. **Mark:** Different logo each year.

COYE, BILL
PO Box 470684, Tulsa, OK 74147, Phone: 918-232-5721, info@coyeknives.com; Web: www.coyeknives.com
Specialties: Tactical and utility knives. **Patterns:** Fighters and utility. **Technical:** Grinds CPM154CM, 154CM, CTS-XHP and Elmax stainless steels. **Prices:** $210 to $320. **Remarks:** Part-time maker. First knife sold in 2009. **Mark:** COYE.

CRADDOCK, MIKE
300 Blythe Dr., Thomasville, NC 27360, Phone: 336-382-8461, ncbladesmith@gmail.com
Specialties: Fighters, bowies. **Patterns:** Hunters and working knives. **Technical:** Forges and grinds high-carbon steel, and does own damascus. **Prices:** $350 to $1,500. **Mark:** CRADDOCK.

CRAIG, ROGER L
2617 SW Seabrook Ave, Topeka, KS 66614, Phone: 785-249-4109
Specialties: Working and camp knives, some fantasy; all his design. **Patterns:** Fighters, hunter. **Technical:** Grinds 1095 and 5160. Most knives have file work. **Prices:** $50 to $250. **Remarks:** Part-time maker; first knife sold in 1991. Doing business as Craig Knives. **Mark:** Last name-Craig.

CRAIN, JACK W
PO Box 212, Granbury, TX 76048, jack@jackcrainknives.com Web: www.jackcrainknives.com
Specialties: Fantasy and period knives; combat and survival knives. **Patterns:** One-of-a-kind art or fantasy daggers, swords and Bowies; survival knives. **Technical:** Forges Damascus; grinds stainless steel. Carves. **Prices:** $350 to $2500; some to $20,000. **Remarks:** Full-time maker; first knife sold in 1969. Designer and maker of the knives seen in the films Dracula 2000, Executive Decision, Demolition Man, Predator I and II, Commando, Die Hard I and II, Road House, Ford Fairlane and Action Jackson, and television shows War of the Worlds, Air Wolf, Kung Fu: The Legend Cont. and Tales of the Crypt. **Mark:** Stylized crane.

CRAMER, BRENT
PO BOX 99, Wheatland, IN 47597, Phone: 812-881-9961, Bdcramer@juno.com Web: BDCramerKnives.com
Specialties: Traditional and custom working and using knives. **Patterns:** Traditional single blade slip-joint folders and standard fixed blades. **Technical:** Stock removal only. Pivot bushing construction on folders. Steel: D-2, 154 CM, ATS-34, CPM-D2, CPM-154CM, O-1, 52100, A-2. All steels heat treated in shop with LN Cryo. Handle Material: Stag, Bone, Wood, Ivory, and Micarta. **Prices:** $150 - $550. **Remarks:** Part-time maker. First fixed blade sold in 2003. First folder sold in 2007. **Mark:** BDC and B.D.Cramer.

CRAWFORD, PAT AND WES
205 N. Center, West Memphis, AR 72301, Phone: 870-732-2452, patcrawford1@earthlink.net; Web: www.crawfordknives.com
Specialties: Stainless steel Damascus. High-tech working self-defense and combat types and folders. **Patterns:** Tactical-more fancy knives now. **Technical:** Grinds S30V. **Prices:** $400 to $2000. **Remarks:** Full-time maker; first knife sold in 1973. **Mark:** Last name.

CRAWLEY, BRUCE R
16 Binbrook Dr, Croydon, VIC, AUSTRALIA 3136
Specialties: Folders. **Patterns:** Hunters, lockback folders and Bowies. **Technical:** Grinds 440C, ATS-34 and commercial Damascus. Offers filework and mirror polish. **Prices:** $160 to $3500. **Remarks:** Part-time maker; first knife sold in 1990. **Mark:** Initials.

CRENSHAW, AL
Rt 1 Box 717, Eufaula, OK 74432, Phone: 918-452-2128
Specialties: Folders of his design and in standard patterns. **Patterns:** Hunters, locking folders, slip-joint folders, multi blade folders. **Technical:** Grinds 440C, D2 and ATS-34. Does filework on back springs and blades; offers scrimshaw on some handles. **Prices:** $150 to $300; some higher. **Remarks:** Full-time maker; first knife sold in 1981. Doing

business as A. Crenshaw Knives. **Mark:** First initial, last name, Lake Eufaula, state stamped; first initial last name in rainbow; Lake Eufaula across bottom with Okla. in middle.

CREWS, RANDY
627 Cricket Trail Rd., Patriot, OH 45658, Phone: 740-379-2329, randy.crews@sbcglobal.net

Specialties: Fixed blades, bowies and hunters. **Technical:** 440C, Alabama Damascus, 1095 with file work. Stock removal method. **Prices:** Start at $150. **Remarks:** Collected knives for 30 years. Part-time maker; first knife made in 2002. **Mark:** Crews Patriot OH.

CRIST, ZOE
2274 Deep Gap Rd., Flat Rock, NC 28731, Phone: 828-275-6689, zoe@zoecristknives.com Web: www.zoecristknives.com

Specialties: San mai and stainless steel. Custom damascus and traditional damascus working and art knives. Also makes Mokume. Works to customer specs. **Patterns:** All damascus hunters, bowies, fighters, neck, boot and high-end art knives. **Technical:** Makes all his own damascus steel from 1095, L6, 15n20. Forges all knives, heat treats, filework, differential heat treating. **Prices:** $150 - $2500. **Remarks:** Full-time maker, has been making knives since 1988, went full-time 2009. Also makes own leather sheaths. **Mark:** Small "z" with long tail on left side of blade at ricasso.

CROCKFORD, JACK
1859 Harts Mill Rd, Chamblee, GA 30341, Phone: 770-457-4680

Specialties: Lockback folders. **Patterns:** Hunters, fishing and camp knives, traditional folders. **Technical:** Grinds A2, D2, ATS-34 and 440C. Engraves and scrimshaws. **Prices:** Start at $175. **Remarks:** Part-time maker; first knife sold in 1975. **Mark:** Name.

CROSS, KEVIN
5 Pear Orchard Rd., Portland, CT 06480, Phone: 860-894-2385, kevincross@comcast.net; Web: www.kevincrossknives.com

Specialties: Working/using and presentation grade fixed-blade knives and custom kitchen knives. **Patterns:** Hunters, skinners, fighters. Bowies, camp knives. **Technical:** Stock removal maker. Uses O1, 1095, 154 CPM as well as Damascus from Eggerling, Ealy, Donnelly, Nichols, Thomas and others. Most handles are natural materials such as burled and spalted woods, stag and ancient ivory. **Prices:** $200 - $1,200. **Remarks:** Part-time maker. First knife sold around 1997. **Mark:** Name.

CROSS, ROBERT
RMB 200B, Manilla Rd, Tamworth, NSW, AUSTRALIA 2340, Phone: 067-618385

CROTTS, DAN
PO Box 68, Elm Springs, AR 72728, Phone: 479-422-7874, dancrottsknives@yahoo.com Web: www.facebook.com/dancrottsknives

Specialties: User grade, hunting, tactical and folders. **Technical:** High-end tool steel. **Prices:** $2200. **Remarks:** Specializes in making performance blades. **Mark:** Crotts.

CROUCH, BUBBA
POB 461, Pleasanton, TX 78064, Phone: 210-846-6890, tommycrouch69@gmail.com; Web: FaceBook Crouch Custom Knives

Specialties: Slip joints, straight blades. **Patterns:** Case style. Offers filework. **Technical:** ATS-34, CPM 154 and commercial damascus. Using stag, bone and mammoth ivory handle material. **Prices:** $250 to $1,200. **Remarks:** Part-time maker, first knife sold in 2010. **Mark:** Crouch.

CROWDER, GARY L
112480 S. 4614 Rd.., Sallisaw, OK 74955, Phone: 918-775-9009, gcrowder99@yahoo.com

Specialties: Folders, multi-blades. **Patterns:** Traditional with a few sheath knives. **Technical:** Flat grinds ATS-34, D2 and others, as well as Damascus via stock-removal. **Prices:** $150 to $600. **Remarks:** Retired, part-time maker. First knife sold in 1994. **Mark:** small acid-etched "Crowder" on blade.

CROWDER, ROBERT
Box 1374, Thompson Falls, MT 59873, Phone: 406-827-4754

Specialties: Traditional working knives to customer specs. **Patterns:** Hunters, Bowies, fighters and fillets. **Technical:** Grinds ATS-34, 154CM, 440C, Vascowear and commercial Damascus. **Prices:** $225 to $500; some to $2500. **Remarks:** Full-time maker; first knife sold in 1985. **Mark:** R Crowder signature & Montana.

CROWELL, JAMES L
676 Newnata Cutoff, Mtn. View, AR 72560, Phone: 870-746-4215, crowellknives@yahoo.com; Web: www.crowellknives.com

Specialties: Bowie knives; fighters and working knives. **Patterns:** Hunters, fighters, Bowies, daggers and folders. Period pieces: War hammers, Japanese and European. **Technical:** Forges 10 series carbon steels as well as O1, L6, W2 and his own damascus. "Flame painted" hamons (temper lines). **Prices:** $525 to $5,500; some to $8,500. **Remarks:** Full-time maker; first knife sold in 1980. Earned ABS Master Bladesmith in 1986. 2016 Marked 30 years as an ABS master smith. **Mark:** A shooting star.

CROWL, PETER
5786 County Road 10, Waterloo, IN 46793, Phone: 260-488-2532, pete@petecrowlknives.com; Web: www.petecrowlknives.com

Specialties: Bowie, hunters. **Technical:** Forges 5160, 1080, W2, 52100. **Prices:** $200 and up. **Remarks:** ABS Journeyman smith. **Mark:** Last name in script.

CROWNER, JEFF
2621 Windsor Pl., Plano, TX 75075, Phone: 541-201-3182, Fax: 541-579-3762

Specialties: Custom knife maker. I make some of the following: wilderness survival blades, martial art weapons, hunting blades. **Technical:** I differentially heat treat every knife. I use various steels like 5160, L-6, Cable Damascus, 52100, 6150, and some stainless types. I use the following for handle materials: TeroTuf by Columbia Industrial products and exotic hardwoods and horn. I make my own custom sheaths as well with either kydex or leather.

CROWTHERS, MARK F
PO Box 4641, Rolling Bay, WA 98061-0641, Phone: 206-842-7501

CUCCHIARA, MATT
387 W. Hagler, Fresno, CA 93711, Phone: 559-917-2328, matt@cucchiaraknives.com Web: www.cucchiaraknives.com

Specialties: I make large and small, plain or hand carved Ti handled Tactical framelock folders. All decoration and carving work done by maker. Also known for my hand carved Ti pocket clips. **Prices:** Start at around $400 and go as high as $1500 or so.

CULHANE, SEAN K.
8 Ranskroon Dr., Horizon, Roodepoort, 1740, SOUTH AFRICA, Phone: +27 82 453-1741, sculhane@wbs.co.za; www.culhaneknives.co.za

Specialties: Traditional working straight knives and folders in standard patterns and to customer specifications. **Patterns:** Fighters, hunters, kitchen cutlery, utility and Scottish dirks and sgian dubhs. **Technical:** Hollow grinding Sandvik 12C27 and commercial damascus. Full process, including heat treating and sheaths done by maker. **Prices:** From $180 up, depending on design and materials. **Remarks:** Part-time maker; first knife sold in 1988. **Mark:** First and surname in Gothic script curved over the word "Maker."

CULVER, STEVE
5682 94th St, Meriden, KS 66512, Phone: 785-230-2505, Web: www.culverart.com; Facebook: Steve Culver Knives; YouTube: SteveCulverMS1

Specialties: Edged weapons. Spiral-welded damascus gun barrels, collectible and functional. **Patterns:** Bowies, daggers, hunters, folders and combination weapons. **Technical:** Forges carbon steels and his own damascus. Stock removal of stainless steel for some folders. **Prices:** $500 to $50,000. **Remarks:** Full-time maker; also builds muzzle-loading pistols. **Mark:** Last name, MS.

CUMMING, BOB
CUMMING KNIVES, 35 Manana Dr, Cedar Crest, NM 87008, Phone: 505-286-0509, cumming@comcast.net; Web: www.cummingknives.com

Specialties: One-of-a-kind exhibition grade custom Bowie knives, exhibition grade and working hunters, bird & trout knives, salt and fresh water fillet knives. Low country oyster knives, custom tanto's plains Indian style sheaths & custom leather, all types of exotic handle materials, scrimshaw and engraving. Added folders in 2006. Custom oyster knives. **Prices:** $95 to $3500 and up. **Remarks:** Mentored by the late Jim Nolen, sold first knife in 1978 in Denmark. Retired U.S. Foreign Service Officer. Member NCCKG. **Mark:** Stylized CUMMING.

CURTISS, DAVID
Curtiss Knives, PO Box 902, Granger, IN 46530, Phone: 574-651-2158, david@curtissknives.com; Web: www.curtissknives.com

Specialties: Specialize in custom tactical-style folders and flipper folders, with some of the best sellers being in the Nano and Cruze series. The Nano is now being produced by Boker Knives. Many new knife designs coming soon.

CURTISS, STEVE L
PO Box 448, Eureka, MT 59914, Phone: 406-889-5510, Fax: 406-889-5510, slc@bladerigger.com; Web: http://www.bladerigger.com

Specialties: True custom and semi-custom production (SCP), specialized concealment blades; advanced sheaths and tailored body harnessing systems. **Patterns:** Tactical/personal defense fighters, swords, utility and custom patterns. **Technical:** Grinds A2 and Talonite®; heat-treats. Sheaths: Kydex or Kydex-lined leather laminated or Kydex-lined with Rigger Coat™. Exotic materials available. **Prices:** $50 to $10,000. **Remarks:** Full-time maker. Doing business as Blade Rigger L.L.C. Martial artist and unique defense industry tools and equipment. **Mark:** For true custom: Initials and for SCP: Blade Rigger.

D

DAILEY, G E
577 Lincoln St, Seekonk, MA 02771, Phone: 508-336-5088, gedailey@msn.com; Web: www.gedailey.com

Specialties: One-of-a-kind exotic designed edged weapons. **Patterns:** Folders, daggers and swords. **Technical:** Reforges and grinds Damascus; prefers hollow-grinding. Engraves, carves, offers filework and sets stones and uses exotic gems and gold. **Prices:** Start at $1100. **Remarks:** Full-time maker. First knife sold in 1982. **Mark:** Last name or stylized initialed logo.

DAKE, C M
19759 Chef Menteur Hwy, New Orleans, LA 70129-9602, Phone: 504-254-0357, Fax: 504-254-9501

Specialties: Fancy working folders. **Patterns:** Front-lock lockbacks, button-lock folders. **Technical:** Grinds ATS-34 and Damascus. **Prices:** $500 to $2500; some higher. **Remarks:** Full-time maker; first knife sold in 1988. Doing business as Bayou Custom Cutlery. **Mark:** Last name.

DAKE, MARY H
Rt 5 Box 287A, New Orleans, LA 70129, Phone: 504-254-0357

DALEY, MARK
P.O. Box 427, Waubaushene, Ontario, CANADA L0K 2C0, Phone: 705-543-1080, mark@markdaleyknives.com

Specialties: Art knives with handles made of stainless steel, bronze, gold, silver, pearl and Shibuichi. Many of the maker's knives are also textured and/or carved. **Mark:** Engraved "Mark Daley" or chiseled initials "MD."

DALLYN, KELLY

124 Deerbrook Place S.E., Calgary, AB, CANADA T2J 6J5, Phone: 403-475-3056, info@dallyn-knives.com Web: dallyn-knives.com
Specialties: Kitchen, utility, and hunting knives

DALY, MICHAEL

9728 3rd Ave., Brooklyn, NY 11209, Phone: 718-748-7796, sifubayridge@aol.com
Specialties: Tactical/utility and EDC (everyday carry) fixed blades. **Technical:** Stock removal method of blade making using ATS-34 and 154CM steels, and linen and paper Micarta handles. **Remarks:** Began making knives as a hobby in 2009 under the guidance of Marcus Clinco and Bill Herndon. Member of the California Knifemakers Association. **Mark:** Last name in a Chinese seal.

DAMLOVAC, SAVA

10292 Bradbury Dr, Indianapolis, IN 46231, Phone: 317-839-4952
Specialties: Period pieces, fantasy, Viking, Moran type all Damascus daggers. **Patterns:** Bowies, fighters, daggers, Persian-style knives. **Technical:** Uses own Damascus, some stainless, mostly hand forges. **Prices:** $150 to $2500; some higher. **Remarks:** Full-time maker; first knife sold in 1993. Specialty, Bill Moran all Damascus dagger sets, in Moran-style wood case. **Mark:** "Sava" stamped in Damascus or etched in stainless.

D'ANDREA, JOHN

8517 N Linwood Loop, Citrus Springs, FL 34433-5045, Phone: 352-489-2803, shootist1@tampabay.rr.com
Specialties: Fancy working straight knives and folders with filework and distinctive leatherwork. **Patterns:** Hunters, fighters, daggers, folders and an occasional sword. **Technical:** Grinds ATS-34, 154CM, 440C and D2. **Prices:** $220 to $1000. **Remarks:** Part-time maker; first knife sold in 1986. **Mark:** First name, last initial imposed on samurai sword.

D'ANGELO, LAURENCE

14703 NE 17th Ave, Vancouver, WA 98686, Phone: 360-573-0546
Specialties: Straight knives of his design. **Patterns:** Bowies, hunters and locking folders. **Technical:** Grinds D2, ATS-34 and 440C. Hand makes all sheaths. **Prices:** $100 to $200. **Remarks:** Full-time maker; first knife sold in 1987. **Mark:** Football logo—first and middle initials, last name, city, state, Maker.

DANIEL, TRAVIS E

PO Box 1223, Thomaston, GA 30286, Phone: 706-601-6418, dtravis405@gmail.com
Specialties: Traditional working straight knives of his design or to customer specs. **Patterns:** Hunters, fighters and utility/camp knives. **Technical:** Grinds ATS-34, 440-C, 154CM, forges his own Damascus. Stock removal. **Prices:** $125 to $500. **Remarks:** Full-time maker; first knife sold in 1976. **Mark:** TED.

DANIELS, ALEX

1416 County Rd 415, Town Creek, AL 35672, Phone: 256-685-0943, akdknives@gmail.com; Web: http://alexdanielscustomknives.com
Specialties: Working and using straight knives and folders; period pieces, reproduction Bowies. **Patterns:** Mostly reproduction Bowies but offers full line of knives. **Technical:** BG-42, 440C, 1095, 52100 forged blades. **Prices:** $350 to $5500. **Remarks:** Full-time maker; first knife sold in 1963. **Mark:** First and middle initials, last name, city and state.

DARBY, DAVID T

30652 S 533 Rd, Cookson, OK 74427, Phone: 918-457-4868, knfmkr@fullnet.net
Specialties: Forged blades only, all styles. **Prices:** $350 and up. **Remarks:** ABS Journeyman Smith. **Mark:** Stylized quillion dagger incorporates last name (Darby).

DARBY, JED

7878 E Co Rd 50 N, Greensburg, IN 47240, Phone: 812-663-2696
Specialties: Traditional working/using straight knives of his design and to customer specs. **Patterns:** Bowies, hunters and utility/camp knives. **Technical:** Grinds 440C, ATS-34 and Damascus. **Prices:** $70 to $550; some to $1000. **Remarks:** Full-time maker; first knife sold in 1992. Doing business as Darby Knives. **Mark:** Last name and year.

DARBY, RICK

71 Nestingrock Ln, Levittown, PA 19054
Specialties: Working straight knives. **Patterns:** Boots, fighters and hunters with mirror finish. **Technical:** Grinds 440C and CPM440V. **Prices:** $125 to $300. **Remarks:** Part-time maker; first knife sold in 1974. **Mark:** First and middle initials, last name.

DARCEY, CHESTER L

1608 Dominik Dr, College Station, TX 77840, Phone: 979-696-1656, DarceyKnives@yahoo.com
Specialties: Lockback, LinerLock® and scale release folders. **Patterns:** Bowies, hunters and utilities. **Technical:** Stock removal on carbon and stainless steels, forge own Damascus. **Prices:** $200 to $1000. **Remarks:** Part-time maker, first knife sold in 1999. **Mark:** Last name in script.

DARK, ROBERT

2218 Huntington Court, Oxford, AL 36203, Phone: 256-831-4645, dark@darkknives.com; Web: www.darkknives.com
Specialties: Fixed blade working knives of maker's designs. Works with customer designed specifications. **Patterns:** Hunters, Bowies, camp knives, kitchen/utility, bird and trout. Standard patterns and customer designed. **Technical:** Forged and stock removal. Works with high carbon, stainless and Damascus steels. Hollow and flat grinds. **Prices:** $175 to $750. **Remarks:** Sole authorship knives and custom leather sheaths. Full-time maker. **Mark:** "R Dark" on left side of blade.

DARPINIAN, DAVE

PO Box 2643, Olathe, KS 66063, Phone: 913-244-7114, darpo1956@yahoo.com

Web: www.kansasknives.org
Specialties: Hunters and Persian fighters with natural handle materials. **Patterns:** Full range of straight knives including art daggers. **Technical:** Art grinds own damascus and purchased damascus. Creates clay-tempered hamon on 1095 blade steel. **Prices:** $300 to $1000. **Remarks:** First knife sold in 1986, part-time maker, member of ABS and KCKA. **Mark:** Last name on the spline.

DAVIDSON, EDMUND

3345 Virginia Ave, Goshen, VA 24439, Phone: 540-997-5651, davidson.edmund@gmail.com; Web: www.edmunddavidson.com
Specialties: High class art integrals. **Patterns:** Many hunters and art models. **Technical:** CPM 154-CM. **Prices:** $100 to infinity. **Remarks:** Full-time maker; first knife sold in 1986. **Mark:** Name in deer head or custom logos.

DAVIDSON, SCOTT

SOLID ROCK KNIVES, 149 Pless Cir., Alto, GA 30510, Phone: 678-316-1318, Fax: 770-869-0882, solidrockknives@bellsouth.net
Specialties: Tactical knives, some hunters, skinners, bird-and-trout and neck knives. **Technical:** Stock-removal method of blade making, using CPM S30V, 440C and ATS-34 steels, also O1 and 1095HC tool steels. **Prices:** $100 to $1,200, depending on materials used. **Remarks:** Part-time maker; first knife made in 1996. **Mark:** "Ichthys," the Christian fish, with maker's name and address in or around the fish.

DAVIS, BARRY L

4262 US 20, Castleton, NY 12033, Phone: 518-477-5036, daviscustomknives@yahoo.com
Specialties: Collector grade Damascus folders. Traditional designs with focus on turn-of-the-century techniques employed. Sole authorship. Forges own Damascus, does all carving, filework, gold work and piquet. Uses only natural handle material. Enjoys doing multi-blade as well as single blade folders and daggers. **Prices:** Prices range from $2000 to $7000. **Remarks:** First knife sold in 1980.

DAVIS, CHARLIE

ANZA KNIVES, PO Box 457, Lakeside, CA 92040-9998, Phone: 619-561-9445, Fax: 619-390-6283, sales@anzaknives.com; Web: www.anzaknives.com
Specialties: Fancy and embellished working straight knives of his design. **Patterns:** Hunters, camp and utility knives. **Technical:** Grinds high-carbon files. **Prices:** $20 to $185, custom depends. **Remarks:** Full-time maker; first knife sold in 1980. Now offers custom. **Mark:** ANZA U.S.A.

DAVIS, DON

8415 Coyote Run, Loveland, CO 80537-9665, Phone: 970-669-9016, Fax: 970-669-8072
Specialties: Working straight knives in standard patterns or to customer specs. **Patterns:** Hunters, utility knives, skinners and survival knives. **Technical:** Grinds 440C, ATS-34. **Prices:** $75 to $250. **Remarks:** Full-time maker; first knife sold in 1985. **Mark:** Signature, city and state.

DAVIS, JESSE W

3853 Peyton Rd., Coldwater, MS 38618, Phone: 901-849-7250, jessewdavis@yahoo.com
Specialties: Working straight knives and boots in standard patterns and to customer specs. **Patterns:** Boot knives, daggers, fighters, subhilts & Bowies. **Technical:** Grinds A2, D2, 440C and commercial Damascus. **Prices:** $125 to $1000. **Remarks:** Full-time maker; first knife sold in 1977. Former member Knifemakers Guild (in good standing). **Mark:** Name or initials.

DAVIS, JOEL

74538 165th, Albert Lea, MN 56007, Phone: 507-377-0808, joelknives@yahoo.com
Specialties: Complete sole authorship presentation grade highly complex pattern-welded mosaic Damascus blade and bolster stock. **Patterns:** To date Joel has executed over 900 different mosaic Damascus patterns in the past four years. Anything conceived by maker's imagination. **Technical:** Uses various heat colorable "high vibrancy" steels, nickel 200 and some powdered metal for bolster stock only. Uses 1095, 1075 and 15N20. High carbon steels for cutting edge blade stock only. **Prices:** 15 to $50 per square inch and up depending on complexity of pattern. **Remarks:** Full-time mosaic Damascus metal smith focusing strictly on never-before-seen mosaic patterns. Most of maker's work is used for art knives ranging between $1500 to $4500.

DAVIS, JOHN

235 Lampe Rd, Selah, WA 98942, Phone: 509-697-3845, 509-945-4570, jdwelds@charter.net
Specialties: Damascus and mosaic Damascus, working knives, working folders, art knives and art folders. **Technical:** Some ATS-34 and stainless Damascus. Embellishes with fancy stabilized wood, mammoth and walrus ivory. **Prices:** Start at $150. **Remarks:** Part-time maker; first knife sold in 1996. **Mark:** Name city and state on Damascus stamp initials; name inside back RFR.

DAVIS, JOHN H.

33842 Picciola Dr., Fruitland Park, FL 34731, Phone: 209-740-7125, jdavis@custom-knifemaker.com; Web: www.custom-knifemaker.com
Patterns: Daggers, bowies, drop-point hunters, bird & trout knives, folding knives and custom orders. **Technical:** Forged knives primarily, but does some stock removal, makes own damascus steel using 1095 and 15N20, and also uses 52100, W2, CPM 154 stainless steel and 440C. **Prices:** $250 and up. **Remarks:** Part-time maker; first knife made in high school in 1977. Voting member of the Knifemakers' Guild and an ABS member, also president and treasurer for the Florida Knifemakers' Association. **Mark:** JD with a cross bar for the "H" between the "JD" and "Davis" under it.

DAVIS, STEVE
3370 Chatsworth Way, Powder Springs, GA 30127, Phone: 770-427-5740, bsdavis@bellsouth.net
Specialties: Gents and ladies folders. **Patterns:** Straight knives, slip-joint folders, locking-liner folders. **Technical:** Grinds ATS-34 forges own Damascus. Offers filework; prefers hand-rubbed finishes and natural handle materials. Uses pearl, ivory, stag and exotic woods. **Prices:** $250 to $800; some to $1500. **Remarks:** Full-time maker; first knife sold in 1988. Doing business as Custom Knives by Steve Davis. **Mark:** Name engraved on blade.

DAVIS JR., JIM
5129 Ridge St, Zephyrhills, FL 33541, Phone: 813-779-9213 813-469-4241 Cell, jimdavisknives@aol.com
Specialties: Presentation-grade fixed blade knives w/composite hidden tang handles. Employs a variety of ancient and contemporary ivories. **Patterns:** One-of-a-kind gents, personal, and executive knives and hunters w/unique cam-lock pouch sheaths and display stands. **Technical:** Flat grinds ATS-34 and stainless Damascus w/most work by hand w/assorted files. **Prices:** $300 and up. **Remarks:** Full-time maker, first knives sold in 2000. **Mark:** Signature w/printed name over "HANDCRAFTED."

DAVISON, TODD A.
230 S. Wells St., Kosciusko, MS 39090, Phone: 662-739-7440, crazyknifeblade@yahoo.com; Web: www.tadscustomknives.com
Specialties: Making working/using and collector folders of his design. All knives are truly made one of a kind. Each knife has a serial number inside the liner. **Patterns:** Single and double blade traditional slip-joint pocket knives. **Technical:** Free hand hollow ground blades, hand finished. Using only the very best materials possible. Holding the highest standards to fit & finish and detail. Does his own heat treating. ATS34 and D2 steel. **Prices:** $450 to $900, some higher. **Remarks:** Full time maker, first knife sold in 1981. **Mark:** T.A. DAVISON USA.

DAWKINS, DUDLEY L
221 NW Broadmoor Ave., Topeka, KS 66606-1254, Phone: 785-817-9343, dawkind@reagan.com or dawkind@sbcglobal.net
Specialties: Stylized old or "Dawkins Forged" with anvil in center. New tang stamps. **Patterns:** Straight knives. **Technical:** Mostly carbon steel; some Damascus-all knives forged. **Prices:** Knives: $275 and up; Sheaths: $95 and up. **Remarks:** All knives supplied with wood-lined sheaths. ABS Member, sole authorship. **Mark:** Stylized "DLD or Dawkins Forged with anvil in center.

DAWSON, BARRY
7760 E Hwy 69, Prescott Valley, AZ 86314, Phone: 928-255-9830, dawsonknives@yahoo.com; Web: www.dawsonknives.com
Specialties: Samurai swords, combat knives, collector daggers, tactical, folding and hunting knives. **Patterns:** Offers over 60 different models. **Technical:** Grinds 440C, ATS-34, own heat-treatment. **Prices:** $75 to $1500; some to $5000. **Remarks:** Full-time maker; first knife sold in 1975. **Mark:** Last name, USA in print or last name in script.

DAWSON, LYNN
7760 E Hwy 69 #C-5 157, Prescott Valley, AZ 86314, Phone: 928-713-2812, lynnknives@yahoo.com; Web: www.lynnknives.com
Specialties: Swords, hunters, utility, and art pieces. **Patterns:** Over 25 patterns to choose from. **Technical:** Grinds 440C, ATS-34, own heat treating. **Prices:** $80 to $1000. **Remarks:** Custom work and her own designs. **Mark:** The name "Lynn" in print or script.

DE BRAGA, JOSE C.
1341 9e Rue, Trois Rivieres, QC, CANADA G8Y 2Z2, Phone: 418-948-5864, josedebraga@cgocable.ca
Specialties: Art knives, fantasy pieces and working knives of his design or to customer specs. **Patterns:** Knives with sculptured or carved handles, from miniatures to full-size working knives. **Technical:** Grinds and hand-files 440C and ATS-34. A variety of steels and handle materials available. Offers lost wax casting. **Prices:** Start at $300. **Remarks:** Full-time maker; wax modeler, sculptor and knifemaker; first knife sold in 1984. **Mark:** Initials in stylized script and serial number.

DE MARIA JR., ANGELO
12 Boronda Rd, Carmel Valley, CA 93924, Phone: 831-659-3381, Fax: 831-659-1315, angelodemaria1@mac.com
Specialties: Damascus, fixed and folders, sheaths. **Patterns:** Mosaic and random. **Technical:** Forging 5160, 1084 and 15N20. **Prices:** $200+. **Remarks:** Part-time maker. **Mark:** Angelo de Maria Carmel Valley, CA etch or AdM stamp.

DE MESA, JOHN
1565 W. Main St., STE. 208 #229, Lewisville, TX 75057, Phone: 972-310-3877, TogiArts@me.com; Web: http://togiarts.com/ and http://togiarts.com/CSC/index.html
Specialties: Japanese sword polishing. **Technical:** Traditional sword polishing of Japanese swords made by sword makers in Japan and U.S. **Prices:** Starting at $75 per inch. **Remarks:** Custom Swords Collaborations IN collaboration with Jose De Braga, we can mount Japanese style sword with custom carved handles, sword fittings and scabbards to customer specs.

DE WET, KOBUS
2601 River Road, Yakima, WA 98902, Phone: 509-728-3736, kobus@moderndamascus.com, Web: www.moderndamascus.com
Specialties: Working and art knives **Patterns:** Every knife is unique. Fixed blades and folders. Hunting, Bowie, Tactical and Utility knives. **Technical:** I enjoy forging my own damascus steel, mainly from 15N20 and 1084. I also use stock removal and stainless steels. **Prices:** Starting at $200 **Remarks:** Part time maker, started in 2007 **Mark:** Circled "K" / Modern Damascus - Kobus de Wet

DEAN, HARVEY J
3266 CR 232, Rockdale, TX 76567, Phone: 512-446-3111, Fax: 512-446-5060, dean@tex1.net; Web: www.harveydean.com
Specialties: Collectible, functional knives. **Patterns:** Bowies, hunters, folders, daggers, swords, battle axes, camp and combat knives. **Technical:** Forges 1095, O1 and his Damascus. **Prices:** $350 to $10,000. **Remarks:** Full-time maker; first knife sold in 1981. **Mark:** Last name and MS.

DEBAUD, JAKE
1309 Glyndon Dr., Plano, TX 75034, Phone: 972-741-6280, jake@debaudblades.com; Web: www.debaudknives.com
Specialties: Custom damascus art knives, hunting knives and tactical knives. **Technical:** A2, D2, 01, 1095 and some stainless if requested ATS-34 or 154CM and S30V. **Remarks:** Full-time maker. Have been making knives for three years.

DEBRAGA, JOVAN
141 Notre Dame des Victoir, Quebec, CANADA G2G 1J3, Phone: 418-997-0819/418-877-1915, jovancdebraga@msn.com
Specialties: Art knives, fantasy pieces and working knives of his design or to customer specs. **Patterns:** Knives with sculptured or carved handles, from miniatures to full-sized working knives. **Technical:** Grinds and hand-files 440C, and ATS-34. A variety of steels and handle materials available. **Prices:** Start at $300. **Remarks:** Full time maker. Sculptor and knifemaker. First knife sold in 2003. **Mark:** Initials in stylized script and serial number.

DEIBERT, MICHAEL
7570 Happy Hollow Rd., Trussville, AL 35173, Phone: 205-612-2359, mike@deibertknives.com; Web: deibertknives.com
Specialties: Working straight knives in full or hidden tangs, in mono or damascus steel. **Patterns:** Choppers, bowies, hunters and bird-and-trout knives. **Technical:** Makes own damascus, forges all blades and does own heat treating. **Remarks:** ABS journeyman smith, part-time maker. **Mark:** Flaming "D" over an anvil.

DEL RASO, PETER
28 Mayfield Dr, Mt. Waverly, VIC, AUSTRALIA 3149, Phone: 613 98060644, delraso@optusnet.com.au
Specialties: Fixed blades, some folders, art knives. **Patterns:** Daggers, Bowies, tactical, boot, personal and working knives. **Technical:** Grinds ATS-34, commercial Damascus and any other type of steel on request. **Prices:** $100 to $1500. **Remarks:** Part-time maker, first show in 1993. **Mark:** Maker's surname stamped.

DELAROSA, JIM
502 Fairview Cir., Waterford, WI 53185, Phone: 262-422-8604, D-knife@hotmail.com
Specialties: Working straight knives and folders of his design or customer specs. **Patterns:** Hunters, skinners, fillets, utility and locking folders. **Technical:** Grinds ATS-34, 440-C, D2, O1 and commercial Damascus. **Prices:** $100 to $500; some higher. **Remarks:** Part-time maker. **Mark:** First and last name.

DELL, WOLFGANG
Am Alten Berg 9, Owen-Teck, GERMANY D-73277, Phone: 49-7021-81802, wolfgang@dell-knives.de; Web: www.dell-knives.de
Specialties: Fancy high-art straight of his design and to customer specs. **Patterns:** Fighters, hunters, Bowies and utility/camp knives. **Technical:** Grinds ATS-34, RWL-34, Elmax, Damascus (Fritz Schneider). Offers high gloss finish and engraving. **Prices:** $500 to $1000; some to $1600. **Remarks:** Full-time maker; first knife sold in 1992. **Mark:** Hopi hand of peace.

DELLANA
STARLANI INT'L INC, 1135 Terminal Way Ste #209, Reno, NV 89502, Phone: 304-727-5512; 702-569-7827, 1dellana@gmail.com; Web: www.dellana.cc
Specialties: Collector grade fancy/embellished high art folders and art daggers. **Patterns:** Locking folders and art daggers. **Technical:** Forges her own Damascus and W-2. Engraves, does stone setting, filework, carving and gold/platinum fabrication. Prefers exotic, high karat gold, platinum, silver, gemstone and mother-of-pearl handle materials. **Prices:** Upscale. **Remarks:** Sole authorship, full-time maker, first knife sold in 1994. Also does one high art collaboration a year with Van Barnett. Member: Art Knife Invitational and ABS. **Mark:** First name.

DELONG, DICK
PO Box 1024, Centerville, TX 75833-1024, Phone: 903-536-1454
Specialties: Fancy working knives and fantasy pieces. **Patterns:** Hunters and small skinners. **Technical:** Grinds and files O1, D2, 440C and Damascus. Offers cocobolo and Osage orange for handles. **Prices:** Start at $50. **Remarks:** Part-time maker. Member of Art Knife Invitational. Voting member of Knifemakers Guild. Member of ABS. **Mark:** Last name; some unmarked.

DEMENT, LARRY
PO Box 1807, Prince Fredrick, MD 20678, Phone: 410-586-9011
Specialties: Fixed blades. **Technical:** Forged and stock removal. **Prices:** $75 to $200. **Remarks:** Affordable, good feelin', quality knives. Part-time maker.

DENNEHY, JOHN D
1142 52 Ave. Ct., Greeley, CO 80634, Phone: 970-218-7128, jddennehy@yahoo.com; Web: www.thewildirishrose.com
Specialties: Working straight knives, throwers, and leatherworker's knives. **Technical:** 440C, & O1, heat treats own blades, part-time maker, first knife sold in 1989. **Patterns:** Small hunting to presentation Bowies, leatherworks round and head knives. **Prices:** $200 and up. **Remarks:** Custom sheath maker, sheath making seminars at the Blade Show.

DENNING, GENO

CAVEMAN ENGINEERING, 135 Allenvalley Rd, Gaston, SC 29053, Phone: 803-794-6067, cden101656@aol.com; Web: www.cavemanengineering.com

Specialties: Mirror finish. **Patterns:** Hunters, fighters, folders. **Technical:** ATS-34, 440V, S-30-V D2. **Prices:** $100 and up. **Remarks:** Full-time maker since 1996. Sole income since 1999. Instructor at Montgomery Community College (Grinding Blades). A director of SCAK: South Carolina Association of Knifemakers. **Mark:** Troy NC.

DERESPINA, RICHARD

derespinaknives@yahoo.com; Web: www.derespinaknives.com

Specialties: Custom fixed blades and folders, Kris and Karambit. **Technical:** I use the stock removal method. Steels I use are S30V, 154CM, D2, 440C, BG42. Handles made of G10 particularly Micarta, etc. **Prices:** $150 to $550 depending on model. **Remarks:** Full-time maker. **Mark:** My etched logos are two, my last name and Brooklyn NY mark as well as the Star/Yin Yang logo. The star being both representative of various angles of attack common in combat as well as being three triangles, each points to levels of metaphysical understanding. The Yin and Yang have my company initials on each side D & K. Yin and Yang shows the ever present physics of life.

DERINGER, CHRISTOPH

625 Chemin Lower, Cookshire, QC, CANADA J0B 1M0, Phone: 819-345-4260, cdsab@sympatico.ca

Specialties: Traditional working/using straight knives and folders of his design and to customer specs. **Patterns:** Boots, hunters, folders, art knives, kitchen knives and utility/camp knives. **Technical:** Forges 5160, O1 and Damascus. Offers a variety of filework. **Prices:** Start at $250. **Remarks:** Full-time maker; first knife sold in 1989. **Mark:** Last name stamped/engraved.

DERR, HERBERT

413 Woodland Dr, St. Albans, WV 25177, Phone: 304-727-3866

Specialties: Damascus one-of-a-kind knives, carbon steels also. **Patterns:** Birdseye, ladder back, mosaics. **Technical:** All styles functional as well as artistically pleasing. **Prices:** $90 to $175 carbon, Damascus $250 to $800. **Remarks:** All Damascus made by maker. **Mark:** H.K. Derr.

DESAULNIERS, ALAIN

100 Pope Street, Cookshire, QC, CANADA J0B 1M0, pinklaperez@sympatico.ca Web: www.desoknives.com

Specialties: Mostly Loveless style knives. **Patterns:** Double grind fighters, hunters, daggers, etc. **Technical:** Stock removal, ATS-34, CPM. High-polished blades, tapered tangs, high-quality handles. **Remarks:** Full-time. Collaboration with John Young. **Prices:** $425 and up. **Mark:** Name and city in logo.

DESROSIERS, ADAM

PO Box 1954, Petersburg, AK 99833, Phone: 907-518-4570, adam@alaskablades.com Web: www.alaskablades.com

Specialties: High performance, forged, carbon steel and damascus camp choppers, and hunting knives. Hidden tang, full tang, and full integral construction. High performance heat treating. Knife designs inspired by life in Alaskan bush. **Technical:** Hand forges tool steels and damascus. Sole authorship. Full range of handle materials, micarta to Ivory. Preferred steels: W-2, O-1, L-6, 15n20, 1095. **Prices:** $200 - $3000. **Remarks:** ABS member. Has trained with Masters around the world. **Mark:** DrsRosiers over Alaska, underlined with a rose.

DESROSIERS, HALEY

PO Box 1954, Petersburg, AK 99833, Phone: 907-518-1416, haley@alaskablades.com Web: www.alaskablades.com

Specialties: Hunting knives, integrals and a few choppers, high performance.**Technical:** Hand forged blades designed for hard use, exotic wood, antler and ivory handles. **Prices:** $300 - $1500. **Remarks:** Forged first knife in 2001. Part-time bladesmith all year except for commercial fishing season. **Mark:** Capital HD.

DETMER, PHILLIP

14140 Bluff Rd, Breese, IL 62230, Phone: 618-526-4834, jpdetmer@att.net

Specialties: Working knives. **Patterns:** Bowies, daggers and hunters. **Technical:** Grinds ATS-34 and D2. **Prices:** $60 to $400. **Remarks:** Part-time maker; first knife sold in 1977. **Mark:** Last name with dagger.

DEUBEL, CHESTER J.

6211 N. Van Ark Rd., Tucson, AZ 85743, Phone: 520-440-7255, cjdeubel@yahoo.com; Web: www.cjdeubel.com

Specialties: Fancy working straight knives and folders of his or customer design, with intricate file work. **Patterns:** Fighters, Bowies, daggers, hunters, camp knives, and cowboy. **Technical:** Flat guard, hollow grind, antiqued, all types Damascus, 154cpm Stainsteel, high carbon steel, 440c Stainsteel. **Prices:** From $250 to $3500. **Remarks:** Started making part-time in 1980; went to full-time in 2000. Don Patch is my engraver. **Mark:** C.J. Deubel.

DEVERAUX, BUTCH

PO Box 1356, Riverton, WY 82501, Phone: 307-851-0601, bdeveraux@wyoming.com; Web: www.deverauxknives.com

Specialties: High-performance working straight knives. **Patterns:** Hunters, fighters, EDC's, miniatures and camp knives. **Technical:** Forged 52100 blade steel, brass guards, sheep-horn handles, as well as stag, cocobolo, she-oak and ironwood. **Prices:** $400 to $3,000. **Remarks:** Part-time maker; first knife sold in 2005. **Mark:** Deveraux on right ricasso.

DEYONG, CLARENCE

8716 Camelot Trace, Sturtevant, WI 53177, Phone: 630-465-6761, cmdeyong@yahoo.com; Web: www.deyongknives.com

Patterns: Mainly creates full-tang hunters, skinners and fighters. **Technical:** Stock removal with some forging, using rasps and files for blade stock with an emphasis on natural handle materials. **Prices:** $150 to $300 with custom sheaths. **Remarks:** Making knives since 1981. **Mark:** DeYong and blade # engraved on the blade.

DIAZ, JOSE

409 W. 12th Ave, Ellensburg, WA 98926, jose@diaztools.com Web: www.diaztools.com

Specialties: Affordable custom user-grade utility and camp knives. Also makes competition cutting knives. **Patterns:** Mas. **Technical:** Blade materials range from high carbon steels and Damascus to high performance tool and stainless steels. Uses both forge and stock removal methods in shaping the steel. Handle materials include Tero Tuf, Black Butyl Burl, Micarta, natural woods and G10. **Prices:** $65-$700. **Remarks:** Part-time knife maker; made first knife in 2008. **Mark:** Reclining tree frog with a smile, and "Diaz Tools."

DICK, DAN

P.O. Box 2303, Hutchinson, KS 67504-2303, Phone: 620-669-6805, Dan@DanDickKnives.com; Web: www.dandickknives.com

Specialties: Traditional working/using fixed bladed knives of maker's design. **Patterns:** Hunters, skinners and utility knives. **Technical:** Stock removal maker using CTS-XHP and D2. Prefers such materials as exotic and fancy burl woods. Makes his own sheaths, all leather with tooling. **Prices:** $150 and up. **Remarks:** Part-time maker since 2006. **Marks:** Name in outline border of Kansas.

DICKERSON, GAVIN

15 Anzac St., Primrose Ext. 2, Germiston, Gauteng, SOUTH AFRICA, Phone: +27 011-927-2469, Fax: +27 011-965-0988, gavind@denelaviation.co.za

Specialties: Straight knives of his design or to customer specs. **Patterns:** Hunters, skinners, fighters and Bowies. **Technical:** Hollow-grinds D2, 440C, ATS-34, 12C27 and Damascus upon request. Prefers natural handle materials; offers synthetic handle materials. **Prices:** $190 to $2500. **Remarks:** Part-time maker; first knife sold in 1982. **Mark:** Name in full.

DICKISON, SCOTT S

179 Taylor Rd, Portsmouth, RI 02871, Phone: 401-847-7398, squared22@cox .net; Web: http://sqauredknives.com

Specialties: Straight knives, locking folders and slip joints of his design. **Patterns:** Sgain dubh, bird and trout knives. **Technical:** Forges and grinds commercial Damascus, D2, O1 and sandvik stainless. **Prices:** $400 to $1000; some higher. **Remarks:** Part-time maker; first knife sold in 1989. **Mark:** Stylized initials.

DICRISTOFANO, ANTHONY P

10519 Nevada Ave., Melrose Park, IL 60164, Phone: 847-845-9598, sukemitsu@sbcglobal.net Web: www.namahagesword.com or www.sukemitsu.com

Specialties: Japanese-style swords. **Patterns:** Katana, Wakizashi, Otanto, Kozuka. **Technical:** Tradition and some modern steels. All clay tempered and traditionally hand polished using Japanese wet stones. **Remarks:** Part-time maker. **Prices:** Varied, available on request. **Mark:** Blade tang signed in "SUKEMITSU."

DIETZ, HOWARD

421 Range Rd, New Braunfels, TX 78132, Phone: 830-885-4662

Specialties: Lock-back folders, working straight knives. **Patterns:** Folding hunters, high-grade pocket knives. ATS-34, 440C, CPM 440V, D2 and stainless Damascus. **Prices:** $300 to $1000. **Remarks:** Full-time gun and knifemaker; first knife sold in 1995. **Mark:** Name, city, and state.

DIETZEL, BILL

779 Baycove Ct., Middleburg, FL 32068, Phone: 904-282-1091, wdms97@bellsouth.net

Specialties: Forged straight knives and folders. **Patterns:** His interpretations. **Technical:** Forges his Damascus and other steels. **Prices:** Middle ranges. **Remarks:** Likes natural materials; uses titanium in folder liners. Master Smith (1997). **Mark:** Name.

DIGANGI, JOSEPH M

PO Box 257, Los Ojos, NM 87551, Phone: 505-929-2987, Fax: 505-753-8144, Web: www.digangidesigns.com

Specialties: Kitchen and table cutlery. **Patterns:** French chef's knives, carving sets, steak knife sets, some camp knives and hunters. Holds patents and trademarks for "System II" kitchen cutlery set. **Technical:** Grinds ATS-34. **Prices:** $150 to $595; some to $1200. **Remarks:** Full-time maker; first knife sold in 1983. **Mark:** DiGangi Designs.

DILL, ROBERT

1812 Van Buren, Loveland, CO 80538, Phone: 970-667-5144, Fax: 970-667-5144, dillcustomknives@msn.com

Specialties: Fancy and working knives of his design. **Patterns:** Hunters, Bowies and fighters. **Technical:** Grinds 440C and D2. **Prices:** $100 to $800. **Remarks:** Full-time maker; first knife sold in 1984. **Mark:** Logo stamped into blade.

DINTRUFF, CHUCK

306 East S.R. 60, Plant City, FL 33567, Phone: 813-381-6916, DINTRUFFKNIVES@aol.com; Web: dintruffknives.com and spinwellfab.com

DION, GREG

3032 S Jackson St, Oxnard, CA 93033, Phone: 519-981-1033

Specialties: Working straight knives, some fancy. Welcomes special orders. **Patterns:** Hunters, fighters, camp knives, Bowies and tantos. **Technical:** Grinds ATS-34, 154CM and 440C. **Prices:** $85 to $300; some to $600. **Remarks:** Part-time maker; first knife sold in 1985. **Mark:** Name.

DIONATAM, FRANCO
Sebastiao Jacinto de Amorim goncalves n 277, Filadelfia, Ibitinga-SP, BRAZIL 14940-000, francofacasartesanais@hotmail.com
Patterns: Bowies, hunters, camp knives, utilitarian and chef's knives. **Technical:** Uses 5160, 1070, 52100 and several damascus steel patterns. Knife handle materials include stabilized wood, natural wood, mammoth ivory, deer horn and exotic materials. **Prices:** $700 to $6,000. **Remarks:** ABS journeyman smith who prefers working from orders. **Mark:** Franco.

DIOTTE, JEFF
DIOTTE KNIVES, 159 Laurier Dr, LaSalle, ON, CANADA N9J 1L4, Phone: 519-978-2764

DIPPOLD, AL
90 Damascus Ln, Perryville, MO 63775, Phone: 573-547-1119, adippold@midwest.net
Specialties: Fancy one-of-a-kind locking folders. **Patterns:** Locking folders. **Technical:** Forges and grinds mosaic and pattern welded Damascus. Offers filework on all folders. **Prices:** $500 to $3500; some higher. **Remarks:** Full-time maker; first knife sold in 1980. **Mark:** Last name in logo inside of liner.

DISKIN, MATT
PO Box 653, Freeland, WA 98249, Phone: 360-730-0451, info@volcanknives.com; Web: www.volcanknives.com
Specialties: Damascus autos. **Patterns:** Dirks and daggers. **Technical:** Forges mosaic Damascus using 15N20, 1084, 02, 06, L6; pure nickel. **Prices:** Start at $500. **Remarks:** Full-time maker. **Mark:** Last name.

DIXON JR., IRA E
PO Box 26, Cave Junction, OR 97523, irasknives@yahoo.com
Specialties: Straight knives of his design. **Patterns:** All patterns include art knives. **Technical:** Grinds CPM materials, Damascus and some tool steels. **Prices:** $275 to $2000. **Remarks:** Full-time maker; first knife sold in 1993. **Mark:** First name, Handmade.

DOBRATZ, ERIC
25371 Hillary Lane, Laguna Hills, CA 92653, Phone: 949-233-5170, knifesmith@gmail.com
Specialties: Differentially quenched blades with Hamon of his design or with customer input. **Patterns:** Hunting, camp, kitchen, fighters, bowies, traditional tanto, and unique fixed blade designs. **Technical:** Hand-forged high carbon and damascus. Prefers natural material for handles; rare/exotic woods and stag, but also uses micarta and homemade synthetic materials. **Prices:** $150 - $1500. **Remarks:** Part-time maker; first knife made in 1995. **Mark:** Stylized Scarab beetle.

DODD, ROBERT F
4340 E Canyon Dr, Camp Verde, AZ 86322, Phone: 928-567-3333, rfdknives@commspeed.net; Web: www.rfdoddknives.com
Specialties: Folders, fixed blade hunter/skinners, Bowies, daggers. **Patterns:** Drop point. **Technical:** ATS-34 and Damascus. **Prices:** $250 and up. **Remarks:** Hand tooled leather sheaths. **Mark:** R. F. Dodd, Camp Verde AZ.

DOIRON, DONALD
6 Chemin Petit Lac des Ced, Messines, QC, CANADA J0X-2J0, Phone: 819-465-2489

DOMINY, CHUCK
PO Box 593, Colleyville, TX 76034, Phone: 817-498-4527
Specialties: Titanium LinerLock® folders. **Patterns:** Hunters, utility/camp knives and LinerLock® folders. **Technical:** Grinds 440C and ATS-34. **Prices:** $250 to $3000. **Remarks:** Full-time maker; first knife sold in 1976. **Mark:** Last name.

DOOLITTLE, MIKE
13 Denise Ct, Novato, CA 94947, Phone: 415-897-3246
Specialties: Working straight knives in standard patterns. **Patterns:** Hunters and fishing knives. **Technical:** Grinds 440C, 154CM and ATS-34. **Prices:** $125 to $200; some to $750. **Remarks:** Part-time maker; first knife sold in 1981. **Mark:** Name, city and state.

DORNELES, DAVE
7404 NW 30th St, Bethany, OK 73008, Phone: 405-789-0750
Specialties: Folders of his design. **Patterns:** Various patterns. **Technical:** Hand-grinds 440C, ATS-34. Offers engraving and filework on all folders. **Prices:** Starting at $450. **Remarks:** Full-time maker; first knife sold in 1987. **Mark:** First initial, last name.

DORNELES, LUCIANO OLIVERIRA
Rua 15 De Novembro 2222, Nova Petropolis, RS, BRAZIL 95150-000, Phone: 011-55-54-303-303-90, tchebufalo@hotmail.com
Specialties: Traditional "true" Brazilian-style working knives and to customer specs. **Patterns:** Brazilian hunters, utility and camp knives, Bowies, Dirk. A master of the making of the true "Faca Campeira Gaucha," the true camp knife of the famous Brazilian Gauchos. A Dorneles knife is 100 percent hand-forged with sledge hammers only. Can make spectacular Damascus hunters/daggers. **Technical:** Forges only 52100 and his own Damascus, can put silver wire inlay on customer design handles on special orders; uses only natural handle materials. **Prices:** $250 to $1000. **Mark:** Symbol with L. Dorneles.

DOTSON, TRACY
1280 Hwy C-4A, Baker, FL 32531, Phone: 850-537-2407
Specialties: Folding fighters and small folders. **Patterns:** LinerLock® and lockback folders. **Technical:** Hollow-grinds ATS-34 and commercial Damascus. **Prices:** Start at $250. **Remarks:** Part-time maker; first knife sold in 1995. **Mark:** Last name.

DOUCETTE, R
CUSTOM KNIVES, 19 Evelyn St., Brantford, ON, CANADA N3R 3G8, Phone: 519-756-9040, randy@randydoucetteknives.com; Web: www.randydoucetteknives.com
Specialties: High-end tactical folders with filework and multiple grinds. **Patterns:** Tactical folders. **Technical:** All knives are handmade. The only outsourcing is heat treatment. **Prices:** $900 to $2,500. **Remarks:** Full-time knifemaker; 2-year waiting list. Maker is proud to produce original knife designs every year!Im **Mark:** R. Doucette

DOURSIN, GERARD
Chemin des Croutoules, Pernes les Fontaines, FRANCE 84210
Specialties: Period pieces. **Patterns:** Liner locks and daggers. **Technical:** Forges mosaic Damascus. **Prices:** $600 to $4000. **Remarks:** First knife sold in 1983. **Mark:** First initial, last name and I stop the lion.

DOUSSOT, LAURENT
1008 Montarville, St. Bruno, QC, CANADA J3V 3T1, Phone: 450-441-3298, doussot@skalja.com; Web: www.skalja.com, www.doussot-knives.com
Specialties: Fancy and embellished folders and fantasy knives. **Patterns:** Fighters and locking folders. **Technical:** Grinds ATS-34 and commercial Damascus. Scale carvings on all knives; most bolsters are carved titanium. **Prices:** $350 to $3000. **Remarks:** Part-time maker; first knife was sold in 1992. **Mark:** Stylized initials inside circle.

DOWNIE, JAMES T
1295 Sandy Ln., Apt. 1208, Sarnia, Ontario, CANADA N7V 4K5, Phone: 519-491-8234
Specialties: Serviceable straight knives and folders; period pieces. **Patterns:** Hunters, Bowies, camp knives, fillet and miniatures. **Technical:** Grinds D2, 440C and ATS-34, Damasteel, stainless steel Damascus. **Prices:** $195 and up. **Remarks:** Full-time maker, first knife sold in 1978. **Mark:** Signature of first and middle initials, last name.

DOWNING, LARRY
12268 State Route 181 N, Bremen, KY 42325, Phone: 270-525-3523, larrydowning@bellsouth.net; Web: www.downingknives.com
Specialties: Working straight knives and folders. **Patterns:** From mini-knives to daggers, folding lockers to interframes. **Technical:** Forges and grinds 154CM, ATS-34 and his own Damascus. **Prices:** $195 to $950; some higher. **Remarks:** Part-time maker; first knife sold in 1979. **Mark:** Name in arrowhead.

DOWNING, TOM
2675 12th St, Cuyahoga Falls, OH 44223, Phone: 330-923-7464
Specialties: Working straight knives; period pieces. **Patterns:** Hunters, fighters and tantos. **Technical:** Grinds 440C, ATs-34 and CPM-T-440V. Prefers natural handle materials. **Prices:** $150 to $900, some to $1500. **Remarks:** Part-time maker; first knife sold in 1979. **Mark:** First and middle initials, last name.

DOWNS, JAMES F
2247 Summit View Rd, Powell, OH 43065, Phone: 614-766-5350, jfdowns1@yahoo.com; Web: www.downshandmadeknives.com
Specialties: Working straight knives of his design or to customer specs. **Patterns:** Folders, Bowies, boot, hunters, utility. **Technical:** Grinds 440C and other steels. Prefers mastodon ivory, all pearls, stabilized wood and elephant ivory. **Prices:** $75 to $1200. **Remarks:** Full-time maker; first knife sold in 1980. **Mark:** Last name.

DOX, JAN
Zwanebloemlaan 27, Schoten, BELGIUM B 2900, Phone: 32 3 658 77 43, jan.dox@scarlet.be; Web: doxblades.weebly.com
Specialties: Working/using knives, from kitchen to battlefield. **Patterns:** Own designs, some based on traditional ethnic patterns (Scots, Celtic, Scandinavian and Japanese) or to customer specs. **Technical:** Grinds D2/A2 and stainless, forges carbon steels, convex edges. Handles: Wrapped in modern or traditional patterns, resin impregnated if desired. Natural or synthetic materials, some carved. **Prices:** $50 and up. **Remarks:** Spare-time maker, first knife sold 2001. **Mark:** Name or stylized initials.

DOYLE, JOHN
4779 W. M-61, Gladwin, MI 48624, Phone: 989-802-9470, jdoyleknives@gmail.com
Specialties: Hunters, camp knives and bowies. **Technical:** Forges 1075, 1080, 1084, 1095 and 5160. Will practice stock-removal method of blademaking on small knives at times. **Remarks:** Full-time maker; first knife made in 2009. **Mark:** J. Doyle in "Invitation" style print font

DOZIER, BOB
Dozier Knives and Arkansas Made Dozier, PO Box 1941, Springdale, AR 72765, Phone: 888-823-0023/479-756-0023, Fax: 479-756-9139, info@dozierknives.com; Web www.dozierknives.com
Specialties: Folding knives and collector-grade knives (Dozier Knives) and hunting and tactical fixed blades (Arkansas Dozier Made). **Technical:** Uses D2. **Prices:** Start at $205 (Arkansas Made Dozier) or $500 (Dozier Knives). **Remarks:** Full-time maker; first knife sold in 1965. **Mark:** Dozier with an arrow through the D and year over arrow for foldiers, or R.L. Dozier, maker, St. Paul, AR in an oval for the collector-grad knives (Dozier Knives); and Arkansas, Made, Dozier in a circle (Arkansas Dozier Made).

DRAPER, AUDRA
#10 Creek Dr, Riverton, WY 82501, Phone: 307-856-6807 or 307-851-0426 cell, adraper@wyoming.com; Web: www.draperknives.com
Specialties: One-of-a-kind straight and folding knives. Also pendants, earring and bracelets of Damascus. **Patterns:** Design custom knives, using, Bowies, and minis. **Technical:** Forge Damascus; heat-treats all knives. **Prices:** Vary depending on item. **Remarks:** Full-time maker; master bladesmith in the ABS. Member of the PKA; first knife sold in 1995. **Mark:** Audra.

DRAPER, MIKE
#10 Creek Dr, Riverton, WY 82501, Phone: 307-856-6807, adraper@wyoming.com
Specialties: Mainly folding knives in tactical fashion, occasonal fixed blade. **Patterns:**

Hunters, Bowies and camp knives, tactical survival. **Technical:** Grinds S30V stainless steel. **Prices:** Starting at $250+. **Remarks:** Full-time maker; first knife sold in 1996. **Mark:** Initials M.J.D. or name, city and state.

DREW, GERALD

213 Hawk Ridge Dr, Mill Spring, NC 28756, Phone: 828-713-4762
    Specialties: Blade ATS-34 blades. Straight knives. **Patterns:** Hunters, camp knives, some Bowies and tactical. **Technical:** ATS-34 preferred. **Prices:** $65 to $400. **Mark:** GL DREW.

DRISCOLL, MARK

4115 Avoyer Pl, La Mesa, CA 91941, Phone: 619-670-0695, markdriscoll91941@yahoo.com
    Specialties: High-art, period pieces and working/using knives of his design or to customer specs; some fancy. **Patterns:** Swords, Bowies, fighters, daggers, hunters and primitive (mountain man-styles). **Technical:** Forges 52100, 5160, O1, L6, 1095, 15n20, W-2 steel and makes his own Damascus and mokume; also does multiple quench heat treating. Uses exotic hardwoods, ivory and horn, offers fancy file work, carving, scrimshaws. **Prices:** $150 to $550; some to $1500. **Remarks:** Part-time maker; first knife sold in 1986. Doing business as Mountain Man Knives. **Mark:** Double "M."

DROST, JASON D

Rt 2 Box 49, French Creek, WV 26218, Phone: 304-472-7901
    Specialties: Working/using straight knives of his design. **Patterns:** Hunters and utility/camp knives. **Technical:** Grinds 154CM and D2. **Prices:** $125 to $5000. **Remarks:** Spare-time maker; first knife sold in 1995. **Mark:** First and middle initials, last name, maker, city and state.

DROST, MICHAEL B

Rt 2 Box 49, French Creek, WV 26218, Phone: 304-472-7901
    Specialties: Working/using straight knives and folders of all designs. **Patterns:** Hunters, locking folders and utility/camp knives. **Technical:** Grinds ATS-34, D2 and CPM-T-440V. Offers dove-tailed bolsters and spacers, filework and scrimshaw. **Prices:** $125 to $400; some to $740. **Remarks:** Full-time maker; first knife sold in 1990. Doing business as Drost Custom Knives. **Mark:** Name, city and state.

DRUMM, ARMIN

Lichtensteinstrasse 33, Dornstadt, GERMANY 89160, Phone: 49-163-632-2842, armin@drumm-knives.de; Web: www.drumm-knives.de
    Specialties: One-of-a-kind forged and Damascus fixed blade knives and folders. **Patterns:** Classic Bowie knives, daggers, fighters, hunters, folders, swords. **Technical:** Forges own Damascus and carbon steels, filework, carved handles. **Prices:** $250 to $800, some higher. **Remarks:** First knife sold in 2001, member of the German Knifemakers Guild. **Mark:** First initial, last name.

DUCKER, BRIAN

Lamorna Cottage, Common End, Colkirk, ENGLAND NR21 7JD, Phone: 01-328-856-183, admin@grommitbaileyknives.com; Web: www.grommitbaileyknives.com
    Specialties: Hunters, utility pieces, bowies, camp knives, fighters and folders. **Technical:** Stock removal and forged 1095, 1075 and 80CrV2. Forging own damascus, using exotic and native hardwoods, stag, leather, Micarta and other synthetic materials, with brass and 301 stainless steel fittings. Own leatherwork and heat treating. **Remarks:** Part-time maker since 2009, full time Dec. 2013. All knives and sheaths are sole authorship. **Mark:** GROMMIT UK MAKER & BAILEY GROMMIT MAKERS.

DUFF, BILL

2801 Ash St, Poteau, OK 74953, Phone: 918-647-4458
    Specialties: Straight knives and folders, some fancy. **Patterns:** Hunters, folders and miniatures. **Technical:** Grinds 440-C and commercial Damascus. **Prices:** $250 and up. **Remarks:** First knife sold in 1976. **Mark:** Bill Duff.

DUFOUR, ARTHUR J

8120 De Armoun Rd, Anchorage, AK 99516, Phone: 907-345-1701
    Specialties: Working straight knives from standard patterns. **Patterns:** Hunters, Bowies, camp and fishing knives—grinded thin and pointed. **Technical:** Grinds 440C, ATS-34, AEB-L. Tempers 57-58R; hollow-grinds. **Prices:** $135; some to $250. **Remarks:** Part-time maker; first knife sold in 1970. **Mark:** Prospector logo.

DUGDALE, DANIEL J.

11 Eleanor Road, Walpole, MA 02081, Phone: 508-404-6509, dlpdugdale@comcast.net
    Specialties: Button-lock and straight knives of his design. **Patterns:** Utilities, hunters, skinners, and tactical. **Technical:** Falt grinds D-2 and 440C, aluminum handles with anodized finishes. **Prices:** $150 to $500. **Remarks:** Part-time maker since 1977. **Mark:** Deer track with last name, town and state.

DUNCAN, RON

5090 N. Hwy. 63, Cairo, MO 65239, Phone: 660-263-8949, www.duncanmadeknives.com
    Remarks: Duncan Made Knives

DUNKERLEY, RICK

PO Box 601, Lincoln, MT 59639, Phone: 406-210-4101, dunkerleyknives@gmail.com Web: www.dunkerleyknives.com
    Specialties: Mosaic Damascus folders and carbon steel utility knives. **Patterns:** One-of-a-kind folders, standard hunters and utility designs. **Technical:** Forges 52100, Damascus and mosaic Damascus. Prefers natural handle materials. **Prices:** $200 and up. **Remarks:** Full-time maker; first knife sold in 1984, ABS Master Smith. Doing business as Dunkerley Custom Knives. Dunkerley handmade knives, sole authorship. **Mark:** Dunkerley, MS.

DUNLAP, JIM

800 E. Badger Lee Rd., Sallisaw, OK 74955, Phone: 918-774-2700, dunlapknives@gmail.com
    Specialties: Traditional slip-joint folders. **Patterns:** Single- and multi-blade traditional slip joints. **Technical:** Grinds ATS-34, CPM-154 and damascus. **Prices:** $250 and up. **Remarks:** Part-time maker; first knife sold in 2009. **Mark:** Dunlap.

DUNN, STEVE

376 Biggerstaff Rd, Smiths Grove, KY 42171, Phone: 270-563-9830, dunnknives@windstream.net; Web: www.stevedunnknives.com
    Specialties: Working and using straight knives of his design; period pieces. Offers engraving and gold inlay. **Patterns:** Hunters, skinners, Bowies, fighters, camp knives, folders, swords and battle axes. **Technical:** Forges own Damascus, 1075, 15N20, 52100, 1084, L6. **Prices:** Moderate to upscale. **Remarks:** Full-time maker; first knife sold in 1990. **Mark:** Last name and MS.

DURAN, JERRY T

PO Box 9753, Albuquerque, NM 87119, Phone: 505-873-4676, jtdknives@hotmail.com; Web: http://www.google.com/profiles/jtdknivesLLC
    Specialties: Tactical folders, Bowies, fighters, liner locks, autopsy and hunters. **Patterns:** Folders, Bowies, hunters and tactical knives. **Technical:** Forges own Damascus and forges carbon steel. **Prices:** Moderate to upscale. **Remarks:** Full-time maker; first knife sold in 1978. **Mark:** Initials in elk rack logo.

DURHAM, KENNETH

BUZZARD ROOST FORGE, 10495 White Pike, Cherokee, AL 35616, Phone: 256-359-4287, www.home.hiwaay.net/~jamesd/
    Specialties: Bowies, dirks, hunters. **Patterns:** Traditional patterns. **Technical:** Forges 1095, 5160, 52100 and makes own Damascus. **Prices:** $85 to $1600. **Remarks:** Began making knives about 1995. Received Journeyman stamp 1999. Got Master Smith stamp in 2004. **Mark:** Bull's head with Ken Durham above and Cherokee AL below.

DURIO, FRED

144 Gulino St, Opelousas, LA 70570, Phone: 337-948-4831/cell 337-351-2652, fdurio@yahoo.com
    Specialties: Folders. **Patterns:** Liner locks; plain and fancy. **Technical:** Makes own Damascus. **Prices:** Moderate to upscale. **Remarks:** Full-time maker. **Mark:** Last name-Durio.

DUVALL, FRED

10715 Hwy 190, Benton, AR 72015, Phone: 501-778-9360
    Specialties: Working straight knives and folders. **Patterns:** Locking folders, slip joints, hunters, fighters and Bowies. **Technical:** Grinds D2 and CPM440V; forges 5160. **Prices:** $100 to $400; some to $800. **Remarks:** Part-time maker; first knife sold in 1973. **Mark:** Last name.

DWYER, DUANE

565 Country Club Dr., Escondido, CA 92029, Phone: 760-471-8275, striderguys@striderknives.com; Web: www.striderknives.com
    Specialties: Primarily tactical. **Patterns:** Fixed and folders. **Technical:** Primarily stock removal specializing in highly technical materials. **Prices:** $100 and up, based on the obvious variables. **Remarks:** Full-time maker since 1996.

DYER, DAVID

4531 Hunters Glen, Granbury, TX 76048, Phone: 817-573-1198
    Specialties: Working skinners and early period knives. **Patterns:** Customer designs, his own patterns. **Technical:** Coal forged blades; 5160 and 52100 steels. Grinds D2, 1095, L6. **Prices:** $150 for neck knives and small (3" to 3-1/2"). To $600 for large blades and specialty blades. **Mark:** Last name DYER electro etched.

DYESS, EDDIE

1005 Hamilton, Roswell, NM 88201, Phone: 505-623-5599, eddyess@msn.com
    Specialties: Working and using straight knives in standard patterns. **Patterns:** Hunters and fighters. **Technical:** Grinds 440C, 154CM and D2 on request. **Prices:** $150 to $300, some higher. **Remarks:** Spare-time maker; first knife sold in 1980. **Mark:** Last name.

E

EAKER, ALLEN L

416 Clinton Ave Dept KI, Paris, IL 61944, Phone: 217-466-5160
    Specialties: Traditional straight knives and folders of his design. **Patterns:** Hunters, locking folders and slip-joint folders. **Technical:** Grinds 440C; inlays. **Prices:** $200 to $500. **Remarks:** Spare-time maker; first knife sold in 1994. **Mark:** Initials in tankard logo stamped on tang, serial number and surname on back.

EALY, DELBERT

PO Box 121, Indian River, MI 49749, Phone: 231-238-4705

EATON, FRANK L JR

5365 W. Meyer Rd., Farmington, MO 63640, Phone: 703-314-8708, eatontactical@me.com; Web: www.frankeatonknives.com
    Specialties: Full tang/hidden tang fixed working and art knives of his own design. **Patterns:** Hunters, skinners, fighters, Bowies, tacticals and daggers. **Technical:** Stock removal maker, prefer using natural materials. **Prices:** $175 to $400. **Remarks:** Part-time maker - Active Duty Airborn Ranger-Making 4 years. **Mark:** Name over 75th Ranger Regimental Crest.

EATON, RICK

313 Dailey Rd, Broadview, MT 59015, Phone: 406-667-2405, rick@eatonknives.com; Web: www.eatonknives.com
    Specialties: Interframe folders and one-hand-opening side locks. **Patterns:** Bowies, daggers, fighters and folders. **Technical:** Grinds 154CM, ATS-34, 440C and other maker's Damascus. Makes own mosaic Damascus. Offers high-quality hand engraving, Bulino and gold inlay. **Prices:** Upscale. **Remarks:** Full-time maker; first knife sold in 1982. **Mark:** Full name or full name and address.

custom knifemakers

EBISU, HIDESAKU
3-39-7 Koi Osako, Nishi Ku, Hiroshima, JAPAN 733 0816

ECHOLS, RODGER
2853 Highway 371 W, Nashville, AR 71852-7577, Phone: 870-845-9173 or 870-845-0400, blademanechols@aol.com; Web: www.echolsknives.com
Specialties: Liner locks, auto-scale release, lock backs. **Patterns:** His or yours. **Technical:** Autos. **Prices:** $500 to $1700. **Remarks:** Likes to use pearl, ivory and Damascus the most. Made first knife in 1984. Part-time maker; tool and die maker by trade. **Mark:** Name.

EDDY, HUGH E
211 E Oak St, Caldwell, ID 83605, Phone: 208-459-0536

EDGE, TOMMY
1244 County Road 157, Cash, AR 72421, Phone: 870-897-6150, tedge@tex.net
Specialties: Fancy/embellished working knives of his design. **Patterns:** Bowies, hunters and utility/camping knives. **Technical:** Grinds 440C, ATS-34 and D2. Makes own cable Damascus; offers filework. **Prices:** $70 to $250; some to $1500. **Remarks:** Part-time maker; first knife sold in 1973. **Mark:** Stamped first initial, last name and stenciled name, city and state in oval shape.

EDMONDS, WARRICK
Adelaide Hills, SOUTH AUSTRALIA, Phone: 61-8-83900339, warrick@riflebirdknives.com Web: www.riflebirdknives.com
Specialties: Fixed blade knives with select and highly figured exotic or unique Australian wood handles. Themed collectors knives to individually designed working knives from Damascus, RWL34, 440C or high carbon steels. **Patterns:** Hunters, utilities and workshop knives, cooks knives with a Deco to Modern flavour. Hand sewn individual leather sheaths. **Technical:** Stock removal using only steel from well known and reliable sources. **Prices:** $250Aust to $1000Aust. **Remarks:** Part-time maker since 2004. **Mark:** Name stamped into sheath.

EDWARDS, MITCH
303 New Salem Rd, Glasgow, KY 42141, Phone: 270-404-0758 / 270-404-0758, medwards@glasgow-ky.com; Web: www.traditionalknives.com
Specialties: Period pieces. **Patterns:** Neck knives, camp, rifleman and Bowie knives. **Technical:** All hand forged, forges own Damascus O1, 1084, 1095, L6, 15N20. **Prices:** $200 to $1000. **Remarks:** Journeyman Smith. **Mark:** Broken heart.

EHRENBERGER, DANIEL ROBERT
1213 S Washington St, Mexico, MO 65265, Phone: 573-633-2010
Specialties: Affordable working/using straight knives of his design and to custom specs. **Patterns:** 10" western Bowie, fighters, hunting and skinning knives. **Technical:** Forges 1085, 1095, his own Damascus and cable Damascus. **Prices:** $80 to $500. **Remarks:** Full-time maker, first knife sold 1994. **Mark:** Ehrenberger JS.

EKLUND, MAIHKEL
Fone Stam V9, Farila, SWEDEN 82041, info@art-knives.com; Web: www.art-knives.com
Specialties: Collector-grade working straight knives. **Patterns:** Hunters, Bowies and fighters. **Technical:** Grinds ATS-34, Uddeholm and Dama steel. Engraves and scrimshaws. **Prices:** $200 to $2000. **Remarks:** Full-time maker; first knife sold in 1983. **Mark:** Initials or name.

ELDRIDGE, ALLAN
7731 Four Winds Dr, Ft. Worth, TX 76133, Phone: 817-370-7778; Cell: 817-296-3528
Specialties: Fancy classic straight knives in standard patterns. **Patterns:** Hunters, Bowies, fighters, folders and miniatures. **Technical:** Grinds O1 and Damascus. Engraves silver-wire inlays, pearl inlays, scrimshaws and offers filework. **Prices:** $50 to $500; some to $1200. **Remarks:** Spare-time maker; first knife sold in 1965. **Mark:** Initials.

ELISHEWITZ, ALLEN
875 Hwy. 321 N, Ste. 600, #212, Lenoir City, TN 37771, Phone: 865-816-3309, allen@elishewitzknives.com; Web: elishewitzknives.com
Specialties: Collectible high-tech working straight knives and folders of his design. **Patterns:** Working, utility and tactical knives. **Technical:** Designs and uses innovative locking mechanisms. All designs drafted and field-tested. **Prices:** $600 to $1000. **Remarks:** Full-time maker; first knife sold in 1989. **Mark:** Gold medallion inlaid in blade.

ELLEFSON, JOEL
PO Box 1016, 310 S 1st St, Manhattan, MT 59741, Phone: 406-284-3111
Specialties: Working straight knives, fancy daggers and one-of-a-kinds. **Patterns:** Hunters, daggers and some folders. **Technical:** Grinds A2, 440C and ATS-34. Makes own mokume in bronze, brass, silver and shibuishi; makes brass/steel blades. **Prices:** $100 to $500; some to $2000. **Remarks:** Part-time maker; first knife sold in 1978. **Mark:** Stylized last initial.

ELLERBE, W B
3871 Osceola Rd, Geneva, FL 32732, Phone: 407-349-5818
Specialties: Period and primitive knives and sheaths. **Patterns:** Bowies to patch knives, some tomahawks. **Technical:** Grinds Sheffield O1 and files. **Prices:** Start at $35. **Remarks:** Full-time maker; first knife sold in 1971. Doing business as Cypress Bend Custom Knives. **Mark:** Last name or initials.

ELLIOTT, JERRY
4507 Kanawha Ave, Charleston, WV 25304, Phone: 304-925-5045, elliottknives@gmail.com
Specialties: Classic and traditional straight knives and folders of his design and to customer specs. **Patterns:** Hunters, locking folders and Bowies. **Technical:** Grinds ATS-34, 154CM, O1, D2 and T-440-V. All guards silver-soldered; bolsters are pinned on straight knives, spot-welded on folders. **Prices:** $80 to $265; some to $1000. **Remarks:** Full-time maker; first knife sold in 1972. **Mark:** First and middle initials, last name, knife maker, city, state.

ELLIS, WILLIAM DEAN
2767 Edgar Ave, Sanger, CA 93657, Phone: 559-314-4459, urleebird@comcast.net; Web: www.billysblades.com
Specialties: Classic and fancy knives of his design. **Patterns:** Boots, fighters and utility knives. **Technical:** Grinds ATS-34, D2 and Damascus. Offers tapered tangs and six patterns of filework; tooled multi-colored sheaths. **Prices:** $250 to $1500 **Remarks:** Part-time maker; first knife sold in 1991. Doing business as Billy's Blades. Also make shave-ready straight razors for actual use. **Mark:** "B" in a five-point star next to "Billy," city and state within a rounded-corner rectangle.

ELLIS, WILLY B
1025 Hamilton Ave., Tarpon Springs, FL 34689, Phone: 727-942-6420, Web: www.willyb.com
Specialties: One-of-a-kind high art and fantasy knives of his design. Occasional customs full size and miniatures. **Patterns:** Bowies, fighters, hunters and others. **Technical:** Grinds 440C, ATS-34, 1095, carbon Damascus, ivory bone, stone and metal carving. **Prices:** $175 to $15,000. **Remarks:** Full-time maker, first knife made in 1973. Member Knifemakers Guild and FEGA. Jewel setting inlays. **Mark:** Willy B. or WB'S C etched or carved.

ELROD, ROGER R
58 Dale Ave, Enterprise, AL 36330, Phone: 334-347-1863

EMBRETSEN, KAJ
FALUVAGEN 67, Edsbyn, SWEDEN 82830, Phone: 46-271-21057, Fax: 46-271-22961, kay.embretsen@telia.com Web:www.embretsenknives.com
Specialties: Damascus folding knives. **Patterns:** Uses mammoth ivory and some pearl. **Technical:** Uses own Damascus steel. **Remarks:** Full time since 1983. **Prices:** $2500 to $8000. **Mark:** Name inside the folder.

EMERSON, ERNEST R
1234 W. 254th, Harbor City, CA 90710, Phone: 310-539-5633, info@emersonknives.com; Web: www.emersonknives.com
Specialties: High-tech folders and combat fighters. **Patterns:** Fighters, LinerLock® combat folders and SPECWAR combat knives. **Technical:** Grinds 154CM and Damascus. Makes folders with titanium fittings, liners and locks. Chisel grind specialist. **Prices:** $550 to $850; some to $10,000. **Remarks:** Full-time maker; first knife sold in 1983. **Mark:** Last name and Specwar knives.

EMMERLING, JOHN
POB 2080, Gearheart, OR 97138, Phone: 503-738-5434, gearhartironwerks@gmail.com; Web: www.gearhartironwerks.com

ENCE, JIM
145 S 200 East, Richfield, UT 84701, Phone: 435-896-6206
Specialties: High-art period pieces (spec in California knives) art knives. **Patterns:** Art, boot knives, fighters, Bowies and occasional folders. **Technical:** Grinds 440C for polish and beauty boys; makes own Damascus. **Prices:** Upscale. **Remarks:** Full-time maker; first knife sold in 1977. Does own engraving, gold work and stone work. Guild member since 1977. Founding member of the AKI. **Mark:** Ence, usually engraved.

ENGLAND, VIRGIL
1340 Birchwood St, Anchorage, AK 99508, Phone: 907-274-9494, hardfistdown@gmail.com; Web: www.virgilenglandshetlandarmory.com
Specialties: Edged weapons and equipage, one-of-a-kind only. **Patterns:** Axes, swords, lances and body armor. **Technical:** Forges and grinds as pieces dictate. Offers stainless and Damascus. **Prices:** Upscale. **Remarks:** A veteran knifemaker. No commissions. **Mark:** Stylized initials.

ENGLE, WILLIAM
16608 Oak Ridge Rd, Boonville, MO 65233, Phone: 816-882-6277
Specialties: Traditional working and using straight knives of his design. **Patterns:** Hunters, Bowies and fighters. **Technical:** Grinds 440C, ATS-34 and 154 CM. **Prices:** $250 to $500; some higher. **Remarks:** Part-time maker; first knife sold in 1982. All knives come with certificate of authenticity. **Mark:** Last name in block lettering.

ENGLISH, JIM
14586 Olive Vista Dr, Jamul, CA 91935, Phone: 619-669-0833
Specialties: Traditional working straight knives to customer specs. **Patterns:** Hunters, bowies, fighters, tantos, daggers, boot and utility/camp knives. **Technical:** Grinds 440C, ATS-34, commercial Damascus and customer choice. **Prices:** $130 to $350. **Remarks:** Part-time maker; first knife sold in 1985. In addition to custom line, also does business as Mountain Home Knives. **Mark:** Double "A," Double "J" logo.

ENNIS, RAY
1220S 775E, Ogden, UT 84404, Phone: 800-410-7603, Fax: 501-621-2683, nifmakr@hotmail.com; Web:www.ennis-entrekusa.com

ENOS III, THOMAS M
12302 State Rd 535, Orlando, FL 32836, Phone: 407-239-6205, tmenos3@att.net
Specialties: Heavy-duty working straight knives; unusual designs. **Patterns:** Swords, machetes, daggers, skinners, filleting, period pieces. **Technical:** Grinds 440C. **Prices:** $75 to $1500. **Remarks:** Full-time maker; first knife sold in 1972. No longer accepting custom requests. Will be making his own designs. Send SASE for listing of items for sale. **Mark:** Name in knife logo and year, type of steel and serial number.

EPTING, RICHARD
4976 Drake Dr., College Station, TX 77845-7176, Phone: 979-255-2161, rgeknives@hotmail.com; Web: www.eptingknives.com
Specialties: Folders and working straight knives. **Patterns:** Hunters, Bowies, and locking folders. **Technical:** Forges high-carbon steel and his own Damascus. **Prices:** $200 to $800; some to $1800. **Remarks:** Part-time maker, first knife sold 1996. **Mark:** Name in arch logo.

ERICKSON, DANIEL
Ring Of Fire Forge, 20011 Welch Rd., Snohomish, WA 98296, Phone: 206-355-1793, Web: www.ringoffireforge.com
Specialties: Likes to fuse traditional and functional with creative concepts. **Patterns:** Hunters, fighters, bowies, folders, slip joints, art knives, the Phalanx. **Technical:** Forges own pattern-welded damascus blades (1080/15N20), 5160, CruForgeV, 52100 and W2. Uses figured burls, stabilized woods, fossil ivories and natural and unique materials for handles. Custom stands and sheaths. **Prices:** $250 to $1,500. **Remarks:** Sole authorship, designer and inventor. Started making in 2003; first knife sold in 2004. ABS journeyman smith. **Mark:** "Ring of Fire" with Erickson moving through it.

ERICKSON, L.M.
1379 Black Mountain Cir, Ogden, UT 84404, Phone: 801-737-1930
Specialties: Straight knives; period pieces. **Patterns:** Bowies, fighters, boots and hunters. **Technical:** Grinds 440C, 154CM and commercial Damascus. **Prices:** $200 to $900; some to $5000. **Remarks:** Part-time maker; first knife sold in 1981. **Mark:** Name, city, state.

ERICKSON, WALTER E.
22280 Shelton Tr, Atlanta, MI 49709, Phone: 989-785-5262, wberic@src-milp.com
Specialties: Unusual survival knives and high-tech working knives. **Patterns:** Butterflies, hunters, tantos. **Technical:** Grinds ATS-34 or customer choice. **Prices:** $150 to $500; some to $1500. **Remarks:** Full-time maker; first knife sold in 1981. **Mark:** Using pantograph with assorted fonts (no longer stamping).

ERIKSEN, JAMES THORLIEF
dba VIKING KNIVES, 3830 Dividend Dr, Garland, TX 75042, Phone: 972-494-3667, Fax: 972-235-4932, VikingKnives@aol.com
Specialties: Heavy-duty working and using straight knives and folders utilizing traditional, Viking original and customer specification patterns. Some high-tech and fancy/embellished knives available. **Patterns:** Bowies, hunters, skinners, boot and belt knives, utility/camp knives, fighters, daggers, locking folders, slip-joint folders and kitchen knives. **Technical:** Hollow-grinds 440C, D2, ASP-23, ATS-34, 154CM, Vascowear. **Prices:** $150 to $300; some to $600. **Remarks:** Full-time maker; first knife sold in 1985. Doing business as Viking Knives. For a color catalog showing 50 different models, mail $5 to above address. **Mark:** VIKING or VIKING USA for export.

ERNEST, PHIL (PJ)
PO Box 5240, Whittier, CA 90607-5240, Phone: 562-556-2324, hugger883562@yahoo.com; Web:www.ernestcustomknives.com
Specialties: Fixed blades. **Patterns:** Wide range. Many original as well as hunters, camp, fighters, daggers, bowies and tactical. Specialzin in Wharncliff's of all sizes. **Technical:** Grinds commercial Damascus, Mosaid Damascus. ATS-34, and 440C. Full Tangs with bolsters. Handle material includes all types of exotic hardwood, abalone, peal mammoth tooth, mammoth ivory, Damascus steel and Mosaic Damascus. **Remarks:** Full time maker. First knife sold in 1999. **Prices:** $200 to $1800. Some to $2500. **Mark:** Owl logo with PJ Ernest Whittier CA or PJ Ernest.

ESPOSITO, EMMANUEL
Via Reano 70, Buttigliera Alta TO, ITALY 10090, Phone: 39-011932-16-21, www.emmanuelmaker.it
Specialties: Folding knife with his patent system lock mechanism with mosaic inlay.

ESSEGIAN, RICHARD
7387 E Tulare St, Fresno, CA 93727, Phone: 309-255-5950
Specialties: Fancy working knives of his design; art knives. **Patterns:** Bowies and some small hunters. **Technical:** Grinds A2, D2, 440C and 154CM. Engraves and inlays. **Prices:** Start at $600. **Remarks:** Part-time maker; first knife sold in 1986. **Mark:** Last name, city and state.

ESTABROOK, ROBBIE
1014 Madge Ct., Conway, SC 29526, Phone: 843-489-2331, r1956e@hotmail.com
Specialties: Traditional working straight knives. **Patterns:** Hunters and fishing knives. **Technical:** Hand grinds ATS 34 and D2. **Prices:** $100 and up. **Remarks:** Part-time maker. **Mark:** ESTABROOK.

ETZLER, JOHN
11200 N Island, Grafton, OH 44044, Phone: 440-748-2460, jetzler@bright.net; Web: members.tripod.com/~etzlerknives/
Specialties: High-art and fantasy straight knives and folders of his design and to customer specs. **Patterns:** Folders, daggers, fighters, utility knives. **Technical:** Forges and grinds nickel Damascus and tool steel; grinds stainless steels. Prefers exotic, natural materials. **Prices:** $250 to $1200; some to $6500. **Remarks:** Full-time maker; first knife sold in 1992. **Mark:** Name or initials.

EVANS, BRUCE A
409 CR 1371, Booneville, MS 38829, Phone: 662-720-0193, beknives@avsia.com; Web: www.bruceevans.homestead.com/open.html
Specialties: Forges blades. **Patterns:** Hunters, Bowies, or will work with customer. **Technical:** 5160, cable Damascus, pattern welded Damascus. **Prices:** $200 and up. **Mark:** Bruce A. Evans Same with JS on reverse of blade.

EVANS, CARLTON
PO Box 72, Fort Davis, TX 79734, Phone: 817-223-8556, carlton@carltonevans.com; Web: www.carltonevans.com
Specialties: High end folders and fixed blades. **Technical:** Uses the stock removal methods. The materials used are of the highest quality. **Remarks:** Full-time knifemaker, voting member of Knifemakers Guild, member of the Texas Knifemakers and Collectors Association.

EVANS, PHIL
594 SE 40th, Columbus, KS 66725, Phone: 620-249-0639, phil@glenviewforge.com
Web: www.glenviewforge.com
Specialties: Working knives, hunters, skinners, also enjoys making Bowies and fighters, high carbon or Damascus. **Technical:** Forges own blades and makes own Damascus. Uses all kinds of ancient Ivory and bone. Stabilizes own native hardwoods. **Prices:** $150 - $1,500. **Remarks:** Part-time maker. Made first knife in 1995. **Mark:** EVANS.

EVANS, RONALD B
209 Hoffer St, Middleton, PA 17057-2723, Phone: 717-944-5464

EVANS, VINCENT K AND GRACE
PO Box 3604, Show Low AZ 85902, Phone: 809-443-8198, evansvk@gmail.com
Web: www.picturetrail.com/vevans
Specialties: Period pieces; swords. **Patterns:** Scottish, Viking, central Asian. **Technical:** Forges 5160 and his own Damascus. **Prices:** $700 to $4000; some to $8000. **Remarks:** Full-time maker; first knife sold in 1983. **Mark:** Last initial with fish logo.

EWING, JOHN H
3276 Dutch Valley Rd, Clinton, TN 37716, Phone: 865-457-5757, johnja@comcast.net
Specialties: Working straight knives, hunters, camp knives. **Patterns:** Hunters. **Technical:** Grinds 440-D2. Forges 5160, 1095 prefers forging. **Prices:** $150 and up. **Remarks:** Part-time maker; first knife sold in 1985. **Mark:** First initial, last name, some embellishing done on knives.

F

FAIRLY, DANIEL
2209 Bear Creek Canyon Rd, Bayfield, CO 81122, danielfairlyknives@gmail.com; Web: www.danielfairlyknives.com
Specialties: "Craftsmanship without compromise. **Patterns:** Ultralight titanium utilities, everyday carry, folders, kitchen knives, Japanese-influenced design. **Technical:** Grinds mostly tool steel and carbidized titanium in .050" to .360" thick material. Uses heavy duty handle materials and flared test tube fasteners or epoxy soaked wrapped handles. Most grinds are chisel; flat convex and hollow grinds used. **Prices:** $85 to $1,850. **Remarks:** Full-time maker since first knife sold in Feb. 2011. **Mark:** Fairly written in all capitals with larger F.

FANT JR., GEORGE
1983 CR 3214, Atlanta, TX 75551-6515, Phone: (903) 846-2938

FARID, MEHR R
8 Sidney Close, Tunbridge Wells, Kent, ENGLAND TN2 5QQ, Phone: 011-44-1892 520345, farid@faridknives.com; Web: www.faridknives.com
Specialties: Hollow handle survival knives. High tech folders. **Patterns:** Flat grind blades & chisel ground LinerLock® folders. **Technical:** Grinds 440C, CPMT-440V, CPM-420V, CPM-15V, CPM5125V, and T-1 high speed steel. **Prices:** $550 to $5000. **Remarks:** Full-time maker; first knife sold in 1991. **Mark:** First name stamped.

FARR, DAN
6531 E. Poleline Ave., Post Falls, ID 83854, Phone: 585-721-1388
Specialties: Hunting, camping, fighting and utility. **Patterns:** Fixed blades. **Technical:** Forged or stock removal. **Prices:** $150 to $750.

FASSIO, MELVIN G
420 Tyler Way, Lolo, MT 59847, Phone: 406-544-1391, fassiocustomknives@gmail.com; Web: www.fassiocustomknives.com
Specialties: Working folders to customer specs. **Patterns:** Locking folders, hunters and traditional-style knives. **Technical:** Grinds 440C. **Prices:** $125 to $350. **Remarks:** Part-time maker; first knife sold in 1975. **Mark:** Name and city, dove logo.

FAUCHEAUX, HOWARD J
PO Box 206, Loreauville, LA 70552, Phone: 318-229-6467
Specialties: Working straight knives and folders; period pieces. Also a hatchet with capping knife in the handle. **Patterns:** Traditional locking folders, hunters, fighters and Bowies. **Technical:** Forges W2, 1095 and his own Damascus; stock removal D2. **Prices:** Start at $200. **Remarks:** Full-time maker; first knife sold in 1969. **Mark:** Last name.

FAUST, JOACHIM
Kirchgasse 10, Goldkronach, GERMANY 95497

FELIX, ALEXANDER
PO Box 4036, Torrance, CA 90510, Phone: 310-320-1836, sgiandubh@dslextreme.com
Specialties: Straight working knives, fancy ethnic designs. **Patterns:** Hunters, Bowies, daggers, period pieces. **Technical:** Forges carbon steel and Damascus; forged stainless and titanium jewelry, gold and silver casting. **Prices:** $110 and up. **Remarks:** Jeweler, ABS Journeyman Smith. **Mark:** Last name.

FELLOWS, MIKE
P.O. Box 184, Riversdale 6670, SOUTH AFRICA, Phone: 27 82 960 3868, karatshin@gmail.com
Specialties: Miniatures, art knives and folders with occasional hunters and skinners. **Patterns:** Own designs. **Technical:** Uses own damascus. **Prices:** Upon request.

custom knifemakers

Remarks: Uses only indigenous materials. Exotic hardwoods, horn and ivory. Does all own embellishments. **Mark:** "SHIN" letter from Hebrew alphabet over Hebrew word "Karat." Other: Member of Knifemakers Guild of South Africa.

FERGUSON, JIM
4652 Hackett St., Lakewood, CA 90713, Phone: 562-342-4890, jim@twistednickel.com; Web: www.twistednickel.com, www.howtomakeaknife.net

Specialties: Bowies and push blades. **Patterns:** All styles. **Technical:** Flat and hollow grinds. Sells in U.S. and Canada. **Prices:** $100 to $1,200. **Mark:** Push blade with "Ferguson-USA." Also makes swords, battle axes and utilities.

FERGUSON, JIM
3543 Shadyhill Dr, San Angelo, TX 76904, Phone: 325-655-1061

Specialties: Straight working knives and folders. **Patterns:** Working belt knives, hunters, Bowies and some folders. **Technical:** Grinds ATS-34, D2 and Vascowear. Flat-grinds hunting knives. **Prices:** $200 to $600; some to $1000. **Remarks:** Full-time maker; first knife sold in 1987. **Mark:** First and middle initials, last name.

FERGUSON, LEE
1993 Madison 7580, Hindsville, AR 72738, Phone: 479-443-0084, info@fergusonknives.com; Web: www.fergusonknives.com

Specialties: Straight working knives and folders, some fancy. **Patterns:** Hunters, daggers, swords, locking folders and slip-joints. **Technical:** Grinds D2, 440C and ATS-34; heat-treats. **Prices:** $50 to $600; some to $4000. **Remarks:** Full-time maker; first knife sold in 1977. **Mark:** Full name.

FERRIER, GREGORY K
3119 Simpson Dr, Rapid City, SD 57702, Phone: 605-342-9280

FERRY, TOM
16005 SE 322nd St, Auburn, WA 98092, Phone: 253-939-4468, tomferryknives@Q.com; Web: tomferryknives.com

Specialties: Presentation grade knives. **Patterns:** Folders and fixed blades. **Technical:** Specialize in Damascus and engraving. **Prices:** $500 and up. **Remarks:** DBA: Soos Creek Ironworks. ABS Master Smith. **Mark:** Combined T and F in a circle and/or last name.

FINCH, RICKY D
1179 Hwy 844, West Liberty, KY 41472, Phone: 606-743-7151, finchknives@mrtc.com; Web: www.finchknives.com

Specialties: Traditional working/using straight knives of his design or to customer spec. **Patterns:** Hunters, skinners and utility/camp knives. LinerLock® of his design. **Technical:** Grinds 440C, ATS-34 and CPM154, hand rubbed stain finish, use Micarta, stabilized wood, natural and exotic. **Prices:** $85 to $225. **Remarks:** Part-time maker, first knife made 1994. Doing business as Finch Knives. **Mark:** Last name inside outline of state of Kentucky.

FINLEY, JON M.
3921 W. 142nd Dr., Leawood, KS 66224, Phone: 913-707-0016, jon66224@hotmail.com

Specialties: Fancy hunters with mosaic handles and channel inlays, with much use of exotic woods, mammoth ivory and gemstones. **Technical:** Stock-removal method of blade making using high-carbon damascus steel. **Prices:** $200 to $1,000. **Remarks:** Part-time maker; first knife made in 2012. **Mark:** Logo and last name.

FINNEY, GARETT
7181 Marcob Way, Loomis, CA 95650, Phone: 650-678-7332, garett@finneyknives.com; Web: www.finneyknives.com

Specialties: Customizes knives utilizing materials that couldn't be used for handle materials until the maker casts them into acrylic. He then combines the cast items with exotic natural materials via inlays in order to create unique, one-of-a-kind works of art. **Technical:** Most knives are mirror polished with fileworked blade spines and engraved bolsters. **Prices:** $80 to $900, depending on knife and materials. **Remarks:** Full-time maker. **Mark:** Maker signs his name via engraving, and also uses a stamp for stock-removal or forged pieces.

FISHER, JAY
1405 Edwards, Clovis, NM 88101, jayfisher@jayfisher.com Web: www.JayFisher.com

Specialties: High-art, working and collector's knives of his design and client's designs. Military working and commemoratives. Gemstone handles. Locking combat sheaths. **Patterns:** Hunters, daggers, folding knives, museum pieces and high-art sculptures. **Technical:** 440C, ATS-34, CPMS30V, D2, O1, CPM154CM, CPMS35VN. Prolific maker of stone-handled knives and swords. **Prices:** $850 to $150,000. **Remarks:** Full-time maker; first knife sold in 1980. High resolution etching, computer and manual engraving. **Mark:** Signature "JaFisher"

FISHER, JOSH
JN Fisher Knives, 8419 CR 3615, Murchison, TX 75778, Phone: 903-203-2130, fisherknives@aol.com; Web: www.jnfisherknives.com

Specialties: Frame-handle fighters. **Technical:** Forge 5160 and 1084 blade steels. **Prices:** $125 to $1,000. **Remarks:** Part-time maker; first knife made in 2007. ABS journeyman smith. **Mark:** Josh Fisher etched. "JS" also etched on the reverse.

FISHER, LANCE
9 Woodlawn Ave., Pompton Lakes, NJ 07442, Phone: 973-248-8447, lance.fisher@sandvik.com

Specialties: Wedding cake knives and servers, forks, etc. Including velvet lined wood display cases. **Patterns:** Drop points, upswept skinners, Bowies, daggers, fantasy, medieval, San Francisco style, chef or kitchen cutlery. **Technical:** Stock removal method only. Steels include but are not limited to CPM 154, D2, CPM S35VN, CPM S90V and Sandvik 13C26. Handle materials include stag, sheep horn, exotic woods, micarta, and G10 as well as reconstituted stone. **Prices:** $350 - $2000. **Remarks:** Part-time maker, will become full-time on retirement. Made and sold first knife in 1981 and has never looked back. **Mark:** Tang stamp.

FISK, JERRY
10095 Hwy 278 W, Nashville, AR 71852, Phone: 870-845-4456, jerry@jerryfisk.com; Web: www.jerryfisk.com or Facebook: Jerry Fisk, MS Custom Knives

Specialties: Edged weapons, collectible and functional. **Patterns:** Bowies, daggers, swords, hunters, camp knives and others. **Technical:** Forges carbon steels and his own pattern welded steels. **Prices:** $1100 to $20,000. **Remarks:** National living treasure. **Mark:** Name, MS.

FISTER, JIM
PO Box 307, Simpsonville, KY 40067

Specialties: One-of-a-kind collectibles and period pieces. **Patterns:** Bowies, camp knives, hunters, buckskinners, and daggers. **Technical:** Forges, 1085, 5160, 52100, his own Damascus, pattern and turkish. **Prices:** $150 to $2500. **Remarks:** Part-time maker; first knife sold in 1982. **Mark:** Name and MS.

FITCH, JOHN S
45 Halbrook Rd, Clinton, AR 72031-8910, Phone: 501-893-2020

FITZ, ANDREW A. SR. AND JR.
63 Bradford Hwy., Milan, TN 38358, Phone: 731-420-0139, fitzknives@yahoo.com

Specialties: Tactical utility flipper folders and fixed blades of the makers' designs. **Patterns:** High-tech utility/defense folders and fixed blades. **Technical:** Grinds CPM 154, CTS B75P, PSF27, Elmax and CTS XHP. Titanium and carbon fiber handles, or G-10 on tactical utility folders. **Prices:** $600 to $1,300 (Andrew Sr.) and $200 to $500 (Andrew Jr.). **Remarks:** Fitz Sr. made and sold first knife in 2002. Fitz Jr. made first knife in 2013 and sold first knife in 2014. **Mark:** Fitz Sr.: Last name Fitz; and Fitz Jr.: Last name with Jr. in the Z.

FITZGERALD, DENNIS M
4219 Alverado Dr, Fort Wayne, IN 46816-2847, Phone: 219-447-1081

Specialties: One-of-a-kind collectibles and period pieces. **Patterns:** Skinners, fighters, camp and utility knives; period pieces. **Technical:** Forges 1085, 1095, L6, 5160, 52100, his own pattern and Turkish Damascus. **Prices:** $100 to $500. **Remarks:** Part-time maker; first knife sold in 1985. Doing business as The Ringing Circle. **Mark:** Name and circle logo.

FLINT, ROBERT
2902 Aspen, Anchorage, AK 99517, Phone: 907-243-6706

Specialties: Working straight knives and folders. **Patterns:** Utility, hunters, fighters and gents. **Technical:** Grinds ATS-34, BG-42, D2 and Damascus. **Prices:** $150 and up. **Remarks:** Part-time maker, first knife sold in 1998. **Mark:** Last name; stylized initials.

FLOURNOY, JOE
5750 Lisbon Rd, El Dorado, AR 71730, Phone: 870-863-7208, flournoy@ipa.net

Specialties: Working straight knives and folders. **Patterns:** Hunters, Bowies, camp knives, folders and daggers. **Technical:** Forges only high-carbon steel, steel cable and his own Damascus. **Prices:** $350 Plus. **Remarks:** First knife sold in 1977. **Mark:** Last name and MS in script.

FLUDDER, KEITH
3 Olive Ln., Tahmoor, New South Wales, AUSTRALIA 2573, Phone: 612 46843236 or 61 412687868, keith@knifemaker.com.au; Web: www.bladesmith.com.au

Specialties: Damascus and carbon steel fixed blades and art knives. **Patterns:** Bowies, fighters, hunters, tantos, wakizashis, katanas and kitchen knives. **Technical:** Forges and makes own damascus, including mosaics and multi-bars from 1075 and 15N20. Also uses 1084, W2, O1, 52100 and 5160. **Prices:** $275 to $3,000. **Remarks:** Full-time maker since 2000; ABS journeyman smith since 2014; first knife made in 1989. **Mark:** Reverse K on F centered in Southern Cross constellation. Fludder on spine.

FLYNT, ROBERT G
15173 Christy Lane, Gulfport, MS 39503, Phone: 228-832-3378 or cell: 228-265-0410, robertflynt@cableone.net; Web: www.flyntstoneknifeworks.com

Specialties: All types of fixed blades: drop point, clip point, trailing point, bull-nose hunters, tactical, fighters and bowies. LinerLock, slip-joint and lockback folders. **Technical:** Using 154CM, CPM-154, ATS-34, 440C, CPM-3V and 52100 steels. Most blades made by stock removal, hollow and flat grind methods. Forges some cable damascus and uses numerous types of damascus purchased in billets from various makers. All filework and bluing done by the maker. Various wood handles, bone and horn materials, including some with wire inlay and other embellishments. Most knives sold with custom-fit leather sheaths, most include exotic skin inlay when appropriate. **Prices:** $150 and up, depending on embellishments on blade and sheath. **Remarks:** Full-time maker; first knife made in 1966. Knifemakers' Guild member. **Mark:** Last name in cursive letters or a knife striking a flint stone.

FOGARIZZU, BOITEDDU
via Crispi 6, Pattada, ITALY 07016

Specialties: Traditional Italian straight knives and folders. **Patterns:** Collectible folders. **Technical:** forges and grinds 12C27, ATS-34 and his Damascus. **Prices:** $200 to $3000. **Remarks:** Full-time maker; first knife sold in 1958. **Mark:** Full name and registered logo.

FONTENOT, GERALD J
901 Maple Ave, Mamou, LA 70554, Phone: 318-468-3180

FORREST, BRIAN
FORREST KNIVES, PO Box 611, Descanso, CA 91916, Phone: 619-445-6343, forrestforge@gmail.com; Web: www.forrestforge.biz

Specialties: Forged tomahawks, working knives, big Bowies. **Patterns:** Traditional and extra large Bowies. **Technical:** Hollow grinds: 440C, 1095, S160 Damascus. **Prices:** $125 and up. **Remarks:** Member of California Knifemakers Association. Full-time maker. First knife sold in 1971. **Mark:** Forrest USA/Tomahawks marked FF (Forrest Forge).

FORTHOFER, PETE

5535 Hwy 93S, Whitefish, MT 59937, Phone: 406-862-2674

Specialties: Interframes with checkered wood inlays; working straight knives. **Patterns:** Traditional-style hunting knives. **Technical:** Grinds D2, 440C, 154CM and ATS-34, and prefers mammoth ivory handles and mokume guards. **Prices:** $650 to $850. **Remarks:** Part-time maker; full-time gunsmith. First knife sold in 1979. **Mark:** Name and logo.

FOSTER, AL

118 Woodway Dr, Magnolia, TX 77355, Phone: 936-372-9297

Specialties: Straight knives and folders. **Patterns:** Hunting, fishing, folders and Bowies. **Technical:** Grinds 440-C, ATS-34 and D2. **Prices:** $100 to $1000. **Remarks:** Full-time maker; first knife sold in 1981. **Mark:** Scorpion logo and name.

FOSTER, BURT

23697 Archery Range Rd, Bristol, VA 24202, Phone: 276-669-0121, burt@burtfoster.com; Web:www.burtfoster.com

Specialties: Working straight knives, laminated blades, and some art knives of his design. **Patterns:** Bowies, hunters, daggers. **Technical:** Forges 52100, W-2 and makes own Damascus. Does own heat treating. **Remarks:** ABS MasterSmith. Full-time maker, believes in sole authorship. **Mark:** Signed "BF" initials.

FOSTER, NORVELL C

7945 Youngsford Rd, Marion, TX 78124-1713, Phone: 830-914-2078

Specialties: Engraving; ivory handle carving. **Patterns:** American-large and small scroll-oak leaf and acorns. **Prices:** $25 to $400. **Remarks:** Have been engraving since 1957. **Mark:** N.C. Foster - Marion - Tex and current year.

FOSTER, RONNIE E

95 Riverview Rd., Morrilton, AR 72110, Phone: 501-354-5389

Specialties: Working, using knives, some period pieces, work with customer specs. **Patterns:** Hunters, fighters, Bowies, liner-lock folders, camp knives. **Technical:** Forge-5160, 1084, O1, 15N20-makes own Damascus. **Prices:** $200 (start). **Remarks:** Part-time maker. First knife sold 1994. **Mark:** Ronnie Foster MS.

FOSTER, TIMOTHY L

723 Sweet Gum Acres Rd, El Dorado, AR 71730, Phone: 870-863-6188

FOWLER, CHARLES R

226 National Forest Rd 48, Ft McCoy, FL 32134-9624, Phone: 904-467-3215

FOWLER, ED A.

Willow Bow Ranch, PO Box 1519, Riverton, WY 82501, Phone: 307-856-9815

Specialties: High-performance working and using straight knives. **Patterns:** Hunter, camp, bird, and trout knives and Bowies. New model, the gentleman's Pronghorn. **Technical:** Low temperature forged 52100 from virgin 5-1/2 round bars, multiple quench heat treating, engraves all knives, all handles domestic sheep horn processed and aged at least 5 years. Makes heavy duty hand-stitched waxed harness leather pouch type sheathes. **Prices:** $800 to $7000. **Remarks:** Full-time maker. First knife sold in 1962. **Mark:** Initials connected.

FOWLER, STEPHAN

1142 Reading Dr. NW, Acworth, GA 30102, Phone: 770-726-9706, stephan@fowlerblades.com; Web: www.fowlerblades.com

Specialties: Bowies. **Patterns:** Bowies, hunters, chef's knives (American and Japanese style). **Technical:** Primarily W2 blade steel, also 52100, 1084, 1095 and various damascus patterns. **Prices:** $200 and up. **Remarks:** Part-time maker since 2004. **Mark:** Fowler.

FRALEY, D B

1355 Fairbanks Ct, Dixon, CA 95620, Phone: 707-678-0393, dbtfnives@sbcglobal.net; Web:www.dbfraleyknives.com

Specialties: Usable gentleman's fixed blades and folders. **Patterns:** Four locking-liner and frame-lock folders in four different sizes. **Technical:** Grinds CPM S30V, 154CM and 6K Stellite. **Prices:** $250 and up. **Remarks:** Part-time maker. First knife sold in 1990. **Mark:** First and middle initials, last name over a buffalo.

FRAMSKI, WALTER P

24 Rek Ln, Prospect, CT 06712, Phone: 203-758-5634

FRANCE, DAN

Box 218, Cawood, KY 40815, Phone: 606-573-6104

Specialties: Traditional working and using straight knives of his design. **Patterns:** Hunters, Bowies and utility/camp knives. **Technical:** Forges and grinds O1, 5160 and L6. **Prices:** $35 to $125; some to $350. **Remarks:** Spare-time maker; first knife sold in 1985. **Mark:** First name.

FRANCIS, JOHN D

FRANCIS KNIVES, 18 Miami St., Ft. Loramie, OH 45845, Phone: 937-295-3941, jdfrancis72@gmail.com

Specialties: Utility and hunting-style fixed bladed knives of 440 C and ATS-34 steel; Micarta, exotic woods, and other types of handle materials. **Prices:** $90 to $150 range. **Remarks:** Exceptional quality and value at factory prices. **Mark:** Francis-Ft. Loramie, OH stamped on tang.

FRANK, HEINRICH H

3323 N.E. Avery St., Newport, OR 97365, Phone: 541-265-8683

Specialties: High-art investor-class folders, handmade and engraved. **Patterns:** Folding daggers, hunter-size folders and gents. **Technical:** Grinds 07 and O1. **Prices:** $2,100 to $16,000. **Remarks:** Full-time maker; first knife sold in 1965. Doing business as H.H. Frank Knives. **Mark:** Name, address and date.

FRANKLIN, LARRY

Mya Knives, 418 S. 7th St., Stoughton, WI 53589, Phone: 608-719-2758

Specialties: Fixed-blade hunters, kitchen knives and bird-and-trout knives. **Technical:** Forges 20 percent of blades and uses stock-removal method of blade making on the other 80 percent, with favorite steels being 1095, D2, 440C and 14-4 CrMo steels. **Prices:** $85 to $500. **Remarks:** Started making knives around 2005. **Mark:** Daughter's name with a leaf for her favorite season.

FRANKLIN, MIKE

12040 Garnet Dr., Clermont, FL 34711, Phone: 606-407-0029, mikefranklin2013@gmail.com

Specialties: Hunters of all sizes, neck knives and tacticals ranging from small to fighter size. **Patterns:** Hunters with all blade shapes, lots of tactical tanto blades, some radical. **Technical:** Mostly full-tang knives, some with tapered tangs and others narrow tangs. **Prices:** $150 to $1,000+. **Remarks:** Retired to Florida and makes knives he desires to make on a limited basis. **Mark:** Franklin made (with an Old English "F.")

FRAPS, JOHN R

3810 Wyandotte Tr, Indianapolis, IN 46240-3422, Phone: 317-849-9419, jfraps@att.net; Web: www.frapsknives.com

Specialties: Working and collector grade LinerLock® and slip joint folders. **Patterns:** One-of-a kind linerlocks and traditional slip joints. **Technical:** Flat and hollow grinds ATS-34, Damascus, Talonite, CPM S30V, 154Cm, Stellite 6K; hand rubbed or mirror finish. **Prices:** $200 to $1500, some higher. **Remarks:** Voting member of the Knifemaker's Guild; Full-time maker; first knife sold in 1997. **Mark:** Cougar Creek Knives and/or name.

FRAZIER, JIM

6315 Wagener Rd., Wagener, SC 29164, Phone: 803-564-6467, jbfrazierknives@gmail.com; Web: www.jbfrazierknives.com

Specialties: Hunters, semi skinners, oyster roast knives, bird and trout, folders, many patterns of own design with George Herron/Geno Denning influence. **Technical:** Stock removal maker using CPM-154, ATS-34, CPM-S30V and D2. Hollow grind, mainly mirror finish, some satin finish. Prefer to use natural handle material such as stag, horn, mammoth ivory, highly figured woods, some Micarta, others on request. Makes own leather sheaths on 1958 straight needle stitcher. **Prices:** $125 to $600. **Remarks:** Part-time maker since 1989. **Mark:** JB Frazier in arch with Knives under it. Stamp on sheath is outline of state of SC, JB Frazier Knives Wagener SC inside outline.

FRED, REED WYLE

3149 X S, Sacramento, CA 95817, Phone: 916-739-0237

Specialties: Working using straight knives of his design. **Patterns:** Hunting and camp knives. **Technical:** Forges any 10 series, old files and carbon steels. Offers initialing upon request; prefers natural handle materials. **Prices:** $30 to $300. **Remarks:** Part-time maker; first knife sold in 1994. Doing business as R.W. Fred Knifemaker. **Mark:** Engraved first and last initials.

FREDEEN, GRAHAM

5121 Finadene Ct., Colorado Springs, CO 80916, Phone: 719-331-5665, fredeenblades@hotmail.com Web: www.fredeenblades.com

Specialties: Working class knives to high-end custom knives. Traditional pattern welding and mosaic Damascus blades.**Patterns:** All types: Bowies, fighters, hunters, skinners, bird and trout, camp knives, utility knives, daggers, etc. Occasionally swords, both European and Asian.**Technical:** Differential heat treatment and Hamon. Damascus steel rings and jewelry. Hand forged blades and Damascus steel. High carbon blade steels: 1050, 1075/1080, 1084, 1095, 5160, 52100, W1, W2, O1, 15n20 **Prices:** $100 - $2,000. **Remarks:** Sole authorship. Part-time maker. First blade produced in 2005. Member of American Bladesmith Society and Professional Knifemaker's Association **Mark:** "Fredeen" etched on the ricasso or on/along the spine of the blade.

FREDERICK, AARON

272 Brooks Ln, West Liberty, KY 41472-8961, Phone: 606-743-2015, aaronf@mrtc.com; Web: www.frederickknives.com

Specialties: Makes most types of knives, but as for now specializes in the Damascus folder. Does all own Damascus and forging of the steel. Also prefers natural handle material such as ivory and pearl. Prefers 14k gold screws in most of the knives he do. Also offer several types of file work on blades, spacers, and liners. Has just recently started doing carving and can do a limited amount of engraving.

FREEMAN, MATT

Fresno, CA 93720, Phone: 559-375-4408, cmftwknives@gmail.com; Web: www.youtube.com/cmftwknives

Specialties: Fixed blades and butterfly knives. **Technical:** Using mostly 1084, 154CM, D2 and file steel, works in any requested materials via stock removal. Also does knife modifications and leather/Kydex work. Three months or less waiting list. **Prices:** $75+. **Mark:** CMFTW.

FREER, RALPH

114 12th St, Seal Beach, CA 90740, Phone: 562-493-4925, Fax: same, ralphfreer@adelphia.net

Specialties: Exotic folders, liner locks, folding daggers, fixed blades. Patters: All original. **Technical:** Lots of Damascus, ivory, pearl, jeweled, thumb studs, carving ATS-34, 420V, 530V. **Prices:** $400 to $2500 and up. **Mark:** Freer in German-style text, also Freer shield.

FREY JR., W FREDERICK

305 Walnut St, Milton, PA 17847, Phone: 570-742-9576, wffrey@ptd.net

Specialties: Working straight knives and folders, some fancy. **Patterns:** Wide range miniatures, boot knives and lock back folders. **Technical:** Grinds A2, O1 and D2; vaseo wear, cru-wear and CPM S90V. **Prices:** $100 to $250; some to $1200. **Remarks:** Spare-time maker; first knife sold in 1983. All knives include quality hand stitched leather sheaths. **Mark:** Last name in script.

custom knifemakers

FRIEDLY, DENNIS E

12 Cottontail Lane E, Cody, WY 82414, Phone: 307-527-6811, friedlyknives@hotmail.com Web: www.friedlyknives.com

Specialties: Fancy working straight knives and daggers, lock back folders and liner locks. Also embellished bowies. **Patterns:** Hunters, fighters, short swords, minis and miniatures; new line of full-tang hunters/boots. **Technical:** Grinds 440C, commercial Damascus, mosaic Damascus and ATS-34 blades; prefers hidden tangs and full tangs. Both flat and hollow grinds. **Prices:** $350 to $2500. Some to $10,000. **Remarks:** Full-time maker; first knife sold in 1972. **Mark:** D.E. Friedly-Cody, WY. Friedly Knives

FRIESEN, DAVE J

Qualicum Beach, British Columbia, CANADA, Phone: 250-927-4113, info@islandblacksmith.ca; Web: www.islandblacksmith.ca

Specialties: Charcoal-forged classical tanto and fusion-style takedown knives crafted by hand from reclaimed and natural materials using traditional techniques.

FRIGAULT, RICK

1189 Royal Pines Rd, Golden Lake, ON, CANADA K0J 1X0, Phone: 613-401-2869, Web: www.rfrigaultknives.ca

Specialties: Fixed blades. **Patterns:** Hunting, tactical and large Bowies. **Technical:** Grinds ATS-34, 440-C, D-2, CPMS30V, CPMS60V, CPMS90V, BG42 and Damascus. Use G-10, Micarta, ivory, antler, ironwood and other stabilized woods for carbon fiber handle material. Makes leather sheaths by hand. Tactical blades include a Concealex sheath made by "On Scene Tactical." **Remarks:** Sold first knife in 1997. Member of Canadian Knifemakers Guild. **Mark:** RFRIGAULT.

FRITZ, ERIK L

837 River St Box 1203, Forsyth, MT 59327, Phone: 406-351-1101, tacmedic45@yahoo.com

Specialties: Forges carbon steel 1084, 5160, 52100 and Damascus. **Patterns:** Hunters, camp knives, bowies and folders as well as forged tactical. **Technical:** Forges own Mosaic and pattern welded Damascus as well as doing own heat treat. **Prices:** A$200 and up. **Remarks:** Sole authorship knives and sheaths. Part time maker first knife sold in 2004. ABS member. **Mark:** E. Fritz in arc on left side ricasso.

FRITZ, JESSE

900 S. 13th St, Slaton, TX 79364, Phone: 806-828-5083

Specialties: Working and using straight knives in standard patterns. **Patterns:** Hunters, utility/camp knives and skinners with gut hook, Bowie knives, kitchen carving sets by request. **Technical:** Grinds 440C, O1 and 1095. Uses 1095 steel. Fline-napped steel design, blued blades, filework and machine jewelling. Inlays handles with turquoise, coral and mother-of-pearl. Makes sheaths. **Prices:** $85 to $275; some to $500. **Mark:** Last name only (FRITZ).

FRIZZELL, TED

14056 Low Gap Rd, West Fork, AR 72774, Phone: 501-839-2516, mmhwaxes@aol.com Web: www.mineralmountain.com

Specialties: Swords, axes and self-defense weapons. **Patterns:** Small skeleton knives to large swords. **Technical:** Grinds 5160 almost exclusively—1/4" to 1/2"— bars some O1 and A2 on request. All knives come with Kydex sheaths. **Prices:** $45 to $1200. **Remarks:** Full-time maker; first knife sold in 1984. Doing business as Mineral Mountain Hatchet Works. Wholesale orders welcome. **Mark:** A circle with line in the middle; MM and HW within the circle.

FRIZZI, LEONARDO

Via Kyoto 31, Firenze, ITALY 50126, Phone: 335-344750, postmaster@frizzi-knives.com; Web: www.frizzi-knives.com

Specialties: Fancy handmade one-of-a kind folders of his own design, some fixed blade and dagger. **Patterns:** Folders liner loch and back locks. **Technical:** Grinds rwl 34, cpm 154, cpm s30v, stainless damascus and the best craft damascus, own heat treating. I usually prefer satin finish the flat of the blade and mirror polish the hollow grind; special 18k gold, filework. **Prices:** $600 to $4,000. **Remarks:** Part-time maker, first knife sold in 2003. **Mark:** Full name, city, country, or initial, last name and city, or initial in square logo.

FRONEFIELD, DANIEL

20270 Warriors Path, Peyton, CO 80831, Phone: 719-749-0226, dfronfld@hiwaay.com **Specialties:** Fixed and folding knives featuring meteorites and other exotic materials. **Patterns:** San-mai Damascus, custom Damascus. **Prices:** $500 to $3000.

FROST, DEWAYNE

1016 Van Buren Rd, Barnesville, GA 30204, Phone: 770-358-1426, lbrtyhill@aol.com **Specialties:** Working straight knives and period knives. **Patterns:** Hunters, Bowies and utility knives. **Technical:** Forges own Damascus, cable, etc. as well as stock removal. **Prices:** $150 to $500. **Remarks:** Part-time maker ABS Journeyman Smith. **Mark:** Liberty Hill Forge Dewayne Frost w/liberty bell.

FRUHMANN, LUDWIG

Stegerwaldstr 8, Burghausen, GERMANY 84489

Specialties: High-tech and working straight knives of his design. **Patterns:** Hunters, fighters and boots. **Technical:** Grinds ATS-34, CPM-T-440V and Schneider Damascus. Prefers natural handle materials. **Prices:** $200 to $1500. **Remarks:** Spare-time maker; first knife sold in 1990. **Mark:** First initial and last name.

FRY, DEAN

1569 Balsam Rd., Wellsboro, PA 16901, Phone: 570-948-9019, fireflycollection@yahoo.com; Web: www.balsamridgeknives.com

Specialties: User-type fixed blades, including hunters, bird & trout, neck knives, drop points and everyday carry pieces. **Technical:** Hollow, Scandi and flat grinds using CPM 154 and Alabama Damascus steels. Exotic wood, antler and composite handles, and

leather and Kydex sheaths made in house. **Prices:** $95 to $250. **Remarks:** Part-time maker; first knife sold in 2007. **Mark:** Initials in script stamped on blade.

FRY, JASON

7310 County Rd. 324, Hawley, TX 79525, Phone: 325-669-4805, frycustomknives@gmail.com; Web: www.frycustomknives.com

Specialties: Traditional hunting patterns in native Texas materials. **Patterns:** Primarily EDC and hunting/skinning knives under 8 inches, slip-joint folders and art knives. **Technical:** Stock removal and forging of 1080 carbon steel, D2 tool steel and 154CM stainless. **Prices:** $150 to $3,000. **Remarks:** Part-time maker since July 2008, and 2015 voting member of the Knifemakers' Guild. 2015 president of the Texas Knifemakers Guild. **Mark:** Jason Fry over Abilene, TX (2015 and prior), and Jason Fry over Hawley, TX (2015 and forward).

FUEGEN, LARRY

617 N Coulter Circle, Prescott, AZ 86303, Phone: 928-776-8777, fuegen@cableone.net; Web: www.larryfuegen.com

Specialties: High-art folders and classic and working straight knives. **Patterns:** Forged scroll folders, lockback folders and classic straight knives. **Technical:** Forges 5160, 1095 and his own Damascus. Works in exotic leather; offers elaborate filework and carving; likes natural handle materials, now offers own engraving. **Prices:** $1,200 to $26,000. **Remarks:** Full-time maker; first knife sold in 1975. Sole authorship on all knives. ABS Mastersmith. **Mark:** Initials connected or last name engraved.

FUJIKAWA, SHUN

Sawa 1157, Kaizuka, Osaka, JAPAN 597 0062, Phone: 81-724-23-4032, Fax: 81-726-23-9229

Specialties: Folders of his design and to customer specs. **Patterns:** Locking folders. **Technical:** Grinds his own steel. **Prices:** $450 to $2500; some to $3000. **Remarks:** Part-time maker.

FUKUTA, TAK

38-Umeagae-cho, Seki-City, Gifu, JAPAN, Phone: 0575-22-0264

Specialties: Bench-made fancy straight knives and folders. **Patterns:** Sheffield-type folders, Bowies and fighters. **Technical:** Grinds commercial Damascus. **Prices:** Start at $300. **Remarks:** Full-time maker. **Mark:** Name in knife logo.

FULLER, BRUCE A

3366 Ranch Rd. 32, Blanco, TX 78606, Phone: 832-262-0529, fullcoforg@aol.com **Specialties:** One-of-a-kind working/using straight knives and folders of his designs. **Patterns:** Bowies, hunters, folders, and utility/camp knives. **Technical:** Forges high-carbon steel and his own Damascus. Prefers El Solo Mesquite and natural materials. Offers filework. **Prices:** $200 to $500; some to $1800. **Remarks:** Spare-time maker; first knife sold in 1991. Doing business as Fullco Forge. **Mark:** Fullco, M.S.

FULLER, JACK A

7103 Stretch Ct, New Market, MD 21774, Phone: 719-395-3374, coloradojack2003@yahoo.com

Specialties: Straight working knives of his design and to customer specs. **Patterns:** Fighters, camp knives, hunters, tomahawks and art knives. **Technical:** Forges 5160, O1, W2 and his own Damascus. Does silver wire inlay and own leather work, wood lined sheaths for big camp knives. **Prices:** $400 and up. **Remarks:** Part-time maker. Master Smith in ABS; first knife sold in 1979. **Mark:** Fuller's Forge, MS.

FULTON, MICKEY

406 S Shasta St, Willows, CA 95988, Phone: 530-934-5780

Specialties: Working straight knives and folders of his design. **Patterns:** Hunters, Bowies, lockback folders and steak knife sets. **Technical:** Hand-filed, sanded, buffed ATS-34, 440C and A2. **Prices:** $65 to $600; some to $1200. **Remarks:** Full-time maker; first knife sold in 1979. **Mark:** Signature.

G

GADBERRY, EMMET

82 Purple Plum Dr, Hattieville, AR 72063, Phone: 501-354-4842

GADDY, GARY LEE

205 Ridgewood Lane, Washington, NC 27889, Phone: 252-946-4359

Specialties: Working/using straight knives of his design; period pieces. **Patterns:** Bowies, hunters, utility/camp knives, oyster knives. **Technical:** Grinds ATS-34, O1; forges 1095. **Prices:** $175+ **Remarks:** Spare-time maker; first knife sold in 1991. No longer accepts orders. **Mark:** Quarter moon stamp.

GAETA, ANGELO

Rua: Saldanha Marinho, 1281, Centro Jau, SP-CEP: 14.201310, BRAZIL 17201-310, e.a.gaeta@gmail.com; Facebook: cutelaria.a.gaeta@gmail.com

Specialties: Straight using knives to customers' specs. **Patterns:** Hunters, fighters, daggers, belt push daggers. **Technical:** Grinds ATS-34 and 440C stainless steel. All knives are unique pieces. **Prices:** $400 and up. **Remarks:** Full-time maker; first knife sold in 1992. **Mark:** First initial, last name.

GAHAGAN, KYLE

200 Preachers Bottom Dr., Moravian Falls, NC 28654, Phone: 919-359-9220, kylegahagan78@yahoo.com; Web: www.gahaganknives.com

Specialties: Bowies and fighters. **Patterns:** Custom designs from maker or customer. **Technical:** Forges 1095, W2, 1075, 1084 and damascus blade steels. **Prices:** $200 and up. **Remarks:** Full-time bladesmith; sold first knife in 2011. **Mark:** Gahagan crest with Gahagan underneath.

GAINES, BUDDY

GAINES KNIVES, 155 Red Hill Rd., Commerce, GA 30530, Web: www.gainesknives.com

Specialties: Collectible and working folders and straight knives. **Patterns:** Folders, hunters, Bowies, tactical knives. **Technical:** Forges own Damascus, grinds ATS-34, D2, commercial Damascus. Prefers mother-of-pearl and stag. **Prices:** Start at $200. **Remarks:** Part-time maker, sold first knife in 1985. **Mark:** Last name.

GAINEY, HAL
904 Bucklevel Rd, Greenwood, SC 29649, Phone: 864-223-0225, Web: www.scak.org
Specialties: Traditional working and using straight knives and folders. **Patterns:** Hunters, slip-joint folders and utility/camp knives. **Technical:** Hollow-grinds ATS-34 and D2; makes sheaths. **Prices:** $95 to $145; some to $500. **Remarks:** Full-time maker; first knife sold in 1975. **Mark:** Eagle head and last name.

GALLAGHER, BARRY
POB 892, 130 Main St., Lincoln, MT 59639, Phone: 406-366-6248, Web: www.gallagherknives.com
Specialties: One-of-a-kind Damascus folders. **Patterns:** Folders, utility to high art, some straight knives, hunter, Bowies, and art pieces. **Technical:** Forges own mosaic Damascus and carbon steel, some stainless. **Prices:** $400 to $5000+. **Remarks:** Full-time maker; first knife sold in 1993. Doing business as Gallagher Custom Knives. **Mark:** Last name.

GALLAGHER, SCOTT
335 Winston Manor Rd., Santa Rosa Beach, FL 32459, Phone: 850-865-8264, scottgallagher04@gmail.com; Facebook: SGallagherKnives
Specialties: Traditional hunters, bowies, fighters and camp knives. **Technical:** Forged-to-shape 1075, 80CrV2, 5160 and W2 blade steels. **Prices:** $300 to $1,500. **Remarks:** Serious part-time maker; first knife sold in 2014. **Mark:** S. Gallagher (with Anvil & Hammer).

GAMBLE, ROGER
18515 N.W. 28th Pl., Newberry, FL 32669, ROGERLGAMBLE@COX.NET
Specialties: Traditional working/using straight knives and folders of his design. **Patterns:** Liner locks and hunters. **Technical:** Grinds ATS-34 and Damascus. **Prices:** $150 to $2000. **Remarks:** Part-time maker; first knife sold in 1982. Doing business as Gamble Knives. **Mark:** First name in a fan of cards over last name.

GANN, TOMMY
2876 State Hwy. 198, Canton, TX 75103, Phone: 903-848-9375
Specialties: Art and working straight knives of my design or customer preferences/design. **Patterns:** Bowie, fighters, hunters, daggers. **Technical:** Forges Damascus 52100 and grinds ATS-34 and D2. **Prices:** $200 to $2500. **Remarks:** Full-time knifemaker, first knife sold in 2002. ABS journey bladesmith. **Mark:** TGANN.

GANSHORN, CAL
123 Rogers Rd., Regina, SK, CANADA S4S 6T7, Phone: 306-584-0524, cganshorn@accesscomm.ca or cganshorn@myaccess.ca
Specialties: Working and fancy fixed blade knives. **Patterns:** Bowies, hunters, daggers, and filleting. **Technical:** Makes own forged Damascus billets, ATS, salt heat treating, and custom forges and burners. **Prices:** $250 to $1500. **Remarks:** Part-time maker. **Mark:** Last name etched in ricasso area.

GARAU, MARCELLO
Via Alagon 42, Oristano, ITALY 09170, Phone: 00393479073454, marcellogarau@libero.it Web: www.knifecreator.com
Specialties: Mostly lock back folders with interframe. **Technical:** Forges own damascus for both blades and frames. **Prices:** 200 - 2,700 Euros. **Remarks:** Full-time maker; first knife made in 1995. Attends Milano Knife Show and ECCKSHOW yearly. **Mark:** M.Garau inside handle.

GARCIA, MARIO EIRAS
Rua Edmundo Scannapieco 300, Caxingui, SP, BRAZIL 05516-070, Phone: 011-37218304, Fax: 011-37214528
Specialties: Fantasy knives of his design; one-of-a-kind only. **Patterns:** Fighters, daggers, boots and two-bladed knives. **Technical:** Forges car leaf springs. Uses only natural handle material. **Prices:** $100 to $200. **Remarks:** Part-time maker; first knife sold in 1976. **Mark:** Two "B"s, one opposite the other.

GARDNER, ROBERT
13462 78th Pl. N, West Palm Beach, FL 33412
Specialties: Straight blades, forged and clay hardened or differentialy heat treated. Kydex and leather sheath making. **Patterns:** Working/using knives, some to customer specs, and high-end knives, daggers, bowies, ethnic knives, and Steelhead and Lil' Chub woodland survival/bushcraft knife set with an elaborate, versatile sheath system. Affordable hard-use production line of everyday carry belt knives, and less-expensive forged knives, neck knives and "wrench" knives. **Technical:** Grinds, forges and heat treats high-carbon 1084, 1095, 1075, W1, W2, 5160 and 52100 steels, some natural handle materials and Micarta for full-tang knives. **Prices:** $60 and up; sheaths $30 and up. **Remarks:** Full-time maker since 2010; first knife sold in 1986. **Mark:** Initials in angular script, stamped, engraved or etched.

GARNER, GEORGE
7527 Calhoun Dr. NE, Albuquerque, NM 87109, Phone: 505-797-9317, razorbackblades@msn.com Web: www.razorbackblades.com
Specialties: High art locking liner folders and Daggers of his own design. Working and high art straight knives. **Patterns:** Bowies, daggers, fighters and locking liner folders. **Technical:** Grinds 440C, CPM-154, ATS34 and others. Damascus, Mosaic Damascus and Mokume. Makes own custom leather sheaths. **Prices:** $150 - $2,500. **Remarks:** Part-time maker since 1993. Full-time maker as of 2011. Company name is Razorback Blades. **Mark:** GEORGE GARNER.

GARNER, LARRY W
13069 FM 14, Tyler, TX 75706, Phone: 903-597-6045, lwgarner@classicnet.net
Specialties: Fixed blade hunters and Bowies. **Patterns:** His designs or yours. **Technical:** Hand forges 5160. **Prices:** $200 to $500. **Remarks:** Apprentice bladesmith. **Mark:** Last name.

GARVOCK, MARK W
RR 1, Balderson, ON, CANADA K1G 1A0, Phone: 613-833-2545, Fax: 613-833-2208, garvock@travel-net.com
Specialties: Hunters, Bowies, Japanese, daggers and swords. **Patterns:** Cable Damascus, random pattern welded or to suit. **Technical:** Forged blades; hi-carbon. **Prices:** $250 to $900. **Remarks:** CKG member and ABS member. Shipping and taxes extra. **Mark:** Big G with M in middle.

GATLIN, STEVE
3812 Arroyo Seco, Schwartz, TX 78154, Phone: 229-328-5074, stevegatlinknives@hotmail.com; Web: www.stevegatlinknives.com
Specialties: Loveless-style knives, double-ground fighters and traditional hunters. Some tactical models of maker's design. Fixed blades only. **Technical:** Grinds CPM-154, ATS-34 and 154CM. **Prices:** $450 to $1,500 on base models. **Remarks:** Voting member of Knifemakers' Guild since 2009; first knife sold in 2008. **Mark:** Typical football shape with name on top and city below.

GEDRAITIS, CHARLES J
GEDRAITIS HAND CRAFTED KNIVES, 444 Shrewsbury St, Holden, MA 01520, Phone: 508-963-1861, gedraitisknives@yahoo.com; Web: www.gedraitisknives.com
Specialties: One-of-a-kind folders & automatics of his own design. **Patterns:** One-of-a-kind. **Technical:** Forges to shape mostly stock removal. **Prices:** $300 to $2500. **Remarks:** Full-time maker. **Mark:** 3 scallop shells with an initial inside each one: CJG.

GENOVESE, RICK
PO Box 226, 182 Purtill Tr., Tonto Basin, AZ 85553, Phone: 916-693-3979, genoveseknives@hotmail.com; Web: www.rickgenoveseknives.com
Specialties: Interframe-style folders. **Patterns:** Sleek folders in gentleman's designs. Also folding dirks and daggers. **Technical:** Main blade material is CPM 154. Also uses damascus by Devin Thomas and Jerry Rados. Inlays gemstones such as lapis lazuli, jade, opal, dinosaur bone, tiger eye, jasper, agate, malachite, petrified wood, as well as various pearls. **Prices:** $1,500-$10,000. **Remarks:** Full-time maker; first knife sold in 1975. **Mark:** Genovese in stylized letters.

GEORGE, HARRY
3137 Old Camp Long Rd, Aiken, SC 29805, Phone: 803-649-1963, hdkk-george@scescape.net
Specialties: Working straight knives of his design or to customer specs. **Patterns:** Hunters, skinners and utility knives. **Technical:** Grinds ATS-34. Prefers natural handle materials, hollow-grinds and mirror finishes. **Prices:** Start at $70. **Remarks:** Part-time maker; first knife sold in 1985. Trained under George Herron. Member SCAK. Member Knifemakers Guild. **Mark:** Name, city, state.

GEORGE, LES
6537 S. Staples St., Ste. 125 #406, Corpus Christi, TX 78413, Phone: 361-288-9777, les@georgeknives.com; Web: www.georgeknives.com
Specialties: Tactical frame locks and fixed blades. **Patterns:** Folders, balisongs, and fixed blades. **Technical:** CPM154, S30V, Chad Nichols Damascus. **Prices:** $200 to $800. **Remarks:** Full-time maker, first knife sold in 1992. Doing business as www.georgeknives.com. **Mark:** Last name over logo.

GEORGE, TOM
550 Aldbury Dr, Henderson, NV 89014, tagmaker@aol.com
Specialties: Working straight knives, display knives, custom meat cleavers, and folders of his design. **Patterns:** Hunters, Bowies, daggers, buckskinners, swords and folders. **Technical:** Uses D2, 440C, ATS-34 and 154CM. **Prices:** $500 to $13,500. **Remarks:** Custom orders not accepted "at this time". Full-time maker. First knife1982; first 350 knives were numbered; after that no numbers. Almost all his knives today are Bowies and swords. Creator and maker of the "Past Glories" series of knives. **Mark:** Tom George maker.

GEPNER, DON
2615 E Tecumseh, Norman, OK 73071, Phone: 405-364-2750
Specialties: Traditional working and using straight knives of his design. **Patterns:** Bowies and daggers. **Technical:** Forges his Damascus, 1095 and 5160. **Prices:** $100 to $400; some to $1000. **Remarks:** Spare-time maker; first knife sold in 1991. Has been forging since 1954; first edged weapon made at 9 years old. **Mark:** Last initial.

GERNER, THOMAS
PO Box 301, Walpole, WA, AUSTRALIA 6398, gerner@bordernet.com.au; Web: www.deepriverforge.com
Specialties: Forged working knives; plain steel and pattern welded. **Patterns:** Tries most patterns heard or read about. **Technical:** 5160, L6, O1, 52100 steels; Australian hardwood handles. **Prices:** $220 and up. **Remarks:** Achieved ABS Master Smith rating in 2001. **Mark:** Like a standing arrow and a leaning cross, T.G. in the Runic (Viking) alphabet.

GHIO, PAOLO
4330 Costa Mesa, Pensacola, FL 32504-7849, Phone: 850-393-0135, paologhio@hotmail.com
Specialties: Folders, fillet knives and skinners. **Patterns:** Maker's own design, or will work from a customer's pattern. **Technical:** Stock removal, all work in house, including heat treat. **Prices:** $200 to $500. **Mark:** PKG.

GIAGU, SALVATORE AND DEROMA MARIA ROSARIA
Via V Emanuele 64, Pattada (SS), ITALY 07016, Phone: 079-755918, Fax: 079-755918, coltelligiagupattada@tiscali.it Web: www.culterpattada.it
Specialties: Using and collecting traditional and new folders from Sardegna. **Patterns:** Folding, hunting, utility, skinners and kitchen knives. **Technical:** Forges ATS-34, 440, D2 and Damascus. **Prices:** $200 to $2000; some higher. **Mark:** First initial, last name and name of town and muflon's head.

GIBERT, PEDRO
Los Alamos 410, San Martin de los Andes, Neuquen, ARGENTINA 8370, Phone: 054-2972-410868, rosademayo@infovia.com.ar
Specialties: Hand forges: Stock removal and integral. High quality artistic knives of his design and to customer specifications. **Patterns:** Country (Argentine gaucho-style), knives, folders, Bowies, daggers, hunters. Others upon request. **Technical:** Blade: Bohler k110 Austrian steel (high resistance to waste). Handles: (Natural materials) ivory elephant, killer whale, hippo, walrus tooth, deer antler, goat, ram, buffalo horn, bone, rhea, sheep, cow, exotic woods (South America native woods) hand carved and engraved guards and blades. Stainless steel guards, finely polished: semi-matte or shiny finish. Sheaths: Raw or tanned leather, hand-stitched; rawhide or cotton yarn embroidered. Box: One wood piece, hand carved. Wooden hinges and locks. **Prices:** $600 and up. **Remarks:** Full-time maker. Made first knife in 1987. **Mark:** Only a rose logo. Buyers initials upon request.

GIBO, GEORGE
PO Box 4304, Hilo, HI 96720, Phone: 808-987-7002, geogibo@hilo808.net
Specialties: Straight knives and folders. **Patterns:** Hunters, bird and trout, utility, gentlemen and tactical folders. **Technical:** Grinds ATS-34, BG-42, Talonite, Stainless Steel Damascus. **Prices:** $250 to $1000. **Remarks:** Spare-time maker; first knife sold in 1995. **Mark:** Name, city and state around Hawaiian "Shaka" sign.

GILBERT, CHANTAL
291 Rue Christophe-Colomb est #105, Quebec City, QC, CANADA G1K 3T1, Phone: 418-525-6961, Fax: 418-525-4666, gilbertc@medion.qc.ca; Web:www.chantalgilbert.com
Specialties: Straight art knives that may resemble creatures, often with wings, shells and antennae, always with a beak of some sort, fixed blades in a feminine style. **Technical:** ATS-34 and Damascus. Handle materials usually silver that she forms to shape via special molds and a press; ebony and fossil ivory. **Prices:** Range from $500 to $4000. **Remarks:** Often embellishes her art knives with rubies, meteorite, 18k gold and similar elements.

GILBREATH, RANDALL
55 Crauswell Rd, Dora, AL 35062, Phone: 205-648-3902
Specialties: Damascus folders and fighters. **Patterns:** Folders and fixed blades. **Technical:** Forges Damascus and high-carbon; stock removal stainless steel. **Prices:** $300 to $1500. **Remarks:** Full-time maker; first knife sold in 1979. **Mark:** Name in ribbon.

GILJEVIC, BRANKO
35 Hayley Crescent, Queanbeyan 2620, New South Wales, AUSTRALIA 0262977613
Specialties: Classic working straight knives and folders of his design. **Patterns:** Hunters, Bowies, skinners and locking folders. **Technical:** Grinds 440C. Offers acid etching, scrimshaw and leather carving. **Prices:** $150 to $1500. **Remarks:** Part-time maker; first knife sold in 1987. Doing business as Sambar Custom Knives. **Mark:** Company name in logo.

GINGRICH, JUSTIN
5329 Anna Belle Ln., Wade, NC 28395, Phone: 507-230-0398, justin@gingrichtactical.com Web: www.gingrichtactical.com
Specialties: Anything from bushcraft to tactical, heavy on the tactical. **Patterns:** Fixed blades and folders. **Technical:** Uses all types of steel and handle material, method is stock-removal. **Prices:** $30 - $1000. **Remarks:** Full-time maker. **Mark:** Tang stamp is the old Ranger Knives logo.

GIRTNER, JOE
409 Catalpa Ave, Brea, CA 92821, Phone: 714-529-2388, conceptsinknives@aol.com
Specialties: Art knives and miniatures. **Patterns:** Mainly Damascus (some carved). **Technical:** Many techniques and materials combined. Wood carving knives and tools, hunters, custom orders. **Prices:** $55 to $3000. **Mark:** Name.

GITTINGER, RAYMOND
6940 S Rt 100, Tiffin, OH 44883, Phone: 419-397-2517

GLASSER, ROGER CESAR
Av. Ceci, 679 - Sao Paulo - SP, BRAZIL 04065-001, Phone: +55-11-974615357, roger.glasser@gmail.com; Web: www.mostrainternacionaldecutelaria.com
Specialties: Fixed blades, military knives, fighters and hunters. **Prices:** $300 to $1,000. **Remarks:** Part-time maker, IBO founder, ABS member, SBC member and CKCA member. Creator and manager of the biggest knife show in Latin America: Mostra Internacional de Cutelaria, a.k.a. Brazil Knife Show. **Mark:** R.Glasser.

GLOVER, RON
5896 Thornhill Ave., Cincinnati, OH 45224, Phone: 513-404-7107, r.glover@zoomtown.com
Specialties: High-tech working straight knives and folders. **Patterns:** Hunters to Bowies; some interchangeable blade models; unique locking mechanisms. **Technical:** Grinds 440C, 154CM; buys Damascus. **Prices:** $70 to $500; some to $800. **Remarks:** Part-time maker; first knife sold in 1981. **Mark:** Name in script.

GLOVER, WARREN D
dba BUBBA KNIVES, PO Box 475, Cleveland, GA 30528, Phone: 706-865-3998, Fax: 706-348-7176, warren@bubbaknives.net; Web: www.bubbaknives.net
Specialties: Traditional and custom working and using straight knives of his design and to customer request. **Patterns:** Hunters, skinners, bird and fish, utility and kitchen knives. **Technical:** Grinds 440, ATS-34 and stainless steel Damascus. **Prices:** $75 to $400 and up. **Remarks:** Full-time maker; sold first knife in 1995. **Mark:** Bubba, year, name, state.

GODDARD, WAYNE
473 Durham Ave, Eugene, OR 97404, Phone: 541-689-8098, wgoddard44@comcast.net
Specialties: Working/using straight knives and folders. **Patterns:** Hunters and folders. **Technical:** Works exclusively with wire Damascus and his own-pattern welded material. **Prices:** $250 to $4000. **Remarks:** Full-time maker; first knife sold in 1963. **Mark:** Blocked initials on forged blades; regular capital initials on stock removal.

GODLESKY, BRUCE F.
1002 School Rd., Apollo, PA 15613, Phone: 724-840-5786, brucegodlesky@yahoo.com; Web: www.birdforge.com
Specialties: Working/using straight knives and tomahawks, mostly forged. **Patterns:** Hunters, birds and trout, fighters and tomahawks. **Technical:** Most forged, some stock removal. Carbon steel only. 5160, O-1, W2, 10xx series. Makes own Damascus and welded cable. **Prices:** Starting at $75. **Mark:** BIRDOG FORGE.

GOERS, BRUCE
3423 Royal Ct S, Lakeland, FL 33813, Phone: 941-646-0984
Specialties: Fancy working and using straight knives of his design and to customer specs. **Patterns:** Hunters, fighters, Bowies and fantasy knives. **Technical:** Grinds ATS-34, some Damascus. **Prices:** $195 to $600; some to $1300. **Remarks:** Part-time maker; first knife sold in 1990. Doing business as Vulture Cutlery. **Mark:** Buzzard with initials.

GOLDBERG, DAVID
321 Morris Rd, Ft Washington, PA 19034, Phone: 215-654-7117, david@goldmountainforge.com; Web: www.goldmountainforge.com
Specialties: Japanese-style designs, will work with special themes in Japanese genre. **Patterns:** Kozuka, Tanto, Wakazashi, Katana, Tachi, Sword canes, Yari and Naginata. **Technical:** Forges his own Damascus and makes his own handmade tamehagane steel from straw ash, iron, carbon and clay. Uses traditional materials, carves fittings handles and cases. Hardens all blades in traditional Japanese clay differential technique. **Remarks:** Full-time maker; first knife sold in 1987. Japanese swordsmanship teacher (jaido) and Japanese self-defense teach (aikido). **Mark:** Name (kinzan) in Japanese Kanji on Tang under handle.

GOLDEN, RANDY
6492 Eastwood Glen Dr, Montgomery, AL 36117, Phone: 334-271-6429, rgolden1@mindspring.com
Specialties: Collectable quality hand rubbed finish, hunter, camp, Bowie straight knives, custom leather sheaths with exotic skin inlays and tooling. **Technical:** Stock removal ATS-34, CPM154, S30V and BG-42. Natural handle materials primarily stag and ivory. **Prices:** $500 to $1500. **Remarks:** Full-time maker, member Knifemakers Guild, first knife sold in 2000. **Mark:** R. R. Golden Montgomery, AL.

GONCALVES, LUIZ GUSTAVO
R Alberto Gebara, 124A -Sao Paulo - SP, BRAZIL 04611-060, Phone: +55-11-98336-0001, lgustavo@lgustavo.com; Web: www.lgustavo.com
Specialties: Most types of fixed blades of his own designs or to customer specs. **Patterns:** Hunters, fighters, bowies, gaucho, utility, camp and kitchen knives. **Technical:** Forges and grinds carbon steel (5160, 52100, 01) and his own damascus in random, ladder, raindrop, W's and other patterns. Heat treatment in electronically controlled kiln to obtain maximum control. Natural handle materials, including hardwood, stabilized wood, giraffe bone, deer stag, merino horn and others. Flat and hollow grinds. **Prices:** $400 to $1,300. **Remarks:** Part-time maker, ABS apprentice; first knife sold in 2012. **Mark:** LGustavo.

GONZALEZ, LEONARDO WILLIAMS
Ituzaingo 473, Maldonado, URUGUAY 20000, Phone: 598 4222 1617, Fax: 598 4222 1617, willyknives@hotmail.com; Web: www.willyknives.com
Specialties: Classic high-art and fantasy straight knives; traditional working and using knives of his design, in standard patterns or to customer specs. **Patterns:** Hunters, Bowies, daggers, fighters, boots, swords and utility/camp knives. **Technical:** Forges and grinds high-carbon and stainless Bohler steels. **Prices:** $100 to $2500. **Remarks:** Full-time maker; first knife sold in 1985. **Mark:** Willy, whale, R.O.U.

GOO, TAI
5920 W Windy Lou Ln, Tucson, AZ 85742, Phone: 520-744-9777, taigoo@msn.com; Web: www.taigoo.com
Specialties: High art, neo-tribal, bush and fantasy. **Technical:** Hand forges, does own heat treating, makes own Damascus. **Prices:** $150 to $500 some to $10,000. **Remarks:** Full-time maker; first knife sold in 1978. **Mark:** Chiseled signature.

GOOD, D.R.
Custom Knives and Weaponry, 6125 W. 100 S., Tipton, IN 46072, Phone: 765-963-6971, drntammigood@bluemarble.net
Specialties: Working knives, own design, Scagel style, "critter" knives, carved handles. **Patterns:** Bowies, large and small, neck knives and miniatures. Offers carved handles, snake heads, eagles, wolves, bear, skulls. **Technical:** Damascus, some stelite, 6K, pearl, ivory, moose. **Prices:** $150 - $1500. **Remarks:** Full-time maker. First knife was Bowie made from a 2-1/2 truck bumper in military. **Mark:** D.R. Good in oval and for minis, DR with a buffalo skull.

GOODE, BEAR
BEAR KNIVES, PO Box 6474, Navajo Dam, NM 87419, Phone: 505-632-8184, beargood58@gmail.com

Specialties: Working/using straight knives of his design and in standard patterns. **Patterns:** Bowies, hunters and utility/camp knives. **Technical:** Grinds 440C, ATS-34, 154-CM; forges and grinds 1095, 5160 and other steels on request; uses Damascus. **Prices:** $150 and up. **Remarks:** Full-time maker since 2010; first knife made in 1975 and first knife sold in 1993. Doing business as Bear Knives. **Mark:** First and last name with a three-toed paw print.

GOODE, BRIAN
203 Gordon Ave, Shelby, NC 28152, Phone: 704-434-6496, web:www.bgoodeknives.com
Specialties: Flat ground working knives with etched/antique or brushed finish. **Patterns:** Field, camp, hunters, skinners, survival, kitchen, maker's design or yours. Currently full tang only with supplied leather sheath. **Technical:** 0-1, D2 and other ground flat stock. Stock removal and differential heat treat preferred. Etched antique/etched satin working finish preferred. Micarta and hardwoods for strength. **Prices:** $150 to $700. **Remarks:** Part-time maker and full-time knife lover. First knife sold in 2004. **Mark:** B. Goode with NC separated by a feather.

GOODPASTURE, TOM
13432 Farrington Road, Ashland, VA 23005, Phone: 804-752-8363, rtg007@aol.com; web: goodpastureknives.com
Specialties: Working/using straight knives of his own design, or customer specs. File knives and primative reproductions. **Patterns:** Hunters, bowies, small double-edge daggers, kitchen, custom miniatures and camp/utility. **Technical:** Stock removal, D-2, 0-1, 12C27, 420 HC, 52100. Forged blades of W-2, 1084, and 1095. Flat grinds only. **Prices:** $60 - $300. **Remarks:** Part-time maker, first knife sold at Blade Show 2005. Lifetime guarantee and sharpening. **Mark:** Early mark were initials RTG, current **mark:** Goodpasture.

GORDON, LARRY B
23555 Newell Cir W, Farmington Hills, MI 48336, Phone: 248-477-5483, lbgordon1@aol.com
Specialties: Folders, small fixed blades. New design rotating scale release automatic. **Patterns:** Rotating handle locker. Ambidextrous fire (R&L) **Prices:** $450 minimum. **Remarks:** High line materials preferred. **Mark:** Gordon.

GORENFLO, JAMES T (JT)
9145 Sullivan Rd, Baton Rouge, LA 70818, Phone: 225-261-5868
Specialties: Traditional working and using straight knives of his design. **Patterns:** Bowies, hunters and utility/camp knives. **Technical:** Forges 5160, 1095, 52100 and his own Damascus. **Prices:** Start at $200. **Remarks:** Part-time maker; first knife sold in 1992. **Mark:** Last name or initials, J.S. on reverse.

GOSHOVSKYY, VASYL
BL.4, C. San Jaime 65, Torreblanca 12596, Castellon de la Plana, SPAIN, Phone: +34-664-838-882, baz_knife@mail.ru; Web: www.goshovskyy-knives.com
Specialties: Presentation and working fixed-blade knives. **Patterns:** R.W. Loveless-pattern knives, primarily hunters and skinners. **Technical:** Stock-removal method. Prefers natural materials for handle scales. Uses primarily RWL-34, CPM-154, N690 or similar blade steel. **Remarks:** Full-time maker.

GOSSMAN, SCOTT
PO Box 41, Whiteford, MD 21160, Phone: 443-617-2444, scogos@peoplepc.com; Web:www.gossmanknives.com
Specialties: Heavy duty knives for big-game hunting and survival. **Patterns:** Modified clip-point/spear-point blades, bowies, hunters and bushcraft. **Technical:** Grinds A2, O1, CPM-154, CPM-3V, S7, flat/convex grinds and convex micro-bevel edges. **Prices:** $65 to $500. **Remarks:** Full-time maker doing business as Gossman Knives. **Mark:** Gossman and steel type.

GOTTAGE, DANTE
43227 Brooks Dr, Clinton Twp., MI 48038-5323, Phone: 586-286-7275
Specialties: Working knives of his design or to customer specs. **Patterns:** Large and small skinners, fighters, Bowies and fillet knives. **Technical:** Grinds O1, 440C and 154CM and ATS-34. **Prices:** $150 to $600. **Remarks:** Part-time maker; first knife sold in 1975. **Mark:** Full name in script letters.

GOTTAGE, JUDY
43227 Brooks Dr, Clinton Twp., MI 48038-5323, Phone: 810-343-4662, jgottage@remaxmetropolitan.com
Specialties: Custom folders of her design or to customer specs. **Patterns:** Interframes or integral. **Technical:** Stock removal. **Prices:** $300 to $3000. **Remarks:** Full-time maker; first knife sold in 1980. **Mark:** Full name, maker in script.

GOTTSCHALK, GREGORY J
12 First St. (Ft. Pitt), Carnegie, PA 15106, Phone: 412-279-6692
Specialties: Fancy working straight knives and folders to customer specs. **Patterns:** Hunters to tantos, locking folders to minis. **Technical:** Grinds 440C, 154CM, ATS-34. Now making own Damascus. Most knives have mirror finishes. **Prices:** Start at $150. **Remarks:** Part-time maker; first knife sold in 1977. **Mark:** Full name in crescent.

GOUKER, GARY B
PO Box 955, Sitka, AK 99835, Phone: 907-747-3476
Specialties: Hunting knives for hard use. **Patterns:** Skinners, semi-skinners, and such. **Technical:** Likes natural materials, inlays, stainless steel. **Prices:** Moderate. **Remarks:** New Alaskan maker. **Mark:** Name.

GRAHAM, GORDON
3145 CR 4008, New Boston, TX 75570, Phone: 903-293-2610, Web: www.grahamknives.com
Prices: $325 to $850. **Mark:** Graham.

GRAHAM, LEVI
6296 W. 3rd St., Greeley, CO 80634, Phone: 970-371-0477, lgknives@hotmail.com; www.levigrahamknives.com
Specialties: Forged frontier/period/Western knives. **Patterns:** Hunters, patch knives, skinners, camp, belt and bowies. **Technical:** Forges high-carbon steels and some stock removal in 1095, 1084, 5160, L6, 80CRV2 and 52100. Handle materials include antler, bone, ivory, horn, hardwoods, Micarta and G-10. Rawhide-covered, vegetable-tanned sheaths decorated with deer fringe, quill work for a band or medicine wheel, beads, cones, horse hair, etc. Custom orders welcome. **Prices:** $300 and up. **Remarks:** Member of ABS and PKA. **Mark:** "lg" stamped in lower case letters.

GRANGER, PAUL J
704 13th Ct. SW, Largo, FL 33770-4471, Phone: 727-953-3249, grangerknives@live.com Web: http://palehorsefighters.blogspot.com
Specialties: Working straight knives of his own design and a few folders. **Patterns:** 2.75" to 4" work knives, tactical knives and Bowies from 5"-9." **Technical:** Grinds CPM154-CM, ATS-34 and forges 52100 and 1084. Offers filework. **Prices:** $95 to $500. **Remarks:** Part-time maker since 1997. Sold first knife in 1997. Doing business as Granger Knives and Pale Horse Fighters. Member of ABS and Florida Knifemakers Association. **Mark:** "Granger" or "Palehorse Fighters."

GRANGETTE, ALAIN
7, Erenas, 23210 Azat-Chatenet, FRANCE, Phone: 05-55-81-32-64, alain.grangette@gmail.com; Web: www.alaingrangette.com
Specialties: Art knives and folders with precise, complex folding mechanisms and tight fits and finishes. **Patterns:** Art folders, fixed blades and cutlery. **Technical:** Uses Pantograph and includes mirror finishing, engraving and contemporary materials. Every knife realized is a unique piece, and every blade, mechanism, screw and all other parts are handmade.

GRAVELINE, PASCAL AND ISABELLE
38 Rue de Kerbrezillic, Moelan-sur-Mer, FRANCE 29350, Phone: 33 2 98 39 73 33, atelier.graveline@wanadoo.fr; Web: www.graveline-couteliers.com
Specialties: French replicas from the 17th, 18th and 19th centuries. **Patterns:** Traditional folders and multi-blade pocket knives; traveling knives, fruit knives and fork sets; puzzle knives and friend's knives; rivet less knives. **Technical:** Grind 12C27, ATS-34, Damascus and carbon steel. **Prices:** $500 to $5000. **Remarks:** Full-time makers; first knife sold in 1992. **Mark:** Last name over head of ram.

GRAVES, DAN
4887 Dixie Garden Loop, Shreveport, LA 71105, Phone: 318-865-8166, Web: wwwtheknifemaker.com
Specialties: Traditional forged blades and Damascus. **Patterns:** Bowies (D guard also), fighters, hunters, large and small daggers. **Remarks:** Full-time maker. **Mark:** Initials with circle around them.

GRAY, BOB
8206 N Lucia Court, Spokane, WA 99208, Phone: 509-468-3924
Specialties: Straight working knives of his own design or to customer specs. **Patterns:** Hunter, fillet and carving knives. **Technical:** Forges 5160, L6 and some 52100; grinds 440C. **Prices:** $100 to $600. **Remarks:** Part-time knifemaker; first knife sold in 1991. Doing business as Hi-Land Knives. **Mark:** HI-L.

GRAY, DANIEL
GRAY KNIVES, POB 718, Brownville, ME 04414, Phone: 207-965-2191, mail@grayknives.com; Web: www.grayknives.com
Specialties: Straight knives, fantasy, folders, automatics and traditional of his own design. **Patterns:** Automatics, fighters, hunters. **Technical:** Grinds O1, 154CM and D2. **Prices:** From $155 to $750. **Remarks:** Full-time maker; first knife sold in 1974. **Mark:** Gray Knives.

GRAY, ROBB
6026 46th Ave. SW, Seattle, WA 98136, Phone: 206-280-7622, robb.gray@graycloud-designs.com; Web: www.graycloud-designs.com
Specialties: Hunting, fishing and leather-workers' knives, along with daggers and utility ranch knives. **Technical:** Stock-removal maker using 440C, CPM-S30V, CPM-154, CPM-12C27, CPM-13C26 and CPM-19C27 stainless steels. Also engraves knives in Sheridan, single point and Western bright cut styles. Owner of "Resinwood," a certified wood fiber product sold to knifemaker supply companies for handle material. **Remarks:** Full-time artist/maker; first knife made in 2009. **Mark:** A rain cloud with name "Graycloud" next to it, surrounded by an oval.

GRAYMAN, MIKE
GRAYMAN KNIVES, POB 50, PMB 132, Lake Arrowhead, CA 92352, info@graymanknives.com; Web: www.graymanknives.com
Specialties: Single-bevel fixed blades and hard-use frame-lock folders. **Technical:** Hand grinds fixed blades using 1095 steel with GunKote finishes, G-10 handles, Cordura sheaths and free personalized hand engraving on blade spines. Precision-machined folders include CPM 20CV and CPM S30V blade steels with titanium handles. **Prices:** $160 to $425. **Remarks:** Started making knives in 2004. **Mark:** "Grayman" hand engraved on the spine of each knife.

GRECO, JOHN
100 Mattie Jones Rd, Greensburg, KY 42743, Phone: 270-932-3335
Specialties: Folders. **Patterns:** Tactical, fighters, camp knives, short swords. **Technical:** Stock removal carbon steel. **Prices:** Affordable. **Remarks:** Full-time maker since 1979. First knife sold in 1979. **Mark:** GRECO

GREEN, BILL
6621 Eastview Dr, Sachse, TX 75048, Phone: 972-463-3147

Specialties: High-art and working straight knives and folders of his design and to customer specs. **Patterns:** Bowies, hunters, kitchen knives and locking folders. **Technical:** Grinds ATS-34, D2 and 440V. Hand-tooled custom sheaths. **Prices:** $70 to $350; some to $750. **Remarks:** Part-time maker; first knife sold in 1990. **Mark:** Last name.

GREEN, WILLIAM (BILL)
46 Warren Rd, View Bank, VIC, AUSTRALIA 3084, Fax: 03-9459-1529

Specialties: Traditional high-tech straight knives and folders. **Patterns:** Japanese-influenced designs, hunters, Bowies, folders and miniatures. **Technical:** Forges O1, D2 and his own Damascus. Offers lost wax castings for bolsters and pommels. Likes natural handle materials, gems, silver and gold. **Prices:** $400 to $750; some to $1200. **Remarks:** Full-time maker. **Mark:** Initials.

GREENAWAY, DON
3325 Dinsmore Tr, Fayetteville, AR 72704, Phone: 501-521-0323

Specialties: Liner locks and bowies. **Prices:** $150 to $1500. **Remarks:** 20 years experience.**Mark:** Greenaway over Fayetteville, Ark.

GREENE, CHRIS
707 Cherry Lane, Shelby, NC 28150, Phone: 704-434-5620

GREENE, DAVID
570 Malcom Rd, Covington, GA 30209, Phone: 770-784-0657

Specialties: Straight working using knives. **Patterns:** Hunters. **Technical:** Forges mosaic and twist Damascus. Prefers stag and desert ironwood for handle material.

GREENE, STEVE
DUNN KNIVES INC, PO Box 307 1449 Nocatee St., Intercession City, FL 33848, Phone: 800-245-6483, s.greene@earthlink.net; Web: www.dunnknives.com

Specialties: Skinning & fillet knives. **Patterns:** Skinners, drop points, clip points and fillets. **Technical:** CPM-S30V powdered metal steel manufactured by Niagara Specialty Metals. **Prices:** $100 to $350. **Mark:** Dunn by Greene and year. **Remarks:** Full-time knifemaker. First knife sold in 1972. Each knife is handcrafted and includes holster-grade leather sheath.

GREENFIELD, G O
2605 15th St #310, Everett, WA 98201, Phone: 425-232-6011, garyg1946@yahoo.com

Specialties: High-tech and working straight knives and folders of his design. **Patterns:** Boots, daggers, hunters and one-of-a-kinds. **Technical:** Grinds ATS-34, D2, 440C and T-440V. Makes sheaths for each knife. **Prices:** $100 to $800; some to $10,000. **Remarks:** Part-time maker; first knife sold in 1978. **Mark:** Springfield®, serial number.

GREGORY, MATTHEW M.
74 Tarn Tr., Glenwood, NY 14069, Phone: 716-863-1215, mgregoryknives@yahoo.com; Web: www.mgregoryknives.com

Patterns: Wide variation of styles, as I make what I like to make. Bowies, fighters, Neo-American/Japanese-inspired blades, occasionally kitchen knives. **Technical:** Forging and stock removal, using forging steels such as 1084, 1095, W2 and CruForgeV, as well as high-alloy steels like CPM-3V and CPM-S110V. Hamon (blade temper line) development and polishing. **Prices:** $350 and up. **Remarks:** Part-time maker since 2005. **Mark:** M. Gregory.

GREGORY, MICHAEL
211 Calhoun Rd, Belton, SC 29627, Phone: 864-338-8898, gregom.123@charter.net

Specialties: Interframe folding knives, working hunters and period pieces. Hand rubbed finish, engraving by maker. **Patterns:** Hunters, bowies, daggers and folding knives. **Technical:** Grinds ATS-34 and other makers' damascus. **Prices:** $200 and up. **Remarks:** Full-time maker; first knife sold in 1980. **Mark:** Name, city in logo.

GREINER, RICHARD
1073 E County Rd 32, Green Springs, OH 44836, Phone: 419-483-4613, rgreiner7295@yahoo.com

Specialties: High-carbon steels, edge hardened. **Patterns:** Most. **Technical:** Hand forged. **Prices:** $125 and up. **Remarks:** Have made knives for 30 years. **Mark:** Maple leaf.

GREISS, JOCKL
Herrenwald 15, Schenkenzell, GERMANY 77773, Phone: +49 7836 95 71 69 or +49 7836 95 55 76, www.jocklgreiss@yahoo.com

Specialties: Classic and working using straight knives of his design. **Patterns:** Bowies, daggers and hunters. **Technical:** Uses only Jerry Rados Damascus. All knives are one-of-a-kind made by hand; no machines are used. **Prices:** $700 to $2000; some to $3000. **Remarks:** Full-time maker; first knife sold in 1984. **Mark:** An "X" with a long vertical line through it.

GREY, PIET
PO Box 363, Naboomspruit, LP, SOUTH AFRICA 0560, Phone: 014-743-3613

Specialties: Fancy working and using straight knives of his design. **Patterns:** Fighters, hunters and utility/camp knives. **Technical:** Grinds ATS-34 and AEB-L; forges and grinds Damascus. Solder less fitting of guards. Engraves and scrimshaws. **Prices:** $125 to $750; some to $1500. **Remarks:** Part-time maker; first knife sold in 1970. **Mark:** Last name.

GRIFFIN, JOHN
26101 Pine Shadows, Hockley, TX 77447, Phone: 281-414-7111, griff6363@yahoo.com; Web: www.griffinknives.us

Specialties: Push button automatics. **Patterns:** All patterns, including custom-designed pieces. **Technical:** Stainless and damascus blade steels with differing textured designs on stainless steel bolsters. **Prices:** Start at $800. **Remarks:** Guaranteed for life, very durable and unique designs.

GRIFFIN JR., HOWARD A
14299 SW 31st Ct, Davie, FL 33330, Phone: 954-474-5406, mgriffin18@aol.com

Specialties: Working straight knives and folders. **Patterns:** Hunters, Bowies, locking folders with his own push-button lock design. **Technical:** Grinds 440C. **Prices:** $100 to $200; some to $500. **Remarks:** Part-time maker; first knife sold in 1983. **Mark:** Initials.

GRIMES, MARK
PO BOX 1293, Bedford, TX 76095, Phone: 817-320-7274, ticktock107@gmail.com

Specialties: Qs. **Patterns:** Hunters, fighters, bowies. **Technical:** Custom hand forged 1084 steel blades full and hidden tang, heat treating, sheathes. **Prices:** $150-$400. **Remarks:** Part-time maker, first knife sold in 2009. **Mark:** Last name.

GRIZZARD, JIM
3626 Gunnels Ln., Oxford, AL 36203, Phone: 256-403-1232, grizzardforgiven@aol.com

Specialties: Hand carved art knives inspired by sole authorship. **Patterns:** Fixedblades, folders, and swords. **Technical:** Carving handles, artgrinding, forged and stock removal. **Prices:** Vary. **Remarks:** Uses knives mostly as a ministry to bless others. **Mark:** FOR HIS GLORY CUSTOM KNIVES OR j grizzard in a grizzly bear.

GROSPITCH, ERNIE
18440 Amityville Dr, Orlando, FL 32820, Phone: 407-568-5438, shrpknife@aol.com; Web: www.erniesknives.com

Specialties: Bowies, hunting, fishing, kitchen, lockback folders, leather craft and knifemaker logo stenciling/blue lightning stencil. **Patterns:** My design or customer's. **Technical:** Stock removal using most available steels. **Prices:** Vary. **Remarks:** Full-time maker, sold first knife in 1990. Blue Lightning stencils. **Mark:** Etched name over Thunderbird image.

GROSS, W W
109 Dylan Scott Dr, Archdale, NC 27263-3858

Specialties: Working knives. **Patterns:** Hunters, boots, fighters. **Technical:** Grinds. **Prices:** Moderate. **Remarks:** Full-time maker. **Mark:** Name.

GROSSMAN, STEWART
24 Water St #419, Clinton, MA 01510, Phone: 508-365-2291; 800-mysword

Specialties: Miniatures and full-size knives and swords. **Patterns:** One-of-a-kind miniatures—jewelry, replicas—and wire-wrapped figures. Full-size art, fantasy and combat knives, daggers and modular systems. **Technical:** Forges and grinds most metals and Damascus. Uses gems, crystals, electronics and motorized mechanisms. **Prices:** $20 to $300; some to $4500 and higher. **Remarks:** Full-time maker; first knife sold in 1985. **Mark:** G1.

GROVES, GARY
P.O. Box 101, Canvas, WV 26662, ggroves51@gmail.com

Specialties: Fixed blades and hidden-tang knives. **Patterns:** Hunters, skinners and bowies. **Technical:** Stock-removal method using ATS 34 and 154CM steels. Handles are mainly natural materials such as bone, horn, stag and wood, with filework on just about all knives. Every knife comes with a made-to-fit sheath. **Prices:** $350 to $1,200. **Remarks:** Full-time knifemaker; first knife sold in 2007. **Mark:** Last name over an anvil and a capital G in the middle of the anvil.

GRUSSENMEYER, PAUL G
310 Kresson Rd, Cherry Hill, NJ 08034, Phone: 856-428-1088, pgrussentne@comcast.net; Web: www.pgcarvings.com

Specialties: Assembling fancy and fantasy straight knives with his own carved handles. **Patterns:** Bowies, daggers, folders, swords, hunters and miniatures. **Technical:** Uses forged steel and Damascus, stock removal and knapped obsidian blades. **Prices:** $250 to $4000. **Remarks:** Spare-time maker; first knife sold in 1991. **Mark:** First and last initial hooked together on handle.

GUARNERA, ANTHONY R
42034 Quail Creek Dr, Quartzhill, CA 93536, Phone: 661-722-4032

Patterns: Hunters, camp, Bowies, kitchen, fighter knives. **Technical:** Forged and stock removal. **Prices:** $100 and up.

GUINN, TERRY
13026 Hwy 6 South, Eastland, TX 76448, Phone: 254-629-8603, Web: www.terryguinn.com

Specialties: Working fixed blades and balisongs. **Patterns:** Almost all types of folding and fixed blades, from patterns and "one of a kind". **Technical:** Stock removal all types of blade steel with preference for air hardening steel. Does own heat treating, all knives Rockwell tested in shop. **Prices:** $200 to $2,000. **Remarks:** Part time maker since 1982, sold first knife 1990. **Mark:** Full name with cross in the middle.

GUNTER, BRAD
13 Imnaha Rd., Tijeras, NM 87059, Phone: 505-281-8080

GUNTHER, EDDIE
11 Nedlands Pl Burswood, Auckland, NEW ZEALAND 2013, Phone: 006492722373, eddit.gunther49@gmail.com

Specialties: Drop point hunters, boot, Bowies. All mirror finished. **Technical:** Grinds D2, 440C, 12c27. **Prices:** $250 to $800. **Remarks:** Part-time maker, first knife sold in 1986. **Mark:** Name, city, country.

H

HAAS, RANDY
HHH Knives, 3875 Vandyke Rd., Marlette, MI 48453, Phone: 989-635-7059, Web: www.hhhcustomknives.com

Specialties: Handmade custom kitchen and culinary knives, hunters, fighters, folders and art knives. **Technical:** Damascus maker and sales. **Remarks:** Full-time maker for 10 years. **Mark:** Three H's with a knife behind the HHH.

HACKNEY, DANA A.

787 Mountain Meadows Rd., Naples, ID 83847-5044, Phone: 719-481-3940; Cell: 719-651-5634, danahackneyknives@gmail.com and dshackney@Q.com

Specialties: Hunters, bowies and everyday carry knives, and some kitchen cutlery. **Technical:** ABS journeyman smith who forges 1080 series, 5160, 52100, 01, W2 and his own damascus. Uses CPM-154 mostly for stainless knives. **Prices:** $150 and up. **Remarks:** Sole ownership knives and sheaths. Full-time maker as of July 2012. Sold first knife in 2005. ABS, MKA and PKA member. **Mark:** Last name, HACKNEY on left-side ricasso.

HAGEN, DOC

POB 58, 702 5th St. SE, Pelican Rapids, MN 56572, Phone: 218-863-8503, dochagen@gmail.com; Web: www.dochagencustomknives.com

Specialties: Folders. Autos:bolster release-dual action. Slipjoint folders**Patterns:** Defense-related straight knives; wide variety of folders. **Technical:** Dual action release, bolster release autos. **Prices:** $300 to $800; some to $3000. **Remarks:** Full-time maker; first knife sold in 1975. Makes his own Damascus. **Mark:** DOC HAGEN in shield, knife, banner logo; or DOC.

HAGGERTY, GEORGE S

PO Box 88, Jacksonville, VT 05342, Phone: 802-368-7437, swewater@sover.net

Specialties: Working straight knives and folders. **Patterns:** Hunters, claws, camp and fishing knives, locking folders and backpackers. **Technical:** Forges and grinds W2, 440C and 154CM. **Prices:** $85 to $300. **Remarks:** Part-time maker; first knife sold in 1981. **Mark:** Initials or last name.

HAGUE, GEOFF

Unit 5, Project Workshops, Lains Farm, Quarley, Hampshire, UNITED KINGDOM SP11 8PX, Phone: (+44) 01672-870212, Fax: (+44) 01672 870212, geoff@ hagueknives.com; Web: www.hagueknives.com

Specialties: Fixed blade and folding knives. **Patterns:** Back lock, locking liner, slip joint, and friction folders. **Technical:** Grinds D2, RWL-34 and damascus. Mainly natural handle materials. **Prices:** $500 to $2,000. **Remarks:** Full-time maker. **Mark:** Last name.

HAINES, JEFF

Haines Custom Knives, W3678 Bay View Rd., Mayville, WI 53050, Phone: 920-387-0212, knifeguy95@gmail.com; Web: www.hainescustom.com

Patterns: Hunters, skinners, camp knives, customer designs welcome. **Technical:** Forges 1095, 5160, and Damascus, grinds A2. **Prices:** $75 and up. **Remarks:** Part-time maker since 1995. **Mark:** Last name.

HALE, LLOYD

7593 Beech Hill Rd., Pulaski, TN 38478, Phone: 931-424-5846, lloydahale@gmail.com

Specialties: Museum-grade, one-of-a-kind daggers, folders and sub-hilt fighting knives. **Remarks:** Full-time maker for 44+ years. Spent 20+ years creating a one-of-a-kind knife collection for Owsley Brown Frazier of Louisville, KY. I don't accept orders anymore.

HALFRICH, JERRY

340 Briarwood, San Marcos, TX 78666, Phone: 512-353-2582, jerryhalfrich@ grandecom.net; Web: www.halfrichknives.com

Specialties: Working knives and specialty utility knives for the professional and serious hunter. Uses proven designs in both straight and folding knives. Pays close attention to fit and finish. Art knives on special request. **Patterns:** Hunters, skinners, and lockback, LinerLock and slip-joint folders. **Technical:** Grinds both flat and hollow D2, Damasteel and CPM 154, makes high precision folders. **Prices:** $450 to $1,500. **Remarks:** Full-time maker since 2000. DBA Halfrich Custom Knives. **Mark:** HALFRICH.

HALL, JEFF

179 Niblick Rd., # 180, Paso Robles, CA 93446, Phone: 562-594-4740, info@ nemesis-knives.com; Web: www.nemisis-knives.com

Specialties: Collectible and working folders and fixed blades of his design. **Technical:** Grinds CPM-S35VN, CPM-154, and various makers' damascus. **Patterns:** Fighters, gentleman's, hunters and utility knives. **Prices:** $100 and up. **Remarks:** Full-time maker. First knife sold 1998. **Mark:** Last name.

HALL, KEN

606 Stevenson Cove Rd., Waynesville, NC 28785, Phone: 828-627-2135, khall@ hallenergyconsulting.com; Web: www.kenhallknives.com

Specialties: Standard and one-of-a-kind fixed-blade knives with leather sheaths. **Patterns:** Hunters, bowies, fighters, chef's knives and tantos. **Technical:** Forges high-carbon steel, flat grinds. **Prices:** $300 to $1,500. **Remarks:** Part-time maker; first knives sold in 2010. **Mark:** Etched "Ken Hall" or "KHall JS."

HALL, SCOTT M.

5 Hickory Hts., Geneseo, IL 61254, Phone: 309-945-2184, smhall@theinter.com; www.hallcustomknives.com

Specialties: Fixed-blade, hollow-ground working knives of his own design and to customer specs. **Patterns:** Designs catering to soldiers and outdoorsmen, including variations of hunters, bowies, fighters and occasionally fillet and kitchen knives. **Technical:** Usually grinds CPM S30V and 154CM, but uses other steels upon request. Handle materials include G-10, Micarta, stag, horn and exotic woods. Most knives are offered with hand-tooled and stitched leather sheaths or Spec Ops sheaths. **Prices:** $150 to $350+. **Remarks:** Part-time maker; first knife sold in 2000. **Mark:** Last name.

HAMLET JR., JOHNNY

300 Billington, Clute, TX 77531, Phone: 979-265-6929, nifeman@swbell.net; Web:

www.hamlets-handmade-knives.com

Specialties: Working straight knives and folders. **Patterns:** Hunters, fighters, fillet and kitchen knives, locking folders. Likes upswept knives and trailing-points. **Technical:** Grinds 440C, D2, ATS-34. Makes sheaths. **Prices:** $125 and up. **Remarks:** Full-time maker; sold first knife in 1988. **Mark:** Hamlet's Handmade in script.

HAMMOND, HANK

189 Springlake Dr, Leesburg, GA 31763, Phone: 229-434-1295, godogs57@ bellsouth.net

Specialties: Traditional hunting and utility knives of his design. Will also design and produce knives to customer's specifications. **Patterns:** Straight or sheath knives, hunters skinners as well as Bowies and fighters. **Technical:** Grinds (hollow and flat grinds) CPM 154CM, ATS-34. Also uses Damascus and forges 52100. Offers filework on blades. Handle materials include all exotic woods, red stag, sambar stag, deer, elk, oosic, bone, fossil ivory, Micarta, etc. All knives come with sheath handmade for that individual knife. **Prices:** $100 up to $500. **Remarks:** Part-time maker. Sold first knife in 1981. Doing business as Double H Knives. **Mark:** "HH" inside 8 point deer rack.

HAMMOND, JIM

104 Owens Parkway, Ste. M, Birmingham, AL 35244, Phone: 256-651-1376, jim@ jimhammondknives.com; Web: www.jimhammondknives.com

Specialties: High-tech fighters and folders. **Patterns:** Proven-design fighters. **Technical:** Grinds 440C, 440V, S30V and other specialty steels. **Prices:** $385 to $1200; some to $9200. **Remarks:** Full-time maker; first knife sold in 1977. Designer for Columbia River Knife and Tool. **Mark:** Full name, city, state in shield logo.

HAMMOND, RAY

Hammond Knives, LLC, 3750 Quail Creek Dr., Buford, GA 30519, Phone: 678-300-2883, rayhammond01@yahoo.com; Web: www.biggamehuntingblades.com

Specialties: Fixed blades, primarily hunting knives, utility knives and bowies. **Technical:** Stock removal and forged blades, including 5160, 1095, CPM-154 and damascus blade steels. **Prices:** Start at $300. **Remarks:** Part-time maker; first knife built in 2008. **Mark:** Capital letters RH surrounded by a broken circle, pierced by a knife silhouette, atop the circle is my name, and below the circle the words "custom knives." Will soon alter this to simply my last name.

HANCOCK, TIM

29125 N. 153rd St., Scottsdale, AZ 85262, Phone: 480-998-8849, westernbladesmith@gmail.com

Specialties: High-art and working straight knives and folders of his design and to customer preferences. **Patterns:** Bowies, fighters, daggers, tantos, swords, folders. **Technical:** Forges damascus and 52100; grinds ATS-34. Makes damascus. Silver-wire inlays; offers carved fittings and file work. **Prices:** $1,000 to $50,000. **Remarks:** Full-time maker; first knife sold in 1988. ABS master smith and AKI member. No longer taking orders. **Mark:** Last name or heart.

HAND, BILL

PO Box 717, 1103 W. 7th St., Spearman, TX 79081, Phone: 806-659-2967, Fax: 806-659-5139, klinker43@yahoo.com

Specialties: Traditional working and using straight knives and folders of his design or to customer specs. **Patterns:** Hunters, Bowies, folders and fighters. **Technical:** Forges 5160, 52100 and Damascus. **Prices:** Start at $150. **Remarks:** Part-time maker; Journeyman Smith. Current delivery time 12 to 16 months. **Mark:** Stylized initials.

HANKALA, JUKKA

Tuhkurintie 225, 39580 Riitiala, FINLAND, Phone: +358-400-684-625, jukka@ hankala.com; www.hankala.com

Specialties: Traditional puukkos and maker's own knife models. **Patterns:** Maker's own puukko models, hunters, folders and ART-knives. **Technical:** Forges Silversteel, Bohler K510, Damasteel stainless damascus and RWL-34 blade steels, as well as his own 15N20-and-1.2842 damascus, mosaic damascus and color damascus. **Prices:** Start at $300. **Remarks:** Full-time maker since 1985. **Mark:** J. Hankala.

HANSEN, LONNIE

PO Box 4956, Spanaway, WA 98387, Phone: 253-847-4632, lonniehansen@msn. com; Web: lchansen.com

Specialties: Working straight knives of his design. **Patterns:** Tomahawks, tantos, hunters, fillet. **Technical:** Forges 1086, 52100, grinds 440V, BG-42. **Prices:** Starting at $300. **Remarks:** Part-time maker since 1989. **Mark:** First initial and last name. Also first and last initial.

HANSEN, ROBERT W

405 357th Ave. NE, Cambridge, MN 55008, Phone: 763-689-3242

Specialties: Working straight knives, folders and integrals. **Patterns:** From hunters to minis, camp knives to miniatures; folding lockers and slip-joints in original styles. **Technical:** Grinds 01, 440C and 154CM; likes filework. **Prices:** $100 to $450; some to $600. **Remarks:** Part-time maker; first knife sold in 1983. **Mark:** Fish w/h inside surrounded by Bob Hansen maker.

HANSON, KYLE S.

POB 12, Success, MO 65570, Phone: 573-674-3045, khansonknives@gmail.com; https://kylehansonknives.wordpress.com/

Specialties: W2 fixed blades with striking hamons and one-of-a-kind, handforged damascus, as well as damascus bolsters and guards on many knives. **Patterns:** Utility knives, hunters, fighters, bowies and the occasional tactical piece. Fixed blades only, with full or hidden tangs. **Technical:** Forges his own damascus, though he can't help dig into his father's, Don Hanson III's, stash once in a while, and is particularly fond of intricate hamons on W2 blades. Also fond of walrus ivory, mother-of-pearl, curly koa and desert ironwood handles. **Remarks:** Full-time maker, first knife sold in 2012. Learned everything he knows from his father and couldn't ask for a better teacher in the world of custom knives. **Mark:** KYLE HANSON.

HANSON III, DON L.

Sunfish Forge, PO Box 13, Success, MO 65570-0013, Phone: 573-674-3045, Web: www.sunfishforge.com; Web: www.donhansonknives.com

Specialties: One-of-a-kind damascus folders, slip joints and forged fixed blades. **Patterns:** Small, fancy pocket knives, large folding fighters and Bowies. **Technical:** Forges own pattern welded Damascus, file work and carving also carbon steel blades with hamons. **Prices:** $800 and up. **Remarks:** Full-time maker, first knife sold in 1984. ABS mastersmith. **Mark:** Sunfish.

HARA, KOJI

292-2 Osugi, Seki-City, Gifu, JAPAN 501-3922, Phone: 0575-24-7569, Fax: 0575-24-7569, info@knifehousehara.com; Web: www.knifehousehara.com

Specialties: High-tech and working straight knives of his design; some folders. **Patterns:** Hunters, locking folders and utility/camp knives. **Technical:** Grinds Cowry X, Cowry Y and ATS-34. Prefers high mirror polish; pearl handle inlay. **Prices:** $400 to $2500. **Remarks:** Full-time maker; first knife sold in 1980. Doing business as Knife House "Hara." **Mark:** First initial, last name in fish.

HARDING, CHAD

12365 Richland Ln, Solsberry, IN 47459, hardingknives@yahoo.com; www.hardingknives.net

Specialties: Hunters and camp knives, occasional fighters or bowies. No folders. **Technical:** Hand forge 90% of work. Prefer 10XX steels and tool steels. Makes own damascus and cable and chainsaw chain damascus. 100% sole authorship on knives and sheaths. Mostly natural handle material, prefer wood and stag. **Prices:** $150 to $1,000. **Remarks:** Part-time maker, member of ABS. First knife sold in 2005. **Mark:** Last name.

HARDING, JACOB

POB 10451, Fairbanks, AK 99710, Phone: 907-347-2961, harding-jake@hotmail.com, www.etsy.com/shop/hardingjm9, Facebook at Walking Stick Arts

Specialties: Blacksmith making handforged blades, including hunting and camp knives, black powder patch knives and collector pieces. **Technical:** Forges high-carbon 5160 steel, and likes to use recycled materials whenever possible, including leaf springs, files, railroad spikes, ammo casings for brass work and handle parts. **Prices:** $80 to $500. **Mark:** Harding, and location: ALASKA.

HARDY, DOUGLAS E

114 Cypress Rd, Franklin, GA 30217, Phone: 706-675-6305

HARDY, SCOTT

639 Myrtle Ave, Placerville, CA 95667, Phone: 530-622-5780, Web: www.innercite.com/~shardy

Specialties: Traditional working and using straight knives of his design. **Patterns:** Most anything with an edge. **Technical:** Forges carbon steels. Japanese stone polish. Offers mirror finish; differentially tempers. **Prices:** $100 to $1000. **Remarks:** Part-time maker; first knife sold in 1982. **Mark:** First initial, last name and Handmade with bird logo.

HARKINS, J A

PO Box 218, Conner, MT 59827, Phone: 406-821-1060, kutter@customknives.net; Web: customknives.net

Specialties: OTFs. **Patterns:** OTFs, Automatics, Folders. **Technical:** Grinds ATS-34. Engraves; offers gem work. **Prices:** $1500 and up. **Remarks:** Celebrating 20th year as full-time maker . **Mark:** First and middle initials, last name.

HARLEY, LARRY W

348 Deerfield Dr, Bristol, TN 37620, Phone: 423-878-5368 (shop); cell: 423-530-1133, Web: www.lonesomepineknives.com

Specialties: One-of-a-kind Persian in one-of-a-kind Damascus. Working knives, period pieces. **Technical:** Forges and grinds ATS-34, 440c, L6, 15, 20, 1084, and 52100. **Patterns:** Full range of straight knives, tomahawks, razors, buck skinners and hog spears. **Prices:** $200 and up. **Mark:** Pine tree.

HARLEY, RICHARD

609 Navaho Trl., Bristol, VA 24201, Phone: 423-878-5368; cell: 423-408-5720

Specialties: Hunting knives, Bowies, friction folders, one-of-a-kind. **Technical:** Forges 1084, S160, 52100, Lg. **Prices:** $150 to $1000. **Mark:** Pine tree with name.

HARM, PAUL W

818 N. Young Rd, Attica, MI 48412, Phone: 810-724-5582, harm@blclinks.net

Specialties: Early American working knives. **Patterns:** Hunters, skinners, patch knives, fighters, folders. **Technical:** Forges and grinds 1084, O1, 52100 and own Damascus. **Prices:** $75 to $1000. **Remarks:** First knife sold in 1990. **Mark:** Connected initials.

HARNER III, "BUTCH" LLOYD R.

745 Kindig Rd., Littlestown, PA 17340, butch@harnerknives.com; Web: www.harnerknives.com

Specialties: Kitchen knives and straight razors. **Technical:** CPM-3V, CPM-154 and various Carpenter powdered steel alloys. **Remarks:** Full-time maker since 2007. **Mark:** L.R. Harner (2005-Sept. 2012) and Harner III (after Oct. 2012)

HARRINGTON, ROGER

P.O. Box 157, Battle, East Sussex, ENGLAND TN 33 3 DD, Phone: 0854-838-7062, info@bisonbushcraft.co.uk; Web: www.bisonbushcraft.co.uk

Specialties: Working straight knives to his or customer's designs, flat saber Scandinavia-style grinds on full tang knives, also hollow and convex grinds. **Technical:** Grinds O1,

D2, Damascus. **Prices:** $200 to $800. **Remarks:** First knife made by hand in 1997 whilst traveling around the world. **Mark:** Bison with bison written under.

HARRIS, CASS

19855 Fraiser Hill Ln, Bluemont, VA 20135, Phone: 540-554-8774, Web: www.tdogforge.com

Prices: $160 to $500.

HARRIS, JAY

991 Johnson St, Redwood City, CA 94061, Phone: 415-366-6077

Specialties: Traditional high-tech straight knives and folders of his design. **Patterns:** Daggers, fighters and locking folders. **Technical:** Uses 440C, ATS-34 and CPM. **Prices:** $250 to $850. **Remarks:** Spare-time maker; first knife sold in 1980.

HARRIS, JOHN

PO Box 2466, Quartzsite, AZ 85346, Phone: 951-653-2755, johnharrisknives@yahoo.com; Web: www.johnharrisknives.com

Specialties: Hunters, daggers, Bowies, bird and trout, period pieces, Damascus and carbon steel knives, forged and stock removal. **Prices:** $200 to $1000.

HARRISON, BRIAN

BFH KNIVES, 2359 E Swede Rd, Cedarville, MI 49719, Phone: 906-430-0720, bfh_knives@yahoo.com

Specialties: High grade fixed blade knives. **Patterns:** Many sizes & variety of patterns from small pocket carries to large combat and camp knives. Mirror and bead blast finishes. All handles of high grade materials from ivory to highly figured stabilized woods to stag, deer & moose horn and Micarta. Hand sewn fancy sheaths for pocket or belt. **Technical:** Flat & hollow grinds usually ATS-34 but some O1, L6 and stellite 6K. **Prices:** $150 to $1200. **Remarks:** Full-time maker, sole authorship. Made first knife in 1980, sold first knife in 1999. Received much knowledge from the following makers: George Young, Eric Erickson, Webster Wood, Ed Kalfayan who are all generous men. **Mark:** Engraved blade outline w/ BFH Knives over the top edge, signature across middle & Cedarville, MI underneath.

HARRISON, JIM (SEAMUS)

721 Fairington View Dr, St. Louis, MO 63129, Phone: 314-791-6350, jrh@seamusknives.com; Web: www.seamusknives.com

Specialties: "Crossover" folders, liner-locks and frame-locks. **Patterns:** Uber, Author, Skyyy Folders, Ryan, Landon, Connor and flipper folders. **Technical:** Uses CPM S30V and 154, Stellite 6k and stainless damascus by Norris, Thomas, Nichols and Damasteel. **Prices:** Folders $550 to $1,400. **Remarks:** Full-time maker since 2008, maker since 1999. **Mark:** Seamus

HARSEY, WILLIAM H

82710 N. Howe Ln, Creswell, OR 97426, Phone: 541-510-8707, billharsey@gmail.com

Specialties: High-tech kitchen and outdoor knives. **Patterns:** Folding hunters, trout and bird folders; straight hunters, camp knives and axes. **Technical:** Grinds; etches. **Prices:** $125 to $300; some to $1500. Folders start at $350. **Remarks:** Full-time maker; first knife sold in 1979. **Mark:** Full name, state, U.S.A.

HART, BILL

647 Cedar Dr, Pasadena, MD 21122, Phone: 410-255-4981

Specialties: Fur-trade era working straight knives and folders. **Patterns:** Springback folders, skinners, Bowies and patch knives. **Technical:** Forges and stock removes 1095 and 5160 wire Damascus. **Prices:** $100 to $600. **Remarks:** Part-time maker; first knife sold in 1986. **Mark:** Name.

HARTMAN, ARLAN (LANNY)

6102 S Hamlin Cir, Baldwin, MI 49304, Phone: 231-745-4029

Specialties: Working straight knives and folders. **Patterns:** Drop-point hunters, coil spring lockers, slip-joints. **Technical:** Flat-grinds D2, 440C and ATS-34. **Prices:** $300 to $2000. **Remarks:** Part-time maker; first knife sold in 1982. **Mark:** Last name.

HARTMAN, TIM

3812 Pedroncelli Rd NW, Albuquerque, NM 87107, Phone: 505-385-6924, tbonz1@comcast.net

Specialties: Exotic wood scales, sambar stag, filework, hunters. **Patterns:** Fixed blade hunters, skinners, utility and hiking. **Technical:** 154CM, Ats-34 and D2. Mirror finish and contoured scales. **Prices:** Start at $200-$450. **Remarks:** Started making knives in 2004. **Mark:** 3 lines Ti Hartman, Maker, Albuquerque NM

HARVEY, KEVIN

HEAVIN FORGE, PO Box 768, Belfast, LP, SOUTH AFRICA 1100, Phone: 27-13-253-0914, info@heavinforge.co.za; Web: www.heavinforge.co.za

Specialties: Large knives of presentation quality and creative art knives. **Patterns:** Fixed blades of Bowie, dagger and fighter-styles, occasionally folders and swords. **Technical:** Stock removal of stainless and forging of carbon steel and own Damascus. Indigenous African handle materials preferred. Own engraving Often collaborate with wife, Heather (ABS MS) under the logo "Heavin." **Prices:** $500 to $5000 average $850. **Remarks:** Full-time maker and knifemaking instructor. Master bladesmith with ABS. First knife sold in 1984. **Mark:** First name and surname, oval with "M S" in the middle.

HARVEY, MAX

6 Winchester Way, Leeming, Perth, Western Australia 6149, AUSTRALIA, Phone: 61 (8) 93101103 or 61-478-633-356, mcharveyknives@outlook.com; http://mcharveycustomknives.com/wordpress/?page_id=84

Specialties: Fixed-blade knives of all styles. **Patterns:** Camp knives, skinners, bowies, daggers and high-end art knives. **Technical:** Stock-removal using ATS-34, 154CM, 440C and damascus. Do all my own faceting of gem stones in the high-end knives. **Prices:** $250 to $5,000. **Remarks:** Full-time maker; first knife sold in 1981, and founding member of the Australian Knife Makers Guild. **Mark:** First and middle initials, and surname (M C Harvey)

HARVEY, MEL

P.O. Box 176, Nenana, AK 99760, Phone: 907-832-5660, tinker1mh@gmail.com
Specialties: Fixed blade knives for hunting and fishing. **Patterns:** Hunters, skinners. **Technical:** Stock removal on ATS-34, 440C, O1, 1095; Damascus blades using 1095 and 15N20. **Prices:** Starting at $350. **Remarks:** ABS member, attended Bill Moran School; 50+ knives sold since 2007. **Mark:** Mel Harvey over serial number over Nenana, AK.

HASLINGER, THOMAS

6460 Woodland Dr., British Columbia V1B 3G7, CANADA, Phone: 778-212-6300, Web: www.haslinger-knives.com / www.haslinger-culinary.com
Specialties: One-of-a-kind using, working and art knives HCK signature sweeping grind lines. Maker of New Generation and Evolution Chef series. Differential heat treated stainless steel. **Patterns:** Likes to work with customers on design. **Technical:** Grinds various specialty alloys, including Damascus, High end satin finish. Prefers natural handle materials e.g. ancient ivory stag, pearl, abalone, stone and exotic woods. Does inlay work with stone, some sterling silver, niobium and gold wire work. Custom sheaths using matching woods or hand stitched with unique leather. Offers engraving. **Prices:** $300 and up. **Remarks:** Full-time maker; first knife sold in 1994. Doing business as Haslinger Custom Knives. **Mark:** Two marks used, high end work uses stylized initials, other uses elk antler with Thomas Haslinger, Canada, handcrafted above.

HAWES, CHUCK

HAWES FORGE, PO Box 176, Weldon, IL 61882, Phone: 217-736-2479
Specialties: 95 percent of all work in own Damascus. **Patterns:** Slip-joints liner locks, hunters, Bowie's, swords, anything in between. **Technical:** Forges everything, uses all high-carbon steels, no stainless. **Prices:** $150 to $4000. **Remarks:** Like to do custom orders, his style or yours. Sells Damascus. Full-time maker since 1995. **Mark:** Small football shape. Chuck Hawes maker Weldon, IL.

HAWK, GRANT AND GAVIN

Box 401, Idaho City, ID 83631, Phone: 208-392-4911, blademaker25@msn.com; www.hawkknifedesigns.com, @hawkknives on Instagram
Specialties: Grant and Gavin Hawk make custom knives, mid-tech knives and have had designs with Kershaw, CRKT, Boker, Buck, Camillus, Chris Reeve Knives, Mantis Knives, Millit Knives and Quartermaster. Specialize in folders with innovative locking systems, such as their new Deadlock OTF (out the front auto) with zero blade play. **Technical:** Grind 204P, Elmax, CPM S35VN, CPM 530V, ATS-34, BG-42 and XHP, and use titanium and carbon fiber folder parts. **Prices:** $450 and up. **Remarks:** Full-time makers. **Mark:** G&G Hawk, Hawk Designs.

HAWKINS, BUDDY

PO Box 5969, Texarkana, TX 75505-5969, Phone: 903-838-7917, buddyhawkins@cableone.net

HAWKINS JR., CHARLES R.

2764 Eunice, San Angelo, TX 76901, Phone: 325-947-7875, chawk12354@aol.com; Web: www.hawkcustomknives.com
Specialties: Custom knives, fixed blades, railroad spike knives and rasp file knives. **Technical:** Stock removal and some forging, using 1095 and 440C steel. **Prices:** $135 and up. **Remarks:** Part-time maker; first knife sold in 2008. **Mark:** Full name, city and state.

HAWLEY, TROY G.

THAWLEY KNIVES, 226 CR 2036, Ivanhoe, TX 75447, Phone: 903-664-4568, thawley123@gmail.com
Specialties: Hunting and fishing knives, kitchen cutlery, tacticals, fighters, tactical machetes and art knives of his own design. **Technical:** Stock removal method of blade making primarily working with 440C, CPM 154 and damascus, with other steels upon request. Forges high-carbon steels, such as 5160 spring steel, to create one-of-a-kind bowies, sabers and hunting knives. **Prices:** Start at $180 and up. **Remarks:** First knife sold in 2014. Member of the Texas Knifemakers Guild. **Mark:** "T."

HAYES, WALLY

9960, 9th Concession, RR#1, Essex, ON, CANADA N8M-2X5, Phone: 226-787-4289, hayesknives@hayesknives.com; Web: www.hayesknives.com
Specialties: Classic and fancy straight knives and folders. **Patterns:** Daggers, Bowies, fighters, tantos. **Technical:** Forges own Damascus and O1; engraves. **Prices:** $150 to $14,000. **Mark:** Last name, M.S. and serial number.

HAYNES, JERRY

260 Forest Meadow Dr, Gunter, TX 75058, Phone: 903-433-1424, jhaynes@arrow-head.com; Web: http://www.arrow-head.com
Specialties: Working straight knives and folders of his design, also historical blades. **Patterns:** Hunters, skinners, carving knives, fighters, renaissance daggers, locking folders and kitchen knives. **Technical:** Grinds ATS-34, CPM, Stellite 6K, D2 and acquired Damascus. Prefers exotic handle materials. Has B.A. in design. Studied with R. Buckminster Fuller. **Prices:** $200 to $1200. **Remarks:** Part-time maker. First knife sold in 1953. **Mark:** Arrowhead and last name.

HAYS, MARK

HAYS HANDMADE KNIVES, 1008 Kavanagh Dr., Austin, TX 78748, Phone: 512-292-4410, markhays@austin.rr.com
Specialties: Working straight knives and folders. Patterns inspired by Randall and Stone. **Patterns:** Bowies, hunters and slip-joint folders. **Technical:** 440C stock removal. Repairs and restores Stone knives. **Prices:** Start at $200. **Remarks:** Part-time maker, brochure available, with Stone knives 1974-1983, 1990-1991. **Mark:** First initial, last name, state and serial number.

HAZE, JEFF

JEFF HAZE CUSTOM KNIVES, 1703 E. 168th St. N, Skiatook, OK 74070, Phone: 918-855-5330, jeffhaze@rocketmail.com; facebook.com/jeffhazecustoms
Specialties: Bushcraft, hunting and everyday carry (EDC) knives. **Technical:** Scandi, saber and flat grinds using the stock-removal method of blade making, and with 1084 high-carbon and 80CrV2 steels. **Prices:** $100 to $250. **Remarks:** Full-time maker; first knife made in 2013. **Mark:** HAZE.

HEADRICK, GARY

122 Wilson Blvd, Juan Les Pins, FRANCE 06160, Phone: 033 610282885, headrick-gary@wanadoo.fr; Web: garyheadrick.free.fr
Specialties: Hi-tech folders with natural furnishings. Back lock & back spring. **Patterns:** Damascus and mokumes. **Technical:** Forges damascus using all steel (no nickel). All frames are titanium, and has a new tactical flipper folder model. **Prices:** $500 to $2,000. **Remarks:** Full-time maker for last eight years, active maker for the past 18 years. German Guild-French Federation, 10 years active, member of the ABS and Italian Corporation. **Mark:** HEADRICK on ricosso is new marking.

HEANEY, JOHN D

9 Lefe Court, Haines City, FL 33844, Phone: 863-422-5823, jdh199@msn.com; Web: www.heaneyknives.com
Specialties: Forged 5160, O1 and Damascus. Prefers using natural handle material such as bone, stag and oosic. Plans on using some of the various ivories on future knives. **Prices:** $250 and up. **Remarks:** ABS member. Received journeyman smith stamp in June. **Mark:** Heaney JS.

HEARD, TOM

Turning Point Knives, 2240 Westwood Dr., Waldorf, MD 20601, Phone: 301-843-8626; cell: 301-752-1944, turningpointknives@comcast.net
Specialties: Gent's working/using LinerLocks, automatics and flipper folders of his design. **Patterns:** Fixed blades of varying styles, folders and neck knives. **Technical:** Flat grinds 1095, O1, damascus and 154CM. Offers acid-etched blade embellishments, scrimshaw and hand-tooled custom leather sheaths. Does own heat-treating. **Prices:** $100 to $700. **Remarks:** Full-time maker since retiring; first knife sold in 2012. **Mark:** TH over last name.

HEATH, WILLIAM

PO Box 131, Bondville, IL 61815, Phone: 217-863-2576
Specialties: Classic and working straight knives, folders. **Patterns:** Hunters and Bowies LinerLock® folders. **Technical:** Grinds ATS-34, 440C, 154CM, Damascus, handle materials Micarta, woods to exotic materials snake skins cobra, rattle snake, African flower snake. Does own heat treating. **Prices:** $75 to $300 some $1000. **Remarks:** Full-time maker. First knife sold in 1979. **Mark:** W. D. HEATH.

HEBEISEN, JEFF

310 19th Ave N, Hopkins, MN 55343, Phone: 952-935-4506, jhebeisen@peoplepc.com
Specialties: One of a kind fixed blade of any size up to 16". **Patterns:** Miniature, Hunters, Skinners, Daggers, Bowies, Fighters and Neck knives. **Technical:** Stock removal using CPM-154, D2, 440C. Handle mterial varies depending on intended use, mostly natural materials such as bone, horn, antler, and wood. Filework on many. Heavy duty sheaths made to fit. **Prices:** From $100 to $750. **Remarks:** Full-time maker. First knife sold in 2007. **Mark:** Started new mark in 2012: J. Hebeisen, Hopkins, MN. Older **mark:** arched name over buffalo skull.

HEDGES, DEE

192 Carradine Rd., Bedfordale, WA, AUSTRALIA 6112, dark_woods_forge@yahoo.com.au; Web: www.darkwoodsforge.com
Patterns: Makes any and all patterns and style of blades from working blades to swords to Japanese inspired. Favors exotic and artistic variations and unique one-off pieces. **Technical:** Forges all blades from a range of steels, favoring 1084, W2, 52100, 5160 and Damascus steels she makes from a 1084/15n20 mix. **Prices:** Start at $200. **Remarks:** Full-time bladesmith and jeweller. Started making blades professionally in 1999, earning my Journeyman Smith rating in 2010. **Mark:** "Dark Woods" atop an ivy leaf, with "Forge" underneath.

HEDLUND, ANDERS

Samstad 400, Brastad, SWEDEN 45491, Phone: 46-523-139 48, anderskniv@passagen.se; Web: http://hem.passagen.se/anderskniv
Specialties: Fancy high-end collectible folders, high-end collectible Nordic hunters with leather carvings on the sheath. Carvings combine traditional designs with own designs. **Patterns:** Own designs. **Technical:** Grinds most steels, but prefers mosaic Damascus and RWL-34. Prefers mother-of-pearl, mammoth, and mosaic steel for folders. Prefers desert ironwood, mammoth, stabilized arctic birch, willow burl, and Damascus steel or RWL-34 for stick tang knives. **Prices:** Starting at $750 for stick tang knives and staring at $1500 for folders. **Remarks:** Part-time maker, first knife sold in 1988. Nordic champion (five countries) several times and Swedish champion 20 times in different classes. **Mark:** Stylized initials or last name.

HEDRICK, DON

131 Beechwood Hills, Newport News, VA 23608, Phone: 757-877-8100, donaldhedrick@cox.net; Web: www.donhedrickknives.com
Specialties: Working straight knives; period pieces and fantasy knives. **Patterns:** Hunters, boots, Bowies and miniatures. **Technical:** Grinds 440C and commercial Damascus. Also makes micro-mini Randall replicas. **Prices:** $150 to $550; some to $1200. **Remarks:** Part-time maker; first knife sold in 1982. **Mark:** First initial, last name in oval logo.

custom knifemakers

HEETER, TODD S.
9569 Polo Place N., Mobile, AL 36695, Phone: 251-490-5107, toddheeter78@yahoo.com; Web: www.heeterknifeworks.com
Specialties: Complete range of handforged knives, one-of-a-kind custom pieces. **Patterns:** Military-style frame-lock folders, neck knives, railroad spike folders. **Technical:** Handforged blades, including 1095 and D2, stainless steel, Alabama Damascus, doing one-sided chisel grinds and all ranges of flat grinds. Specializes in war-torn look, hand-hammered copper, pattern etching, antique copper and brass handle scales. **Prices:** $150 to $950. **Remarks:** Part-time maker, full-time fabricator and machinist, tool and die maker; first knife sold in 2009. **Mark:** Stamped first initial, middle initial and full last name, logo: HK with a dagger crossing letters.

HEGE, JOHN B.
P.O. Box 316, Danbury, NC 27106, Phone: 336-593-8324, jbhege@embarqmail.com; www.jbhegecustomknives.com
Specialties: Period-style knives and traditional bowies, utility hunters and fancy pieces. **Technical:** Forges larger pieces and often uses stock removal for knives 6 inches and smaller. **Remarks:** ABS journeyman smith since 2013.

HEGWALD, J L
1106 Charles, Humboldt, KS 66748, Phone: 316-473-3523
Specialties: Working straight knives, some fancy. **Patterns:** Makes Bowies, miniatures. **Technical:** Forges or grinds O1, L6, 440C; mixes materials in handles. **Prices:** $35 to $200; some higher. **Remarks:** Part-time maker; first knife sold in 1983. **Mark:** First and middle initials.

HEHN, RICHARD KARL
Lehnmuehler Str 1, Dorrebach, GERMANY 55444, Phone: 06724 3152
Specialties: High-tech, full integral working knives. **Patterns:** Hunters, fighters and daggers. **Technical:** Grinds CPM T-440V, CPM T-420V, forges his own stainless Damascus. **Prices:** $1000 to $10,000. **Remarks:** Full-time maker; first knife sold in 1963. **Mark:** Runic last initial in logo.

HEIMDALE, J E
7749 E 28 CT, Tulsa, OK 74129, Phone: 918-640-0784, heimdale@sbcglobal.net
Specialties: Art knives **Patterns:** Bowies, daggers **Technical:** Makes allcomponents and handles - exotic woods and sheaths. Uses Damascus blades by other Blademakers, notably R.W. Wilson. **Prices:** $300 and up. **Remarks:** Part-time maker. First knife sold in 1999. **Marks:** JEHCO

HEINZ, JOHN
611 Cafferty Rd, Upper Black Eddy, PA 18972, Phone: 610-847-8535, Web: www.herugrim.com
Specialties: Historical pieces / copies. **Technical:** Makes his own steel. **Prices:** $150 to $800. **Mark:** "H."

HEITLER, HENRY
8106 N Albany, Tampa, FL 33604, Phone: 813-933-1645
Specialties: Traditional working and using straight knives of his design and to customer specs. **Patterns:** Fighters, hunters, utility/camp knives and fillet knives. **Technical:** Flat-grinds ATS-34; offers tapered tangs. **Prices:** $135 to $450; some to $600. **Remarks:** Part-time maker; first knife sold in 1990. **Mark:** First initial, last name, city, state circling double H's.

HELSCHER, JOHN W
2645 Highway 1, Washington, IA 52353, Phone: 319-653-7310

HELTON, ROY
HELTON KNIVES, 2941 Comstock St., San Diego, CA 92111, Phone: 858-277-5024

HEMPERLEY, GLEN
13322 Country Run Rd, Willis, TX 77318, Phone: 936-228-5048, hemperley.com
Specialties: Specializes in hunting knives, does fixed and folding knives.

HENDRICKS, SAMUEL J
2162 Van Buren Rd, Maurertown, VA 22644, Phone: 703-436-3305
Specialties: Integral hunters and skinners of thin design. **Patterns:** Boots, hunters and locking folders. **Technical:** Grinds ATS-34, 440C and D2. Integral liners and bolsters of N-S and 7075 T6 aircraft aluminum. Does leatherwork. **Prices:** $50 to $250; some to $500. **Remarks:** Full-time maker; first knife sold in 1992. **Mark:** First and middle initials, last name, city and state in football-style logo.

HENDRICKSON, E JAY
4204 Ballenger Creek Pike, Frederick, MD 21703, Phone: 301-663-6923, Fax: 301-663-6923, ejayhendrickson@comcast.net
Specialties: Specializes in silver wire inlay. **Patterns:** Bowies, Kukri's, camp, hunters, and fighters. **Technical:** Forges 06, 1084, 5160, 52100, D2, L6 and W2; makes Damascus. Moran-styles on order. **Prices:** $400 to $8,000. **Remarks:** Full-time maker; first knife made in 1972; first knife sold in 1974. **Mark:** Last name, M.S.

HENDRICKSON, SHAWN
2327 Kaetzel Rd, Knoxville, MD 21758, Phone: 301-432-4306
Specialties: Hunting knives. **Patterns:** Clip points, drop points and trailing point hunters. **Technical:** Forges 5160, 1084 and L6. **Prices:** $175 to $400.

HENDRIX, JERRY
HENDRIX CUSTOM KNIVES, 17 Skyland Dr. Ext., Clinton, SC 29325, Phone: 864-833-2659
Specialties: Traditional working straight knives of all designs. **Patterns:** Hunters, utility, boot, bird and fishing. **Technical:** Grinds ATS-34 and 440C. **Prices:** $85 to $275. **Remarks:** Full-time maker. Hand stitched, waxed leather sheaths. **Mark:** Full name in shape of knife.

HENDRIX, WAYNE
9636 Burton's Ferry Hwy, Allendale, SC 29810, Phone: 803-584-3825, Fax: 803-584-3825, whendrixknives@gmail.com Web: www.hendrixknives.com
Specialties: Working/using knives of his design. **Patterns:** Hunters and fillet knives. **Technical:** Grinds ATS-34, D2 and 440C. **Prices:** $100 and up. **Remarks:** Full-time maker; first knife sold in 1985. **Mark:** Last name.

HENNINGSSON, MICHAEL
Klingkarrsvagen 8, 430 83 Vrango (Gothenburg), SWEDEN, Phone: +46 76 626 06 51, michael.henningsson@gmail.com; Web: henningssonknives.com
Specialties: Handmade folding knives, mostly tactical linerlocks and framelocks. **Patterns:** Own design in both engravings and knife models. **Technical:** All kinds of stee; such as Damascus, but prefer clean RWL-43. Tweaking a lot with hand engraving and therefore likes clean steel mostly. Work a lot with inlays of various materials. **Prices:** Starting at $1200 and up, depending on decoration and engravings. **Remarks:** Part-time maker, first knife sold in 2010. **Mark:** Hand engraved name or a Viking sail with initials in runes

HENSLEY, WAYNE
PO Box 904, Conyers, GA 30012, Phone: 770-483-8938, rebwayhe@bellsouth.net
Specialties: Period pieces and fancy working knives. **Patterns:** Boots to bowies, locking folders to miniatures. Large variety of straight knives. **Technical:** Grinds ATS-34, 440C, D2 and commercial damascus. **Prices:** $175 and up. **Remarks:** Full-time maker; first knife sold in 1974. **Mark:** Hensley USA.

HERBST, GAWIE
PO Box 59158, Karenpark, Akasia, GT, SOUTH AFRICA 0118, Phone: +27 72 060 3687, Fax: +27 12 549 1876, gawie@herbst.co.za Web: www.herbst.co.za
Specialties: Hunters, Utility knives, Art knives and Liner lock folders.

HERBST, PETER
Komotauer Strasse 26, Lauf a.d. Pegn., GERMANY 91207, Phone: 09123-13315, Fax: 09123-13379
Specialties: Working/using knives and folders of his design. **Patterns:** Hunters, fighters and daggers; interframe and integral. **Technical:** Grinds CPM-T-440V, UHB-Elmax, ATS-34 and stainless Damascus. **Prices:** $300 to $3000; some to $8000. **Remarks:** Full-time maker; first knife sold in 1981. **Mark:** First initial, last name.

HERBST, THINUS
PO Box 59158, Karenpark, Akasia, GT, SOUTH AFRICA 0118, Phone: +27 82 254 8016, thinus@herbst.co.za; Web: www.herbst.co.za
Specialties: Plain and fancy working straight knives of own design and liner lock folders. **Patterns:** Hunters, utility knives, art knives, and liner lock folders. **Technical:** Prefer exotic materials for handles. Most knives embellished with file work, carving and scrimshaw. **Prices:** $200 to $2000. **Remarks:** Full-time maker, member of the Knifemakers Guild of South Africa.

HERMAN, TIM
517 E. 126 Terrace, Olathe, KS 66061-2731, Phone: 913-839-1924, HermanKnives@comcast.net
Specialties: Investment-grade folders of his design; interframes and bolster frames. **Patterns:** Interframes and new designs in carved stainless. **Technical:** Grinds ATS-34 and damasteel Damascus. Engraves and gold inlays with pearl, jade, lapis and Australian opal. **Prices:** $1500 to $20,000 and up. **Remarks:** Full-time maker; first knife sold in 1978. Inventor of full-color bulino engraving since 1993. **Mark:** Etched signature.

HERNDON, WM R "BILL"
32520 Michigan St, Acton, CA 93510, Phone: 661-269-5860, bherndons1@roadrunner.com
Specialties: Straight knives, plain and fancy. **Technical:** Carbon steel (white and blued), Damascus, stainless steels. **Prices:** Start at $175. **Remarks:** Full-time maker; first knife sold in 1972. American Bladesmith Society journeyman smith. **Mark:** Signature and/or helm logo.

HERRING, MORRIS
Box 85 721 W Line St, Dyer, AR 72935, Phone: 501-997-8861, morrish@ipa.com

HETHCOAT, DON
Box 1764, Clovis, NM 88101, Phone: 575-762-5721, dhethcoat@plateautel.net; Web: www.donhethcoat.com
Specialties: Liner locks, lock backs and multi-blade folder patterns. **Patterns:** Hunters, Bowies. **Technical:** Grinds stainless; forges Damascus. **Prices:** Moderate to upscale. **Remarks:** Full-time maker; first knife sold in 1969. **Mark:** Last name on all.

HEWITT, RONALD "COTTON"
P.O. Box 326, Adel, GA 31620, Phone: 229-896-6366 or 229-237-4378, gobbler12@msn.com; www.hewittknives.com
Specialties: LinerLock folders and assisted flippers. **Technical:** Grinds CPM 154, CPM S35VN, CPM 3V and 52100 blade steels. Assisted flippers all have thrust bearings. **Prices:** $350 and up. **Remarks:** Full-time maker; first knife sold in 1975. **Mark:** Last name.

HIBBEN, DARYL
PO Box 172, LaGrange, KY 40031-0172, Phone: 502-222-0983, dhibben1@bellsouth.net
Specialties: Working straight knives, some fancy to customer specs. **Patterns:** Hunters, fighters, Bowies, short sword, art and fantasy. **Technical:** Grinds 440C, ATS-34, 154CM, Damascus; prefers hollow-grinds. **Prices:** $275 and up. **Remarks:** Full-time maker; first knife sold in 1979. Retired, part time. **Mark:** Etched full name in script.

HIBBEN, GIL

PO Box 13, LaGrange, KY 40031, Phone: 502-222-1397, Fax: 502-222-2676, gil@hibbenknives.com Web: www.hibbenknives.com

Specialties: Working knives and fantasy pieces to customer specs. **Patterns:** Full range of straight knives, including swords, axes and miniatures; some locking folders. **Technical:** Grinds ATS-34, 440C and D2. **Prices:** $300 to $2000; some $10,000. **Remarks:** Full-time maker; first knife sold in 1957. Maker and designer of Rambo III knife; made swords for movie Marked for Death and throwing knife for movie Under Seige; made belt buckle knife and knives for movie Perfect Weapon; made knives featured in movie Star Trek the Next Generation, Star Trek Nemesis. 1990 inductee Cutlery Hall of Fame; designer for United Cutlery. Official klingon armourer for Star Trek. Knives also for movies of the Expendables and the Expendables sequel. Over 37 movies and TV productions. Past president of the Knifemakers' Guild. Celebrating 59 years since first knife sold. **Mark:** Hibben Knives. City and state, or signature.

HIBBEN, WESTLEY G

14101 Sunview Dr, Anchorage, AK 99515

Specialties: Working straight knives of his design or to customer specs. **Patterns:** Hunters, fighters, daggers, combat knives and some fantasy pieces. **Technical:** Grinds 440C mostly. Filework available. **Prices:** $200 to $400; some to $3000. **Remarks:** Part-time maker; first knife sold in 1988. **Mark:** Signature.

HICKS, GARY

341 CR 275, Tuscola, TX 79562, Phone: 325-554-9762

Hielscher, Guy

PO Box 992, 6550 Otoe Rd., Alliance, NE 69301, Phone: 308-762-4318, g-hielsc@bbcwb.net Web: www.ghknives.com

Specialties: Working Damascus fixed blade knives. **Patterns:** Hunters, fighters, capers, skinners, bowie, drop point. **Technical:** Forges own Damascus using 1018 and 0-1 tool steels. **Prices:** $285 and up. **Remarks:** Member of PKA. Part-time maker; sold first knife in 1988. **Mark:** Arrowhead with GH inside.

HIGH, TOM

5474 S 1128 Rd, Alamosa, CO 81101, Phone: 719-589-2108, www.rockymountainscrimshaw.com

Specialties: Hunters, some fancy. **Patterns:** Drop-points in several shapes; some semi-skinners. Knives designed by and for top outfitters and guides. **Technical:** Grinds ATS-34; likes hollow-grinds, mirror finishes; prefers scrimable handles. **Prices:** $300 to $8000.. **Remarks:** Full-time maker; first knife sold in 1965. Limited edition wildlife series knives. **Mark:** Initials connected; arrow through last name.

HILL, RICK

20 Nassau, Maryville, IL 62062-5618, Phone: 618-288-4370

Specialties: Working knives and period pieces to customer specs. **Patterns:** Hunters, locking folders, fighters and daggers. **Technical:** Grinds D2, 440C and 154CM; forges his own Damascus. **Prices:** $75 to $500; some to $3000. **Remarks:** Part-time maker; first knife sold in 1983. **Mark:** Full name in hill shape logo.

HILL, STEVE E

217 Twin Lake Tr., Spring Branch, TX 78070, Phone: 830-624-6258 (cell) or 830-885-6108 (home), kingpirateboy2@juno.com or kingpirateboy2@gvtc.com; Web: www.stevehillknives.com

Specialties: Fancy manual and automatic LinerLock folders, small fixed blades and classic bowie knives. **Patterns:** Classic to cool folding and fixed blade designs. **Technical:** Grinds damascus fabricated in the U.S.A. and occasional high-carbon 1095, etc. Prefers natural handle materials, and offers elaborate filework, carving and inlays. **Prices:** $250 to $6,000, some higher. **Remarks:** Knifemaker to rock stars, Hollywood celebrities and occasional riff raff. Full-time maker; first knife sold in 1978. **Mark:** S. Hill Spring Branch Texas hand inscribed on inside of folder handle, spine or on a fixed blade spine.

HILLMAN, CHARLES

225 Waldoboro Rd, Friendship, ME 04547, Phone: 207-832-4634

Specialties: Working knives of his own or custom design. Heavy Scagel influence. **Patterns:** Hunters, fishing, camp and general utility. Occasional folders. **Technical:** Grinds D2 and 440C. File work, blade and handle carving, engraving. Natural handle materials-antler, bone, leather, wood, horn. Sheaths made to order. **Prices:** $60 to $500. **Remarks:** Part-time maker; first knife sold 1986. **Mark:** Last name in oak leaf.

HINDERER, RICK

5373 Columbus Rd., Shreve, OH 44676, Phone: 330-317-2964, rhind64@earthlink.net; Web: www.rickhindererknives.com

Specialties: Working tactical knives, and some one-of-a kind. **Patterns:** Makes his own. **Technical:** Grinds Duratech 20 CV and CPM S30V. **Prices:** $150 to $4000. **Remarks:** Full-time maker doing business as Rick Hinderer Knives, first knife sold in 1988. **Mark:** R. Hinderer.

HINDMARCH, GARTH

PO Box 135, Carlyle, SK, CANADA S0C 0R0, Phone: 306-453-2568

Specialties: Working and fancy straight knives, bowies. **Patterns:** Hunters, skinners, bowies. **Technical:** Grinds 440C, ATS 34, some damascus. **Prices:** $250 to $1,100. **Remarks:** Part-time maker; first knife sold 1994. All knives satin finished. Does filework, offers engraving, stabilized wood, giraffe bone, some Micarta. **Mark:** First initial, last name, city, province.

HINK III, LES

1599 Aptos Lane, Stockton, CA 95206, Phone: 209-547-1292

Specialties: Working straight knives and traditional folders in standard patterns or to customer specs. **Patterns:** Hunting and utility/camp knives; others on request. **Technical:** Grinds carbon and stainless steels. **Prices:** $80 to $200; some higher. **Remarks:** Part-time maker; first knife sold in 1980. **Mark:** Last name, or last name 3.

HINMAN, THEODORE

186 Petty Plain Road, Greenfield, MA 01301, Phone: 413-773-0448, armenemargosian@verizon.net

Specialties: Tomahawks and axes. Offers classes in bladesmithing and toolmaking.

HINSON AND SON, R

2419 Edgewood Rd, Columbus, GA 31906, Phone: 706-327-6801

Specialties: Working straight knives and folders. **Patterns:** Locking folders, liner locks, combat knives and swords. **Technical:** Grinds 440C and commercial Damascus. **Prices:** $200 to $450; some to $1500. **Remarks:** Part-time maker; first knife sold in 1983. Son Bob is co-worker. **Mark:** HINSON, city and state.

HINTZ, GERALD M

5402 Sahara Ct, Helena, MT 59602, Phone: 406-458-5412

Specialties: Fancy, high-art, working/using knives of his design. **Patterns:** Bowies, hunters, daggers, fish fillet and utility/camp knives. **Technical:** Forges ATS-34, 440C and D2. Animal art in horn handles or in the blade. **Prices:** $75 to $400; some to $1000. **Remarks:** Part-time maker; first knife sold in 1980. Doing business as Big Joe's Custom Knives. Will take custom orders. **Mark:** F.S. or W.S. with first and middle initials and last name.

HIRAYAMA, HARUMI

4-5-13 Kitamachi, Warabi City, Saitama, JAPAN 335-0001, Phone: 048-443-2248, Fax: 048-443-2248, swanbird3@gmail.com; Web: www.ne.jp/asahi/harumi/knives

Specialties: High-tech working knives of her design. **Patterns:** Locking folders, interframes, straight gents and slip-joints. **Technical:** Grinds 440C or equivalent; uses natural handle materials and gold. **Prices:** Start at $2500. **Remarks:** Part-time maker; first knife sold in 1985. **Mark:** First initial, last name.

HIROTO, FUJIHARA

2-34-7 Koioosako, Nishi-ku, Hiroshima, JAPAN, Phone: 082-271-8389, fjhr8363@crest.ocn.ne.jp

HOBART, GENE

100 Shedd Rd, Windsor, NY 13865, Phone: 607-655-1345

HOCKENSMITH, DAN

104 North Country Rd 23, Berthoud, CO 80513, Phone: 970-231-6506, blademan@skybeam.com; Web: www.dhockensmithknives.com

Specialties: Traditional working and using straight knives of his design. **Patterns:** Hunters, Bowies, folders and utility/camp knives. **Technical:** Uses his Damascus, 5160, carbon steel, 52100 steel and 1084 steel. Hand forged. **Prices:** $250 to $1500. **Remarks:** Part-time maker; first knife sold in 1987. **Mark:** Last name or stylized "D" with H inside.

HODGE III, JOHN

422 S 15th St, Palatka, FL 32177, Phone: 904-328-3897

Specialties: Fancy straight knives and folders. **Patterns:** Various. **Technical:** Pattern-welded Damascus—"Southern-style." **Prices:** To $1000. **Remarks:** Part-time maker; first knife sold in 1981. **Mark:** JH3 logo.

HOEL, STEVE

PO Box 283, Pine, AZ 85544-0283, Phone: 928-476-6523

Specialties: Investor-class folders, straight knives and period pieces of his design. **Patterns:** Folding interframes lockers and slip-joints; straight Bowies, boots and daggers. **Technical:** Grinds 154CM, ATS-34 and commercial Damascus. **Prices:** $600 to $1200; some to $7500. **Remarks:** Full-time maker. **Mark:** Initial logo with name and address.

HOFER, LOUIS

BOX 125, Rose Prairie, BC, CANADA V0C 2H0, Phone: 250-827-3999, anvil_needles@hotmail.cq; www.anvilandneedles.com

Specialties: Damascus knives, working knives, fixed blade bowies, daggers. **Patterns:** Hunting, skinning, custom. **Technical:** Wild damascus, random damascus. **Prices:** $450 and up. **Remarks:** Part-time maker since 1995. **Mark:** Logo of initials.

HOFFMAN, JAY

Hoffman Haus + Heraldic Device, 911 W Superior St., Munising, MI 49862, Phone: 906-387-3440, hoffmanhaus1@yahoo.com; Web: www.hoffmanhausknives.com

Technical: Scrimshaw, metal carving, own casting of hilts and pommels, etc. Most if not all leather work for sheaths. **Remarks:** Has been making knives for 50 + years. Professionally since 1991. **Mark:** Early knives marked "Hoffman Haus" and year. Now marks "Hoffman Haus Knives" on the blades. Starting in 2010 uses heraldic device. Will build to your specs. Lag time 1-2 months.

HOFFMAN, JESS

W7089 Curt Black Rd., Shawano, WI 54166, Phone: 715-584-2466, mooseyard@gmail.com; Web: www.jhoffmanknives.com

Specialties: Working fixed blades. **Technical:** Stock removal of carbon, stainless and damascus steels. Handles range from paper Micarta to exotic hardwoods. **Prices:** Start at $75. **Remarks:** Part-time knifemaker. **Mark:** Ancestral lower-case "h" and/or J. Hoffman.

HOFFMAN, KEVIN L

28 Hopeland Dr, Savannah, GA 31419, Phone: 912-920-3579, Fax: 912-920-3579, kevh052475@aol.com; Web: www.KLHoffman.com

Specialties: Distinctive folders and fixed blades. **Patterns:** Titanium frame lock folders. **Technical:** Sculpted guards and fittings cast in sterling silver and 14k gold. Grinds ATS-34, CPM S30V damascus. Makes kydex sheaths for his fixed blade working knives. **Prices:** $400 and up. **Remarks:** Full-time maker since 1981. **Mark:** KLH.

custom knifemakers

HOFFMAN, LIAM

POB 1584, Newland, NC 28657, Phone: 828-260-4593, liam@hoffmanblacksmithing.com; Web: www.hoffmanblacksmithing.com

Specialties: Handforged one-off knives and axes. **Technical:** Full-tang knives and integral knives out of high-carbon steel or damascus, generally preferring to use wood handles. Also utilitarian-type working axes. **Prices:** $170 to $400 (axes) and $400 to $1,500 (knives). **Remarks:** Full-time 19-year-old maker who made his first knife at 13 years old, a bladesmith by trade. Axes are some of the finest in the world, in comparison with known smiths Autine, John Neeman and Gansfors bruk, working axes with functionality over aesthetics in mind, and quality over quantity. Nearly all knives are one of a kind, preferring to make integral knives. Everything made in the U.S.A. **Mark:** Knife touch mark is a Japanese hammer with "Hoffman" underneath, and the axe touch mark reads NC, LH, USA.

HOGAN, THOMAS R

2802 S. Heritage Ave, Boise, ID 83709, Phone: 208-362-7848

HOGSTROM, ANDERS T

P.O. Box 72, 37011 Backaryd, SWEDEN, Phone: 46 702 674 574, andershogstrom@hotmail.com or info@andershogstrom.com; Web: www.andershogstrom.com

Specialties: Short and long daggers, fighters and swords For select pieces makes wooden display stands. **Patterns:** Daggers, fighters, short knives and swords and an occasional sword. **Technical:** Grinds 1050 High Carbon, Damascus and stainless, forges own Damasus on occasion, fossil ivories. Does clay tempering and uses exotic hardwoods. **Prices:** Start at $850. **Marks:** Last name in maker's own signature.

HOKE, THOMAS M

3103 Smith Ln, LaGrange, KY 40031, Phone: 502-222-0350

Specialties: Working/using knives, straight knives. Own designs and customer specs. **Patterns:** Daggers, Bowies, hunters, fighters, short swords. **Technical:** Grind 440C, Damascus and ATS-34. Filework on all knives. Tooling on sheaths (custom fit on all knives). Any handle material, mostly exotic. **Prices:** $100 to $700; some to $1500. **Remarks:** Full-time maker, first knife sold in 1986. **Mark:** Dragon on banner which says T.M. Hoke.

HOLBROOK, H L

PO Box 483, Sandy Hook, KY 41171, Phone: Cell: 606-794-1497, hhknives@mrtc.com

Specialties: Traditional working using straight knives of his design, to customer specs and in standard patterns. Stabilized wood. **Patterns:** Hunters, mild tacticals and neck knives with kydex sheaths. **Technical:** Grinds CPM154CM, 154CM. Blades have hand-rubbed satin finish. Uses exotic woods, stag, G-10 and Micarta. Hand-sewn sheath with each straight knife. **Prices:** $165 to $485. **Remarks:** Part-time maker; first knife sold in 1983. Doing business as Holbrook Knives. **Mark:** Name, city, state.

HOLDER, D'ALTON

18910 McNeil Rd., Wickenburg, AZ 85390, Phone: 928-684-2025, Fax: 623-878-3964, dholderknives@commspeed.net; Web: dholder.com

Specialties: Deluxe working knives and high-art hunters. **Patterns:** Drop-point hunters, fighters, Bowies. **Technical:** Grinds ATS-34; uses amber and other materials in combination on stick tangs. **Prices:** $400 to $1000; some to $2000. **Remarks:** Full-time maker; first knife sold in 1966. **Mark:** D'HOLDER, city and state.

HOLLOWAY, PAUL

714 Burksdale Rd, Norfolk, VA 23518, Phone: 757-547-6025, houdini969@yahoo.com

Specialties: Working straight knives and folders to customer specs. **Patterns:** Lockers, fighters and boots, push knives, from swords to miniatures. **Technical:** Grinds A2, D2, 154CM, 440C and ATS-34. **Prices:** $210 to $1,200; some to $1,500, higher. **Remarks:** Retired; first knife sold in 1981. USN 28 years, deputy sheriff 16 years. **Mark:** Name and city in logo.

HOOK, BOB

3247 Wyatt Rd, North Pole, AK 99705, Phone: 907-488-8886, grayling@alaska.net; Web: www.alaskaknifeandforge.com

Specialties: Forged carbon steel. Damascus blades. **Patterns:** Pronghorns, bowies, drop point hunters and knives for the kitchen. **Technical:** 5160, 52100, carbon steel and 1084 and 15N20 pattern welded steel blades are hand forged. Heat treated and ground by maker. Handles are natural materials from Alaska. I favor sole authorship of each piece. **Prices:** $300-$1000. **Remarks:** Journeyman smith with ABS. I have attended the Bill Moran School of Bladesmithing. Knife maker since 2000. **Mark:** Hook.

HORN, DES

PO Box 322, Onrusrivier, WC, SOUTH AFRICA 7201, Phone: 27283161795, Fax: +27866280824, deshorn@usa.net

Specialties: Folding knives. **Patterns:** Ball release side lock mechanism and interframe automatics. **Technical:** Prefers working in totally stainless materials. **Prices:** $800 to $7500. **Remarks:** Full-time maker. Enjoys working in gold, titanium, meteorite, pearl and mammoth. **Mark:** Des Horn.

HORN, JESS

2526 Lansdown Rd, Eugene, OR 97404, Phone: 541-463-1510, jandahorn@earthlink.net

Specialties: Investor-class working folders; period pieces; collectibles. **Patterns:** High-tech design and finish in folders; liner locks, traditional slip-joints and featherweight models. **Technical:** Grinds ATS-34, 154CM. **Prices:** Start at $1000. **Remarks:** Full-time maker; first knife sold in 1968. **Mark:** Full name or last name.

HORNE, GRACE

The Old Public Convenience, 469 Fulwood Road, Sheffield, UNITED KINGDOM S10 3QA, gracehorne@hotmail.co.uk Web: www.gracehorn.co.uk

Specialties: Knives of own design, mainly slip-joint folders. **Technical:** Grinds RWL34, Damasteel and own Damascus for blades. Scale materials vary from traditional (coral, wood, precious metals, etc) to unusual (wool, fabric, felt, etc), **Prices:** $500 - $1500**Remarks:** Part-time maker. **Mark:** 'gH' and 'Sheffield'.

HORRIGAN, JOHN

433 C.R. 200 D, Burnet, TX 78611, Phone: 512-756-7545 or 512-636-6562, jhorrigan@yahoo.com Web: www.eliteknives.com

Specialties: High-end custom knives. **Prices:** $450 - $12,500. **Remarks:** Part-time maker. Obtained Mastersmith stamp 2005. First knife made in 1982. **Mark:** Horrigan M.S.

HORTON, SCOT

PO Box 451, Buhl, ID 83316, Phone: 208-543-4222

Specialties: Traditional working stiff knives and folders. **Patterns:** Hunters, skinners, utility, hatchets and show knives. **Technical:** Grinds ATS-34 and D-2 tool steel. **Prices:** $400 to $2500. **Remarks:** First knife sold in 1990. **Mark:** Full name in arch underlined with arrow, city, state.

HOSSOM, JERRY

3585 Schilling Ridge, Duluth, GA 30096, Phone: 770-449-7809, jerry@hossom.com; Web: www.hossom.com

Specialties: Working straight knives of his own design. **Patterns:** Fighters, combat knives, modern Bowies and daggers, modern swords, concealment knives for military and LE uses. **Technical:** Grinds 154CM, S30V, CPM-3V, CPM-154 and stainless Damascus. Uses natural and synthetic handle materials. **Prices:** $350-1500, some higher. **Remarks:** Full-time maker since 1997. First knife sold in 1983. **Mark:** First initial and last name, includes city and state since 2002.

HOSTETLER, LARRY

10626 Pine Needle Dr., Fort Pierce, FL 34945, Phone: 772-465-8352, hossknives@bellsouth.net Web: www.hoss-knives.com

Specialties: EDC working knives and custom collector knives. Utilizing own designs and customer designed creations. Maker uses a wide variety of exotic materials. **Patterns:** Bowies, hunters and folders. **Technical:** Stock removal, grinds ATS-34, carbon and stainless Damascus, embellishes most pieces with file work. **Prices:** $200 - $1500. Some custom orders higher. **Remarks:** Motto: "EDC doesn't have to be ugly." First knife made in 2001, part-time maker, voting member in the Knife Maker's Guild. Doing business as "Hoss Knives." **Mark:** "Hoss" etched into blade with a turn of the century fused bomb in place of the "O" in Hoss.

HOSTETTER, WALLY

P.O. Box 404, San Mateo, FL 32187, Phone: 386-649-0731, shiningmoon_13@yahoo.com; www.shiningmoon13.com

Specialties: Japanese swords and pole arms, and all their mountings from different time periods, other sword styles. **Technical:** Hand forges 1075 on up to 1095 steels, some with vanadium alloys. **Prices:** $1,200 to $6,500. **Remarks:** Full-time maker; first sword was a katana in 1999. **Mark:** Signature on tang in Japanese kanji is Wally San.

HOUSE, CAMERON

2001 Delaney Rd Se, Salem, OR 97306, Phone: 503-585-3286, chouse357@aol.com

Specialties: Working straight knives. **Patterns:** Hunters, Bowies, fighters. **Technical:** Grinds ATS-34, 530V, 154CM. **Remarks:** Part-time maker, first knife sold in 1993. **Prices:** $150 and up. **Mark:** HOUSE.

HOUSE, GARY

2851 Pierce Rd, Ephrata, WA 98823, Phone: 509-754-3272, spindry101@aol.com

Specialties: Bowies, hunters, daggers and some swords. **Patterns:** Unlimited, SW Indian designs, geometric patterns, bowies, hunters and daggers. **Technical:** Mosaic damascus bar stock, forged blades, using 1084, 15N20 and some nickel. Forged company logos and customer designs in mosaic damascus. **Prices:** $500 & up. **Remarks:** Some of the finest and most unique patterns available. ABS master smith. **Marks:** Initials GTH, G hanging T, H.

HOWARD, DURVYN M.

4220 McLain St S, Hokes Bluff, AL 35903, Phone: 256-504-1853

Specialties: Collectible upscale folders; one-of-a-kind, gentlemen's folders. Unique mechanisms and multiple patents. **Patterns:** Conceptual designs; each unique and different. **Technical:** Uses natural and exotic materials and precious metals. **Prices:** $7,500 to $35,000. **Remarks:** Full-time maker; 52 years experience. **Mark:** Howard.

HOWE, TORI

30020 N Stampede Rd, Athol, ID 83801, Phone: 208-449-1509, wapiti@knifescales.com; Web:www.knifescales.com

Specialties: Custom knives, knife scales & Damascus blades. **Remarks:** Carry James Luman polymer clay knife scales.

HOWELL, JASON G

1112 Sycamore, Lake Jackson, TX 77566, Phone: 979-297-9454, tinyknives@yahoo.com; Web:www.howellbladesmith.com

Specialties: Fixed blades and LinerLock® folders. Makes own Damascus. **Patterns:** Clip and drop point. **Prices:** $150 to $750. **Remarks:** Likes making Mosaic Damascus out of the ordinary stuff. Member of TX Knifemakers and Collectors Association; apprentice in ABS; working towards Journeyman Stamp. **Mark:** Name, city, state.

HOWELL, KEITH A.

67 Hidden Oaks Dr., Oxford, AL 36203, Phone: 256-283-3269, keith@howellcutlery.com; Web: www.howellcutlery.com

Specialties: Working straight knives and folders of his design or to customer specs. **Patterns:** Hunters, utility pieces, neck knives, everyday carry knives and friction folders. **Technical:** Grinds damascus, 1095 and 154CM. **Prices:** $100 to $250. **Remarks:** Part-time maker; first knife sold in 2007. **Mark:** Last name.

HOWELL, LEN
550 Lee Rd 169, Opelika, AL 36804, Phone: 334-749-1942
Specialties: Traditional and working knives of his design and to customer specs. Patterns: Buckskinner, hunters and utility/camp knives. Technical: Forges cable Damascus, 1085 and 5160; makes own Damascus. Mark: Engraved last name.

HOWELL, TED
1294 Wilson Rd, Wetumpka, AL 36092, Phone: 205-569-2281, Fax: 205-569-1764
Specialties: Working/using straight knives and folders of his design; period pieces. Patterns: Bowies, fighters, hunters. Technical: Forges 5160, 1085 and cable. Offers light engraving and scrimshaw; filework. Prices: $75 to $250; some to $450. Remarks: Part-time maker; first knife sold in 1991. Doing business as Howell Co. Mark: Last name, Slapout AL.

HOY, KEN
54744 Pinchot Dr, North Fork, CA 93643, Phone: 209-877-7805

HRISOULAS, JIM
SALAMANDER ARMOURY, 284-C Lake Mead Pkwy #157, Henderson, NV 89105, Phone: 702-566-8551, www.atar.com
Specialties: Working straight knives; period pieces. Patterns: Swords, daggers and sgian dubhs. Technical: Double-edged differential heat treating. Prices: $85 to $175; some to $600 and higher. Remarks: Full-time maker; first knife sold in 1973. Author of The Complete Bladesmith, The Pattern Welded Blade and The Master Bladesmith. Doing business as Salamander Armory. Mark: 8R logo and sword and salamander.

HUCKABEE, DALE
254 Hwy 260, Maylene, AL 35114, Phone: 205-664-2544, huckabeeknives@hotmail.com; Web: http://dalehuckabeeknives.weebly.com
Specialties: Fixed-blade knives and tomahawks of his design. Technical: Steel used: 5160, 1084, and Damascus. Prices: $225 and up, depending on materials used. Remarks: Hand forged. Journeyman Smith. Part-time maker. Mark: Stamped Huckabee J.S.

HUCKS, JERRY
KNIVES BY HUCKS, 1807 Perch Road, Moncks Corner, SC 29461, Phone: 843-761-6481, Fax: Cell: 843-708-1649, knivesbyhucks@gmail.com
Specialties: Drop points, bowies and oyster knives. Patterns: To customer specs or maker's own design. Technical: CPM-154, ATS-34, 5160, 15N20, D2 and 1095 mostly for damascus billets. Prices: $200 and up. Remarks: Full-time maker, retired as a machinist in 1990. Makes sheaths sewn by hand with some carving. Will custom make to order or by sketch. Will also make a miniature bowie on request. Thirty years making knives. Mark: Robin Hood hat with Moncks Corner under.

HUDSON, C ROBBIN
116 Hansonville Rd., Rochester, NH 03839, Phone: 603-786-9944, bladesmith8@gmail.com
Specialties: High-art working knives. Patterns: Hunters, Bowies, fighters and kitchen knives. Technical: Forges W2, nickel steel, pure nickel steel, composite and mosaic Damascus; makes knives one-at-a-time. Prices: 500 to $1200; some to $5000. Remarks: Full-time maker; first knife sold in 1970. Mark: Last name and MS.

HUDSON, ROBERT
3802 Black Cricket Ct, Humble, TX 77396, Phone: 713-454-7207
Specialties: Working straight knives of his design. Patterns: Bowies, hunters, skinners, fighters and utility knives. Technical: Grinds D2, 440C, 154CM and commercial Damascus. Prices: $85 to $350; some to $1500. Remarks: Part-time maker; first knife sold in 1980. Mark: Full name, handmade, city and state.

HUGHES, DAN
301 Grandview Bluff Rd, Spencer, TN 38585, Phone: 931-946-3044
Specialties: Working straight knives to customer specs. Patterns: Hunters, fighters, fillet knives. Technical: Grinds 440C and ATS-34. Prices: $55 to $175; some to $300. Remarks: Part-time maker; first knife sold in 1984. Mark: Initials.

HUGHES, DARYLE
10979 Leonard, Nunica, MI 49448, Phone: 616-837-6623, hughes.builders@verizon.net
Specialties: Working knives. Patterns: Buckskinners, hunters, camp knives, kitchen and fishing knives. Technical: Forges and grinds 52100 and Damascus. Prices: $125 to $1000. Remarks: Part-time maker; first knife sold in 1979. Mark: Name and city in logo.

HUGHES, ED
280 1/2 Holly Lane, Grand Junction, CO 81503, Phone: 970-243-8547, edhughes26@msn.com
Specialties: Working and art folders. Patterns: Buys Damascus. Technical: Grinds stainless steels. Engraves. Prices: $300 and up. Remarks: Full-time maker; first knife sold in 1978. Mark: Name or initials.

HUGHES, LAWRENCE
207 W Crestway, Plainview, TX 79072, Phone: 806-293-5406
Specialties: Working and display knives. Patterns: Bowies, daggers, hunters, buckskinners. Technical: Grinds D2, 440C and 154CM. Prices: $125 to $300; some to $2000. Remarks: Full-time maker; first knife sold in 1979. Mark: Name with buffalo skull in center.

HUGHES, TONY
Tony Hughes Forged Blades, 7536 Trail North Dr., Littleton, CO 80125, Phone: 303-941-1092, tonhug@msn.com
Specialties: Fixed blades, bowies/fighters and hunters of maker's own damascus steel. Technical: Forges damascus and mosaic-damascus blades. Fittings are 416 stainless steel, 1095-and-nickel damascus, 1080-and-15N20 damascus or silicon bronze.

Prefers ivory, desert ironwood, blackwood, ebony and other burls. Prices: $450 and up. Remarks: Full-time ABS journeyman smith forging knives for 20 years. Mark: Tony Hughes and JS on the other side.

HULETT, STEVE
115 Yellowstone Ave, West Yellowstone, MT 59758-0131, Phone: 406-646-4116, blade1231@msn.com; Web: www.seldomseenknives.com
Specialties: Classic, working/using knives, straight knives, folders. Your design, custom specs. Patterns: Utility/camp knives, hunters, and LinerLock folders, lock back pocket knives. Technical: Grinds 440C stainless steel, O1 Carbon, 1095. Shop is retail and knife shop; people watch their knives being made. We do everything in house: "all but smelt the ore, or tan the hide." Prices: Strarting $250 to $7000. Remarks: Full-time maker; first knife sold in 1994. Mark: Seldom seen knives/West Yellowstone Montana.

HULSEY, HOYT
379 Shiloh, Attalla, AL 35954, Phone: 256-538-6765
Specialties: Traditional working straight knives and folders of his design. Patterns: Hunters and utility/camp knives. Technical: Grinds 440C, ATS-34, O1 and A2. Prices: $75 to $250. Remarks: Part-time maker; first knife sold in 1989. Mark: Hoyt Hulsey Attalla AL.

HUMENICK, ROY
PO Box 55, Rescue, CA 95672, rhknives@gmail.com; Web: www.humenick.com
Specialties: Traditional multiblades and tactical slipjoints. Patterns: Original folder and fixed blade designs, also traditional patterns. Technical: Grinds premium steels and Damascus. Prices: $350 and up; some to $1500. Remarks: First knife sold in 1984. Mark: Last name in ARC.

HUMPHREY, LON
4 Western Ave., Newark, OH 43055, Phone: 740-644-1137, lonhumphrey@gmail.com
Specialties: Hunters, tacticals, and bowie knives. Prices: I make knives that start in the $150 range and go up to $1000 for a large bowie. Remarks: Has been blacksmithing since age 13 and progressed to the forged blade.

HUMPHREYS, JOEL
90 Boots Rd, Lake Placid, FL 33852, Phone: 863-773-0439
Specialties: Traditional working/using straight knives and folders of his design and in standard patterns. Patterns: Hunters, folders and utility/camp knives. Technical: Grinds ATS-34, D2, 440C. All knives have tapered tangs, mitered bolster/handle joints, handles of horn or bone fitted sheaths. Prices: $135 to $225; some to $350. Remarks: Part-time maker; first knife sold in 1990. Doing business as Sovereign Knives. Mark: First name or "H" pierced by arrow.

HUNT, RAYMON E.
3H's KNIVES, LLC, 600 Milam Ct., Irving, TX 75038, Phone: 214-507-0896, Fax: 972-887-9931, Web: www.3hsknives.com
Specialties: Forged and stock removal for both using and collector-grade knives. Patterns: Kitchen cutlery, bowies, daggers, hunters, tactical, utility, slip joints and straight razors. Technical: Steels include 5160, 1075, 1084, 1095, O1, CPM 154, CTS XHP and damascus. Heat treating in-house using oven and torch edge hardening. Uses his own damascus of 1095 and 15N20 and purchases damascus. Engraving and gold inlay by Steve Dunn, filework, peined and polished pins of sterling silver and gold, fire and niter bluing. Remarks: American Bladesmith Society, apprentice. Mark: 3Hs on left side of blade near the grind line.

HUNTER, HYRUM
285 N 300 W, PO Box 179, Aurora, UT 84620, Phone: 435-529-7244
Specialties: Working straight knives of his design or to customer specs. Patterns: Drop and clip, fighters dagger, some folders. Technical: Forged from two-piece Damascus. Prices: Prices are adjusted according to size, complexity and material used. Remarks: Will consider any design you have. Part-time maker; first knife sold in 1990. Mark: Initials encircled with first initial and last name and city, then state. Some patterns are numbered.

HUNTER, RICHARD D
7230 NW 200th Ter, Alachua, FL 32615, Phone: 386-462-3150
Specialties: Traditional working/using knives of his design or customer suggestions; filework. Patterns: Folders of various types, Bowies, hunters, daggers. Technical: Traditional blacksmith; hand forges high-carbon steel (5160, 1084, 52100) and makes own Damascus; grinds 440C and ATS-34. Prices: $200 and up. Remarks: Part-time maker; first knife sold in 1992. Mark: Last name in capital letters.

HURST, JEFF
PO Box 247, Rutledge, TN 37861, Phone: 865-828-5729, jhurst@esper.com
Specialties: Working straight knives and folders of his design. Patterns: Tomahawks, hunters, boots, folders and fighters. Technical: Forges W2, O1 and his own Damascus. Makes mokume. Prices: $250 to $600. Remarks: Full-time maker; first knife sold in 1984. Doing business as Buzzard's Knob Forge. Mark: Last name; partnered knives are marked with Newman L. Smith, handle artisan, and SH in script.

HUSE, JAMES D. II
P.O. Box 1753, Buda, TX 78610, Phone: 512-296-9888, huseknives@gmail.com; Web: www.huseknives.com
Specialties: Texas-legal carry knives, hunters and utility knives, and large camp knives and bowies on request. Patterns: Clip points, drop points, Puma-style trailing points and fighter styles. Technical: Makes most knives using the stock-removal method of blade making with A2 tool steel, hardening and tempering it to 60-61 HRC on the Rockwell Hardness Scale. Does forge some knives, and when forging, uses 1084, 52100, 1095 and 15N20 damascus, as well as CruForge V. Prices: $150 to $700. Remarks: Part-time maker; first knife made in 2001. Member of Texas Knifemakers' Guild (secretary) and American Bladesmith Society (apprentice).

HUSIAK, MYRON
PO Box 238, Altona, VIC, AUSTRALIA 3018, Phone: 03-315-6752
Specialties: Straight knives and folders of his design or to customer specs. **Patterns:** Hunters, fighters, lock-back folders, skinners and boots. **Technical:** Forges and grinds his own Damascus, 440C and ATS-34. **Prices:** $200 to $900. **Remarks:** Part-time maker; first knife sold in 1974. **Mark:** First initial, last name in logo and serial number.

HUTCHESON, JOHN
SURSUM KNIFE WORKS, 1237 Brown's Ferry Rd., Chattanooga, TN 37419, Phone: 423-667-6193, sursum5071@aol.com; Web: www.sursumknife.com
Specialties: Straight working knives, hunters. **Patterns:** Customer designs, hunting, speciality working knives. **Technical:** Grinds D2, S7, O1 and 5160, ATS-34 on request. **Prices:** $100 to $300, some to $600. **Remarks:** First knife sold 1985, also produces a mid-tech line. Doing business as Sursum Knife Works. **Mark:** Family crest boar's head over 3 arrows.

HUTCHINSON, ALAN
315 Scenic Hill Road, Conway, AR 72034, Phone: 501-470-9653, hutchinsonblades@yahoo.com
Specialties: Hunters, bowies, fighters, combat/survival knives. **Patterns:** Traditional edged weapons and tomahawks, custom patterns. **Technical:** Forges 10 series, 5160, L6, O1, CruForge V, damascus and his own patterns. **Prices:** $250 and up. **Remarks:** Prefers natural handle materials, part-time maker. **Mark:** Last name.

HYTOVICK, JOE "HY"
14872 SW 111th St, Dunnellon, FL 34432, Phone: 800-749-5339, Fax: 352-489-3732, hyclassknives@aol.com
Specialties: Straight, folder and miniature. **Technical:** Blades from Wootz, Damascus and Alloy steel. **Prices:** To $5000. **Mark:** HY.

I

IKOMA, FLAVIO
R Manoel Rainho Teixeira 108, Presidente Prudente, SP, BRAZIL 19031-220, Phone: 0182-22-0115, fikoma@itelesonica.com.br
Specialties: Tactical fixed blade knives, LinerLock® folders and balisongs. **Patterns:** Utility and defense tactical knives built with hi-tech materials. **Technical:** Grinds S30V and Damasteel. **Prices:** $500 to $1000. **Mark:** Ikoma hand made beside Samurai

IMBODEN II, HOWARD L.
620 Deauville Dr, Dayton, OH 45429, Phone: 513-439-1536
Specialties: One-of-a-kind hunting, flint, steel and art knives. **Technical:** Forges and grinds stainless, high-carbon and Damascus. Uses obsidian, cast sterling silver, 14K and 18K gold guards. Carves ivory animals and more. **Prices:** $65 to $25,000. **Remarks:** Full-time maker; first knife sold in 1986. Doing business as Hill Originals. **Mark:** First and last initials, II.

IMEL, BILLY MACE
1616 Bundy Ave, New Castle, IN 47362, Phone: 765-529-1651
Specialties: High-art working knives, period pieces and personal cutlery. **Patterns:** Daggers, fighters, hunters; locking folders and slip-joints with interframes. **Technical:** Grinds D2, 440C and 154CM. **Prices:** $300 to $2000; some to $6000. **Remarks:** Part-time maker; first knife sold in 1973. **Mark:** Name in monogram.

IOANNIS-MINAS, FILIPPOU
5, Krinis Str, Nea Smyrni, Athens, GREECE 171 22, Phone: (1) 210-9352093, kamami53@yahoo.gr

IRIE, MICHAEL L
MIKE IRIE HANDCRAFT, 1606 Auburn Dr., Colorado Springs, CO 80909, Phone: 719-572-5330, mikeirie@aol.com
Specialties: Working fixed blade knives and handcrafted blades for the do-it-yourselfer. **Patterns:** Twenty standard designs along with custom. **Technical:** Blades are ATS-34, BG-43, 440C with some outside Damascus. **Prices:** Fixed blades $95 and up, blade work $45 and up. **Remarks:** Formerly dba Wood, Irie and Co. with Barry Wood. Full-time maker since 1991. **Mark:** Name.

ISAO, OHBUCHI
702-1 Nouso, Yame-City, Fukuoka, JAPAN, Phone: 0943-23-4439, www.5d.biglobe.ne.jp/~ohisao/

ISHIHARA, HANK
86-18 Motomachi, Sakura City, Chiba, JAPAN, Phone: 043-485-3208, Fax: 043-485-3208
Specialties: Fantasy working straight knives and folders of his design. **Patterns:** Boots, Bowies, daggers, fighters, hunters, fishing, locking folders and utility camp knives. **Technical:** Grinds ATS-34, 440C, D2, 440V, CV-134, COS25 and Damascus. Engraves. **Prices:** $250 to $1000; some to $10,000. **Remarks:** Full-time maker; first knife sold in 1987. **Mark:** HANK.

J

JACKS, JIM
344 S. Hollenbeck Ave, Covina, CA 91723-2513, Phone: 626-331-5665
Specialties: Working straight knives in standard patterns. **Patterns:** Bowies, hunters, fighters, fishing and camp knives, miniatures. **Technical:** Grinds Stellite 6K, 440C and ATS-34. **Prices:** Start at $100. **Remarks:** Spare-time maker; first knife sold in 1980. **Mark:** Initials in diamond logo.

JACKSON, CHARLTON R
6811 Leyland Dr, San Antonio, TX 78239, Phone: 210-601-5112

JACKSON, DAVID
214 Oleander Ave, Lemoore, CA 93245, Phone: 559-925-8247, jnbcrea@lemoorenet.com
Specialties: Forged steel. **Patterns:** Hunters, camp knives and bowies. **Prices:** $300 and up. **Mark:** G.D. Jackson - Maker - Lemoore CA.

JACKSON, LARAMIE
POB 442, Claysprings, AZ 85923, Phone: 480-747-3804, ljacksonknives@yahoo.com
Specialties: Traditional hunting and working knives and folders, chef's knives. **Patterns:** Bowies, fighters, hunters, daggers and skinners. **Technical:** Grinds 440C, CPM D2, CPM S30V, W2, O1, 52100, 5160, L6, 1095, damascus and whatever customer wants. Offers sheaths. **Prices:** $100-$450+. **Remarks:** Full-time maker; first knife sold in 2010. **Mark:** First initial and last name.

JACQUES, ALEX
332 Williams St., Warwick, RI 02906, Phone: 617-771-4441, customrazors@gmail.com Web: www.customrazors.com
Specialties: One-of-a-kind, heirloom quality straight razors … functional art. **Technical:** Damascus, O1, CPM154, and various other high-carbon and stainless steels. **Prices:** $450 and up. **Remarks:** First knife sold in 2008. **Mark:** Jack-O-Lantern logo with "A. Jacques" underneath.

JAKSIK JR., MICHAEL
427 Marschall Creek Rd, Fredericksburg, TX 78624, Phone: 830-997-1119
Mark: MJ or M. Jaksik.

JANGTANONG, SUCHAT
10901 W. Cave Blvd., Dripping Springs, TX 78620, Phone: 512-264-1501, shakeallpoints@yahoo.com; Web: www.mrdamascusknives.com
Specialties: One-of-a-kind handmade art knives, carving pearl and titanium. **Patterns:** Folders (lock back and LinerLock), some fixed blades and butterfly knives. **Technical:** Grinds ATS-34 and damascus steels. **Prices:** $500 to $3,000. **Remarks:** Third-generation, began making knives in 1982; full-time maker who lives in Uthai Thani Province of Thailand. **Mark:** Name (Suchat) on blade.

JANSEN VAN VUUREN, LUDWIG
311 Brighton Rd., Waldronville 9018, Dunedin, NEW ZEALAND, Phone: 64-3-7421012, ludwig@nzhandmadeknives.co.nz; Web: www.nzhandmadeknives.co.nz
Specialties: Fixed-blade knives of his design or custom specifications. **Patterns:** Hunting, fishing, bird-and-trout and chef's knives. **Technical:** Stock-removal maker; Elmax, Sandvik 12C27 and other blade steels on request. Handle material includes Micarta, antler and a wide selection of woods. **Prices:** Starting at $250. **Remarks:** Part-time maker since 2008. **Mark:** L J van Vuuren.

JARVIS, PAUL M
30 Chalk St, Cambridge, MA 02139, Phone: 617-547-4355 or 617-661-3015
Specialties: High-art knives and period pieces of his design. **Patterns:** Japanese and Mid-Eastern knives. **Technical:** Grinds Myer Damascus, ATS-34, D2 and O1. Specializes in height-relief Japanese-style carving. Works with silver, gold and gems. **Prices:** $200 to $17,000. **Remarks:** Part-time maker; first knife sold in 1978.

JEAN, GERRY
25B Cliffside Dr, Manchester, CT 06040, Phone: 860-649-6449
Specialties: Historic replicas. **Patterns:** Survival and camp knives. **Technical:** Grinds A2, 440C and 154CM. Handle slabs applied in unique tongue-and-groove method. **Prices:** $125 to $250; some to $1000. **Remarks:** Spare-time maker; first knife sold in 1973. **Mark:** Initials and serial number.

JEFFRIES, MIKE
1015 Highland Ave., Louisville, KY 40204, Phone: 502-592-4240, 2birdsmetalworks@gmail.com; Facebook.com/2BirdsMetalWorks, Instagram @2Birdsmetalworks
Specialties: Handmade custom knives, mostly drop-point and wharncliffe-style blades. **Patterns:** Outdoor, camping, hiking, hunting and bushcraft knives. **Technical:** Stock removal of high-carbon and tool steels, as well as damascus. Prefers stabilized wood and synthetic handles, the latter including G-10, carbon fiber and Thunderstorm Kevlar. **Prices:** $150 to $800. **Remarks:** Three years making knives, two years full time. **Mark:** MJK.

JEFFRIES, ROBERT W
Route 2 Box 227, Red House, WV 25168, Phone: 304-586-9780, wvknifeman@hotmail.com; Web: www.jeffriesknivesvv.tripod.com
Specialties: Hunters, Bowies, daggers, lockback folders and LinerLock push buttons. **Patterns:** Skinning types, drop points, typical working hunters, folders one-of-a-kind. **Technical:** Grinds all types of steel. Makes his own Damascus. **Prices:** $125 to $600. Private collector pieces to $3000. **Remarks:** Starting engraving. Custom folders of his design. Part-time maker since 1988. **Mark:** Name etched or on plate pinned to blade.

JENKINS, MITCH
194 East 500 South, Manti, Utah 84642, Phone: 435-813-2532, mitch.jenkins@gmail.com Web: MitchJenkinsKnives.com
Specialties: Hunters, working knives. **Patterns:** Johnson and Loveless Style. Drop points, skinners and semi-skinners, Capers and utilities. **Technical:** 154CM and ATS-34. Experimenting with S30V and love working with Damascus on occasion. **Prices:** $150 and up. **Remarks:** Slowly transitioning to full-time maker; first knife made in 2008. **Mark:** Jenkins Manti, Utah and M. Jenkins, Utah.

JENSEN, ELI

525 Shalimar Dr., Prescott, AZ 86303, Phone: 928-606-0373, ej89@nau.edu

Specialties: Fixed blades, mostly small and mid-size drop-points. **Technical:** Stock-removal method of blade making, preferring interesting natural materials, including burls, roots and uncommon species. **Prices:** $400 and up. **Remarks:** Part-time maker; first knife made in 2010. **Mark:** First and last name in cursive.

JENSEN, JOHN LEWIS

JENSEN KNIVES, 146 W. Bellevue Dr. #7, Pasadena, CA 91105, Phone: 626-773-0296, john@jensenknives.com; Web: www.jensenknives.com

Specialties: Designer and fabricator of modern, original one-of-a-kind, hand crafted, custom ornamental edged weaponry. Combines skill, precision, distinction and the finest materials, geared toward the discriminating art collector. **Patterns:** Folding knives and fixed blades, daggers, fighters and swords. **Technical:** High embellishment, BFA 96 Rhode Island School of Design: jewelry and metalsmithing. Grinds carbon and stainless, and carbon/stainless damascus. Works with custom made Damascus to his specs. Uses gold, silver, gemstones, pearl, titanium, fossil mastodon and walrus ivories. Carving, file work, soldering, deep etches Damascus, engraving, layers, bevels, blood grooves. Also forges his own Damascus. **Prices:** Start at $10,000. **Remarks:** Available on a first come basis and via commission based on his designs. **Mark:** Maltese cross/butterfly shield.

JERNIGAN, STEVE

3082 Tunnel Rd., Milton, FL 32571, Phone: 850-994-0802, Fax: 850-994-0802, jerniganknives@att.net

Specialties: Investor-class folders and various theme pieces. **Patterns:** Array of models and sizes in side plate locking interframes and conventional liner construction, including tactical and automatics. **Technical:** Grinds ATS-34, CPM-T-440V and damascus. Inlays mokume (and minerals) in blades and sculpts marble cases. **Prices:** $650 to $1,800; some to $6,000. **Remarks:** Full-time maker; first knife sold in 1982. **Mark:** Last name.

JOBIN, JACQUES

46 St Dominique, Levis, QC, CANADA G6V 2M7, Phone: 418-833-0283, Fax: 418-833-8378

Specialties: Fancy and working straight knives and folders; miniatures. **Patterns:** Minis, fantasy knives, fighters and some hunters. **Technical:** ATS-34, some Damascus and titanium. Likes native snake wood. Heat-treats. **Prices:** Start at $250. **Remarks:** Full-time maker; first knife sold in 1986. **Mark:** Signature on blade.

JOEHNK, BERND

Posadowskystrasse 22, Kiel, GERMANY 24148, Phone: 0431-7297705, Fax: 0431-7297705

Specialties: One-of-a-kind fancy/embellished and traditional straight knives of his design and from customer drawing. **Patterns:** Daggers, fighters, hunters and letter openers. **Technical:** Grinds and file 440C, ATS-34, powder metal orgical, commercial Damascus and various stainless and corrosion-resistant steels. **Prices:** Upscale. **Remarks:** Likes filework. Leather sheaths. Offers engraving. Part-time maker; first knife sold in1990. Doing business as metal design kiel. All knives made by hand. **Mark:** From 2005 full name and city, with certificate.

JOHANNING CUSTOM KNIVES, TOM

1735 Apex Rd, Sarasota, FL 34240 9386, Phone: 941-371-2104, Fax: 941-378-9427, Web: www.survivalknives.com

Specialties: Survival knives. **Prices:** $375 to $775.

JOHANSSON, ANDERS

Konstvartarevagen 9, Grangesberg, SWEDEN 77240, Phone: 46 240 23204, Fax: +46 21 358778, www.scrimart.u.se

Specialties: Scandinavian traditional and modern straight knives. **Patterns:** Hunters, fighters and fantasy knives. **Technical:** Grinds stainless steel and makes own Damascus. Prefers water buffalo and mammoth for handle material. **Prices:** Start at $100. **Remarks:** Spare-time maker; first knife sold in 1994. Works together with scrimshander Viveca Sahlin. **Mark:** Stylized initials.

JOHNSON, C E GENE

1240 Coan Street, Chesterton, IN 46304, Phone: 219-787-8324, ddjlady55@aol.com

Specialties: Lock-back folders and springers of his design or to customer specs. **Patterns:** Hunters, Bowies, survival lock-back folders. **Technical:** Grinds D2, 440C, A18, O1, Damascus; likes filework. **Prices:** $100 to $2000. **Remarks:** Full-time maker; first knife sold in 1975. **Mark:** Gene.

JOHNSON, DAVID A

1791 Defeated Creek Rd, Pleasant Shade, TN 37145, Phone: 615-774-3596, artsmith@mwsi.net

JOHNSON, GORDON A.

981 New Hope Rd, Choudrant, LA 71227, Phone: 318-768-2613

Specialties: Using straight knives and folders of my design, or customers. Offering filework and hand stitched sheaths. **Patterns:** Hunters, bowies, folders and miniatures. **Technical:** Forges 5160, 1084, 52100 and my own Damascus. Some stock removal on working knives and miniatures. **Prices:** Mid range. **Remarks:** First knife sold in 1990. ABS apprentice smith. **Mark:** Interlocking initials G.J. or G. A. J.

JOHNSON, JERRY

PO Box 491, Spring City, Utah 84662, Phone: 435-851-3604 or 435-462-3688, Web: sanpetesilver.com

Specialties: Hunter, fighters, camp. **Patterns:** Multiple. **Prices:** $225 - $3000. **Mark:** Jerry E. Johnson Spring City, UT in several fonts.

JOHNSON, JERRY L

29847 260th St, Worthington, MN 56187, Phone: 507-376-9253; Cell: 507-370-3523, doctorj55@yahoo.com

Specialties: Straight knives, hunters, bowies, and fighting knives. **Patterns:** Drop points, trailing points, bowies, and some favorite Loveless patterns. **Technical:** Grinds ATS 34, 440C, S30V, forges own damascus, mirror finish, satin finish, file work and engraving done by self. **Prices:** $250 to $1500. **Remarks:** Part-time maker since 1991, member of knifemakers guild since 2009. **Mark:** Name over a sheep head or elk head with custom knives under the head.

JOHNSON, JOHN R

PO Box 246, New Buffalo, PA 17069, Phone: 717-834-6265, jrj@jrjknives.com; Web: www.jrjknives.com

Specialties: Working hunting and tactical fixed blade sheath knives. **Patterns:** Hunters, tacticals, Bowies, daggers, neck knives and primitives. **Technical:** Flat, convex and hollow grinds. ATS-34, CPM154CM, L6, O1, D2, 5160, 1095 and Damascus. **Prices:** $60 to $700. **Remarks:** Full-time maker, first knife sold in 1996. Doing business as JRJ Knives. Custom sheath made by maker for every knife, **Mark:** Initials connected.

JOHNSON, JOHN R

5535 Bob Smith Ave, Plant City, FL 33565, Phone: 813-986-4478, rottyjohn@msn.com

Specialties: Hand forged and stock removal. **Technical:** High tech. Folders. **Mark:** J.R. Johnson Plant City, FL.

JOHNSON, KEITH R.

9179 Beltrami Line Rd. SW, Bemidji, MN 56601, Phone: 218-368-7482, keith@greatriverforge.com; www.greatriverforge.com

Specialties: Slip-joint and lockback folders. **Patterns:** Mostly traditional patterns but with customer preferences, some of maker's own patterns. **Technical:** Mainly uses CTS XHP, sometimes other high-quality stainless steels, Damasteel. Variety of handle materials, including bone, mammoth ivory, Micarta, G-10 and carbon fiber. **Remarks:** Full-time maker; first knife sold in 1986. **Mark:** K.R. JOHNSON (arched) over BEMIDJI.

JOHNSON, MIKE

38200 Main Rd, Orient, NY 11957, Phone: 631-323-3509, mjohnsoncustomknives@hotmail.com

Specialties: Large Bowie knives and cutters, fighters and working knives to customer specs. **Technical:** Forges 5160, O1. **Prices:** $325 to $1200. **Remarks:** Full-time bladesmith. **Mark:** Johnson.

JOHNSON, R B

Box 11, Clearwater, MN 55320, Phone: 320-558-6128, Fax: 320-558-6128, rb@rbjohnsonknives.com; Web: rbjohnsonknives.com

Specialties: Liner locks with titanium, mosaic Damascus. **Patterns:** LinerLock® folders, skeleton hunters, frontier Bowies. **Technical:** Damascus, mosaic Damascus, A-2, O1, 1095. **Prices:** $200 and up. **Remarks:** Full-time maker since 1973. Not accepting orders. **Mark:** R B Johnson (signature).

JOHNSON, RANDY

2575 E Canal Dr, Turlock, CA 95380, Phone: 209-632-5401

Specialties: Folders. **Patterns:** Locking folders. **Technical:** Grinds Damascus. **Prices:** $200 to $400. **Remarks:** Spare-time maker; first knife sold in 1989. Doing business as Puedo Knifeworks. **Mark:** PUEDO.

JOHNSON, RICHARD

W165 N10196 Wagon Trail, Germantown, WI 53022, Phone: 262-251-5772, rlj@execpc.com; Web: http://www.execpc.com/~rlj/index.html

Specialties: Custom knives and knife repair.

JOHNSON, RYAN M

3103 Excelsior Ave., Signal Mountain, TN 37377, Phone: 866-779-6922, contact@rmjtactical.com; Web: www.rmjforge.com www.rmjtactical.com

Specialties: Historical and Tactical Tomahawks. Some period knives and folders. **Technical:** Forges a variety of steels including own Damascus. **Prices:** $500 - $1200 **Remarks:** Full-time maker began forging in 1986. **Mark:** Sledge-hammer with halo.

JOHNSON, STEVEN R

202 E 200 N, PO Box 5, Manti, UT 84642, Phone: 435-835-7941, srj@mail.manti.com; Web: www.srjknives.com

Specialties: Investor-class working knives. **Patterns:** Hunters, fighters, boots. **Technical:** Grinds CPM-154CM and CTS-XHP. **Prices:** $1,500 to $20,000. Engraved knives up to $50,000. **Remarks:** Full-time maker; first knife sold in 1972. Also see SR Johnson forum on www.knifenetwork.com. **Mark:** Registered trademark, including name, city, state, and optional signature mark.

JOHNSON, TIMOTHY A.

Worcester, MA, tim@blackstoneknife.com

Specialties: Custom kitchen knives. **Technical:** Stock removal of stainless, high carbon, san mai and damascus blade steels. **Prices:** $250 to $800. **Remarks:** Part-time maker, first knife made around 1994. **Mark:** Stylized initials TAJ.

JOHNSON, TOMMY

144 Poole Rd., Troy, NC 27371, Phone: 910-975-1817, tommy@tjohnsonknives.com Web: www.tjohnsonknives.com

Specialties: Straight knives for hunting, fishing, utility, and linerlock and slip joint folders since 1982.

JOHNSON, WM. C. "BILL"

225 Fairfield Pike, Enon, OH 45323, Phone: 937-864-7802, wjohnson64@woh.RR.com

custom knifemakers

Patterns: From hunters to art knives as well as custom canes, some with blades. **Technical:** Stock removal method utilizing 440C, ATS34, 154CPM, and custom Damascus. **Prices:** $175 to over $2500, depending on design, materials, and embellishments. **Remarks:** Full-time maker. First knife made in 1978. Member of the Knifemakers Guild since 1982. **Mark:** Crescent shaped WM. C. "BILL" JOHNSON, ENON OHIO. Also uses an engraved or electro signature on some art knives and on Damascus blades.

JOHNSTON, DR. ROBT
PO Box 9887 1 Lomb Mem Dr, Rochester, NY 14623

JOKERST, CHARLES
9312 Spaulding, Omaha, NE 68134, Phone: 402-571-2536
Specialties: Working knives in standard patterns. **Patterns:** Hunters, fighters and pocketknives. **Technical:** Grinds 440C, ATS-34. **Prices:** $90 to $170. **Remarks:** Spare-time maker; first knife sold in 1984. **Mark:** Early work marked RCJ; current work marked with last name and city.

JONAS, ZACHARY
204 Village Rd., Wilmot, NH 03287, Phone: 603-877-0128, zack@jonasblade.com; www.jonasblade.com
Specialties: Custom high-carbon damascus, sporting knives, kitchen knives and art knives. Always interested in adding to the repertoire. **Patterns:** Kitchen and bowie knives, hunters, daggers, push daggers, tantos, boot knives, all custom. **Technical:** Forges all damascus blades, works with high-carbon steels to suit the client's individual tastes and needs. **Remarks:** Full-time maker, ABS journeyman smith trained by ABS master smith J.D. Smith, juried member of League of New Hampshire Craftsmen. **Mark:** Sytlized "Z" symbol on one side, "JS" on other, either stamped, engraved or etched.

JONES, BARRY M AND PHILLIP G
221 North Ave, Danville, VA 24540, Phone: 804-793-5282
Specialties: Working and using straight knives and folders of their design and to customer specs; combat and self-defense knives. **Patterns:** Bowies, fighters, daggers, swords, hunters and LinerLock® folders. **Technical:** Grinds 440C, ATS-34 and D2; flat-grinds only. All blades hand polished. **Prices:** $100 to $1000, some higher. **Remarks:** Part-time makers; first knife sold in 1989. **Mark:** Jones Knives, city, state.

JONES, ENOCH
7278 Moss Ln, Warrenton, VA 20187, Phone: 540-341-0292
Specialties: Fancy working straight knives. **Patterns:** Hunters, fighters, boots and Bowies. **Technical:** Forges and grinds O1, W2, 440C and Damascus. **Prices:** $100 to $350; some to $1000. **Remarks:** Part-time maker; first knife sold in 1982. **Mark:** First name.

JONES, JACK P.
17670 Hwy. 2 East, Ripley, MS 38663, Phone: 662-837-3882, jacjones@ripleycable.net
Specialties: Working knives in classic design. **Patterns:** Hunters, fighters, and Bowies. **Technical:** Grinds D2, A2, CPM-154, CTS-XHP and ATS-34. **Prices:** $200 and up. **Remarks:** Full-time maker since retirement in 2005, first knife sold in 1976. **Mark:** J.P. Jones, Ripley, MS.

JONES, ROGER MUDBONE
GREENMAN WORKSHOP, 320 Prussia Rd, Waverly, OH 45690, Phone: 740-739-4562, greenmanworkshop@yahoo.com
Specialties: Working in cutlery to suit working woodsman and fine collector. **Patterns:** Bowies, hunters, folders, hatchets in both period and modern style, scale miniatures a specialty. **Technical:** All cutlery hand forged to shape with traditional methods; multiple quench and draws, limited Damascus production hand carves wildlife and historic themes in stag/antler/ivory, full line of functional and high art leather. All work sole authorship. **Prices:** $50 to $5000 **Remarks:** Full-time maker/first knife sold in 1979. **Mark:** Stamped R. Jones hand made or engraved sig. W/Bowie knife mark.

JORGENSEN, CARSON
1805 W Hwy 116, Mt Pleasant, UT 84647, tcjorgensenknife@gmail.com; Web: tcjknives.com
Specialties: Stock removal, Loveless Johnson and young styles. **Prices:** Most $100 to $800.

K

K B S, KNIVES
RSD 181, North Castlemaine, VIC, AUSTRALIA 3450, Phone: 0011 61 3 54 705864
Specialties: Historically inspired bowies, and restoration of fixed and folding knives. **Patterns:** Bowies and folders. **Technical:** Flat and hollow grinds, filework. **Prices:** $500 and up. **Remarks:** First knife sold in 1983, foundation member of Australian Knife Guild. **Mark:** Initials and address within Southern cross.

KACZOR, TOM
375 Wharncliffe Rd N, Upper London, ON, CANADA N6G 1E4, Phone: 519-645-7640

KAGAWA, KOICHI
1556 Horiyamashita, Hatano-Shi, Kanagawa, JAPAN
Specialties: Fancy high-tech straight knives and folders to customer specs. **Patterns:** Hunters, locking folders and slip-joints. **Technical:** Uses 440C and ATS-34. **Prices:** $500 to $2000; some to $20,000. **Remarks:** Part-time maker; first knife sold in 1986. **Mark:** First initial, last name-YOKOHAMA.

KAIN, CHARLES
KAIN DESIGNS, 1736 E. Maynard Dr., Indianapolis, IN 46227, Phone: 317-781-9549, Fax: 317-781-8521, charles@kaincustomknives.com; Web: www.kaincustomknives.com
Specialties: Unique Damascus art folders. **Patterns:** Any. **Technical:** Specialized & patented mechanisms. **Remarks:** Unique knife & knife mechanism design. **Mark:** Kain and Signet stamp for unique pieces.

KANKI, IWAO
691-2 Tenjincho, Ono-City, Hyogo, JAPAN 675-1316, Phone: 07948-3-2555, Web: www.chiyozurusadahide.jp
Specialties: Plane, knife. **Prices:** Not determined yet. **Remarks:** Masters of traditional crafts designated by the Minister of International Trade and Industry (Japan). **Mark:** Chiyozuru Sadahide.

KANSEI, MATSUNO
109-8 Uenomachi, Nishikaiden, Gifu, JAPAN 501-1168, Phone: 81-58-234-8643
Specialties: Folders of original design. **Patterns:** LinerLock® folder. **Technical:** Grinds VG-10, Damascus. **Prices:** $350 to $2000. **Remarks:** Full-time maker. First knife sold in 1993. **Mark:** Name.

KANTER, MICHAEL
ADAM MICHAEL KNIVES, 14550 West Honey Ln., New Berlin, WI 53151, Phone: 262-860-1136, mike@adammichaelknives.com; Web: www.adammichaelknives.com
Specialties: Fixed blades and folders. **Patterns:** Drop point hunters, Bowies and fighters. **Technical:** Jerry Rados Damascus, BG42, CPM, S60V and S30V. **Prices:** $375 and up. **Remarks:** Ivory, mammoth ivory, stabilized woods, and pearl handles. **Mark:** Engraved Adam Michael.

KARP, BOB
PO Box 47304, Phoenix, AZ 85068, Phone: 602 870-1234, Fax: 602-331-0283
Remarks: Bob Karp "Master of the Blade."

KATO, SHINICHI
Rainbow Amalke 402, Moriyama-ku Nagoya, Aichi, JAPAN 463-0002, Phone: 81-52-736-6032, skato-402@u0l.gate01.com
Specialties: Flat grind and hand finish. **Patterns:** Bowie, fighter. Hunting and folding knives. **Technical:** Hand forged,flat grind. **Prices:** $100 to $2000. **Remarks:** Part-time maker. **Mark:** Name.

KATSUMARO, SHISHIDO
2-6-11 Kamiseno, Aki-ku, Hiroshima, JAPAN, Phone: 090-3634-9054, Fax: 082-227-4438, shishido@d8.dion.ne.jp

KAUFFMAN, DAVE
158 Jackson Creek Rd., Clancy, MT 59634, Phone: 406-431-8435
Specialties: Field grade and exhibition grade hunting knives and ultra light folders. **Patterns:** Fighters, Bowies and drop-point hunters. **Technical:** S30V and SS Damascus. **Prices:** $155 to $1200. **Remarks:** Full-time maker; first knife sold in 1989. On the cover of Knives '94. **Mark:** First and last name, city and state.

KAY, J WALLACE
332 Slab Bridge Rd, Liberty, SC 29657

KAZSUK, DAVID
27789 Ethanac Rd., Menifee, CA 92585, Phone: 951-216-0883, ddkaz@hotmail.com
Specialties: Hand forged. **Prices:** $150+. **Mark:** Last name.

KEARNEY, JAROD
1505 Parkersburg Turnpike, Swoope, VA 24479, jarodkearney@gmail.com Web: www.jarodkearney.com
Patterns: Bowies, skinners, hunters, Japanese blades, Sgian Dubhs

KEESLAR, JOSEPH F
391 Radio Rd, Almo, KY 42020, Phone: 270-753-7919, Fax: 270-753-7919, suzjoe.kees@gmail.com
Specialties: Classic and contemporary Bowies, combat, hunters, daggers and folders. **Patterns:** Decorative filework, engraving and custom leather sheaths available. **Technical:** Forges 5160, 52100 and his own Damascus steel. **Prices:** $300 to $3000. **Remarks:** Full-time maker; first knife sold in 1976. ABS Master Smith, and 50 years as a bladesmith (1962-2012). **Mark:** First and middle initials, last name in hammer, knife and anvil logo, M.S.

KEESLAR, STEVEN C
115 Lane 216 Hamilton Lake, Hamilton, IN 46742, Phone: 260-488-3161, sskeeslar@hotmail.com
Specialties: Traditional working/using straight knives of his design and to customer specs. **Patterns:** Bowies, hunters, utility/camp knives. **Technical:** Forges 5160, files 52100 Damascus. **Prices:** $100 to $600; some to $1500. **Remarks:** Part-time maker; first knife sold in 1976. ABS member. **Mark:** Fox head in flames over Steven C. Keeslar.

KEETON, WILLIAM L
6095 Rehobeth Rd SE, Laconia, IN 47135-9550, Phone: 812-969-2836, wlkeeton@hughes.net; Web: www.keetoncustomknives.com
Specialties: Plain and fancy working knives. **Patterns:** Hunters and fighters; locking folders and slip-joints. Names patterns after Kentucky Derby winners. **Technical:** Grinds any of the popular alloy steels. **Prices:** $250 to $8,000. **Remarks:** Full-time maker; first knife sold in 1971. **Mark:** Logo of key.

KEHIAYAN, ALFREDO
Cuzco 1455 Ing., Maschwitz, Buenos Aires, ARGENTINA B1623GXU, Phone: 540-348-4442212, Fax: 54-077-75-4493-5359, alfredo@kehiayan.com.ar; Web: www.kehiayan.com.ar
Specialties: Functional straight knives. **Patterns:** Utility knives, skinners, hunters and boots. **Technical:** Forges and grinds SAE 52.100, SAE 6180, SAE 9260, SAE 5160, 440C and ATS-34, titanium with nitride. All blades mirror-polished; makes leather sheath and wood cases. **Prices:** From $350 up. **Remarks:** Full-time maker; first knife sold in 1983. Some knives are satin finish (utility knives). **Mark:** Name.

KEISUKE, GOTOH
105 Cosumo-City Otozu 202, Oita-city, Oita, JAPAN, Phone: 097-523-0750, k-u-an@ki.rim.or.jp

KELLER, BILL
12211 Las Nubes, San Antonio, TX 78233, Phone: 210-653-6609
Specialties: Primarily folders, some fixed blades. **Patterns:** Autos, liner locks and hunters. **Technical:** Grinds stainless and Damascus. **Prices:** $400 to $1000, some to $4000. **Remarks:** Part-time maker, first knife sold 1995. **Mark:** Last name inside outline of Alamo.

KELLEY, GARY
17485 SW Pheasant Lane, Aloha, OR 97006, Phone: 503-649-7867, garykelley@thebladermaker.com; Web: wwwthebladermaker.com
Specialties: Primitive knives and blades. **Patterns:** Fur trade era rifleman's knives, tomahawks, and hunting knives. **Technical:** Hand-forges and precision investment casts. **Prices:** $35 to $125. **Remarks:** Family business. Doing business as The Blademaker. **Mark:** Fir tree logo.

KELLY, DAVE
865 S. Shenandoah St., Los Angeles, CA 90035, Phone: 310-657-7121, dakcon@sbcglobal.net
Specialties: Collector and user one-of-a-kind (his design) fixed blades, liner lock folders, and leather sheaths. **Patterns:** Utility and hunting fixed blade knives with hand-sewn leather sheaths, Gentleman liner lock folders. **Technical:** Grinds carbon steels, hollow, convex, and flat. Offers clay differentially hardened blades, etched and polished. Uses Sambar stag, mammoth ivory, and high-grade burl woods. Hand-sewn leather sheaths for fixed blades and leather pouch sheaths for folders. **Prices:** $250 to $750, some higher. **Remarks:** Full-time maker, first knife made in 2003. **Mark:** First initial, last name with large K.

KELLY, STEVEN
11407 Spotted Fawn Ln., Bigfork, MT 59911, Phone: 406-212-2195, steve@skknives.com; Web: www.skknives.com
Specialties: Tactical-style folders. **Technical:** Damascus from 1084 or 1080 and 15n20. 52100.

KELSEY, NATE
3867 N. Forestwood Dr., Palmer, AK 99645, Phone: 907-360-4469, edgealaska@mac.com; Web: www.edgealaska.com
Specialties: Forges high-performance 52100, stock removal on 154CM for Extreme Duty Worldwide. **Patterns:** Hunters, fighters, bowies and neck knives. **Technical:** Forges own damascus, 52100 and W2 blade steels, and stock removal of XHP and 154CM. **Prices:** $250 to $5,000. **Remarks:** Maker since 1990, member ABS. **Mark:** EDGE ALASKA or last name and Palmer AK.

KELSO, JIM
577 Collar Hill Rd, Worcester, VT 05682, Phone: 802-229-4254, Fax: 802-229-0595, kelsomaker@gmail.com; Web:www.jimkelso.com
Specialties: Fancy high-art straight knives and folders that mix Eastern and Western influences. Only uses own designs. **Patterns:** Daggers, swords and locking folders. **Technical:** Works with top bladesmiths. **Prices:** $15,000 to $60,000. **Remarks:** Full-time maker; first knife sold in 1980. **Mark:** Stylized initials.

KEMP, LAWRENCE
8503 Water Tower Rd, Ooltewah, TN 37363, Phone: 423-344-2357, larry@kempknives.com Web: www.kempknives.com
Specialties: Bowies, hunters and working knives. **Patterns:** Bowies, camp knives, hunters and skinners. **Technical:** Forges carbon steel, and his own Damascus. **Prices:** $250 to $1500. **Remarks:** Part-time maker, first knife sold in 1991. ABS Journeyman Smith since 2006. **Mark:** L.A. Kemp.

KENNEDY JR., BILL
PO Box 850431, Yukon, OK 73085, Phone: 405-354-9150, bkfish1@gmail.com; www.billkennedyjrknives.com
Specialties: Working straight knives and folders. **Patterns:** Hunters, minis, fishing, and pocket knives. **Technical:** Grinds D2, 440C, ATS-34, BG42. **Prices:** $110 and up. **Remarks:** Part-time maker; first knife sold in 1980. **Mark:** Last name and year made.

KERANEN, PAUL
4122 S. E. Shiloh Ct., Tacumseh, KS 66542, Phone: 785-220-2141, pk6269@yahoo.com
Specialties: Specializes in Japanese style knives and swords. Most clay tempered with hamon. **Patterns:** Does bowies, fighters and hunters. **Technical:** Forges and grinds carbons steel only. Make my own Damascus. **Prices:** $75 to $800. **Mark:** Keranen arched over anvil.

KEYES, DAN
6688 King St, Chino, CA 91710, Phone: 909-628-8329

KEYES, GEOFF P.
13027 Odell Rd NE, Duvall, WA 98019, Phone: 425-844-0758, 5ef@polarisfarm.com; Web: www5elementsforge.com
Specialties: Working grade fixed blades, 19th century style gents knives. **Patterns:** Fixed blades, your design or mine. **Technical:** Hnad-forged 5160, 1084, and own Damascus. **Prices:** $200 and up. **Remarks:** Geoff Keyes DBA 5 Elements Forge, ABS Journeyman Smith. **Mark:** Early mark KEYES etched in script. New mark as of 2009: pressed GPKeyes.

KHALSA, JOT SINGH
368 Village St, Millis, MA 02054, Phone: 508-376-8162, Fax: 508-532-0517, jotkhalsa@comcast.net; Web: www.khalsakirpans.com, www.lifeknives.com, and www.thekhalsaraj.com
Specialties: Liner locks, one-of-a-kind daggers, swords, and kirpans (Sikh daggers) all original designs. **Technical:** Forges own Damascus, uses others high quality Damascus including stainless, and grinds stainless steels. Uses natural handle materials frequently unusual minerals. Pieces are frequently engraved and more recently carved. **Prices:** Start at $700.

KHARLAMOV, YURI
Oboronnay 46, Tula, RUSSIA 300007
Specialties: Classic, fancy and traditional knives of his design. **Patterns:** Daggers and hunters. **Technical:** Forges only Damascus with nickel. Uses natural handle materials; engraves on metal, carves on nut-tree; silver and pearl inlays. **Prices:** $600 to $2380; some to $4000. **Remarks:** Full-time maker; first knife sold in 1988. **Mark:** Initials.

KI, SHIVA
5222 Ritterman Ave, Baton Rouge, LA 70805, Phone: 225-356-7274, shivakicustomknives@netzero.net; Web: www.shivakicustomknives.com
Specialties: Working straight knives and folders. **Patterns:** Emphasis on personal defense knives, martial arts weapons. **Technical:** Forges and grinds; makes own Damascus; prefers natural handle materials. **Prices:** $550 to $10,000. **Remarks:** Full-time maker; first knife sold in 1981. **Mark:** Name with logo.

KIEFER, TONY
112 Chateaugay Dr, Pataskala, OH 43062, Phone: 740-927-6910
Specialties: Traditional working and using straight knives in standard patterns. **Patterns:** Bowies, fighters and hunters. **Technical:** Grinds 440C and D2; forges D2. Flat-grinds Bowies; hollow-grinds drop-point and trailing-point hunters. **Prices:** $110 to $300; some to $200. **Remarks:** Spare-time maker; first knife sold in 1988. **Mark:** Last name.

KILBY, KEITH
1902 29th St, Cody, WY 82414, Phone: 307-587-2732
Specialties: Works with all designs. **Patterns:** Mostly Bowies, camp knives and hunters of his design. **Technical:** Forges 52100, 5160, 1095, Damascus and mosaic Damascus. **Prices:** $250 to $3500. **Remarks:** Part-time maker; first knife sold in 1974. Doing business as Foxwood Forge. **Mark:** Name.

KILEY, MIKE AND JANDY
ROCKING K KNIVES, 1325 Florida, Chino Valley, AZ 86323, Phone: 928-910-2647
Specialties: Period knives for cowboy action shooters and mountain men. **Patterns:** Bowies, drop-point hunters, skinners, sheepsfoot blades and spear points. **Technical:** Steels are 1095, 0-1, Damascus and others upon request. Handles include all types of wood, with cocobolo, ironwood, rosewood, maple and bacote being favorites as well as buffalo horn, stag, elk antler, mammoth ivory, giraffe boon, sheep horn and camel bone. **Prices:** $100 to $500 depending on style and materials. Hand-tooled leather sheaths by Jan and Mike. **Mark:** Stylized K on one side; Kiley on the other.

KILPATRICK, CHRISTIAN A
6925 Mitchell Ct, Citrus Heights, CA 95610, Phone: 916-729-0733, crimsonkil@gmail.com; Web:www.crimsonknives.com
Specialties: All forged weapons (no firearms) from ancient to modern. All blades produced are first and foremost useable tools, and secondly but no less importantly, artistic expressions. **Patterns:** Hunters, bowies, daggers, swords, axes, spears, boot knives, bird knives, ethnic blades and historical reproductions. Customer designs welcome. **Technical:** Forges and grinds, makes own Damascus. Does file work. **Prices:** $125 to $3200. **Remarks:** 26 year part time maker. First knife sold in 2002.

KILROY, KYLE
POB 24655, Knoxville, TN 37933, Phone: 843-729-5141, kylekilroy@yahoo.com; Web: www.kylekilroy.com
Specialties: Traditional forged knives in a mixture of traditional and modern materials. Professional chemical engineering background in polymers allows the exclusive use of many unique handle materials. **Patterns:** Bowie/fighting knife patterns, hunting knives, chef's knives and modern bearing flipper folders. **Technical:** Forges D2, 1090, 1095 and several other carbon steels depending on application. Forges own damascus and can produce stainless blades via stock removal. **Prices:** $80 and up. **Remarks:** Professional engineer; first knife sold in 1996. **Mark:** Name above Charleston SC, with earlier stamp being "Chicora Gun Works" in three lines.

KIMBERLEY, RICHARD L.
86-B Arroyo Hondo Rd, Santa Fe, NM 87508, Phone: 505-820-2727
Specialties: Fixed-blade and period knives. **Technical:** O1, 52100, 9260 steels. **Remarks:** Member ABS. Marketed under "Kimberleys of Santa Fe." **Mark:** "By D. KIMBERLEY SANTA FE NM."

KIMSEY, KEVIN
198 Cass White Rd. NW, Cartersville, GA 30121, Phone: 770-387-0779 and 770-655-8879
Specialties: Tactical fixed blades and folders. **Patterns:** Fighters, folders, hunters and utility knives. **Technical:** Grinds 440C, ATS-34 and D2 carbon. **Prices:** $100 to $400; some to $600. **Remarks:** Three-time Blade magazine award winner, knifemaker since 1983. **Mark:** Rafter and stylized KK.

KING, BILL
14830 Shaw Rd, Tampa, FL 33625, Phone: 813-961-3455, billkingknives@yahoo.com
Specialties: Folders, lockbacks, liner locks, automatics and stud openers. **Patterns:** Wide varieties; folders. **Technical:** ATS-34 and some Damascus; single and double grinds. Offers filework and jewel embellishment; nickel-silver Damascus and mokume bolsters. **Prices:** $150 to $475; some to $850. **Remarks:** Full-time maker; first knife sold in 1976. All titanium fitting on liner-locks; screw or rivet construction on lock-backs. **Mark:** Last name in crown.

KING, FRED

430 Grassdale Rd, Cartersville, GA 30120, Phone: 770-382-8478, Web: http://www. fking83264@aol.com

Specialties: Fancy and embellished working straight knives and folders. Patterns: Hunters, Bowies and fighters. Technical: Grinds ATS-34 and D2: forges 5160 and Damascus. Offers filework. Prices: $100 to $3500. Remarks: Spare-time maker; first knife sold in 1984. Mark: Kings Edge.

KING JR., HARVEY G

32170 Hwy K4, Alta Vista, KS 66834, Phone: 785-499-5207, Web: www. harveykingknives.com

Specialties: Traditional working and using straight knives of his design and to customer specs. Patterns: Hunters, Bowies and fillet knives. Technical: Grinds O1, A2 and D2. Prefers natural handle materials; offers leatherwork. Prices: Start at $150. Remarks: Full-time maker; first knife sold in 1988. Mark: Name, city, state, and serial number.

KINKER, MIKE

8755 E County Rd 50 N, Greensburg, IN 47240, Phone: 812-663-5277, kinkercustomknives@gmail.com

Specialties: Working/using knives, straight knives. Starting to make folders. Your design. Patterns: Boots, daggers, hunters, skinners, hatchets. Technical: Grind 440C and ATS-34, others if required. Damascus, dovetail bolsters, jeweled blade. Prices: $125 to 375; some to $1000. Remarks: Part-time maker; first knife sold in 1991. Doing business as Kinker Custom Knives. Mark: Kinker

KINNIKIN, TODD

EUREKA FORGE, 7 Capper Dr., Pacific, MO 63069-3603, Phone: 314-938-6248

Specialties: Mosaic Damascus. Patterns: Hunters, fighters, folders and automatics. Technical: Forges own mosaic Damascus with tool steel Damascus edge. Prefers natural, fossil and artifact handle materials. Prices: $1200 to $2400. Remarks: Full-time maker; first knife sold in 1994. Mark: Initials connected.

KIRK, RAY

PO Box 1445, Tahlequah, OK 74465, Phone: 918-207-8076, ray@rakerknives.com; Web: www.rakerknives.com

Specialties: Folders, skinners fighters, and Bowies. Patterns: Neck knives and small hunters and skinners. Full and hidden-tang integrals from 52100 round bar. Technical: Forges all knives from 52100 and own damascus. Prices: $65 to $3000. Remarks: Started forging in 1989; makes own Damascus. Mark: Stamped "Raker" on blade.

KIRKES, BILL

235 Oaklawn Cir., Little Rock, AR 72206, Phone: 501-551-0135, bill@kirkesknives. com; Web: www.kirkesknives.com

Specialties: Handforged fixed blades. Technical: High-carbon 5160 and 1084 blade steels. Will build to customer's specs, prefers to use natural handle material. Remarks: ABS Journeyman smith. Mark: Kirkes.

KISLINGER, MILOS

KISLINGER KNIVES, Dobronin 314 58812, CZECH REPUBLIC, Phone: +420724570451, kislinger.milos@centrum.cz; Web: http://kislingerknives.blogspot. cz/ or Facebook.com/KislingerKnives

Specialties: Fine folders, daggers, automatic knives, flipper folders and bowies. Technical: Forges own damascus steel, and uses ivory, pearl and more luxurious handle materials. Prices: $400 and up. Remarks: Knifemaker and blacksmith since 2005, with first knife made eight years ago.

KISTNER, DEE

107 Whitecrest Dr., Crossville, TN 38571, Phone: 931-200-1233, dkknives@gmail. com; Web: www.kistnerknives.com

Specialties: Working knives. Patterns: Everyday carry, hunting and outdoor knives, military knives. Technical: Flat grinds 1075 steel, differentially heat treated. Prices: $100 and up. Remarks: Full-time maker, sole authorship. Mark: KISTNER.

KITSMILLER, JERRY

67277 Las Vegas Dr, Montrose, CO 81401, Phone: 970-249-4290

Specialties: Working straight knives in standard patterns. Patterns: Hunters, boots. Technical: Grinds ATS-34 and 440C only. Prices: $75 to $200; some to $300. Remarks: Spare-time maker; first knife sold in 1984. Mark: JandS Knives.

KLAASEE, TINUS

PO Box 10221, George, WC, SOUTH AFRICA 6530

Specialties: Hunters, skinners and utility knives. Patterns: Uses own designs and client specs. Technical: N690 stainless steel 440C Damascus. Prices: $700 and up. Remarks: Use only indigenous materials. Hardwood, horns and ivory. Makes his own sheaths and boxes. Mark: Initials and sur name over warthog.

KLEIN, KEVIN

129 Cedar St., Apt. 2, Boston, MA 02119, Phone: 609-937-8949, kevin.a.klein779@ gmail.com

Specialties: Forged damascus blades using 15N20 and 1084. Remarks: Full-time maker; first knife made in 2012. Apprentice to J.D. Smith starting in 2012. Mark: KAK? or ?, depending on piece.

KLEIN, KIERAN

2436 Stonewall Rd. NE, Check, VA 24072, Phone: 540-651-2454, hammerdownkjk@ gmail.com; Web: www.hammerdownforge.com

Specialties: Large chopping blades as well as camping and EDC (everyday carry) styles. Patterns: Custom khukuri styles, drop points, sheepsfoot, etc. Technical: Stock removal method of blade making using 80CrV2, 52100, 1075, W2 and CPM 3V blade steels, and high-quality stabilized burl wood, carbon fiber, G-10 and Micarta handles. Prices: $125 to $1,200. Remarks: Full-time maker since 2013; first knife made in 2012. Mark: Mountain range profile over HDF initials with Virginia, USA under that.

KNAPP, MARK

Mark Knapp Custom Knives, 1971 Fox Ave, Fairbanks, AK 99701, Phone: 907-452-7477, info@markknappcustomknives.com; Web: www.markknappcustomknives.com

Specialties: Mosaic handles of exotic natural materials from Alaska and around the world. Folders, fixed blades, full and hidden tangs. Patterns: Folders, hunters, skinners, and camp knives. Technical: Forges own Damascus, uses both forging and stock removal with ATS-34, 154CM, stainless Damascus, carbon steel and carbon Damascus. Prices: $800-$3000. Remarks: Full time maker, sold first knife in 2000. Mark: Mark Knapp Custom Knives Fairbanks, AK.

KNAPTON, CHRIS C.

76 Summerland Dr., Henderson, Aukland, NEW ZEALAND, Phone: 09-835-3598, knaptch76@gmail.com; Web: www.knappoknives.com

Specialties: Working and fancy straight and folding knives of his own design. Patterns: Tactical, utility, hunting fixed and folding knives. Technical: Predominate knife steels are Elmax, CPM-154 and D2. All blades made via the stock removal method. Prices: $120 - $500. Remarks: Part-time maker. Mark: Stylized letter K, country name and Haast eagle.

KNICKMEYER, HANK

6300 Crosscreek, Cedar Hill, MO 63016, Phone: 636-285-3210

Specialties: Complex mosaic Damascus constructions. Patterns: Fixed blades, swords, folders and automatics. Technical: Mosaic Damascus with all tool steel Damascus edges. Prices: $500 to $2000; some $3000 and higher. Remarks: Part-time maker; first knife sold in 1989. Doing business as Dutch Creek Forge and Foundry. Mark: Initials connected.

KNICKMEYER, KURT

6344 Crosscreek, Cedar Hill, MO 63016, Phone: 314-274-0481

KNIGHT, JASON

110 Paradise Pond Ln, Harleyville, SC 29448, Phone: 843-452-1163, jasonknightknives.com

Specialties: Bowies. Patterns: Bowies and anything from history or his own design. Technical: 1084, 5160, O1, 52102, Damascus/forged blades. Prices: $200 and up. Remarks: Bladesmith. Mark: KNIGHT.

KNIPSCHIELD, TERRY

808 12th Ave NE, Rochester, MN 55906, Phone: 507-288-7829, terry@knipknives. com; Web: www.knipknives.com

Specialties: Folders and fixed blades and leather working knives. Patterns: Variations of traditional patterns and his own new designs. Technical: Stock removal. Grinds CPM-154CM, ATS-34, stainless Damascus, 01.Prices: $60 to $1200 and higher for upscale folders. Mark: Etchd logo on blade, KNIP with shield image.

KNOTT, STEVE

KNOTT KNIVES, 203 Wild Rose, Guyton, GA 31312, Phone: 912-536-7651, knottknives@yahoo.com; FaceBook: Knott Knives/Steve Knott

Technical: Uses ATS-34/440C and some commercial Damascus, single and double grinds with mirror or satin finishes. Patterns: Hunters, boot knives, bowies, and tantos, slip joint, LinerLock and lock-back folders. Uses a wide variety of handle materials to include ironwood, coca-bola and colored stabilized wood, also horn, bone and ivory upon customer request. Remarks: First knife sold in 1991. Part-time maker.

KNOWLES, SHAWN

750 Townsbury Rd, Great Meadows, NJ 07838, Phone: 973-670-3307, skcustomknives@gmail.com Web: shawnknowlescustomknives.com

KOHLS, JERRY

N4725 Oak Rd, Princeton, WI 54968, Phone: 920-295-3648

Specialties: Working knives and period pieces. Patterns: Hunters-boots and Bowies, your designs or his. Technical: Grinds, ATS-34 440c 154CM and 1095 and commercial Damascus. Remarks: Part-time maker. Mark: Last name.

KOJETIN, W

20 Bapaume Rd Delville, Germiston, GT, SOUTH AFRICA 1401, Phone: 27118733305/ mobile 27836256208

Specialties: High-art and working straight knives of all designs. Patterns: Daggers, hunters and his own Man hunter Bowie. Technical: Grinds D2 and ATS-34; forges and grinds 440B/C. Offers "wrap-around" pava and abalone handles, scrolled wood or ivory, stacked filework and setting of faceted semi-precious stones. Prices: $185 to $600; some to $11,000. Remarks: Spare-time maker; first knife sold in 1962. Mark: Billy K.

KOLENKO, VLADIMIR

505 Newell Dr., Huntingdon Valley, PA 19006, Phone: 617-501-8366, kolenkv@yahoo. com; Web: www.kolenko.com

Specialties: Daggers and fighters. Patterns: Art knives. Technical: Typically uses custom mosaic damascus blades forged by various bladesmiths and commercial damascus makers. Prices: $1,000 to $2,500. Remarks: Making jewelry and fashioning knives have been longstanding hobbies, so the maker combined them and says he enjoys the whole process, not just the end product. He guesses that makes the difference between a hobby and business.

KOLITZ, ROBERT

W9342 Canary Rd, Beaver Dam, WI 53916, Phone: 920-887-1287

Specialties: Working straight knives to customer specs. Patterns: Bowies, hunters, bird and trout knives, boots. Technical: Grinds O1, 440C; commercial Damascus. Prices: $50 to $100; some to $500. Remarks: Spare-time maker; first knife sold in 1979. Mark: Last initial.

KOMMER, RUSS

4609 35th Ave N, Fargo, ND 58102, Phone: 701-281-1826, russkommer@yahoo.com Web: www.russkommerknives.com

Specialties: Working straight knives with the outdoorsman in mind. **Patterns:** Hunters, semi-skinners, fighters, folders and utility knives, art knives. **Technical:** Hollow-grinds ATS-34, 440C and 440V. **Prices:** $125 to $850; some to $3000. **Remarks:** Full-time maker; first knife sold in 1995. **Mark:** Bear paw—full name, city and state or full name and state.

KOPP, TODD M

PO Box 3474, Apache Jct., AZ 85217, Phone: 480-983-6143, tmkopp@msn.com

Specialties: Classic and traditional straight knives. Fluted handled daggers. **Patterns:** Bowies, boots, daggers, fighters, hunters, swords and folders. **Technical:** Grinds 5160, 440C, ATS-34. All Damascus steels, or customers choice. Some engraving and filework. **Prices:** $200 to $1200; some to $4000. **Remarks:** Part-time maker; first knife sold in 1989. **Mark:** Last name in Old English, some others name, city and state.

KOSTER, DANIEL

KOSTER KNIVES, 1711 Beverly Ct., Bentonville, AR 72712, Phone: 479-366-7794, dan@kosterknives.com; www.kosterknives.com

Patterns: Bushcraft, survival, outdoor and utility knives. **Technical:** Stock-removal method of blade making, using CPM 3V steel. **Prices:** $150 to $300. **Remarks:** Full-time knifemaker in business since 2005. **Mark:** "K" in a circle, negative shape.

KOSTER, STEVEN C

16261 Gentry Ln, Huntington Beach, CA 92647, Phone: 714-907-7250, kosterknives@verizon.net Web: www.kosterhandforgedknives.com

Specialties: Walking sticks, hand axes, tomahawks, Damascus.**Patterns:** Ladder, twists, round horn. **Technical:** Use 5160, 52100, 1084, 1095 steels. Ladder, twists, **Prices:** $200 to $1000. **Remarks:** Wood and leather sheaths with silver furniture. ABS Journeyman 2003. California knifemakers member. **Mark:** Koster squeezed between lines.

KOVACIK, ROBERT

Zavadska 122, Tomasovce 98401, SLOVAKIA, Phone: Mobil: 00421907644800, kovacikart@gmail.com Web: www.robertkovacik.com

Specialties: Engraved hunting knives, guns engraved; Knifemakers. **Technical:** Fixed blades, folder knives, miniatures. **Prices:** $350 to $10,000 U.S. **Mark:** R.

KOVAR, EUGENE

2626 W 98th St., Evergreen Park, IL 60642, Phone: 708-636-3724/708-790-4115, baldemaster333@aol.com

Specialties: One-of-a-kind miniature knives only. **Patterns:** Fancy to fantasy miniature knives; knife pendants and tie tacks. **Technical:** Files and grinds nails, nickel-silver and sterling silver. **Prices:** $5 to $35; some to $100. **Mark:** GK.

KOYAMA, CAPTAIN BUNSHICHI

3-23 Shirako-cho, Nakamura-ku, Nagoya, Aichi, JAPAN City 453-0817, Phone: 052-461-7070, Fax: 052-461-7070

Specialties: Innovative folding knife. **Patterns:** General purpose one hand. **Technical:** Grinds ATS-34 and Damascus. **Prices:** $400 to $900; some to $1500. **Remarks:** Part-time maker; first knife sold in 1994. **Mark:** Captain B. Koyama and the shoulder straps of CAPTAIN.

KRAFT, STEVE

408 NE 11th St, Abilene, KS 67410, Phone: 785-263-1411

Specialties: Folders, lockbacks, scale release auto, push button auto. **Patterns:** Hunters, boot knives and fighters. **Technical:** Grinds ATS-34, Damascus; uses titanium, pearl, ivory etc. **Prices:** $500 to $2500. **Remarks:** Part-time maker; first knife sold in 1984. **Mark:** Kraft.

KRAMMES, JEREMY

138 W. Penn St., Schuylkill Haven, PA 17972, Phone: 570-617-5753, blade@jkknives.com; Web: www.jkknives.com

Specialties: Working folders and collectible art knives. **Technical:** Stock removal, hollow grinding, carving and engraving. **Prices:** $550+ for working knives, and $1,000+ for art knives. **Remarks:** Part-time maker; first knife sold in 2004. **Mark:** Stylized JK on blade.

KRAPP, DENNY

1826 Windsor Oak Dr, Apopka, FL 32703, Phone: 407-880-7115

Specialties: Fantasy and working straight knives of his design. **Patterns:** Hunters, fighters and utility/camp knives. **Technical:** Grinds ATS-34 and 440C. **Prices:** $85 to $300; some to $800. **Remarks:** Spare-time maker; first knife sold in 1988. **Mark:** Last name.

KRAUSE, JIM

3272 Hwy H, Farmington, MO 63640, Phone: 573-756-7388 or 573-701-7047, james_krause@sbcglobal.net

Specialties: Folders, fixed blades and neck knives. **Patterns:** New pattern for each knife. **Technical:** CPM steels or high-carbon steel on request. **Prices:** $125 and up for neck knives, $250 and up for fixed blades and $250 to $1,000 for folders and damascus pieces. **Remarks:** Full-time maker; first knife made in 2000. Makes one knife at a time with the best materials the maker can find. **Mark:** Krause Handmade with Christian fish.

KREGER, THOMAS

1996 Dry Branch Rd., Lugoff, SC 29078, Phone: 803-438-4221, tdkreger@bellsouth.net

Specialties: South Carolina/George Herron style working/using knives. Customer designs considered. **Patterns:** Hunters, skinners, fillet, liner lock folders, kitchen, and camp knives. **Technical:** Hollow and flat grinds of ATS-34, CPM154CM, and 5160. **Prices:** $100 and up. **Remarks:** Full-time maker. President of the South Carolina Association of Knifemakers 2002-2006, and current president since 2013. **Mark:** TDKreger.

KREH, LEFTY

210 Wichersham Way, "Cockeysville", MD 21030

KREIBICH, DONALD L.

1638 Commonwealth Circle, Reno, NV 89503, Phone: 775-746-0533, dmkreno@sbcglobal.net

Specialties: Working straight knives in standard patterns. **Patterns:** Bowies, boots and daggers; camp and fishing knives. **Technical:** Grinds 440C, 154CM and ATS-34; likes integrals. **Prices:** $100 to $200; some to $500. **Remarks:** Part-time maker; first knife sold in 1980. **Mark:** First and middle initials, last name.

KREIN, TOM

P.O. Box 994, 337 E. Main St., Gentry, AR 72734, Phone: 479-233-0508, kreinknives@gmail.com; www.kreinknives.net

Specialties: LinerLock folders and fixed blades designed to be carried and used. **Technical:** Stock removal using D2, A2, CPM 3V, CPM 154, CPM M4, Stellite 6K and damascus, and makes his own sheaths. **Prices:** $250 to $500 and up. **Remarks:** Full-time maker; first knife made in 1993. **Mark:** Last name and the year the knife was made in the shape of a circle, with a bulldog in the middle.

KRESSLER, D F

Mittelweg 31 i, D-28832 Achim, GERMANY 28832, Phone: +49 (0) 42 02/76-5742, Fax: +49 (0) 42 02/7657 41, info@kresslerknives.com; Web: www.kresslerknives.com

Specialties: High-tech integral and interframe knives. **Patterns:** Hunters, fighters, daggers. **Technical:** Grinds new state-of-the-art steels; prefers natural handle materials. **Prices:** Upscale. **Mark:** Name in logo.

KUBASEK, JOHN A

74 Northhampton St, Easthampton, MA 01027, Phone: 413-527-7917, jaknife01@yahoo.com

Specialties: Left- and right-handed LinerLock® folders of his design or to customer specs. Also new knives made with Ripcord patent. **Patterns:** Fighters, tantos, drop points, survival knives, neck knives and belt buckle knives. **Technical:** Grinds 154CM, S30 and Damascus. **Prices:** $395 to $1500. **Remarks:** Part-time maker; first knife sold in 1985. **Mark:** Name and address etched.

KULIS, DAVID S.

10741 S. Albany Ave., Chicago, IL 60655, windycitywoodworks@hotmail.com

Patterns: Folding LinerLocks, frame locks, straight hunters, fighters and kitchen knives. **Technical:** Stock removal method of making blades with hollow grinds and using CPM S30V, CPM 154, O1 and damascus steels. Handle materials include everything from stabilized wood to carbon fiber. **Prices:** $150 to $1,000. **Remarks:** Part-time maker; first knife sold in 2015. **Mark:** Stylized "DK" etched into blade.

KURT, DAVID

POB 1377, Molalla, OR 97038, Phone: 503-871-5420, dkurtknives@aol.com; Web: www.dkurtknives.com

Specialties: Fixed blades. **Patterns:** Tactical, utility and hunting knives. **Technical:** Stock removal method of blade making using primarily 154CM steel or to customers' preferences. **Remarks:** Full-time maker. **Mark:** Bear skull with maker's full name.

L

LAINSON, TONY

114 Park Ave, Council Bluffs, IA 51503, Phone: 712-322-5222

Specialties: Working straight knives, liner locking folders. **Technical:** Grinds 154CM, ATS-34, 440C buys Damascus. Handle materials include Micarta, carbon fiber G-10 ivory pearl and bone. **Prices:** $95 to $600. **Remarks:** Part-time maker; first knife sold in 1987. **Mark:** Name and state.

LAIRSON SR., JERRY

H C 68 Box 970, Ringold, OK 74754, Phone: 580-876-3426, bladesmt@brightok.net; Web: www.lairson-custom-knives.net

Specialties: Damascus collector grade knives & high performance field grade hunters & cutting competition knives. **Patterns:** Damascus, random, raindrop, ladder, twist and others. **Technical:** All knives hammer forged. Mar Tempering**Prices:** Field grade knives $300. Collector grade $400 & up. **Mark:** Lairson. **Remarks:** Makes any style knife but prefer fighters and hunters. ABS Mastersmith, AKA member, KGA member. Cutting competition competitor.

LAKE, RON

3360 Bendix Ave, Eugene, OR 97401, Phone: 541-484-2683

Specialties: High-tech knives; inventor of the modern interframe folder. **Patterns:** Hunters, boots, etc.; locking folders. **Technical:** Grinds 154CM and ATS-34. Patented interframe with special lock release tab. **Prices:** $2200 to $3000; some higher. **Remarks:** Full-time maker; first knife sold in 1966. **Mark:** Last name.

LALA, PAULO RICARDO P AND LALA, ROBERTO P.

R Daniel Martins 636, Presidente Prudente, SP, BRAZIL 19031-260, Phone: 0182-210125, korthknives@terra.com.br; Web: www.ikbsknifetech.com

Specialties: Straight knives and folders of all designs to customer specs. **Patterns:** Bowies, daggers fighters, hunters and utility knives. **Technical:** Grinds and forges D6, 440C, high-carbon steels and Damascus. **Prices:** $60 to $400; some higher. **Remarks:** Full-time makers; first knife sold in 1991. All stainless steel blades are ultra sub-zero quenched. **Mark:** Sword carved on top of anvil under KORTH.

LAMB, CURTIS J

3336 Louisiana Ter, Ottawa, KS 66067-8996, Phone: 785-242-6657

LAMBERT, KIRBY

2131 Edgar St, Regina, SK, CANADA S4N 3K8, kirby@lambertknives.com; Web: www.lambertknives.com

Specialties: Tactical/utility folders. Tactical/utility Japanese style fixed blades. **Prices:** $200 to $1500 U.S. **Remarks:** Full-time maker since 2002. **Mark:** Black widow spider and last name Lambert.

LAMEY, ROBERT M

15800 Lamey Dr, Biloxi, MS 39532, Phone: 228-396-9066, Fax: 228-396-9022, rmlamey@ametro.net; Web: www.lameyknives.com

Specialties: Bowies, fighters, hard use knives. **Patterns:** Bowies, fighters, hunters and camp knives. **Technical:** Forged and stock removal. **Prices:** $125 to $350. **Remarks:** Lifetime reconditioning; will build to customer designs, specializing in hard use, affordable knives. **Mark:** LAMEY.

LAMOTHE, JORDAN

1317 County Rte. 31, Granville, NY 12832, Phone: 518-368-5147, jgl2@williams.edu; Web: www.jordanlamothe.com

Specialties: Handforged fixed blades and stock-removal folders. **Patterns:** Chef's, utility, paring, boning, fillet, hunting and camp knives, fighters and lockback folders. **Technical:** Forges W1, W2, 1084, 1095 and 1075 blade steels, grinding folder blades from 154CM and 440C. **Prices:** $100 to $600. **Remarks:** Part-time maker; first knife sold in 2014. **Mark:** Stamped JL.

LANCASTER, C G

No 2 Schoonwinkel St, Parys, Free State, SOUTH AFRICA, Phone: 0568112090

Specialties: High-tech working and using knives of his design and to customer specs. **Patterns:** Hunters, locking folders and utility/camp knives. **Technical:** Grinds Sandvik 12C27, 440C and D2. Offers anodized titanium bolsters. **Prices:** $450 to $750; some to $1500. **Remarks:** Part-time maker; first knife sold in 1990. **Mark:** Etched logo.

LANCE, BILL

12820 E. Scott Rd., Palmer, AK 99645-8863, Phone: 907-694-1487, Web: www.lanceknives.com

Specialties: Ulu sets and working straight knives; limited issue sets. **Patterns:** Several ulu patterns, drop-point skinners. **Technical:** Uses ATS-34 and AEBL; ivory, horn and high-class wood handles. **Prices:** $145 to $500; art sets to $7,500. **Remarks:** First knife sold in 1981. **Mark:** Last name over a lance.

LANCE, DAN

889 Pamela Kay Ln., Weatherford, TX 76088, Phone: 940-682-5381, dan@danlanceknives.com; Web: www.danlanceknives.com

Specialties: High-end locking knives of maker's own designs. **Patterns:** Locking folders, fighters, skinners, hunting and camp knives. **Technical:** Stock removal using stainless damascus, CPM 154 and PSF-27 primarily. Performs own heat treating. Handle materials consist of mammoth ivory, stag, exotic woods, Kirinite, carbon fiber and various bones and horns. **Prices:** $250 to $1,250, some higher. **Remarks:** Full-time maker; first knife made and sold in 2014. Member of the ABS and Knifemakers' Guild. **Mark:** Dan Lance over a lance with a broken shaft.

LANCE, LUCAS

3600 N. Charley, Wasilla, AK 99654, Phone: 907-357-0349, lucas@lanceknives.com; Web: www.lanceknives.com

Specialties: Working with materials native to Alaska such as fossilized ivory, bone, musk ox bone, sheep horn, moose antler, all combined with exotic materials from around the world. **Patterns:** Fully functional knives of my own design. **Technical:** Mainly stock removal, flat grinds in ATS-34, 440C, 5160 and various makes of American-made damascus. **Prices:** $165 to $850. **Remarks:** Second-generation knifemaker who grew up and trained in father, Bill Lance's, shop. First knife designed and made in 1994. **Mark:** Last name over a lance.

LANDERS, JOHN

758 Welcome Rd, Newnan, GA 30263, Phone: 404-253-5719

Specialties: High-art working straight knives and folders of his design. **Patterns:** Hunters, fighters and slip-joint folders. **Technical:** Grinds 440C, ATS-34, 154CM and commercial Damascus. **Prices:** $85 to $250; some to $500. **Remarks:** Part-time maker; first knife sold in 1989. **Mark:** Last name.

LANDIS, DAVID E. SR.

4544 County Rd. 29, Galion, OH 44833, Phone: 419-946-3145, del@redbird.net

Specialties: Damascus knives in ladder, twist, double-twist and "W's" patterns. Makes leather sheaths and forges his own damascus. **Prices:** $250 to $500. **Remarks:** Retiree who says knifemaking keeps him learning with new challenges and meeting a lot of great people. **Mark:** DEL.

LANG, DAVID

6153 Cumulus Circle, Kearns, UT 84118, Phone: 801-809-1241, dknifeguy@msn.com

Specialties: Art knives, metal sheaths, push daggers, fighting knives, hunting knives, camp knives, skinning knives, pocketknives, utility knives and three-finger knives. **Patterns:** Prefers to work with own patterns, but will consider other designs. **Technical:** Flat grinds, hollow grinds, hand carving on the blades and handles, and gold and silver casting. **Remarks:** Will work from his designs or to customer specifications. Has been making knives for over 20 years and has learned from some of the best. **Prices:** $250 to $3,000, with most work ranging from $750 to $1,500. **Mark:** Dlang over UTAH.

LANGLEY, GENE H

1022 N. Price Rd, Florence, SC 29506, Phone: 843-669-3150

Specialties: Working knives in standard patterns. **Patterns:** Hunters, boots, fighters,

locking folders and slip-joints. **Technical:** Grinds 440C, 154CM and ATS-34. **Prices:** $125 to $450; some to $1000. **Remarks:** Part-time maker; first knife sold in 1979. **Mark:** Name.

LANGLEY, MICK

1015 Centre Crescent, Qualicum Beach, BC, CANADA V9K 2G6, Phone: 250-752-4261

Specialties: Period pieces and working knives. **Patterns:** Bowies, push daggers, fighters, boots. Some folding lockers. **Technical:** Forges 5160, 1084, W2 and his own Damascus. **Prices:** $250 to $2500; some to $4500. **Remarks:** Full-time maker, first knife sold in 1977. **Mark:** Langley with M.S. (for ABS Master Smith)

LANKTON, SCOTT

8065 Jackson Rd. R-11, Ann Arbor, MI 48103, Phone: 313-426-3735

Specialties: Pattern welded swords, krisses and Viking period pieces. **Patterns:** One-of-a-kind. **Technical:** Forges W2, L6 nickel and other steels. **Prices:** $600 to $12,000. **Remarks:** Part-time bladesmith, full-time smith; first knife sold in 1976. **Mark:** Last name logo.

LAPEN, CHARLES

Box 529, W. Brookfield, MA 01585

Specialties: Chef's knives for the culinary artist. **Patterns:** Camp knives, Japanese-style swords and wood working tools, hunters. **Technical:** Forges 1075, car spring and his own Damascus. Favors narrow and Japanese tangs. **Prices:** $200 to $400; some to $2000. **Remarks:** Part-time maker; first knife sold in 1972. **Mark:** Last name.

LAPLANTE, BRETT

4545 CR412, McKinney, TX 75071, Phone: 972-838-9191, blap007@aol.com

Specialties: Working straight knives and folders to customer specs. **Patterns:** Survival knives, Bowies, skinners, hunters. **Technical:** Grinds D2 and 440C. Heat-treats. **Prices:** $200 to $800. **Remarks:** Part-time maker; first knife sold in 1987. **Mark:** Last name in Canadian maple leaf logo.

LARGIN, KEN

KELGIN Knifemakers Co-Op, 2001 S. State Rd. 1, Connersville, IN 47331, Phone: 765-969-5012, kelginfinecutlery@gmail.com; Web: www.kelgin.com

Specialties: Retired from general knifemaking. Only take limited orders in meteorite damascus or solid meteorite blades. **Patterns:** Any. **Technical:** Stock removal or forged. **Prices:** $500 & up. **Remarks:** Travels the U.S. full time teaching hands-on "History Of Cutting Tools" to Scouts and any interested group. Participants flint knap, forge and keep three tools they make! **Mark:** K.C. Largin (Kelgin mark retired in 2004).

LARK, DAVID

6641 Schneider Rd., Kingsley, MI 49649, Phone: 231-342-1076, dblark58@yahoo.com

Specialties: Traditional straight knives, art knives, folders. **Patterns:** All types. **Technical:** Grinds all types of knife making steel and makes damascus. **Prices:** $600 and up. **Remarks:** Full-time maker, custom riflemaker, and engraver. **Mark:** Lark in script and DBL on engraving.

LAROCHE, JEAN-MARC

16 rue Alexandre Dumas, 78160 Marly le Roi, FRANCE, Phone: +33 1 39 16 16 58, infojmlaroche@orange.fr; Web: www.jmlaroche.com

Specialties: Fantasy pieces to customer specs. **Patterns:** Straight knives and folding knives. **Technical:** Stainless or damascus blade steels. **Prices:** $800 to $4,000, some to $10,000. **Remarks:** Full-time sculptor; full-time knifemaker for 12 years from 1992 to 2004. Awards won include BLADEhandmade "Best In Show" Award in 1997 and "Best Fantasy Knife" at the 1998 BLADE Show West. Artistic design knives are influenced by fantasy movies and comics with handles in bronze, silver or resin, including animal skulls, bones and natural stones. Collaborations with Gil Hibben and Roger Bergh. Recently created a knife capable of mechanical movement: "The Living Knife" with a blade by Bergh. **Mark:** Logo, + name sometimes.

LARSON, RICHARD

549 E Hawkeye Ave, Turlock, CA 95380, Phone: 209-668-1615, lebatardknives@aol.com

Specialties: Sound working knives, lightweight folders, practical tactical knives. **Patterns:** Hunters, trout and bird knives, fish fillet knives, Bowies, tactical sheath knives, one- and two-blade folders. **Technical:** Grinds ATS-34, A2, D2, CPM 3V and commercial Damascus; forges and grinds 52100, O1 and 1095. Machines folder frames from aircraft aluminum. **Prices:** $40 to $650. **Remarks:** Full-time maker. First knife made in 1974. Offers knife repair, restoration and sharpening. All knives are serial numbered and registered in the name of original purchaser. **Mark:** Stamped last name or etched logo of last name, city, and state.

LARY, ED

951 Rangeline Rd., Mosinee, WI 54455, Phone: 715-630-6202, laryblades@hotmail.com

Specialties: Upscale hunters and art knives with display presentations. **Patterns:** Hunters, period pieces. **Technical:** Grinds all steels, heat treats, fancy filework and engraving. **Prices:** Upscale. **Remarks:** Full-time maker since 1974. **Mark:** Hand engraved "Ed Lary" in script.

LAURENT, KERMIT

1812 Acadia Dr, LaPlace, LA 70068, Phone: 504-652-5629

Specialties: Traditional and working straight knives and folders of his design. **Patterns:** Bowies, hunters, utilities and folders. **Technical:** Forges own Damascus, plus uses most tool steels and stainless. Specializes in altering cable patterns. Uses stabilized handle materials, especially select exotic woods. **Prices:** $100 to $2500; some to $50,000. **Remarks:** Full-time maker; first knife sold in 1982. Doing business as Kermit's Knife Works. Favorite material is meteorite Damascus. **Mark:** First name.

LAURENT, VERONIQUE

Avenue du Capricorne, 53, 1200 Brussels, BELGIUM, Phone: 0032 477 48 66 73, whatsonthebench@gmail.com

Specialties: Fixed blades and friction folders. Patterns: Bowies, camp knives, "ladies knives" and maker's own designs. Technical: Makes own san mai steel with the edges in blue paper steel and the sides in pure nickel and O2, called "Nickwich," meaning nickel in a sandwich. Makes own damascus, numerical milling embellishment, inlays and sheaths. Prices: Start at $350. Remarks: Part-time knifemaker since 2005 and ABS journeyman smith since 2013.

LAWRENCE, ALTON
201 W Stillwell, De Queen, AR 71832, Phone: 870-642-7643, Fax: 870-642-4023, uncle21@riversidemachine.net; Web: riversidemachine.net
Specialties: Classic straight knives and folders to customer specs. Patterns: Bowies, hunters, folders and utility/camp knives. Technical: Forges 5160, 1095, 1084, Damascus and railroad spikes. Prices: Start at $100. Remarks: Part-time maker; first knife sold in 1988. Mark: Last name inside fish symbol.

LAY, L J
602 Mimosa Dr, Burkburnett, TX 76354, Phone: 940-569-1329
Specialties: Working straight knives in standard patterns; some period pieces. Patterns: Drop-point hunters, Bowies and fighters. Technical: Grinds ATS-34 to mirror finish; likes Micarta handles. Prices: Moderate. Remarks: Full-time maker; first knife sold in 1985. Mark: Name or name with ram head and city or stamp L J Lay.

LAY, R J (BOB)
Box 1225, Logan Lake, BC, CANADA V0K 1W0, Phone: 250-523-9923, rjlay@telus.net
Specialties: Traditional-styled, fancy straight knifes of his design. Specializing in hunters. Patterns: Bowies, fighters and hunters. Technical: Grinds high-performance stainless and tool steels. Uses exotic handle and spacer material. File cut, prefers narrow tang. Sheaths available. Prices: $200 to $500, some to $5000. Remarks: Full-time maker, first knife sold in 1976. Doing business as Lay's Custom Knives. Mark: Signature acid etched.

LEAVITT JR., EARL F
Pleasant Cove Rd Box 306, E. Boothbay, ME 04544, Phone: 207-633-3210
Specialties: 1500-1870 working straight knives and fighters; pole arms. Patterns: Historically significant knives, classic/modern custom designs. Technical: Flat-grinds O1; heat-treats. Filework available. Prices: $90 to $350; some to $1000. Remarks: Full-time maker; first knife sold in 1981. Doing business as Old Colony Manufactory. Mark: Initials in oval.

LEBATARD, PAUL M
14700 Old River Rd, Vancleave, MS 39565, Phone: 228-826-4137, Fax: Cell phone: 228-238-7461, lebatardknives@aol.com
Specialties: Sound working hunting and fillet knives, folding knives, practical tactical knives. Patterns: Hunters, trout and bird knives, fish fillet knives, kitchen knives, Bowies, tactical sheath knives,one- and two-blade folders. Technical: Grinds ATS-34, D-2, CPM 3-V, CPM-154CM, and commercial Damascus; forges and grinds 1095, 01, and 52100. Prices: $75 to $850; some to $1,200. Remarks: Full-time maker, first knife made in 1974. Charter member Gulf Coast Custom Knifemakers; Voting member Knifemaker's Guild. Mark: Stamped last name, or etched logo of last name, city, and state. Other: All knives are serial numbered and registered in the name of the original purchaser.

LEBER, HEINZ
Box 446, Hudson's Hope, BC, CANADA V0C 1V0, Phone: 250-783-5304
Specialties: Working straight knives of his design. Patterns: 20 models, from capers to Bowies. Technical: Hollow-grinds D2 and M2 steel; mirror-finishes and full tang only. Likes moose, elk, stone sheep for handles. Prices: $175 to $1000. Remarks: Full-time maker; first knife sold in 1975. Mark: Initials connected.

LEBLANC, GARY E
1403 Fairview Ln., Little Falls, MN 56345, Phone: 320-232-0245, butternutcove@hotmail.com
Specialties: Hunting and fishing, some kitchen knives and the Air Assualt tactical knife. Does own leather and Kydex work. Technical: Stock removal. Mostly ATS34 for spec knives--orders, whatever the customer desires. Prices: Full range $85 for parring knife, up $4000 plus fro collector grade hunter and fillet set. Remarks: First knife in 1998. Mark: Circular with star in center and LEBLANC on upper curve and KNIFEWORKS on lower curve.

LECK, DAL
Box 1054, Hayden, CO 81639, Phone: 970-276-3663
Specialties: Classic, traditional and working knives of his design and in standard patterns; period pieces. Patterns: Boots, daggers, fighters, hunters and push daggers. Technical: Forges O1 and 5160; makes his own Damascus. Prices: $175 to $700; some to $1500. Remarks: Part-time maker; first knife sold in 1990. Doing business as The Moonlight Smithy. Mark: Stamped: hammer and anvil with initials.

LEE, ETHAN
17200 N. Tucker School Rd., Sturgeon, MO 65284, Phone: 573-682-4364, elee4364@aol.com; Facebook page: ELEE Knives
Specialties: Practical, usable, quality-crafted custom knives. Technical: Primarily damascus and hand-forged high-carbon steel, as well as 440C or 154CM stainless. Prices: $200-$500. Remarks: Part-time knifemaker; first knife made in 2007. Mark: ELEE.

LEE, RANDY
PO Box 1873, St. Johns, AZ 85936, Phone: 928-337-2594, randylee.knives@yahoo.com; Web.www.randyleeknives.com
Specialties: Traditional working and using straight knives of his design. Patterns: Bowies, fighters, hunters, daggers. Technical: Grinds ATS-34, 440C Damascus, and 154CPM. Offers sheaths. Prices: $325 to $2500. Remarks: Full-time maker; first knife sold in 1979. Mark: Full name, city, state.

LEEPER, DAN
10344 Carney Dr. SE, Olympia, WA 98501, Phone: 360-250-2130, leeperd@ymail.com; Web: www.leeperknives.com
Specialties: Hunters, fighters, bowies and chef's knives. Technical: Forges 52100, W2, 1084 and 5160 blade steels. Stock removal using CPM 154 stainless and other modern alloy steels. Does own heat treating and leather work. Prices: Start at $200. Remarks: ABS member. Mark: Dan Leeper Olympia WA.

LELAND, STEVE
2300 Sir Francis Drake Blvd, Fairfax, CA 94930-1118, Phone: 415-457-0318, Fax: 415-457-0995, Web: www.stephenleland@comcast.net
Specialties: Traditional and working straight knives and folders of his design. Patterns: Hunters, fighters, Bowies, chefs. Technical: Grinds O1, ATS-34 and 440C. Does own heat treat. Makes nickel silver sheaths. Prices: $150 to $750; some to $1500. Remarks: Part-time maker; first knife sold in 1987. Doing business as Leland Handmade Knives. Mark: Last name.

LEMAIRE, RYAN M.
14045 Leon Rd., Abbeville, LA 70510, Phone: 337-893-1937, ryanlemaire@yahoo.com
Specialties: All styles. Enjoys early American and frontier styles. Also, office desk sets for hunters and fishermen. Patterns: Hunters, camp knives, miniatures and period styles. Technical: Stock removal, carbon steel, stainless steel and damascus. Some forging of guards. Leather and wooden sheaths. Prices: Vary. Remarks: Member of American Bladesmith Society and Louisiana Craft Guild. Mark: First name, city and state in oval.

LEMCKE, JIM L
10649 Haddington Ste 180, Houston, TX 77043, Phone: 888-461-8632, Fax: 713-461-8221, jimll@hal-pc.org; Web: www.texasknife.com
Specialties: Large supply of custom ground and factory finished blades; knife kits; leather sheaths; in-house heat treating and cryogenic tempering; exotic handle material (wood, ivory, oosik, horn, stabilized woods); machines and supplies for knifemaking; polishing and finishing supplies; heat treat ovens; etching equipment; bar, sheet and rod material (brass, stainless steel, nickel silver); titanium sheet material. Catalog. $4.

LEMELIN, STEPHANIE
3495 Olivier St., Brossard, CANADA J4Y 2J9, Phone: 514-462-1322, stephlemelin@hotmail.com
Specialties: Art knives, mostly ornate. Patterns: Knives with sculptured or carved handles. Straight knives and folders. Technical: Grinds 440C, CPM 154 and ATS-34, all knives hand filed and flat ground. Remarks: Part-time maker, jeweler and knifemaker; first knife sold in 2013. Mark: Lemelin.

LEMOINE, DAVID C
239 County Rd. 637, Mountain Home, AR 72653, Phone: 870-656-4730, dlemoine@davidlemoineknives.com; Web: davidlemoineknives.com
Specialties: Superior edge geometry on high performance custom classic and tactical straight blades and liner lock folders. Patterns: Hunters, skinners, bird and trout, fillet, camp, tactical, and military knives. Some miniatures. Technical: Flat and hollow grinds, CPMS90V, CPMS35V, CPMS30V, D2, A2, O1, 440C, ATS34, 154cm,Damasteel, Chad Nichols, Devin Thomas, and Robert Eggerling Damascus. Hidden and full tapered tangs, ultra-smooth folding mechanisms. File work, will use most all handle materials, does own professional in-house heat treatment and Rockwell testing. Hot blueing. Prices: $250 and up. Remarks: Part-time maker, giving and selling knives since 1986. Each patron receives a NIV Sportsman's Field Bible. Mark: Name, city and state in full oval with cross in the center. Reverse image on other side. The cross never changes.

LENNON, DALE
459 County Rd 1554, Alba, TX 75410, Phone: 903-765-2392, devildaddy1@netzero.net
Specialties: Working / using knives. Patterns: Hunters, fighters and Bowies. Technical: Grinds high carbon steels, ATS-34, forges some. Prices: Starts at $120. Remarks: Part-time maker, first knife sold in 2000. Mark: Last name.

LEONARD, RANDY JOE
188 Newton Rd, Sarepta, LA 71071, Phone: 318-994-2712

LEONE, NICK
9 Georgetown Dr, Pontoon Beach, IL 62040, Phone: 618-792-0734, nickleone@sbcglobal.net
Specialties: 18th century period straight knives. Patterns: Fighters, daggers, bowies. Besides period pieces makes modern designs. Technical: Forges 5160, W2, O1, 1098, 52100 and his own Damascus. Prices: $100 to $1000; some to $3500. Remarks: Full-time maker; first knife sold in 1987. Doing business as Anvil Head Forge. Mark: AHF, Leone, NL

LERCH, MATTHEW
N88 W23462 North Lisbon Rd, Sussex, WI 53089, Phone: 262-246-6362, Web: www.lerchcustomknives.com
Specialties: Folders and folders with special mechanisms. Patterns: Interframe and integral folders; lock backs, assisted openers, side locks, button locks and liner locks. Technical: Grinds ATS-34, 1095, 440 and Damascus. Offers filework and embellished bolsters. Prices: $900 and up. Remarks: Full-time maker; first knife made in 1986. Mark: Last name.

LESSWING, KEVIN
29A East 34th St, Bayonne, NJ 07002, Phone: 551-221-1841, klesswing@excite.com
Specialties: Traditonal working and using straight knives of his design or to customer specs. A few folders. Makes own leather sheaths. Patterns: Hunters, daggers, bird and trout. Technical: Forges high carbon and tool steels, makes own Damascus, grinds CPM154CM, Damasteel, and other stainless steels. Does own heat treating. Remarks: Voting member of Knifemakers Guild, part-time maker. Mark: KL on early knives, LESSWING on Current knives.

LEU, POHAN

PO BOX 15423, Rio Rancho, NM 87174, Phone: 949-300-6412, pohanleu@hotmail.com Web: www.leucustom.com

Specialties: Japanese influenced fixed blades made to your custom specifications. Knives and swords. A2 tool steel, Stock Removal. **Prices:** $180 and up. **Remarks:** Full-time; first knife sold in 2003. **Mark:** LEU or PL.

LEVENGOOD, BILL

15011 Otto Rd, Tampa, FL 33624, Phone: 813-961-5688, bill.levengood@verison.net; Web: www.levengoodknives.com

Specialties: Working straight knives and folders. **Patterns:** Hunters, Bowies, folders and collector pieces. **Technical:** Grinds ATS-34, S-30V, CPM-154 and Damascus. **Prices:** $175 to $1500. **Remarks:** Full time maker; first knife sold in 1983. **Mark:** Last name, city, state.

LEVIN, JACK

201 Brighton 1st Road, Suite 3R, Brooklyn, NY 11235, Phone: 718-415-7911, jacklevin1@yahoo.com

Specialties: Folders with mechanisms.

LEVINE, BOB

101 Westwood Dr, Tullahoma, TN 37388, Phone: 931-454-9943, levineknives@msn.com

Specialties: Working left- and right-handed LinerLock® folders. **Patterns:** Hunters and folders. **Technical:** Grinds ATS-34, 440C, D2, O1 and some Damascus; hollow and some flat grinds. Uses fossil ivory, Micarta and exotic woods. Provides custom leather sheath with each fixed knife. **Prices:** Starting at $135. **Remarks:** Full-time maker; first knife sold in 1984. Voting member Knifemakers Guild, German Messermaher Guild. **Mark:** Name and logo.

LEWIS, BILL

PO Box 63, Riverside, IA 52327, Phone: 319-461-1609, kalewis52@exede.net

Specialties: Folders of all kinds including those made from one-piece of white tail antler with or without the crown. **Patterns:** Hunters, folding hunters, fillet, Bowies, push daggers, etc. **Prices:** $20 to $200. **Remarks:** Full-time maker; first knife sold in 1978. **Mark:** W.E.L.

LEWIS, MIKE

94134 Covey Ln., Coquille, OR 97423-6736, Phone: 386-753-0936, mikeswords@outlook.com

Specialties: Traditional straight knives. **Patterns:** Swords and daggers. **Technical:** Grinds 440C, ATS-34 and 5160. Frequently uses cast bronze and cast nickel guards and pommels. **Prices:** $100 to $750. **Remarks:** Part-time maker; first knife sold in 1988. **Mark:** Mike Lewis.

LEWIS, TOM R

1613 Standpipe Rd, Carlsbad, NM 88220, Phone: 575-885-3616, lewisknives@gmail.com

Specialties: Traditional working straight knives. **Patterns:** Outdoor knives, hunting knives and Bowies. **Technical:** Grinds ATS-34 and CPM-154, forges 5168, W2, 1084 and O1. Makes wire, pattern welded and chainsaw Damascus. **Prices:** $140 to $1500. **Remarks:** Full-time maker; first knife sold in 1980. Doing business as TR Lewis Handmade Knives. **Mark:** Lewis family crest.

LICATA, STEVEN

LICATA CUSTOM KNIVES, 146 Wilson St. 1st Floor, Boonton, NJ 07005, Phone: 973-588-4909, kniveslicata@aol.com; Web: www.licataknives.com

Specialties: Fantasy swords and knives. One-of-a-kind sculptures in steel. **Prices:** $200 to $25,000.

LIEBENBERG, ANDRE

8 Hilma Rd, Bordeaux, Randburg, GT, SOUTH AFRICA 2196, Phone: 011-787-2303

Specialties: High-art straight knives of his design. **Patterns:** Daggers, fighters and swords. **Technical:** Grinds 440C and 12C27. **Prices:** $250 to $500; some $4000 and higher. Giraffe bone handles with semi-precious stones. **Remarks:** Spare-time maker; first knife sold in 1990. **Mark:** Initials.

LIEGEY, KENNETH R

288 Carney Dr, Millwood, WV 25262, Phone: 304-273-9545

Specialties: Traditional working/using straight knives of his design and to customer specs. **Patterns:** Hunters, utility/camp knives, miniatures. **Technical:** Grinds 440C. **Prices:** $125 and up. **Remarks:** Spare-time maker; first knife sold in 1977. **Mark:** First and middle initials, last name.

LIGHTFOOT, GREG

RR #2, Kitscoty, AB, CANADA T0B 2P0, Phone: 780-846-2812; 780-800-1061, Pitbull@lightfootknives.com; Web: www.lightfootknives.com

Specialties: Stainless steel and Damascus. **Patterns:** Boots, fighters and locking folders. **Technical:** Grinds BG-42, 440C, D2, CPM steels, Stellite 6K. Offers engraving. **Prices:** $500 to $2000. **Remarks:** Full-time maker; first knife sold in 1988. Doing business as Lightfoot Knives. **Mark:** Shark with Lightfoot Knives below.

LIN, MARCUS

26825 Morena Dr., Mission Viejo, CA 92691, Phone: 310-720-4368, marcuslin7@gmail.com; Web: www.linknives.com

Specialties: Working knives in the Loveless tradition. **Patterns:** Original patterns direct from the Loveless Shop, designed by R.W. Loveless and, on special request, maker's own patterns. **Technical:** Main blade material is Hitachi's ATS-34; other steels available. Please inquire. **Prices:** $550 to $1,750. **Remarks:** Part-time maker since 2004. Mentored by R.W. Loveless and Jim Merritt. Sole authorship work: knives and sheaths, except for heat treat (which goes to Paul Bos Heat Treat). **Mark:** Main logo is "Marcus Lin, maker, Loveless Design."

LINKLATER, STEVE

8 Cossar Dr, Aurora, ON, CANADA L4G 3N8, Phone: 905-727-8929, knifman@sympatico.ca

Specialties: Traditional working/using straight knives and folders of his design. **Patterns:** Fighters, hunters and locking folders. **Technical:** Grinds ATS-34, 440V and D2. **Prices:** $125 to $350; some to $600. **Remarks:** Part-time maker; first knife sold in 1987. Doing business as Links Knives. **Mark:** LINKS.

LISCH, DAVID K

16948 Longmire Rd., Yelm, WA 98597, Phone: 206-919-5431, Web: www.davidlisch.com

Specialties: One-of-a-kind collectibles, straight knives and custom kitchen knives of own design and to customer specs. **Patterns:** Hunters, bowies and fighters. **Technical:** Forges all his own Damascus under 360-pound air hammer. Forges and chisels wrought iron, pure iron, and bronze butt caps. **Prices:** Starting at $1,000. **Remarks:** Full-time blacksmith, part-time bladesmith. **Mark:** D. Lisch M.S.

LISTER JR., WELDON E

116 Juniper Ln, Boerne, TX 78006, Phone: 210-269-0102, wlister@grtc.com; Web: www.weldonlister.com

Specialties: One-of-a-kind fancy and embellished folders. **Patterns:** Locking and slip-joint folders. **Technical:** Commercial Damascus and O1. All knives embellished. Engraves, inlays, carves and scrimshaws. **Prices:** Upscale. **Remarks:** Spare-time maker; first knife sold in 1991. **Mark:** Last name.

LITTLE, GARY M

94716 Conklin Meadows Ln, PO Box 156, Broadbent, OR 97414, Phone: 503-572-2656

Specialties: Fancy working knives. **Patterns:** Hunters, tantos, Bowies, axes and buckskinners; locking folders and interframes. **Technical:** Forges and grinds O1, L6m, 1095, and 15N20; makes his own Damascus; bronze fittings. **Prices:** $120 to $1500. **Remarks:** Full-time maker; first knife sold in 1979. Doing business as Conklin Meadows Forge. **Mark:** Name, city and state.

LITTLE, LARRY

1A Cranberry Ln, Spencer, MA 01562, Phone: 508-885-2301, littcran@aol.com

Specialties: Working straight knives of his design or to customer specs. Likes Scagel-style. **Patterns:** Hunters, fighters, Bowies, folders. **Technical:** Grinds and forges L6, O1, 5160, 1095, 1080. Prefers natural handle material especially antler. Uses nickel silver. Makes own heavy duty leather sheath. **Prices:** Start at $125. **Remarks:** Part-time maker. First knife sold in 1985. Offers knife repairs. **Mark:** Little on one side, LL brand on the other.

LIVESAY, NEWT

3306 S. Dogwood St, Siloam Springs, AR 72761, Phone: 479-549-3356, Fax: 479-549-3357, newt@newtlivesay.com; Web:www.newtlivesay.com

Specialties: Combat utility knives, hunting knives, titanium knives, swords, axes, KYDWX sheaths for knives and pistols, custom orders.

LIVINGSTON, ROBERT C

PO Box 6, Murphy, NC 28906, Phone: 704-837-4155

Specialties: Art letter openers to working straight knives. **Patterns:** Minis to machetes. **Technical:** Forges and grinds most steels. **Prices:** Start at $20. **Remarks:** Full-time maker; first knife sold in 1988. Doing business as Mystik Knifeworks. **Mark:** MYSTIK.

LOCKETT, LOWELL C.

344 Spring Hill Dr., Canton, GA 30115, Phone: 770-846-8114, lcl1932@gmail.com or spur1932@windstream.net

Technical: Forges 5160, 1095 and other blade steels, and uses desert ironwood, ivory and other handle materials. **Prices:** $150 to $1,500. **Remarks:** ABS journeyman smith.

LOCKETT, STERLING

527 E Amherst Dr, Burbank, CA 91504, Phone: 818-846-5799

Specialties: Working straight knives and folders to customer specs. **Patterns:** Hunters and fighters. **Technical:** Grinds. **Prices:** Moderate. **Remarks:** Spare-time maker. **Mark:** Name, city with hearts.

LOERCHNER, WOLFGANG

WOLFE FINE KNIVES, PO Box 255, Bayfield, ON, CANADA N0M 1G0, Phone: 519-565-2196

Specialties: Traditional straight knives, mostly ornate. **Patterns:** Small swords, daggers and stilettos; locking folders and miniatures. **Technical:** Grinds D2, 440C and 154CM; all knives hand-filed and flat-ground. **Prices:** Vary. **Remarks:** Full-time maker; first knife sold in 1983. Doing business as Wolfe Fine Knives. **Mark:** WOLFE.

LOGAN, IRON JOHN

4260 Covert, Leslie, MI 49251, ironjohnlogan@gmail.com; www.ironjohnlogan.com

Patterns: Hunting, camping, outdoor sheath knives, folding knives, axes, tomahawks, historical knives. swords, working chef's knives, and woodwork and leather work knives. **Technical:** Forges low-alloy steels, wrought iron, bloom and hearth materials, or high-alloy steel as the job insists. Makes own damascus and San Mai seel, modern materials and stainlesses. Vegetable-tanned leather sheaths, and American hardwood handles like hickory, walnut and cherry. **Prices:** $200 to $2,000. **Remarks:** Full-time bladesmith; first knife made in 1998. **Mark:** Two horizontal lines crossed by one vertical line and an angle off the bottom to creat a "J."

LONEWOLF, J AGUIRRE

481 Hwy 105, Demorest, GA 30535, Phone: 706-754-4660, Fax: 706-754-8470, lonewolfandsons@windstream.net, Web: www.knivesbylonewolf.com www.eagleswinggallery.com

Specialties: High-art working and using straight knives of his design. **Patterns:** Bowies, hunters, utility/camp knives and fine steel blades. **Technical:** Forges Damascus and high-carbon steel. Most knives have hand-carved moose antler handles. **Prices:** $55 to $500; some to $2000. **Remarks:** Full-time maker; first knife sold in 1980. Doing business as Lonewolf and Sons LLC. **Mark:** Stamp.

LONG, GLENN A
10090 SW 186th Ave, Dunnellon, FL 34432, Phone: 352-489-4272, galong99@att.net
Specialties: Classic working and using straight knives of his design and to customer specs. **Patterns:** Hunters, Bowies, utility. **Technical:** Grinds 440C D2 and 440V. **Prices:** $85 to $300; some to $800. **Remarks:** Part-time maker; first knife sold in 1990. **Mark:** Last name inside diamond.

LONGWORTH, DAVE
1200 Red Oak Ridge, Felicity, OH 45120, Phone: 513-876-2372
Specialties: High-tech working knives. **Patterns:** Locking folders, hunters, fighters and elaborate daggers. **Technical:** Grinds O1, ATS-34, 440C; buys Damascus. **Prices:** $125 to $600; some higher. **Remarks:** Part-time maker; first knife sold in 1980. **Mark:** Last name.

LOOS, HENRY C
210 Ingraham, New Hyde Park, NY 11040, Phone: 516-354-1943, hcloos@optonline.net
Specialties: Miniature fancy knives and period pieces of his design. **Patterns:** Bowies, daggers and swords. **Technical:** Grinds O1 and 440C. Uses sterling, 18K, rubies and emeralds. All knives come with handmade hardwood cases. **Prices:** $90 to $195; some to $250. **Remarks:** Spare-time maker; first knife sold in 1990. **Mark:** Script last initial.

LOUKIDES, DAVID E
76 Crescent Circle, Cheshire, CT 06410, Phone: 203-271-3023, Loussharp1@sbcglobal.net; Web: www.prayerknives.com
Specialties: Hand forged working blades and collectible pieces. **Patterns:** Chef knives, bowies, and hunting knives. . **Technical:** Uses 1084, 1095, 5160, W2, O1 and 1084-and-15N20 damascus. **Prices:** Normally $200 to $1,000. **Remarks:** part-time maker, Journeyman Bladesmith, Full-time Journeyman Toolmaker. **Mark:** Loukides JS.

LOVE, ED
19443 Mill Oak, San Antonio, TX 78258, Phone: 210-497-1021, Fax: 210-497-1021, annaedlove@sbcglobal.net
Specialties: Hunting, working knives and some art pieces. **Technical:** Grinds ATS-34, and 440C. **Prices:** $150 and up. **Remarks:** Part-time maker. First knife sold in 1980. **Mark:** Name in a weeping heart.

LOVESTRAND, SCHUYLER
1136 19th St SW, Vero Beach, FL 32962, Phone: 772-778-0282, Fax: 772-466-1126, lovestranded@aol.com
Specialties: Fancy working straight knives of his design and to customer specs; unusual fossil ivories. **Patterns:** Hunters, fighters, Bowies and fishing knives. **Technical:** Grinds stainless steel. **Prices:** $550 to $2,500. **Remarks:** Part-time maker; first knife sold in 1982. **Mark:** Name in logo.

LOVETT, MICHAEL
PO Box 121, Mound, TX 76558, Phone: 254-865-9956, michaellovett@embarqmail.com
Specialties: The Loveless Connection Knives as per R.W. Loveless-Jim Merritt. **Patterns:** All Loveless Patterns and Original Lovett Patterns. **Technical:** Complicated double grinds and premium fit and finish. **Prices:** $1000 and up. **Remarks:** High degree of fit and finish - Authorized collection by R. W. Loveless **Mark:** Loveless Authorized football or double nude.

LOZIER, DON
5394 SE 168th Ave, Ocklawaha, FL 32179, Phone: 352-625-3576
Specialties: Tactical folders, collaborative art pieces and sole authorship fixed blades. **Patterns:** Various. **Technical:** Grinds CPM 154, 440C and stainless damascus. **Prices:** $350 to $15,000. **Remarks:** Full-time maker and dealer. **Mark:** Name or DLFF.

LUCHAK, BOB
15705 Woodforest Blvd, Channelview, TX 77530, Phone: 281-452-1779
Specialties: Presentation knives; start of The Survivor series. **Patterns:** Skinners, Bowies, camp axes, steak knife sets and fillet knives. **Technical:** Grinds 440C. Offers electronic etching; filework. **Prices:** $50 to $1500. **Remarks:** Full-time maker; first knife sold in 1983. Doing business as Teddybear Knives. **Mark:** Full name, city and state with Teddybear logo.

LUCHINI, BOB
1220 Dana Ave, Palo Alto, CA 94301, Phone: 650-321-8095, rwluchin@bechtel.com

LUCIE, JAMES R
9100 Calera Dr., Unit 9, Austin, TX 78735, Phone: 512-436-9202 or 231-557-3084, scagel@netonecom.net
Specialties: William Scagel-style knives. **Patterns:** Authentic scagel-style knives and miniatures. **Technical:** Forges 1084 steel. **Prices:** $1,200 and up. **Remarks:** Full-time maker; first knife sold in 1975. Believes in sole authorship of his work. ABS Journeyman Smith. **Mark:** Scagel-style Kris stamp and maker's name and address.

LUCKETT, BILL
108 Amantes Ln, Weatherford, TX 76088, Phone: 817-320-1568, luckettknives@gmail.com Web: www.billluckettcustomknives.com
Specialties: Uniquely patterned robust straight knives. **Patterns:** Fighters, Bowies, hunters. **Technical:** 154CM stainless.**Prices:** $550 to $1500. **Remarks:** Part-time maker; first knife sold in 1975. Knifemakers Guild Member. **Mark:** Last name over Bowie logo.

LUDWIG, RICHARD O
57-63 65 St, Maspeth, NY 11378, Phone: 718-497-5969
Specialties: Traditional working/using knives. **Patterns:** Boots, hunters and utility/camp knives folders. **Technical:** Grinds 440C, ATS-34 and BG42. File work on guards

and handles; silver spacers. Offers scrimshaw. **Prices:** $325 to $400; some to $2000. **Remarks:** Full-time maker. **Mark:** Stamped first initial, last name, state.

LUI, RONALD M
4042 Harding Ave, Honolulu, HI 96816, Phone: 808-734-7746
Specialties: Working straight knives and folders in standard patterns. **Patterns:** Hunters, boots and liner locks. **Technical:** Grinds 440C and ATS-34. **Prices:** $100 to $700. **Remarks:** Spare-time maker; first knife sold in 1988. **Mark:** Initials connected.

LUNDSTROM, JAN-AKE
Mastmostigen 8, Dals-Langed, SWEDEN 66010, Phone: 0531-40270
Specialties: Viking swords, axes and knives in cooperation with handle makers. **Patterns:** All traditional-styles, especially swords and inlaid blades. **Technical:** Forges his own Damascus and laminated steel. **Prices:** $200 to $1000. **Remarks:** Full-time maker; first knife sold in 1985; collaborates with museums. **Mark:** Runic.

LUNDSTROM, TORBJORN (TOBBE)
Norrskenet 4, Are, SWEDEN 83013, 9lundstrm@telia.com Web: http://tobbeiare.se/site/
Specialties: Hunters and collectible knives. **Patterns:** Nordic-style hunters and art knives with unique materials such as mammoth and fossil walrus ivory. **Technical:** Uses forged blades by other makers, particularly Mattias Styrefors who mostly uses 15N20 and 20C steels and is a mosaic blacksmith. **Remarks:** First knife made in 1986.

LUNN, GAIL
434 CR 1422, Mountain Home, AR 72653, Phone: 870-424-2662, gail@lunnknives.com; Web: www.lunnknives.com
Specialties: Fancy folders and double action autos, some straight blades. **Patterns:** One-of-a-kind, all types. **Technical:** Stock removal, hand made. **Prices:** $300 and up. **Remarks:** Fancy file work, exotic materials, inlays, stone etc. **Mark:** Name in script.

LUNN, LARRY A
434 CR 1422, Mountain Home, AR 72653, Phone: 870-424-2662, larry@lunnknives.com; Web: www.lunnknives.com
Specialties: Fancy folders and double action autos; some straight blades. **Patterns:** All types; his own designs. **Technical:** Stock removal; commercial Damascus. **Prices:** $125 and up. **Remarks:** File work inlays and exotic materials. **Mark:** Name in script.

LUPOLE, JAMIE G
KUMA KNIVES, 285 Main St., Kirkwood, NY 13795, Phone: 607-775-9368, jlupole@stny.rr.com
Specialties: Working and collector grade fixed blades, ethnic-styled blades. **Patterns:** Fighters, Bowies, tacticals, hunters, camp, utility, personal carry knives, some swords. **Technical:** Forges and grinds 10XX series and other high-carbon steels, grinds ATS-34 and 440C, will use just about every handle material available. **Prices:** $100 to $500 and up. **Remarks:** Part-time maker since 1999. **Mark:** "KUMA" and/or name, city, state etched, or "Daiqoma saku" in Kanji.

LURQUIN, SAMUEL
Hameau Du Bois, Hoyaux 10, 7133 Buvrinnes Belgique, Binches, BELGIUM, Phone: 0032-478-349-051, knifespirit@hotmail.com; Web: www.samuel-lurquin.com
Specialties: Forged bowies, fighters, hunters and working knives. **Technical:** Uses, but is not limited to, W1, W2 and L6 blade steels, creates own pattern-welded steel. Commonly uses wood, walrus ivory, mammoth ivory and stag for handles. **Prices:** $500 and up. **Remarks:** Full-time maker beginning in 2014, ABS master smith as of 2015.

LUTZ, GREG
127 Crescent Rd, Greenwood, SC 29646, Phone: 864-229-7340
Specialties: Working and using knives and period pieces of his design and to customer specs. **Patterns:** Fighters, hunters and swords. **Technical:** Forges 1095 and O1; grinds ATS-34. Differentially heat-treats forged blades; uses cryogenic treatment on ATS-34. **Prices:** $50 to $350; some to $1200. **Remarks:** Part-time maker; first knife sold in 1986. Doing business as Scorpion Forge. **Mark:** First initial, last name.

LYLE III, ERNEST L
LYLE KNIVES, PO Box 1755, Chiefland, FL 32644, Phone: 352-490-6693, ernestlyle@msn.com
Specialties: Fancy period pieces; one-of-a-kind and limited editions. **Patterns:** Arabian/Persian influenced fighters, military knives, Bowies and Roman short swords; several styles of hunters. **Technical:** Grinds 440C, D2 and 154 CM. Engraves. **Prices:** $200 - $7500. **Remarks:** Full-time maker; first knife sold in 1972. **Mark:** Lyle Knives over Chiefland, Fla.

LYNCH, TAD
140 Timberline Dr., Beebe, AR 72012, Phone: 501-626-1647, lynchknives@yahoo.com Web: lynchknives.com
Specialties: Forged fixed blades. **Patterns:** Bowies, choppers, fighters, hunters. **Technical:** Hand-forged W-2, 1084, 1095 clay quenched 52100, 5160. **Prices:** Starting at $250. **Remarks:** Part-time maker, also offers custom leather work via wife Amy Lynch. **Mark:** T.D. Lynch over anvil.

LYNN, ARTHUR
29 Camino San Cristobal, Galisteo, NM 87540, Phone: 505-466-3541, amyandarthur@aol.com
Specialties: Handforged Damascus knives. **Patterns:** Folders, hunters, Bowies, fighters, kitchen. **Technical:** Forges own Damascus. **Prices:** Moderate.

LYONS, WILLIAM R. (BILL)
7287 Ave. 354, Palisade, NE 69040, Phone: 970-219-1600, wrlyons@lyonsknives.com; Web: www.lyonsknives.com
Specialties: Scrimshaw, ivory inlay, silver wire inlay, hand-carved wood handles and leather handles. **Patterns:** Fighters, bowies, camp knives, integrals, and Moran and

custom knifemakers

Scagel styles. **Technical:** Heat treating to very precise levels, makes own damascus and forges O1, O6, W2, 5160, 1084, 1095, 15N20 and L6. **Prices:** $250 to $3,000. **Remarks:** Full-time maker; member of ABS since 1990. Antique reproductions, all natural handle material, leather sheaths. **Mark:** LYONS.

M

MACCAUGHTRY, SCOTT F.
Fullerton Forge, 1824 Sorrel St, Camarillo, CA 93010, Phone: 805-750-2137, smack308@hotmail.com
   Specialties: Fixed blades and folders. **Technical:** Forges 5160, 52100, W2 and his own damascus using 1084 and 15N20 steels. **Prices:** $275 and up. **Remarks:** ABS journeyman smith. **Mark:** S. MacCaughtry in script, and J.S. on the back side.

MACDONALD, DAVID
2824 Hwy 47, Los Lunas, NM 87031, Phone: 505-866-5866

MACKIE, JOHN
13653 Lanning, Whittier, CA 90605, Phone: 562-945-6104
   Specialties: Forged. **Patterns:** Bowie and camp knives. **Technical:** Attended ABS Bladesmith School. **Prices:** $75 to $500. **Mark:** Oval JOHN MACKIE over FORGED with an anvil and thistle in the middle.

MACKRILL, STEPHEN
PO Box 1580, Pinegowrie, Johannesburg, GT, SOUTH AFRICA 2123, Phone: 27-11-474-7139, Fax: 27-11-474-7139, info@mackrill.co.za; Web: www.mackrill.net
   Specialties: Art fancy, historical, collectors and corporate gifts cutlery. **Patterns:** Fighters, hunters, camp, custom lock back and LinerLock® folders. **Technical:** N690, 12C27, ATS-34, silver and gold inlay on handles; wooden and silver sheaths. **Prices:** $330 and upwards. **Remarks:** First knife sold in 1978. **Mark:** Mackrill fish with country of origin.

MADRULLI, MME JOELLE
Residence Ste Catherine B1, Salon De Provence, FRANCE 13330

MAESTRI, PETER A
S11251 Fairview Rd, Spring Green, WI 53588, Phone: 608-546-4481
   Specialties: Working straight knives in standard patterns. **Patterns:** Camp and fishing knives, utility green-river-styled. **Technical:** Grinds 440C, 154CM and 440A. **Prices:** $15 to $45; some to $150. **Remarks:** Full-time maker; first knife sold in 1981. Provides professional cutler service to professional cutters. **Mark:** CARISOLO, MAESTRI BROS., or signature.

MAGEE, JIM
741 S. Ohio St., Salina, KS 67401, Phone: 785-820-6928, jimmagee@cox.net
   Specialties: Working and fancy folding knives. **Patterns:** Liner locking folders, favorite is his Persian. **Technical:** Grinds ATS-34, Devin Thomas & Eggerling Damascus, titanium. Liners Prefer mother-of-pearl handles. **Prices:** Start at $225 to $1200. **Remarks:** Part-time maker, first knife sold in 2001. Purveyor since 1982. Past president of the Professional Knifemakers Association **Mark:** Last name.

MAGRUDER, JASON
3700 Bellinger Ln. #13, Medford, OR 97501, Phone: 719-210-1579, jason@magruderknives.com; web: MagruderKnives.com
   Specialties: Unique and innovative designs combining the latest modern materials with traditional hand craftsmanship. **Patterns:** Fancy neck knives. Tactical gents folders. Working straight knives. **Technical:** Flats grinds CPM3v, CPM154, ATS34, 1080, and his own forged damascus. Hand carves carbon fiber, titanium, wood, ivory, and pearl handles. Filework and carving on blades. **Prices:** $150 and up. **Remarks:** Part-time maker; first knife sold in 2000. **Mark:** Last name.

MAHOMEDY, A R
PO Box 76280, Marble Ray, KZN, SOUTH AFRICA 4035, Phone: +27 31 577 1451, arm-koknives@mweb.co.za; Web: www.arm-koknives.co.za
   Specialties: Daggers and elegant folders of own design finished with finest exotic materials currently available. **Technical:** Via stock removal, grinds Damasteel, Damascus and the famous hardenable stainless steels. **Prices:** U.S. $650 and up. **Remarks:** Part-time maker. First knife sold in 1995. Voting member knifemakers guild of SA, FEGA member starting out Engraving. **Mark:** Initials A R M crowned with a "Minaret."

MAHOMEDY, HUMAYD A.R.
PO BOX 76280, Marble Ray, KZN, SOUTH AFRICA 4035, Phone: +27 31 577 1451, arm-koknives@mweb.co.za
   Specialties: Tactical folding and fixed blade knives. **Patterns:** Fighters, utilities, tacticals, folders and fixed blades, daggers, modern interpretation of Bowies. **Technical:** Stock-removal knives of Bohler N690, Bohler K110, Bohler K460, Sandvik 12C27, Sandvik RWL 34. Handle materials used are G10, Micarta, Cape Buffalo horn, Water Buffalo horn, Kudu horn, Gemsbok horn, Giraffe bone, Elephant ivory, Mammoth ivory, Arizona desert ironwood, stabilised and dyed burls. **Prices:** $250 - $1000. **Remarks:** First knife sold in 2002. Full-time knifemaker since 2002. First person of color making knives full-time in South Africa. Doing business as HARM EDGED TOOLS. **Mark:** HARM and arrow over EDGED TOOLS.

MAIENKNECHT, STANLEY
38648 S R 800, Sardis, OH 43946

MAINES, JAY
SUNRISE RIVER CUSTOM KNIVES, 5584 266th St., Wyoming, MN 55092, Phone: 651-462-5301, jaymaines@fronternet.net; Web: http://www.sunrisecustomknives.com
   Specialties: Heavy duty working, classic and traditional fixed blades. Some high-tech and fancy embellished knives available. **Patterns:** Hunters, including wild boar hunting knives

and spears, skinners, fillet knives, bowies tantos, boot daggers, barbecue implements and cutlery sets. **Technical:** Hollow ground, stock removal blades of 440C, ATS-34 and CPM S-90V. Prefers natural handle materials, exotic hard woods, and stag, rams and buffalo horns. Offers dovetailed bolsters in brass, stainless steel and nickel silver. Custom sheaths from matching wood or hand-stitched from heavy duty water buffalo hide. **Prices:** Moderate to up-scale. **Remarks:** Part-time maker; first knife sold in 1992. Doing business as Sunrise River Custom Knives. Offers fixed blade repair and handle conversions, and custom leather sheaths. **Mark:** Full name under a Rising Sun logo.

MAINOLFI, DR. RICCARDO
Via Pastiniello, 6-84017, Positano (SA), ITALY, Phone: +39 3338128775 OR +39 3493586416, riccardomainolfi@gmail.com; Web: www.mainolfiknife.com, Instagram @ riccardomainolfi, Facebook @ Riccardo Mainolfi
   Specialties: Handmade hunting and tactical knives, as well as art knives and collaborative pieces with famous engravers. **Technical:** Stock removal method of blade making using RWL-34, CPM 154 and Elmax steel, and occasionally CPM S30V, CPM S35V or Sleipner steels. Heat treats own blades in furnace with electronically controlled temperature. Uses AISI 416 and AISI 304 for bolsters and pins. **Prices:** $200 and up. **Remarks:** Part-time maker; first knife made in 2003, purchasing his first belt sander in 2004. **Mark:** Stylized blade in which is written the maker's name, with the beautiful city in which he resides.

MAISEY, ALAN
PO Box 197, Vincentia, NSW, AUSTRALIA 2540, Phone: 2-4443 7829, tosanaji@excite.com
   Specialties: Daggers, especially krisses; period pieces. **Technical:** Offers knives and finished blades in Damascus and nickel Damascus. **Prices:** $75 to $2000; some higher. **Remarks:** Part-time maker; provides complete restoration service for krisses. Trained by a Japanese Kris smith. **Mark:** None, triangle in a box, or three peaks.

MAJORS, CHARLIE
1911 King Richards Ct, Montgomery, TX 77316, Phone: 713-826-3135, charliemajors@sbcglobal.net
   Specialties: Fixed-blade hunters and slip-joint and lock-back folders. **Technical:** Practices stock removal method, preferring CPM154 steel and natural handle materials such as ironwood, stag, and mammoth ivory. Also takes customer requests. Does own heat treating and cryogenic quenching. **Remarks:** First knife made in 1980.

MAKOTO, KUNITOMO
3-3-18 Imazu-cho, Fukuyama-city, Hiroshima, JAPAN, Phone: 084-933-5874, kunitomo@po.iijnet.or.jp

MALABY, RAYMOND J
835 Calhoun Ave, Juneau, AK 99801, Phone: 907-586-6981, Fax: 907-523-8031, malaby@gci.net
   Specialties: Straight working knives. **Patterns:** Hunters, skiners, Bowies, and camp knives. **Technical:** Hand forged 1084, 5160, O1 and grinds ATS-34 stainless. **Prices:** $195 to $400. **Remarks:** First knife sold in 1994. **Mark:** First initial, last name, city, and state.

MALLOY, JOE
1039 Schwabe St, Freeland, PA 18224, Phone: 570-436-6416, jdmalloy@msn.com
   Specialties: Working straight knives of his own design or to customers' specs. **Patterns:** Full-tang hunters, bird & trout knives, neck knives, folders (plain or fancy), fighters, camp knives, khukuris and tomahawks. DEA specs. Each knife comes with a custom leather or Kydex sheath. **Technical:** Hollow or flat grinds CPM 154, D2, A2, 440C and damascus. Titanium on fancy folders with multi-color anodizing and filework. **Prices:** $200 to $1,800. **Remarks:** Part-time maker; first knife sold in 1982. Voting member of the Knifemakers' Guild since 1990. **Mark:** First and middle initials and last name, city and state.

MANARO, SAL
10 Peri Ave., Holbrook, NY 11741, Phone: 631-737-1180, maker@manaroknives.com
   Specialties: Tactical folders, bolstered titanium LinerLocks, handmade folders, and fixed blades with hand-checkered components. **Technical:** Compound grinds, hidden fasteners and welded components, with blade steels including CPM-154, damascus, Stellite, D2, S30V and O-1 by the stock-removal method of blade making. **Prices:** $500 and up. **Remarks:** Part-time maker, made first knife in 2001. **Mark:** Last name with arrowhead underline.

MANDT, JOE
3735 Overlook Dr. NE, St. Petersburg, FL 33703, Phone: 813-244-3816, jmforge@mac.com
   Specialties: Forged Bowies, camp knives, hunters, skinners, fighters, boot knives, military style field knives. **Technical:** Forges plain carbon steel and high carbon tool steels, including W2, 1084, 5160, O1, 9260, 15N20, cable Damascus, pattern welded Damascus, flat and convex grinds. Prefers natural handle materials, hand-rubbed finishes, and stainless low carbon steel, Damascus and wright iron fittings. Does own heat treat. **Prices:** $150 to $750. **Remarks:** Part-time maker, first knife sold in 206. **Mark:** "MANDT".

MANEKER, KENNETH
RR 2, Galiano Island, BC, CANADA V0N 1P0, Phone: 604-539-2084
   Specialties: Working straight knives; period pieces. **Patterns:** Camp knives and hunters; French chef knives. **Technical:** Grinds 440C, 154CM and Vascowear. **Prices:** $50 to $200; some to $300. **Remarks:** Part-time maker; first knife sold in 1981. Doing business as Water Mountain Knives. **Mark:** Japanese Kanji of initials, plus glyph.

MANLEY, DAVID W
3270 Six Mile Hwy, Central, SC 29630, Phone: 864-654-1125, dmanleyknives@bellsouth.net

Specialties: Working straight knives of his design or to custom specs. **Patterns:** Hunters, boot and fighters. **Technical:** Grinds 440C and ATS-34. **Prices:** $80 to $400. **Remarks:** Part-time maker; first knife sold in 1994. **Mark:** First initial, last name, year and serial number.

MANN, MICHAEL L

IDAHO KNIFE WORKS, PO Box 144, Spirit Lake, ID 83869, Phone: 509 994-9394, Web: www.idahoknifeworks.com

Specialties: Good working blades, historical reproductions, modern or custom designs. **Patterns:** Cowboy bowies, mountain man period blades, old-style folders, designer and maker of "The Cliff Knife," hunting and fillet knives. **Technical:** Forges 5160 high-carbon steel blades. Stock removal of 15N20. **Prices:** $200 to $730. **Remarks:** Made first knife in 1965. Full-time making knives as Idaho Knife Works since 1989. Functional as well as collectible. Each knife is truly unique! **Mark:** Four mountain peaks are his initials MM.

MANN, TIM

BLADEWORKS, PO Box 1196, Honokaa, HI 96727, Phone: 808-775-0949, Fax: 808-775-0949, birdman@shaka.com

Specialties: Hand-forged knives and swords. **Patterns:** Bowies, tantos, pesh kabz, daggers. **Technical:** Use 5160, 1050, 1075, 1095 and ATS-34 steels, cable Damascus. **Prices:** $200 to $800. **Remarks:** Just learning to forge Damascus. **Mark:** None yet.

MARAGNI, DAN

RD 1 Box 106, Georgetown, NY 13072, Phone: 315-662-7490

Specialties: Heavy-duty working knives, some investor class. **Patterns:** Hunters, fighters and camp knives, some Scottish types. **Technical:** Forges W2 and his own Damascus; toughness and edge-holding a high priority. **Prices:** $125 to $500; some to $1000. **Remarks:** Full-time maker; first knife sold in 1975. **Mark:** Celtic initials in circle.

MARCHAND, RICK

Wildertools, 69 Maple Ave., POB 1635, Lunenburg, Nova Scotia, CANADA B0J 2C0, Phone: 226-783-8771, rickmarchand@wildertools.com; Web: www.wildertools.com

Specialties: Specializing in multicultural, period stylized blades and accoutrements. **Technical:** Hand forged from 1070/84/95, L6 and 52100 steel. **Prices:** $175 - $1,500. **Remarks:** Maker since 2007. ABS apprentice smith. **Mark:** Tang stamp: "MARCHAND" along with two Japanese-style characters resembling "W" and "M."

MARINGER, TOM

2692 Powell St., Springdale, AR 72764, maringer@arkansas.net; Web: shirepost.com/cutlery.

Specialties: Working straight and curved blades with stainless steel furniture and wire-wrapped handles. **Patterns:** Subhilts, daggers, boots, swords. **Technical:** Grinds D-2, A-2, ATS-34. May be safely disassembled by the owner via pommel screw or pegged construction. **Prices:** $2000 to $3000, some to $20,000. **Remarks:** Former full-time maker, now part-time. First knife sold in 1975. **Mark:** Full name, year, and serial number etched on tang under handle.

MARKLEY, KEN

7651 Cabin Creek Lane, Sparta, IL 62286, Phone: 618-443-5284

Specialties: Traditional working and using knives of his design and to customer specs. **Patterns:** Fighters, hunters and utility/camp knives. **Technical:** Forges 5160, 1095 and L6; makes his own Damascus; does file work. **Prices:** $150 to $800; some to $2000. **Remarks:** Part-time maker; first knife sold in 1991. Doing business as Cabin Creek Forge. **Mark:** Last name, JS.

MARLOWE, CHARLES

10822 Poppleton Ave, Omaha, NE 68144, Phone: 402-933-5065, cmarlowe1@cox.net; Web: www.marloweknives.com

Specialties: Folding knives and balisong. **Patterns:** Tactical pattern folders. **Technical:** Grind ATS-34, S30V, CPM154, 154CM, Damasteel, others on request. Forges/grinds 1095 on occasion. **Prices:** Start at $450. **Remarks:** First knife sold in 1993. Full-time since 1999. **Mark:** Turtle logo with Marlowe above, year below.

MARLOWE, DONALD

2554 Oakland Rd, Dover, PA 17315, Phone: 717-764-6055

Specialties: Working straight knives in standard patterns. **Patterns:** Bowies, fighters, boots and utility knives. **Technical:** Grinds D2 and 440C. Integral design hunter models. **Prices:** $130 to $850. **Remarks:** Spare-time maker; first knife sold in 1977. **Mark:** Last name.

MARSH, JEREMY

6169 3 Mile NE, Ada, MI 49301, Phone: 616-889-1945, steelbean@hotmail.com; Web: www.marshcustomknives.com

Specialties: Locking liner folders, dressed-up gents knives, tactical knives, and dress tacticals. **Technical:** CPM S30V stainless and Damascus blade steels using the stock-removal method of bladesmithing. **Prices:** $450 to $1500. **Remarks:** Self-taught, part-time knifemaker; first knife sold in 2004. **Mark:** Maker's last name and large, stylized M.

MARSHALL, REX

1115 State Rte. 380, Wilmington, OH 45177, Phone: 937-604-8430, rexmarshall@hotmail.com; www.rexmarshallcustomknives.com

Specialties: Handforged fixed-blade traditional hunters, bowies and fighters. **Technical:** Forges and stock removal, using 5160, 1080, 1095 and 52100 high carbon steels, with stainless steels on request. Will custom build to customer's specifications. **Prices:** $125 and up. **Remarks:** Offers custom plain and lined sheaths, decorative filework. First knife made in 2011. **Mark:** Rex Marshall over eagle.

MARTIN, CORY

4249 Taylor Harbor #7, Racine, WI 53403, Phone: 262-352-5392, info@corymartinimaging.com; Web: www.corymartinimaging.com, Facebook: Cory Martin Imaging, Instagram: corymartinimaging

Specialties: Unique high-tech folders using a wide variety of materials. CNC skills used to create inlays, textures and patterns. **Technical:** Forges own damascus as well as his own unique "reverse san mai damascus." **Prices:** Moderate. **Remarks:** Part-time maker and son of Peter Martin, Cory is establishing his own unique style with creative designs and unmatched fit and finish. **Mark:** "CMD" and "C. Martin."

MARTIN, GENE

PO Box 396, Williams, OR 97544, Phone: 541-846-6755, bladesmith@customknife.com

Specialties: Straight knives and folders. **Patterns:** Fighters, hunters, skinners, boot knives, spring back and lock back folders. **Technical:** Grinds ATS-34, 440C, Damascus and 154CM. Forges; makes own Damascus; scrimshaws. **Prices:** $150 to $2500. **Remarks:** Full-time maker; first knife sold in 1993. Doing business as Provision Forge. **Mark:** Name and/or crossed staff and sword.

MARTIN, HAL W

781 Hwy 95, Morrilton, AR 72110, Phone: 501-354-1682, hal.martin@sbcglobal.net

Specialties: Hunters, Bowies and fighters. **Prices:** $250 and up. **Mark:** MARTIN.

MARTIN, HERB

2500 Starwood Dr, Richmond, VA 23229, Phone: 804-747-1675, hamjlm@hotmail.com

Specialties: Working straight knives. **Patterns:** Skinners, hunters and utility. **Technical:** Hollow grinds ATS-34, and Micarta handles. **Prices:** $125 to $200. **Remarks:** Part-time Maker. First knife sold in 2001. **Mark:** HA MARTIN.

MARTIN, MICHAEL W

Box 572, Jefferson St, Beckville, TX 75631, Phone: 903-678-2161

Specialties: Classic working/using straight knives of his design and in standard patterns. **Patterns:** Hunters. **Technical:** Grinds ATS-34, 440C, O1 and A2. Bead blasted, Parkerized, high polish and satin finishes. Sheaths are handmade. Also hand forges cable Damascus. **Prices:** $185 to $280 some higher. **Remarks:** Part-time maker; first knife sold in 1995. Doing business as Michael W. Martin Knives. **Mark:** Name and city, state in arch.

MARTIN, PETER

28220 N. Lake Dr, Waterford, WI 53185, Phone: 262-706-3076, Web: www.petermartinknives.com

Specialties: Fancy, fantasy and working straight knives and folders of his design and in standard patterns. **Patterns:** Bowies, fighters, hunters, locking folders and liner locks. **Technical:** Forges own Mosaic Damascus, powdered steel and his own Damascus. Prefers natural handle material; offers file work and carved handles. **Prices:** Moderate. **Remarks:** Full-time maker; first knife sold in 1988. Doing business as Martin Custom Products. **Mark:** Martin Knives.

MARTIN, RANDALL J

51 Bramblewood St, Bridgewater, MA 02324, Phone: 508-279-0682

Specialties: High tech folding and fixed blade tactical knives employing the latest blade steels and exotic materials. Employs a unique combination of 3d-CNC machining and hand work on both blades and handles. All knives are designed for hard use. Clean, radical grinds and ergonomic handles are hallmarks of RJ's work, as is his reputation for producing "Scary Sharp" knives. **Technical:** Grinds CPM30V, CPM 3V, CPM154CM, A2 and stainless Damascus. Other CPM alloys used on request. Performs all heat treating and cryogenic processing in-house. **Remarks:** Full-time maker since 2001 and materials engineer. Former helicopter designer. First knife sold in 1976.

MARTIN, TONY

PO Box 10, Arcadia, MO 63621, Phone: 573-546-2254, arcadian@charter.net; Web: www.arcadianforge.com

Specialties: Specializes in historical designs, esp. puukko, skean dhu. **Remarks:** Premium quality blades, exotic wood handles, unmatched fit and finish. **Mark:** AF.

MARTIN, JOHN ALEXANDER

821 N Grand Ave, Okmulgee, OK 74447, Phone: 918-758-1099, jam@jamblades.com; Web: www.jamblades.com

Specialties: Inlaid and engraved handles. **Patterns:** Bowies, fighters, hunters and traditional patterns. Swords, fixed blade knives, folders and axes. **Technical:** Forges 5160, 1084, 10XX, O1, L6 and his own Damascus. **Prices:** Start at $300. **Remarks:** Part-time maker. **Mark:** Two initials with last name and MS or 5 pointed star.

MARZITELLI, PETER

19929 35A Ave, Langley, BC, CANADA V3A 2R1, Phone: 604-532-8899, info@marzknives.com; Web: www.marzknives.com

Specialties: Specializes in unique functional knife shapes and designs using natural and synthetic handle materials. **Patterns:** Fixed blades: hunting, tactical, utility and art knives. **Technical:** Grinds 154CM, CPM steels, damascus and more. **Prices:** $220 to $1000 (average $375). **Remarks:** Full-time maker; first knife sold in 1984. **Mark:** Stylized logo reads "Marz."

MASON, BILL

9306 S.E. Venns St., Hobe Sound, FL 33455, Phone: 772-545-3649

Specialties: Combat knives; some folders. **Patterns:** Fighters to match knife types in book Cold Steel. **Technical:** Grinds O1, 440C and ATS-34. **Prices:** $115 to $250; some to $350. **Remarks:** Spare-time maker; first knife sold in 1979. **Mark:** Initials connected.

MASSEY, AL

Box 14 Site 15 RR#2, Mount Uniacke, NS, CANADA B0N 1Z0, Phone: 902-866-4754, armjan@eastlink.ca

Specialties: Working knives and period pieces. **Patterns:** Swords and daggers of Celtic to medieval design, Bowies. **Technical:** Forges 5160, 1084 and 1095. Makes own Damascus. **Prices:** $200 to $500, damascus $300-$1000. **Remarks:** Part-time maker, first blade sold in 1988. **Mark:** Initials and JS on Ricasso.

custom knifemakers

MASSEY, ROGER
4928 Union Rd, Texarkana, AR 71854, Phone: 870-779-1018, rmassey668@aol.com
Specialties: Traditional and working straight knives and folders of his design and to customer specs. **Patterns:** Bowies, hunters, daggers and utility knives. **Technical:** Forges 1084 and 52100, makes his own Damascus. Offers filework and silver wire inlay in handles. **Prices:** $200 to $1500; some to $2500. **Remarks:** Part-time maker; first knife sold in 1991. **Mark:** Last name, M.S.

MASSEY, RON
61638 El Reposo St., Joshua Tree, CA 92252, Phone: 760-366-9239 after 5 p.m., Fax: 763-366-4620
Specialties: Classic, traditional, fancy/embellished, high art, period pieces, working/using knives, straight knives, folders, and automatics. Your design, customer specs, about 175 standard patterns. **Patterns:** Automatics, hunters and fighters. All folders are side-locking folders. Unless requested as lock books slip joint he specializes or custom designs. **Technical:** ATS-34, 440C, D-2 upon request. Engraving, filework, scrimshaw, most of the exotic handle materials. All aspects are performed by him: inlay work in pearls or stone, handmade Pem' work. **Prices:** $110 to $2500; some to $6000. **Remarks:** Part-time maker; first knife sold in 1976.

MATA, LEONARD
3583 Arruza St, San Diego, CA 92154, Phone: 619-690-6935

MATHEWS, CHARLIE AND HARRY
TWIN BLADES, 121 Mt Pisgah Church Rd., Statesboro, GA 30458, Phone: 912-865-9098, twinblades@bulloch.net; Web: www.twinxblades.com
Specialties: Working straight knives, carved stag handles. **Patterns:** Hunters, fighters, bowies and period pieces. **Technical:** Grinds D2, CPM S30V, CPM 3V, ATS-34 and commercial damascus; handmade sheaths some with exotic leather, filework. **Prices:** Starting at $200. **Remarks:** Twin brothers making knives full-time under the label of Twin Blades. Charter members Georgia Custom Knifemakers Guild. Members of The Knifemakers Guild. Charlie is secretary/treasurer of the Knifemakers' Guild. **Mark:** Twin Blades over crossed knives, reverse side steel type.

MATSUNO, KANSEI
109-8 Uenomachi, Nishikaiden, Gifu-City, JAPAN 501-1168, Phone: 81 58 234 8643

MATSUOKA, SCOT
94-415 Ukalialii Place, Mililani, HI 96789, Phone: 808-625-6658, Fax: 808-625-6658, scottym@hawaii.rr.com; Web: www.matsuokaknives.com
Specialties: Folders, fixed blades with custom hand-stitched sheaths. **Patterns:** Gentleman's knives, hunters, tactical folders. **Technical:** CPM 154CM, 440C, 154, BG42, bolsters, file work, and engraving. **Prices:** Starting price $350. **Remarks:** Part-time maker, first knife sold in 2002. **Mark:** Logo, name and state.

MATSUSAKI, TAKESHI
MATSUSAKI KNIVES, 151 Ono-Cho, Sasebo-shi, Nagasaki, JAPAN, Phone: 0956-47-2938, Fax: 0956-47-2938
Specialties: Working and collector grade front look and slip joint. **Patterns:** Sheffierd type folders. **Technical:** Grinds ATS-34 k-120. **Prices:** $250 to $1000, some to $8000. **Remarks:** Part-time maker, first knife sold in 1990. **Mark:** Name and initials.

MAXEN, MICK
2 Huggins Welham Green, Hatfield, Herts, UNITED KINGDOM AL97LR, Phone: 01707 261213, mmaxen@aol.com
Specialties: Damascus and Mosaic. **Patterns:** Medieval-style daggers and Bowies. **Technical:** Forges CS75 and 15N20 / nickel Damascus. **Mark:** Last name with axe above.

MAXFIELD, LYNN
382 Colonial Ave, Layton, UT 84041, Phone: 801-544-4176, lcmaxfield@msn.com
Specialties: Sporting knives, some fancy. **Patterns:** Hunters, fishing, fillet, special purpose; some locking folders. **Technical:** Grinds 440-C, 154-CM, CPM154, D2, CPM S30V, and Damascus. **Prices:** $125 to $400; some to $900. **Remarks:** Part-time maker; first knife sold in 1979. **Mark:** Name, city and state.

MAXWELL, DON
1484 Celeste Ave, Clovis, CA 93611, Phone: 559-299-2197, maxwellknives@aol.com; Web: maxwellknives.com
Specialties: Fancy folding knives and fixed blades of his design. **Patterns:** Hunters, fighters, utility/camp knives, LinerLock® folders, flippers and fantasy knives. **Technical:** Grinds 440C, ATS-34, D2, CPM 154, and commercial Damascus. **Prices:** $250 to $1000; some to $2500. **Remarks:** Full-time maker; first knife sold in 1987. **Mark:** Last name only or Maxwell MAX-TAC.

MAY, CHARLES
10024 McDonald Rd., Aberdeen, MS 39730, Phone: 662-369-0404, charlesmayknives@yahoo.com; Web: charlesmayknives.blademakers.com
Specialties: Fixed-blade sheath knives. **Patterns:** Hunters and fillet knives. **Technical:** Scandinavian-ground D2 and S30V blades, black micarta and wood handles, nickel steel pins with maker's own pocket carry or belt-loop pouches. **Prices:** $215 to $495. **Mark:** "Charles May Knives" and a knife in a circle.

MAYNARD, LARRY JOE
PO Box 493, Crab Orchard, WV 25827
Specialties: Fancy and fantasy straight knives. **Patterns:** Big knives; a Bowie with a full false edge; fighting knives. **Technical:** Grinds standard steels. **Prices:** $350 to $500; some to $1000. **Remarks:** Full-time maker; first knife sold in 1986. **Mark:** Middle and last initials.

MAYNARD, WILLIAM N.
2677 John Smith Rd, Fayetteville, NC 28306, Phone: 910-425-1615
Specialties: Traditional and working straight knives of all designs. **Patterns:** Combat, Bowies, fighters, hunters and utility knives. **Technical:** Grinds 440C, ATS-34 and commercial Damascus. Offers fancy filework; handmade sheaths. **Prices:** $100 to $300; some to $750. **Remarks:** Full-time maker; first knife sold in 1988. **Mark:** Last name.

MAYO JR., HOMER
18036 Three Rivers Rd., Biloxi, MS 39532, Phone: 228-326-8298
Specialties: Traditional working straight knives, folders and tactical. **Patterns:** Hunters, fighters, tactical, bird, Bowies, fish fillet knives and lightweight folders. **Technical:** Grinds 440C, ATS-34, D-2, Damascus, forges and grinds 52100 and custom makes sheaths. **Prices:** $100 to $1000. **Remarks:** Part-time maker **Mark:** All knives are serial number and registered in the name of the original purchaser, stamped last name or etched.

MAYO JR., TOM
67 412 Alahaka St, Waialua, HI 96791, Phone: 808-637-6560, mayot001@hawaii.rr.com; Web: www.mayoknives.com
Specialties: Framelocks/tactical knives. **Patterns:** Combat knives, hunters, Bowies and folders. **Technical:** Titanium/stellite/S30V. **Prices:** $500 to $1000. **Remarks:** Full-time maker; first knife sold in 1982. **Mark:** Volcano logo with name and state.

MAYVILLE, OSCAR L
2130 E. County Rd 910S, Marengo, IN 47140, Phone: 812-338-4159
Specialties: Working straight knives; period pieces. **Patterns:** Kitchen cutlery, Bowies, camp knives and hunters. **Technical:** Grinds A2, O1 and 440C. **Prices:** $50 to $350; some to $500. **Remarks:** Full-time maker; first knife sold in 1984. **Mark:** Initials over knife logo.

MCABEE, WILLIAM
27275 Norton Grade, Colfax, CA 95713, Phone: 530-389-8163
Specialties: Working/using knives. **Patterns:** Fighters, Bowies, Hunters. **Technical:** Grinds ATS-34. **Prices:** $75 to $200; some to $350. **Remarks:** Part-time maker; first knife sold in 1990. **Mark:** Stylized WM stamped.

MCCALLEN JR., HOWARD H
110 Anchor Dr, So Seaside Park, NJ 08752

MCCARLEY, JOHN
4165 Harney Rd, Taneytown, MD 21787
Specialties: Working straight knives; period pieces. **Patterns:** Hunters, Bowies, camp knives, miniatures, throwing knives. **Technical:** Forges W2, O1 and his own Damascus. **Prices:** $150 to $300; some to $1000. **Remarks:** Part-time maker; first knife sold in 1977. **Mark:** Initials in script.

MCCARTY, HARRY
1479 Indian Ridge Rd, Blaine, TN 37709, harry@indianridgeforge.com; Web: www.indianridgeforge.com
Specialties: Period pieces. **Patterns:** Trade knives, Bowies, 18th and 19th century folders and hunting swords. **Technical:** Forges and grinds high-carbon steel. **Prices:** $75 to $1300. **Remarks:** Full-time maker; first knife sold in 1977. Doing business as Indian Ridge Forge. **Mark:** Stylized initials inside a shamrock.

MCCLURE, JERRY
3052 Isim Rd, Norman, OK 73026, Phone: 405-321-3614, jerry@jmccclureknives.net; Web: www.jmccclureknives.net
Specialties: Gentleman's folder, linerlock with my jeweled pivot system of eight rubies, forged one-of-a-kind Damascus Bowies, and a line of hunting/camp knives. **Patterns:** Folders, Bowie, and hunting/camp **Technical:** Forges own Damascus, also uses Damasteel and does own heat treating. **Prices:** $500 to $3,000 and up **Remarks:** Full-time maker, made first knife in 1965. **Mark:** J.MCCLURE

MCCLURE, MICHAEL
803 17th Ave, Menlo Park, CA 94025, Phone: 650-323-2596, mikesknives@att.net; Web: www.customknivesbymike.com
Specialties: Working/using straight knives of his design and to customer specs. **Patterns:** Bowies, hunters, skinners, utility/camp, tantos, fillets and boot knives. **Technical:** Forges high-carbon and Damascus; also grinds stainless, all grades. **Prices:** Start at $300. **Remarks:** Part-time maker; first knife sold in 1991. ABS Journeyman Smith. **Mark:** Mike McClure.

MCCONNELL JR., LOYD A
309 County Road 144-B, Marble Falls, TX 78654, Phone: 830-596-3488, ccknives@ccknives.com; Web: www.ccknives.com
Specialties: Working straight knives and folders, some fancy. **Patterns:** Hunters, boots, Bowies, locking folders and slip-joints. **Technical:** Grinds CPM Steels, ATS-34 and BG-42 and commercial Damascus. **Prices:** $450 to $10,000. **Remarks:** Full-time maker; first knife sold in 1975. Doing business as Cactus Custom Knives. Markets product knives under name: Lone Star Knives. **Mark:** Name, city and state in cactus logo.

MCCORNOCK, CRAIG
MCC MTN OUTFITTERS, 4775 Rt. 212/PO 162, Willow, NY 12495, Phone: 845-679-9758, Mccmtn@aol.com; Web: www.mccmtn.com
Specialties: Carry, utility, hunters, defense type knives and functional swords. **Patterns:** Drop points, hawkbills, tantos, waklzashis, katanas **Technical:** Stock removal, forged and Damascus, (yes, he still flints knap). **Prices:** $200 to $2000. **Mark:** McM.

MCCOUN, MARK
14212 Pine Dr, DeWitt, VA 23840, Phone: 804-469-7631, mccounandsons@live.com
Specialties: Working/using straight knives of his design and in standard patterns; custom miniatures. **Patterns:** Locking liners, integrals. **Technical:** Grinds Damascus,

ATS-34 and 440C. **Prices:** $150 to $500. **Remarks:** Part-time maker; first knife sold in 1989. **Mark:** Name, city and state.

MCCRACKIN, KEVIN

3720 Hess Rd, House Springs, MO 63051, Phone: 636-677-6066

MCCRACKIN AND SON, V J

3720 Hess Rd, House Springs, MO 63051, Phone: 636-677-6066
Specialties: Working straight knives in standard patterns. **Patterns:** Hunters, Bowies and camp knives. **Technical:** Forges L6, 5160, his own Damascus, cable Damascus. **Prices:** $125 to $700; some to $1500. **Remarks:** Part-time maker; first knife sold in 1983. Son Kevin helps make the knives. **Mark:** Last name, M.S.

MCCULLOUGH, JERRY

274 West Pettibone Rd, Georgiana, AL 36033, Phone: 334-382-7644, ke4er@alaweb.com
Specialties: Standard patterns or custom designs. **Technical:** Forge and grind scrap-tool and Damascus steels. Use natural handle materials and turquoise trim on some. Filework on others. **Prices:** $65 to $250 and up. **Remarks:** Part-time maker. **Mark:** Initials (JM) combined.

MCDONALD, RICH

5010 Carmel Rd., Hillboro, OH 45133, Phone: 937-466-2071, rmclongknives@aol.com; Web: www.longknivesandleather.com
Specialties: Traditional working/using and art knives of his design. **Patterns:** Bowies, hunters, folders, primitives and tomahawks. **Technical:** Forges 5160, 1084, 1095, 52100 and his own Damascus. Fancy filework. **Prices:** $200 to $1500. **Remarks:** Full-time maker; first knife sold in 1994. **Mark:** First and last initials connected.

MCDONALD, ROBERT J

14730 61 Court N, Loxahatchee, FL 33470, Phone: 561-790-1470
Specialties: Traditional working straight knives to customer specs. **Patterns:** Fighters, swords and folders. **Technical:** Grinds 440C, ATS-34 and forges own Damascus. **Prices:** $150 to $1000. **Remarks:** Part-time maker; first knife sold in 1988. **Mark:** Electro-etched name.

MCDONALD, W.J. "JERRY"

7173 Wickshire Cove E, Germantown, TN 38138, Phone: 901-756-9924, wjmcdonaldknives@msn.com; Web: www.mcdonaldknives.com
Specialties: Classic and working/using straight knives of his design and in standard patterns. **Patterns:** Bowies, hunters kitchen and traditional spring back pocket knives. **Technical:** Grinds ATS-34, 154CM, D2, 440V, BG42 and 440C. **Prices:** $125 to $1000. **Remarks:** Full-time maker; first knife sold in 1989. **Mark:** First and middle initials, last name, maker, city and state. Some of his knives are stamped McDonald in script.

MCFALL, KEN

PO Box 458, Lakeside, AZ 85929, Phone: 928-537-2026, Fax: 928-537-8066, knives@citlink.net
Specialties: Fancy working straight knives and some folders. **Patterns:** Daggers, boots, tantos, Bowies; some miniatures. **Technical:** Grinds D2, ATS-34 and 440C. Forges his own Damascus. **Prices:** $200 to $1200. **Remarks:** Part-time maker; first knife sold in 1984. **Mark:** Name, city and state.

MCFARLIN, ERIC E

PO Box 2188, Kodiak, AK 99615, Phone: 907-486-4799, e2mc@reagan.com
Specialties: Working knives of his design. **Patterns:** Bowies, skinners, camp knives and hunters. **Technical:** Flat and convex grinds 440C, A2 and AEB-L. **Prices:** Start at $350. **Remarks:** Part-time maker; first knife sold in 1989. **Mark:** Name and city and Old Goat logo.

MCFARLIN, J W

3331 Pocohantas Dr, Lake Havasu City, AZ 86404, Phone: 928-453-7612, Fax: 928-453-7612, aztheedge@NPGcable.com
Technical: Flat grinds, D2, ATS-34, 440C, Thomas and Peterson Damascus. **Remarks:** From working knives to investment. Customer designs always welcome. 100 percent handmade. Made first knife in 1972. **Prices:** $150 to $3000. **Mark:** Hand written in the blade.

MCGHEE, E. SCOTT

7136 Lisbon Rd., Clarkton, NC 28433, Phone: 910-448-2224, guineahogforge@gmail.com; Web: www.guineahogforge.com
Specialties: Hunting knives, kitchen blades, presentation blades, tactical knives and sword canes. **Technical:** Forge and stock removal, all flat-ground blades, including 1080-and-15N20 damascus, 1084, O1 and W2. **Prices:** $200 to $3,500. **Remarks:** Full-time maker; first knife sold in 2009. Currently an ABS journeyman smith. **Mark:** E. Scott McGhee (large print) above Guinea Hog Forge (small print).

MCGILL, JOHN

PO Box 302, Blairsville, GA 30512, Phone: 404-745-4686
Specialties: Working knives. **Patterns:** Traditional patterns; camp knives. **Technical:** Forges L6 and 9260; makes Damascus. **Prices:** $50 to $250; some to $500. **Remarks:** Full-time maker; first knife sold in 1982. **Mark:** XYLO.

MCGOWAN, FRANK E

12629 Howard Lodge Rd., Sykesville, MD 21784, Phone: 443-745-2611, lizmcgowan31@gmail.com
Specialties: Fancy working knives and folders to customer specs. **Patterns:** Survivor knives, fighters, fishing knives, folders and hunters. **Technical:** Grinds and forges O1, 440C, 5160, ATS-34, 52100, or customer choice. **Prices:** $100 to $1000; some more. **Remarks:** Full-time maker; first knife sold in 1986. **Mark:** Last name.

MCGRATH, PATRICK T

8343 Kenyon Ave, Westchester, CA 90045, Phone: 310-338-8764, hidinginLA@excite.com

MCGRODER, PATRICK J

5725 Chapin Rd, Madison, OH 44057, Phone: 216-298-3405, Fax: 216-298-3405

Specialties: Traditional working/using knives of his design. **Patterns:** Bowies, hunters and utility/camp knives. **Technical:** Grinds ATS-34, D2 and customer requests. Does reverse etching; heat-treats; prefers natural handle materials; custom made sheath with each knife. **Prices:** $125 to $250. **Remarks:** Part-time maker. **Mark:** First and middle initials, last name, maker, city and state.

MCGUANE IV, THOMAS F

410 South 3rd Ave, Bozeman, MT 59715, Phone: 406-586-0248, Web: http://www.thomasmcguane.com
Specialties: Multi metal inlaid knives of handmade steel. **Patterns:** Lock back and LinerLock® folders, fancy straight knives. **Technical:** 1084/1SN20 Damascus and Mosaic steel by maker. **Prices:** $1000 and up. **Mark:** Surname or name and city, state.

MCHENRY, WILLIAM JAMES

Box 67, Wyoming, RI 02898, Phone: 401-539-8353
Specialties: Fancy high-tech folders of his design. **Patterns:** Locking folders with various mechanisms. **Technical:** One-of-a-kind only, no duplicates. Inventor of the Axis Lock. Most pieces disassemble and feature top-shelf materials including gold, silver and gems. **Prices:** Upscale. **Remarks:** Full-time maker; first knife sold in 1988. Former goldsmith. **Mark:** Last name or first and last initials.

MCINTYRE, SHAWN

71 Leura Grove, Hawthornm, E VIC, AUSTRALIA 3123, Phone: 61 3 9813 2049/Cell 61 412 041 062, macpower@netspace.net.au; Web: www.mcintyreknives.com
Specialties: Damascus & CS fixed blades and art knives. **Patterns:** Bowies, hunters, fighters, kukris, integrals. **Technical:** Forges, makes own Damascus including pattern weld, mosaic, and composite multi-bars form O1 & 15N20 Also uses 1084, W2, and 52100. **Prices:** $275 to $2000. **Remarks:** Full-time maker since 1999. **Mark:** Mcintyre in script.

MCKEE, NEIL

674 Porter Hill Rd., Stevensville, MT 59870, Phone: 406-777-3507, mckeenh@wildblue.net
Specialties: Early American. **Patterns:** Nessmuk, DeWeese, French folders, art pieces. **Technical:** Engraver. **Prices:** $150 to $1000. **Mark:** Oval with initials.

MCKENZIE, DAVID BRIAN

2311 B Ida Rd, Campbell River, BC, CANADA V9W-4V7

MCKIERNAN, STAN

11751 300th St, Lamoni, IA 50140, Phone: 641-784-6873/641-781-0368, slmck@hotmailc.om
Specialties: Self-sheathed knives and miniatures. **Patterns:** Daggers, ethnic designs and individual styles. **Technical:** Grinds Damascus and 440C. **Prices:** $200 to $500, some to $1500. **Mark:** "River's Bend" inside two concentric circles.

MCLUIN, TOM

36 Fourth St, Dracut, MA 01826, Phone: 978-957-4899, tmcluin@comcast.net
Specialties: Working straight knives and folders of his design. **Patterns:** Boots, hunters and folders. **Technical:** Grinds ATS-34, 440C, O1 and Damascus; makes his own mokume. **Prices:** $100 to $400; some to $700. **Remarks:** Part-time maker; first knife sold in 1991. **Mark:** Last name.

MCLURKIN, ANDREW

2112 Windy Woods Dr, Raleigh, NC 27607, Phone: 919-834-4693, mclurkincustomknives.com
Specialties: Collector grade folders, working folders, fixed blades, and miniatures. Knives made to order and to his design. **Patterns:** Locking liner and lock back folders, hunter, working and tactical designs. **Technical:** Using patterned Damascus, Mosaic Damascus, ATS-34, BG-42, and CPM steels. Prefers natural handle materials such as pearl, ancient ivory and stabilized wood. Also using synthetic materials such as carbon fiber, titanium, and G10. **Prices:** $250 and up. **Mark:** Last name. Mark is often on inside of folders.

MCNABB, TOMMY

CAROLINA CUSTOM KNIVES, PO Box 327, Bethania, NC 27010, Phone: 336-924-6053, tommy@tmcnabb.com; Web: carolinaknives.com
Specialties: Classic and working knives of his own design or to customer's specs. **Patterns:** Traditional bowies. Tomahawks, hunters and customer designs. **Technical:** Forges his own Damascus steel, hand forges or grinds ATS-34 and other hi-tech steels. Prefers mirror finish or satin finish on working knives. Uses exotic or natural handle material and stabilized woods. **Prices:** $300-$3500. **Remarks:** Full time maker. Made first knife in 1982. **Mark:** "Carolina Custom Knives" on stock removal blades "T. McNabb" on custom orders and Damascus knives.

MCNEES, JONATHAN

15203 Starboard Pl, Northport, AL 35475, Phone: 205-391-8383, jmackusmc@yahoo.com; Web: www.mcneescustomknives.com
Specialties: Tactical, outdoors, utility. **Technical:** Stock removal method utilizing carbon and stainless steels to include 1095, cpm154, A2, cpms35v. **Remarks:** Part-time maker, first knife made in 2007. **Mark:** Jmcnees

MCRAE, J MICHAEL

6100 Lake Rd, Mint Hill, NC 28227, Phone: 704-545-2929, scotia@carolina.rr.com; Web: www.scotiametalwork.com
Specialties: Scottish dirks, sgian dubhs, broadswords. **Patterns:** Traditional blade styles with traditional and slightly non-traditional handle treatments. **Technical:** Forges 5160 and his own Damascus. Prefers stag and exotic hardwoods for handles, many intricately carved. **Prices:** Starting at $125, some to $3500. **Remarks:** Journeyman Smith in ABS, member of ABANA. Full-time maker, first knife sold in 1982. Doing business as Scotia Metalwork. **Mark:** Last name underlined with a claymore.

MCWILLIAMS, SEAN

PO Box 1685, Carbondale, CO 81623, Phone: 970-618-0198, info@
seanmcwilliamsforge.com; Web: www.seanmcwilliamsforge.com

Specialties: Tactical, survival and working knives in Kydex-and-nylon sheaths. **Patterns:** Fighters, bowies, hunters and sports knives, period pieces, swords, martial arts blades and some folders, including Panama Folder linerlocks. **Technical:** Forges only CPM T440V, CPM S90V and CPM S35VN. **Prices:** $230 to $2,500. **Remarks:** Full-time maker; first knife sold in 1972. **Mark:** Stylized bear paw.

MEERDINK, KURT

248 Yulan Barryville Rd., Barryville, NY 12719-5305, Phone: 845-557-0783

Specialties: Working straight knives. **Patterns:** Hunters, Bowies, tactical and neck knives. **Technical:** Grinds ATS-34, 440C, D2, Damascus. **Prices:** $95 to $1100. **Remarks:** Full-time maker, first knife sold in 1994. **Mark:** Meerdink Maker, Rio NY.

MEERS, ANDREW

1100 S Normal Ave., Allyn Bldg MC 4301, Carbondale, IL 62901, Phone: 774-217-3574, namsuechool@gmail.com

Specialties: Pattern welded blades, in the New England style. **Patterns:** Can do open or closed welding and fancies middle eastern style blades. **Technical:** 1095, 1084, 15n20, 5160, w1, w2 steels **Remarks:** Part-time maker attending graduate school at SIUC; looking to become full-time in the future as well as earn ABS Journeyman status. **Mark:** Korean character for south.

MEIER, DARYL

75 Forge Rd, Carbondale, IL 62903, Phone: 618-549-3234, Web: www.meiersteel.com

Specialties: One-of-a-kind knives and swords. **Patterns:** Collaborates on blades. **Technical:** Forges his own Damascus, W1 and A203E, 440C, 431, nickel 200 and clad steel. **Prices:** $500 and up. **Remarks:** Full-time smith and researcher since 1974; first knife sold in 1974. **Mark:** Name.

MELIN, GORDON C

14207 Coolbank Dr, La Mirada, CA 90638, Phone: 562-946-5753

MELOY, SEAN

7148 Rosemary Lane, Lemon Grove, CA 91945-2105, Phone: 619-465-7173

Specialties: Traditional working straight knives of his design. **Patterns:** Bowies, fighters and utility/camp knives. **Technical:** Grinds 440C, ATS-34 and D2. **Prices:** $125 to $300. **Remarks:** Part-time maker; first knife sold in 1985. **Mark:** Broz Knives.

MENEFEE, RICKY BOB

2440 County Road 1322, Blanchard, OK 73010, rmenefee@pldi.net; Web: www.menefeeknives.com

Specialties: Working straight knives and pocket knives. **Patterns:** Hunters, fighters, minis & Bowies. **Technical:** Grinds 154CM, A2 and CPM S90V. **Prices:** $200 to $2,000. **Remarks:** Part-time maker, first knife sold in 1996. Member of KGA of Oklahoma, also Knifemakers Guild. **Mark:** Menefee made or Menefee stamped in blade.

MENSCH, LARRY C

Larry's Knife Shop, 578 Madison Ave, Milton, PA 17847, Phone: 570-742-9554

Specialties: Custom orders. **Patterns:** Bowies, daggers, hunters, tantos, short swords and miniatures. **Technical:** Grinds ATS-34, stainless steel Damascus; blade grinds hollow, flat and slack. Filework; bending guards and fluting handles with finger grooves. **Prices:** $200 and up. **Remarks:** Full-time maker; first knife sold in 1993. Doing business as Larry's Knife Shop. **Mark:** Connected capital "L" and small "m" in script.

MERCER, MIKE

149 N. Waynesville Rd, Lebanon, OH 45036, Phone: 513-932-2837, mmercer08445@roadrunner.com

Specialties: Miniatures and autos. **Patterns:** All folder patterns. **Technical:** Diamonds and gold, one-of-a-kind, Damascus, O1, stainless steel blades. **Prices:** $500 to $5000. **Remarks:** Carved wax - lost wax casting. **Mark:** Stamp - Mercer.

MERCHANT, TED

7 Old Garrett Ct, White Hall, MD 21161, Phone: 410-343-0380

Specialties: Traditional and classic working knives. **Patterns:** Bowies, hunters, camp knives, fighters, daggers and skinners. **Technical:** Forges W2 and 5160; makes own Damascus. Makes handles with wood, stag, horn, silver and gem stone inlay; fancy filework. **Prices:** $125 to $600; some to $1500. **Remarks:** Full-time maker; first knife sold in 1985. **Mark:** Last name.

MEROLA, JIM

6648 Ridge Blvd., Brooklyn, NY 11220, Phone: 347-342-6923, jimolds@earthlink.net; Web: www.jimmerola.com

Specialties: Folders and fixed blades, including antique bowie reproductions, all in stainless steel and damascus. **Technical:** Stock removal method of blade making, using the finest steels and handle materials. **Prices:** $400 to $1,500. **Remarks:** Part-time maker since 1998.

MERZ III, ROBERT L

1447 Winding Canyon, Katy, TX 77493, Phone: 281-391-2897, bobmerz@consolidated.net; Web: www.merzknives.com

Specialties: Folders. **Prices:** $400 to $2,000. **Remarks:** Full-time maker; first knife sold in 1974. **Mark:** MERZ.

MESENBOURG, NICK

2545 Upper 64th Ct. E, Inver Grove Heights, MN 55076, Phone: 651-457-2753 or 651-775-7505, mesenbourg_nicholas@hotmail.com; www.ndmknives.com

Specialties: Working straight knives of his design or to customer specs, also sport-themed knives. **Patterns:** Hunters, skinners, bowies, fighters, utility and fillet knives.

Technical: Grinds 440C stainless steel and commercial damascus. **Prices:** $175-$450, special knives higher. **Remarks:** Part-time maker; first knife sold in 2008. **Mark:** Encircled N D M capital letters.

MESHEJIAN, MARDI

5 Bisbee Court 109 PMB 230, Santa Fe, NM 87508, Phone: 505-310-7441, toothandnail13@yahoo.com

Specialties: One-of-a-kind art knives, folders and kitchen knives. **Patterns:** Swords, daggers, folders and other weapons. **Technical:** Forged steel Damascus and titanium Damascus. **Prices:** $300 to $5000 some to $7000. **Mark:** Stamped stylized "M."

METHENY, H A "WHITEY"

7750 Waterford Dr, Spotsylvania, VA 22551, Phone: 540842-1440, Fax: 540-582-3095, hametheny@aol.com; Web: www methenyknives.com

Specialties: Working and using straight knives of his design and to customer specs. **Patterns:** Hunters and kitchen knives. **Technical:** Grinds 440C and ATS-34. Offers filework; tooled custom sheaths. **Prices:** $350 to $450. **Remarks:** Spare-time maker; first knife sold in 1990. **Mark:** Initials/full name football logo.

METSALA, ANTHONY

30557 103rd St. NW, Princeton, MN 55371, Phone: 763-389-2628, acmetsala@izoom.net; Web: www.metsalacustomknives.com

Specialties: Sole authorship one-off mosaic Damascus liner locking folders, sales of makers finished one-off mosaic Damascus blades. **Patterns:** Except for a couple EDC folding knives, maker does not use patterns. **Technical:** Forges own mosaic Damascus carbon blade and bolster material. All stainless steel blades are heat treated by Paul Bos. **Prices:** $250 to $1500. **Remarks:** Full-time knifemaker and Damascus steel maker, first knife sold in 2005. **Mark:** A.C. Metsala or Metsala.

METZ, GREG T

c/o Yellow Pine Bar HC 83, BOX 8080, Cascade, ID 83611, Phone: 208-382-4336, metzenterprise@yahoo.com

Specialties: Hunting and utility knives. **Prices:** $350 and up. **Remarks:** Natural handle materials; hand forged blades; 1084 and 1095. **Mark:** METZ (last name).

MEYER, CHRISTOPHER J

737 Shenipsit Lake Rd, Tolland, CT 06084, Phone: 860-875-1826, shenipsitforge.cjm@gmail.com

Specialties: Handforged tool steels. **Technical:** Forges tool steels, grinds stainless. **Remarks:** Spare-time maker; sold first knife in 2003. **Mark:** Name and/or "Shenipsit Forge."

MICHINAKA, TOSHIAKI

I-679 Koyamacho-nishi, Tottori-shi, Tottori, JAPAN 680-0947, Phone: 0857-28-5911

Specialties: Art miniature knives. **Patterns:** Bowies, hunters, fishing, camp knives & miniatures. **Technical:** Grinds ATS-34 and 440C. **Prices:** $300 to $900 some higher. **Remarks:** Part-time maker. First knife sold in 1982. **Mark:** First initial, last name.

MICKLEY, TRACY

42112 Kerns Dr, North Mankato, MN 56003, Phone: 507-947-3760, tracy@mickleyknives.com; Web: www.mickleyknives.com

Specialties: Working and collectable straight knives using mammoth ivory or burl woods, LinerLock® folders. **Patterns:** Custom and classic hunters, utility, fighters and Bowies. **Technical:** Grinding 154-CM, BG-42 forging O1 and 52100. **Prices:** Starting at $325 **Remarks:** Part-time since 1999. **Mark:** Last name.

MIDGLEY, BEN

PO Box 577, Wister, OK 74966, Phone: 918-655-6701, mauricemidgley@windstream.net

Specialties: Multi-blade folders, slip-joints, some lock-backs and hunters. File work, engraving and scrimshaw. **Patterns:** Reproduce old patterns, trappers, muskrats, stockman, whittlers, lockbacks an hunters. **Technical:** Grinds ATS-34, 440C, 12-C-27, CPM-154, some carbon steel, and commercial Damascus. **Prices:** $385 to $1875. **Remarks:** Full-time maker, first knife sold in 2002. **Mark:** Name, city, and state stamped on blade.

MIKOLAJCZYK, GLEN

4650 W. 7 Mile Rd., Caledonia, WI 53108, Phone: 414-791-0424, Fax: 262-835-9697, glenmikol@aol.com Web: www.customtomahawk.com

Specialties: Pipe hawks, fancy folders, bowies, long blades, hunting knives, all of his own design. **Technical:** Sole-author, forges own Damascus and powdered steel. Works with ivory, bone, tortoise, horn and antlers, tiger maple, pearl for handle materials. Designs and does intricate file work and custom sheaths. Enjoys exotic handle materials. **Prices:** Moderate. **Remarks:** Founded Weg Von Wennig Forge in 2003, first knife sold in 2004. Also, designs and builds mini-forges. Will build upon request. International sales accepted. **Mark:** Tomahawk and name.

MILES JR., C R "IRON DOCTOR"

1541 Porter Crossroad, Lugoff, SC 29078, Phone: 803-600-9397

Specialties: Traditional working straight knives of his design or made to custom specs. **Patterns:** Hunters, fighters, utility camp knives and hatches. **Technical:** Grinds O1, D2, ATS-34, 440C, 1095, and 154 CPM. Forges 18th century style cutlery of high carbon steels. Also forges and grinds old files and farrier's rasps to make knives. Custom leather sheaths. **Prices:** $100 and up. **Remarks:** Part-time maker, first knife sold in 1997. **Mark:** Iron doctor plus name and serial number.

MILITANO, TOM

CUSTOM KNIVES, 77 Jason Rd., Jacksonville, AL 36265-6655, Phone: 256-435-7132, jeffkin57@aol.com

Specialties: Fixed blade, one-of-a-kind knives. **Patterns:** Bowies, fighters, hunters and tactical knives. **Technical:** Grinds 440C, CPM 154CM, A2, and Damascus. Hollow grinds, flat grinds, and decorative filework. **Prices:** $150 plus. **Remarks:** Part-time maker. Sold first knives in the mid-to-late 1980s. **Mark:** Name engraved in ricasso area - type of steel on reverse side.

MILLARD, FRED G
27627 Kopezyk Ln, Richland Center, WI 53581, Phone: 608-647-5376
Specialties: Working/using straight knives of his design or to customer specs. **Patterns:** Bowies, hunters, utility/camp knives, kitchen/steak knives. **Technical:** Grinds ATS-34, O1, D2 and 440C. Makes sheaths. **Prices:** $110 to $300. **Remarks:** Full-time maker; first knife sold in 1993. Doing business as Millard Knives. **Mark:** Mallard duck in flight with serial number.

MILLER, CHELSEA GRACE
80 Ainslie St., Brooklyn, NY 11211, Phone: 917-623-7804, chelsea@chelseamillerknives.com; Web: www.chelseamillerknives.com
Specialties: Selection of rustic cheese knives and kitchen knives. **Technical:** Uses recycled tool steel, such as mechanic's files, wood files and rasps. Forges cheese and smaller kitchen knives, using stock removal to preserve the rasp pattern on large kitchen knives. All the wood for handles is collected from the maker's family farm in Vermont, including spalted maple, apple and walnut. **Prices:** $200 to $500. **Remarks:** Full-time maker; first knife made in 2011. Maker often examines that first knife and admires its simplicity, though it lacks functionality, and uses it as inspiration to remain as imaginative as possible.

MILLER, HANFORD J
1751 Mountain Ranch Rd., Lakespur, CO 80118, Phone: 719-999-2551, hanford.miller@gmail.com
Specialties: Working knives in Moran styles, Bowie, period pieces, Cinquedea. **Patterns:** Daggers, Bowies, working knives. **Technical:** All work forged: W2, 1095, 5160 and Damascus. ABS methods; offers fine silver repousse, scabboard mountings and wire inlay, oak presentation cases. **Prices:** $400 to $1000; some to $3000 and up. **Remarks:** Full-time maker; first knife sold in 1968. **Mark:** Initials or name within Bowie logo.

MILLER, JAMES P
9024 Goeller Rd, RR 2, Box 28, Fairbank, IA 50629, Phone: 319-635-2294, Web: www.damascusknives.biz
Specialties: All tool steel Damascus; working knives and period pieces. **Patterns:** Hunters, Bowies, camp knives and daggers. **Technical:** Forges and grinds 1095, 52100, 440C and his own Damascus. **Prices:** $175 to $500; some to $1500. **Remarks:** Full-time maker; first knife sold in 1970. **Mark:** First and middle initials, last name with knife logo.

MILLER, LEVI
8065 N. 450 West, Howe, IN 46746, Phone: 260-562-2724, lmcustomknives@gmail.com; Facebook.com/Lmknives
Specialties: Traditional knives. **Patterns:** Slip joints, hunters, camp knives and hoof knives. **Technical:** Forges 52100 and 80CrV2. **Prices:** $200 and up. **Remarks:** Part-time maker; first knife sold in 2009. ABS journeyman smith. **Mark:** LRMiller Howe IN JS.

MILLER, M A
11625 Community Center Dr, Unit #1531, Northglenn, CO 80233, Phone: 303-280-3816
Specialties: Using knives for hunting. 3-1/2"-4" Loveless drop-point. Made to customer specs. **Patterns:** Skinners and camp knives. **Technical:** Grinds 440C, D2, O1 and ATS-34 Damascus miniatures. **Prices:** $225 to $350; miniatures $75 to $150. **Remarks:** Part-time maker; first knife sold in 1988. **Mark:** Last name stamped in block letters or first and middle initials, last name, maker, city and state with triangles on either side etched.

MILLER, MICHAEL
3030 E Calle Cedral, Kingman, AZ 86401, Phone: 928-757-1359, mike@mmilleroriginals.com
Specialties: Hunters, Bowies, and skinners with exotic burl wood, stag, ivory and gemstone handles. **Patterns:** High carbon steel knives. **Technical:** High carbon and nickel alloy Damascus and high carbon and meteorite Damascus. Also mosaic Damascus. **Prices:** $235 to $4500. **Remarks:** Full-time maker since 2002, first knife sold 2000; doing business as M Miller Originals. **Mark:** First initial and last name with 'handmade' underneath.

MILLER, MICHAEL E
910146 S. 3500 Rd., Chandler, OK 74834, Phone: 918-377-2411, mimiller1@cotc.net
Specialties: Traditional working/using knives of his design. **Patterns:** Bowies, hunters and kitchen knives. **Technical:** Grinds ATS-34, CPM 440V; forges Damascus and cable Damascus and 52100. Prefers scrimshaw, fancy pins, basket weave and embellished sheaths. **Prices:** $130 to $500. **Remarks:** Part-time maker; first knife sold in 1984. Doing business as Miller Custom Knives. Member of Knife Group Of Oklahoma. **Mark:** First and middle initials, last name, maker.

MILLER, NATE
Sportsman's Edge, 1075 Old Steese Hwy N, Fairbanks, AK 99712, Phone: 907-460-4718, sportsmansedge@gci.net Web: www.alaskasportsmansedge.com
Specialties: Fixed blade knives for hunting, fishing, kitchen and collector pieces. **Patterns:** Hunters, skinners, utility, tactical, fishing, camp knives-your pattern or mine. **Technical:** Stock removal maker, ATS-34, 154CM, 440C, D2, 1095, other steels on request. Handle material includes micarta, horn, antler, fossilized ivory and bone, wide selection of woods. **Prices:** $225-$800. **Remarks:** Full time maker since 2002. **Mark:** Nate Miller, Fairbanks, AK.

MILLER, RICK
516 Kanaul Rd, Rockwood, PA 15557, Phone: 814-926-2059
Specialties: Working/using straight knives of his design and in standard patterns.

Patterns: Bowies, daggers, hunters and friction folders. **Technical:** Grinds L6. Forges 5160, L6 and Damascus. Patterns for Damascus are random, twist, rose or ladder. **Prices:** $75 to $250; some to $400. **Remarks:** Part-time maker; first knife sold in 1982. **Mark:** Script stamp "R.D.M."

MILLER, RONALD T
12922 127th Ave N, Largo, FL 34644, Phone: 813-595-0378 (after 5 p.m.)
Specialties: Working straight knives in standard patterns. **Patterns:** Combat knives, camp knives, kitchen cutlery, fillet knives, locking folders and butterflies. **Technical:** Grinds D2, 440C and ATS-34; offers brass inlays and scrimshaw. **Prices:** $45 to $325; some to $750. **Remarks:** Part-time maker; first knife sold in 1984. **Mark:** Name, city and state in palm tree logo.

MILLER, STEVE
1376 Pine St., Clearwater, FL 33756, Phone: 727-461-4180, millknives@aol.com; Web: www.millerknives.com
Patterns: Bowies, hunters, skinners, folders. **Technical:** Primarily uses CPM 154, 440C, ATS-34, CPM S30V, damascus and Sandvik stainless steels. Exotic hardwoods, bone, horn, antler, ivory, synthetics. All leather work and sheaths made by me and handstitched. **Remarks:** Have been making custom knives for sale since 1990. Part-time maker, hope to go full time in about five and a half years (after retirement from full-time job). **Mark:** Last name inside a pentagram.

MILLER, TERRY
P.O. Box 262, Healy, AK 99743, Phone: 907-683-1239, terry@denalidomehome.com
Specialties: Alaskan ulus with wood or horn. **Remarks:** New to knifemaking (7 years).

MILLER, WILLIAM (BILL)
21937 Holiday Ln., Warsaw, MO 65355, Phone: 660-723-1866, wmknives@hotmail.com
Specialties: Uses own handforged high-carbon damascus for bowies, daggers, push daggers and hunters. **Patterns:** All different styles. **Prices:** $250 to $3,000. **Remarks:** Uses exotic hardwood, stag, fossil ivory and fossil bone as handle materials. **Mark:** "W" over "M" in an oval.

MILLS, LOUIS G
9450 Waters Rd, Ann Arbor, MI 48103, Phone: 734-668-1839
Specialties: High-art Japanese-style period pieces. **Patterns:** Traditional tantos, daggers and swords. **Technical:** Makes steel from iron; makes his own Damascus by traditional Japanese techniques. **Prices:** $900 to $2000; some to $8000. **Remarks:** Spare-time maker. **Mark:** Yasutomo in Japanese Kanji.

MILLS, MICHAEL
151 Blackwell Rd, Colonial Beach, VA 22443-5054, Phone: 804-224-0265
Specialties: Working knives, hunters, skinners, utility and Bowies. **Technical:** Forge 5160 differential heat-treats. **Prices:** $300 and up. **Remarks:** Part-time maker, ABS Journeyman. **Mark:** Last name in script.

MINCHEW, RYAN
2101 Evans Ln., Midland, TX 79705, Phone: 806-752-0223, ryan@minchewknives.com Web: www.minchewknives.com
Specialties: Hunters and folders. **Patterns:** Standard hunters and bird-and-trout knives. **Prices:** $150 to $500. **Mark:** Minchew.

MINNICK, JIM & JOYCE
144 North 7th St, Middletown, IN 47356, Phone: 765-354-4108, jmjknives@aol.com; Web: www.minnickknives@aol.com
Specialties: Lever-lock folding art knives, liner-locks. **Patterns:** Stilettos, Persian and one-of-a-kind folders. **Technical:** Grinds and carves Damascus, stainless, and high-carbon. **Prices:** $950 to $7000. **Remarks:** Part-time maker; first knife sold in 1976. Husband and wife team. **Mark:** Minnick and JMJ.

MIRABILE, DAVID
PO BOX 20417, Juneau, AK 99802, Phone: 907-321-1103, dmirabile02@gmail.com; Web: www.mirabileknives.com
Specialties: Elegant edged weapons and hard use Alaskan knives. **Patterns:** Fighters, personal carry knives, special studies of the Tlinget dagger. **Technical:** Uses W-2, 1080, 15n20, 1095, 5160, and his own Damascus, and stainless/high carbon San Mai.

MITCHELL, ALAN
133 Standard Dr., Blairgowrie, Randburg, Gauteng, SOUTH AFRICA, Phone: +27(83) 501 0944, alspostbox@hotmail.com; Facebook.com/mitchellhandmade
Specialties: Forged working and using knives. **Patterns:** Hunters, utility knives and bowies. **Technical:** Forges high-carbon steels with flat and hollow grinds and hamons (temper lines). **Prices:** $100 to $1,000. **Remarks:** Member of Knife Makers Guild of South Africa. **Mark:** Mitchell.

MITCHELL, JAMES A
PO Box 4646, Columbus, GA 31904, Phone: 404-322-8582
Specialties: Fancy working knives. **Patterns:** Hunters, fighters, Bowies and locking folders. **Technical:** Grinds D2, 440C and commercial Damascus. **Prices:** $100 to $400; some to $900. **Remarks:** Part-time maker; first knife sold in 1976. Sells knives in sets. **Mark:** Signature and city.

MITCHELL, MAX DEAN AND BEN
3803 VFW Rd, Leesville, LA 71440, Phone: 318-239-6416
Specialties: Hatchet and knife sets with folder and belt and holster all match. **Patterns:** Hunters, 200 L6 steel. **Technical:** L6 steel; soft back, hand edge. **Prices:** $300 to $500. **Remarks:** Part-time makers; first knife sold in 1965. Custom orders only; no stock. **Mark:** First names.

MITCHELL, WM DEAN
2405 County Rd. 1550, Warren, TX 77664, Phone: 409-547-0420, wmdeanmitchell@gmail.com
Specialties: Functional and collectable cutlery. Patterns: Personal and collector's designs. Technical: Forges own Damascus and carbon steels. Prices: Determined by the buyer. Remarks: Gentleman knifemaker. ABS Master Smith 1994. Mark: Full name with anvil and MS or WDM and MS.

MITSUYUKI, ROSS
PO Box 29577, Honolulu, HI 96820, Phone: 808-778-5907, Fax: 808-671-3335, r.p.mitsuyuki@gmail.com; Web:www.picturetrail.com/homepage/mrbing
Specialties: Working straight knives and folders/engraving titanium & 416 S.S. Patterns: Hunting, fighters, utility knives and boot knives. Technical: 440C, BG42, ATS-34, S30V, CPM154, and Damascus. Prices: $150 and up. Remarks: Spare-time maker, first knife sold in 1998. Mark: (Honu) Hawaiian sea turtle.

MIVILLE-DESCHENES, ALAIN
1952 Charles A Parent, Quebec, CANADA G2B 4B2, Phone: 418-845-0950, Fax: 418-845-0950, amd@miville-deschenes.com; Web: www.miville-deschenes.com
Specialties: Working knives of his design or to customer specs and art knives. Patterns: Bowies, skinner, hunter, utility, camp knives, fighters, art knives. Technical: Grinds ATS-34, CPMS30V, 0-1, D2, and sometime forge carbon steel. Prices: $250 to $700; some higher. Remarks: Part-time maker; first knife sold in 2001. Mark: Logo (small hand) and initials (AMD).

MOELLER, HARALD
#17-493 Pioneer Crescent, Parksville, BC, CANADA V9P 1V2, Phone: 250-248-0391, moeknif@shaw.ca; Web: www.collectiblecustomknives.com
Specialties: Collector grade San Fransisco Dagger; small fighters, Fantasy Axes, Bowies, Survival Knives. Special design award winning liner lock folders; Viper throwing knives. Technical: Steels - 440-C, ATS34, damascus, etc. Materials: mammoth, Abalone, MOP, Black Water Buffalo, 14K Gold, rubies, diamonds, etc. Prices: Throwing knives - $80 to $350; Fighters - $400 to $600; Axe - $3200; Folders - $600 to $3400; Dagger - Up to $9,000 Remarks: Now part time maker, first knife sold in 1979. member Southern California Blades; Member Oregon Knife Collectors Assoc. Mark: Moeller

MOEN, JERRY
4478 Spring Valley Rd., Dallas, TX 75244, Phone: 972-839-1609, jmoen@moencustomknives.com Web: moencustomknives.com
Specialties: Hunting, pocket knives, fighters tactical, and exotic. Prices: $500 to $5,000.

MOIZIS, STAN
8213 109B St., Delta, British Columbia (BC), CANADA V4C 4G9, Phone: 604-597-8929, moizis@telus.net
Specialties: Automatic and spring-assist folding knives and soon to come out-the-fronts. Patterns: Well-made carry knives with some upper-end materials available for steel and handles. All patterns are freehand, and thus each knife is unique. Marks: "SM" on blade with date and place of manufacture on inside of spacer. On knives with professionally out-of-house machined parts, mark is "BRNO BORN."

MOJZIS, JULIUS
B S Timravy 6, 98511 Halic, SLOVAKIA, julius.mojzis@gmail.com; Web: www.juliusmojzis.com
Specialties: Art Knives. Prices: USD 2000. Mark: MOJZIS.

MONCUS, MICHAEL STEVEN
1803 US 19 N, Smithville, GA 31787, Phone: 912-846-2408

MONTANO, GUS A
P.O. Box 501264, San Diego, CA 92150, Phone: 619-273-5357
Specialties: Traditional working/using straight knives of his design. Patterns: Boots, Bowies and fighters. Technical: Grinds 1095 and 5160; grinds and forges cable. Double or triple hardened and triple drawn; hand-rubbed finish. Prefers natural handle materials. Prices: $200 to $400; some to $600. Remarks: Spare-time maker; first knife sold in 1997. Mark: First initial and last name.

MONTEIRO, VICTOR
31 Rue D'Opprebais, Maleves Ste Marie, BELGIUM 1360, Phone: 010 88 0441, victor.monteiro@skynet.be
Specialties: Working and fancy straight knives, folders and integrals of his design. Patterns: Fighters, hunters and kitchen knives. Technical: Grinds ATS-34, 440C, D2, Damasteel and other commercial Damascus, embellishment, filework and domed pins. Prices: $300 to $1000, some higher. Remarks: Part-time maker; first knife sold in 1989. Mark: Logo with initials connected.

MONTELL, TY
PO BOX 1312, Thatcher, AZ 85552, Phone: 575-538-1610, Fax: Cell: 575-313-4373, montellfamily@aol.com
Specialties: Automatics, slip-joint folders, hunting and miniatures. Technical: Stock removal. Steel of choice is CPM-154, Devin Thomas Damascus. Prices: $250 and up. Remarks: First knife made in 1980. Mark: Tang stamp - Montell.

MONTENEGRO, FACUNDO
777 Jorge L. Borges St., Merlo (5881) San Luis, ARGENTINA, Phone: 005492664759472, faca32@yahoo.com.ar; Web: www.montenegroknives.com.ar
Specialties: Bowies, hunters, gaucho knives and integrals. Technical: Forges own damascus and O1, specializing in Turkish and mosaic damascus on gaucho knives and hunting swords. Prices: $400 and up, with most pieces around $850 to $2,000. Remarks: First ABS journeyman smith from Argentina, and considered one of the best knifemakers of Argentina. Mark: Montenegro JS.

MONTGOMERY, STEPHEN R.
4621 Crescent Rd., Madison, WI 53711, Phone: 608-658-2623, smontgomery2211@gmail.com
Specialties: Working hunters, bowies and Scottish knives. Patterns: Small hunters of the maker's design. Technical: Forges and grinds 1095, CVR 80 and 154CM steels. Prices: $65 to $300. Remarks: Uses what he makes, as he is a hunter, archer and armored combat fighter. Mark: sm.

MOONEY, MIKE
19432 E. Cloud Rd., Queen Creek, AZ 85142, Phone: 480-244-7768, mike@moonblades.com; Web: www.moonblades.com
Specialties: Hand-crafted high-performing straight knives of his or customer's design. Patterns: Bowies, fighters, hunting, camp and kitchen users or collectible. Technical: Flat-grind, hand-rubbed finish. S30V, CPM 154, Damascus, any steel. Prices: $300 to $3000. Remarks: Doing business as moonblades.com. Commissions are welcome. Mark: M. Mooney followed by crescent moon.

MOORE, DAVY
Moyriesk, Quin, Co Clare, IRELAND, Phone: 353 (0)65 6825975, davy@mooreireland.com; Web: http://www.mooreireland.com
Specialties: Traditional and Celtic outdoor hunting and utility knives. Patterns: Traditional hunters and skinners, Celtic pattern hunting knives, Bushcrafting, fishing, utility/camp knives. Technical: Stock removal knives 01, D2, RWL 34, ATS 34, CPM 154, Damasteel (various). Prices: 250-1700 Euros. Remarks: Full-time maker, first knife sold in 2004. Mark: Three stars over rampant lion / MOORE over Ireland.

MOORE, JAMES B
1707 N Gillis, Ft. Stockton, TX 79735, Phone: 915-336-2113
Specialties: Classic working straight knives and folders of his design. Patterns: Hunters, Bowies, daggers, fighters, boots, utility/camp knives, locking folders and slip-joint folders. Technical: Grinds 440C, ATS-34, D2, L6, CPM and commercial Damascus. Prices: $85 to $700; exceptional knives to $1500. Remarks: Full-time maker; first knife sold in 1972. Mark: Name, city and state.

MOORE, JON P
304 South N Rd, Aurora, NE 68818, Phone: 402-849-2616, Web: www.sharpdecisionknives.com
Specialties: Working and fancy straight knives using antler, exotic bone, wood and Micarta. Will use customers' antlers on request. Patterns: Hunters, skinners, camp and bowies. Technical: Hand-forged high carbon steel. Makes his own damascus. Prices: Start at $125. Remarks: Full-time maker, sold first knife in 2003. Does on-location knife forging demonstrations. Mark: Sword through anvil with name.

MOORE, MARVE
HC 89 Box 393, Willow, AK 99688, Phone: 907-232-0478, marvemoore@aol.com
Specialties: Fixed blades forged and stock removal. Patterns: Hunter, skinners, fighter, short swords. Technical: 100 percent of his work is done by hand. Prices: $100 to $500. Remarks: Also makes his own sheaths. Mark: -MM-.

MOORE, MICHAEL ROBERT
70 Beauliew St, Lowell, MA 01850, Phone: 978-479-0589, Fax: 978-441-1819

MOORE, TED
340 E Willow St, Elizabethtown, PA 17022, Phone: 717-367-3939, tedmoore@tedmooreknives.com; Web: www.tedmooreknives.com
Specialties: Damascus folders, cigar cutters, high art. Patterns: Slip joints, linerlock, cigar cutters. Technical: Grinds Damascus and stainless steels. Prices: $250 and up. Remarks: Part-time maker; first knife sold 1993. Mark: Moore U.S.A.

MORALES, RAMON
LP-114, Managua, NICARAGUA, Phone: 011-505-824-8950, nicaraguabladesmith@gmail.com
Specialties: Forges knives and enjoys making brut de forge pieces. Patterns: Choppers, bowies and hunters. Technical: Does all his own blade heat treating in house and makes his own damascus. Remarks: Only ABS journeyman smith in Central America. Mark: Initials "RM" inside the outline of Nicaragua.

MORETT, DONALD
116 Woodcrest Dr, Lancaster, PA 17602-1300, Phone: 717-746-4888

MORGAN, JEFF
9200 Arnaz Way, Santee, CA 92071, Phone: 619-448-8430
Specialties: Early American style knives. Patterns: Hunters, bowies, etc. Technical: Carbon steel and carbon steel damascus. Prices: $60 to $400

MORGAN, TOM
14689 Ellett Rd, Beloit, OH 44609, Phone: 330-537-2023
Specialties: Working straight knives and period pieces. Patterns: Hunters, boots and presentation tomahawks. Technical: Grinds O1, 440C and 154CM. Prices: Knives, $65 to $200; tomahawks, $100 to $325. Remarks: Full-time maker; first knife sold in 1977. Mark: Last name and type of steel used.

MORO, CORRADO
Via Omegna, 22 - Rivoli 10098, Torino, ITALY, Phone: +39 3472451255, info@moroknives.com; Web: www.moroknives.com
Specialties: High-end folders of his own design and to customer specs, unique locking and pivoting systems. Patterns: Inspired by nature and technology. Technical: Uses ATS 34, 916 and 904L blade steels, and titanium, carbon-lip inlays, precious metals and diamonds. Prices: $3,500 to $11,000 and above. Remarks: Full-time maker; first knife sold in 2011. Mark: MORO on blade.

MORRIS, C H
1590 Old Salem Rd, Frisco City, AL 36445, Phone: 334-575-7425
Specialties: LinerLock® folders. **Patterns:** Interframe liner locks. **Technical:** Grinds 440C and ATS-34. **Prices:** Start at $350. **Remarks:** Full-time maker; first knife sold in 1973. Doing business as Custom Knives. **Mark:** First and middle initials, last name.

MORRIS, ERIC
306 Ewart Ave, Beckley, WV 25801, Phone: 304-255-3951

MORRIS, MICHAEL S.
609 S. Main St., Yale, MI 48097, Phone: 810-887-7817, michaelmorrisknives@gmail.com
Specialties: Hunting and Tactical fixed blade knives of his design made from files. **Technical:** All knives hollow ground on 16" wheel. Hand stitches his own sheaths also. **Prices:** From $60 to $350 with most in the $90 to $125 range. **Remarks:** Machinist since 1980, made his first knife in 1984, sold his first knife in 2004. Now full-time maker. **Mark:** Last name with date of manufacture.

MOSES, STEVEN
1610 W Hemlock Way, Santa Ana, CA 92704

MOSIER, DAVID
1725 Millburn Ave., Independence, MO 64056, Phone: 816-796-3479, dmknives@aol.com Web: www.dmknives.com
Specialties: Tactical folders and fixed blades. **Patterns:** Fighters and concealment blades. **Technical:** Uses S35VN, CPM 154, S30V, 154CM, ATS-34, 440C, A2, D2, Stainless damascus, and Damasteel. Fixed blades come with Kydex sheaths made by maker. **Prices:** $150 to $1000. **Remarks:** Full-time maker, business name is DM Knives. **Mark:** David Mosier Knives encircling sun.

MOULTON, DUSTY
135 Hillview Lane, Loudon, TN 37774, Phone: 865-408-9779, Web: www.moultonknives.com
Specialties: Fancy and working straight knives. **Patterns:** Hunters, fighters, fantasy and miniatures. **Technical:** Grinds ATS-34 and Damascus. **Prices:** $300 to $2000. **Remarks:** Full-time maker; first knife sold in 1991. Now doing engraving on own knives as well as other makers. **Mark:** Last name.

MOYER, RUSS
1266 RD 425 So, Havre, MT 59501, Phone: 406-395-4423
Specialties: Working knives to customer specs. **Patterns:** Hunters, Bowies and survival knives. **Technical:** Forges W2 & 5160. **Prices:** $150 to $350. **Remarks:** Part-time maker; first knife sold in 1976. **Mark:** Initials in logo.

MULKEY, GARY
533 Breckenridge Rd, Branson, MO 65616, Phone: 417-335-0123, gary@mulkeyknives.com; Web: www.mulkeyknives.com
Specialties: Sole authorship damascus and high-carbon steel hunters, bowies and fighters. **Patterns:** Fixed blades (hunters, bowies, and fighters). **Prices:** $450 and up. **Remarks:** Full-time maker since 1997. **Mark:** MUL above skeleton key.

MULLER, JODY
3359 S. 225th Rd., Goodson, MO 65663, Phone: 417-752-3260, mullerforge2@hotmail.com; Web: www.mullerforge.com
Specialties: Hand engraving, carving and inlays, fancy folders and oriental styles. **Patterns:** One-of-a-kind fixed blades and folders in all styles. **Technical:** Forges own Damascus and high carbon steel. **Prices:** $300 and up. **Remarks:** Full-time knifemaker, does hand engraving, carving and inlay. All work done by maker. **Mark:** Muller

MUNJAS, BOB
600 Beebe Rd., Waterford, OH 45786, Phone: 740-336-5538, Web: hairofthebear.com
Specialties: Damascus and carbon steel sheath knives. **Patterns:** Hunters and neck knives. **Technical:** My own Damascus, 5160, 1095, 1984, L6, and W2. Forge and stock removal. Does own heat treating and makes own sheaths **Prices:** $100 to $500. **Remarks:** Part-time maker. **Mark:** Moon Munjas.

MURA, DENIS
Via Pesciule 15 56021, Cascina (Pi), ITALY, Phone: +39 3388365277, zeb1d@libero.it; Web: www.denismura.com
Specialties: Straight knives. **Patterns:** Hunters, bowies, camp knives and everyday carry (EDC) knives. **Technical:** Grinds A2, D2, W2; 440C, RWL 34; CPM 154, Sleipner, Niolox, 1095, 1084, 1070, C145SC, Becut, damascus and san mai steels. **Prices:** Start at $250. **Remarks:** Part-time maker; first knife made in 2006. **Mark:** MD.

MURSKI, RAY
12129 Captiva Ct, Reston, VA 22091-1204, Phone: 703-264-1102, rmurski@gmail.com
Specialties: Fancy working/using folders of his design. **Patterns:** Hunters, slip-joint folders and utility/camp knives. **Technical:** Grinds CPM-3V **Prices:** $125 to $500. **Remarks:** Spare-time maker; first knife sold in 1996. **Mark:** Engraved name with serial number under name.

MUTZ, JEFF
8210 Rancheria Dr. Unit 7, Rancho Cucamonga, CA 91730, Phone: 909-559-7129, jmutzknives@hotmail.com; Web: www.jmutzknives.com
Specialties: Traditional working/using fixed blade and slip-jointed knives of own design and customer specs. **Patterns:** Hunters, skinners, and folders. **Technical:** Forges and grinds all steels Offers scrimshaw. **Prices:** $225 to $800. **Remarks:** Full-time maker, first knife sold in 1998. **Mark:** First initial, last name over "maker."

MYERS, PAUL
644 Maurice St, Wood River, IL 62095, Phone: 618-258-1707
Specialties: Fancy working straight knives and folders. **Patterns:** Full range of folders, straight hunters and Bowies; tie tacks; knife and fork sets. **Technical:** Grinds D2, 440C, ATS-34 and 154CM. **Prices:** $100 to $350; some $3000. **Remarks:** Full-time maker; first knife sold in 1974. **Mark:** Initials with setting sun on front; name and number on back.

MYERS, STEVE
1045 Marshall St., Carlinville, IL 62626-1048, Phone: 217-416-0800, myersknives@ymail.com
Specialties: Working straight knives and integrals. **Patterns:** Camp knives, hunters, skinners, Bowies, and boot knives. **Technical:** Forges own Damascus and high carbon steels. **Prices:** $250 to $1,000. **Remarks:** Full-time maker, first knife sold in 1985. **Mark:** Last name in logo.

N

NADEAU, BRIAN
SHARPBYDESIGN LLC, 8 Sand Hill Rd., Stanhope, NJ 07874, Phone: 862-258-0792, nadeau@sharpbydesign.com; Web: www.sharpbydesign.com
Specialties: High-quality tactical fixed blades and folders, collector and working blades. All blades and sheaths of maker's own design. Designs, writes programs and machines all components on CNC equipment, nothing water jet, everything hand finished. **Technical:** Works with new CPM steels, but loves to get an order for a W2 blade with a nice hamon or temper line. **Prices:** $100 and up. **Remarks:** Part-time maker. **Mark:** Name in script, or initials "BN" skewed on top of one another.

NARASADA, MAMORU
9115-8 Nakaminowa, Minowa-machi, Kamiina-gun, NAGANO, JAPAN 399-4601, Phone: 81-265-79-3960, Fax: 81-265-79-3960
Specialties: Utility working straight knife. **Patterns:** Hunting, fishing, and camping knife. **Technical:** Grind and forges / ATS34, VG10, 440C, CRM07.**Prices:** $150 to $500, some higher. **Remarks:** First knife sold in 2003. **Mark:** M.NARASADA with initial logo.

NATEN, GREG
1804 Shamrock Way, Bakersfield, CA 93304-3921
Specialties: Fancy and working/using folders of his design. **Patterns:** Fighters, hunters and locking folders. **Technical:** Grinds 440C, ATS-34 and CPM440V. Heat-treats; prefers desert ironwood, stag and mother-of-pearl. Designs and sews leather sheaths for straight knives. **Prices:** $175 to $600; some to $950. **Remarks:** Spare-time maker; first knife sold in 1992. **Mark:** Last name above battle-ax, handmade.

NAUDE, LOUIS
P.O. Box 1103, Okahandja, Namibia, AFRICA 7560, Phone: +264 (0)81-38-36-285, info@louisnaude.co.za Web: www.louisnaude.co.za
Specialties: Folders, Hunters, Custom.. **Patterns:** See Website. **Technical:** Stock removal, African materials.**Prices:** See website. **Remarks:** Still the tool! **Mark:** Louis Naude Knives with family crest.

NAZZ, THEO "ROCK"
159 2nd Ave., Apt. 12, New York, NY 10003, Phone: 917-532-7291, theorocknazz@gmail.com; Web: www.theorocknazz.com
Specialties: Knives, daggers and swords with 3-D-printed cast metal components that increase the ability to grip while offering extensive customization. **Technical:** Monosteel bades are CruForgeV, 80CrV2 and W2; san mai is typically one of the aforementioned steels with a stainless, pattern-welded or wrought iron shell. Pattern-welded blades are 1080, W2, 80CrV2 and/or 15N20 for the cutting edge, and wrought iron, pure nickel, stainless and/or 15N20 for the shell/spine if applicable. Does own heat treat to form a variety of hamons (temper lines). **Prices:** $400 to $1,500, or $1,000 to $8,000 for swords. **Remarks:** Part-time maker since 2007. **Mark:** "N" fileworked on the spine, or "N" incorporated in a 3-D printed metal component.

NEALY, BUD
125 Raccoon Way, Stroudsburg, PA 18360, Phone: 570-402-1018, Fax: 570-402-1018, bnealy@ptd.net; Web: www.budnealyknifemaker.com
Specialties: Original design concealment knives with designer multi-concealment sheath system. **Patterns:** Fixed Blades and Folders **Technical:** Grinds CPM 154, XHP, and Damascus. **Prices:** $200 to $2500. **Remarks:** Full-time maker; first knife sold in 1980. **Mark:** Name, city, state or signature.

NEASE, WILLIAM
2336 Front Rd., LaSalle, ON, CANADA Canada N9J 2C4, wnease@hotmail.com Web: www.unsubtleblades.com
Specialties: Hatchets, choppers, and Japanese-influenced designs. **Technical:** Stock removal. Works A-2, D-2, S-7, O-1, powder stainless alloys, composite laminate blades with steel edges. **Prices:** $125 to $2200. **Remarks:** Part-time maker since 1994. **Mark:** Initials W.M.N. engraved in cursive on exposed tangs or on the spine of blades.

NEDVED, DAN
206 Park Dr, Kalispell, MT 59901, bushido2222@yahoo.com
Specialties: Slip joint folders, liner locks, straight knives. **Patterns:** Mostly traditional or modern blend with traditional lines. **Technical:** Grinds ATS-34, 440C, 1095 and uses other makers Damascus. **Prices:** $95 and up. Mostly in the $150 to $200 range. **Remarks:** Part-time maker, averages 2 a month. **Mark:** Dan Nedved or Nedved with serial # on opposite side.

NEELY, GREG
5419 Pine St, Bellaire, TX 77401, Phone: 713-991-2677, gtneely64@comcast.net
Specialties: Traditional patterns and his own patterns for work and/or collecting. **Patterns:** Hunters, Bowies and utility/camp knives. **Technical:** Forges own Damascus, 1084, 5160 and some tool steels. Differentially tempers. **Prices:** $225 to $5000. **Remarks:** Part-time maker; first knife sold in 1987. **Mark:** Last name or interlocked initials, MS.

NEELY, JONATHAN
JAECO KNIVES, 2401 N. Beech Ln., Greensboro, NC 27455, Phone: 336-540-4925, jaecoknives@gmail.com; Web: http://www.jaecoknives.com
Specialties: Fixed-blade hunters, EDC (everyday carry) and utility-style knives. **Technical:** Stock removal maker using 1084 steel. **Prices:** Start at $25 to $30 per inch. **Remarks:** Part-time maker and full-time stay-at-home dad who feels confident he will be making knives for the rest of his life; first knife made in 2014. **Mark:** "Jaeco" (Jon and Erin's Company) with a mountain range logo.

NEILSON, J
187 Cistern Ln., Towanda, PA 18848, Phone: 570-721-0470, Web: www.mountainhollow.net
Specialties: Working and collectable fixed blade knives. **Patterns:** Hunter/fighters, Bowies, neck knives and daggers. **Technical:** Multiple high-carbon steels as well as maker's own damascus. **Prices:** $100 to $7,500. **Remarks:** ABS Master Smith, full-time maker, judge on History Channel's "Forged In Fire" program, doing business as Neilson's Mountain Hollow. Each knife comes with a sheath. **Mark:** J. Neilson MS.

NELL, CHAD
2424 E. 2070 S, St. George, UT 84790, Phone: 435-229-6442, chad@nellknives.com; Web: www.nellknives.com
Specialties: Frame-lock folders and fixed blades. **Patterns:** Templar, ESG, Hybrid and Loveless patterns. **Technical:** Grinds CPM-154, ATS-34. **Prices:** Starting at $300. **Remarks:** Full-time maker since Sep 2011, First knife made in May 2010. **Mark:** C. Nell Utah, USA or C. Nell Kona, Hawaii.

NELSON, KEN
2712 17th St., Racine, WI 53405, Phone: 262-456-7519 or 262-664-5293, ken@ironwolfonline.com Web: www.ironwolfonline.com
Specialties: Working straight knives, period pieces. **Patterns:** Utility, hunters, dirks, daggers, throwers, hawks, axes, swords, pole arms and blade blanks as well. **Technical:** Forges 5160, 52100, W2, 10xx, L6, carbon steels and own Damascus. Does his own heat treating. **Prices:** $50 to $350, some to $3000. **Remarks:** Part-time maker. First knife sold in 1995. Doing business as Iron Wolf Forge. **Mark:** Stylized wolf paw print.

NETO JR.,, NELSON AND DE CARVALHO, HENRIQUE M.
R. Joao Margarido No 20-V, Braganca Paulista, SP, BRAZIL 12900-000, Phone: 011-7843-6889, Fax: 011-7843-6889
Specialties: Straight knives and folders. **Patterns:** Bowies, katanas, jambyias and others. **Technical:** Forges high-carbon steels. **Prices:** $70 to $3000. **Remarks:** Full-time makers; first knife sold in 1990. **Mark:** HandN.

NEVLING, MARK
BURR OAK KNIVES, 3567 N. M52, Owosso, MI 48867, Phone: 989-472-3167, burroakknives@aol.com; Web: www.burroakknives.com
Specialties: Tactical folders using stainless over high-carbon San Mai. **Patterns:** Hunters, fighters, bowies, folders and small executive knives. **Technical:** Convex grinds, forges, uses only high-carbon and damascus. **Prices:** $200 to $4,000. **Remarks:** Full-time maker, first knife sold 1988. Apprentice damascus smith to George Werth and Doug Ponzio.

NEWBERRY, ALLEN
PO BOX 301, Lowell, AR 72745, Phone: 479-530-6439, newberry@newberryknives.com Web: www.newberryknives.com
Specialties: Fixed blade knives both forged and stock removal. **Patterns:** Traditional patterns as well as newer designs inspired by historical and international blades. **Technical:** Uses 1095, W2, 5160, 154-CM, other steels by request. **Prices:** $150 to $450+. **Remarks:** Many of the knives feature hamons. **Mark:** Newberry with a capital N for forged pieces and newberry with a lower case n for stock removal pieces.

NEWCOMB, CORBIN
628 Woodland Ave, Moberly, MO 65270, Phone: 660-263-4639
Specialties: Working straight knives and folders; period pieces. **Patterns:** Hunters, axes, Bowies, folders, buckskinned blades and boots. **Technical:** Hollow-grinds D2, 440C and 154CM; prefers natural handle materials. Makes own Damascus; offers cable Damascus. **Prices:** $100 to $500. **Remarks:** Full-time maker; first knife sold in 1982. Doing business as Corbin Knives. **Mark:** First name and serial number.

NEWHALL, TOM
3602 E 42nd Stravenue, Tucson, AZ 85713, Phone: 520-721-0562, gggaz@aol.com

NEWTON, LARRY
1758 Pronghorn Ct, Jacksonville, FL 32225, Phone: 904-537-2066, lnewton1@comcast.net; Web: larrynewtonknives.com
Specialties: Traditional and slender high-grade gentlemen's automatic folders, locking liner type tactical, and working straight knives. **Patterns:** Front release locking folders, interframes, hunters, and skinners. **Technical:** Grinds Damascus, ATS-34, 440C and D2. **Prices:** Folders start at $350, straights start at $150. **Remarks:** Retired teacher. Full-time maker. First knife sold in 1989. Won Best Folder for 2008 - Blade Magazine.**Mark:** Last name.

NEWTON, RON
223 Ridge Ln, London, AR 72847, Phone: 479-293-3001, rnewton@centurylink.net
Specialties: All types of folders and fixed blades. Blackpowder gun knife combos. **Patterns:** Traditional slip joint, multi-blade patterns, antique bowie repros. **Technical:** Forges traditional and mosaid damascus. Performs engraving and gold inlay. **Prices:** $500 and up. **Remarks:** Creates hidden mechanisms in assisted opening folders. **Mark:** NEWTON M.S. in a western invitation font."

NGUYEN, MIKE
213 Fawn Ct., Pittsburgh, PA 15239, Phone: 949-812-2749, mike12_nguyen@yahoo.com; Instagram.com: mike12_nguyen

Patterns: Folders, flipper folders and fixed blades. **Technical:** Stock-removal maker using no smart-controlled machines, sole authorship, in-house heat-treating and custom one-off designs. Uses all types of stainless steels such as CPM 154, CTS-XHP, CPM S90V, as well as high-carbon and damascus. Any materials available, such as carbon fiber, Micarta, copper, zirconium and titanium. **Prices:** $850 to $1,300 and up. **Remarks:** Part-time maker working on one knife at a time. Does not have bookings, but rather holds a lotto for the next build spot at the end of his current build. **Mark:** "M" with extended horizontal lines at end, but maker never puts mark on the blade or anywhere visible.

NICHOLS, CALVIN
710 Colleton Rd., Raleigh, NC 27610, Phone: 919-523-4841, calvin.nichols@nicholsknives.com; Web: http://nicholsknives.com
Specialties: Flame-colored high carbon damascus. **Patterns:** Fixed blades or folders, bowies and daggers. **Technical:** Stock removal. **Prices:** Start at $200. **Remarks:** Full-time maker, 22 years experience, own heat treating, 2012 Best Custom and High Art winner, National and North Carolina Knifemakers Guild member. **Mark:** First, last name-city, state.

NICHOLS, CHAD
1125 Cr 185, Blue Springs, MS 38828, Phone: 662-538-5966, chadn28@hotmail.com Web: chadnicholsdamascus.com
Specialties: Gents folders and everyday tactical/utility style knives and fixed hunters. **Technical:** Makes own stainless damascus, mosaic damascus, and high carbon damascus. **Prices:** $450 - $1000. **Mark:** Name and Blue Springs.

NICHOLSON, R. KENT
16502 Garfield Ave., Monkton, MD 21111, Phone: 410-323-6925
Specialties: Large using knives. **Patterns:** Bowies and camp knives in the Moran-style. **Technical:** Forges W2, 9260, 5160; makes Damascus. **Prices:** $150 to $995. **Remarks:** Part-time maker; first knife sold in 1984. **Mark:** Name.

NIELSON, JEFF V
1060 S Jones Rd, Monroe, UT 84754, Phone: 435-527-4242, jvn1u205@hotmail.com
Specialties: Classic knives of his design and to customer specs. **Patterns:** Fighters, hunters; miniatures. **Technical:** Grinds 440C stainless and Damascus. **Prices:** $100 to $1200. **Remarks:** Part-time maker; first knife sold in 1991. **Mark:** Name, location.

NIEMUTH, TROY
3143 North Ave, Sheboygan, WI 53083, Phone: 414-452-2927
Specialties: Period pieces and working/using straight knives of his design and to customer specs. **Patterns:** Hunters and utility/camp knives. **Technical:** Grinds 440C, 1095 and A2. **Prices:** $85 to $350; some to $500. **Remarks:** Full-time maker; first knife sold in 1995. **Mark:** Etched last name.

NILSSON, JONNY WALKER
Akkavare 16, 93391 Arvidsjaur, SWEDEN, Phone: +46 702144207, 0960.13048@telia.com; Web: www.jwnknives.com
Specialties: High-end collectible Nordic hunters, engraved reindeer antler. World class freehand engravings. Matching engraved sheaths in leather, bone and Arctic wood with inlays. Combines traditional techniques and design with his own innovations. Master Bladesmith who specializes in forging mosaic Damascus. Sells unique mosaic Damascus bar stock to folder makers. **Patterns:** Own designs and traditional Sami designs. **Technical:** Mosaic Damascus of UHB 20 C 15N20 with pure nickel, hardness HRC 58-60. **Prices:** $1500 to $6000. **Remarks:** Full-time maker since 1988. Nordic Champion (5 countries) numerous times, 50 first prizes in Scandinavian shows. Yearly award in his name in Nordic Championship. Knives inspired by 10,000 year old indigenous Sami culture. **Mark:** JN on sheath, handle, custom wood box. JWN on blade.

NIRO, FRANK
1948 Gloaming Dr, Kamloops, B.C., CANADA V1S1P8, Phone: 250-372-8332, niro@telus.net
Specialties: Liner locking folding knives in his designs in what might be called standard patterns. **Technical:** Enjoys grinding mosaic Damascus with pure nickel of the make up for blades that are often double ground; as well as meteorite for bolsters which are then etched and heat colored. Uses 416 stainless for spacers with inlays of natural materials, gem stones with also file work. Liners are made from titanium are most often fully file worked and anodized. Only uses natural materials particularly mammoth ivory for scales. **Prices:** $500 to $1500 **Remarks:** Full time maker. Has been selling knives for over thirty years. **Mark:** Last name on the inside of the spacer.

NISHIUCHI, MELVIN S
6121 Forest Park Dr, Las Vegas, NV 89156, Phone: 702-501-3724, msnknives@yahoo.com
Specialties: Collectable quality using/working knives. **Patterns:** Locking liner folders, fighters, hunters and fancy personal knives. **Technical:** Grinds ATS-34 and Devin Thomas Damascus; prefers semi-precious stone and exotic natural handle materials. **Prices:** $375 to $2000. **Remarks:** Part-time maker; first knife sold in 1985. **Mark:** Circle with a line above it.

NOLEN, STEVE
3325 Teton, Longmont, CO 80504-6251, Phone: 720-334-1801, stevenolen1@msn.com; Web: www.nolenknives.org
Specialties: Working knives and hunters. **Patterns:** Wide variety of straight knives and neck knives. **Technical:** Grinds D2, ATS-34 and 440C. Offers filework and makes exotic handles. **Prices:** $75 to $1,000, some higher. **Remarks:** Part-time maker, third generation, and still has quite a few of R.D. Nolen's collection. **Mark:** NK in oval logo and NOLEN-Steve Nolen knives have hardness and steel engraved by logo.

NOLTE, BARBIE
10801 Gram B Cir., Lowell, AR 72745, Phone: 479-283-2095, barbie.b@gmail.com
Specialties: Collector-grade high art knives. **Technical:** Hollow grinds high-carbon, mosaic-damascus blades. Limited supply. **Prices:** Start at $600. All prices include handmade exotic leather sheaths. **Mark:** B Bell and B Nolte.

NOLTE, STEVE
10801 Gram B Cir., Lowell, AR 72745, Phone: 479-629-1676, snolte@alertalarmsys. com; Web: www.snolteknives.com
Specialties: Fancy hunters and skinners, a few fighters, some collector-grade, high-art knives. One-of-a-kind mosaic handle creations including exotic stone work. **Technical:** Mostly high-carbon damascus, some stainless damascus with very few straight stainless blades. Hollow grinds. **Prices:** Start at $400. All prices include handmade sheaths, mostly exotic leathers. **Mark:** S.Nolte.

NORDELL, INGEMAR
SkarpŒvagen 5, FŠrila, SWEDEN 82041, Phone: 0651-23347, ingi@ingemarnordell. se; Web: www.ingemarnordell.se
Specialties: Classic working and using straight knives. **Patterns:** Hunters, Bowies and fighters. **Technical:** Forges and grinds ATS-34, D2 and Sandvik. **Prices:** $300 to $3,000. **Remarks:** Part-time maker; first knife sold in 1985. **Mark:** Initials or name.

NOREN, DOUGLAS E
14676 Boom Rd, Springlake, MI 49456, Phone: 616-842-4247, gnoren@ icsworldmail.com
Specialties: Hand forged blades, custom built and made to order. Hand filework, carving and casting. Stag and stacked handles. Replicas of Scagel and Joseph Rogers pieces, as well as American bowies. Hand-tooled custom made sheaths. **Technical:** Master smith, 5160, 52100 and 1084 steel. **Prices:** $400 and up. **Remarks:** Sole authorship, works in all mediums, ABS Mastersmith, all knives come with a custom hand-tooled sheath. Enjoys the challenge and meeting people.

NORFLEET, ROSS W
4110 N Courthouse Rd, Providence Forge, VA 23140-3420, Phone: 804-966-2596, rossknife@aol.com
Specialties: Classic, traditional and working/using knives of his design or in standard patterns. **Patterns:** Hunters and folders. **Technical:** Hollow-grinds 440C and ATS-34. **Prices:** $150 to $550. **Remarks:** Part-time maker; first knife sold in 1992. **Mark:** Last name.

NORTON, DON
95N Wilkison Ave, Port Townsend, WA 98368-2534, Phone: 306-385-1978
Specialties: Fancy and plain straight knives. **Patterns:** Hunters, small Bowies, tantos, boot knives, fillets. **Technical:** Prefers 440C, Micarta, exotic woods and other natural handle materials. Hollow-grinds all knives except fillet knives. **Prices:** $185 to $2800; average is $200. **Remarks:** Full-time maker; first knife sold in 1980. **Mark:** Full name, Hsi Shuai, city, state.

NOWACKI, STEPHEN R.
167 King Georges Ave, Regents Park, Southampton, Hampshire, ENGLAND SO154LD, Phone: 023 81 785 630 or 079 29 737 872, forgesmith9@gmail.com; Web: www.whitetigerknives.com
Specialties: Hand-forged, bowies, daggers, tactical blades, hunters and mountain-man style folders. **Technical:** Hitachi white paper steel and stainless carbon San Mai. Heat treats and uses natural handle materials. **Prices:** $200 - $1500. **Remarks:** Full-time maker. First knife sold in 2000. Doing business as White Tiger Knives. **Mark:** Stylized W T.

NOWLAND, RICK
3677 E Bonnie Rd, Waltonville, IL 62894, Phone: 618-279-3170, ricknowland@ frontiernet.net
Specialties: Slip joint folders in traditional patterns. **Patterns:** Trapper, whittler, sowbelly, toothpick and copperhead. **Technical:** Uses ATS-34, bolsters and liners have integral construction. **Prices:** $225 to $1000. **Remarks:** Part-time maker. **Mark:** Last name.

NUCKELS, STEPHEN J
1105 Potomac Ave, Hagerstown, MD 21742, Phone: 301-739-1287, sgnucks@ myactv.net
Specialties: Traditional using/working/everyday carry knives and small neck knives. **Patterns:** Hunters, bowies, Drop and trailing point knives, frontier styles. **Technical:** Hammer forges carbon steels, stock removal. Modest silver wire inlay and file work. Sheath work. **Remarks:** Spare-time maker forging under Potomac Forge, first knife made in 2008. Member W.F. Moran Jr. Foundation, American Bladesmith Society. **Mark:** Initials.

NUNN, GREGORY
HC64 Box 2107, Castle Valley, UT 84532, Phone: 435-259-8607
Specialties: High-art working and using knives of his design; new edition knife with handle made from anatomized dinosaur bone, first ever made. **Patterns:** Flaked stone knives. **Technical:** Uses gem-quality agates, jaspers and obsidians for blades. **Prices:** $250 to $2300. **Remarks:** Full-time maker; first knife sold in 1989. **Mark:** Name, knife and edition numbers, year made.

NYLUND, ERIK
Kyrontie 31, 65320 Vaasa, FINLAND, Phone: +358456349392, erik.nylund@pp2.inet. fi; Web: http://personal.inet.fi/koti/erik.nylund/
Specialties: Art knives. **Patterns:** Art knives, hunters and leuku knives. **Technical:** Forges Silversteel and 52100, and grinds RWL-34, Damasteel and 13C26. **Prices:** Start at $250. **Remarks:** Part-time maker. **Mark:** Erik Nylund, or earlier knives marked EN.

O

OATES, LEE
PO BOX 214, Bethpage, TN 37022, Phone: 281-838-0480 or 281-838-0468, bearoates89@comcast.net; Web: www.bearclawknives.com
Specialties: Friction folders, period correct replicas, traditional, working and primitive knives of my design or to customer specs. **Patterns:** Bowies, teflon-coated fighters, daggers, hunters, fillet and kitchen cutlery. **Technical:** Heat treating service for other makers. Teaches blacksmithing/bladesmithing classes. Forges carbon, 440C, D2, and makes own Damascus, stock removal on SS and kitchen cutlery, Teflon coatings available on custom hunters/fighters, makes own sheaths. **Prices:** $150 to $2500. **Remarks:** Full-time maker and heat treater since 1996. First knive sold in 1988. **Mark:** Harmony (yin/yang) symbol with two bear tracks inside all forged blades; etched "Commanche Cutlery" on SS kitchen cutlery.

O'BRIEN, MIKE J.
3807 War Bow, San Antonio, TX 78238, Phone: 210-256-0673, obrien8700@att.net
Specialties: Quality straight knives of his design. **Patterns:** Mostly daggers (safe queens), some hunters. **Technical:** Grinds 440c, ATS-34, and CPM-154. Emphasis on clean workmanship and solid design. Likes hand-rubbed blades and fittings, exotic woods. **Prices:** $300 to $700 and up. **Remarks:** Part-time maker, made first knife in 1988. **Mark:** O'BRIEN in semi-circle.

OCHS, CHARLES F
124 Emerald Lane, Largo, FL 33771, Phone: 727-536-3827, Fax: 727-536-3827, charlesox@oxforge.com; Web: www.oxforge.com
Specialties: Working knives; period pieces. **Patterns:** Hunters, fighters, Bowies, buck skinners and folders. **Technical:** Forges 52100, 5160 and his own Damascus. **Prices:** $150 to $1800; some to $2500. **Remarks:** Full-time maker; first knife sold in 1978. **Mark:** OX Forge.

OCHS, ERIC
PO BOX 1311, Sherwood, OR 97140, Phone: 503-925-9790, Fax: 503-925-9790, eric@ochs.com Web: www.ochssherworx.com
Specialties: Tactical folders and flippers, as well as fixed blades for tactical, hunting and camping. **Patterns:** Tactical liner- and frame-lock folders with texture in various synthetic and natural materials. **Technical:** Focus on powder metals, including CPM-S30V, Elmax, CPM-154, CPM-3V and CPM-S35VN, as well as damascus steels. Flat, hollow, compound and Loveless-style grinds. **Prices:** $300 - $2,500. **Remarks:** Part-time maker; made first knife in 2008 and started selling knives in mid-2009. **Mark:** The words "Ochs Sherworx" separated by an eight point compass insignia was used through 2013. Beginning in January 2014, "Ochs Worx" separated by navigation star compass insignia.

ODOM JR., VICTOR L.
PO Box 572, North, SC 29112, Phone: 803-247-2749, cell 803-608-0829, vlodom3@ tds.net; Web: www.odomforge.com
Specialties: Forged knives and tomahawks; stock removal knives. **Patterns:** Hunters, Bowies, George Herron patterns, and folders. **Technical:** Use 1095, 5160, 52100 high carbon and alloy steels, ATS-34, and 154 CM. **Prices:** Straight knives $60 and up. Folders $250 and up. **Remarks:** Student of Mr. George Herron. SCAK.ORG. **Mark:** Steel stamp "ODOM" and etched "Odom Forge North, SC" plus year.

OELOFSE, TINUS
P.O. Box 33879, Glenstantia, Pretoria, SOUTH AFRICA 0100, Phone: +27-82-3225090, tinusoelofseknives@gmail.com
Specialties: Top-class folders, mainly LinerLocks, and practical fixed blades. **Technical:** Using damascus, mostly Damasteel, and blade billets. Mammoth ivory, mammoth tooth, mother-of-pearl, gold and black-lip-pearl handles for folders. Giraffe bone, warthog ivory, horn and African hardwoods for hunters. Deep relief engraving, mostly leaf and scroll, and daughter Mariscke's scrimshaw. Likes to work on themed knives and special projects. Hand-stitched sheaths by Kitty. **Prices:** $350 to $1,500. **Mark:** Tinus Oelofse in an oval logo with a dagger outline used for the "T."

OGDEN, BILL
OGDEN KNIVES, PO Box 52, Avis
AVIS, PA 17721, Phone: 570-974-9114
Specialties: One-of-a-kind, liner-lock folders, hunters, skinners, minis. **Technical:** Grinds ATS-34, 440-C, D2, 52100, Damascus, natural and unnatural handle materials, hand-stitched custom sheaths. **Prices:** $50 and up. **Remarks:** Part-time maker since 1992. Marks: Last name or "OK" stamp (Ogden Knives).

OGLETREE JR., BEN R
2815 Israel Rd, Livingston, TX 77351, Phone: 409-327-8315
Specialties: Working/using straight knives of his design. **Patterns:** Hunters, kitchen and utility/camp knives. **Technical:** Grinds ATS-34, W1 and 1075; heat-treats. **Prices:** $200 to $400. **Remarks:** Part-time maker; first knife sold in 1955. **Mark:** Last name, city and state in oval with a tree on either side.

O'HARE, SEAN
1831 Rte. 776, Grand Manan, NB, CANADA E5G 2H9, Phone: 506-662-8524, sean@ oharecustomknives.com; Web: www.oharecustomknives.com
Specialties: Fixed blade hunters and folders. **Patterns:** Fixed and folding knives, daily carry to collectible art. **Technical:** Stock removal, flat ground. **Prices:** $250 USD to $2,000 USD. **Remarks:** Strives to balance aesthetics, functionality and durability. **Mark:** O'Hare.

custom knifemakers

OHLEMANN, BOB

RANGERMADE KNIVES, Phone: 832-549-7218, ohlemannr@hotmail.com; Web: www.rangermadeknives.com, Facebook.com/rangermadeknives

Specialties: Texas-based maker of custom LinerLocks and fixed blades. **Technical:** Forges and stock removal working primarily in W2, CPM 154 and damascus, with other materials including zirconium, meteorite, Timascus, stag, mammoth ivory and precious metals and gems. **Prices:** Fixed blades start at $350 and folders start at $700. **Remarks:** Full-time maker who has been making knives since 2014.

OLIVE, MICHAEL E

6388 Angora Mt Rd, Leslie, AR 72645, Phone: 870-363-4668

Specialties: Fixed blades. **Patterns:** Bowies, camp knives, fighters and hunters. **Technical:** Forged blades of 1084, W2, 5160, Damascus of 1084, and1572. **Prices:** $250 and up. **Remarks:** Received J.S. stamp in 2005. **Mark:** Olive.

OLIVER, TODD D

OLIVER CUSTOM BLADES, 7430 Beckle Rd., Cheyenne, WY 82009, Phone: 812-821-5928, tdblues7@aol.com

Specialties: Damascus hunters and daggers. High-carbon as well. **Patterns:** Ladder, twist random. **Technical:** Sole author of all his blades. **Prices:** $350 and up. **Remarks:** Learned bladesmithing from Jim Batson at the ABS school and Damascus from Billy Merritt in Indiana. **Mark:** T.D. Oliver Spencer IN. Two crossed swords and a battle ax.

OLSON, DARROLD E

PO Box 1182, McMinnville, OR 97128, Phone: 541-285-1412

Specialties: Straight knives and folders of his design and to customer specs. **Patterns:** Hunters, liner locks and slip joints. **Technical:** Grinds ATS-34, 154CM and 440C. Uses anodized titanium; sheaths wet-molded. **Prices:** $125 to $550 and up. **Remarks:** Part-time maker; first knife sold in 1989. **Mark:** Name, type of steel and year.

OLSON, JOE

2008 4th Ave., #8, Great Falls, MT 59405, Phone: 406-735-4404, olsonhandmade@hotmail.com; Web: www.olsonhandmade.com

Specialties: Theme based art knives specializing in mosaic Damascus autos, folders, and straight knives, all sole authorship. **Patterns:** Mas. **Technical:** Foix. **Prices:** $300 to $5000 with most in the $3500 range. **Remarks:** Full-time maker for 15 years. **Mark:** Folders marked OLSON relief carved into back bar. Carbon steel straight knives stamped OLSON, forged hunters also stamped JS on reverse side.

OLSON, ROD

Box 373, Nanton, AB, CANADA T0L 1R0, Phone: 403-646-5838, rod.olson@hotmail.com

Patterns: Button lock folders. **Technical:** Grinds RWL 34 blade steel, titanium frames. **Prices:** Mid range. **Remarks:** Part-time maker; first knife sold in 1979. **Mark:** Last name.

OLSZEWSKI, STEPHEN

1820 Harkney Hill Rd, Coventry, RI 02816, Phone: 401-397-4774, blade5377@yahoo.com; Web: www.olszewskiknives.com

Specialties: Lock back, liner locks, automatics (art knives). **Patterns:** One-of-a-kind art knives specializing in figurals. **Technical:** Damascus steel, titanium file worked liners, fossil ivory and pearl. Double actions. **Prices:** $400 to $20,000. **Remarks:** Will custom build to your specifications. Quality work with guarantee. **Mark:** SCO inside fish symbol. Also "Olszewski."

O'MACHEARLEY, MICHAEL

129 Lawnview Dr., Wilmington, OH 45177, Phone: 937-728-2818, omachearleycustomknives@yahoo.com

Specialties: Forged and Stock removal; hunters, skinners, bowies, plain to fancy. **Technical:** ATS-34 and 5160, forges own Damascus. **Prices:** $180-$1000 and up. **Remarks:** Full-time maker, first knife made in 1999. **Mark:** Last name and shamrock.

O'MALLEY, DANIEL

4338 Evanston Ave N, Seattle, WA 98103, Phone: 206-261-1735

Specialties: Custom chef's knives. **Remarks:** Making knives since 1997.

ONION, KENNETH J

47-501 Hui Kelu St, Kaneohe, HI 96744, Phone: 808-239-1300, shopjunky@aol.com; Web: www.kenonionknives.com

Specialties: Folders featuring speed safe as well as other invention gadgets. **Patterns:** Hybrid, art, fighter, utility. **Technical:** S30V, CPM 154V, Cowry Y, SQ-2 and Damascus. **Prices:** $500 to $20,000. **Remarks:** Full-time maker; designer and inventor. First knife sold in 1991. **Mark:** Name and state.

O'QUINN, W. LEE

2654 Watson St., Elgin, SC 29045, Phone: 803-438-8322, wleeoquinn@bellsouth.net; Web: www.creativeknifeworks.com

Specialties: Hunters, utility, working, tactical and neck knives. **Technical:** Grinds ATS-34, CPM-154, 5160, D2, 1095 and damascus steels. **Prices:** Start at $100. **Remarks:** Member of South Carolina Association of Knifemakers. **Mark:** O'Quinn.

ORFORD, BEN

Nethergreen Farm, Ridgeway Cross, Malvern, Worcestershire, ENGLAND WR13 5JS, Phone: 44 01886 880410, web: www.benorford.com

Specialties: Working knives for woodcraft and the outdoorsman, made to his own designs. **Patterns:** Mostly flat Scandinavian grinds, full and partial tang. Also makes specialist woodcraft tools and hook knives. Custom leather sheaths by Lois, his wife. **Technical:** Grinds and forges 01, EN9, EN43, EN45 plus recycled steels. Heat treats. **Prices:** $25 - $650. **Remarks:** Full-time maker; first knife made in 1997. **Mark:** Celtic knot with name underneath.

ORTON, RICH

1218 Cary Ave.r., Wilmington, CA 90744, Phone: 310-549-2990, rorton2@ca.rr.com

Specialties: Straight knives only. **Patterns:** Fighters, hunters, skinners. **Technical:** Grinds ATS-34. Heat treats by Paul Bos. **Prices:** $100 to $1000. **Remarks:** Full-time maker; first knife sold in 1992. Doing business as Orton Knife Works. **Mark:** Rich Orton/Maker/Wilmington, CA./Orton Knifeworks.

OSBORNE, DONALD H

5840 N McCall, Clovis, CA 93611, Phone: 559-299-9483, Fax: 559-298-1751, oforge@sbcglobal.net

Specialties: Traditional working using straight knives and folder of his design. **Patterns:** Working straight knives, Bowies, hunters, camp knives and folders. **Technical:** Forges carbon steels and makes Damascus. Grinds ATS-34, 154CM, and 440C. **Prices:** $150 and up. **Remarks:** Part-time maker. **Mark:** Last name logo and J.S.

OTT, FRED

1257 Rancho Durango Rd, Durango, CO 81303, Phone: 970-375-9669, fredsknives@wildblue.net

Patterns: Bowies, hunters tantos and daggers. **Technical:** Forges 1086M, W2 and Damascus. **Prices:** $250 to $2,000. **Remarks:** Full-time maker. **Mark:** Last name.

OTT, TED

154 Elgin Woods Ln., Elgin, TX 78621, Phone: 512-413-2243, tedottknives@aol.com

Specialties: Fixed blades, chef knives, butcher knives, bowies, fillet and hunting knives. **Technical:** Use mainly CPM powder steel, also ATS-34 and D-2. **Prices:** $250 - $1000, depending on embellishments, including scrimshaw and engraving. **Remarks:** Part-time maker; sold first knife in 1993. Won world cutting competition title in 2010 and 2012, along with the Bladesports championship. **Mark:** Ott Knives Elgin Texas.

OUYE, KEITH

PO Box 25307, Honolulu, HI 96825, Phone: 808-395-7000, keith@keithouyeknives.com; Web: www.keithouyeknives.com

Specialties: Folders with 1/8 blades and titanium handles. **Patterns:** Tactical design with liner lock and flipper. **Technical:** Blades are stainless steel ATS 34, CPM154 and S30V. Titanium liners (.071) and scales 3/16 pivots and stop pin, titanium pocket clip. Heat treat by Paul Bos. **Prices:** $495 to $995, with engraved knives starting at $1,200. **Remarks:** Engraving done by C.J. Cal, Bruce Shaw, Lisa Tomlin and Tom Ferry. Retired, so basically a full time knifemaker. Sold first fixed blade in 2004 and first folder in 2005. **Mark:** Ouye/Hawaii with steel type on back side Other: Selected by Blade Magazine (March 2006 issue) as one of five makers to watch in 2006.

OVERALL, JASON

111 Golfside Cir., Sanford, FL 32773, Phone: 407-883-5800, Larevo@gmail.com; Web: www.larevoknives.com, Instagram: larevoknives

Specialties: High-grade tactical and dress tactical folders and fixed blades. **Technical:** Stock removal method of blade making with various stainless steels and stainless damascus, and uses titanium, zirconium, Timascus, Mokuti, Mokume and other high-performance alloys. Manmade and natural handle materials used, and offers custom-designed pocket clips. **Prices:** $650 and up, depending on materials and details. **Mark:** Combined L and K.

OVEREYNDER, T R

1800 S. Davis Dr, Arlington, TX 76013, Phone: 817-277-4812, trovereynder@gmail.com or tom@overeynderknives.com; Web: www.overeynderknives.com

Specialties: Highly finished collector-grade knives. Multi-blades. **Patterns:** Fighters, Bowies, daggers, locking folders, 70 percent collector-grade multi blade slip joints, 25 percent interframe, 5 percent fixed blade **Technical:** Grinds CPM-D2, CPM-S60V, CPM-S30V, CPM-154, CPM-M4, BG-42, CTS-XHP, PSF27, RWL-34 and vendor supplied damascus. Has been making titanium-frame folders since 1977. **Prices:** $800 to $2,500, some to $9,000. **Remarks:** Full-time maker; first knife sold in 1977. Doing business as TRO Knives. **Mark:** T.R. OVEREYNDER KNIVES, city and state.

OWEN, DAVID J.A.

30 New Forest Rd., Forest Town, Johannesburg, SOUTH AFRICA, Phone: +27-11-486-1086; cell: +27-82-990-7178, djaowen25@gmail.com

Specialties: Steak knife sets, carving sets, bird-and-trout knives, top-end hunting knives, LinerLock folders. **Patterns:** Variety of knives and techniques. **Technical:** Stock-removal method, freehand hollow and flat grinds, exotic handle materials such as African hardwoods, giraffe bone, hippo tooth and warthog tusk. **Prices:** $150 and up. **Remarks:** Full-time maker since 1993. **Mark:** Two knives back-to-back with words "Owen" and "original" acid etched above and below the knives.

OWENS, DONALD

2274 Lucille Ln, Melbourne, FL 32935, Phone: 321-254-9765

OWENS, JOHN

P.O. Box 455, Buena Vista, CO 81211, Phone: 719-207-0067

Specialties: Hunters. **Prices:** $225 to $425 some to $700. **Remarks:** Spare-time maker. **Mark:** Last name.

OWNBY, JOHN C

708 Morningside Tr., Murphy, TX 75094-4365, Phone: 972-442-7352, john@johnownby.com; Web: www.johnownby.com

Specialties: Hunters, utility/camp knives. **Patterns:** Hunters, locking folders and utility/camp knives. **Technical:** 440C, D2 and ATS-34. All blades are flat ground. Prefers natural materials for handles—exotic woods, horn and antler. **Prices:** $150 to $350; some to $500. **Remarks:** Part-time maker; first knife sold in 1993. Doing business as John C. Ownby Handmade Knives. **Mark:** Name, city, state.

OYSTER, LOWELL R
543 Grant Rd, Corinth, ME 04427, Phone: 207-884-8663
Specialties: Traditional and original designed multi-blade slip-joint folders. **Patterns:** Hunters, minis, camp and fishing knives. **Technical:** Grinds O1; heat-treats. **Prices:** $55 to $450; some to $750. **Remarks:** Full-time maker; first knife sold in 1981. **Mark:** A scallop shell.

P

PACKARD, RONNIE
301 White St., Bonham, TX 75418, Phone: 903-227-3131, packardknives@gmail.com; Web: www.packardknives.com
Specialties: Bowies, folders (lockback, slip joint, frame lock, Hobo knives) and hunters of all sizes. **Technical:** Grinds 440C, ATS-34, D2 and stainless damascus. Makes own sheaths, does heat treating and sub-zero quenching in shop. **Prices:** $160 to $2,000. **Remarks:** Part-time maker; first knife sold in 1975. **Mark:** Last name over year.

PADILLA, GARY
PO Box 5706, Bellingham, WA 98227, Phone: 360-756-7573, gkpadilla@yahoo.com
Specialties: Unique knives of all designs and uses. **Patterns:** Hunters, kitchen knives, utility/camp knives and obsidian ceremonial knives. **Technical:** Grinds 440C, ATS-34 and damascus, with limited flintknapped obsidian. **Prices:** Discounted from $50 to $200 generally. **Remarks:** Retired part-time maker; first knife sold in 1977. **Mark:** Stylized name.

PAGE, LARRY
1200 Mackey Scott Rd, Aiken, SC 29801-7620, Phone: 803-648-0001
Specialties: Working knives of his design. **Patterns:** Hunters, boots and fighters. **Technical:** Grinds ATS-34. **Prices:** Start at $85. **Remarks:** Part-time maker; first knife sold in 1983. **Mark:** Name, city and state in oval.

PAGE, REGINALD
6587 Groveland Hill Rd, Groveland, NY 14462, Phone: 716-243-1643
Specialties: High-art straight knives and one-of-a-kind folders of his design. **Patterns:** Hunters, locking folders and slip-joint folders. **Technical:** Forges O1, 5160 and his own Damascus. Prefers natural handle materials but will work with Micarta. **Remarks:** Sparetime maker; first knife sold in 1985. **Mark:** First initial, last name.

PAINTER, TONY
87 Fireweed Dr, Whitehorse, YT, CANADA Y1A 5T8, Phone: 867-633-3323, yukonjimmies@gmail.com; Web: www.tonypainterdesigns.com
Specialties: One-of-a-kind using knives, some fancy, fixed and folders. **Patterns:** No fixed patterns. **Technical:** Grinds ATS-34, D2, O1, S30V, Damascus satin finish. Prefers to use exotic woods and other natural materials. Micarta and G10 on working knives. **Prices:** Starting at $200. **Remarks:** Full-time knifemaker and carver. First knife sold in 1996. **Mark:** Two stamps used: initials TP in a circle and painter.

PALIKKO, J-T
B30 B1, Suomenlinna, 00190 Helsinki, FINLAND, Phone: +358-400-699687, jt@kp-art.fi; Web: www.art-helsinki.com
Specialties: One-of-a-kind knives and swords. **Patterns:** Own puukko models, hunters, integral & semi-integral knives, swords & other historical weapons and friction folders. **Technical:** Forges 52100 & other carbon steels, Damasteel stainless damascus & RWL-34, makes own damascus steel, makes carvings on walrus ivory and antler. **Prices:** Starting at $250. **Remarks:** Full-time maker; first knife sold in 1989. **Mark:** JT

PALM, RIK
10901 Scripps Ranch Blvd, San Diego, CA 92131, Phone: 858-530-0407, rikpalm@knifesmith.com; Web: www.knifesmith.com
Specialties: Sole authorship of one-of-a-kind unique art pieces, working/using knives and sheaths. **Patterns:** Carved nature themed knives, camp, hunters, friction folders, tomahawks, and small special pocket knives. **Technical:** Makes own Damascus, forges 5160H, 1084, 1095, W2, O1. Does his own heat treating including clay hardening. **Prices:** $80 and up. **Remarks:** American Bladesmith Society Journeyman Smith. First blade sold in 2000. **Mark:** Stamped, hand signed, etched last name signature.

PALMER, TAYLOR
TAYLOR-MADE SCENIC KNIVES INC., 1607 E. 450 S, Blanding, UT 84511, Phone: 435-678-2523, taylormadewoodeu@citlink.net
Specialties: Bronze carvings inside of blade area. **Prices:** $250 and up. **Mark:** Taylor Palmer Utah.

PANAK, PAUL S
6103 Leon Rd., Andover, OH 44003, Phone: 330-442-2724, burn@burnknives.com; Web: www.burnknives.com
Specialties: Italian-styled knives. DA OTF's, Italian style stilettos. **Patterns:** Vintage-styled Italians, fighting folders and high art gothic-styles all with various mechanisms. **Technical:** Grinds ATS-34, 154 CM, 440C and Damascus. **Prices:** $800 to $3000. **Remarks:** Full-time maker, first knife sold in 1998. **Mark:** "Burn."

PANCHENKO, SERGE
5927 El Sol Way, Citrus Heights, CA 95621, Phone: 916-588-8821, serge@sergeknives.com Web: www.sergeknives.com
Specialties: Unique art knives using natural materials, copper and carbon steel for a rustic look. **Patterns:** Art knives, tactical folders, Japanese- and relic-style knives. **Technical:** Forges carbon steel, grinds carbon and stainless steels. **Prices:** $100 to $800. **Remarks:** Part-time maker, first knife sold in 2008. **Mark:** SERGE

PARDUE, JOE
PO Box 569, Hillister, TX 77624, Phone: 409-429-7074, Fax: 409-429-5657, joepardue@hughes.net; Web: www.melpardueknives.com/Joeparadueknives/index.htm

PARDUE, MELVIN M
4461 Jerkins Rd., Repton, AL 36475, Phone: 251-248-2686, mpardue@frontiernet.net; Web: www.pardueknives.com
Specialties: Folders, collectable, combat, utility and tactical. **Patterns:** Lockback, liner lock, push button; all blade and handle patterns. **Technical:** Grinds 154CM, 440C, 12C27. Forges mokume and Damascus. Uses titanium. **Prices:** $400 to $1600. **Remarks:** Full-time maker, Guild member, ABS member, AFC member. First knife made in 1957; first knife sold professionally in 1974. **Mark:** Mel Pardue.

PARKER, CLIFF
6350 Tulip Dr, Zephyrhills, FL 33544, Phone: 813-973-1682, cooldamascus@aol.com Web: cliffparkerknives.com
Specialties: Damascus gent knives. **Patterns:** Locking liners, some straight knives. **Technical:** Mostly use 1095, 1084, 15N20, 203E and powdered steel. **Prices:** $700 to $2100. **Remarks:** Making own Damascus and specializing in mosaics; first knife sold in 1996. Full-time beginning in 2000. **Mark:** CP.

PARKER, J E
11 Domenica Cir, Clarion, PA 16214, Phone: 814-226-4837, jimparkerknives@hotmail.com Web:www.jimparkerknives.com
Specialties: Fancy/embellished, traditional and working straight knives of his design and to customer specs. Engraving and scrimshaw by the best in the business. **Patterns:** Bowies, hunters and LinerLock® folders. **Technical:** Grinds 440C, 440V, ATS-34 and nickel Damascus. Prefers mastodon, oosik, amber and malachite handle material. **Prices:** $75 to $5200. **Remarks:** Full-time maker; first knife sold in 1991. Doing business as Custom Knife. **Mark:** J E Parker and Clarion PA stamped or etched in blade.

PARKER, ROBERT NELSON
1527 E Fourth St, Royal Oak, MI 48067, Phone: 248-545-8211, rnparkerknives@gmail.com or rnparkerknives@wowway.com; Web: www.classicknifedesign.com
Specialties: Traditional working and using straight knives of his design. **Patterns:** Chutes, subhilts, hunters, and fighters. **Technical:** Grinds CPM-154, CPM-D2, BG-42 and ATS-34, no forging, hollow and flat grinds, full and hidden tangs. Hand-stitched leather sheaths. **Prices:** $400 to $2,000, some to $3,000. **Remarks:** Full-time maker; first knife sold in 1986. I do forge elements. **Mark:** Full name.

PARKINSON, MATTHEW
DRAGON'S BREATH FORGE, 10 Swiss Ln., Wolcott, CT 06716, Phone: 203-879-1786, swordmatt@yahoo.com and info@fallinghammerproductions.com; Web: www.dragonsbreathforge.com
Specialties: Knives, swords and axes from the 7th-19th centuries, as well as kitchen knives. **Technical:** Forges blades in a number of steels, including 1084, W1, 80CrV2, L6 and his own damascus in 1095/15N20 and 8670/1095. Specializes in the low-layer, multi-bar Viking style of pattern welding. **Prices:** Knives start at $200 and swords at $1,000. **Remarks:** First knife made in 1990, "Forged In Fire" champion, winning the first aired episode (katana making) on History Channel. **Mark:** Connected MP in a shield, and in the past used simply a connected MP. Viking-era blades are marked with the runes for M&P.

PARKS, BLANE C
15908 Crest Dr, Woodbridge, VA 22191, Phone: 703-221-4680
Specialties: Knives of his design. **Patterns:** Boots, Bowies, daggers, fighters, hunters, kitchen knives, locking and slip-joint folders, utility/camp knives, letter openers and friction folders. **Technical:** Grinds ATS-34, 440C, D2 and other carbon steels. Offers filework, silver wire inlay and wooden sheaths. **Prices:** Start at $250 to $650; some to $1000. **Remarks:** Part-time maker; first knife sold in 1993. Doing business as B.C. Parks Knives. **Mark:** First and middle initials, last name.

PARKS, JOHN
3539 Galilee Church Rd, Jefferson, GA 30549, Phone: 706-367-4916
Specialties: Traditional working and using straight knives of his design. **Patterns:** Hunters, integral bolsters, and personal knives. **Technical:** Forges 1095 and 5168. **Prices:** $275 to $600; some to $800. **Remarks:** Part-time maker; first knife sold in 1989. **Mark:** Initials.

PARLER, THOMAS O
11 Franklin St, Charleston, SC 29401, Phone: 803-723-9433

PARRISH, ROBERT
271 Allman Hill Rd, Weaverville, NC 28787, Phone: 828-645-2864
Specialties: Heavy-duty working knives of his design or to customer specs. **Patterns:** Survival and duty knives; hunters and fighters. **Technical:** Grinds 440C, D2, O1 and commercial Damascus. **Prices:** $200 to $300; some to $6000. **Remarks:** Part-time maker; first knife sold in 1970. **Mark:** Initials connected, sometimes with city and state.

PARRISH III, GORDON A
940 Lakloey Dr, North Pole, AK 99705, Phone: 907-488-0357, ga-parrish@gci.net
Specialties: Classic and high-art straight knives of his design and to customer specs; working and using knives. **Patterns:** Bowies and hunters. **Technical:** Grinds tool steel and ATS-34. Uses mostly Alaskan handle materials. **Prices:** Starting at $300. **Remarks:** Spare-time maker; first knife sold in 1980. **Mark:** Last name, FBKS. ALASKA

PARSONS, LARRY
539 S. Pleasant View Dr., Mustang, OK 73064, Phone: 405-376-9408, l.j.parsons@sbcglobal.net; parsonssaddleshop.com
Specialties: Variety of sheaths from plain leather, geometric stamped, also inlays of various types. **Prices:** Starting at $35 and up

PARSONS, PETE

5905 High Country Dr., Helena, MT 59602, Phone: 406-202-0181, Parsons14@ MT.net; Web: www.ParsonsMontanaKnives.com

Specialties: Forged utility blades in straight steel or Damascus (will grind stainless on customer request). Folding knives of my own design. **Patterns:** Hunters, fighters, Bowies, hikers, camp knives, everyday carry folders, tactical folders, gentleman's folders. Some customer designed pieces. **Technical:** Forges carbon steel, grinds carbon steel and some stainless. Forges own Damascus. **Mark:** Left side of blade PARSONS stamp or Parsons Helena, MT etch.

PARTRIDGE, JERRY D.

P.O. Box 977, DeFuniak Springs, FL 32435, Phone: 850-520-4873, jerry@ partridgeknives.com; Web: www.partridgeknives.com

Specialties: Fancy and working straight knives and straight razors of his designs. **Patterns:** Hunters, skinners, fighters, chef's knives, straight razors, neck knives, and miniatures. **Technical:** Grinds 440C, ATS-34, carbon Damascus, and stainless Damascus. **Prices:** $250 and up, depending on materials used. **Remarks:** Part-time maker, first knife sold in 2007. **Mark:** Partridge Knives logo on the blade; Partridge or Partridge Knives engraved in script.

PASSMORE, JIMMY D

316 SE Elm, Hoxie, AR 72433, Phone: 870-886-1922

PATRICK, BOB

12642 24A Ave, S. Surrey, BC, CANADA V4A 8H9, Phone: 604-538-6214, Fax: 604-888-2683, bob@knivesonnet.com; Web: www.knivesonnet.com

Specialties: Maker's designs only, No orders. **Patterns:** Bowies, hunters, daggers, throwing knives. **Technical:** D2, 5160, Damascus. **Prices:** Good value. **Remarks:** Full-time maker; first knife sold in 1987. Doing business as Crescent Knife Works. **Mark:** Logo with name and province or Crescent Knife Works.

PATRICK, CHUCK

4650 Pine Log Rd., Brasstown, NC 28902, Phone: 828-837-7627, chuckandpeggypatrick@gmail.com Web: www.chuckandpeggypatrick.com

Specialties: Period pieces. **Patterns:** Hunters, daggers, tomahawks, pre-Civil War folders. **Technical:** Forges hardware, his own cable and Damascus, available in fancy pattern and mosaic. **Prices:** $150 to $1000; some higher. **Remarks:** Full-time maker. **Mark:** Hand-engraved name or flying owl.

PATRICK, PEGGY

4650 Pine Log Rd., Brasstown, NC 28902, Phone: 828-837-7627, chuckandpeggypatrick@gmail.com Web: www.chuckandpeggypatrick.com

Specialties: Authentic period and Indian sheaths, braintan, rawhide, beads and quill work. **Technical:** Does own braintan, rawhide; uses only natural dyes for quills, old color beads.

PATRICK, WILLARD C

PO Box 5716, Helena, MT 59604, Phone: 406-458-6552, wilamar@mt.net

Specialties: Working straight knives and one-of-a-kind art knives of his design or to customer specs. **Patterns:** Hunters, Bowies, fish, patch and kitchen knives. **Technical:** Grinds ATS-34, 1095, O1, A2 and Damascus. **Prices:** $100 to $2000. **Remarks:** Full-time maker; first knife sold in 1989. Doing business as Wil-A-Mar Cutlery. **Mark:** Shield with last name and a dagger.

PATTAY, RUDY

8739 N. Zurich Way, Citrus Springs, FL 34434, Phone: 516-318-4538, dolphin51@ att.net; Web: www.pattayknives.com

Specialties: Fancy and working straight knives of his design. **Patterns:** Bowies, hunters, utility/camp knives, drop point, skinners. **Technical:** Hollow-grinds ATS-34, 440C, O1. Offers commercial Damascus, stainless steel soldered guards; fabricates guard and butt cap on lathe and milling machine. Heat-treats. Prefers synthetic handle materials. Offers hand-sewn sheaths. **Prices:** $100 to $350; some to $500. **Remarks:** Full-time maker; first knife sold in 1990. **Mark:** First initial, last name in sorcerer logo.

PATTERSON, PAT

Box 246, Barksdale, TX 78828, Phone: 830-234-3586, pat@pattersonknives.com

Specialties: Traditional fixed blades and LinerLock folders. **Patterns:** Hunters and folders. **Technical:** Grinds 440C, ATS-34, D2, O1 and Damascus. **Prices:** $250 to $1000. **Remarks:** Full-time maker. First knife sold in 1991. **Mark:** Name and city.

PATTON, DICK AND ROB

6803 View Ln., Nampa, ID 83687, Phone: 208-468-4123, grpatton@pattonknives.com; Web: www.pattonknives.com

Specialties: Custom Damascus, hand forged, fighting knives, Bowie and tactical. **Patterns:** Mini Bowie, Merlin Fighter, Mandrita Fighting Bowie. **Prices:** $100 to $2000.

PATTON, PHILLIP

PO BOX 113, Yoder, IN 46798, phillip@pattonblades.com Web: www.pattonblades.com

Specialties: Tactical fixed blades, including fighting, camp, and general utility blades. Also makes Bowies and daggers. Known for leaf and recurve blade shapes. **Technical:** Forges carbon, stainless, and high alloy tool steels. Makes own damascus using 1084/15n20 or O1/L6. Makes own carbon/stainless laminated blades. For handle materials, prefers high end woods and sythetics. Uses 416 ss and bronze for fittings. **Prices:** $175 - $1000 for knives; $750 and up for swords. **Remarks:** Full-time maker since 2005. Two-year backlog. ABS member. **Mark:** "Phillip Patton" with Phillip above Patton.

PAULO, FERNANDES R

Raposo Tavares No 213, Lencois Paulista, SP, BRAZIL 18680, Phone: 014-263-4281

Specialties: An apprentice of Jose Alberto Paschoarelli, his designs are heavily based on the later designs. **Technical:** Grinds tool steels and stainless steels. Part-time knifemaker. **Prices:** Start from $100. **Mark:** P.R.F.

PAWLOWSKI, JOHN R

19380 High Bluff Ln., Barhamsville, VA 23011, Phone: 757-870-4284 or 804-843-2223, Fax: 757-223-5935, bigjohnknives@yahoo.com; Web: www.bigjohnknives.com

Specialties: Traditional working and using straight knives and folders. **Patterns:** Hunters, Bowies, fighters and camp knives. **Technical:** Stock removal, grinds 440C, ATS-34, 154CM and buys Damascus. **Prices:** $400 and up. **Remarks:** Part-time maker, first knife sold in 1983, Knifemaker Guild Member. **Mark:** Big John, Virginia.

PAYNE, TRAVIS

T-BONE'S CUSTOM CREATIONS, 1588 CR 2655, Telephone, TX 75488, Phone: 903-640-6484, tbone7599@yahoo.com; Web: tbonescustomcreations.com

Specialties: Full-time maker of fixed blades, specializing in a unique style of castration knives, but also hunting and everyday carry (EDC's). **Technical:** Prefers 440C, PSF27, CPM 154 and Damasteel blade steels. **Prices:** $200 to $1,000. **Remarks:** Full-time maker since 1993.

PEAGLER, RUSS

PO Box 1314, Moncks Corner, SC 29461, Phone: 803-761-1008 or 843-312-7371, rpeagler1@homesc.com or rfpeagler1@gmail.com

Specialties: Traditional working straight knives of his design and to customer specs. **Patterns:** Hunters, fighters, boots. **Technical:** Hollow-grinds 440C, ATS-34 and O1; uses Damascus steel. Prefers bone handles. **Prices:** $85 to $300; some to $500. **Remarks:** Spare-time maker; first knife sold in 1983. **Mark:** Initials.

PEARCE, LOGAN

1013 Dogtown Rd, De Queen, AR 71832, Phone: 580-212-0995, night_everclear@ hotmail.com; Web: www.pearceknives.com

Specialties: Edged weapons, art knives, stright working knives. **Patterns:** Bowie, hunters, tomahawks, fantasy, utility, daggers, and slip-joint. **Technical:** Fprges 1080, L6, 5160, 440C, steel cable, and his own Damascus. **Prices:** $35 to $500. **Remarks:** Full-time maker, first knife sold in 1992. Doing business as Pearce Knives **Mark:** Name

PEASE, W D

657 Cassidy Pike, Ewing, KY 41039, Phone: 606-845-0387, Web: www.wdpeaseknives.com

Specialties: Display-quality working folders. **Patterns:** Fighters, tantos and boots; locking folders and interframes. **Technical:** Grinds ATS-34 and commercial Damascus; has own side-release lock system. **Prices:** $500 to $1000; some to $3000. **Remarks:** Full-time maker; first knife sold in 1970. **Mark:** First and middle initials, last name and state. W. D. Pease Kentucky.

PEDERSEN, OLE

23404 W. Lake Kayak Dr., Monroe, WA 98272, Phone: 425-931-5750, ole@ pedersenknives.com; www.pedersenknives.com

Specialties: Fixed blades of own design. **Patterns:** Hunters, working and utility knives. **Technical:** Stock removal, hollow grinds CPM 154 and stainless steel, 416 stainless fittings, makes own custom sheaths. Handles are mostly stabilized burl wood, some G-10. Heat treats and tempers own knives. **Prices:** $275 to $500. **Remarks:** Full-time maker; sold first knife in 2012. **Mark:** Ole Pedersen - Maker.

PEELE, BRYAN

219 Ferry St, PO Box 1363, Thompson Falls, MT 59873, Phone: 406-827-4633, banana_peele@yahoo.com

Specialties: Fancy working and using knives of his design. **Patterns:** Hunters, Bowies and fighters. **Technical:** Grinds 440C, ATS-34, D2, O1 and commercial Damascus. **Prices:** $110 to $300; some to $900. **Remarks:** Part-time maker; first knife sold in 1985. **Mark:** The Elk Rack, full name, city, state.

PELLEGRIN, MIKE

MP3 Knives, 107 White St., Troy, IL 62294-1126, Phone: 618-667-6777, Web: MP3knives.com

Specialties: Lockback folders with stone inlays, and one-of-a-kind art knives with stainless steel or damascus handles. **Technical:** Stock-removal method of blade making using 440C, Damasteel or high-carbon damascus blades. **Prices:** $800 and up. **Remarks:** Making knives since 2000. **Mark:** MP (combined) 3.

PENDRAY, ALFRED H

13950 NE 20th St, Williston, FL 32696, Phone: 352-528-6124

Specialties: Working straight knives and folders; period pieces. **Patterns:** Fighters and hunters, axes, camp knives and tomahawks. **Technical:** Forges Wootz steel; makes his own Damascus; makes traditional knives from old files and rasps. **Prices:** $125 to $1000; some to $3500. **Remarks:** Part-time maker; first knife sold in 1954. **Mark:** Last initial in horseshoe logo.

PENNINGTON, C A

163 Kainga Rd, Kainga Christchurch, NEW ZEALAND 8009, Phone: 03-3237292, capennington@xtra.co.nz

Specialties: Classic working and collectors knives. Folders a specialty. **Patterns:** Classical styling for hunters and collectors. **Technical:** Forges his own all tool steel Damascus. Grinds D2 when requested. **Prices:** $240 to $2000. **Remarks:** Full-time maker; first knife sold in 1988. Color brochure $3. **Mark:** Name, country.

PEPIOT, STEPHAN

73 Cornwall Blvd, Winnipeg, MB, CANADA R3J-1E9, Phone: 204-888-1499

Specialties: Working straight knives in standard patterns. **Patterns:** Hunters and camp knives. **Technical:** Grinds 440C and industrial hack-saw blades. **Prices:** $75 to $125. **Remarks:** Spare-time maker; first knife sold in 1982. Not currently taking orders. **Mark:** PEP.

PERRY, CHRIS
1654 W. Birch, Fresno, CA 93711, Phone: 559-246-7446, chris.perry4@comcast.net
Specialties: Traditional working/using straight knives of his design. **Patterns:** Boots, hunters and utility/camp knives. **Technical:** Grinds ATS-34, Damascus, 416ss fittings, silver and gold fittings, hand-rubbed finishes. **Prices:** Starting at $250. **Remarks:** Part-time maker, first knife sold in 1995. **Mark:** Name above city and state.

PERRY, JIM
Hope Star PO Box 648, Hope, AR 71801, jenn@comfabinc.com

PERRY, JOHN
9 South Harrell Rd, Mayflower, AR 72106, Phone: 501-470-3043, jpknives@cyberback.com
Specialties: Investment grade and working folders; Antique Bowies and slip joints. **Patterns:** Front and rear lock folders, liner locks, hunters and Bowies. **Technical:** Grinds CPM440V, D2 and making own Damascus. Offers filework. **Prices:** $375 to $1200; some to $3500. **Remarks:** Part-time maker; first knife sold in 1991. Doing business as Perry Custom Knives. **Mark:** Initials or last name in high relief set in a diamond shape.

PERRY, JOHNNY
PO Box 35, Inman, SC 29349, Phone: 864-431-6390, perr3838@bellsouth.net
Mark: High Ridge Forge.

PERSSON, CONNY
PL 588, Loos, SWEDEN 82050, Phone: +46 657 10305, Fax: +46 657 413 435, connyknives@swipnet.se; Web: www.connyknives.com
Specialties: Mosaic Damascus. **Patterns:** Mosaic Damascus. **Technical:** Straight knives and folders. **Prices:** $1000 and up. **Mark:** C. Persson.

PETEAN, FRANCISCO AND MAURICIO
R. Dr. Carlos de Carvalho Rosa 52, Birigui, SP, BRAZIL 16200-000, Phone: 0186-424786
Specialties: Classic knives to customer specs. **Patterns:** Bowies, boots, fighters, hunters and utility knives. **Technical:** Grinds D6, 440C and high-carbon steels. Prefers natural handle material. **Prices:** $70 to $500. **Remarks:** Full-time maker; first knife sold in 1985. **Mark:** Last name, hand made.

PETERS, DANIEL
5101 Flager St., El Paso, TX 79938, Phone: 360-451-9386, dan@danpeterscustomknives.com; www.danpeterscustomknives.com
Specialties: Hunters, skinners, tactical and combat knives. **Patterns:** Drop points, daggers, folders, hunters, skinners, Kukri style and fillet knives, often to customer's specs. **Technical:** CPM S35VN, CPM 3V, CPM 154 and a few other high-end specialty steels. **Prices:** $75 for bottle openers, and $150 and up on all others. **Remarks:** Part-time maker, full-time military. Member of Georgia Custom Knifemakers Guild and The Knifemakers' Guild. **Mark:** Peters USA etched or engraved with crossed knives.

PETERSEN, DAN L
10610 SW 81st, Auburn, KS 66402, Phone: 785-220-8043, dan@petersenknives.com; Web: www.petersenknives.com
Specialties: Period pieces and forged integral hilts on hunters and fighters. Vitreous enameling on guards and buttcaps. **Patterns:** Texas-style Bowies, boots and hunters in high-carbon and Damascus steel. **Technical:** Precision heat treatments. Bainite blades with mantensite cores. **Prices:** $800 to $10,000. **Remarks:** First knife sold in 1978. ABS Master Smith. **Mark:** Stylized initials.

PETERSON, CHRIS
Box 143, 2175 W Rockyford, Salina, UT 84654, Phone: 435-529-7194
Specialties: Working straight knives of his design. **Patterns:** Large fighters, boots, hunters and some display pieces. **Technical:** Forges O1 and meteor. Makes and sells his own Damascus. Engraves, scrimshaws and inlays. **Prices:** $150 to $600; some to $1500. **Remarks:** Full-time maker; first knife sold in 1986. **Mark:** A drop in a circle with a line through it.

PETERSON, LLOYD (PETE) C
64 Halbrook Rd, Clinton, AR 72031, Phone: 501-893-0000, wmblade@cyberback.com
Specialties: Miniatures and mosaic folders. **Prices:** $250 and up. **Remarks:** Lead time is 6-8 months. **Mark:** Pete.

PFANENSTIEL, DAN
1824 Lafayette Ave, Modesto, CA 95355, Phone: 209-575-5937, dpfan@sbcglobal.net
Specialties: Japanese tanto, swords. One-of-a-kind knives. **Technical:** Forges simple carbon steels, some Damascus. **Prices:** $200 to $1000. **Mark:** Circle with wave inside.

PHILIPPE, D A
3024 Stepping Stone Path, The Villages, FL 32163, Phone: 352-633-9676, dave.philippe@yahoo.com
Specialties: Traditional working straight knives. **Patterns:** Hunters, trout and bird, camp knives etc. **Technical:** Grinds ATS-34, 440C, A-2, Damascus, flat and hollow ground. Exotic woods and antler handles. Brass, nickel silver and stainless components. **Prices:** $125 to $800. **Remarks:** Full-time maker, first knife sold in 1984. **Mark:** First initial, last name.

PHILLIPS, ALISTAIR
Amaroo, ACT, AUSTRALIA 2914, alistair.phillips@knives.mutantdiscovery.com; Web: http://knives.mutantdiscovery.com
Specialties: Slipjoint folders, forged or stock removal fixed blades. **Patterns:** Single blade slipjoints, smaller neck knives, and hunters. **Technical:** Flat grnds O1, ATS-34, and forged 1055. **Prices:** $80 to $400. **Remarks:** Part-time maker, first knife made in 2005. **Mark:** Stamped signature.

PHILLIPS, DENNIS
16411 West Bennet Rd, Independence, LA 70443, Phone: 985-878-8275
Specialties: Specializes in fixed blade military combat tacticals.

PHILLIPS, DONAVON
905 Line Prairie Rd., Morton, MS 39117, Phone: 662-907-0322, bigdknives@gmail.com
Specialties: Flat ground, tapered tang working/using knives. **Patterns:** Hunters, Capers, Fillet, EDC, Field/Camp/Survival, Competition Cutters. Will work with customers on custom designs or changes to own designs. **Technical:** Stock removal maker using CPM-M4, CPM-154, and other air-hardening steels. Will use 5160 or 52100 on larger knives. G-10 or rubber standard, will use natural material if requested including armadillo. Kydex sheath is standard, outsourced leather available.†Heat treat is done by maker. **Prices:** $100 - $1000 **Remarks:** Part-time/hobbyist maker. First knife made in 2004; first sold 2007. **Mark:** Mark is etched, first and last name forming apex of triangle, city and state at the base, D in center.

PICA, DANIEL
SCREECH OWL KNIVES, 109 Olde Farm Rd., Pittsboro, NC 27312, Phone: 919-542-2335, screechowlknives@gmail.com; Web: www.screechowlknives.com
Specialties: Outdoor/sportsman's blades and tactical/EDC knives, also folders, excelling in fit and finish, and making each knife an heirloom tool to be passed down from generation to generation. **Patterns:** Wharncliffe blades, small EDC/neck knives, Bushcrafter, bird & trout knives, skinners and two sizes of fillet knives for large- and medium-sized fish. **Technical:** Stock removal maker using mainly CPM 154, O1 and CPM 3V steels, all work done by hand, in-house heat-treating and sheath work. **Prices:** $200 to $1,000-plus. **Remarks:** Full-time maker as of January 2015; first knife made in 2013. **Mark:** Side profile of an owl head looking down the blade of the knife.

PICKENS, SELBERT
2295 Roxalana Rd, Dunbar, WV 25064, Phone: 304-744-4048
Specialties: Using knives. **Patterns:** Standard sporting knives. **Technical:** Stainless steels; stock removal method. **Prices:** Moderate. **Remarks:** Part-time maker. **Mark:** Name.

PICKETT, TERRELL
66 Pickett Ln, Lumberton, MS 39455, Phone: 601-794-6125, pickettfence66@bellsouth.net
Specialties: Fix blades, camp knives, Bowies, hunters, & skinners. Forge and stock removal and some firework. **Technical:** 5160, 1095, 52100, 440C and ATS-34. **Prices:** Range from $150 to $550. **Mark:** Logo on stock removal T.W. Pickett and on forged knives Terrell Pickett's Forge.

PIENAAR, CONRAD
19A Milner Rd, Bloemfontein, Free State, SOUTH AFRICA 9300, Phone: 027 514364180, Fax: 027 514364180
Specialties: Fancy working and using straight knives and folders of his design, to customer specs and in standard patterns. **Patterns:** Hunters, locking folders, cleavers, kitchen and utility/camp knives. **Technical:** Grinds 12C27, D2 and ATS-34. Uses some Damascus. Embellishments; scrimshaws; inlays gold. Knives come with wooden box and custom-made leather sheath. **Prices:** $300 to $1000. **Remarks:** Part-time maker; first knife sold in 1981. Doing business as C.P. Knifemaker. Makes slip joint folders and liner locking folders. **Mark:** Initials and serial number.

PIERCE, HAROLD L
106 Lyndon Lane, Louisville, KY 40222, Phone: 502-429-5136
Specialties: Working straight knives, some fancy. **Patterns:** Big fighters and Bowies. **Technical:** Grinds D2, 440C, 154CM; likes sub-hilts. **Prices:** $150 to $450; some to $1200. **Remarks:** Full-time maker; first knife sold in 1982. **Mark:** Last name with knife through the last initial.

PIERCE, RANDALL
903 Wyndam, Arlington, TX 76017, Phone: 817-468-0138

PIERGALLINI, DANIEL E
4011 N. Forbes Rd, Plant City, FL 33565, Phone: 813-754-3908 or 813-967-1471, coolnifedad@wildblue.net; Web: www.piergalliniknives.com
Specialties: Traditional and fancy straight knives and folders of his design or to customer's specs. **Patterns:** Hunters, fighters, skinners, working and camp knives. **Technical:** Grinds 440C, O1, D2, ATS-34, some Damascus; forges his own mokume. Uses natural handle material. **Prices:** $450 to $800; some to $1800. **Remarks:** Full-time maker; sold first knife in 1994. **Mark:** Last name, city, state or last name in script.

PIESNER, DEAN
1786 Sawmill Rd, Conestogo, ON, CANADA N0B 1N0, Phone: 519-664-3648, dean47@rogers.com
Specialties: Classic and period pieces of his design and to customer specs. **Patterns:** Bowies, skinners, fighters and swords. **Technical:** Forges 5160, 52100, steel Damascus and nickel-steel Damascus. Makes own mokume gane with copper, brass and nickel silver. Silver wire inlays in wood. **Prices:** Start at $150. **Remarks:** Full-time maker; first knife sold in 1990. **Mark:** First initial, last name, JS.

PITMAN, DAVID
PO Drawer 2566, Williston, ND 58802, Phone: 701-572-3325

custom knifemakers

PITT, DAVID F

Anderson, CA 96007, Phone: 530-357-2393, handcannons@tds.net; Web: www.bearpawcustoms.blademakers.com

Specialties: Fixed blade, hunters and hatchets. Flat ground mirror finish. **Patterns:** Hatchets with gut hook, small gut hooks, guards, bolsters or guard less. **Technical:** Grinds A2, 440C, 154CM, ATS-34, D2. **Prices:** $150 to $1,000. **Remarks:** All work done in-house including heat treat, and all knives come with hand-stitched, wet-fromed sheaths. **Mark:** Bear paw with David F. Pitt Maker.

PLOPPERT, TOM

1407 2nd Ave. SW, Cullman, AL 35055, Phone: 256-962-4251, tomploppert3@bellsouth.net

Specialties: Highly finished single- to multiple-blade slip-joint folders in standard and traditional patterns, some lockbacks. **Technical:** Hollow grinds CPM-154, 440V, damascus and other steels upon customer request. Uses elephant ivory, mammoth ivory, bone and pearl. **Mark:** Last name stamped on main blade.

PLUNKETT, RICHARD

29 Kirk Rd, West Cornwall, CT 06796, Phone: 860-672-3419; Toll free: 888-KNIVES-8

Specialties: Traditional, fancy folders and straight knives of his design. **Patterns:** Slip-joint folders and small straight knives. **Technical:** Grinds O1 and stainless steel. Offers many different file patterns. **Prices:** $150 to $450. **Remarks:** Full-time maker; first knife sold in 1994. **Mark:** Signature and date under handle scales.

PODMAJERSKY, DIETRICH

9219 15th Ave NE, Seattle, WA 98115, Phone: 206-552-0763, podforge@gmail.com; Web: podforge.com

Specialties: Straight and folding knives that use fine engraving and materials to create technically intricate, artistic visions. **Technical:** Stainless and carbon steel blades, with titanium and precious metal fittings, including Japanese ornamental alloys. **Prices:** $500 and up.

POIRIER, RICK

1149 Sheridan Rd., McKees Mills, New Brunswick E4V 2W7, CANADA, Phone: 506-525-2818, ripknives@gmail.com; Web: www.ripcustomknives.com

Specialties: Working straight knives of his design or to customer specs, hunters, fighters, bowies, utility, camp, tantos and short swords. **Technical:** Forges own damascus and cable damascus using 1084, 15N20, O1 and mild steel. Forges/grinds mostly O1 and W2. Varied handle materials inlcude G-10, Micarta, wood, bone, horn and Japanese cord wrap. **Prices:** $200 and up. **Remarks:** Full-time maker, apprenticed under ABS master smith Wally Hayes; first knife sold in 1998. **Marks:** R P (pre. 2007), RIP (2007 on), also etches gravestone RIP.

POLK, CLIFTON

4625 Webber Creek Rd, Van Buren, AR 72956, Phone: 479-474-3828, cliffpolkknives1@aol.com; Web: www.polkknives.com

Specialties: Fancy working folders. **Patterns:** One blades spring backs in five sizes, LinerLock®, automatics, double blades spring back folder with standard drop & clip blade or bird knife with drop and vent hook or cowboy's knives with drop and hoof pick and straight knives. **Technical:** Uses D2 & ATS-34. Makes all own Damascus using 1084, 1095, O1, 15N20, 5160. Using all kinds of exotic woods. Stag, pearls, ivory, mastodon ivory and other bone and horns. **Prices:** $200 to $3000. **Remarks:** Retired fire fighter, made knives since 1974. **Mark:** Polk.

POLK, RUSTY

5900 Wildwood Dr, Van Buren, AR 72956, Phone: 870-688-3009, polkknives@yahoo.com; Web: www.facebook.com/polkknives

Specialties: Skinners, hunters, Bowies, fighters and forging working knives fancy Damascus, daggers, boot knives, survival knives, and folders. **Patterns:** Drop point, and forge to shape. **Technical:** ATS-34, 440C, Damascus, D2, 51/60, 1084, 15N20, does all his forging. **Prices:** $200 to $2000. **Mark:** R. Polk.

POLLOCK, WALLACE J

806 Russet Valley Dr., Cedar Park, TX 78613, Phone: 512-918-0528, jarlsdad@gmail.com; Web: www.pollacknives.com

Specialties: Using knives, skinner, hunter, fighting, camp knives. **Patterns:** Use his own patterns or yours. Traditional hunters, daggers, fighters, camp knives. **Technical:** Grinds ATS-34, D-2, BG-42, makes own Damascus, D-2, O-1, ATS-34, prefer D-2, handles exotic wood, horn, bone, ivory. **Remarks:** Full-time maker, sold first knife 1973. **Prices:** $250 to $2500. **Mark:** Last name, maker, city/state.

POLZIEN, DON

1912 Inler Suite-L, Lubbock, TX 79407, Phone: 806-791-0766, blindinglightknives.net

Specialties: Traditional Japanese-style blades; restores antique Japanese swords, scabbards and fittings. **Patterns:** Hunters, fighters, one-of-a-kind art knives. **Technical:** 1045-1050 carbon steels, 440C, D2, ATS-34, standard and cable Damascus. **Prices:** $150 to $2500. **Remarks:** Full-time maker. First knife sold in 1990. **Mark:** Oriental characters inside square border.

PONZIO, DOUG

10219 W State Rd 81, Beloit, WI 53511, Phone: 608-313-3223, prfgdoug@hughes.net; Web: www.ponziodamascus.com

Specialties: Mosaic Damascus, stainless Damascus. **Mark:** P.F.

POOLE, MARVIN O

PO Box 552, Commerce, GA 30529, Phone: 803-225-5970

Specialties: Traditional working/using straight knives and folders of his design and in standard patterns. **Patterns:** Bowies, fighters, hunters, locking folders, bird and trout

knives. **Technical:** Grinds 440C, D2, ATS-34. **Prices:** $50 to $150; some to $750. **Remarks:** Part-time maker; first knife sold in 1980. **Mark:** First initial, last name, year, serial number.

POTIER, TIMOTHY F

PO Box 711, Oberlin, LA 70655, Phone: 337-639-2229, tpotier@hotmail.com

Specialties: Classic working and using straight knives to customer specs; some collectible. **Patterns:** Hunters, Bowies, utility/camp knives and belt axes. **Technical:** Forges carbon steel and his own Damascus; offers filework. **Prices:** $300 to $1800; some to $4000. **Remarks:** Part-time maker; first knife sold in 1981. **Mark:** Last name, MS.

POTTER, BILLY

6323 Hyland Dr., Dublin, OH 43017, Phone: 614-589-8324, potterknives@yahoo.com; Web: www.potterknives.com

Specialties: Working straight knives; his design or to customers patterns. **Patterns:** Bowie, fighters, utilities, skinners, hunters, folding lock blade, miniatures and tomahawks. **Technical:** Grinds and forges, carbon steel, L6, O-1, 1095, 5160, 1084 and 52000. Grinds 440C stainless. Forges own Damascus. Handles: prefers exotic hardwood, curly and birdseye maples. Bone, ivory, antler, pearl and horn. Some scrimshaw. **Prices:** Start at $100 up to $800. **Remarks:** Part-time maker; first knife sold 1996. **Mark:** First and last name (maker).

POWELL, ROBERT CLARK

PO Box 321, 93 Gose Rd., Smarr, GA 31086, Phone: 478-994-5418

Specialties: Composite bar Damascus blades. **Patterns:** Art knives, hunters, combat, tomahawks. **Patterns:** Hand forges all blades. **Prices:** $300 and up. **Remarks:** ABS Journeyman Smith. **Mark:** Powell.

POWERS, WALTER R.

PO BOX 82, Lolita, TX 77971, Phone: 361-874-4230, carlyn@laward.net Web: waltscustomknives.blademakers.com

Specialties: Skinners and hunters. **Technical:** Uses mainly CPM D2, CPM 154, CPM S35VN and 52010, but will occasionally use 3V. Stock removal. **Prices:** $160 - $225. **Remarks:** Part-time maker; first knife made in 2002. **Mark:** WP

PRATER, MIKE

PRATER AND COMPANY, 81 Sanford Ln., Flintstone, GA 30725, Phone: 706-820-7300, cmprater@aol.com; Web: www.pratercustoms.com

Specialties: Customizing factory knives. **Patterns:** Buck knives, case knives, hen and rooster knives. **Technical:** Manufacture of mica pearl. **Prices:** Varied. **Remarks:** First knife sold in 1980. **Mark:** Mica pearl.

PRESSBURGER, RAMON

59 Driftway Rd, Howell, NJ 07731, Phone: 732-363-0816

Specialties: BG-42. Only knifemaker in U.S.A. that has complete line of affordable hunting knives made from BG-42. **Patterns:** All types hunting styles. **Technical:** Uses all steels; main steels are D-2 and BG-42. **Prices:** $75 to $500. **Remarks:** Full-time maker; has been making hunting knives for 30 years. Makes knives to your patterning. **Mark:** NA.

PRESTI, MATT

5280 Middleburg Rd, Union Bridge, MD 21791, Phone: 410-775-1520; Cell: 240-357-3592

Specialties: Hunters and chef's knives, fighters, bowies, and period pieces. **Technical:** Forges 5160, 52100, 1095, 1080, W2, and O1 steels as well as his own Damascus. Does own heat treating and makes sheaths. Prefers natural handle materials, particularly antler and curly maple. **Prices:** $150 and up. **Remarks:** Part-time knifemaker who made his first knife in 2001. **Mark:** MCP.

PRICE, DARRELL MORRIS

92 Union, Plymouth, Devon, ENGLAND PL1 3EZ, Phone: 0752 223546

Specialties: Traditional Japanese knives, Bowies and high-art knives. **Technical:** Nickel Damascus and mokume. **Prices:** $1000 to $4000. **Remarks:** Part-time maker; first knife sold in 1990. **Mark:** Initials and Japanese name—Kuni Shigae.

PRICE, TIMMY

PO Box 906, Blairsville, GA 30514, Phone: 706-745-5111

PRIDGEN JR., LARRY

PO Box 127, Davis, OK 73030, Phone: 229-457-6522, pridgencustomknives@gmail.com Web: www.pridgencustomknives.com

Specialties: Custom folders. **Patterns:** Bowie, fighter, skinner, trout, liner lock, and custom orders. **Technical:** I do stock removal and use carbon and stainless Damascus and stainless steel. **Prices:** $300 and up. **Remarks:** Each knife comes with a hand-crafted custom sheath and life-time guarantee. **Mark:** Distinctive logo that looks like a brand with LP and a circle around it.

PRIMOS, TERRY

932 Francis Dr, Shreveport, LA 71118, Phone: 318-686-6625, tprimos@sport.rr.com or terry@primosknives.com; Web: www.primosknives.com

Specialties: Traditional forged straight knives. **Patterns:** Hunters, Bowies, camp knives, and fighters. **Technical:** Forges primarily 1084 and 5160; also forges Damascus. **Prices:** $250 to $600. **Remarks:** Full-time maker; first knife sold in 1993. **Mark:** Last name.

PRINSLOO, THEUNS

PO Box 2263, Bethlehem, Free State, SOUTH AFRICA 9700, Phone: 27824663885, theunsmes@yahoo.com; Web: www.theunsprinsloo.co.za

Specialties: Handmade folders and fixed blads. **Technical:** Own Damascus and mokume. I try to avoid CNC work, laser cutting and machining as much as possible. **Prices:** $650 and up. **Mark:** Handwritten name with bushman rock art and mountain scene.

PRITCHARD, RON

613 Crawford Ave, Dixon, IL 61021, Phone: 815-284-6005

Specialties: Plain and fancy working knives. **Patterns:** Variety of straight knives, locking folders, interframes and miniatures. **Technical:** Grinds 440C, 154CM and commercial Damascus. **Prices:** $100 to $200; some to $1500. **Remarks:** Part-time maker; first knife sold in 1979. **Mark:** Name and city.

PROVENZANO, JOSEPH D

39043 Dutch Lane, Ponchatoula, LA 70454, Phone: 225-615-4846, gespro61@gmail.com

Specialties: Working straight knives and folders in standard patterns. **Patterns:** Hunters, Bowies, folders, camp and fishing knives. **Technical:** Grinds ATS-34, 440C, 154CM, CPM-S60V, CPM-S90V, CPM-3V and damascus. Hollow-grinds hunters. **Prices:** $125 to $300; some to $1,000. **Remarks:** Part-time maker; first knife sold in 1980. **Mark:** Joe-Pro.

PROVOST, J.C.

1634 Lakeview Dr., Laurel, MS 39440, Phone: 601-498-1143, jcprovost2@gmail.com; Web: www.jcprovost.com

Specialties: Classic working straight knives and folders. **Patterns:** Hunters, skinners, bowies, daggers, fighters, fillet knives, chef's and steak knives, folders and customs. **Technical:** Grinds 440C, CPM-154 and commercial damascus. **Prices:** $175 and up. **Remarks:** Part-time maker; first knife made in 1979. Taught by R.W. Wilson. **Mark:** Name, city and state.

PRUYN, PETER

Brothersville Custom Knives, 110 Reel La., Grants Pass, OR 97527, Phone: 631-793-9052, Fax: 541-479-1889, brothersvilleknife@gmail.com Web: brothersvilleknife.com

Specialties: Chef knives and fighters in damascus and san mai, as well as stainless steels. **Patterns:** Fixed-blade knives of all styles, some folding models. **Technical:** Damascus, high-carbon and stainless steels; does own heat treating. **Prices:** $200 to $2,000, with a discount to active and retired military personnel. **Remarks:** Full-time maker, first knife sold in 2009. **Mark:** Anvil with "Brothersville" crested above.

PUDDU, SALVATORE

Via Lago Bunnari #12, 09045 Quartu Sant 'Elena, (Cagliari) Sardinia, ITALY, Phone: 0039-070-892208, salvatore.puddu@tin.it

Specialties: Custom knives. **Remarks:** Full-time maker.

PULIS, VLADIMIR

CSA 230-95, 96701 Kremnica, SLOVAKIA, Phone: 00421 903 340076, vpulis@gmail.com; Web: www.vpulis.host.sk

Specialties: Fancy and high-art straight knives of his design. **Patterns:** Daggers and hunters. **Technical:** Forges Damascus steel. All work done by hand. **Prices:** $250 to $3000; some to $10,000. **Remarks:** Full-time maker; first knife sold in 1990. **Mark:** Initials in sixtagon.

PURSLEY, AARON

8885 Coal Mine Rd, Big Sandy, MT 59520, Phone: 406-378-3200

Specialties: Fancy working knives. **Patterns:** Locking folders, straight hunters and daggers, personal wedding knives and letter openers. **Technical:** Grinds O1 and 440C; engraves. **Prices:** $900 to $2500. **Remarks:** Full-time maker; first knife sold in 1975. **Mark:** Initials connected with year.

PURVIS, BOB AND ELLEN

2416 N Loretta Dr, Tucson, AZ 85716, Phone: 520-795-8290, repknives2@cox.net

Specialties: Hunter, skinners, Bowies, using knives, gentlemen folders and collectible knives. **Technical:** Grinds ATS-34, 440C, Damascus, Dama steel, heat-treats and cryogenically quenches. We do gold-plating, salt bluing, scrimshawing, filework and fashion handmade leather sheaths. Materials used for handles include exotic woods, mammoth ivory, mother-of-pearl, G-10 and Micarta. **Prices:** $165 to $800. **Remarks:** Knifemaker since retirement in 1984. Selling them since 1993. **Mark:** Script or print R.E. Purvis ~ Tucson, AZ or last name only.

Q

QUAKENBUSH, THOMAS C

2426 Butler Rd, Ft Wayne, IN 46808, Phone: 219-483-0749

QUARTON, BARR

PO Box 4335, McCall, ID 83638, Phone: 208-634-3641

Specialties: Plain and fancy working knives; period pieces. **Patterns:** Hunters, tantos and swords. **Technical:** Forges and grinds 154CM, ATS-34 and his own Damascus. **Prices:** $180 to $450; some to $4500. **Remarks:** Part-time maker; first knife sold in 1978. Doing business as Barr Custom Knives. **Mark:** First name with bear logo.

QUESENBERRY, MIKE

110 Evergreen Cricle, Blairsden, CA 96103, Phone: 775-233-1527, quesenberryknives@gmail.com; Web: www.quesenberryknives.com

Specialties: Hunters, daggers, bowies and integrals. **Technical:** Forges 52100 and W2. Makes own damascus. Will use stainless on customer requests. Does own heat-treating and own leather work. **Prices:** Starting at $400. **Remarks:** Part-time maker. ABS member since 2006. ABS master bladesmith. **Mark:** Last name.

R

RABUCK, JASON

W3080 Hay Lake Road, Springbrook, WI 54875, Phone: 715-766-8220, sales@rabuckhandmadeknives.com; web: www.rabuckhandmadeknives.com

Patterns: Hunters, skinners, camp knives, fighters, survival/tactical, neck knives, kitchen knives. Include whitetail antler, maple, walnut, as well as stabilized woods and micarta.

Technical: Flat grinds 1095, 5160, and 0-1 carbon steels. Blades are finished with a hand-rubbed satin blade finish. Hand stitched leather sheaths specifically fit to each knife. Boot clips, swivel sheaths, and leg ties include some of the available sheath options. **Prices:** $140 - $560. **Remarks:** Also knife restoration (handle replacement, etc.) Custom and replacement sheath work available for any knife. **Mark:** "RABUCK" over a horseshoe

RACHLIN, LESLIE S

412 Rustic Ave., Elmira, NY 14905, Phone: 607-733-6889, lrachlin@stry.rr.com

Specialties: Classic and working kitchen knives, carving sets and outdoors knives. **Technical:** Grinds 440C or cryogenically heat-treated A2. **Prices:** $65 to $1,400. **Remarks:** Spare-time maker; first knife sold in 1989. Doing business as Tinkermade Knives. **Mark:** LSR

RADER, MICHAEL

23706 7th Ave. SE, Ste. D, Bothell, WA 98021, michael@raderblade.com; Web: www.raderblade.com

Specialties: Swords, kitchen knives, integrals. **Patterns:** Non traditional designs. Inspired by various cultures. **Technical:** Damascus is made with 1084 and 15N-20, forged blades in 52100, W2 and 1084. **Prices:** $350 - $5,000 **Remarks:** ABS Journeyman Smith **Mark:** ABS Mastersmith Mark "Rader" on one side, "M.S." on other

RADOS, JERRY F

134 Willie Nell Rd., Columbia, KY 42728, Phone: 606-303-3334, jerry@radosknives.com Web: www.radosknives.com

Specialties: Deluxe period pieces. **Patterns:** Hunters, fighters, locking folders, daggers and camp knives. **Technical:** Forges and grinds his own Damascus which he sells commercially; makes pattern-welded Turkish Damascus. **Prices:** Start at $900. **Remarks:** Full-time maker; first knife sold in 1981. **Mark:** Last name.

RAFN, DAN C.

Norholmvej 46, 7400 Herning, DENMARK, contact@dcrknives.com Web: www.dcrknives.com

Specialties: One of a kind collector art knives of own design. **Patterns:** Mostly fantasy style fighters and daggers. But also swords, hunters, and folders. **Technical:** Grinds RWL-34, sleipner steel, damasteel, and hand forges Damascus. **Prices:** Start at $500. **Remarks:** Part-time maker since 2003. **Mark:** Rafn. or DCR. or logo.

RAGSDALE, JAMES D

160 Clear Creek Valley Tr., Ellijay, GA 30536, Phone: 706-636-3180, jimmarrags@etcmail.com

Specialties: Fancy and embellished working knives of his design or to customer specs. **Patterns:** Hunters, folders and fighters. **Technical:** Grinds 440C, ATS-34 and A2. Uses some Damascus **Prices:** $150 and up. **Remarks:** Full-time maker; first knife sold in 1984. **Mark:** Fish symbol with name above, town below.

RAINVILLE, RICHARD

126 Cockle Hill Rd, Salem, CT 06420, Phone: 860-859-2776, w1jo@comcast.net

Specialties: Traditional working straight knives. **Patterns:** Outdoor knives, including fishing knives. **Technical:** L6, 400C, ATS-34. **Prices:** $100 to $800. **Remarks:** Full-time maker; first knife sold in 1982. **Mark:** Name, city, state in oval logo.

RALEY, R. WAYNE

825 Poplar Acres Rd, Collierville, TN 38017, Phone: 901-853-2026

RALPH, DARREL

DDR CUSTOM KNIVES, 12034 S. Profit Row, Forney, TX 75126, Phone: 469-728-7242, ddr@darrelralph.com; Web: www.darrelralph.com

Specialties: Tactical and tactical dress folders and fixed blades. **Patterns:** Daggers, fighters and swords. **Technical:** High tech. Forges his own damascus, nickel and high-carbon. Uses mokume and damascus, mosaics and special patterns. Engraves and heat treats. Prefers pearl, ivory and abalone handle material; uses stones and jewels. **Prices:** $600 to $30,000. **Remarks:** Full-time maker; first knife sold in 1987. Doing business as Briar Knives. **Mark:** DDR.

RAMONDETTI, SERGIO

VIA MARCONI N 24, CHIUSA DI PESIO (CN), ITALY 12013, Phone: 0171 734490, Fax: 0171 734490, info@ramon-knives.com Web: www.ramon-knives.com

Specialties: Folders and straight knives of his design. **Patterns:** Utility, hunters and skinners. **Technical:** Grinds RWL-34 and Damascus. **Prices:** $500 to $2000. **Remarks:** Part-time maker; first knife sold in 1999. **Mark:** Logo (S.Ramon) with last name.

RAMOS, STEVEN

2466 Countryside Ln., West Jordan, UT 84084, Phone: 801-913-1696, srknives88@gmail.com; Web: www.stevenramosknives.com

Specialties: Mirror finishes, complex filework, tapered tangs, genuine polished gemstone handles, all original and unique blade designs. **Patterns:** Fixed, full-tang hunters/utility, fighters, modified bowies, daggers, cooking and chef's knives, personalized wedding cake knives and art pieces. **Technical:** Stock removal, predominantly using CPM 154 stainless steel, but also 440C, D2, 154CM and others. Mostly polished gemstone handles, but also Micarta, G-10 and various woods. Sheaths and custom display stands with commemorative engravings also available. **Prices:** $400 to $3,000. **Remarks:** Full-time maker. **Mark:** Signature "Steven Ramos" laser etched on blade.

RAMSEY, RICHARD A

8525 Trout Farm Rd, Neosho, MO 64850, Phone: 417-592-1494, rams@hughes.net or ramseyknives@gmail.com; Web: www.ramseyknives.com

Specialties: Drop point hunters. **Patterns:** Various Damascus. **Prices:** $125 to $1500. **Mark:** RR double R also last name-RAMSEY.

RANDALL, PATRICK
Patrick Knives, 160 Mesa Ave., Newbury Park, CA 91320, Phone: 805-390-5501, pat@patrickknives.com; Web: www.patrickknives.com
Specialties: Chef's and kitchen knives, bowies, hunters and utility folding knives. **Technical:** Preferred materials include 440C, 154CM, CPM-3V, 1084, 1095 and ATS-34. Handle materials include stabilized wood, Micarta, stag and jigged bone. **Prices:** $125 to $225. **Remarks:** Part-time maker since 2005.

RANDALL, STEVE
3438 Oak Ridge Cir., Lincolnton, NC 28092, Phone: 704-472-4957, steve@ksrblades.com; Web: www.ksrblades.com
Specialties: Mostly working straight knives and one-of-a-kind pieces, some fancy fixed blades. **Patterns:** Bowies, hunters, choppers, camp and utility knives. **Technical:** Forged high-carbon-steel blades: 5160, 52100, W2 and damascus patterns. **Prices:** $275 and up. **Remarks:** Part-time maker, first knife sold in 2009. Earned journeyman smith rating in 2012. Doing business as Knives By Steve Randall or KSR Blades. **Mark:** KS Randall on left side, JS on right side.

RANDALL JR., JAMES W
11606 Keith Hall Rd, Keithville, LA 71047, Phone: 318-925-6480, Fax: 318-925-1709, jw@jwrandall.com; Web: www.jwrandall.com
Specialties: Collectible and functional knives. **Patterns:** Bowies, hunters, daggers, swords, folders and combat knives. **Technical:** Forges 5160, 1084, O1 and his Damascus. **Prices:** $400 to $8000. **Remarks:** Part-time. First knife sold in 1998. **Mark:** JW Randall, MS.

RANDALL MADE KNIVES
4857 South Orange Blossom Trail, Orlando, FL 32839, Phone: 407-855-8075, Fax: 407-855-9054, Web: http://www.randallknives.com
Specialties: Working straight knives. **Patterns:** Hunters, fighters and Bowies. **Technical:** Forges and grinds O1 and 440B. **Prices:** $170 to $550; some to $450. **Remarks:** Full-time maker; first knife sold in 1937. **Mark:** Randall made, city and state in scimitar logo.

RANDOW, RALPH
7 E. Chateau Estates Dr., Greenbrier, AR 72058, Phone: 318-729-3368, randow3368@gmail.com

RANKL, CHRISTIAN
Possenhofenerstr 33, Munchen, GERMANY 81476, Phone: 0049 01 71 3 66 26 79, Fax: 0049 8975967265, Web: http://www.german-knife.com/german-knifemakers-guild.html
Specialties: Tail-lock knives. **Patterns:** Fighters, hunters and locking folders. **Technical:** Grinds ATS-34, D2, CPM1440V, RWL 34 also stainless Damascus. **Prices:** $450 to $950; some to $2000. **Remarks:** Part-time maker; first knife sold in 1989. **Mark:** Electrochemical etching on blade.

RAPP, STEVEN J
8033 US Hwy 25-70, Marshall, NC 28753, Phone: 828-649-1092
Specialties: Gold quartz; mosaic handles. **Patterns:** Daggers, Bowies, fighters and San Francisco knives. **Technical:** Hollow- and flat-grinds 440C and Damascus. **Prices:** Start at $500. **Remarks:** Full-time maker; first knife sold in 1981. **Mark:** Name and state.

RAPPAZZO, RICHARD
142 Dunsbach Ferry Rd, Cohoes, NY 12047, Phone: 518-783-6843
Specialties: Damascus locking folders and straight knives. **Patterns:** Folders, dirks, fighters and tantos in original and traditional designs. **Technical:** Hand-forges all blades; specializes in Damascus; uses only natural handle materials. **Prices:** $400 to $1500. **Remarks:** Part-time maker; first knife sold in 1985. **Mark:** Name, date, serial number.

RARDON, A D
1589 SE Price Dr, Polo, MO 64671, Phone: 660-354-2330
Specialties: Folders, miniatures. **Patterns:** Hunters, buck skinners, Bowies, miniatures and daggers. **Technical:** Grinds O1, D2, 440C and ATS-34. **Prices:** $150 to $2000; some higher. **Remarks:** Full-time maker; first knife sold in 1954. **Mark:** Fox logo.

RARDON, ARCHIE F
1589 SE Price Dr, Polo, MO 64671, Phone: 660-354-2330
Specialties: Working knives. **Patterns:** Hunters, Bowies and miniatures. **Technical:** Grinds O1, D2, 440C, ATS-34, cable and Damascus. **Prices:** $50 to $500. **Remarks:** Part-time maker. **Mark:** Boar hog.

RASSENTI, PETER
218 Tasse, St-Eustache, Quebec J7P 4C2, CANADA, Phone: 450-598-6250, guireandgimble@hotmail.com
Specialties: Tactical mono-frame folding knives.

RAY, ALAN W
1287 FM 1280 E, Lovelady, TX 75851, awray@rayzblades.com; Web: www.rayzblades.com
Specialties: Working straight knives of his design. **Patterns:** Hunters. **Technical:** Forges O1, L6 and 5160 for straight knives. **Prices:** $200 to $1000. **Remarks:** Full-time maker; first knife sold in 1979. **Mark:** Stylized initials.

RAYMOND, MICHAEL
4000 Weber Rd., Malabar, FL 32950, Phone: 321-300-5515, michael@michaelraymondknives.com; Web: www.michaelraymondknives.com
Specialties: Integral folding knives with bushings and washer pivot construction. All parts made in-house. **Technical:** Uses Bohler M390, Crucible 20CV and Uddeholm Elmax steels. **Prices:** $1,200+. **Remarks:** Full-time maker; first folder made in late 2011, graduate of machinist school and apprentice tool & die maker.

REBELLO, INDIAN GEORGE
358 Elm St, New Bedford, MA 02740-3837, Phone: 508-999-7090, indgeo@juno.com; Web: www.indiangeorgesknives.com
Specialties: One-of-a-kind fighters and Bowies. **Patterns:** To customer's specs, hunters and utilities. **Technical:** Forges his own Damascus, 5160, 52100, 1084, 1095, cable and O1. Grinds S30V, ATS-34, 154CM, 440C, D2 and A2. **Prices:** Starting at $250. **Remarks:** Full-time maker, first knife sold in 1991. Doing business as Indian George's Knives. Founding father and President of the Southern New England Knife-Makers Guild. Member of the N.C.C.A. **Mark:** Indian George's Knives.

RED, VERNON
2020 Benton Cove, Conway, AR 72034, Phone: 501-450-7284, knivesvr@conwaycorp.net
Specialties: Lock-blade folders, as well as fixed-blade knives of maker's own design or customer's. **Patterns:** Hunters, fighters, Bowies, folders. **Technical:** Hollow grind, flat grind, stock removal and forged blades. Uses 440C, D-2, A-2, ATS-34, 1084, 1095, and Damascus. **Prices:** $225 and up. **Remarks:** Made first knife in 1982, first folder in 1992. Member of (AKA) Arkansas Knives Association. **Mark:** Last name.

REDD, BILL
2647 West 133rd Circle, Broomfield, Colorado 80020, Phone: 303-469-9803, unlimited_design@msn.com
Prices: Contact maker. **Remarks:** Full-time custom maker, member of PKA and RMBC (Rocky Mountain Blade Collectors). **Mark:** Redd Knives, Bill Redd.

REDDIEX, BILL
27 Galway Ave, Palmerston North, NEW ZEALAND, Phone: 06-357-0383, Fax: 06-358-2910
Specialties: Collector-grade working straight knives. **Patterns:** Traditional-style Bowies and drop-point hunters. **Technical:** Grinds 440C, D2 and O1; offers variety of grinds and finishes. **Prices:** $130 to $750. **Remarks:** Full-time maker; first knife sold in 1980. **Mark:** Last name around kiwi bird logo.

REEVES, J.R.
5181 South State Line, Texarkana, AR 71854, Phone: 870-773-5777, jos123@netscape.com
Specialties: Working straight knives of my design or customer design if a good flow. **Patterns:** Hunters, fighters, bowies, camp, bird, and trout knives. **Technical:** Forges and grinds 5160, 1084, 15n20, L6, 52100 and some damascus. Also some stock removal 440C, O1, D2, and 154 CM steels. I offer flat or hollow grinds. Natural handle material to include Sambar stag, desert Ironwood, sheep horn, other stabilized exotic woods and ivory. Custom filework offered. **Prices:** $200 - $1500. **Remarks:** Full-time maker, first knife sold in 1985. **Mark:** JR Reeves.

REGEL, JEAN-LOUIS
les ichards, Saint Leger de Fougeret, FRANCE 58120, Phone: 0033-66-621-6185, jregel2@hotmail.com
Specialties: Bowies, camp knives, swords and folders. **Technical:** Forges own Wootz steel by hand, and damascus and high-carbon blade steels. **Remarks:** American Bladesmith Society journeyman smith. **Mark:** Jean-louis on right side of blade.

REGGIO JR., SIDNEY J
PO Box 851, Sun, LA 70463, Phone: 985-886-1397
Specialties: Miniature classic and fancy straight knives of his design or in standard patterns. **Patterns:** Fighters, hunters and utility/camp knives. **Technical:** Grinds 440C, ATS-34 and commercial Damascus. Engraves; scrimshaws; offers filework. Hollow grinds most blades. Prefers natural handle material. Offers handmade sheaths. **Prices:** $85 to $250; some to $500. **Remarks:** Part-time maker; first knife sold in 1988. Doing business as Sterling Workshop. **Mark:** Initials.

REID, JIM
6425 Cranbrook St. NE, Albuquerque, NM 87111, jhrabq7@Q.com
Specialties: Fixed-blade knives. **Patterns:** Hunting, neck, and cowboy bowies. **Technical:** A2, D2, and damascus, stock removal. **Prices:** $125 to $300. **Mark:** Jim Reid over New Mexico zia sign.

RENNER, TERRY
TR Blades, Inc., 707 13th Ave. Cir. W, Palmetto, FL 34221, Phone: 941-729-3226; 941-545-6320, terrylmusic@gmail.com Web: www.trblades.com
Specialties: High art folders and straight-blades, specialty locking mechanisms. Designer of the Neckolas knife by CRKT. Deep-relief carving. **Technical:** Prefer CPM154, S30V, 1095 carbon, damascus by Rob Thomas, Delbert Ealey, Bertie Reitveld, Todd Fischer, Joel Davis. Does own heat treating. **Remarks:** Full-time maker as of 2005. Formerly in bicylce manufacturing business, with patents for tooling and fixtures. President of the Florida Knifemaker's Association since 2009. **Mark:** TR* stylized

REPKE, MIKE
4191 N. Euclid Ave., Bay City, MI 48706, Phone: 517-684-3111
Specialties: Traditional working and using straight knives of his design or to customer specs; classic knives; display knives. **Patterns:** Hunters, Bowies, skinners, fighters boots, axes and swords. **Technical:** Grind 440C. Offer variety of handle materials. **Prices:** $99 to $1500. **Remarks:** Full-time makers. Doing business as Black Forest Blades. **Mark:** Knife logo.

REVERDY, NICOLE AND PIERRE
5 Rue de L'egalite', Romans, FRANCE 26100, Phone: 334 75 05 10 15, Web: http://www.reverdy.com
Specialties: Art knives; legend pieces. Pierre and Nicole, his wife, are creating knives of

art with combination of enamel on pure silver (Nicole) and poetic Damascus (Pierre) such as the "La dague a la licorne." **Patterns:** Daggers, folding knives Damascus and enamel, Bowies, hunters and other large patterns. **Technical:** Forges his Damascus and "poetic Damascus"; where animals such as unicorns, stags, dragons or star crystals appear, works with his own EDM machine to create any kind of pattern inside the steel with his own touch. **Prices:** $2000 and up. **Remarks:** Full-time maker since 1989; first knife sold in 1986. Nicole (wife) collaborates with enamels. **Mark:** Reverdy.

REVISHVILI, ZAZA
2102 Linden Ave, Madison, WI 53704, Phone: 608-243-7927
Specialties: Fancy/embellished and high-art straight knives and folders of his design. **Patterns:** Daggers, swords and locking folders. **Technical:** Uses Damascus; silver filigree, silver inlay in wood; enameling. **Prices:** $1000 to $9000; some to $15,000. **Remarks:** Full-time maker; first knife sold in 1987. **Mark:** Initials, city.

REXFORD, TODD
4531 W. Hwy. 24, Florissant, CO 80816, Phone: 719-492-2282, rexfordknives@gmail.com; Web: www.rexfordknives.com
Specialties: Dress tactical and tactical folders and fixed blades. **Technical:** I work in stainless steels, stainless damascus, titanium, Stellite and other high performance alloys. All machining and part engineering is done in house.

REXROAT, KIRK
12 Crow Ln., Banner, WY 82832, Phone: 307-689-5430, rexroatknives@gmail.com; Web: www.rexroatknives.com
Specialties: Using and collectible straight knives and folders of his design or to customer specs. **Patterns:** Bowies, hunters, folders. **Technical:** Forges damascus patterns, mosaic and 52100. Does own engraving. **Prices:** $400 and up. **Remarks:** Part-time maker, master smith in the ABS; first knife sold in 1984. Doing business as Rexroat Knives. Designs and builds prototypes for Al Mar Knives. **Mark:** Last name.

REYNOLDS, DAVE
1404 Indian Creek, Harrisville, WV 26362, Phone: 304-643-2889, wvreynolds@zoomintevnet.net
Specialties: Working straight knives of his design. **Patterns:** Bowies, kitchen and utility knives. **Technical:** Grinds and forges L6, 1095 and 440C. Heat-treats. **Prices:** $50 to $85; some to $175. **Remarks:** Full-time maker; first knife sold in 1980. Doing business as Terra-Gladius Knives. **Mark:** Mark on special orders only; serial number on all knives.

REYNOLDS, JOHN C
#2 Andover HC77, Gillette, WY 82716, Phone: 307-682-6076
Specialties: Working knives, some fancy. **Patterns:** Hunters, Bowies, tomahawks and buck skinners; some folders. **Technical:** Grinds D2, ATS-34, 440C and forges own Damascus and knives. Scrimshaws. **Prices:** $200 to $3000. **Remarks:** Spare-time maker; first knife sold in 1969. **Mark:** On ground blades JC Reynolds Gillette, WY, on forged blades, initials make the mark-JCR.

RHEA, LIN
413 Grant 291020, Prattsville, AR 72129, Phone: 870-942-6419, lwrhea@rheaknives.com; Web: www.rheaknives.com
Specialties: Traditional and early American styled Bowies in high carbon steel or Damascus. **Patterns:** Bowies, hunters and fighters. **Technical:** Filework wire inlay. Sole authorship of construction, Damascus and embellishment. **Prices:** $280 to $1500. **Remarks:** Serious part-time maker and rated as a Master Smith in the ABS.

RHO, NESTOR LORENZO
Primera Junta 589, Junin, Buenos Aires, ARGENTINA CP 6000, Phone: +54-236-15-4670686, info@cuchillosrho.com.ar; Web: www.cuchillosrho.com.ar
Specialties: Classic and fancy straight knives of his design. **Patterns:** Bowies, fighters and hunters. **Technical:** Grinds 420C, 440C, 1084, 5160, 52100, L6 and W1. Offers semi-precious stones on handles, acid etching on blades and blade engraving. **Prices:** $120 to $600, collector's pieces up to $3,000. **Remarks:** Full-time maker; first knife sold in 1975. **Mark:** Name.

RIBONI, CLAUDIO
Via L Da Vinci, Truccazzano (MI), ITALY, Phone: 02 95309010, Web: www.riboni-knives.com

RICARDO ROMANO, BERNARDES
Ruai Coronel Rennò 1261, Itajuba MG, BRAZIL 37500, Phone: 0055-2135-622-5896
Specialties: Hunters, fighters, Bowies. **Technical:** Grinds blades of stainless and tools steels. **Patterns:** Hunters. **Prices:** $100 to $700. **Mark:** Romano.

RICHARD, RAYMOND
31047 SE Jackson Rd., Gresham, OR 97080, Phone: 503-663-1219, rayskee13@hotmail.com; Web: www.hawknknives.com
Specialties: Hand-forged knives, tomahawks, axes, and spearheads, all one-of-a-kind. **Prices:** $200 and up, some to $3000. **Remarks:** Full-time maker since 1994. **Mark:** Name on spine of blades.

RICHARDS, CHUCK
7243 Maple Tree Lane SE, Salem, OR 97317, Phone: 503-569-5549, woodchuckforge@gmail.com; Web: www.acrichardscustomknives.com
Specialties: Fixed blade Damascus. One-of-a-kind. **Patterns:** Hunters, fighters. **Prices:** $300 to $1,500+ **Remarks:** Likes to work with customers on a truly custom knife. **Mark:** A.C. Richards J.S. or ACR J.S.

RICHARDS, RALPH (BUD)
6413 Beech St, Bauxite, AR 72011, Phone: 501-602-5367, DoubleR042@aol.com;

Web: www.ralphrichardscustomknives.com
Specialties: Forges 55160, 1084, and 15N20 for Damascus. S30V, 440C, and others. Wood, mammoth, giraffe and mother of pearl handles.

RICHARDSON, PERCY
1508 Atkinson Dr., Lufkin, TX 75901, Phone: 936-288-1690 or 936-634-1690, richardsonknives@yahoo.com; Web: americasfightingshipsknives.com or richardsonhandmadeknives.com
Specialties: Knives forged from steel off old ships. **Patterns:** Slip joints, lockbacks, hunters, bowies, mostly knives forged from steel from old Navy ships. **Prices:** $300 to $2,000. **Remarks:** Five-year project of ships knives, 2014 until 2019. **Mark:** Richardson over five-point star and Lone Star USA.

RICHARDSON III, PERCY (RICH)
1508 Atkinson Dr., Lufkin, TX 75901, Phone: 318-455-5309 or 936-634-1690, prichardson100@yahoo.com; Web: www.facebook.com/PRichKnives
Specialties: Straight knives of others' damascus, laser etching, some stabilized woods. **Patterns:** Hunters, skinners, small bowies and fighters. **Technical:** Stock removal, hollow grinds using CPM 154, ATS 34, 440C and damascus blade steels. **Prices:** $150 to $600. **Remarks:** Full-time maker, first knife made in 1995. **Mark:** Rich with year after on backbone of blade.

RICHARDSON JR., PERCY
1508 Atkinson Dr., Lufkin, TX 75901, Phone: 936-288-1690, Percy@Richardsonhandmadeknives.com; Web: www.Richardsonhandmadeknives.com
Specialties: Working straight knives and folders. **Patterns:** Hunters, skinners, bowies, fighters and folders. **Technical:** Mostly grinds CPM-154. **Prices:** $175 - $750 some bowies to $1200. **Remarks:** Full-time maker, first knife sold in 1990. Doing business as Richardsons Handmade Knives. **Mark:** Texas star with last name across it.

RICHERSON, RON
P.O. Box 51, Greenburg, KY 42743, Phone: 270-405-0491, Fax: 270-932-5601, RRicherson1@windstream.net
Specialties: Collectible and functional fixed blades, locking liners, and autos of his design. **Technical:** Grinds ATS-34, S30V, S60V, CPM-154, D2, 440, high carbon steel, and his and others' Damascus. Prefers natural materials for handles and does both stock removal and forged work, some with embellishments. **Prices:** $250 to $850, some higher. **Remarks:** Full-time maker. Member American Bladesmith Society. Made first knife in September 2006, sold first knife in December 2006. **Mark:** Name in oval with city and state. Also name in center of oval Green River Custom Knives.

RICKE, DAVE
1209 Adams St, West Bend, WI 53090, Phone: 262-334-5739
Specialties: Working knives; period pieces. **Patterns:** Hunters, boots, Bowies; locking folders and slip joints. **Technical:** Grinds ATS-34, A2, 440C and 154CM. **Prices:** $145 and up. **Remarks:** Full-time maker; first knife sold in 1976. **Mark:** Last name.

RICKS, KURT J.
Darkhammer Forge, 29 N. Center, Trenton, UT 84338, Phone: 435-563-3471, kopsh@hotmail.com; http://darkhammerworks.tripod.com
Specialties: Fixed blade working knives of all designs and to customer specs. **Patterns:** Fighters, daggers, hunters, swords, axes, and spears. **Technical:** Uses a coal fired forge. Forges high carbon, tool and spring steels. Does own heat treat on forge. Prefers natural handle materials. Leather sheaths available. **Prices:** Start at $50 plus shipping. **Remarks:** A knife should be functional first and pretty second. Part-time maker; first knife sold in 1994. **Mark:** Initials.

RIDER, DAVID M
PO Box 5946, Eugene, OR 97405-0911, Phone: 541-343-8747

RIDGE, TIM
SWAMP FOX KNIVES, 1282 W. Creston Rd., Crossville, TN 38571, Phone: 931-484-0216, swampfoxknives@frontiernet.net; www.swampfoxknives.com
Specialties: Handforged historical American knives circa 1700 to 1865, colonial through Civil War eras. **Technical:** Forges 1095, 5160, 1084 and 1075 high-carbon steels. **Prices:** $135 to $2,000, depending on style and size of knife. **Remarks:** Full-time maker for 17 years. **Mark:** Patented running fox with TR in the body.

RIDLEY, ROB
RR1, Sundre, AB, CANADA T0M 1X0, Phone: 405-556-1113, rob@rangeroriginal.com; www.rangeroriginal.com, www.knifemaker.ca
Specialties: The knives I make are mainly fixed blades, though I'm exploring the complex world of folders. **Technical:** I favour high-end stainless alloys and exotic handle materials because a knife should provide both cutting ability and bragging rights. **Remarks:** I made my first knife in 1998 and still use that blade today. I've gone from full time, to part time, to hobby maker, but I still treasure time in the shop or spent with other enthusiasts. Operates Canadian Knifemakers Supply

RIEPE, RICHARD A
17604 E 296 St, Harrisonville, MO 64701

RIETVELD, BERTIE
PO Box 53, Magaliesburg, GT, SOUTH AFRICA 1791, Phone: 2783 232 8766, bertie@rietveldknives.com; Web: www.rietveldknives.com
Specialties: Art daggers, Bolster lock folders, Persian designs, embraces elegant designs. **Patterns:** Mostly one-of-a-kind. **Technical:** Sole authorship, work only in own Damascus, gold inlay, blued stainless fittings. **Prices:** $500 - $8,000 **Remarks:** First knife made in 1979. Annual shows attended: ECCKS, Blade Show, Milan Show, South African Guild Show. **Marks:** Logo is elephant in half circle with name, enclosed in Stanhope lens

RIGNEY JR., WILLIE
191 Colson Dr, Bronston, KY 42518, Phone: 606-679-4227
Specialties: High-tech period pieces and fancy working knives. **Patterns:** Fighters, boots, daggers and push knives. **Technical:** Grinds 440C and 154CM; buys Damascus. Most knives are embellished. **Prices:** $150 to $1500; some to $10,000. **Remarks:** Full-time maker; first knife sold in 1978. **Mark:** First initial, last name.

RINKES, SIEGFRIED
Am Sportpl 2, Markterlbach, GERMANY 91459

RITCHIE, ADAM
Koi Knifeworks, 10925 Sheridan Ave. S, Bloomington, MN 55431, Phone: 651-503-2818, adamkara2@earthlink.net
Specialties: Japanese-influenced fixed blades. **Patterns:** Small utility knives to larger hunter/tactical pieces, Kwaikens, tantos and Kiridashis. **Technical:** Flat and convex grinds O1 tool steel and 1095, differentially heat treated to 58-60 Rockwell hardness. **Prices:** $150-$1,000. **Remarks:** Part-time maker, full-time firefighter/EMT/FEO. **Mark:** Koi Knifeworks in circle around Kanji or Koi.

RIZZI, RUSSELL J
37 March Rd., Ashfield, MA 01330, Phone: 413-625-2842
Specialties: Fancy working and using straight knives and folders of his design or to customer specs. **Patterns:** Hunters, locking folders and fighters. **Technical:** Grinds 440C, D2 and commercial Damascus. **Prices:** $150 to $750; some to $2500. **Remarks:** Part-time maker; first knife sold in 1990. **Mark:** Last name, Ashfield, MA.

ROBBINS, BILL
2160 E. Fry Blvd., Ste. C5, Sierra Vista, AZ 85635-2794, billrknifemaker@aol.com
Specialties: Plain and fancy working straight knives. Makes to his designs and most anything you can draw. **Patterns:** Hunting knives, utility knives, and Bowies. **Technical:** Grinds ATS-34, 440C, tool steel, high carbon, buys Damascus. **Prices:** $70 to $450. **Remarks:** Part-time maker, first knife sold in 2001. **Mark:** Last name or desert scene with name.

ROBBINS, HOWARD P
1310 E. 310th Rd., Flemington, MO 65650, Phone: 417-282-5055, ARobb1407@aol.com
Specialties: High-tech working knives with clean designs, some fancy. **Patterns:** Folders, hunters and camp knives. **Technical:** Grinds 440C. Heat-treats; likes mirror finishes. Offers leatherwork. **Prices:** $100 to $500; some to $1000. **Remarks:** Full-time maker; first knife sold in 1982. **Mark:** Name, city and state.

ROBBINS, LANDON
2370 State Hwy. U, Crane, MO 65633, Phone: 417-207-4290, lwrobbins71@gmail.com
Specialties: Fixed blades using high-carbon damascus. **Patterns:** Hunters, bowies and fighters. **Technical:** Hand-forged, flat-ground 1084, 1074, 5160, 52100 and maker's own damascus. **Prices:** $300 and up. **Remarks:** Part-time maker, ABS journeyman smith. **Mark:** Robbins with an arrow under name.

ROBERTS, CHUCK
PO Box 7174, Golden, CO 80403, Phone: 303-642-2388, chuck@crobertsart.com; Web: www.crobertsart.com
Specialties: Price daggers, large Bowies, hand-rubbed satin finish. **Patterns:** Bowies and California knives. **Technical:** Grinds 440C, 5160 and ATS-34. Handles made of stag, ivory or mother-of-pearl. **Prices:** $1250. **Remarks:** Full-time maker. Company name is C. Roberts - Art that emulates the past. **Mark:** Last initial or last name.

ROBERTS, JACK
10811 Sagebluff Dr, Houston, TX 77089, Phone: 281-481-1784, jroberts59@houston.rr.com
Specialties: Hunting knives and folders, offers scrimshaw by wife Barbara. **Patterns:** Drop point hunters and LinerLock® folders. **Technical:** Grinds 440-C, offers file work, texturing, natural handle materials and Micarta. **Prices:** $200 to $800 some higher. **Remarks:** Part-time maker, sold first knife in 1965. **Mark:** Name, city, state.

ROBERTS, T. C. (TERRY)
142131 Lake Forest Heights Rd., Siloam Springs, AR 72761, Phone: 479-373-6502, carolcroberts@cox.net
Specialties: Working straight knives and folders of the maker's original design. **Patterns:** Bowies, daggers, fighters, locking folders, slip joints to include multiblades and whittlers. **Technical:** Grinds all types of carbon and stainless steels and commercially available Damascus. Works in stone and casts in bronze and silver. Some inlays and engraving. **Prices:** $250 - $3500. **Remarks:** Full-time maker; sold first knife in 1983. **Mark:** Stamp is oval with initials inside.

ROBERTSON, LEO D
3728 Pleasant Lake Dr, Indianapolis, IN 46227, Phone: 317-882-9899, ldr52@juno.com
Specialties: Hunting and folders. **Patterns:** Hunting, fillet, Bowie, utility, folders and tantos. **Technical:** Uses ATS-34, 154CM, 440C, 1095, D2 and Damascus steels. **Prices:** Fixed knives $75 to $350, folders $350 to $600. **Remarks:** Handles made with stag, wildwoods, laminates, mother-of-pearl. Made first knife in 1990. Member of American Bladesmith Society. **Mark:** Logo with full name in oval around logo.

ROBINSON, CALVIN
5501 Twin Creek Circle, Pace, FL 32571, Phone: 850 572 1504, calvin@calvinrobinsonknives.com; Web: www.CalvinRobinsonKnives.com
Specialties: Working knives of my own design. **Patterns:** Hunters, fishing, folding and kitchen and purse knives. **Technical:** Now using 14C28N stainless blade steel, as well as 12C27, 13C26 and D2. **Prices:** $180 to $2500. **Remarks:** Full-time maker. Knifemakers' Guild Board of Directors. **Mark:** Robinson.

ROBINSON, CHUCK
SEA ROBIN FORGE, 1423 Third Ave., Picayune, MS 39466, Phone: 601-798-0060, robi5515@bellsouth.net
Specialties: Deluxe period pieces and working / using knives of his design and to customer specs. **Patterns:** Bowies, fighters, hunters, utility knives and original designs. **Technical:** Forges own damascus, 52100, O1, W2, L6, A2 and 1070 thru 1095. **Prices:** Start at $250. **Remarks:** First knife 1958. **Mark:** Fish logo, anchor and initials C.R.

ROBINSON III, REX R
10531 Poe St, Leesburg, FL 34788, Phone: 352-787-4587
Specialties: One-of-a-kind high-art automatics of his design. **Patterns:** Automatics, liner locks and lock back folders. **Technical:** Uses tool steel and stainless Damascus and mokume; flat grinds. Hand carves folders. **Prices:** $1800 to $7500. **Remarks:** First knife sold in 1988. **Mark:** First name inside oval.

ROCHFORD, MICHAEL R
PO Box 577, Dresser, WI 54009, Phone: 715-755-3520, mrrochford@centurytel.net
Specialties: Working straight knives and folders. Classic Bowies and Moran traditional. **Patterns:** Bowies, fighters, hunters: slip-joint, locking and liner locking folders. **Technical:** Grinds ATS-34, 440C, 154CM and D-2; forges W2, 5160, and his own Damascus. Offers metal and metal and leather sheaths. Filework and wire inlay. **Prices:** $150 to $1000; some to $2000. **Remarks:** Part-time maker; first knife sold in 1984. **Mark:** Name.

RODDENBERRY, CHARLES
SUWANNEE RIVER KNIFE, 160 Elm St. NE, Live Oak, FL 32064, Phone: 386-362-5641, suwanneeknife@yahoo.com; Web: Facebook.com: Suwannee River Knife & Jewelry
Patterns: Small three-finger fixed blades, friction folders and miniatures. **Technical:** Uses forging and stock removal methods of blademaking, with preferred steels currently being 1095, L6, 52100 and D2. **Prices:** $50 to $500. **Remarks:** Full-time knifemaker since 2012; first knife made in 2000 under the tutoring of Paul Martrildonno, with further training by Billy Brown. **Mark:** Simple skull face hot stamped.

RODDY, ROY "TIM"
7640 Hub-Bedford Rd., Hubbard, OH 44425, Phone: 330-770-5921, pfr2rtr@hotmail.com
Specialties: Any type of knife a customer wants, large knives, small knives and anything in between. **Patterns:** Hunters, fighters, martial arts knives, hide-outs, neck knives, throwing darts and locking-liner folders. Leather or Kydex sheaths with exotic-skin inlays. **Technical:** 440C, D2, ATS-34 or damascus blade steels. **Remarks:** Started making knives 25 years ago. **Mark:** Railroad sign (circle with an X inside and an R on either side of the X).

RODEBAUGH, JAMES L
P.O. Box 404, Carpenter, WY 82054, Phone: 307-649-2394, jlrodebaugh@gmail.com

RODEWALD, GARY
447 Grouse Ct, Hamilton, MT 59840, Phone: 406-363-2192
Specialties: Bowies of his design as inspired from historical pieces. **Patterns:** Hunters, Bowies and camp/combat. Forges 5160 1084 and his own Damascus of 1084, 15N20, field grade hunters AT-34-440C, 440V, and BG42. **Prices:** $200 to $1500. **Remarks:** Sole author on knives, sheaths done by saddle maker. **Mark:** Rodewald.

RODKEY, DAN
18336 Ozark Dr, Hudson, FL 34667, Phone: 727-863-8264
Specialties: Traditional straight knives of his design and in standard patterns. **Patterns:** Boots, fighters and hunters. **Technical:** Grinds 440C, D2 and ATS-34. **Prices:** Start at $200. **Remarks:** Full-time maker; first knife sold in 1985. Doing business as Rodkey Knives. **Mark:** Etched logo on blade.

ROEDER, DAVID
426 E. 9th Pl., Kennewick, WA 99336, d.roeder1980@yahoo.com
Specialties: Fixed blade field and exposition grade knives. **Patterns:** Favorite styles are Bowie and hunter. **Technical:** Forges primarily 5160 and 52100. Makes own Damascus. **Prices:** Start at $150. **Remarks:** Made first knife in September, 1996. **Mark:** Maker's mark is a D and R with the R resting at a 45-degree angle to the lower right of the D.

ROGERS, RAY
PO Box 126, Wauconda, WA 98859, Phone: 509-486-8069, knives @rayrogers.com; Web: www.rayrogers.com
Specialties: LinerLock® folders. Asian and European professional chef's knives. **Patterns:** Rayzor folders, chef's knives and cleavers of his own and traditional designs, drop point hunters and fillet knives. **Technical:** Stock removal S30V, 440, 1095, O1 Damascus and other steels. Does all own heat treating, clay tempering, some forging G-10, Micarta, carbon fiber on folders, stabilized burl woods on fixed blades. **Prices:** $300 to $700. **Remarks:** Knives are made one-at-a-time to the customer's order. Happy to consider customizing knife designs to suit your preferences and sometimes create entirely new knives when necessary. As a full-time knifemaker is willing to spend as much time as it takes (usually through email) discussing the options and refining details of a knife's design to insure that you get the knife you really want.

ROGERS, RICHARD
PO Box 769, Magdalena, NM 87825, Phone: 575-838-7237, r.s.rogersknives@gmail.com; Web: www.richardrogersknives.com
Specialties: Folders. **Patterns:** Modern slip joints, LinerLocks and frame-locks. **Prices:** $300 and up. **Mark:** Last name.

ROGHMANS, MARK
607 Virginia Ave., LaGrange, GA 30240, Phone: 706-885-1273

Specialties: Classic and traditional knives of his design. **Patterns:** Bowies, daggers and fighters. **Technical:** Grinds ATS-34, D2 and 440C. **Prices:** $250 to $500. **Remarks:** Part-time maker; first knife sold in 1984. Doing business as LaGrange Knife. **Mark:** Last name and/or LaGrange Knife.

ROHDE, DANIEL S.
25692 County Rd. 9, Winona, MN 55987, Phone: 507-312-6664, rohdeedge@gmail.com; Web: www.rohdeedge.com
Specialties: High performance fixed blades, chef's knives and slip-joint folders. **Patterns:** Loveless- and Fowler-style hunters, SharkTail and other hunting, EDC and chef's knives. **Technical:** Highly thermal cycled and forged 52100 and 1095, and AEB-L for a stainless steel. **Prices:** $100 to $400, some to $1,200, with the typical EDC knife going for about $185. **Remarks:** HEPK apprentice smith, part-time maker, and consistent, repeatable performance is the goal. **Mark:** Electro-etched last name (typically).

ROHN, FRED
7675 W Happy Hill Rd, Coeur d'Alene, ID 83814, Phone: 208-667-0774
Specialties: Hunters, boot knives, custom patterns. **Patterns:** Drop points, double edge, etc. **Technical:** Grinds 440 or 154CM. **Prices:** $85 and up. **Remarks:** Part-time maker. **Mark:** Logo on blade; serial numbered.

ROLLERT, STEVE
PO Box 65, Keenesburg, CO 80643-0065, Phone: 303-732-4858, steve@doveknives.com; Web: www.doveknives.com
Specialties: Highly finished working knives. **Patterns:** Variety of straight knives; locking folders and slip-joints. **Technical:** Forges and grinds W2, 1095, ATS-34 and his pattern-welded, cable Damascus and nickel Damascus. **Prices:** $300 to $1000; some to $3000. **Remarks:** Full-time maker; first knife sold in 1980. Doing business as Dove Knives. **Mark:** Last name in script.

ROMEIS, GORDON
1521 Coconut Dr., Fort Myers, FL 33901, Phone: 239-940-5060, gordonromeis@gmail.com Web: Romeisknives.com
Specialties: Smaller using knives. **Patterns:** I have a number of standard designs that include both full tapered tangs and narrow tang knives. Custom designs are welcome. Many different types. No folders. **Technical:** Standard steel is 440C. Also uses Alabama Damascus steel. **Prices:** Start at $165. **Remarks:** I am a part-time maker however I do try to keep waiting times to a minimum. **Mark:** Either my name, city, and state or simply ROMEIS depending on the knife.

RONZIO, N. JACK
PO Box 248, Fruita, CO 81521, Phone: 970-858-0921

ROOSEVELT, RUSSELL
398 County Rd. 450 E, Albion, IL 62806-4753, Phone: 618-445-3226 or 618-302-7272, rroosevelt02@gmail.com
Specialties: Using straight knives of his design and to customers' specs. **Patterns:** Hunters, utility and camp knives. **Technical:** Forges 1084 and high-carbon damascus. **Prices:** $250 to $1,200. **Remarks:** Part-time maker, first knife sold in 1999. **Mark:** Full name left side, ABS JS stamp right side.

ROOT, GARY
644 East 14th St, Erie, PA 16503, Phone: 814-459-0196
Specialties: Damascus Bowies with hand carved eagles, hawks and snakes for handles. Few folders made. **Patterns:** Daggers, fighters, hunter/field knives. **Technical:** Using handforged Damascus from Ray Bybar Jr (M.S.) and Robert Eggerling. Grinds D2, 440C, 1095 and 5160. Some 5160 is hand forged. **Prices:** $80 to $300 some to $1000. **Remarks:** Full time maker, first knife sold in 1976. **Mark:** Name over Erie, PA.

ROSE, BOB
PO BOX 126, Wagontown, PA 19376, Phone: 484-883-3925, bobmedit8@comcast.net Web: www.bobroseknives.com
Patterns: Bowies, fighters, drop point hunters, daggers, bird and trout, camp, and other fixed blade styles. **Technical:** Mostly using 1095 and damascus steel, desert ironwood and other top-of-the-line exotic woods as well as mammoth tooth. **Prices:** $49 - $300. **Remarks:** Been making and selling knives since 2004. "Knife Making is a meditation technique for me."

ROSE, DEREK W
14 Willow Wood Rd, Gallipolis, OH 45631, Phone: 740-446-4627

ROSE II, DOUN T.
Ltc US Special Operations Command (ret.), 1795/96 W Sharon Rd SW, Fife Lake, MI 49633, Phone: 231-645-1369, rosecutlery@gmail.com; Web: www.rosecutlery.com
Specialties: Straight working, collector and presentation knives to a high level of fit and finish. Design in collaboration with customer. **Patterns:** Field knives, Scagel, bowies, tactical, period pieces, axes and tomahawks, fishing and hunting spears and fine kitchen cutlery. **Technical:** Forged and billet ground, high carbon and stainless steel appropriate to end use. Steel from leading industry sources. Some period pieces from recovered stock. Makes own damascus (to include multi-bar and mosaic) and mokume gane. **Remarks:** Full-time maker, ABS since 2000, William Scagel Memorial Scholarship 2002, Bill Moran School of Blade Smithing 2003, apprentice under Master Blacksmith Dan Nickels at Black Rock Forge current. Working at Crooked Pine Forge. **Mark:** Last name ROSE in block letters with five petal "wild rose" in place of O. Doing business as Rose Cutlery.

ROSENBAUGH, RON
2806 Stonegate Dr, Crystal Lake, IL 60012, Phone: 815-477-9233 or 815-345-1633, ron@rosenbaughknives.com; Web: www.rosenbaughknives.com
Specialties: Fancy and plain working knives using own designs, collaborations,

and traditional patterns. **Patterns:** Bird, trout, boots, hunters, fighters, some Bowies. **Technical:** Grinds high alloy stainless, tool steels, and Damascus; forges 1084, 5160, 52100, carbon and spring steels. **Prices:** $150 to $1000. **Remarks:** Full-time maker, first knife sold in 2004. **Mark:** Last name, logo, city.

ROSS, STEPHEN
534 Remington Dr, Evanston, WY 82930, Phone: 307-799-7653
Specialties: One-of-a-kind collector-grade classic and contemporary straight knives and folders of his design and to customer specs; some fantasy pieces. **Patterns:** Combat and survival knives, hunters, boots and folders. **Technical:** Grinds stainless and tool steels. Engraves, scrimshaws. Makes leather sheaths. **Prices:** $160 to $3000. **Remarks:** Part-time maker; first knife sold in 1971. **Mark:** Last name in modified Roman; sometimes in script.

ROSS, TIM
3239 Oliver Rd, Thunder Bay, ON, CANADA P7G 1S9, Phone: 807-935-2667, Fax: 807-935-3179, rosscustomknives@gmail.com
Specialties: Fixed blades, natural handle material. **Patterns:** Hunting, fishing, Bowies, fighters. **Technical:** 440C, D2, 52100, Cable, 5160, 1084, L6, W2. **Prices:** $150 to $750 some higher. **Remarks:** Forges and stock removal. **Mark:** Ross Custom Knives.

ROSSDEUTSCHER, ROBERT N
133 S Vail Ave, Arlington Heights, IL 60005, Phone: 847-577-0404, Web: www.rnrknives.com
Specialties: Frontier-style and historically inspired knives. **Patterns:** Trade knives, Bowies, camp knives and hunting knives, tomahawks and lances. **Technical:** Most knives are hand forged, a few are stock removal. **Prices:** $135 to $1500. **Remarks:** Journeyman Smith of the American Bladesmith Society. **Mark:** Back-to-back "R's", one upside down and backwards, one right side up and forward in an oval. Sometimes with name, town and state; depending on knife style.

ROTELLA, RICHARD A
643 75th St., Niagara Falls, NY 14304, richarpo@roadrunner.com
Specialties: Highly finished working knives of his own design, as well as some Loveless-style designs. **Patterns:** Hunters, fishing, small game, utility, fighters and boot knives. **Technical:** Grinds ATS-34, 154CM, CPM 154 and 440C. **Prices:** $150 to $600. **Remarks:** Part-time maker; first knife sold in 1977. Sells completed knives only and does not take orders; makes about 70 knives a year. **Mark:** Name and city.

ROUGEAU, DERICK
1465 Cloud Peak Dr., Sparks, NV 89436, Phone: 775-232-6167, derick@rougeauknives.com; Web: www.rougeauknives.com
Specialties: A wide range of original designs from practical to tactical and traditional. **Patterns:** Bowies, hunters, fighters, bushcraft blades, tantos, machetes, chef's knives, tomahawks, hatchets, swords, neck and tool knives. Also makes assorted accessories and other cool items. **Technical:** Using stock-removal process. Flat and hollow grinds using a wide range of steels from damascus to 1080, 1095, 6150, O1, D2, ATS 34, CPM 154 and other CPM stainless steels. Does own heat treating, leather work and Kydex, and uses synthetic materials, stabilized woods and antler. **Prices:** $250 to $650 or more. **Remarks:** Part-time maker, full-time artist/designer. **Mark:** "DR" logo in front of "ROUGEAU."

ROULIN, CHARLES
113 B Rt. de Soral, Geneva, SWITZERLAND 1233, Phone: 022-757-4479, Fax: 079-218-9754, charles.roulin@bluewin.ch; Web: www.coutelier-roulin.com
Specialties: Fancy high-art straight knives and folders of his design. **Patterns:** Bowies, locking folders, slip-joint folders and miniatures. **Technical:** Grinds 440C, ATS-34 and D2. Engraves; carves nature scenes and detailed animals in steel, ivory, on handles and blades. **Prices:** $500 to $3000; some to Euro: 14,600. **Remarks:** Full-time maker; first knife sold in 1988. **Mark:** Symbol of fish with name or name engraved.

ROUSH, SCOTT
Big Rock Forge, 30955 Hove Ln., Washburn, WI 54891, Phone: 715-682-2844, scott@bigrockforge.com; Web: bigrockforge.com
Specialties: Forged blades representing a diversity of styles from trasditional hunters, fighters, camp knives, and EDC's to artistic pieces of cultural and historical inspiration with an emphasis in unique materials. **Technical:** Forges Aldo 1084, W2, low MN 1075, stainless/high carbon san mai, wrought iron/high carbon san mai, damascus. **Prices:** $85 to $1000 **Remarks:** Full-time maker; first knife sold in 2010. **Mark:** Stamped initials (SAR) set in a diamond.

ROWE, FRED
BETHEL RIDGE FORGE, 3199 Roberts Rd, Amesville, OH 45711, Phone: 866-325-2164, fred.rowe@bethelridgeforge.com; Web: www.bethelridgeforge.com
Specialties: Damascus and carbon steel sheath knives. **Patterns:** Bowies, hunters, fillet small kokris. **Technical:** His own Damascus, 52100, O1, L6, 1095 carbon steels, mosaics. **Prices:** $200 to $2000. **Remarks:** All blades are clay hardened. **Mark:** Bethel Ridge Forge.

ROYER, KYLE
9021 State Hwy. M, Clever, MO 65631, Phone: 417-247-5572, royerknifeworks@live.com; Web: www.kyleroyerknives.com
Specialties: Folders and fixed-blade knives. **Technical:** Mosaic damascus and engraving. **Prices:** $350 to $7,500. **Remarks:** ABS master smith. **Mark:** K~ROYER~MS.

ROZAS, CLARK D
1436 W "G" St, Wilmington, CA 90744, Phone: 310-518-0488
Specialties: Hand forged blades. **Patterns:** Pig stickers, toad stabbers, whackers, choppers. **Technical:** Damascus, 52100, 1095, 1084, 5160. **Prices:** $200 to $600. **Remarks:** A.B.S. member; part-time maker since 1995. **Mark:** Name over dagger.

RUA, GARY

400 Snell St., Apt. 2, Fall River, MA 02721, Phone: 508-677-2664
Specialties: Working straight knives of his design. 1800 to 1900 century standard patterns. **Patterns:** Bowies, hunters, fighters, and patch knives. **Technical:** Forges and grinds. Damascus, 5160, 1095, old files. Uses only natural handle material. **Prices:** $350 - $2000. **Remarks:** Part-time maker. (Harvest Moon Forge) **Mark:** Last name.

RUANA KNIFE WORKS

Box 520, Bonner, MT 59823, Phone: 406-258-5368, Fax: 406-258-2895, info@ ruanaknives.com; Web: www.ruanaknives.com
Specialties: Working knives and period pieces. **Patterns:** Variety of straight knives. **Technical:** Forges 5160 chrome alloy for Bowies and 1095. **Prices:** $300 and up. **Remarks:** Full-time maker; first knife sold in 1938. For free catalog email regular mailing address to info@ruanaknives.com **Mark:** Name.

RUCKER, THOMAS

30222 Mesa Valley Dr., Spring, TX 77386, Phone: 832-216-8122, admin@ knivesbythomas.com Web: www.knivesbythomas.com
Specialties: Personal design and custom design. Hunting, tactical, folding knives, and cutlery. **Technical:** Design and grind ATS34, D2, O1, Damascus, and VG10. **Prices:** $150 - $5,000. **Remarks:** Full-time maker and custom scrimshaw and engraving done by wife, Debi Rucker. First knife done in 1969; first design sold in 1975 **Mark:** Etched logo and signature.

RUPERT, BOB

301 Harshaville Rd., Clinton, PA 15026, Phone: 724-573-4569, rbrupert@aol.com
Specialties: Wrought period pieces with natural elements. **Patterns:** Elegant straight blades, friction folders. **Technical:** Forges colonial 7; 1095; 5160; diffuse mokume-gane and Damascus. **Prices:** $150 to $1500; some higher. **Remarks:** Part-time maker; first knife sold in 1980. Evening hours studio since 1980. Likes simplicity that disassembles. **Mark:** R etched in Old English.

RUPLE, WILLIAM H

201 Brian Dr., Pleasanton, TX 78064, Phone: 830-569-0007, bknives@devtex.net
Specialties: Multi-blade folders, slip joints, some lock backs. **Patterns:** Like to reproduce old patterns. Offers filework and engraving. **Technical:** Grinds CPM-154 and other carbon and stainless steel and commercial Damascus. **Prices:** $950 to $2500. **Remarks:** Full-time maker; first knife sold in 1988. **Mark:** Ruple.

RUSNAK, JOSEF

Breclavska 6, 323 00 Plzen, CZECH REPUBLIC, Phone: 00420721329442, rusnak. josef@centrum.cz; Web: http://knife.guaneru.cz
Specialties: Highly artistically designed knives. **Patterns:** Straight knives and folders. Collaboration with Buddy Weston. **Technical:** Engraving in high-quality steel and organic materials (mammoth tusk, giraffe bone, mother-of-pearl, bone), miniature sculpting, casting (Au, Ag, bronze). **Prices:** $1,000 and up. **Remarks:** Part-time maker; first knife sold in 1994. **Mark:** Signature.

RUSS, RON

5351 NE 160th Ave, Williston, FL 32696, Phone: 352-528-2603, RussRs@aol.com
Specialties: Damascus and mokume. **Patterns:** Ladder, rain drop and butterfly. **Technical:** Most knives, including Damascus, are forged from 52100-E. **Prices:** $65 to $2500. **Mark:** Russ.

RUSSELL, MICK

4 Rossini Rd, Pari Park, Port Elizabeth, EC, SOUTH AFRICA 6070
Specialties: Art knives. **Patterns:** Working and collectible bird, trout and hunting knives, defense knives and folders. **Technical:** Grinds D2, 440C, ATS-34 and Damascus. Offers mirror or satin finishes. **Prices:** Start at $100. **Remarks:** Full-time maker; first knife sold in 1986. **Mark:** Stylized rhino incorporating initials.

RUSSELL, TOM

6500 New Liberty Rd, Jacksonville, AL 36265, Phone: 205-492-7866
Specialties: Straight working knives of his design or to customer specs. **Patterns:** Hunters, folders, fighters, skinners, Bowies and utility knives. **Technical:** Grinds D2, 440C and ATS-34; offers filework. **Prices:** $75 to $225. **Remarks:** Part-time maker; first knife sold in 1987. Full-time tool and die maker. **Mark:** Last name with tulip stamp.

RUTH, MICHAEL G

3101 New Boston Rd, Texarkana, TX 75501, Phone: 903-832-7166/cell:903-277-3663, Fax: 903-832-4710, mike@ruthknives.com; Web: www.ruthknives.com
Specialties: Hunters, bowies & fighters. Damascus & carbon steel. **Prices:** $375 & up. **Mark:** Last name.

RUTH, JR., MICHAEL

5716 Wilshire Dr., Texarkana, TX 75503, Phone: 903-293-2663, michael@ ruthlesscustomknives.com; Web: www.ruthlesscustomknives.com
Specialties: Custom hand-forged blades, utilizing high carbon and Damascus steels. **Patterns:** Bowies, hunters and fighters ranging from field to presentation-grade pieces. **Technical:** Steels include 5160, 1084, 15n20, W-2, 1095, and O-1. Handle materials include a variety of premium hardwoods, stag, assorted ivories and micarta.**Mark:** 8-pointed star with capital "R" in center.

RUUSUVUORI, ANSSI

Verkkotie 38, Piikkio, FINLAND 21500, Phone: 358-50-520 8057, anssi.ruusuvuori@ akukon.fi; Web: www.arknives.suntuubi.com
Specialties: Traditional and modern puukko knives and hunters. Sole author except for Damascus steel.**Technical:** Forges mostly 1080 steel and grinds RWL-34. **Prices:** $200 to $500; some to $1200. **Remarks:** Part-time maker.**Mark:** A inside a circle (stamped)

RYBAR JR., RAYMOND B

2328 S. Sunset Dr., Camp Verde, AZ 86322, Phone: 928-567-6372
Specialties: Straight knives or folders with customers name, logo, etc. in mosaic pattern. **Patterns:** Common patterns plus mosaics of all types. **Technical:** Forges own Damascus. Primary forging of self smelted steel - smelting classes. **Prices:** $200 to $1200; Bible blades to $10,000. **Remarks:** Master Smith (A.B.S.) Primary focus toward Biblicaly themed blades **Mark:** Rybar or stone church forge or Rev. 1:3 or R.B.R. between diamonds.

RYDBOM, JEFF

PO Box 548, Annandale, MN 55302, Phone: 320-274-9639, jry1890@hotmail.com
Specialties: Ring knives. **Patterns:** Hunters, fighters, Bowie and camp knives. **Technical:** Straight grinds O1, A2, 1566 and 5150 steels. **Prices:** $150 to $1000. **Remarks:** No pinning of guards or pommels. All silver brazed. **Mark:** Capital "C" with J R inside.

RYUICHI, KUKI

504-7 Tokorozawa-Shinmachi, Tokorozawa-city, Saitama, JAPAN, Phone: 042-943-3451

RZEWNICKI, GERALD

8833 S Massbach Rd, Elizabeth, IL 61028-9714, Phone: 815-598-3239

S

SAINDON, R BILL

233 Rand Pond Rd, Goshen, NH 03752, Phone: 603-863-1874, dayskier71@aol.com
Specialties: Collector-quality folders of his design or to customer specs. **Patterns:** Latch release, LinerLock® and lockback folders. **Technical:** Offers limited amount of own Damascus; also uses Damas makers steel. Prefers natural handle material, gold and gems. **Prices:** $500 to $4000. **Remarks:** Full-time maker; first knife sold in 1981. Doing business as Daynia Forge. **Mark:** Sun logo or engraved surname.

SAKMAR, MIKE

4337 E. Grand River Ave. #113, Howell, MI 48843, Phone: 517-546-6388, Fax: 517-546-6399, sakmarent@yahoo.com; Web: www.sakmarenterprises.com
Specialties: Mokume in various patterns and alloy combinations. **Patterns:** Bowies, fighters, hunters and integrals. **Technical:** Grinds ATS-34, Damascus and high-carbon tool steels. Uses mostly natural handle materials—elephant ivory, walrus ivory, stag, wildwood, oosic, etc. Makes mokume for resale. **Prices:** $250 to $2500; some to $4000. **Remarks:** Part-time maker; first knife sold in 1990. Supplier of mokume. **Mark:** Last name.

SALLEY, JOHN D

3965 Frederick-Ginghamsburg Rd., Tipp City, OH 45371, Phone: 937-698-4588, Fax: 937-698-4131
Specialties: Fancy working knives and art pieces. **Patterns:** Hunters, fighters, daggers and some swords. **Technical:** Grinds ATS-34, 12C27 and W2; buys Damascus. **Prices:** $85 to $1000; some to $6000. **Remarks:** Part-time maker; first knife sold in 1979. **Mark:** First initial, last name.

SALTER, GREGG

Salter Fine Cutlery, POB 384571, Waikoloa, HI 96738-4571, Phone: 808-883-0128, salterfinecutlery@gmail.com; Web: www.salterfinecutlery.com
Specialties: Custom, made-to-order cutlery and custom display boxes, including kitchen knife sets, steak knife sets, carving sets, chef's knives and collectible knives and swords. Work in collaboration with several individual bladesmiths who create blades to our specifications. **Technical:** Variety of steels available, including VG-10, Aogami Super, R2, OU-31, YSS White Paper Shirogami, YSS Aogami Blue Paper and Tamahagane (swords). Damascus patterns, hammered and laser-etched patterns, and, in the case of swords, hand-etched scenes available. **Prices:** Range widely, from approximately $250 to over $1 million in the case of one spectacular collectible. Average price for chef's knives in the $500-$750 range. **Remarks:** Full-time business making a range of products based around knives. **Mark:** Hawaiian koa tree with crossed chef's knives and the outline of a crown between them.

SAMPSON, LYNN

381 Deakins Rd, Jonesborough, TN 37659, Phone: 423-348-8373
Specialties: Highly finished working knives, mostly folders. **Patterns:** Locking folders, slip-joints, interframes and two-blades. **Technical:** Grinds D2, 440C and ATS-34; offers extensive filework. **Prices:** Start at $300. **Remarks:** Full-time maker; first knife sold in 1982. **Mark:** Name and city in logo.

SANDBERG, RONALD B

24784 Shadowland Ln, Brownstown, MI 48134-9560, Phone: 734-671-6866, msc2009@comcast.net
Specialties: Good looking and functional hunting knives, filework, mixing of handle materials. **Patterns:** Hunters, skinners and Bowies. **Prices:** $120 and up. **Remarks:** Full lifetime workmanship guarantee. **Mark:** R.B. SANDBERG

SANDERS, BILL

335 Bauer Ave, PO Box 957, Mancos, CO 81328, Phone: 970-533-7223, Fax: 970-533-7390, billsand@frontier.net; Web: www.billsandershandmadeknives.com
Specialties: Survival knives, working straight knives, some fancy and some fantasy, of his design. **Patterns:** Hunters, boots, utility knives, using belt knives. **Technical:** Grinds 440C, ATS-34 and commercial Damascus. Provides wide variety of handle materials. **Prices:** $170 to $800. **Remarks:** Full-time maker. Formerly of Timberline Knives. **Mark:** Name, city and state.

SANDOW, BRENT EDWARD
50 O'Halloran Road, Howick, Auckland, NEW ZEALAND 2014, Phone: 64 9 537 4166, knifebug@vodafone.co.nz; Web: www.brentsandowknives.com
Specialties: Tactical fixed blades, hunting, camp, Bowie. **Technical:** All blades made by stock removal method. **Prices:** From US $200 upward. **Mark:** Name etched or engraved.

SANDS, SCOTT
2 Lindis Ln, New Brighton, Christchurch 9, NEW ZEALAND
Specialties: Classic working and fantasy swords. **Patterns:** Fantasy, medieval, celtic, viking, katana, some daggers. **Technical:** Forges own Damascus; 1080 and L6; 5160 and L6; O1 and L6. All hand-polished, does own heat-treating, forges non-Damascus on request. **Prices:** $1500 to $15,000+. **Remarks:** Full-time maker; first blade sold in 1996. **Mark:** Stylized Moon.

SANFORD, DICK
151 London Ln., Chehalis, WA 98532, Phone: 360-748-2128, richardsanfo364@centurytel.net
Remarks: Ten years experience hand forging knives

SANGSTER, JOE
POB 312, Vienna, GA 31092, Phone: 229-322-3407, ssangster@sowega.net; Web: www.sangsterknives.com
Specialties Gent's LinerLock folders with filework. Patterns: Traditional LinerLock folders, hunters, skinners and kitchen knives. **Technical:** Grinds ATS-34, CPM 134, 440C and commercial damascus. Handle materials of mammoth ivory, mammoth tooth, pearl, oosic, coral and exotic burl woods. **Prices:** $250 to $500, some up to $1,200. **Remarks:** Full-time maker; first knife sold in 2003. **Mark:** name or name, city and state.

SANTA, LADISLAV "LASKY"
Stara Voda 264/10, 97637 Hrochot, SLOVAKIA, Phone: +421-907-825-2-77, lasky@lasky.sk; Web: www.lasky.sk
Specialties: Damascus hunters, daggers and swords. **Patterns:** Various damascus patterns. **Prices:** $300 to $6,000 U.S. **Mark:** L or Lasky.

SANTIAGO, ABUD
Av Gaona 3676 PB, Buenos Aires, ARGENTINA 1416, Phone: 5411 4612 8396, info@phi-sabud.com; Web: www.phi-sabud.com/blades.html

SANTINI, TOM
101 Clayside Dr, Pikeville, NC 27863, Phone: 586-354-0245, tomsantiniknives@hotmail.com; Web: www.tomsantiniknives.com
Specialties: working/using straight knives, tactical, and some slipjoints **Technical:** Grinds ATS-34, S-90-V, D2, and damascus. I handstitch my leather sheaths. **Prices:** $150 - $500. **Remarks:** Full-time maker, first knife sold in 2004. **Mark:** Full name.

SARGANIS, PAUL
2215 Upper Applegate Rd, Jacksonville, OR 97530, Phone: 541-899-2831, paulsarganis@hotmail.com; Web: www.sarganis.50megs.com
Specialties: Hunters, folders, Bowies. **Technical:** Forges 5160, 1084. Grinds ATS-34 and 440C. **Prices:** $120 to $500. **Remarks:** Spare-time maker, first knife sold in 1987. **Mark:** Last name.

SASS, GARY N
803 W. Main St., Sharpsville, PA 16150, Phone: 724-866-6165, gnsass@yahoo.com
Specialties: Working straight knives of his design or to customer specifications. **Patterns:** Hunters, fighters, utility knives, push daggers. **Technical:** Grinds 440C, ATS-34 and Damascus. Uses exotic wood, buffalo horn, warthog tusk and semi-precious stones. **Prices:** $50 to $250, some higher. **Remarks:** Part-time maker. First knife sold in 2003. **Mark:** Initials G.S. formed into a diamond shape or last name.

SAVIANO, JAMES
124 Wallis St., Douglas, MA 01516, Phone: 508-476-7644, jimsaviano@gmail.com
Specialties: Straight knives. **Patterns:** Hunters, bowies, fighters, daggers, short swords. **Technical:** Hand-forged high-carbon and my own damascus steel. **Prices:** Starting at $300. **Remarks:** ABS mastersmith, maker since 2000, sole authorship. **Mark:** Last name or stylized JPS initials.

SAWBY, SCOTT
480 Snowberry Ln, Sandpoint, ID 83864, Phone: 208-263-4253, scotmar3@gmail.com; Web: www.sawbycustomknives.com
Specialties: Folders, working and fancy. **Patterns:** Locking folders, patent locking systems and interframes. **Technical:** Grinds D2, 440C, CPM154, ATS-34, S30V, and Damascus. **Prices:** $700 to $3000. **Remarks:** Full-time maker; first knife sold in 1974. **Mark:** Last name, city and state.

SCARROW, WIL
c/o Scarrow's Custom Stuff, PO Box 1036, Gold Hill, OR 97525-1036, Phone: 541-855-1236, willsknife@gmail.com
Specialties: Carving knives and tools, and some mini wood lathe tools. **Patterns:** Carving, fishing, hunting, skinning, utility, swords and Bowies. **Technical:** Forges and grinds: A2, W1, O1, 5160 and 1095. Offers some filework. **Prices:** $45 and up. **Remarks:** Spare-time maker; first knife made/sold in 1983. One month turnaround on orders. Doing business as Scarrow's Custom Stuff (Gold Hill, OR, USA). Carving knives available at Raven Dog Enterprises. Contact at Ravedog@aol.com. **Mark:** SC with arrow and year made.

SCHALLER, ANTHONY BRETT
5609 Flint Ct. NW, Albuquerque, NM 87120, Phone: 505-899-0155, brett@schallerknives.com; Web: www.schallerknives.com
Specialties: Straight knives and locking-liner folders of his design and in standard patterns. **Patterns:** Boots, fighters, utility knives and folders. **Technical:** Grinds CPM154, S30V, and stainless Damascus. Offers filework, hand-rubbed finishes and full and narrow tangs. Prefers exotic woods or Micarta for handle materials, G-10 and carbon fiber to handle materials. **Prices:** $100 to $350; some to $500. **Remarks:** Part-time maker; first knife sold in 1990. **Mark:** A.B. Schaller - Albuquerque NM - handmade.

SCHEID, MAGGIE
124 Van Stallen St, Rochester, NY 14621-3557
Specialties: Simple working straight knives. **Patterns:** Kitchen and utility knives; some miniatures. **Technical:** Forges 5160 high-carbon steel. **Prices:** $100 to $200. **Remarks:** Part-time maker; first knife sold in 1986. **Mark:** Full name.

SCHEMPP, ED
PO Box 1181, Ephrata, WA 98823, Phone: 509-754-2963, Fax: 509-754-3212, edschempp@yahoo.com
Specialties: Mosaic Damascus and unique folder designs. **Patterns:** Primarily folders. **Technical:** Grinds CPM440V; forges many patterns of mosaic using powdered steel. **Prices:** $100 to $400; some to $2000. **Remarks:** Part-time maker; first knife sold in 1991. Doing business as Ed Schempp Knives. **Mark:** Ed Schempp Knives over five heads of wheat, city and state.

SCHEMPP, MARTIN
PO Box 1181, 5430 Baird Springs Rd NW, Ephrata, WA 98823, Phone: 509-754-2963, Fax: 509-754-3212
Specialties: Fantasy and traditional straight knives of his design, to customer specs and in standard patterns. Paleolithic-styles. **Patterns:** Fighters and Paleolithic designs. **Technical:** Uses opal, Mexican rainbow and obsidian. Offers scrimshaw. **Prices:** $15 to $100; some to $250. **Remarks:** Spare-time maker; first knife sold in 1995. **Mark:** Initials and date.

SCHEURER, ALFREDO E FAES
Av Rincon de los Arcos 104, Col Bosque Res del Sur, Distrito Federal, MEXICO 16010, Phone: 5676 47 63
Specialties: Fancy and fantasy knives of his design. **Patterns:** Daggers. **Technical:** Grinds stainless steel; casts and grinds silver. Sets stones in silver. **Prices:** $2000 to $3000. **Remarks:** Spare-time maker; first knife sold in 1989. **Mark:** Symbol.

SCHIPPNICK, JIM
PO Box 326, Sanborn, NY 14132, Phone: 716-731-3715, ragnar@ragweedforge.com; Web: www.ragweedforge.com
Specialties: Nordic, early American, rustic. **Mark:** Runic R. **Remarks:** Also imports Nordic knives from Norway, Sweden and Finland.

SCHLUETER, DAVID
2136 Cedar Gate Rd., Madison Heights, VA 24572, Phone: 434-384-8642, drschlueter@hotmail.com
Specialties: Japanese-style swords. **Patterns:** Larger blades. O-tanto to Tachi, with focus on less common shapes. **Technical:** Forges and grinds carbon steels, heat-treats and polishes own blades, makes all fittings, does own mounting and finishing. **Prices:** Start at $3000. **Remarks:** Sells fully mounted pieces only, doing business as Odd Frog Forge. **Mark:** Full name and date.

SCHMITZ, RAYMOND E
PO Box 1787, Valley Center, CA 92082, Phone: 760-749-4318

SCHNEIDER, CRAIG M
5380 N Amity Rd, Claremont, IL 62421, Phone: 217-377-5715, raephtownslam@att.blackberry.net
Specialties: Straight knives and folders of his own design. **Patterns:** Bowies, hunters, tactical, bird & trout. **Technical:** Forged high-carbon steel and Damascus. Flat grind and differential heat treatment use a wide selection of handle, guard and bolster material, also offers leather sheaths. **Prices:** $150 to $3,500. **Remarks:** Part-time maker; first knife sold in 1985. **Mark:** Stylized initials with Schneider Claremont IL.

SCHNEIDER, HERMAN J.
14084 Apple Valley Rd, Apple Valley, CA 92307, Phone: 760-946-9096
Specialties: Presentation pieces, Fighters, Hunters. **Prices:** Starting at $900. **Mark:** H.J. Schneider-Maker or maker's last name.

SCHOEMAN, CORRIE
Box 28596, Danhof, Free State, SOUTH AFRICA 9310, Phone: 027 51 4363528 Cell: 027 82-3750789, corries@intekom.co.za
Specialties: High-tech folders of his design or to customer's specs. **Patterns:** Linerlock folders and automatics. **Technical:** ATS-34, Damascus or stainless Damascus with titanium frames; prefers exotic materials for handles. **Prices:** $650 to $2000. **Remarks:** Full-time maker; first knife sold in 1984. All folders come with filed liners and back and jeweled inserts. **Mark:** Logo in knife shape engraved on inside of back bar.

SCHOENFELD, MATTHEW A
RR #1, Galiano Island, BC, CANADA V0N 1P0, Phone: 250-539-2806
Specialties: Working knives of his design. **Patterns:** Kitchen cutlery, camp knives, hunters. **Technical:** Grinds 440C. **Prices:** $85 to $500. **Remarks:** Part-time maker; first knife sold in 1978. **Mark:** Signature, Galiano Is. B.C., and date.

SCHOENINGH, MIKE
49850 Miller Rd, North Powder, OR 97867, Phone: 541-856-3239

SCHOLL, TIM
1389 Langdon Rd, Angier, NC 27501, Phone: 910-897-2051, tschollknives@live.com; Web: www.timschollcustomknives.com

Specialties: Fancy and working/using straight knives and folders of his design and to customer specs. **Patterns:** Bowies, hunters, tomahawks, daggers & fantasy knives. **Technical:** Forges high carbon and tool steel makes Damascus, grinds ATS-34 and D2 on request. **Prices:** $150 to $6000. **Remarks:** Part-time maker; first knife sold in 1990. Doing business as Tim Scholl Custom Knives. Member North Carolina Custom Knifemakers Guild. American Bladesmith Society journeyman smith. **Mark:** S pierced by arrow.

SCHORSCH, KENDALL
693 Deer Trail Dr., Jourdanton, TX 78026, Phone: 830-770-0205, schorschknives@gmail.com; Web: www.schorschknives.com

Specialties Slip-joint folders and straight blades. **Patterns:** Single- and double-blade trappers and straight hunting knives, all with or without filework. **Technical:** Grinds CPM 154, ATS-34, D2 and damascus. **Prices:** $350 to $750 and up. **Remarks:** Full-time maker; first knife sold in 2010. **Mark:** Stamped SCHORSCH on the tang or Schorsch Knives etched in a circle with an Arrow "S" in the center.

SCHOW, LYLE
2103 Ann Ave., Harrisonville, MO 64701, Phone: 816-738-9849, rocktips17@yahoo.com; Web: www.LDknives.com

Specialties: Bowies, hunters, skinners, camp knives and some folders. **Technical:** Forges hunters and big knives, and practices stock-removal method of blade making on small blades. Uses high-carbon steels such as 1075, 1080, 1084, 1095 and W2, makes his own damascus and stainless/high-carbon San Mai steel. **Prices:** $110 to $2,000. **Remarks:** Part-time maker; started making knives in 2009. **Mark:** Maker's initials LDS configured together in the center, with LYLE D. in an arch on the top and SCHOW in an upward arch on the bottom.

SCHRADER, ROBERT
55532 Gross De, Bend, OR 97707, Phone: 541-598-7301

Specialties: Hunting, utility, Bowie. **Patterns:** Fixed blade. **Prices:** $150 to $600.

SCHRAP, ROBERT G
CUSTOM LEATHER KNIFE SHEATH CO., 7024 W Wells St, Wauwatosa, WI 53213-3717, Phone: 414-771-6472 or 414-379-6819, Fax: 414-479-9765, knifesheaths@aol.com; Web: www.customsheaths.com

Specialties: Leather knife sheaths. **Prices:** $38 to $150. **Mark:** Schrap in oval.

SCHREINER, TERRY
4310 W. Beech St., Duncan, OK 73533, Phone: 580-255-4880, Rhino969@hotmail.com

Specialties Hunters, bird-and-trout knives, handforged, one-of-a-kind bowies. **Patterns:** Hunters and bird-and-trout knives. **Technical:** Stainless damascus, Damasteel, hand-forged carbon damascus and RWL stainless steels, with handle materials mostly natural, including stag, mastodon ivory, horn and wood. **Prices:** $350 to $1,500. **Remarks:** Part-time maker. **Mark:** TerryJack Knives; TSchreiner with interlocking T&S.

SCHROEN, KARL
4042 Bones Rd, Sebastopol, CA 95472, Phone: 707-823-4057, Web: www.schroenknives.com

Specialties: Using knives made to fit. **Patterns:** Sgian dubhs, carving sets, wood-carving knives, fishing knives, kitchen knives and new cleaver design. **Technical:** Forges D2, CPM S30V and 204P. **Prices:** $150 to $6000. **Remarks:** Full-time maker; first knife sold in 1968. Author of The Hand Forged Knife. **Mark:** Last name.

SCHUCHMANN, RICK
1251 Wilson Dunham Hill Rd., New Richmond, OH 45157, Phone: 513-553-4316

Specialties: Replicas of antique and out-of-production Scagels and Randalls, primarily miniatures. **Patterns:** All sheath knives, mostly miniatures, hunting and fighting knives, some daggers and hatchets. **Technical:** Stock removal, 440C and O1 steel. Most knives are flat ground, some convex. **Prices:** $175 to $600 and custom to $4000. **Remarks:** Part-time maker, sold first knife in 1997. Knives on display in the Randall Museum. Sheaths are made exclusively at Sullivan's Holster Shop, Tampa, FL **Mark:** SCAR.

SCHUTTE, NEILL
01 Moffet St., Fichardt Park, Bloemfontein, SOUTH AFRICA 9301, Phone: +27(0) 82 787 3429, neill@schutteknives.co.za; www.schutteknives.co.za

Specialties: Bob Loveless-style knives, George Herron fighters, custom designs and designs/requests from clients. **Technical:** Mainly stock removal of Bohler N690, RWL-34 and ATS-34, if available, blade steels. Uses the materials clients request. **Prices:** $450 to $1,250. **Remarks:** Full-time maker; first knife made at 10 years old, seriously started knifemaking in 2008. **Mark:** Kneeling archer/bowman (maker's surname, Schutte, directly translates to archer or bowman.)

SCHWARTZ, AARON
4745 B Asdee Ln., Woodbridge, VA 22192, Phone: 908-256-3869, big_hammer_forge@yahoo.com; Web: www.bighammerforge.com

Specialties Fantasy custom designs and one-off custom pieces to order. **Technical:** Stock-removal method of blade making. **Remarks:** Made first knife around eight years ago.

SCHWARZER, LORA SUE
POB 6, Crescent City, FL 32112, Phone: 904-307-0872, auntielora57@yahoo.com

Specialties: Scagel style knives. **Patterns:** Hunters and miniatures **Technical:** Forges 1084 and Damascus. **Prices:** Start at $400. **Remarks:** Part-time maker; first knife sold in 1997. Journeyman Bladesmith, American Bladesmith Society. Now working with Steve Schwarzer on some projects.**Mark:** Full name - JS on reverse side.

SCHWARZER, STEPHEN
POB 6, Crescent City, FL 32112, Phone: 904-307-0872, schwarzeranvil@gmail.com; Web: www.steveschwarzer.com

Specialties: Mosaic Damascus and picture mosaic in folding knives. All Japanese

blades are finished working with Wally Hostetter considered the top Japanese lacquer specialist in the U.S.A. Also produces a line of carbon steel skinning knives at $300. **Patterns:** Folders, axes and buckskinner knives. **Technical:** Specializes in picture mosaic Damascus and powder metal mosaic work. Sole authorship; all work including carving done in-house. Most knives have file work and carving. Hand carved steel and precious metal guards. **Prices:** $1500 to $5000, some higher; carbon steel and primitive knives much less. **Remarks:** Full-time maker; first knife sold in 1976, considered by many to be one of the top mosaic Damascus specialists in the world. Mosaic Master level work. I am now working with Lora Schwarzer on some projects. **Mark:** Schwarzer + anvil.

SCIMIO, BILL
4554 Creek Side Ln., Spruce Creek, PA 16683, Phone: 814-632-3751, sprucecreekforge@gmail.com Web: www.sprucecreekforge.com

Specialties: Hand-forged primitive-style knives with curly maple, antler, bone and osage handles.

SCORDIA, PAOLO
Via Terralba 144, Torrimpietra, Roma, ITALY 00050, Phone: 06-61697231, paolo.scordia@uni.net; Web: www.scordia-knives.com

Specialties: Working, fantasy knives, Italian traditional folders and fixed blades of own design. **Patterns:** Any. **Technical:** Forge mosaic Damascus, forge blades, welds own mokume and grinds ATS-34, etc. use hardwoods and Micarta for handles, brass and nickel-silver for fittings. Makes sheaths. **Prices:** $200 to $2000, some to $4000. **Remarks:** Part-time maker; first knife sold in 1988. **Mark:** Sun and moon logo and initials.

SCROGGS, JAMES A
108 Murray Hill Dr, Warrensburg, MO 64093, Phone: 660-747-2568, jscroggsknives@embarqmail.com

Specialties: Straight knives, prefers light weight. **Patterns:** Hunters, hideouts, and fighters. **Technical:** Grinds CPM-154 stainless plus experiments in steel. Prefers handles of walnut in English, bastonge, American black. Also uses myrtle, maple, Osage orange. **Prices:** $200 to $1000. **Remarks:** 1st knife sold in 1985. Full-time maker. Won "Best Hunter Award" at Branson Hammer-In & Knife Show for 2012 and 2014. **Mark:** SCROGGS in block or script.

SCULLEY, PETER E
340 Sunset Dr, Rising Fawn, GA 30738, Phone: 706-398-0169

SEATON, DAVID D
1028 South Bishop Ave, #237, Rolla, MO 65401, Phone: 573-465-3193, aokcustomknives@gmail.com

Specialties: Gentleman's and Lady's folders. **Patterns:** Liner lock folders of own design and to customer specs, lock backs, slip joints, some stright knives, tactical folders, skinners, fighters, and utility knives. **Technical:** Grinds ATS 34, O1, 1095, 154CM, CPM154, commercial Damascus. Blades are mostly flat ground, some hollow ground. Does own heat treating, tempering, and Nitre Bluing. Prefers natural handle materials such as ivory, mother of pearl, bone, and exotic woods, some use of G10 and micarta on hard use knives. Use gem stones, gold, silver on upscale knives, offers some carving, filework, and engrving. **Prices:** $150 to $600 avg; some to $1500 and up depending on materials and embellishments. **Remarks:** First knife sold in 2002, part-time maker, doing business at AOK Custom Knives. **Mark:** full or last name engraved on blade.

SEIB, STEVE
7914 Old State Road, Evansville, IN 47710, Phone: 812-867-2231, sseib@insightbb.com

Specialties: Working straight knives. **Pattern:** Skinners, hunters, bowies and camp knives. **Technical:** Forges high-carbon and makes own damascus. **Remarks:** Part-time maker. ABS member. **Mark:** Last name.

SELF, ERNIE
950 O'Neill Ranch Rd, Dripping Springs, TX 78620-9760, Phone: 512-940-7134, ernieself@yahoo.com

Specialties: Traditional and working straight knives and folders of his design and in standard patterns. **Patterns:** Hunters, locking folders and slip-joints. **Technical:** Grinds 440C, D2, 440V, ATS-34 and Damascus. Offers fancy filework. **Prices:** $250 to $1000; some to $2500. **Remarks:** Full-time maker; first knife sold in 1982. Also customizes Buck 110's and 112's folding hunters. **Mark:** In oval shape - Ernie Self Maker Dripping Springs TX.

SELLEVOLD, HARALD
PO Box 4134, Sandviken S Kleivesmau:2, Bergen, NORWAY N5835, Phone: 47 55-310682, haraldsellevold@gmail.com; Web:knivmakeren.com

Specialties: Norwegian-styles; collaborates with other Norse craftsmen. **Patterns:** Distinctive ferrules and other mild modifications of traditional patterns; Bowies and friction folders. **Technical:** Buys Damascus blades; blacksmiths his own blades. Semi-gemstones used in handles; gemstone inlay. **Prices:** $350 to $2000. **Remarks:** Full-time maker; first knife sold in 1980. **Mark:** Name and country in logo.

SELZAM, FRANK
Martin Reinhard Str 23, Bad Koenigshofen, GERMANY 97631, Phone: 09761-5980, frankselzam.de

Specialties: Hunters, working knives to customers specs, hand tooled and stitched leather sheaths large stock of wood and German stag horn. **Patterns:** Mostly own design. **Technical:** Forged blades, own Damascus, also stock removal stainless. **Prices:** $250 to $1500. **Remarks:** First knife sold in 1978. **Mark:** Last name stamped.

SENTZ, MARK C
4084 Baptist Rd, Taneytown, MD 21787, Phone: 410-756-2018

Specialties: Fancy straight working knives of his design. **Patterns:** Hunters, fighters, folders and utility/camp knives. **Technical:** Forges 1085, 1095, 5160, 5155 and his

Damascus. Most knives come with wood-lined leather sheath or wooden presentation sheath. **Prices:** Start at $275. **Remarks:** Full-time maker; first knife sold in 1989. Doing business as M. Charles Sentz Gunsmithing, Inc. **Mark:** Last name.

SERAFEN, STEVEN E
24 Genesee St, New Berlin, NY 13411, Phone: 607-847-6903
Specialties: Traditional working/using straight knives of his design and to customer specs. **Patterns:** Bowies, fighters, hunters. **Technical:** Grinds ATS-34, 440C, high-carbon steel. **Prices:** $175 to $600; some to $1200. **Remarks:** Part-time maker; first knife sold in 1990. **Mark:** First and middle initial, last name in script.

SEVECEK, PAVEL
Lhota u Konice 7, BRODEK U KONICE, 79845 CZECH REPUBLIC, Phone: 00420 603 545333, seva.noze@seznam.cz; Web: www.sevaknives.cz
Specialties Production of handforged mosaic damascus knives, all including the plastic engravings and sheaths of his own exclusive work. **Prices:** $800 and up. **Remarks:** First knife sold in 2001. **Mark:** Logo SP in blade.

SEVEY CUSTOM KNIFE
94595 Chandler Rd, Gold Beach, OR 97444, Phone: 541-247-2649, sevey@charter.net; Web: www.seveyknives.com
Specialties: Fixed blade hunters. **Patterns:** Drop point, trailing paint, clip paint, full tang, hidden tang. **Technical:** D-2, and ATS-34 blades, stock removal. Heat treatment by Paul Bos. **Prices:** $225 and up depending on overall length and grip material. **Mark:** Sevey Custom Knife.

SEWARD, BEN
471 Dogwood Ln., Austin, AR 72007, Phone: 501-416-1543, sewardsteel@gmail.com; Web: www.bensewardknives.com
Specialties: Forged blades, mostly bowies and fighters. **Technical:** Forges high-carbon steels such as 1075 and W2. **Remarks:** First knife made in 2005; ABS journeyman smith and member Arkansas Knifemakers Association.

SFREDDO, RODRIGO MENEZES
Rua 7 De Setembro 66 Centro, Nova Petropolis, RS, BRAZIL 95150-000, Phone: 011-55-54-303-303-90, r.sfreddoknives@gmail.com; www.sbccutelaria.org.br
Specialties: Integrals, bowies, hunters, dirks & swords. **Patterns:** Forges his own Damascus and 52100 steel. **Technical:** Specialized in integral knives and Damascus. **Prices:** From $350 and up. Most around $750 to $1000. **Remarks:** Considered by many to be the Brazil's best bladesmith. ABS SBC Member. **Mark:** S. Sfreddo on the left side of the blade.

SHADLEY, EUGENE W
209 NW 17th Street, Grand Rapids, MN 55744, Phone: 218-999-7197 or 218-244-8628, Fax: call first, ShadleyKnives@hotmail.com
Specialties: Gold frames are available on some models. **Patterns:** Whittlers, stockman, sowbelly, congress, trapper, etc. **Technical:** Grinds ATS-34, 416 frames. **Prices:** Starts at $600, some models up to $15,000. **Remarks:** Full-time maker; first knife sold in 1985. Doing business as Shadley Knives. **Mark:** Last name.

SHADMOT, BOAZ
MOSHAV PARAN D N, Arava, ISRAEL 86835, srb@arava.co.il

SHARP, DAVID
17485 Adobe St., Hesperia, CA 92345, Phone: 520-370-1899, sharpwerks@gmail.com or david@sharpwerks.com; Web: www.sharpwerks.com
Specialties: Fixed blades. **Patterns:** Original and real Loveless pattern utilities, hunters and fighters. **Technical:** Stock removal, tool steel and stainless steel, hollow grind, machine finish, full polish, various handle materials. **Prices:** $300 to $1,500. **Remarks:** Part-time maker, first knife sold in 2011. **Mark:** "Sharpwerks" on original designs; "D. Sharp" on Loveless designs.

SHARRIGAN, MUDD
111 Bradford Rd, Wiscasset, ME 04578-4457, Phone: 207-882-9820, Fax: 207-882-9835
Specialties: Custom designs; repair straight knives, custom leather sheaths. **Patterns:** Daggers, fighters, hunters, crooked knives and seamen working knives; traditional Scandinavian-styles. **Technical:** Forges 1095, 5160, and W2. **Prices:** $50 to $325; some to $1200. **Remarks:** Full-time maker; first knife sold in 1982. **Mark:** Swallow tail carving. Mudd engraved.

SHEEHY, THOMAS J
4131 NE 24th Ave, Portland, OR 97211-6411, Phone: 503-493-2843
Specialties: Hunting knives and ulus. **Patterns:** Own or customer designs. **Technical:** 1095/01 and ATS-34 steel. **Prices:** $35 to $200. **Remarks:** Do own heat treating; forged or ground blades. **Mark:** Name.

SHEELY, "BUTCH" FOREST
15784 Custar Rd., Grand Rapids, OH 43522, Phone: 419-308-3471, sheelyblades@gmail.com
Specialties: Traditional bowies and pipe tomahawks. **Patterns:** Bowies, hunters, integrals, dirks, axes and hawks. **Technical:** Forges 5160, 52100, 1084, 1095, and Damascus. **Prices:** $150 to $1500; **Remarks:** Full-time bladesmith part-time blacksmith; first knife sold in 1982. ABS Journeysmith, sole author of all knives and hawks including hand sewn leather sheaths, doing business as Beaver Creek Forge. **Mark:** First and last name above Bladesmith.

SHEETS, STEVEN WILLIAM
6 Stonehouse Rd, Mendham, NJ 07945, Phone: 201-543-5882

SHIFFER, STEVE
PO Box 471, Leakesville, MS 39451, Phone: 601-394-4425, aiifish2@yahoo.com; Web: wwwchoctawplantationforge.com
Specialties: Bowies, fighters, hard use knives. **Patterns:** Fighters, hunters, combat/utility knives. Walker pattern LinerLock® folders. Allen pattern scale and bolster release autos. **Technical:** Most work forged, stainless stock removal. Makes own Damascus. 01 and 5160 most used also 1084, 440c, 154cm, s30v. **Prices:** $125 to $1000. **Remarks:** First knife sold in 2000, all heat treatment done by maker. Doing business as Choctaw Plantation Forge. **Mark:** Hot mark sunrise over creek.

SHIGENO, MAMORU
2-12-3 Hirosehigashi, Sayama-shi, Saitama, 350-1320, JAPAN, shigeno-knife@tbc.t-com.ne.jp; Web: http://www2.tbb.t-com.ne.jp/shigeno-knife/
Specialties: Fixed blades. **Patterns:** Hunters, boot knives, fighters, including most Loveless patterns, bowies and others. **Technical:** Stock removal of ATS-34. **Prices:** $700 to $3,000 and up. **Remarks:** Full-time maker; first knife sold in 2003. **Mark:** SHIGENO (last name).

SHINOSKY, ANDY
3117 Meanderwood Dr, Canfield, OH 44406, Phone: 330-702-0299, andrew@shinosky.com; Web: www.shinosky.com
Specialties: Collectable folders and interframes. **Patterns:** Drop point, spear point, trailing point, daggers. **Technical:** Grinds ATS-34 and Damascus. Prefers natural handle materials. Most knives are engraved by Andy himself. **Prices:** Start at $800. **Remarks:** Part-time maker/engraver. First knife sold in 1992. **Mark:** Name.

SHINOZAKI, AKIO
24-10 Jyouseigaoka 2-chome, Munakata-city, Fukuoka-ken, JAPAN 811-3404, Phone: 81-940-32-6768, shinozakiknife4152@ab.auone-net.jp
Specialties: One-of-a-kind straight knives and locking folders. **Patterns:** Hunters, skinners, bowies and utility knives of maker's own design and to customer's specifications. **Technical:** Stock removal method of blade making using ATS-34, CPM S30V, CV134 and SPG2 steels, mirror polishes. Handle materials are stag, exotic woods, Micarta and mammoth ivory. **Prices:** $350 to $800, with bowies and fighters starting at $1,200 and up. **Remarks:** Full-time maker; first knife sold in 1987. **Mark:** Akio S or Akio Shinozaki.

SHIPLEY, STEVEN A
800 Campbell Rd Ste 137, Richardson, TX 75081, Phone: 972-644-7981, Fax: 972-644-7985, steve@shipleysphotography.com
Specialties: Hunters, skinners and traditional straight knives. **Technical:** Hand grinds ATS-34, 440C and Damascus steels. Each knife is custom sheathed by his son, Dan. **Prices:** $175 to $2000. **Remarks:** Part-time maker; like smooth lines and unusual handle materials. **Mark:** S A Shipley.

SHOEMAKER, CARROLL
380 Yellowtown Rd, Northup, OH 45658, Phone: 740-446-6695
Specialties: Working/using straight knives of his design. **Patterns:** Hunters, utility/camp and early American backwoodsmen knives. **Technical:** Grinds ATS-34; forges old files, 01 and 1095. Uses some Damascus; offers scrimshaw and engraving. **Prices:** $100 to $175; some to $350. **Remarks:** Spare-time maker; first knife sold in 1977. **Mark:** Name and city or connected initials.

SHOEMAKER, SCOTT
316 S Main St, Miamisburg, OH 45342, Phone: 513-859-1935
Specialties: Twisted, wire-wrapped handles on swords, fighters and fantasy blades; new line of seven models with quick-draw, multi-carry Kydex sheaths. **Patterns:** Bowies, boots and one-of-a-kinds in his design or to customer specs. **Technical:** Grinds A6 and ATS-34; buys Damascus. Hand satin finish is standard. **Prices:** $100 to $1500; swords to $8000. **Remarks:** Part-time maker; first knife sold in 1984. **Mark:** Angel wings with last initial, or last name.

SHOGER, MARK O
POB 778, Kalama, WA 98625, Phone: 503-816-8615, mosdds@msn.com
Specialties: Working and using straight knives and folders of his design; fancy and embellished knives. **Patterns:** Hunters, Bowies, daggers and folders. **Technical:** Forges 01, W2, 1084, 5160, 52100 and 1084/15n20 pattern weld. **Remarks:** Spare-time maker. **Mark:** Last name "Shoger" or stamped last initial over anvil.

SHROPSHIRE, SHAWN
PO Box 453, Piedmont, OK 73078, Phone: 405-833-5239, shawn@sdsknifeworks.com; Web: www.sdsknifeworks.com
Specialties: Working straight knives and frontier style period pieces. **Patterns:** Bowies, hunters, skinners, fighters, patch/neck knives. **Technical:** Grinds D2, 154CM and some Damascus, forges 1084, 5160. **Prices:** Starting at $125. **Remarks:** Part-time maker; first knife sold in 1997. Doing business at SDS Knifeworks. **Mark:** Etched "SDS Knifeworks - Oklahoma" in an oval or "SDS" tang stamp.

SHULL, JAMES
5146 N US 231 W, Rensselaer, IN 47978, Phone: 219-866-0436, nbjs@netnitco.net Web: www.shullhandforgedknives.com
Specialties: Working knives of hunting, fillet, Bowie patterns. **Technical:** Forges or uses 1095, 5160, 52100 & 01. **Prices:** $100 to $300. **Remarks:** DBA Shull Handforged Knives. **Mark:** Last name in arc.

SIBERT, SHANE
PO BOX 241, Gladstone, OR 97027, Phone: 503-650-2082, shane.sibert@comcast.net Web: www.sibertknives.com
Specialties: Innovative knives designed for hostile environments, lightweight hiking and backpacking knives for outdoorsman and adventurers, progressive fixed blade combat

and fighting knives. One-of-a-kind knives of various configurations. Titanium frame lock folders. **Patterns:** Modern configurations of utility/camp knives, bowies, modified spear points, daggers, tantos, recurves, clip points and spine serrations. **Technical:** Stock removal. Specializes in CPM S30V, CPM S35VN, CPM D2, CPM 3V, stainless damascus. Micarta, G-10, stabilized wood and titanium. **Prices:** $200 - $1000, some pieces $1500 and up. **Remarks:** Full-time maker, first knife sold in 1994. **Mark:** Stamped "SIBERT" and occasionally uses electro-etch with oval around last name.

SIBRIAN, AARON
4308 Dean Dr, Ventura, CA 93003, Phone: 805-642-6950
Specialties: Tough working knives of his design and in standard patterns. **Patterns:** Makes a "Viper utility"—a kukri derivative and a variety of straight using knives. **Technical:** Grinds 440C and ATS-34. Offers traditional Japanese blades; soft backs, hard edges, temper lines. **Prices:** $60 to $100; some to $250. **Remarks:** Spare-time maker; first knife sold in 1989. **Mark:** Initials in diagonal line.

SIMMONS, H R
1100 Bay City Rd, Aurora, NC 27806, Phone: 252-916-2241
Specialties: Working/using straight knives of his design. **Patterns:** Fighters, hunters and utility/camp knives. **Technical:** Forges and grinds Damascus and L6; grinds ATS-34. **Prices:** $150 and up. **Remarks:** Part-time maker; first knife sold in 1987. Doing business as HRS Custom Knives, Royal Forge and Trading Company. **Mark:** HRS.

SIMONELLA, GIANLUIGI
Via Battiferri 33, Maniago, ITALY 33085, Phone: 01139-427-730350
Specialties: Traditional and classic folding and working/using knives of his design and to customer specs. **Patterns:** Bowies, fighters, hunters, utility/camp knives. **Technical:** Forges ATS-34, D2, 440C. **Prices:** $250 to $400; some to $1000. **Remarks:** Full-time maker; first knife sold in 1988. **Mark:** Wilson.

SINCLAIR, J E
520 Francis Rd, Pittsburgh, PA 15239, Phone: 412-793-5778
Specialties: Fancy hunters and fighters, liner locking folders. **Patterns:** Fighters, hunters and folders. **Technical:** Flat-grinds and hollow grind, prefers hand rubbed satin finish. Uses natural handle materials. **Prices:** $185 to $800. **Remarks:** Part-time maker; first knife sold in 1995. **Mark:** First and middle initials, last name and maker.

SINYARD, CLESTON S
27522 Burkhardt Dr, Elberta, AL 36530, Phone: 334-987-1361, nimoforge1@gulftel.com; Web: www.knifemakersguild
Specialties: Working straight knives and folders of his design. **Patterns:** Hunters, buckskinners, Bowies, daggers, fighters and all-Damascus folders. **Technical:** Makes Damascus from 440C, stainless steel, D2 and regular high-carbon steel; forges "forefinger pad" into hunters and skinners. **Prices:** In Damascus $450 to $1500; some $2500. **Remarks:** Full-time maker; first knife sold in 1980. Doing business as Nimo Forge. **Mark:** Last name, U.S.A. in anvil.

SIROIS, DARRIN
Tactical Combat Tools, 6182 Lake Trail Dr., Fayetteville, NC 28304, Phone: 910-730-0536, knives@tctknives.com; www.tctknives.com
Specialties: Tactical fighters, hunters and camp knives. **Technical:** Stock removal method of blade making, using D2 and 154CM steels. Entire process, including heat treat, done in-house. **Prices:** $80 to $750. **Remarks:** Part-time maker; first knife sold in 2008. **Mark:** Letters TCT surrounded by a triangle, or "Delta Tactical Combat Tools."

SISKA, JIM
48 South Maple St, Westfield, MA 01085, Phone: 413-642-3059, siskaknives@comcast.net
Specialties: Traditional working straight knives, no folders. **Patterns:** Hunters, fighters, Bowies and one-of-a-kinds; folders. **Technical:** Grinds D2, A2, 154CM and ATS-34, buys damascus and forges some blades. Likes exotic woods. **Prices:** $300 and up. **Remarks:** Part-time. **Mark:** Siska in Old English, or for forged blades, a hammer over maker's name.

SJOSTRAND, KEVIN
1541 S Cain St, Visalia, CA 93292, Phone: 559-625-5254
Specialties: Traditional and working/using straight knives and folders of his design or to customer specs. **Patterns:** Fixed blade hunters, Bowies, utility/camp knives. **Technical:** Grinds ATS-34, 440C and 1095. Prefers high polished blades and full tang. Natural and stabilized hardwoods, Micarta and stag handle material. **Prices:** $250 to $400. **Remarks:** Part-time maker; first knife sold in 1992. **Mark:** SJOSTRAND

SKIFF, STEVEN
SKIFF MADE BLADES, PO Box 537, Broadalbin, NY 12025, Phone: 518-883-4875, skiffmadeblades @hotmail.com; Web: www.skiffmadeblades.com
Specialties: Custom using/collector grade straight blades and LinerLock® folders of maker's design or customer specifications. **Patterns:** Hunters, utility/camp knives, tactical/fancy art folders. **Prices:** Straight blades $225 and up. Folders $450 and up. **Technical:** Stock removal hollow ground ATS-34, 154 CM, S30V, and tool steel. Damascus-Devon Thomas, Robert Eggerling, Mike Norris and Delbert Ealy. Nickel silver and stainless in-house heat treating. Handle materials: man made and natural woods (stabilized). Horn shells sheaths for straight blades, sews own leather and uses sheaths by "Tree-Stump Leather." **Remarks:** First knife sold 1997. Started making folders in 2000. **Mark:** SKIFF on blade of straight blades and in inside of backspacer on folders.

SLEE, FRED
9 John St, Morganville, NJ 07751, Phone: 732-591-9047
Specialties: Working straight knives, some fancy, to customer specs. **Patterns:** Hunters, fighters, fancy daggers and folders. **Technical:** Grinds D2, 440C and ATS-34. **Prices:** $285 to $1100. **Remarks:** Part-time maker; first knife sold in 1980. **Mark:** Letter "S" in Old English.

SLOAN, DAVID
PO BOX 83, Diller, NE 68342, Phone: 402-793-5755, sigp22045@hotmail.com
Specialties: Hunters, choppers and fighters. **Technical:** Forged blades of W2, 1084 and Damascus. **Prices:** Start at $225. **Remarks:** Part-time maker, made first knife in 2002, received JS stamp 2010. **Mark:** Sloan JS.

SLOAN, SHANE
4226 FM 61, Newcastle, TX 76372, Phone: 940-846-3290
Specialties: Collector-grade straight knives and folders. **Patterns:** Uses stainless Damascus, ATS-34 and 12C27. Bowies, lockers, slip-joints, fancy folders, fighters and period pieces. **Technical:** Grinds D2 and ATS-34. Uses hand-rubbed satin finish. Prefers rare natural handle materials. **Prices:** $250 to $6500. **Remarks:** Full-time maker; first knife sold in 1985. **Mark:** Name and city.

SLOBODIAN, SCOTT
PO Box 1498, San Andreas, CA 95249, Phone: 209-286-1980, Fax: 209-286-1982, info@slobodianswords.com; Web: www.slobodianswords.com
Specialties: Japanese-style knives and swords, period pieces, fantasy pieces and miniatures. **Patterns:** Small kweikens, tantos, wakazashis, katanas, traditional samurai swords. **Technical:** Flat-grinds 1050, commercial Damascus. **Prices:** Prices start at $1500. **Remarks:** Full-time maker; first knife sold in 1987. **Mark:** Blade signed in Japanese characters and various scripts.

SMALE, CHARLES J
509 Grove Ave, Waukegan, IL 60085, Phone: 847-244-8013

SMALL, ED
Rt 1 Box 178-A, Keyser, WV 26726, Phone: 304-298-4254, coldanvil@gmail.com
Specialties: Working knives of his design; period pieces. **Patterns:** Hunters, daggers, buckskinners and camp knives; likes one-of-a-kinds, very primative bowies. **Technical:** Forges and grinds W2, L6 and his own Damascus. **Prices:** $150 to $1500. **Remarks:** Full-time maker; first knife sold in 1978. **Mark:** Script initials connected.

SMART, STEVE
907 Park Row Cir, McKinney, TX 75070-3847, Phone: 214-882-0441, Fax: 972-548-7151
Specialties: Working/using straight knives and folders of his design, to customer specs and in standard patterns. **Patterns:** Bowies, hunters, kitchen knives, locking folders, utility/camp, fishing and bird knives. **Technical:** Grinds ATS-34, D2, 440C and O1. Prefers mirror polish or satin finish; hollow-grinds all blades. All knives come with sheath. Offers some filework. **Prices:** $95 to $225; some to $500. **Remarks:** Spare-time maker; first knife sold in 1983. **Mark:** Name, Custom, city and state in oval.

SMIT, GLENN
627 Cindy Ct, Aberdeen, MD 21001, Phone: 410-272-2959, wolfsknives@comcast.net; Web: www.facebook.com/Wolf'sKnives
Specialties: Working and using straight and folding knives of his design or to customer specs. Customizes and repairs all types of cutlery. Exclusive maker of Dave Murphy Style knives. **Patterns:** Hunters, Bowies, daggers, fighters, utility/camp, folders, kitchen knives and miniatures, Murphy combat, C.H.A.I.K., Little 88 and Tiny 90-styles. **Technical:** Grinds 440C, ATS-34, O1, A2 also grinds 6AL4V titanium allox for blades. Reforges commercial Damascus and makes cast aluminum handles. **Prices:** Miniatures start at $50; full-size knives start at $100. **Remarks:** Spare-time maker; first knife sold in 1986. Doing business as Wolf's Knives. **Mark:** G.P. SMIT, with year on reverse side, Wolf's Knives-Murphy's way with date.

SMITH, CHRIS
POB 351, Burgin, KY 40310, Phone: 859-948-1505, fireman6152000@yahoo.com; Web: Facebook.com: CS&Sons
Technical: Stock removal method of blade making using mainly simple carbon steels like 1080, 1084, 5160 and some damascus, has done a few forged knives. **Prices:** $100 to $500. **Remarks:** Part-time maker since June of 2014. **Mark:** Maker's initials in his own cursive script, the same way he has signed his work since he was in art class in elementary school.

SMITH, J D
22 Ledge St., Melrose, MA 02176, Phone: 857-492-5324, mamboslave@yahoo.com
Specialties: Fighters, Bowies, Persian, locking folders and swords. **Patterns:** Bowies, fighters and locking folders. **Technical:** Forges and grinds D2, his Damascus, O1, 52100 etc. and wootz-pattern hammer steel. **Prices:** $500 to $2000; some to $5000. **Remarks:** Full-time maker; first knife sold in 1987. Doing business as Hammersmith. **Mark:** Last initial alone or in cartouche.

SMITH, J.B.
21 Copeland Rd., Perkinston, MS 39573, Phone: 228-380-1851
Specialties: Traditional working knives for the hunter and fisherman. **Patterns:** Hunters, Bowies, and fishing knives; copies of 1800 period knives. **Technical:** Grinds ATS-34, 440C. **Prices:** $100 to $800. **Remarks:** Full-time maker, first knife sold in 1972. **Mark:** J.B. Smith MAKER PERKINSTON, MS.

SMITH, JERRY W.
Jerry W. Smith Knives, 1950 CR 5120, Willow Springs, MO 65793, Phone: 417-252-7463, jwdeb93@gmail.com; Web: www.jerrywsmith.com
Specialties: Loveless-style knives, folders/slip joints. **Patterns:** Sway backs and drop-point hunters. **Technical:** Steels used D2, A2, O1, 154CM and CPM 154. Stock removal, heat treat in house, all leather work in house. **Prices:** Start at $200. **Remarks:** Full-time knifemaker. First knife made in 2004. **Mark:** Jerry W Smith USA.

SMITH, JOHN M

3450 E Beguelin Rd, Centralia, IL 62801, Phone: 618-249-6444, jknife@frontiernet.net
Specialties: Folders. **Patterns:** Folders. **Prices:** $250 to $2500. **Remarks:** First knife sold in 1980. Not taking orders at this time on fixed blade knives. Part-time maker. **Mark:** Etched signature or logo.

SMITH, JOHN W

1322 Cow Branch Rd, West Liberty, KY 41472, Phone: 606-743-3599, jwsknive@mrtc.com; Web: www.jwsmithknives.com
Specialties: Fancy and working locking folders of his design or to customer specs. **Patterns:** Interframes, traditional and daggers. **Technical:** Grinds 530V and his own Damascus. Offers gold inlay, engraving with gold inlay, hand-fitted mosaic pearl inlay and filework. Prefers hand-rubbed finish. Pearl and ivory available. **Prices:** Utility pieces $375 to $650. Art knives $1200 to $10,000. **Remarks:** Full-time maker. **Mark:** Initials engraved inside diamond.

SMITH, JOSH

Box 753, Frenchtown, MT 59834, Phone: 406-626-5775, joshsmithknives@gmail.com; Web: www.joshsmithknives.com
Specialties: Mosaic, Damascus, LinerLock folders, automatics, Bowies, fighters, etc. **Patterns:** All kinds. **Technical:** Advanced Mosaic and Damascus. **Prices:** $450 and up. **Remarks:** A.B.S. Master Smith. **Mark:** Josh Smith with last two digits of the current year.

SMITH, LACY

PO BOX 188, Jacksonville, AL 36265, Phone: 256-310-4619, sales@smith-knives.com; Web: www.smith-knives.com
Specialties: All styles of fixed-blade knives. **Technical:** Stock removal method of blade making. **Prices:** $100 and up. **Mark:** Circle with three dots and three S's on inside.

SMITH, LENARD C

PO Box D68, Valley Cottage, NY 10989, Phone: 914-268-7359

SMITH, MICHAEL J

1418 Saddle Gold Ct, Brandon, FL 33511, Phone: 813-431-3790, smithknife@hotmail.com; Web: www.smithknife.com
Specialties: Fancy high art folders of his design. **Patterns:** Locking locks and automatics. **Technical:** Uses ATS-34, non-stainless and stainless Damascus; hand carves folders, prefers ivory and pearl. Hand-rubbed satin finish. Liners are 6AL4V titanium. **Prices:** $500 to $3000. **Remarks:** Full-time maker; first knife sold in 1989. **Mark:** Name, city, state.

SMITH, NEWMAN L.

865 Glades Rd Shop #3, Gatlinburg, TN 37738, Phone: 423-436-3322, thesmithshop@aol.com; Web: www.thesmithsshop.com
Specialties: Collector-grade and working knives. **Patterns:** Hunters, slip-joint and lock-back folders, some miniatures. **Technical:** Grinds O1 and ATS-34; makes fancy sheaths. **Prices:** $165 to $750; some to $1000. **Remarks:** Full-time maker; first knife sold in 1984. Partners part-time to handle Damascus blades by Jeff Hurst; marks these with SH connected. **Mark:** First and middle initials, last name.

SMITH, RALPH L

525 Groce Meadow Rd, Taylors, SC 29687, Phone: 864-444-0819, ralph_smith1@charter.net; Web: www.smithhandcraftedknives.com
Specialties: Working knives: straight and folding knives. Hunters, skinners, fighters, bird, boot, Bowie and kitchen knives. **Technical:** Concave Grind D2, ATS 34, 440C, steel hand finish or polished. **Prices:** $125 to $350 for standard models. **Remarks:** First knife sold in 1976. KMG member since 1981. SCAK founding member and past president. **Mark:** SMITH handcrafted knives in SC state outline.

SMITH, RAYMOND L

217 Red Chalk Rd, Erin, NY 14838, Phone: 607-795-5257, Bladesmith@wildblue.net; Web: www.theanvilsedge.com
Specialties: Working/using straight knives and folders to customer specs and in standard patterns; period pieces. **Patterns:** Bowies, hunters, slip joints. **Technical:** Forges 5160, 52100, 1018, 15N20, 1084, ATS 34. Damascus and wire cable Damascus. Filework. **Prices:** $125 to $1500; estimates for custom orders. **Remarks:** Full-time maker; first knife sold in 1991. ABS Master Smith. Doing business as The Anvils Edge. **Mark:** Ellipse with RL Smith, Erin NY MS in center.

SMITH, RICK

BEAR BONE KNIVES, 1843 W Evans Creek Rd., Rogue River, OR 97537, Phone: 541-582-4144, BearBoneSmith@msn.com; Web: www.bearbone.com
Specialties: Classic, historical style Bowie knives, hunting knives and various contemporary knife styles. **Technical:** Blades are either forged or made by stock removal method depending on steel used. Also forge weld wire Damascus. Does own heat treating and tempering using digital even heat kiln. Stainless blades are sent out for cryogenic "freeze treat." Preferred steels are O1, tool, 5160, 1095, 1084, ATS-34, 154CM, 440C and various high carbon Damascus. **Prices:** $350 to $1500. Custom leather sheaths available for knives. **Remarks:** Full-time maker since 1997. Serial numbers no longer put on knives. Official business name is "Bear Bone Knives." **Mark:** Early maker's mark was "Bear Bone" over capital letters "RS" with downward arrow between letters and "Hand Made" underneath letters. Mark on small knives is 3/8 circle containing "RS" with downward arrow between letters. Current mark since 2003 is "R Bear Bone Smith" arching over image of coffin Bowie knife with two shooting stars and "Rogue River, Oregon" underneath.

SMITH, SHAWN

2644 Gibson Ave, Clouis, CA 93611, Phone: 559-323-6234, kslc@sbcglobal.net
Specialties: Working and fancy straight knives. **Patterns:** Hunting, trout, fighters, skinners. **Technical:** Hollow grinds ATS-34, 154CM, A-2. **Prices:** $150.00 and up. **Remarks:** Part time maker. **Mark:** Shawn Smith handmade.

SMITH, STUART

Smith Hand Forged Knives, 32 Elbon Rd., Blairgowrie, Gauteng, SOUTH AFRICA 2123, Phone: +27 84 248 1324, samuraistu@forgedknives.co.za; www.forgedknives.co.za
Specialties: Hand-forged bowie knives and puukos in high-carbon steel and maker's own damascus. **Patterns:** Bowies, puukos, daggers, hunters, fighters, skinners and swords. **Technical:** Forges 5160, 1070, 52100 and SilverSteel, and maker's own damascus from 5160 and Bohler K600 nickel tool steel. Fitted guards and threaded pommels. Own heat treating. Wood and bronze carving. Own sheaths and custom sheaths. **Prices:** $150 to $1,500. **Remarks:** Full-time maker since 2004; first knife sold in 2000. **Mark:** Stamped outline of an anvil with SMITH underneath on right side of knife. For 2014, anvil and surname with 10Yrs.

SMOCK, TIMOTHY E

1105 N Sherwood Dr, Marion, IN 46952, Phone: 765-664-0123

SNODY, MIKE

910 W. Young Ave., Aransas Pass, TX 78336, Phone: 361-443-0161, snodyknives@yahoo.com; Web: www.snodygallery.com
Specialties: High performance straight knives in traditional and Japanese-styles. **Patterns:** Skinners, hunters, tactical, Kwaiken and tantos. **Technical:** Grinds BG42, ATS-34, 440C and A2. Offers full or tapered tangs, upgraded handle materials such as fossil ivory, coral and exotic woods. Traditional diamond wrap over stingray on Japanese-style knives. Sheaths available in leather or Kydex. **Prices:** $100 to $1000. **Remarks:** Part-time maker; first knife sold in 1999. **Mark:** Name over knife maker.

SNOW, BILL

4824 18th Ave, Columbus, GA 31904, Phone: 706-576-4390, tipikw@knology.net
Specialties: Traditional working/using straight knives and folders of his design and to customer specs. Offers engraving and scrimshaw. **Patterns:** Bowies, fighters, hunters and folders. **Technical:** Grinds ATS-34, 440V, 440C, 420V, CPM350, BG42, A2, D2, 5160, 52100 and O1; forges if needed. Cryogenically quenches all steels; inlaid handles; some integrals; leather or Kydex sheaths. **Prices:** $125 to $700; some to $3500. **Remarks:** Now also have 530V, 10V and 3V steels in use. Full-time maker; first knife sold in 1958. Doing business as Tipi Knife works. **Mark:** Old English scroll "S" inside a tipi.

SOAPER, MAX H.

2375 Zion Rd, Henderson, KY 42420, Phone: 270-827-8143
Specialties: Primitive Longhunter knives, scalpers, camp knives, cowboy Bowies, neck knives, working knives, period pieces from the 18th century. **Technical:** Forges 5160, 1084, 1095; all blades differentially heat treated. **Prices:** $80 to $800. **Remarks:** Part-time maker since 1989. **Mark:** Initials in script.

SOILEAU, DAMON

POB 7292, Kingsport, TN 37664, Phone: 423-297-4665, oiseaumetalarts@gmail.com; Web: www.oiseaumetalarts.etsy.com
Specialties: Natural and exotic materials, slip-joint folders, fixed blades, hidden tang and full tang, hand engraving. **Patterns:** Slip-joint folders, hunters, skinners and art knives. **Technical:** Stock removal of damascus, forges W2, O1 and 1084. **Prices:** $150 to $2,000. **Remarks:** Full-time maker and hand engraver. **Mark:** Hand engraved last name on spine of blade, or inside back spring of folders.

SONNTAG, DOUGLAS W

902 N 39th St, Nixa, MO 65714, Phone: 417-693-1640, dougsonntag@gmail.com
Specialties: Working knives; art knives. **Patterns:** Hunters, boots, straight working knives; Bowies, some folders, camp/axe sets. **Technical:** Grinds D2, ATS-34, forges own Damascus; does own heat treating. **Prices:** $225 and up. **Remarks:** Full-time maker; first knife sold in 1986. **Mark:** Etched name in arch.

SONNTAG, JACOB D

14148 Trisha Dr., St. Robert, MO 65584, Phone: 573-336-4082, Jake0372@live.com
Specialties: Working knives, some art knives. **Patterns:** Hunters, bowies, and tomahawks. **Technical:** Grinds D2, ATS34 and Damascus. Forges some Damascus and tomahawks; does own heat treating. **Prices:** $200 and up. **Remarks:** Part-time maker; first knife sold in 2010. **Mark:** Etched name or stamped

SONNTAG, KRISTOPHER D

902 N 39th St, Nixa, MO 65714, Phone: 417-838-8327, kriss@buildit.us
Specialties: Working fixed blades, hunters, skinners, using knives. **Patterns:** Hunters, bowies, skinners. **Technical:** Grinds D2, ATS 34, Damascus. Makes some Damascus; does own heat treating. **Prices:** $200 and up. **Remarks:** Part-time maker; first knife sold in 2010. **Mark:** Etched name or stamped

SONTHEIMER, G DOUGLAS

14821 Dufief Mill Rd., Gaithersburg, MD 20878, Phone: 301-948-5227
Specialties: Fixed blade knives. **Patterns:** Whitetail deer, backpackers, camp, claws, fillet, fighters. **Technical:** Hollow Grinds. **Prices:** $500 and up. **Remarks:** Spare-time maker; first knife sold in 1976. **Mark:** LORD.

SORNBERGER, JIM

25126 Overland Dr, Volcano, CA 95689, Phone: 209-295-7819, sierrajs@volcano.net
Specialties: Master engraver making classic San Francisco-style knives. Collectible straight knives. **Patterns:** Fighters, daggers, bowies, miniatures, hunters, custom canes and LinerLock folders. **Technical:** Grinds 440C, 154CM and ATS-34; engraves, carves and embellishes. **Prices:** $500 to $35,000 in gold with gold quartz inlays. **Remarks:** Full-time maker; first knife sold in 1970. Master engraver. **Mark:** First initial, last name, city and state.

SOWELL, BILL
100 Loraine Forest Ct, Macon, GA 31210, Phone: 478- 994-9863, billsowell@reynoldscable.net

Specialties: Antique reproduction Bowies, forging Bowies, hunters, fighters, and most others. Also folders. **Technical:** Makes own Damascus, using 1084/15N20, also making own designs in powder metals, forges 5160-1095-1084, and other carbon steels, grinds ATS-34. **Prices:** Starting at $150 and up. **Remarks:** Part-time maker. Sold first knife in 1998. Does own leather work. ABS Master Smith. **Mark:** Iron Horse Forge - Sowell - MS.

SPAKE, JEREMY
6128 N. Concord Ave., Portland, OR 97217-4735, jeremy@spakeknife.com; Web: www.spakeknife.com, www.instagram.com/jspake

Specialties: Handmade hidden-tang fixed blade knives. **Patterns:** Utility, hunting and Nordic-influenced knives, kitchen cutlery and others as the occasion arises. **Technical:** Concentration on forged three-layer laminated blades with high-carbon steel cores. Also forges high-carbon mono-steel blades. Stock removal on occasion. For handles, prefers a variety fo stabilized woods and premium natural materials. **Prices:** $350 to $500 and up. **Remarks:** Part-time maker; first knife sold in 2012. American Bladesmith Society member. **Mark:** Last name etched or stamped in Gotham typeface.

SPARKS, BERNARD
PO Box 73, Dingle, ID 83233, Phone: 208-847-1883, dogknifeii@juno.com; Web: www.sparksknives.com

Specialties: Maker engraved, working and art knives. Straight knives and folders of his own design. **Patterns:** Locking inner-frame folders, hunters, fighters, one-of-a-kind art knives. **Technical:** Grinds 530V steel, 440-C, 154CM, ATS-34, D-2 and forges by special order; triple temper, cryogenic soak. Mirror or hand finish. New Liquid metal steel. **Prices:** $300 to $2000. **Remarks:** Full-time maker, first knife sold in 1967. **Mark:** Last name over state with a knife logo on each end of name. Prior 1980, stamp of last name.

SPICKLER, GREGORY NOBLE
5614 Mose Cir, Sharpsburg, MD 21782, Phone: 301-432-2746

SPINALE, RICHARD
4021 Canterbury Ct, Lorain, OH 44053, Phone: 440-282-1565

Specialties: High-art working knives of his design. **Patterns:** Hunters, fighters, daggers and locking folders. **Technical:** Grinds 440C, ATS-34 and 07; engraves. Offers gold bolsters and other deluxe treatments. **Prices:** $300 to $1000; some to $3000. **Remarks:** Spare-time maker; first knife sold in 1976. **Mark:** Name, address, year and model number.

SPIVEY, JEFFERSON
9244 W Wilshire, Yukon, OK 73099, Phone: 405-371-9304, jspivey5@cox.net

Specialties: The Saber tooth: a combination hatchet, saw and knife. **Patterns:** Built for the wilderness, all are one-of-a-kind. **Technical:** Grinds chromemoly steel. The saw tooth spine curves with a double row of biangular teeth. **Prices:** Start at $275. **Remarks:** First knife sold in 1977. As of September 2006 Spivey knives has resumed production of the Sabertooth knife (one word trademark).**Mark:** Name and serial number.

SPRAGG, WAYNE E
252 Oregon Ave, Lovell, WY 82431, Phone: 307-548-7212

Specialties: Working straight knives, some fancy. **Patterns:** Folders. **Technical:** Forges carbon steel and makes Damascus. **Prices:** $200 and up. **Remarks:** All stainless heat-treated by Paul Bos. Carbon steel in shop heat treat. **Mark:** Last name front side w/s initials on reverse side.

SPROKHOLT, ROB
Burgerweg 5, Gatherwood, NETHERLANDS 1754 KB Burgerbrug, Phone: 0031 6 51230225, Fax: 0031 84 2238446, info@gatherwood.nl; Web: www.gatherwood.nl

Specialties: One-of-a-kind knives. Top materials collector grade, made to use. **Patterns:** Outdoor knives (hunting, sailing, hiking), Bowies, man's surviving companions MSC, big tantos, folding knives. **Technical:** Handles mostly stabilized or oiled wood, ivory, Micarta, carbon fibre, G10. Stiff knives are full tang. Characteristic one row of massive silver pins or tubes. Folding knives have a LinerLock® with titanium or Damascus powdersteel liner thumb can have any stone you like. Stock removal grinder: flat or convex. Steel 440-C, RWL-34, ATS-34, PM damascener steel. **Prices:** Start at 320 euro. **Remarks:** Writer of the first Dutch knifemaking book, supply shop for knife enthusiastic. First knife sold in 2000. **Mark:** Gatherwood in an eclipse etched blade or stamped in an intarsia of silver in the spine.

SQUIRE, JACK
350 W. 7th St., McMinnville, OR 97182-5509, Phone: 503-472-7290

ST. AMOUR, MURRAY
2066 Lapasse Rd., Beachburg, Ontario, CANADA K0J 1C0, Phone: 613-587-4194, knives@nrtco.net; Web: www.st-amourknives.com

Specialties: Hunters, fish knives, outdoor knives, bowies and some collectors' pieces. **Technical:** Steels include CPM S30V, CPM S90V, CPM 154, 154CM and ATS 34. **Remarks:** Full-time maker; first knife sold in 1992. **Mark:** St. Amour over Canada or small print st. amour.

ST. CLAIR, THOMAS K
12608 Fingerboard Rd, Monrovia, MD 21770, Phone: 301-482-0264

STAFFORD, RICHARD
104 Marcia Ct, Warner Robins, GA 31088, Phone: 912-923-6372, Fax: Cell: 478-508-5821, rnrstafford@cox.net

Specialties: High-tech straight knives and some folders. **Patterns:** Hunters in several patterns, fighters, boots, camp knives, combat knives and period pieces. **Technical:** Grinds ATS-34 and 440C. Machine satin finish offered. **Prices:** Starting at $150. **Remarks:** Part-timer maker; first knife sold in 1983. **Mark:** R. W. STAFFORD GEORGIA.

STAINTHORP, GUY
4 Fisher St, Brindley Ford, Stroke-on-Trent, ENGLAND ST8 7QJ, Phone: 07946 469 888, guystainthorp@hotmail.com Web: http://stainthorpknives.co.uk/index.html

Specialties: Tactical and outdoors knives to his own design. **Patterns:** Hunting, survival and occasionally folding knives. **Technical:** Grinds RWL-34, O1, S30V, Damasteel. Micarta, G10 and stabilised wood/bone for handles. **Prices:** $200 - $1000. **Remarks:** Full-time knifemaker. **Mark:** Squared stylised GS over "Stainthorp".

STALCUP, EDDIE
PO Box 2200, Gallup, NM 87305, Phone: 505-863-3107, sharon.stalcup@gmail.com

Specialties: Working and fancy hunters, bird and trout. Special custom orders. **Patterns:** Drop point hunters, locking liner and multi blade folders. **Technical:** ATS-34, 154 CM, 440C, CPM 154 and S30V. **Prices:** $150 to $1500. **Remarks:** Scrimshaw, exotic handle material, wet formed sheaths. Membership Arizona Knife Collectors Association. Southern California blades collectors & professional knife makers assoc. **Mark:** E.F. Stalcup, Gallup, NM.

STANCER, CHUCK
62 Hidden Ranch Rd NW, Calgary, AB, CANADA T3A 5S5, Phone: 403-295-7370, stancerc@telusplanet.net

Specialties: Traditional and working straight knives. **Patterns:** Bowies, hunters and utility knives. **Technical:** Forges and grinds most steels. **Prices:** $175 and up. **Remarks:** Part-time maker. **Mark:** Last name.

STANFORD, PERRY
405N Walnut #9, Broken Arrow, OK 74012, Phone: 918-251-7983 or 866-305-5690, stanfordoutdoors@valornet; Web: www.stanfordoutdoors.homestead.com

Specialties: Drop point, hunting and skinning knives, handmade sheaths. **Patterns:** Stright, hunting, and skinners. **Technical:** Grinds 440C, ATS-34 and Damascus. **Prices:** $65 to $275. **Remarks:** Part-time maker, first knife sold in 2007. Knifemaker supplier, manufacturer of paper sharpening systems. Doing business as Stanford Outdoors. **Mark:** Company name and nickname.

STANLEY, JOHN
604 Elm St, Crossett, AR 71635, Phone: 970-304-3005

Specialties: Hand forged fixed blades with engraving and carving. **Patterns:** Scottish dirks, skeans and fantasy blades. **Technical:** Forge high-carbon steel, own Damascus. Prices $70 to $500. **Remarks:** All work is sole authorship. Offers engraving and carving services on other knives and handles. **Mark:** Varies.

STAPLETON, WILLIAM E
BUFFALO 'B' FORGE, 5425 Country Ln, Merritt Island, FL 32953

Specialties: Classic and traditional knives of his design and customer spec. **Patterns:** Hunters and using knives. **Technical:** Forges, O1 and L6 Damascus, cable Damascus and 5160; stock removal on request. **Prices:** $150 to $1000. **Remarks:** Part-time maker, first knife sold 1990. Doing business as Buffalo "B" Forge. **Mark:** Anvil with S initial in center of anvil.

STATES, JOSHUA C
43905 N 16th St, New River, AZ 85087, Phone: 623-826-3809, Web: www.dosgatosforge.com

Specialties: Design and fabrication of forged working and art knives from O1 and my own damascus. Stock removal from 440C and CM154 upon request. Folders from 440C, CM154 and Damascus. Flat and Hollow grinds. Knives made to customer specs and/or design.**Patterns:** Bowies, hunters, daggers, chef knives, and exotic shapes. **Technical:** Damascus is 1095, 1084, O1 and 15N20. Carved or file-worked fittings from various metals including my own mokume gane and Damascus.**Prices:** $250 and up. **Remarks:** Part-time maker with waiting list. First knife sold in 2006. **Mark:** Initials JCS in small oval, or States in italisized script. Unmarked knives come with certificate of authorship.

STECK, VAN R
260 W Dogwood Ave, Orange City, FL 32763, Phone: 407-416-1723, van@thudknives.com

Specialties: Specializing in double-edged grinds. Free-hand grinds: folders, spears, bowies, swords and miniatures. **Patterns:** Tomahawks with a crane for the spike, tactical merged with nature.**Technical:** Hamon lines, folder lock of own design, the arm-lock! **Prices:** $50 - $1500. **Remarks:** Builds knives designed by Laci Szabo or builds to customer design. Studied with Reese Weiland on folders and automatics. **Mark:** GEISHA holding a sword with initials and THUD KNIVES in a circle.

STEGALL, KEITH
701 Outlet View Dr, Wasilla, AK 99654, Phone: 907-376-0703, kas5200@yahoo.com

Specialties: Traditional working straight knives. **Patterns:** Most patterns. **Technical:** Grinds 440C and 154CM. **Prices:** $100 to $300. **Remarks:** Spare-time maker; first knife sold in 1987. **Mark:** Name and state with anchor.

STEGNER, WILBUR G
9242 173rd Ave SW, Rochester, WA 98579, Phone: 360-273-0937, wilbur@wgsk.net; Web: www.wgsk.net

Specialties: Working/using straight knives and folders of his design. **Patterns:** Hunters and locking folders. **Technical:** Makes his own Damascus steel. **Prices:** $100 to $1000; some to $5000. **Remarks:** Full-time maker; first knife sold in 1979. Google search key words-"STEGNER KNIVES." Best folder awards NWKC 2009, 2010 and 2011. **Mark:** First and middle initials, last name in bar over shield logo.

STEIER, DAVID
7722 Zenith Way, Louisville, KY 40219, Phone: 502-969-8409, umag300@aol.com; Web: www.steierknives.com

Specialties: Folding LinerLocks, Bowies, slip joints, lockbacks, and straight hunters. **Technical:** Stock removal blades of 440C, ATS-34, and Damascus from outside sources like Robert Eggerling and Mike Norris. **Prices:** $150 for straight hunters to $1400 for fully decked-out folders. **Remarks:** First knife sold in 1979. **Mark:** Last name STEIER.

STEIGER, MONTE L
Box 186, Genesee, ID 83832, Phone: 208-285-1769, monteshatron@genesee-id.com
Specialties: Traditional working/using straight knives of all designs. **Patterns:** Hunters, utility/camp knives, fillet and chefs. **Technical:** Grinds 1095, O1, 440C, ATS-34. Handles of stacked leather, natural wood, Micarta or pakkawood. Each knife comes with right- or left-handed sheath. **Prices:** $110 to $600. **Remarks:** Spare-time maker; first knife sold in 1988. Retired librarian **Mark:** First initial, last name, city and state.

STEIGERWALT, KEN
507 Savagehill Rd, Orangeville, PA 17859, Phone: 570-683-5156, Web: www.steigerwaltknives.com
Specialties: Elaborate carving and inlays, primarily in Art Deco design. **Patterns:** Folders, button locks and rear locks. **Technical:** Uses CPM 154, CPM S35V, RWL-34 and damascus steels. **Prices:** $500 to $10,000. **Remarks:** Full-time maker; first knife sold in 1981. **Mark:** Kasteigerwalt

STEINAU, JURGEN
Julius-Hart Strasse 44, Berlin, GERMANY 01162, Phone: 372-6452512, Fax: 372-645-2512
Specialties: Fantasy and high-art straight knives of his design. **Patterns:** Boots, daggers and switch-blade folders. **Technical:** Grinds 440B, 2379 and X90 Cr.Mo.V. 78. **Prices:** $1500 to $2500; some to $3500. **Remarks:** Full-time maker; first knife sold in 1984. **Mark:** Symbol, plus year, month day and serial number.

STEINBERG, AL
5244 Duenas, Laguna Woods, CA 92653, Phone: 949-951-2889, lagknife@fea.net
Specialties: Fancy working straight knives to customer specs. **Patterns:** Hunters, Bowies, fishing, camp knives, push knives and high end kitchen knives. **Technical:** Grinds O1, 440C and 154CM. **Prices:** $60 to $2500. **Remarks:** Full-time maker; first knife sold in 1972. **Mark:** Signature, city and state.

STEINBRECHER, MARK W
1122 92nd Place, Pleasant Prairie, WI 53158-4939
Specialties: Working and fancy folders. **Patterns:** Daggers, pocket knives, fighters and gents of his own design or to customer specs. **Technical:** Hollow grinds ATS-34, O1 other makers Damascus. Uses natural handle materials: stag, ivories, mother-of-pearl. File work and some inlays. **Prices:** $500 to $1200, some to $2500. **Remarks:** Part-time maker, first folder sold in 1989. **Mark:** Name etched or handwritten on ATS-34; stamped on Damascus.

STEINGASS, T.K.
334 Silver Lake Rd., Bucksport, ME 04416, Phone: 304-268-1161, tksteingass@frontier.com; Web: http://steingassknives.com
Specialties: Loveless style hunters and fighters and sole authorship knives: Man Knife, Silent Hunter, and Silent Fighter. Harpoon Grind Camp Knife and Harpoon Grind Man Hunter. **Technical:** Stock removal, use CPM 154, S3V and occasionally 1095 or O1 for camp choppers.**Prices:** $200 to $500. **Remarks:** Part-time maker; first knife made in 2010. **Mark:** STEINGASS.

STEKETEE, CRAIG A
871 NE US Hwy 60, Billings, MO 65610, Phone: 417-744-2770, stekknives04@yahoo.com
Specialties: Classic and working straight knives and swords of his design. **Patterns:** Bowies, hunters, and Japanese-style swords. **Technical:** Forges his own Damascus; bronze, silver and Damascus fittings, offers filework. Prefers exotic and natural handle materials. **Prices:** $200 to $4000. **Remarks:** Full-time maker. **Mark:** STEK.

STEPHAN, DANIEL
2201 S Miller Rd, Valrico, FL 33594, Phone: 727-580-8617, knifemaker@verizon.net
Specialties: Art knives, one-of-a-kind.

STERLING, MURRAY
693 Round Peak Church Rd, Mount Airy, NC 27030, Phone: 336-352-5110, Fax: Fax: 336-352-5105, sterck@surry.net; Web: www.sterlingcustomknives.com
Specialties: Single and dual blade folders. Interframes and integral dovetail frames. **Technical:** Grinds ATS-34 or Damascus by Mike Norris and/or Devin Thomas. **Prices:** $400 to $1,200. **Remarks:** Full-time maker; first knife sold in 1991. **Mark:** Last name stamped.

STERLING, THOMAS J
ART KNIVES BY, POB 1621, Coupeville, WA 98239, Phone: 360-678-9269, Fax: 360-678-9269, netsuke@comcast.net; Web: www.sterlingsculptures.com
Specialties: Since 2003, Tom Sterling has created one-of-a-kind, ultra-quality art knives, jewelry and assorted doodads using high-quality precious and semi-precious materials, steel, titanium, shibuichi and shakudo. His work is often influenced by the traditions of Japanese netsuke and a unique fusion of cultures and styles. Tom's highly sought-after engraving skills reflect stylistically integrated choices of materials and contrasting inlays for a unique presentation style. **Prices:** $300 to $14,000. **Remarks:** Limited output ensures highest quality artwork and exceptional levels of craftsmanship. **Mark:** TJSterling.

STEYN, PETER
PO Box 76, Welkom, Freestate, SOUTH AFRICA 9460, Phone: 27573522015, Fax: 27573523566, Web:www.petersteynknives.com email:info@petersteynknives.com
Specialties: Fixed blade knives of own design, all with hand-stitched leather sheaths.

Folding knives of own design supplied with soft pouches. **Patterns:** Fixed blades: hunters and skinners. Folding knives: friction folders, slip joints and lockbacks. **Technical:** Grinds 12C27 and Damasteel. Blades are bead-blasted in plain or patterned finish. Ceramic wash also available in satin or antiqued finish. Grind syle is convex, concave on the obverse, and convex on the reverse. Works with a wide variety of handle materials, prefers exotic woods and synthetics. **Prices:** $150 to $650. **Remarks:** Full-time maker, first knife sold 2005, member of South African Guild. **Mark:** Letter 'S' in shape of pyramid with full name above and 'Handcrafted' below.

STICE, DOUGLAS W
PO Box 12815, Wichita, KS 67277, Phone: 316-295-6855, doug@sticecraft.com; Web: www.sticecraft.com
Specialties: Working fixed blade knives of own design. **Patterns:** Tacticals, hunters, skinners,utility, and camp knives. **Technical:** Grinds CPM154CM, 154CM, CPM3V, Damascus; uses 18" contact grinds where wheel for hollow grinds, also flat. **Prices:** $100 to $750. **Remarks:** Full-time maker; first professional knife made in 2009. All knives have serial numbers and include certificate of authenticity. **Mark:** Stylized "Stice" stamp.

STIDHAM, DANIEL
3106 Mill Cr. Rd., Gallipolis, Ohio 45631, Phone: 740-446-1673, danstidham@yahoo.com
Specialties: Fixed blades, folders, Bowies and hunters. **Technical:** 440C, Alabama Damascus, 1095 with filework. **Prices:** Start at $150. **Remarks:** Has made fixed blades since 1961, folders since 1986. Also sells various knife brands.**Mark:** Stidham Knives Gallipolis, Ohio 45631.

STIMPS, JASON M
374 S Shaffer St, Orange, CA 92866, Phone: 714-744-5866

STIPES, DWIGHT
2651 SW Buena Vista Dr, Palm City, FL 34990, Phone: 772-597-0550, dwightstipes@adelphia.net
Specialties: Traditional and working straight knives in standard patterns. **Patterns:** Boots, Bowies, daggers, hunters and fighters. **Technical:** Grinds 440C, D2 and D3 tool steel. Handles of natural materials, animal, bone or horn. **Prices:** $75 to $150. **Remarks:** Full-time maker; first knife sold in 1972. **Mark:** Stipes.

STOKES, ED
22614 Cardinal Dr, Hockley, TX 77447, Phone: 713-351-1319
Specialties: Working straight knives and folders of all designs. **Patterns:** Boots, Bowies, daggers, fighters, hunters and miniatures. **Technical:** Grinds ATS-34, 440C and D2. Offers decorative butt caps, tapered spacers on handles and finger grooves, nickel-silver inlays, handmade sheaths. **Prices:** $185 to $290; some to $350. **Remarks:** Full-time maker; first knife sold in 1973. **Mark:** First and last name, Custom Knives with Apache logo.

STONE, JERRY
PO Box 1027, Lytle, TX 78052, Phone: 830-709-3042
Specialties: Traditional working and using folders of his design and to customer specs; fancy knives. **Patterns:** Fighters, hunters, locking folders and slip joints. Also make automatics. **Technical:** Grinds 440C and ATS-34. Offers filework. **Prices:** $175 to $1000. **Remarks:** Full-time maker; first knife sold in 1973. **Mark:** Name over Texas star/town and state underneath.

STORCH, ED
RR 4, Mannville, AB, CANADA T0B 2W0, Phone: 780-763-2214, storchknives@gmail.com; Web: www.storchknives.com
Specialties: Working knives, fancy fighting knives, kitchen cutlery and art knives. Knifemaking classes. **Patterns:** Working patterns, Bowies and folders. **Technical:** Forges his own Damascus. Grinds ATS-34. Builds friction folders. Salt heat treating. **Prices:** $100 to $3,000 (U.S.). **Remarks:** Full-time maker; first knife sold in 1984. Classes taught in stock-removal, and damascus and sword making. **Mark:** Last name.

STORMER, BOB
34354 Hwy E, Dixon, MO 65459, Phone: 636-734-2693, bs34354@gmail.com
Specialties: Straight knives, using collector grade. **Patterns:** Bowies, skinners, hunters, camp knives. **Technical:** Forges 5160, 1095. **Prices:** $200 to $500. **Remarks:** Part-time maker, ABS Journeyman Smith 2001. **Mark:** Setting sun/fall trees/initials.

STOUT, CHARLES
RT3 178 Stout Rd, Gillham, AR 71841, Phone: 870-386-5521

STOUT, JOHNNY
1205 Forest Trail, New Braunfels, TX 78132, Phone: 830-606-4067, johnny@stoutknives.com; Web: www.stoutknives.com, Facebook-Johnny Stout, Instagram-Stout Handmade Knives
Specialties: Folders, some fixed blades. Working knives, some fancy. **Patterns:** Hunters, automatics, LinerLocks and slip joints. **Technical:** Grinds stainless and carbon steels; forges some Damascus. **Prices:** $450 to $895; some to $6,500. **Remarks:** Full-time maker; first knife sold in 1983. Hosts semi-annual Guadalupe Forge Hammer-in and Knifemakers Rendezvous. **Mark:** Name and city in logo.

STRAIGHT, KENNETH J
11311 103 Lane N, Largo, FL 33773, Phone: 813-397-9817

STRANDE, POUL
Soster Svenstrup Byvej 16, Viby Sj., Dastrup, DENMARK 4130, Phone: 46 19 43 05, Fax: 46 19 53 19, Web: www.poulstrande.com
Specialties: Classic fantasy working knives; Damasceret blade, Nikkel Damasceret blade, Lamineret: Lamineret blade with Nikkel. **Patterns:** Bowies, daggers, fighters, hunters and

swords. **Technical:** Uses carbon steel and 15C20 steel. **Prices:** NA. **Remarks:** Full-time maker; first knife sold in 1985. **Mark:** First and last initials.

STRAUB, SALEM F.
324 Cobey Creek Rd., Tonasket, WA 98855, Phone: 509-486-2627, vorpalforge@hotmail.com Web: www.prometheanknives.com

Specialties: Elegant working knives, fixed blade hunters, utility, skinning knives; liner locks. Makes own horsehide sheaths. **Patterns:** A wide range of syles, everything from the gentleman's pocket to the working kitchen, integrals, Bowies, folders, check out my website to see some of my work for ideas. **Technical:** Forges several carbon steels, 52100, W1, etc. Grinds stainless and makes/uses own damascus, cable, san mai, stadard patterns. Likes clay quenching, hamons, hand rubbed finishes. Flat, hollow, or convex grinds. Prefers synthetic handle materials. Hidden and full tapered tangs. **Prices:** $150 - $600, some higher. **Remarks:** Full-time maker. Doing what it takes to make your knife ordering and buying experience positive and enjoyable; striving to exceed expectations. All knives backed by lifetime guarantee. **Mark:** "Straub" stamp or "Promethean Knives" etched. Some older pieces stamped "Vorpal" though no longer using this mark. **Other:** Feel free to call or e-mail anytime. I love to talk knives.

STRICKLAND, DALE
1440 E Thompson View, Monroe, UT 84754, Phone: 435-896-8362

Specialties: Traditional and working straight knives and folders of his design and to customer specs. **Patterns:** Hunters, folders, miniatures and utility knives. **Technical:** Grinds Damascus and 440C. **Prices:** $120 to $350; some to $500. **Remarks:** Part-time maker; first knife sold in 1991. **Mark:** Oval stamp of name, Maker.

STRIDER, MICK
STRIDER KNIVES, 565 Country Club Dr., Escondido, CA 92029, Phone: 760-471-8275, Fax: 503-218-7069, striderguys@striderknives.com; Web: www.striderknives.com

STRONG, SCOTT
1599 Beaver Valley Rd, Beavercreek, OH 45434, Phone: 937-426-9290

Specialties: Working knives, some deluxe. **Patterns:** Hunters, fighters, survival and military-style knives, art knives. **Technical:** Forges and grinds O1, A2, D2, 440C and ATS-34. Uses no solder; most knives disassemble. **Prices:** $75 to $450; some to $1500. **Remarks:** Spare-time maker; first knife sold in 1983. **Mark:** Strong Knives.

STROYAN, ERIC
Box 218, Dalton, PA 18414, Phone: 717-563-2603

Specialties: Classic and working/using straight knives and folders of his design. **Patterns:** Hunters, locking folders, slip-joints. **Technical:** Forges Damascus; grinds ATS-34, D2. **Prices:** $200 to $600; some to $2000. **Remarks:** Part-time maker; first knife sold in 1968. **Mark:** Signature or initials stamp.

STUART, MASON
24 Beech Street, Mansfield, MA 02048, Phone: 508-339-8236, smasonknives@verizon.net Web: smasonknives.com, Facebook.com/S. Mason Custom Knives

Specialties: Straight knives of his design, standard patterns. **Patterns:** Bowies, hunters, fighters and neck knives. **Technical:** Forges and grinds. Damascus, 5160, 1095, 1084, old files. Uses only natural handle material. **Prices:** $350 - 2,000. **Remarks:** Part-time maker. **Mark:** First initial and last name.

STUART, STEVE
Box 168, Gores Landing, ON, CANADA K0K 2E0, Phone: 905-440-6910, stevestuart@xplornet.com

Specialties: Straight knives. **Patterns:** Tantos, fighters, skinners, file and rasp knives. **Technical:** Uses 440C, CPM154, CPMS30V, Micarta and natural handle materials. **Prices:** $60 to $400. **Remarks:** Part-time maker. **Mark:** SS.

STUCKY, DANIEL
37924 Shenandoah Loop, Springfield, OR 97478, Phone: 541-747-6496, stuckyj1@msn.com, www.stuckyknives.com

Specialties: Tactical, fancy and everyday carry folders, fixed-blade hunting knives, trout, bird and fillet knives. **Technical:** Stock removal maker. Steels include but are not limited to damascus, CPM 154, CPM S30V, CPM S35VN, 154CM and ATS-34. **Prices:** Start at $300 and can go to thousands, depending on materials used. **Remarks:** Full-time maker; first knife sold in 1999. **Mark:** Name over city and state.

STYREFORS, MATTIAS
Unbyn 23, Boden, SWEDEN 96193, infor@styrefors.com

Specialties: Damascus and mosaic Damascus. Fixed blade Nordic hunters, folders and swords. **Technical:** Forges, shapes and grinds Damascus and mosaic Damascus from mostly UHB 15N20 and 20C with contrasts in nickel and 15N20. Hardness HR 58. **Prices:** $800 to $3000. **Remarks:** Full-time maker since 1999. International reputation for high end Damascus blades. Uses stabilized Arctic birch and willow burl, horn, fossils, exotic materials, and scrimshaw by Viveca Sahlin for knife handles. Hand tools and hand stitches leather sheaths in cow raw hide. Works in well equipped former military forgery in northern Sweden. **Mark:** MS.

SUEDMEIER, HARLAN
762 N 60th Rd, Nebraska City, NE 68410, Phone: 402-873-4372

Patterns: Straight knives. **Technical:** Forging hi carbon Damascus. **Prices:** Starting at $175. **Mark:** First initials & last name.

SUGIHARA, KEIDOH
4-16-1 Kamori-Cho, Kishiwada City, Osaka, JAPAN F596-0042, Fax: 0724-44-2677

Specialties: High-tech working straight knives and folders of his design. **Patterns:** Bowies, hunters, fighters, fishing, boots, some pocket knives and liner-lock folders. **Technical:** Grinds ATS-34, COS-25, buys Damascus and high-carbon steels. Prices $60 to $4000. **Remarks:** Full-time maker, first knife sold in 1980. **Mark:** Initial logo with fish design.

SUGIYAMA, EDDY K
2361 Nagayu, Naoirimachi Naoirigun, Oita, JAPAN, Phone: 0974-75-2050

Specialties: One-of-a-kind, exotic-style knives. **Patterns:** Working, utility and miniatures. **Technical:** CT rind, ATS-34 and D2. **Prices:** $400 to $1200. **Remarks:** Full-time maker. **Mark:** Name or cedar mark.

SUMMERS, ARTHUR L
1310 Hess Rd, Concord, NC 28025, Phone: 704-787-9275 Cell: 704-305-0735, arthursummers88@hotmail.com

Specialties: Drop points, clip points, straight blades. **Patterns:** Hunters, Bowies and personal knives. **Technical:** Grinds ATS-34, CPM-D2, CPM-154 and damascus. **Prices:** $250 to $1000. **Remarks:** Full-time maker; first knife sold in 1988. **Mark:** Serial number is the date.

SUMMERS, DAN
2675 NY Rt. 11, Whitney Pt., NY 13862, Phone: 607-692-2391, dansumm11@gmail.com

Specialties: Period knives and tomahawks. **Technical:** All hand forging. **Prices:** Most $100 to $400.

SUMMERS, DENNIS K
827 E. Cecil St, Springfield, OH 45503, Phone: 513-324-0624

Specialties: Working/using knives. **Patterns:** Fighters and personal knives. **Technical:** Grinds 440C, A2 and D2. Makes drop and clip point. **Prices:** $75 to $200. **Remarks:** Part-time maker; first knife sold in 1995. **Mark:** First and middle initials, last name, serial number.

SUNDERLAND, RICHARD
Av Infraganti 23, Col Lazaro Cardenas, Puerto Escondido, OA, MEXICO 71980, Phone: 011 52 94 582 1451, sunamerica@prodigy.net.mx7

Specialties: Personal and hunting knives with carved handles in oosic and ivory. **Patterns:** Hunters, Bowies, daggers, camp and personal knives. **Technical:** Grinds 440C, ATS-34 and O1. Handle materials of rosewoods, fossil mammoth ivory and oosic. **Prices:** $150 to $1000. **Remarks:** Part-time maker; first knife sold in 1983. Doing business as Sun Knife Co. **Mark:** SUN.

SURLS, W. ALLEN
W.A. SURLS KNIVES, 3889 Duncan Ives Dr., Buford, GA 30519, Phone: 678-897-1624, wasknives@gmail.com

Patterns: Bushcraft knives, traditional fixed blades, Loveless patterns, skinners and gent's knives. **Technical:** Stock removal method of blade making with occasional forging, using CPM 154, A2 and O1 steels. **Prices:** $150 to $1,200. **Remarks:** Full-time maker; first blade ground in May of 2013. Owner and operator of W.A. Surls Knives, and vice president of Fiddleback Forge Inc. **Mark:** Current mark is "W.A. Surls," with early production pieces marked "WAS."

SUTTON, S RUSSELL
4900 Cypress Shores Dr, New Bern, NC 28562, Phone: 252-637-3963, srsutton@suddenlink.net; Web: www.suttoncustomknives.com

Specialties: Straight knives and folders to customer specs and in standard patterns. **Patterns:** Boots, hunters, interframes, slip joints and locking liners. **Technical:** Grinds ATS-34, 440C and stainless Damascus. **Prices:** $220 to $2000. **Remarks:** Full-time maker; first knife sold in 1992. Provides relief engraving on bolsters and guards. **Mark:** Etched last name.

SWARZ-BURT, PETER T.
FALLING HAMMER PRODUCTIONS, LLC, 10 Swiss Ln., Wolcott, CT 06716, Phone: 203-879-1786, dragonsbreathforge@gmail.com; Web: www.fallinghammerproductions.com or www.dragonsbreathforge.com

Specialties: Makes own Wootz and other crucible steels, specializing in unusual blade shapes with a focus on Indian and Middle Eastern weapons; historical reproductions from all regions. **Patterns:** Designs focus on utility and comfort. **Technical:** Uses 5160, L6, 10xx, and his own Wootz and damascus steels. Forges closely to shape. **Prices:** $150 to $2,000 (knives) and $500 to $5,000 (swords). **Remarks:** Full-time blacksmith and bladesmith; first knife made in 1992. **Mark:** PTSB combined to look like a snake twined around a sword on one side of ricasso, and the Dragon's Breath Forge symbol that looks like a talon on the other side.

SWEARINGEN, KURT
22 Calvary Rd., Cedar Crest, NM 87008, Phone: 575-613-0500, kurt@swearingenknife.com; Web: www.swearingenknife.com

Specialties: Traditional hunting and camp knives, as well as slip-joint and lockback folders of classic design with an emphasis on utility. Hand-carved and tooled sheaths accompany each knife. **Patterns:** Loveless-style hunters, Scagel folders, as well as original designs. **Technical:** Grinds CPM 154 for all standard hunting models and D2 for all folders. Smiths W2 for forged hunters, and 5160 or 1084 for camp knives. **Prices:** Standard models in CPM 154 start at $320, including a custom sheath. **Remarks:** Serious part-time maker and ABS journeyman smith, I personally test each knife in my shop and in the field during hunting season (hunters) and in my work as a forester (camp knives).

SWEAZA, DENNIS
4052 Hwy 321 E, Austin, AR 72007, Phone: 501-941-1886, knives4den@aol.com

SWENSON, LUKE
SWENSON KNIVES, 1667 Brushy Creek Dr., Lakehills, TX 78063, Phone: 210-722-3227, luke@swensonknives.com; Web: www.swensonknives.com

Specialties: Small hunting knives, concentrating on traditional multi-blade slip joints. **Technical:** Stock-removal method of blade making. Flat grinds A2 tool steel for fixed blades, and hollow grinds CPM 154 for slip-joint folders. Credits Bill Ruple for mentoring him in the making slip joints. **Prices:** $275 to $675. **Remarks:** Part-time maker/full-time firefighter; first knife made in 2003. Starting to do some traditional lockback patterns also. **Mark:** Name and city where maker lives.

SWYHART, ART

509 Main St, PO Box 267, Klickitat, WA 98628, Phone: 509-369-3451, swyhart@ gorge.net; Web: www.knifeoutlet.com/swyhart.htm
   Specialties: Traditional working and using knives of his design. **Patterns:** Bowies, hunters and utility/camp knives. **Technical:** Forges 52100, 5160 and Damascus 1084 mixed with either 15N20 or O186. Blades differentially heat-treated with visible temper line. **Prices:** $75 to $250; some to $350. **Remarks:** Part-time maker; first knife sold in 1983. **Mark:** First name, last initial in script.

SYLVESTER, DAVID

465 Sweede Rd., Compton, QC, CANADA J0B 1L0, Phone: 819-837-0304, david@ swedevilleforge.com Web: swedevilleforge.com
   Patterns: I hand forge all my knives and I like to make hunters and integrals and some Bowies and fighters. I work with W2, 1084, 1095, and my damascus. **Prices:** $200 - $1500. **Remarks:** Part-time maker. ABS Journeyman Smith. **Mark:** D.Sylvester

SYMONDS, ALBERTO E

Rambla M Gandhi 485, Apt 901, Montevideo, URUGUAY 11300, Phone: 011 598 27103201, Fax: 011 598 2 7103201, albertosymonds@hotmail.com
   Specialties: All kinds including puukos, nice sheaths, leather and wood. **Prices:** $300 to $2200. **Mark:** AESH and current year.

SYSLO, CHUCK

3418 South 116 Ave, Omaha, NE 68144, Phone: 402-333-0647, ciscoknives@cox.net
   Specialties: Hunters, working knives, daggers and misc. **Patterns:** Hunters, daggers and survival knives; locking folders. **Technical:** Flat-grinds D2, 440C and 154CM; hand polishes only. **Prices:** $250 to $1,000; some to $3,000. **Remarks:** Part-time maker; first knife sold in 1978. Uses many natural materials. Making some knives, mainly retired from knifemaking. **Mark:** CISCO in logo.

SZCZERBIAK, MACIEJ

Crusader Forge Knives, PO Box 2181, St. George, UT 84771, Phone: 435-574-2193, crusaderforge@yahoo.com; Web: www.crusaderforge.com
   Patterns: Drop-point, spear-point and tanto fixed blades and tactical folders. **Technical:** Stock removal using CPM-S30V and D2 steels. Knives designed with the technical operator in mind, and maintain an amazing balance in the user's hand. **Prices:** $300 to $2,500. **Remarks:** First knife made in 1999.

SZILASKI, JOSEPH

School of Knifemaking, 52 Woods Dr., Pine Plains, NY 12567, Phone: 518-398-0309, joe@szilaski.com; Web: www.szilaski.com
   Specialties: Straight knives, folders and tomahawks of his design, to customer specs and in standard patterns. Many pieces are one-of-a-kind. Offers knifemaking classes for all levels in 4,000-square-foot shop. Courses are in forging, grinding, damascus, tomahawk engraving and carving. **Patterns:** Bowies, daggers, fighters, hunters, art knives and early American styles. **Technical:** Forges A2, D2, O1 and damascus. **Prices:** $450 to $4,000; some to $10,000. **Remarks:** Full-time maker; first knife sold in 1990. ABS master smith. **Mark:** Snake logo.

T

TABER, DAVID E.

51 E. 4th St., Ste. 300, Winona, MN 55987, Phone: 507-450-1918, dtaber@ qwestoffice.net
   Specialties: Traditional slip joints, primarily using and working knives. **Technical:** Blades are hollow ground on a 20" wheel, ATS-34 and some damascus steel. **Remarks:** Full-time orthodontist, part-time maker; first knife made in January 2011. **Mark:** dr.t.

TABOR, TIM

18925 Crooked Lane, Lutz, FL 33548, Phone: 813-948-6141, taborknives.com
   Specialties: Fancy folders, Damascus Bowies and hunters. **Patterns:** My own design folders & customer requests. **Technical:** ATS-34, hand forged Damascus, 1084, 15N20 mosaic Damascus, 1095, 5160 high carbon blades, flat grind, file work & jewel embellishments. **Prices:** $175 to $1500. **Remarks:** Part-time maker, sold first knife in 2003. **Mark:** Last name

TAKACH, ANDREW

1390 Fallen Timber Rd., Elizabeth, PA 15037, Phone: 724-691-2271, a-takach@ takachforge.com; Web: www.takachforge.com
   Specialties: One-of-a-kind fixed blade working knives (own design or customer's). Mostly all fileworked. **Patterns:** Hunters, skinners, caping, fighters, and designs of own style. **Technical:** Forges mostly 5160, 1090, 01, an down pattern welded Damascus, nickle Damascus, and cable and various chain Damascus. Also do some San Mai. **Prices:** $100 to $350, some over $550. **Remarks:** Doing business as Takach Forge. First knife sold in 2004. **Mark:** Takach (stamped).

TALLY, GRANT

26961 James Ave, Flat Rock, MI 48134, Phone: 313-414-1618
   Specialties: Straight knives and folders of his design. **Patterns:** Bowies, daggers, fighters. **Technical:** Grinds ATS-34, 440C and D2. Offers filework. **Prices:** $250 to $1000. **Remarks:** Part-time maker; first knife sold in 1985. Doing business as Tally Knives. **Mark:** Tally (last name).

TAMATSU, KUNIHIKO

5344 Sukumo, Sukumo City, Kochi-ken, JAPAN 788-0000, Phone: 0880-63-3455,

ktamatsu@mb.gallery.ne.jp; Web: www.knife.tamatu.net
   Specialties: Loveless-style fighters, sub-hilt fighters and hunting knives. **Technical:** Mirror-finished ATS-34, BG-42 and CPM-S30V blades. **Prices:** $400 to $2,500. **Remarks:** Part-time maker, making knives for eight years. **Mark:** Electrical etching of "K. Tamatsu."

TAMBOLI, MICHAEL

12447 N 49 Ave, Glendale, AZ 85304, Phone: 602-978-4308, mnbtamboli@gmail.com
   Specialties: Miniatures, some full size. **Patterns:** Miniature hunting knives to fantasy art knives. **Technical:** ATS-34 & Damascus. **Prices:** $75 to $500; some to $2000. **Remarks:** Full time maker; first knife sold in 1978. **Mark:** Initials, last name, last name city and state, MT Custom Knives or Mike Tamboli in Japanese script.

TASMAN, KERLEY

9 Avignon Retreat, Pt Kennedy, WA, AUSTRALIA 6172, Phone: 61 8 9593 0554, Fax: 61 8 9593 0554, taskerley@optusnet.com.au
   Specialties: Knife/harness/sheath systems for elite military personnel and body guards. **Patterns:** Utility/tactical knives, hunters small game and presentation grade knives. **Technical:** ATS-34 and 440C, Damascus, flat and hollow grids. **Prices:** $200 to $1800 U.S. **Remarks:** Will take presentation grade commissions. Multi award winning maker and custom jeweler. **Mark:** Maker's initials.

TAYLOR, BILLY

10 Temple Rd, Petal, MS 39465, Phone: 601-544-0041
   Specialties: Straight knives of his design. **Patterns:** Bowies, skinners, hunters and utility knives. **Technical:** Flat-grinds 440C, ATS-34 and 154CM. **Prices:** $60 to $300. **Remarks:** Part-time maker; first knife sold in 1991. **Mark:** Full name, city and state.

TAYLOR, C. GRAY

560 Poteat Ln, Fall Branch, TN 37656, Phone: 423-348-8304 or 423-765-6434, graysknives@aol.com; Web: www.cgraytaylor.com
   Specialties: Traditonal multi-blade lobster folders, also art display Bowies and daggers. **Patterns:** Orange Blossom, sleeveboard and gunstocks. **Technical:** Grinds. **Prices:** Upscale. **Remarks:** Full-time maker; first knife sold in 1975. **Mark:** Name, city and state.

TAYLOR, SHANE

42 Broken Bow Ln, Miles City, MT 59301, Phone: 406-234-7175, shane@ taylorknives.com; Web: www.taylorknives.com
   Specialties: One-of-a-kind fancy Damascus straight knives and folders. **Patterns:** Bowies, folders and fighters. **Technical:** Forges own mosaic and pattern welded Damascus. **Prices:** $450 and up. **Remarks:** ABS Master Smith, full-time maker; first knife sold in 1982. **Mark:** First name.

TEDFORD, STEVEN J.

14238 Telephone Rd., Colborne, ON, CANADA K0K 1S0, Phone: 613-689-7569, firebornswords@yahoo.com; Web: www.steventedfordknives.com
   Specialties: Handmade custom fixed blades, specialty outdoors knives. **Patterns:** Swept Survival Bowie, large, medium and small-size field-dressing/hunting knives, drop-point skinners, and world-class fillet knives. **Technical:** Exclusively using ATS-34 stainless steel, Japanese-inspired, free-hand ground, zero-point edge blade design. **Prices:** All knives are sold wholesale directly from the shop starting at $150 to $500+. **Remarks:** Tedford Knives; Function is beauty. Every knife is unconditionally guaranteed for life.

TENDICK, BEN

798 Nadine Ave, Eugene, OR 97404, Phone: 541-912-1280, bentendick@gmail.com; Web: www.brtbladeworks.com
   Specialties: Hunter/utility, tactical, bushcraft, and kitchen. **Technical:** Preferred steel - L6, 5160, and 15N20. Stock Removal. **Prices:** $130 to $700. **Remarks:** Part-time; has been making knives since early 90's but started seriously making knives in 2010. In business at BRT Bladeworks, no website yet but can be found on Facebook. **Mark:** Initials (BRT) with B backwards and T between the B and R, and also use last name.

TERRILL, STEPHEN

16357 Goat Ranch Rd, Springville, CA 93265, Phone: 559-920-2722, steve@ slterrillknives.com; Web: www.slterrillknives.com
   Specialties: Deluxe working straight knives and folders. **Patterns:** Fighters, tantos, boots, locking folders and axes; traditional oriental patterns. **Technical:** Forged and stock removal of 1095, 5160, Damascus, stock removal ATS-34. **Prices:** $400 and up. **Remarks:** Full-time maker, semi-retired; first knife sold in 1972. **Mark:** Name, name-city-state.

TERZUOLA, ROBERT

10121 Eagle Rock NE, Albuquerque, NM 87122, Phone: 505-856-7077, terzuola@ earthlink.net
   Specialties: Working folders of his design; period pieces. **Patterns:** High-tech utility, defense and gentleman's folders. **Technical:** Grinds CPM154 and damascus. Offers titanium, carbon fiber and G10 composite for side-lock folders and tactical folders. **Prices:** $1,200 to $3,000. **Remarks:** Full-time maker; first knife sold in 1980. **Mark:** Mayan dragon head, name.

TESARIK, RICHARD

Pisecnik 87, 614 00 Brno, Czech Republic, Phone: 00420-602-834-726, rtesarik@ gmail.com; Web: www.tesarikknives.com
   Specialties: Handmade art knives. **Patterns:** Daggers, hunters and LinerLock or back-lock folders. **Technical:** Grinds RWL-34, N690 and stainless or high-carbon damascus. Carves on blade, handle and other parts. I prefer fossil material and exotic wood, don't use synthetic material. **Prices:** $600 to $2,000. **Remarks:** Part-time maker, full-time hobby; first knife sold in 2009. **Mark:** TR.

custom knifemakers

THAYER, DANNY O
8908S 100W, Romney, IN 47981, Phone: 765-538-3105, dot61h@juno.com
Specialties: Hunters, fighters, Bowies. **Prices:** $250 and up.

THEVENOT, JEAN-PAUL
16 Rue De La Prefecture, Dijon, FRANCE 21000
Specialties: Traditional European knives and daggers. **Patterns:** Hunters, utility-camp knives, daggers, historical or modern style. **Technical:** Forges own Damascus, 5160, 1084. **Remarks:** Part-time maker. ABS Master Smith. **Mark:** Interlocked initials in square.

THIE, BRIAN
13250 150th St, Burlington, IA 52601, Phone: 319-850-2188, thieknives@gmail.com; Web: www.mepotelco.net/web/tknives
Specialties: Working using knives from basic to fancy. **Patterns:** Hunters, fighters, camp and folders. **Technical:** Forges blades and own Damascus. **Prices:** $250 and up. **Remarks:** ABS Journeyman Smith, part-time maker. Sole author of blades including forging, heat treat, engraving and sheath making. **Mark:** Last name hand engraved into the blade, JS stamped into blade.

THILL, JIM
10242 Bear Run, Missoula, MT 59803, Phone: 406-251-5475, bearrunmt@hotmail.com
Specialties: Traditional and working/using knives of his design. **Patterns:** Fighters, hunters and utility/camp knives. **Technical:** Grinds D2 and ATS-34; forges 10-95-85, 52100, 5160, 10 series, reg. Damascus-mosaic. Offers hand cut sheaths with rawhide lace. **Prices:** $145 to $350; some to $1250. **Remarks:** Full-time maker; first knife sold in 1962. **Mark:** Running bear in triangle.

THOMAS, BOB
Sunset Forge, 3502 Bay Rd., Ferndale, WA 98248, Phone: 360-201-0160, Fax: 360-366-5723, sunsetforge@rockisland.com

THOMAS, DAVID E
8502 Hwy 91, Lillian, AL 36549, Phone: 251-961-7574, redbluff@gulftel.com
Specialties: Bowies and hunters. **Technical:** Hand forged blades in 5160, 1095 and own Damascus. **Prices:** $400 and up. **Mark:** Stylized DT, maker's last name, serial number.

THOMAS, DEVIN
PO Box 568, Panaca, NV 89042, Phone: 775-728-4363, hoss@devinthomas.com; Web: www.devinthomas.com
Specialties: Traditional straight knives and folders in standard patterns. **Patterns:** Bowies, fighters, hunters. **Technical:** Forges stainless Damascus, nickel and 1095. Uses, makes and sells mokume with brass, copper and nickel-silver. **Prices:** $300 to $1200. **Remarks:** Full-time maker; first knife sold in 1979. **Mark:** First and last name, city and state with anvil, or first name only.

THOMAS, KIM
PO Box 531, Seville, OH 44273, Phone: 330-769-9906
Specialties: Fancy and traditional straight knives of his design and to customer specs; period pieces. **Patterns:** Boots, daggers, fighters, swords. **Technical:** Forges own Damascus from 5160, 1010 and nickel. **Prices:** $135 to $1500; some to $3000. **Remarks:** Part-time maker; first knife sold in 1986. Doing business as Thomas Iron Works. **Mark:** KT.

THOMAS, ROCKY
1716 Waterside Blvd, Moncks Corner, SC 29461, Phone: 843-761-7761
Specialties: Traditional working knives in standard patterns. **Patterns:** Hunters and utility/camp knives. **Technical:** ATS-34 and commercial Damascus. **Prices:** $130 to $350. **Remarks:** Spare-time maker; first knife sold in 1986. **Mark:** First name in script and/or block.

THOMPSON, KENNETH
4887 Glenwhite Dr, Duluth, GA 30136, Phone: 770-446-6730
Specialties: Traditional working and using knives of his design. **Patterns:** Hunters, Bowies and utility/camp knives. **Technical:** Forges 5168, O1, 1095 and 52100. **Prices:** $75 to $1500; some to $2500. **Remarks:** Part-time maker; first knife sold in 1990. **Mark:** P/W; or name, P/W, city and state.

THOMPSON, LEON
3400 S.W. Dilley Rd., Forest Grove, OR 97116, Phone: 503-357-2573, lsthomp@msn.com
Specialties: Working knives. **Patterns:** Locking folders, slip-joints and liner locks. **Technical:** Grinds ATS-34, D2 and 440C. **Prices:** $450 to $1000. **Remarks:** Full-time maker; first knife sold in 1976. **Mark:** First and middle initials, last name, city and state.

THOMPSON, LLOYD
PO Box 1664, Pagosa Springs, CO 81147, Phone: 970-264-5837
Specialties: Working and collectible straight knives and folders of his design. **Patterns:** Straight blades, lock back folders and slip joint folders. **Technical:** Hollow-grinds ATS-34, D2 and O1. Uses sambar stag and exotic woods. **Prices:** $150 to upscale. **Remarks:** Full-time maker; first knife sold in 1985. Doing business as Trapper Creek Knife Co. **Remarks:** Offers three-day knife-making classes. **Mark:** Name.

THOMPSON, TOMMY
4015 NE Hassalo, Portland, OR 97232-2607, Phone: 503-235-5762
Specialties: Fancy and working knives; mostly liner-lock folders. **Patterns:** Fighters, hunters and liner locks. **Technical:** Grinds D2, ATS-34, CPM440V and T15. Handles are either hardwood inlaid with wood banding and stone or shell, or made of agate, jasper, petrified woods, etc. **Prices:** $75 to $500; some to $1000. **Remarks:** Part-time maker; first knife sold in 1987. Doing business as Stone Birds. Knife making temporarily stopped due to family obligations. **Mark:** First and last name, city and state.

THOMSEN, LOYD W
25241 Renegade Pass, Custer, SD 57730, Phone: 605-673-2787, loydt@yahoo.com; Web: horseheadcreekknives.com
Specialties: High-art and traditional working/using straight knives and presentation pieces of his design and to customer specs; period pieces. Hand carved animals in crown of stag on handles and carved display stands. **Patterns:** Bowies, hunters, daggers and utility/camp knives. **Technical:** Forges and grinds 1095HC, 1084, L6, 15N20, 440C stainless steel, nickel 200; special restoration process on period pieces. Uses natural materials for handles. **Prices:** $350 to $1000. **Remarks:** Full-time maker; first knife sold in 1995. Doing business as Horsehead Creek Knives. **Mark:** Initials and last name over a horse's head.

THORBURN, ANDRE E.
P.O. Box 1748, Bela Bela, Warmbaths, LP, SOUTH AFRICA 0480, Phone: 27-82-650-1441, Fax: 27-86-750-2765, andrethorburn@gmail.com; Web: www.thorburnknives.co.za
Specialties: Working and fancy folders of own design to customer specs. **Technical:** Uses RWL-34, Damasteel, CPM steels, Bohler N690, and carbon and stainless damascus. **Prices:** Starting at $350. **Remarks:** Full-time maker since 1996; first knife sold in 1990. Member of South African, Italian, and German guilds. **Mark:** Initials and name in a double circle.

THOUROT, MICHAEL W
T-814 Co Rd 11, Napoleon, OH 43545, Phone: 419-533-6832, Fax: 419-533-3516, mike2row@henry-net.com; Web: wwwsafariknives.com
Specialties: Working straight knives to customer specs. Designed two-handled skinning ax and limited edition engraved knife and art print set. **Patterns:** Fishing and fillet knives, Bowies, tantos and hunters. **Technical:** Grinds O1, D2, 440C and Damascus. **Prices:** $200 to $5000. **Remarks:** Part-time maker; first knife sold in 1968. **Mark:** Initials.

THUESEN, ED
21211 Knolle Rd, Damon, TX 77430, Phone: 979-553-1211, Fax: 979-553-1211
Specialties: Working straight knives. **Patterns:** Hunters, fighters and survival knives. **Technical:** Grinds D2, 440C, ATS-34 and Vascowear. **Prices:** $150 to $275; some to $600. **Remarks:** Part-time maker; first knife sold in 1979. Runs knifemaker supply business. **Mark:** Last name in script.

TIENSVOLD, ALAN L
PO Box 355, 3277 U.S. Hwy. 20, Rushville, NE 69360, Phone: 308-360-0613, tiensvoldknives@gpcom.net
Specialties: Working knives, tomahawks and period pieces, high end Damascus knives. **Patterns:** Random, ladder, twist and many more. **Technical:** Hand forged blades, forges own Damascus. **Prices:** Working knives start at $300. **Remarks:** Received Journeyman rating with the ABS in 2002. Does own engraving and fine work. **Mark:** Tiensvold hand made U.S.A. on left side, JS on right.

TIENSVOLD, JASON
PO Box 795, Rushville, NE 69360, Phone: 308-360-2217, jasontiensvoldknives@yahoo.com
Specialties: Working and using straight knives of his design; period pieces. Gentlemen folders, art folders. Single action automatics. **Patterns:** Hunters, skinners, Bowies, fighters, daggers, liner locks. **Technical:** Forges own Damascus using 15N20 and 1084, 1095, nickel, custom file work. **Prices:** $200 to $4000. **Remarks:** Full-time maker, first knife sold in 1994; doing business under Tiensvold Custom Knives. **Mark:** J. Tiensvold on left side, MS on right.

TIGHE, BRIAN
12-111 Fourth Ave, Suite 376 Ridley Square, St. Catharines, ON, CANADA L2S 3P5, Phone: 905-892-2734, Web: www.tigheknives.com
Specialties: Folding knives, bearing pivots. High tech tactical folders. **Patterns:** Boots, daggers and locking. **Technical:** BG-42, RWL-34, Damasteel, 154CM, S30V, CPM 440V and CPM 420V. Prefers natural handle material inlay; hand finishes. **Prices:** $450 to $4000. **Remarks:** Full-time maker; first knife sold in 1989. **Mark:** Etched signature.

TILL, CALVIN E AND RUTH
1010 Maple St., Lot 4, Chadron, NE 69337-6967, Phone: 308-430-2231
Specialties: Straight knives, hunters, Bowies; no folders **Patterns:** Training point, drop point hunters, Bowies. **Technical:** ATS-34 sub zero quench RC59, 61. **Prices:** $700 to $1200. **Remarks:** Sells only the absolute best knives they can make. Manufactures every part in their knives. **Mark:** RC Till. The R is for Ruth, the C for Calvin.

TILTON, JOHN
24041 Hwy 383, Iowa, LA 70647, Phone: 337-582-6785, john@jetknives.com
Specialties: Bowies, camp knives, skinners and folders. **Technical:** All forged blades. Makes own Damascus. **Prices:** $150 and up. **Remarks:** ABS Journeyman Smith. **Mark:** Initials J.E.T.

TINDERA, GEORGE
BURNING RIVER FORGE, 751 Hadcock Rd, Brunswick, OH 44212-2648, Phone: 330-220-6212
Specialties: Straight knives; his designs. **Patterns:** Personal knives; classic Bowies and fighters. **Technical:** Hand-forged high-carbon; his own cable and pattern welded Damascus. **Prices:** $125 to $600. **Remarks:** Spare-time maker; sold first knife in 1995. Natural handle materials.

TINGLE, DENNIS P
19390 E Clinton Rd, Jackson, CA 95642, Phone: 209-223-4586, dtknives@earthlink.net
Specialties: Swords, fixed blades: small to medium, tomahawks. **Technical:** All blades forged. **Remarks:** ABS, JS. **Mark:** D. Tingle over JS.

TIPPETTS, COLTEN
4515 W. Long Meadow Dr., Hidden Springs, ID 83714, Phone: 208-473-1474, coltentippetts@gmail.com; Web: www.ctknives.webs.com
Specialties: Fancy and working fixed blades and folders of his own design or to customer specifications. **Patterns:** Hunters and skinners, fighters, tactical blades and lockback folders. **Technical:** Grinds BG-42 and CPM S30V, and forges O1. **Prices:** $200 to $1,000. **Remarks:** Full-time maker; first knife sold in 1996. **Mark:** Fused initials.

TOBOLAK, LIBOR
NO COMPROMISE DESIGN, 635 N. Twin Oaks Valley Rd., Ste. 20, San Marcos, CA 92069, Phone: 201-668-9885, nocompromisedesign@gmail.com; Web: www.nocompromisedesign.com; Facebook: No Compromise Design

TODD, RICHARD C
375th LN 46001, Chambersburg, IL 62323, Phone: 217-327-4380, ktodd45@yahoo.com
Specialties: Multi blade folders and silver sheaths. **Patterns:** Jewel setting and hand engraving. **Mark:** RT with letter R crossing the T or R Todd.

TOICH, NEVIO
Via Pisacane 9, Rettorgole di Caldogna, Vincenza, ITALY 36030, Phone: 0444-985065, Fax: 0444-301254
Specialties: Working/using straight knives of his design or to customer specs. **Patterns:** Bowies, hunters, skinners and utility/camp knives. **Technical:** Grinds 440C, D2 and ATS-34. Hollow-grinds all blades and uses mirror polish. Offers hand-sewn sheaths. Uses wood and horn. **Prices:** $120 to $300; some to $450. **Remarks:** Spare-time maker; first knife sold in 1989. Doing business as Custom Toich. **Mark:** Initials and model number punched.

TOKAR, DANIEL
Box 1776, Shepherdstown, WV 25443
Specialties: Working knives; period pieces. **Patterns:** Hunters, camp knives, buckskinners, axes, swords and battle gear. **Technical:** Forges L6, 1095 and his Damascus; makes mokume, Japanese alloys and bronze daggers; restores old edged weapons. **Prices:** $25 to $800; some to $3000. **Remarks:** Part-time maker; first knife sold in 1979. Doing business as The Willow Forge. **Mark:** Arrow over rune and date.

TOMBERLIN, BRION R
ANVIL TOP CUSTOM KNIVES, 825 W Timberdell, Norman, OK 73072, Phone: 405-202-6832, anviltopp@aol.com
Specialties: Handforged blades, working pieces, standard classic patterns, some swords and customer designs. **Patterns:** Bowies, hunters, fighters, Persian and eastern-styles. Likes Japanese blades. **Technical:** Forges 1050, 1075, 1084, 1095, 5160, some forged stainless, also does some stock removal in stainless. Also makes own damascus. **Prices:** $350 to $4,000 or higher for swords and custom pieces. **Remarks:** Part-time maker, ABS master smith. Prefers natural handle materials, hand-rubbed finishes. Likes temper lines. **Mark:** BRION with MS.

TOMEY, KATHLEEN
146 Buford Pl, Macon, GA 31204, Phone: 478-746-8454, ktomey@tomeycustomknives.com; Web: www.tomeycustomknives.com
Specialties: Working hunters, skinners, daily users in fixed blades, plain and embellished. Tactical neck and belt carry. Japanese influenced. Bowies. **Technical:** Grinds O1, ATS-34, flat or hollow grind, filework, satin and mirror polish finishes. High quality leather sheaths with tooling. Kydex with tactical. **Prices:** $150 to $500. **Remarks:** Almost full-time maker. **Mark:** Last name in diamond.

TONER, ROGER
531 Lightfoot Pl, Pickering, ON, CANADA L1V 5Z8, Phone: 905-420-5555
Specialties: Exotic sword canes. **Patterns:** Bowies, daggers and fighters. **Technical:** Grinds 440C, D2 and Damascus. Scrimshaws and engraves. Silver cast pommels and guards in animal shapes; twisted silver wire inlays. Uses semi-precious stones. **Prices:** $200 to $2000; some to $3000. **Remarks:** Part-time maker; first knife sold in 1982. **Mark:** Last name.

TORRES, HENRY
2329 Moody Ave., Clovis, CA 93619, Phone: 559-297-9154, Web: www.htknives.com
Specialties: Forged high-performance hunters and working knives, Bowies, and fighters. **Technical:** 52100 and 5160 and makes own Damascus. **Prices:** $350 to $3000. **Remarks:** Started forging in 2004. Has mastersmith with American Bladesmith Association.

TOSHIFUMI, KURAMOTO
3435 Higashioda, Asakura-gun, Fukuoka, JAPAN, Phone: 0946-42-4470

TOWELL, DWIGHT L
2375 Towell Rd, Midvale, ID 83645, Phone: 208-355-2419
Specialties: Solid, elegant working knives; art knives, high quality engraving and gold inlay. **Patterns:** Hunters, Bowies, daggers and folders. **Technical:** Grinds 154CM, ATS-34, 440C and other maker's Damascus. **Prices:** Upscale. **Remarks:** Full-time maker. First knife sold in 1970. Member of AKI. **Mark:** Towell, sometimes hand engraved.

TOWNSEND, ALLEN MARK
6 Pine Trail, Texarkana, AR 71854, Phone: 870-772-8945

TOWNSLEY, RUSSELL
PO BOX 91, Floral, AR 72534-0091, Phone: 870-307-8069, circleTRMtownsley@yahoo.com
Specialties: Using knives of his own design. **Patterns:** Hunters, skinners, folders. **Technical:** Hollow grinds D2 and O1. Handle material - antler, tusk, bone, exotic woods. **Prices:** Prices start at $125. **Remarks:** Arkansas knifemakers association. Sold first knife in 2009. Doing business as Circle-T knives. **Mark:** Encircled T.

TRACE RINALDI CUSTOM BLADES
1470 Underpass Rd, Plummer, ID 83851, Trace@thrblades.com; Web: www.thrblades.com
Technical: Grinds S30V, 3V, A2 and talonite fixed blades. **Prices:** $300-$1000. **Remarks:** Tactical and utility for the most part. **Mark:** Diamond with THR inside.

TRIBBLE, SKYLAR
Cold Handle Custom Knives, 1413 Alabama St., Leakesville, MS 39451, Phone: 601-394-3490, skylartribble@yahoo.com
Specialties: Fixed blades only. **Patterns:** From small neck knives to large bowie knives. **Technical:** Mainly uses repurposed steels from old files and high-carbon steels, and recently started using 154CM and CPM 154 stainless steels that he enjoys working with. Does both stock removal and forging, saying it's up to the customer. **Prices:** $50+ (up to around $600). **Remarks:** Part-time maker and full-time student; first knife made in 2009 at 13 years old. **Mark:** C with H and K on the tail of the C (for Cold Handle Custom Knives).

TRINDLE, BARRY
1660 Ironwood Trail, Earlham, IA 50072-8611, Phone: 515-462-1237
Specialties: Engraved folders. **Patterns:** Mostly small folders, classical-styles and pocket knives. **Technical:** 440 only. Engraves. Handles of wood or mineral material. **Prices:** Start at $1000. **Mark:** Name on tang.

TRISLER, KENNETH W
6256 Federal 80, Rayville, LA 71269, Phone: 318-728-5541

TRITZ, JEAN-JOSE
Pinneberger Chaussee 48, Hamburg, GERMANY 22523, Phone: +49(40) 49 78 21, jeanjosetritz@aol.com; www.tritz-messer.com
Specialties: Scandinavian knives, Japanese kitchen knives, friction folders, swords. **Patterns:** Puukkos, Tollekniven, Hocho, friction folders, swords. **Technical:** Forges tool steels, carbon steels, 52100 Damascus, mokume, San Maj. **Prices:** $200 to $2000; some higher. **Remarks:** Full-time maker; first knife sold in 1989. Does own leatherwork, prefers natural materials. Sole authorship. Speaks French, German, English, Norwegian. **Mark:** Initials in monogram.

TROUT, GEORGE H.
727 Champlin Rd, Wilmington, OH 45177, Phone: 937-382-2331, gandjtrout@msn.com
Specialties: Working knives, some fancy. **Patterns:** Hunters, drop points, Bowies and fighters. **Technical:** Stock removal: ATS-34, 440C Forged: 5160, W2, 1095, O1 Full integrals: 440C, A2, O1. **Prices:** $150 and up. **Remarks:** Makes own sheaths and mosaic pins. Fileworks most knives. First knife 1985. **Mark:** Etched name and state on stock removal. Forged: stamped name and forged.

TRUJILLO, ALBERT M B
2035 Wasmer Cir, Bosque Farms, NM 87068, Phone: 505-869-0428, trujilloscutups@comcast.net
Specialties: Working/using straight knives of his design or to customer specs. **Patterns:** Hunters, skinners, fighters, working/using knives. File work offered. **Technical:** Grinds ATS-34, D2, 440C, S30V. Tapers tangs, all blades cryogenically treated. **Prices:** $75 to $500. **Remarks:** Part-time maker; first knife sold in 1997. **Mark:** First and last name under logo.

TRUNCALI, PETE
966 Harmony Circle, Nevada, TX 75173, Phone: 214-763-7127, truncaliknives@yahoo.com Web:www.truncaliknives.com
Specialties: Lockback folders and automatics. Does business as Truncali Custom Knives.

TSCHAGER, REINHARD
S. Maddalena di Sotto 1a, Bolzano, ITALY 39100, Phone: 0471-975005, Fax: 0471-975005, reinhardtschager@virgilio.it
Specialties: Classic, high-art, collector-grade straight knives of his design. **Patterns:** Jewel knife, daggers, and hunters. **Technical:** Grinds ATS-34, D2 and Damascus. Oval pins. Gold inlay. Offers engraving. **Prices:** $900 to $2000; some to $3000. **Remarks:** Spare-time maker; first knife sold in 1979. **Mark:** Gold inlay stamped with initials.

TUCH, WILLIAM
Troy Studios, 1220 S.W. Morrison St., Lobby A, Portland, OR 97205, Phone: 503-504-1261, tuchknives@gmail.com; Web: www.tuchknives.com
Specialties: Folding knives and daggers, mostly ornate. **Patterns:** One-of-a-kind locking knives, lockbacks, side locks, switchblades, miniatures and more. **Technical:** Flat and hollow grinds, ornate sculpture. All knives are hand filed and hand polished. Materials vary. **Prices:** $1,800 to $10,000 and up. **Remarks:** Full-time maker since 2004. **Mark:** TUCH.

TUOMINEN, PEKKA
Pohjois-Keiteleentie 20, Tossavanlahti, FINLAND 72930, Phone: 358405167853, puukkopekka@luukku.com; Web: www.puukkopekka.com
Specialties: Puukko knives. **Patterns:** Puukkos, hunters, leukus, and folders. **Technical:** Forges silversteel, 1085, 52100, and makes own Damascus 15N20 and 1095. Grinds RWL-34 and ATS-34. **Prices:** Starting at $300. **Remarks:** Full-time maker. **Mark:** PEKKA; earlier whole name.

TURECEK, JIM
12 Elliott Rd, Ansonia, CT 06401, Phone: 203-734-8406, jturecek@sbcglobal.net
Specialties: Exotic folders, art knives and some miniatures. **Patterns:** Trout and bird knives with split bamboo handles and one-of-a-kind folders. **Technical:** Grinds and forges stainless and carbon damascus. All knives are handmade using no computer-controlled machinery. **Prices:** $2,000 to $10,000. **Remarks:** Full-time maker; first knife sold in 1983. **Mark:** Last initial in script, or last name.

TURNBULL, RALPH A

14464 Linden Dr, Spring Hill, FL 34609, Phone: 352-688-7089, tbull2000@bellsouth.net; Web: www.turnbullknives.com

Specialties: Fancy folders. **Patterns:** Primarily gents pocket knives. **Technical:** Wire EDM work on bolsters. **Prices:** $300 and up. **Remarks:** Full-time maker; first knife sold in 1973. **Mark:** Signature or initials.

TURNER, KEVIN

17 Hunt Ave, Montrose, NY 10548, Phone: 914-739-0535

Specialties: Working straight knives of his design and to customer specs; period pieces. **Patterns:** Daggers, fighters and utility knives. **Technical:** Forges 5160 and 52100. **Prices:** $90 to $500. **Remarks:** Part-time maker; first knife sold in 1991. **Mark:** Acid-etched signed last name and year.

TURNER, MIKE

3065 Cedar Flat Rd., Williams, OR 97544, Phone: 541-846-0204, mike@turnerknives.com Web: www.turnerknives.com

Specialties: Forged and stock removed full tang, hidden and thru tang knives. **Patterns:** Hunters, fighters, Bowies, boot knives, skinners and kitchen knives. **Technical:** I make my own damascus. **Prices:** $200 - $1,000. **Remarks:** Part-time maker, sold my first knife in 2008, doing business as Mike Turner Custom Knives. **Mark:** Name, City, & State.

TYRE, MICHAEL A

1219 Easy St, Wickenburg, AZ 85390, Phone: 928-684-9601/602-377-8432, mtyre86@gmail.com; Web: www.mikeytyrecustomknives.com

Specialties: Quality folding knives, upscale gents folders, one-of-a-kind collectable models. **Patterns:** Working fixed blades for hunting, kitchen and fancy bowies. Forging my own damascus patterns. **Technical:** Grinds, prefers hand-rubbed satin finishes and uses natural handle materials. **Prices:** $250 to $1,300. **Remarks:** ABS journeyman smith.

TYSER, ROSS

1015 Hardee Court, Spartanburg, SC 29303, Phone: 864-585-7616

Specialties: Traditional working and using straight knives and folders of his design and in standard patterns. **Patterns:** Bowies, hunters and slip-joint folders. **Technical:** Grinds 440C and commercial Damascus. Mosaic pins; stone inlay. Does filework and scrimshaw. Offers engraving and cut-work and some inlay on sheaths. **Prices:** $45 to $125; some to $400. **Remarks:** Part-time maker; first knife sold in 1995. Doing business as RT Custom Knives. **Mark:** Stylized initials.

U

UCHIDA, CHIMATA

977-2 Oaza Naga Shisui Ki, Kumamoto, JAPAN 861-1204

UPTON, TOM

Little Rabbit Forge, 1414 Feast Pl., Rogers, AR 72758, Phone: 479-636-6755, Web: www.upton-knives.com

Specialties: Working fixed blades. **Patterns:** Hunters, utility, fighters, bowies and small hatchets. **Technical:** Forges 5160, 1084 and W2 blade steels, or stock removal using D2, 440C and 154CM. Performs own heat treat. **Prices:** $150 and up. **Remarks:** Part-time maker; first knife sold in 1977. Member of the Knife Group Association. **Mark:** Name (Small Rabbit logo), city and state, etched or stamped.

URBACH, SCOTT

19135 E. Oxford Dr., Aurora, CO 80013, Phone: 303-882-1875, urbach@comcast.net or laughingcoyoteknives@gmail.com; Web: www.facebook.com/laughingcoyoteknivescolorado

Specialties: Unique hard-use working knives. **Patterns:** Western, cowboy and traditional/historic bowies, fighters, mountain man styles, camp knives and hunters. **Technical:** Customer's choice of steel, from high-end carbon to custom damascus, including natural handle material and leather or Kydex sheaths. Specializes in repurposing discarded steel from old saws, kitchen knives, auto parts, etc., as well as repairing damaged knives that would otherwise be discarded. **Prices:** $50 to $300+. **Remarks:** Part-time maker looking to transition to full time; first knife sold in 2014. **Mark:** Petroglyph Coyote with last name.

V

VAGNINO, MICHAEL

1415 W. Ashland Ave., Visalia, CA 93277, Phone: 559-636-0501; cell: 559-827-7802, mike@mvknives.com; Web: www.mvknives.com

Specialties: Folders and straight knives, working and fancy. **Patterns:** Folders--locking liners, slip joints, lock backs, double and single action autos. Straight knives--hunters, Bowies, camp and kitchen. **Technical:** Forges 52100, W2, 15N20 and 1084. Grinds stainless. Makes own damascus and does engraving. **Prices:** $300 to $4,000 and above. **Remarks:** Full-time maker, ABS Mastersmith. **Mark:** Logo, last name.

VAIL, DAVE

554 Sloop Point Rd, Hampstead, NC 28443, Phone: 910-270-4456

Specialties: Working/using straight knives of his own design or to the customer's specs. **Patterns:** Hunters/skinners, camp/utility, fillet, Bowies. **Technical:** Grinds ATS-34, 440c, 154 CM and 1095 carbon steel. **Prices:** $90 to $450. **Remarks:** Part-time maker. Member of NC Custom Knifemakers Guild. **Mark:** Etched oval with "Dave Vail Hampstead NC" inside.

VALLOTTON, BUTCH AND AREY

621 Fawn Ridge Dr, Oakland, OR 97462, Phone: 541-459-2216, Fax: 541-459-7473

Specialties: Quick opening knives w/complicated mechanisms. **Patterns:** Tactical, fancy, working, and some art knives. **Technical:** Grinds all steels, uses others' Damascus. Uses Spectrum Metal. **Prices:** From $350 to $4500. **Remarks:** Full-time maker since 1984; first

knife sold in 1981. Co-designer, Appelgate Fairbarn folding w/Bill Harsey. **Mark:** Name w/ viper head in the "V."

VALLOTTON, RAINY D

1295 Wolf Valley Dr, Umpqua, OR 97486, Phone: 541-459-0465

Specialties: Folders, one-handed openers and art pieces. **Patterns:** All patterns. **Technical:** Stock removal all steels; uses titanium liners and bolsters; uses all finishes. **Prices:** $350 to $3500. **Remarks:** Full-time maker. **Mark:** Name.

VALLOTTON, SHAWN

621 Fawn Ridge Dr, Oakland, OR 97462, Phone: 503-459-2216

Specialties: Left-hand knives. **Patterns:** All styles. **Technical:** Grinds 440C, ATS-34 and Damascus. Uses titanium. Prefers bead-blasted or anodized finishes. **Prices:** $250 to $1400. **Remarks:** Full-time maker. **Mark:** Name and specialty.

VALLOTTON, THOMAS

621 Fawn Ridge Dr, Oakland, OR 97462, Phone: 541-459-2216

Specialties: Custom autos. **Patterns:** Tactical, fancy. **Technical:** File work, uses Damascus, uses Spectrum Metal. **Prices:** From $350 to $700. **Remarks:** Full-time maker. Maker of ProtŽgé 3 canoe. **Mark:** T and a V mingled.

VAN CLEVE, STEVE

Box 372, Sutton, AK 99674, Phone: 907-745-3038, Fax: 907-745-8770, sucents@mtaonline.net; Web: www.alaskaknives.net

VAN DE MANAKKER, THIJS

Koolweg 34, Holland, NETHERLANDS, Phone: 0493539369, www.ehijsvandemanakker.com

Specialties: Classic high-art knives. **Patterns:** Swords, utility/camp knives and period pieces. **Technical:** Forges soft iron, carbon steel and Bloomery Iron. Makes own Damascus, Bloomery Iron and patterns. **Prices:** $20 to $2000; some higher. **Remarks:** Full-time maker; first knife sold in 1969. **Mark:** Stylized "V."

VAN DEN BERG, NEELS

166 Van Heerdan St., Capital Park, Pretoria, Gauteng, SOUTH AFRICA, Phone: +27(0)12-326-5649 or +27(0)83-451-3105, neels@blackdragonforge.com; Web: http://www.blackdragonforge.com or http://www.facebook.com/neels.vandenberg

Specialties: Handforged damascus and high-carbon steel axes, hunters, swords and art knives. **Patterns:** All my own designs and customer collaborations, from axes, hunters, choppers, bowies, swords and folders to one-off tactical prototypes. **Technical:** Flat and hollow grinding. Handforges high-carbon steels and maker's own damascus. Also works in high-carbon stainless steels. **Prices:** $50 to $1,000. **Remarks:** Part-time maker; first knife sold in Oct. 2009. **Mark:** Stylized capital letter "N" resembling a three-tier mountain, normally hot stamped in forged blades.

VAN DEN ELSEN, GERT

Purcelldreef 83, Tilburg, NETHERLANDS 5012 AJ, Phone: 013-4563200, gvdelsen@home.nl

Specialties: Fancy, working/using, miniatures and integral straight knives of the maker's design or to customer specs. **Patterns:** Bowies, fighters, hunters and Japanese-style blades. **Technical:** Grinds ATS-34 and 440C; forges Damascus. Offers filework, differentially tempered blades and some mokume-gane fittings. **Prices:** $350 to $1000; some to $4000. **Remarks:** Part-time maker; first knife sold in 1982. Doing business as G-E Knives. **Mark:** Initials GE in lozenge shape.

VAN DER WESTHUIZEN, PETER

PO Box 1698, Mossel Bay, SC, SOUTH AFRICA 6500, Phone: 27 446952388, pietvdw@telkomsa.net

Specialties: Working knives, folders, daggers and art knives. **Patterns:** Hunters, skinners, bird, trout and sidelock folders. **Technical:** Sandvik, 12627. Damascus indigenous wood and ivory. **Prices:** From $450 to $5500. **Remarks:** First knife sold in 1987. Full-time since 1996. **Mark:** Initial & surname. Handmade RSA.

VAN DIJK, RICHARD

76 Stepney Ave Rd 2, Harwood Dunedin, NEW ZEALAND, Phone: 0064-3-4780401, Web: www.hoihoknives.com

Specialties: Damascus, Fantasy knives, sgiandubhs, dirks, swords, and hunting knives. **Patterns:** Mostly one-offs, anything from bird and trout to swords, no folders. **Technical:** Forges mainly own Damascus, some 5160, O1, 1095, L6. Prefers natural handle materials, over 40 years experience as goldsmith, handle fittings are often made from sterling silver and sometimes gold, manufactured to cap the handle, use gemstones if required. Makes own sheaths. **Prices:** $300 and up. **Remarks:** Full-time maker, first knife sold in 1980. Doing business as HOIHO KNIVES. **Mark:** Stylized initials RvD in triangle.

VAN EIZENGA, JERRY W

14281 Cleveland, Nunica, MI 49448, Phone: 616-638-2275

Specialties: Hand forged blades, Scagel patterns and other styles. **Patterns:** Camp, hunting, bird, trout, folders, axes, miniatures. **Technical:** 5160, 52100, 1084. **Prices:** Start at $250. **Remarks:** Part-time maker, sole author of knife and sheath. First knife made 1970s. ABS member who believes in the beauty of simplicity. **Mark:** J.S. stamp.

VAN ELDIK, FRANS

Ho Flaan 3, Loenen, NETHERLANDS 3632 BT, Phone: 0031 294 233 095, Fax: 0031 294 233 095

Specialties: Fancy collector-grade straight knives and folders of his design. **Patterns:** Hunters, fighters, boots and folders. **Technical:** Forges and grinds D2, 154CM, ATS-34 and stainless Damascus. **Prices:** Start at $450. **Remarks:** Spare-time maker; first knife sold in 1979. Knifemaker 30 years, 25 year member of Knifemakers Guild. **Mark:** Lion with name and Amsterdam.

VAN HEERDEN, ANDRE
P.O. Box 905-417, Garsfontein, Pretoria, GT, SOUTH AFRICA 0042, Phone: 27 82 566 6030, andrevh@iafrica.com; Web: www.andrevanheerden.com
Specialties: Fancy and working folders of his design to customer specs. **Technical:** Grinds RWL34, 19C27, D2, carbon and stainless Damascus. **Prices:** Starting at $350. **Remarks:** Part-time maker, first knife sold in 2003. **Mark:** Initials and name in a double circle.

VAN REENEN, IAN
6003 Harvard St, Amarillo, TX 79109, Phone: 806-236-8333, ianvanreenen@suddenlink.net Web: www.ianvanreenencustomknives.com
Specialties: Pocketknives and hunting knives. **Patterns:** Tactical pocketknives. **Technical:** 14C28N, 12C27 and ATS-34 blade steels. **Prices:** $600 to $1,500. **Remarks:** Specializing in tactical pocketknives. **Mark:** IVR with TEXAS underneath.

VAN RYSWYK, AAD
AVR KNIVES, Werf Van Pronk 8, Vlaardingen, NETHERLANDS 3134 HE, Phone: +31 10 4742952, info@avrknives.com; Web: www.avrknives.com
Specialties: High-art interframe folders of his design. **Patterns:** Hunters and locking folders. **Technical:** Uses semi-precious stones, mammoth ivory, iron wood, etc. **Prices:** $550 to $3800. **Remarks:** Full-time maker; first knife sold in 1993.

VANCE, DAVID
2646 Bays Bend Rd., West Liberty, KY 41472, Phone: 606-743-1465 and 606-362-8339, dtvance@mrtc.com; Web: www.facebook.com/ddcutlery
Specialties: Custom hunting or collectible knives, folders and fixed blades, also unique bullet casing handle pins and filework. **Patterns:** Maker's design or made to customers' specifications. **Technical:** Uses stock removal method on 1095 steel. **Remarks:** Part-time maker; first knife made in 2006. **Mark:** Cursive D&D.

VANDERFORD, CARL G
2290 Knob Creek Rd, Columbia, TN 38401, Phone: 931-381-1488
Specialties: Traditional working straight knives and folders of his design. **Patterns:** Hunters, Bowies and locking folders. **Technical:** Forges and grinds 440C, O1 and wire Damascus. **Prices:** $60 to $125. **Remarks:** Part-time maker; first knife sold in 1987. **Mark:** Last name.

VANDERKOLFF, STEPHEN
5 Jonathan Crescent, Mildmay, ON, CANADA N0g 2J0, Phone: 519-367-3401, steve@vanderkolffknives.com; Web: www.vanderkolffknives.com
Specialties: Fixed blades from gent's pocketknives and drop hunters to full sized Bowies and art knives. **Technical:** Primary blade steel 440C, Damasteel or custom made Damascus. All heat treat done by maker and all blades hardness tested. Handle material: stag, stabilized woods or MOP. **Prices:** $150 to $1200. **Remarks:** Started making knives in 1998 and sold first knife in 2000. Winner of the best of show art knife 2005 Wolverine Knife Show.

VANDEVENTER, TERRY L
1915 Timberlake Pl., Byram, MS 39272, Phone: 601-371-7414, vandeventerterry@gmail.com; Web: www.vandeventerknives.com
Specialties: Bowies, hunters, camp knives, friction folders. **Technical:** 1084, 1095, 15N20 and L6 steels. Damascus and mokume. Natural handle materials. **Prices:** $600 to $3000. **Remarks:** Sole author; makes everything here. First ABS MS from the state of Mississippi. **Mark:** T.L. Vandeventer (silhouette of snake underneath). MS on ricasso.

VANHOY, ED AND TANYA
24255 N Fork River Rd, Abingdon, VA 24210, Phone: 276-944-4885, vanhoyknives@centurylink.net
Specialties: Traditional and working/using straight knives and folders and innovative locking mechanisms. **Patterns:** Fighters, straight knives, folders, hunters, art knives and Bowies. **Technical:** Grinds ATS-34 and carbon/stainless steel Damascus; forges carbon and stainless Damascus. Offers filework and engraving with hammer and chisel. **Prices:** $250 to $3000. **Remarks:** Full-time maker; first knife sold in 1977. Wife also engraves. Doing business as Van Hoy Custom Knives. **Mark:** Acid etched last name.

VARDAMAN, ROBERT
2406 Mimosa Lane, Hattiesburg, MS 39402, Phone: 601-268-3889, rvx222@gmail.com
Specialties: Working straight knives, mainly integrals, of his design or to customer specs. **Patterns:** Mainly integrals, bowies and hunters. **Technical:** Forges 52100, W2 and 1084. Filework. **Prices:** $250 to $1,000. **Remarks:** Part-time maker. First knife sold in 2004. **Mark:** Last name, last name with Mississippi state logo.

VASQUEZ, JOHNNY DAVID
1552 7th St, Wyandotte, MI 48192, Phone: 734-837-7733, trollhammerv@aol.com

VEIT, MICHAEL
3289 E Fifth Rd, LaSalle, IL 61301, Phone: 815-223-3538, whitebear@starband.net
Specialties: Damascus folders. **Technical:** Engraver, sole author. **Prices:** $2500 to $6500. **Remarks:** Part-time maker; first knife sold in 1985. **Mark:** Name in script.

VELARDE, RICARDO
7240 N Greenfield Dr, Park City, UT 84098, Phone: 435-901-1773, velardeknives@mac.com Web: www.velardeknives.com
Specialties: Investment grade integrals and interframs. **Patterns:** Boots, fighters and hunters; hollow grind. **Technical:** BG on Integrals. **Prices:** $1450 to $5200. **Remarks:** First knife sold in 1992. **Mark:** First initial and last name.

VELICK, SAMMY
3457 Maplewood Ave, Los Angeles, CA 90066, Phone: 310-663-6170, metaltamer@gmail.com
Specialties: Working knives and art pieces. **Patterns:** Hunter, utility and fantasy. **Technical:** Stock removal and forges. **Prices:** $100 and up. **Mark:** Last name.

VENSILD, HENRIK
GI Estrup, Randersvei 4, Auning, DENMARK 8963, Phone: +45 86 48 44 48
Specialties: Classic and traditional working and using knives of his design; Scandinavian influence. **Patterns:** Hunters and using knives. **Technical:** Forges Damascus. Hand makes handles, sheaths and blades. **Prices:** $350 to $1000. **Remarks:** Part-time maker; first knife sold in 1967. **Mark:** Initials.

VERONIQUE, LAURENT
Avenue du Capricorne, 53, 1200 Bruxelles, BELGIUM, Phone: 0032-477-48-66-73, whatsonthebench@gmail.com
Specialties: Fixed blades and friction folders. **Patterns:** Bowies, camp knives, ladies' knives and maker's own designs. **Technical:** Maker's own San Mai steel with a Blue Paper Steel edge and pure-nickel-and-O1 outer layers, called "Nickwich" (nickel in sandwich), and damascus, numerical milling embellishments and inlays, and hand-fashioned sheaths. **Prices:** Start at $350. **Remarks:** Part-time maker since 2005, ABS journeyman smith since 2013.

VESTAL, CHARLES
26662 Shortsville Rd., Abingdon, VA 24210, Phone: 276-492-3262, charles@vestalknives.com; Web: www.vestalknives.com
Specialties: Hunters and double ground fighters in traditional designs and own designs. **Technical:** Grinds CPM-154, ATS-134, 154-CM and other steels. **Prices:** $300 to $1000, some higher. **Remarks:** First knife sold in 1995.

VIALLON, HENRI
Les Belins, Thiers, FRANCE 63300, Phone: 04-73-80-24-03, Fax: 04 73-51-02-02
Specialties: Folders and complex Damascus **Patterns:** His draws. **Technical:** Forge. **Prices:** $1000 to $5000. **Mark:** H. Viallon.

VICKERS, DAVID
11620 Kingford Dr., Montgomery, TX 77316, Phone: 936-537-4900, jdvickers@gmail.com
Specialties: Working/using blade knives especially for hunters. His design or to customer specs. **Patterns:** Hunters, skinners, camp/utility. **Technical:** Grinds ATS-34, 440C, and D-2. Uses stag, various woods, and micarta for handle material. Hand-stitched sheaths. **Remarks:** Full-time maker. **Prices:** $125 - $350. **Mark:** VICKERS

VIELE, H J
88 Lexington Ave, Westwood, NJ 07675, Phone: 201-666-2906, h.viele@verizon.net
Specialties: Folding knives of distinctive shapes. **Patterns:** High-tech folders and one-of-a-kind. **Technical:** Grinds ATS-34 and S30V. **Prices:** Start at $575. **Remarks:** Full-time maker; first knife sold in 1973. **Mark:** Japanese design for the god of war.

VILAR, RICARDO
Al. dos Jasmins 243, Mairipora, SP, BRAZIL 07600-000, Phone: +55 (15) 8133-0196, ricardovilar@gmail.com; Web: rvilarknives.com.br
Specialties: Straight working knives to customer specs. **Patterns:** Bowies, fighters and utility/camp knives. **Technical:** Grinds D6, ATS-34 and 440C stainless. **Prices:** $80 to $200. **Remarks:** Part-time maker; first knife sold in 1993. **Mark:** Percor over sword and circle.

VILAR, RICARDO AUGUSTO FERREIRA
Rua Alemada Dos Jasmins NO 243, Parque Petropolis, Mairipora, SP, BRAZIL 07600-000, Phone: 011-55-11-44-85-43-46, ricardovilar@ig.com.br.
Specialties: Traditional Brazilian-style working knives of the Sao Paulo state. **Patterns:** Fighters, hunters, utility, and camp knives, welcome customer design. Specialize in the "true" Brazilian camp knife "Soracabana." **Technical:** Forges only with sledge hammer to 100 percent shape in 5160 and 52100 and his own Damascus steels. Makes own sheaths in the "true" traditional "Paulista"-style of the state of Sao Paulo. **Remarks:** Full-time maker. **Prices:** $250 to $600. Uses only natural handle materials. **Mark:** Special designed signature styled name R. Vilar.

VILLA, LUIZ
R. Com. Miguel Calfat 398, Itaim Bibi, SP, BRAZIL 04537-081, Phone: 011-8290649
Specialties: One-of-a-kind straight knives and jewel knives of all designs. **Patterns:** Bowies, hunters, utility/camp knives and jewel knives. **Technical:** Grinds D6, Damascus and 440C; forges 5160. Prefers natural handle material. **Prices:** $70 to $200. **Remarks:** Part-time maker; first knife sold in 1990. **Mark:** Last name and serial number.

VILPPOLA, MARKKU
Jaanintie 45, Turku, FINLAND 20540, Phone: +358 (0)50 566 1563, markku@mvforge.fi Web: www.mvforge.fi
Specialties: All kinds of swords and knives. **Technical:** Forges silver steel, CO, 8%, nickel, 1095, A203E, etc. Mokume (sterling silver/brass/copper). Bronze casting (sand casting, lost-wax casting). **Prices:** Starting at $200.

VINING, BILL
9 Penny Lane, Methuen, MA 01844, Phone: 978-688-4729, billv@medawebs.com; Web: www.medawebs.com/knives
Specialties Liner locking folders. Slip joints & lockbacks. Patterns: Likes to make patterns of his own design. **Technical:** S30V, 440C, ATS-34. Damascus from various makers. **Prices:** $450 and up. **Remarks:** Part-time maker. **Mark:** VINING or B. Vining.

VISTE, JAMES
EDGEWISE FORGE, 9745 Dequindre, Hamtramck, MI 48212, Phone: 313-587-8899, edgewiseforge@hotmail.com
Mark: EWF touch mark.

VISTNES, TOR
Svelgen, NORWAY N-6930, Phone: 047-57795572
　　Specialties: Traditional and working knives of his design. **Patterns:** Hunters and utility knives. **Technical:** Grinds Uddeholm Elmax. Handles made of rear burls of different Nordic stabilized woods. **Prices:** $300 to $1100. **Remarks:** Part-time maker; first knife sold in 1988. **Mark:** Etched name and deer head.

VITALE, MACE
925 Rt 80, Guilford, CT 06437, Phone: 203-457-5591, Web: www.laurelrockforge.com
　　Specialties: Hand forged blades. **Patterns:** Hunters, utility, chef, Bowies and fighters. **Technical:** W2, 1095, 1084, L6. Hand forged and finished. **Prices:** $100 to $1000. **Remarks:** American Bladesmith Society, Journeyman Smith. Full-time maker; first knife sold 2001. **Mark:** MACE.

VOGT, DONALD J
9007 Hogans Bend, Tampa, FL 33647, Phone: 813-973-3245, vogtknives@verizon.net
　　Specialties: Art knives, folders, automatics. **Technical:** Uses Damascus steels for blade and bolsters, filework, hand carving on blade bolsters and handles. Other materials used: jewels, gold, mother-of-pearl, gold-lip pearl, black-lip pearl, ivory. **Prices:** $4,000 to $10,000. **Remarks:** Part-time maker; first knife sold in 1997. **Mark:** Last name.

VOGT, PATRIK
Kungsvagen 83, Halmstad, SWEDEN 30270, Phone: 46-35-30977
　　Specialties: Working straight knives. **Patterns:** Bowies, hunters and fighters. **Technical:** Forges carbon steel and own Damascus. **Prices:** From $100. **Remarks:** Not currently making knives. **Mark:** Initials or last name.

VOORHIES, LES
14511 Lk Mazaska Tr, Faribault, MN 55021, Phone: 507-332-0736, lesvor@msn.com; Web: www.lesvoorhiesknives.com
　　Specialties: Steels. **Patterns:** Liner locks & autos. **Technical:** ATS-34 Damascus. **Prices:** $250 to $1200. **Mark:** L. Voorhies.

VOSS, BEN
2212 Knox Rd. 1600 Rd. E, Victoria, IL 61485-9644, Phone: 309-879-2940
　　Specialties: Fancy working knives of his design. **Patterns:** Bowies, fighters, hunters, boots and folders. **Technical:** Grinds 440C, ATS-34 and D2. **Prices:** $35 to $1200. **Remarks:** Part-time maker; first knife sold in 1986. **Mark:** Name, city and state.

VOTAW, DAVID P
305 S State St, Pioneer, OH 43554, Phone: 419-737-2774
　　Specialties: Working knives; period pieces. **Patterns:** Hunters, Bowies, camp knives, buckskinners and tomahawks. **Technical:** Grinds O1 and D2. **Prices:** $100 to $200; some to $500. **Remarks:** Part-time maker; took over for the late W.K. Kneubuhler. Doing business as W-K Knives. **Mark:** WK with V inside anvil.

W

WACHOLZ, DOC
95 Anne Rd, Marble, NC 28905, Phone: 828-557-1543, killdrums@aol.com; web: rackforge.com
　　Specialties: Forged tactical knives and tomahawks. **Technical:** Use 52100 and 1084 high carbon steel; make own Damascus; design and dew own sheaths. Grind up and down fashion on a 3" wheel.**Prices:** $300 to $800. **Remarks:** Part-time maker; started forging in 1999, with ABS master Charles Ochs.. **Mark:** Early knives stamped RACK, newer knives since 2005 stamped WACHOLZ.

WADA, YASUTAKA
2-6-22 Fujinokidai, Nara City, Nara, JAPAN 631-0044, Phone: 0742 46-0689
　　Specialties: Fancy and embellished one-of-a-kind straight knives of his design. **Patterns:** Bowies, daggers and hunters. **Technical:** Grinds ATS-34. All knives hand-filed and flat grinds. **Prices:** $400 to $2500; some higher. **Remarks:** Part-time maker; first knife sold in 1990. **Mark:** Owl eyes with initial and last name underneath or last name.

WAGAMAN, JOHN K
107 E Railroad St, Selma, NC 27576, Phone: 919-965-9659, Fax: 919-965-9901
　　Specialties: Fancy working knives. **Patterns:** Bowies, miniatures, hunters, fighters and boots. **Technical:** Grinds D2, 440C, 154CM and commercial Damascus; inlays mother-of-pearl. **Prices:** $110 to $2000. **Remarks:** Part-time maker; first knife sold in 1975. **Mark:** Last name.

WAIDE, RUSTY
Triple C Knives, PO Box 499, Buffalo, MO 65622, Phone: 417-345-7231, Fax: 417-345-1911, wrrccc@yahoo.com
　　Specialties: Custom-designed hunting knives and cowboy working knives in high-carbon and damascus steels. **Prices:** $150 to $450. **Remarks:** Part-time maker; first knife sold in 2010. **Mark:** Name.

WAITES, RICHARD L
PO Box 188, Broomfield, CO 80038, Phone: 303-324-2905, Fax: 303-465-9971, dickknives@aol.com
　　Specialties: Working fixed blade knives of all kinds including "paddle blade" skinners. Hand crafted sheaths, some upscale and unusual. **Technical:** Grinds 440C, damascus and D2. **Prices:** $100 to $500. **Remarks:** Part-time maker. First knife sold in 1998. Doing business as R.L. Waites Knives. **Mark:** Oval etch with first and middle initial and last name on top and city and state on bottom. Memberships; Professional Knifemakers Association and Rocky Mountain Blade Collectors Club.

WALKER, BILL
431 Walker Rd, Stevensville, MD 21666, Phone: 410-643-5041

WALKER, DON
2850 Halls Chapel Rd, Burnsville, NC 28714, Phone: 828-675-9716, dlwalkernc@gmail.com

WALKER, JIM
22 Walker Ln, Morrilton, AR 72110, Phone: 501-354-3175, jwalker46@att.net
　　Specialties: Period pieces and working/using knives of his design and to customer specs. **Patterns:** Bowies, fighters, hunters, camp knives. **Technical:** Forges 5160, O1, L6, 52100, 1084, 1095. **Prices:** Start at $450. **Remarks:** Full-time maker; first knife sold in 1993. **Mark:** Three arrows with last name/MS.

WALKER, MICHAEL L
925-A Paseo del, Pueblo Sur Taos, NM 87571, Phone: 505-751-3409, Fax: 505-751-3417, metalwerkr@msn.com
　　Specialties: Innovative knife designs and locking systems; titanium and SS furniture and art. **Patterns:** Folders from utility grade to museum quality art; others upon request. **Technical:** State-of-the-art materials: titanium, stainless Damascus, gold, etc. **Prices:** $3500 and above. **Remarks:** Designer/MetalCrafts; full-time professional knifemaker since 1980; four U.S. patents; invented LinerLock® and was awarded registered U.S. trademark no. 1,585,333. **Mark:** Early mark MW, Walker's Lockers by M.L. Walker; current M.L. Walker or Michael Walker.

WALL, GREG
4753 Michie Pebble Hill Rd., Michie, TN 38357, Phone: 662-415-2909, glwall36@hotmail.com, www.wallhandmadeknives.com
　　Specialties: Working straight knives. **Patterns:** Classic hollow-handle survival knives, Ek-style fighters, drop-point hunters and big 7's models. **Technical:** Stock removal method of blade making, convex and flat grinds, using O1 tool steels and 440C stainless steel. **Prices:** $295 to $395. **Remarks:** First knife made and sold in 1983.

WALLINGFORD JR., CHARLES W
9024 Old Union Rd, Union, KY 41091, Phone: 859-384-4141, Web: www.cwknives.com
　　Specialties: 18th and 19th century styles, patch knives, rifleman knives. **Technical:** 1084 and 5160 forged blades. **Prices:** $125 to $300. **Mark:** CW.

WARD, CHUCK
PO Box 2272, 1010 E North St, Benton, AR 72018-2272, Phone: 501-778-4329, chuckbop@aol.com
　　Specialties: Traditional working and using straight knives and folders of his design. **Technical:** Grinds 440C, D2, A2, ATS-34 and O1; uses natural and composite handle materials. **Prices:** $90 to $400, some higher. **Remarks:** Part-time maker; first knife sold in 1990. **Mark:** First initial, last name.

WARD, KEN
1125 Lee Roze Ln, Grants Pass, OR 97527, Phone: 541-956-8864
　　Specialties: Working knives, some to customer specs. **Patterns:** Straight, axes, Bowies, buckskinners and miniatures. **Technical:** Grinds ATS-34, Damascus. **Prices:** $100 to $700. **Remarks:** Part-time maker; first knife sold in 1977. **Mark:** Name.

WARD, RON
PO BOX 21, Rose Hill, VA 24281, Phone: 276-445-4757
　　Specialties: Classic working and using straight knives, fantasy knives. **Patterns:** Bowies, hunter, fighters, and utility/camp knives. **Technical:** Grinds 440C, 154CM, ATS-34, uses composite and natural handle materials. **Prices:** $50 to $750. **Remarks:** Part-time maker, first knife sold in 1992. Doing business as Ron Ward Blades. **Mark:** RON WARD BLADES.

WARD, TOM
204 Village Rd., Wilmot, NH 03287, Phone: 508-277-3190, tempestcraft@gmail.com; Web: www.tempestcraft.com
　　Specialties: Axes and pattern welding, multi-billet twist constructions. Open to all commissions. **Technical:** Forges to shape, generally using 15N20, 1095 and 1084 blade steels. **Prices:** $400 for mono-steel hunting/camping knives to $3,000 and up on elaborate pieces. **Remarks:** Full-time maker; first knife made in 2008. **Mark:** An ornate T.

WARD, W C
817 Glenn St, Clinton, TN 37716, Phone: 615-457-3568
　　Specialties: Working straight knives; period pieces. **Patterns:** Hunters, Bowies, swords and kitchen cutlery. **Technical:** Grinds O1. **Prices:** $85 to $150; some to $500. **Remarks:** Part-time maker; first knife sold in 1969. He styled the Tennessee Knife Maker. **Mark:** TKM.

WARDELL, MICK
20 Clovelly Rd, Bideford, N Devon, ENGLAND EX39 3BU, wardellknives@hotmail.co.uk Web: www.wardellscustomknives.com
　　Specialties: Spring back folders and a few fixed blades. **Patterns:** Locking and slip-joint folders, Bowies. **Technical:** Grinds stainless Damascus and RWL34. Heat-treats. **Prices:** $300 to $2500. **Remarks:** Full-time maker; first knife sold in 1986. Takes limited Comissions. **Mark:** Wardell.

WARDEN, ROY A
275 Tanglewood Rd, Union, MO 63084, Phone: 314-583-8813, rwarden@yhti.net
　　Specialties: Complex mosaic designs of "EDM wired figures" and "stack up" patterns and "lazer cut" and "torch cut" and "sawed" patterns combined. **Patterns:** Mostly "all mosaic" folders, automatics, fixed blades. **Technical:** Mosaic Damascus with all tool steel edges. **Prices:** $100 to $1000. **Remarks:** Part-time maker; first knife sold in 1987. **Mark:** WARDEN stamped or initials connected.

WARE, J.D.

Calle 40 #342 x 47 y 49, Colonia Benito Juarez Norte, Merida, Yucatan, MEXICO 97119, jdware@jdwareknives.com; Web: www.jdwareknives.com

Specialties: Coin knives, slip-joint folders, chef's knives and hunting/camping/fishing knives. **Technical:** Practices stock-removal and forging methods of blade making using O1, 440C and D2 blade steels. **Prices:** Start at $200. **Remarks:** Full-time maker; first knife made in 1976. **Mark:** Usually etched "JD Ware, Artesano, Merida Yucatan, Hecho a Mano, Mexico."

WARE, TOMMY

158 Idlewilde, Onalaska, TX 77360, Phone: 936-646-4649

Specialties: Traditional working and using straight knives, folders and automatics of his design and to customer specs. **Patterns:** Hunters, automatics and locking folders. **Technical:** Grinds ATS-34, 440C and D2. Offers engraving and scrimshaw. **Prices:** $425 to $650; some to $1500. **Remarks:** Full-time maker; first knife sold in 1990. Doing business as Wano Knives. **Mark:** Last name inside oval, business name above, city and state below, year on side.

WARREN, AL

1423 Sante Fe Circle, Roseville, CA 95678, Phone: 916-257-5904, Fax: 215-318-2945, al@warrenknives.com; Web: www.warrenknives.net

Specialties: Working straight knives and folders, some fancy. **Patterns:** Hunters, Bowies, fillets, lockback, folders & multi blade. **Technical:** Grinds ATS-34 and S30V.440V. **Prices:** $225 to $2,500. **Remarks:** Full-time maker; first knife sold in 1978. **Mark:** First and middle initials, last name.

WARREN, ALAN AND CARROLL

6605 S.E. 69th Ave., Portland, OR 97206, Phone: 503-788-6863 or 503-926-3559, alanwarrenknives@yahoo.com

Specialties: Mostly one-of-a-kind straight knives, bird & trout knives, skinners, fighters, bowies, daggers, short swords and LinerLock folders (tactical and gent's). My designs or custom. **Technical:** Hollow and flat grinds 154CM, ATS-34, CPM-S30V, O1, 5160 and others. Uses just about all handle materials available. Makes custom-to-fit, hand-tooled and hand stitched leather sheaths, some with skin inlays or hard inlays to match knife handle materials such as G-10, Micarta, ironwood, ivory, stag, etc. **Prices:** $200 to $1,800, some to $3,595. **Remarks:** Full-time maker for nine years; first knife sold in 1998. **Mark:** Name, state, USA.

WARREN, DANIEL

571 Lovejoy Rd, Canton, NC 28716, Phone: 828-648-7351

Specialties: Using knives. **Patterns:** Drop point hunters. **Prices:** $200 to $500. **Mark:** Warren-Bethel NC.

WASHBURN, ARTHUR D

ADW CUSTOM KNIVES, 211 Hinman St / PO Box 625, Pioche, NV 89043, Phone: 775-962-5463, knifeman@lcturbonet.com; Web: www.adwcustomknives.com

Specialties: Locking liner folders. **Patterns:** Slip joint folders (single and multiplied), lock-back folders, some fixed blades. Do own heat-treating; Rockwell test each blade. **Technical:** Carbon and stainless Damascus, some 1084, 1095, AEBL, 12C27, S30V. **Prices:** $200 to $1000 and up. **Remarks:** Sold first knife in 1997. Part-time maker. **Mark:** ADW enclosed in an oval or ADW.

WASHBURN JR., ROBERT LEE

636 75th St., Tuscaloosa, AL 35405, Phone: 435-619-4432, Fax: 435-574-8554, rlwashburn@excite.com; Web: www.washburnknives.net

Specialties: Hand-forged period, Bowies, tactical, boot and hunters. **Patterns:** Bowies, tantos, loot hunters, tactical and folders. **Prices:** $100 to $2500. **Remarks:** All hand forged. 52100 being his favorite steel. **Mark:** Washburn Knives W.

WATANABE, MELVIN

1297 Kika St., Kailua, HI 96734, Phone: 808-429-9403, meltod808@yahoo.com

Specialties: Fancy folding knives. Some hunters. **Patterns:** Liner-locks and hunters. **Technical:** Grinds ATS-34, stainless Damascus. **Prices:** $350 and up. **Remarks:** Part-time maker, first knife sold in 1985. **Mark:** Name and state.

WATANABE, WAYNE

PO Box 3563, Montebello, CA 90640, wwknives@yahoo.com

Specialties: Straight knives in Japanese-styles. One-of-a-kind designs; welcomes customer designs. **Patterns:** Tantos to katanas, Bowies. **Technical:** Flat grinds A2, O1 and ATS-34. Offers hand-rubbed finishes and wrapped handles. **Prices:** Start at $200. **Remarks:** Part-time maker. **Mark:** Name in characters with flower.

WATERS, GLENN

11 Shinakawa Machi, Hirosaki City, JAPAN 036, Phone: 0172-886741, watersglenn@hotmail.com; Web: www.glennwaters.com

Specialties: One-of-a-kind collector-grade highly embellished art knives. Mostly folders with a few fixed blades and up-market tactical flippers. **Patterns:** Locking-liner folders and collectible flippers and fixed art knives. **Technical:** Grinds blades from Damasteel, VG-10, CowryX, ZDP-189, San Mai from ZDP-189 and VG-10, and Super Gold 2 powdered stainless by Takefu. Does own engraving, gold inlaying and stone setting, filework and carving. Gold and Japanese precious metal fabrication. Prefers exotic material, high karat gold, silver, Shyaku Dou, Shibu Ichi Gin, precious gemstones. **Prices:** Upscale. **Remarks:** Designs and makes one-of-a-kind highly embellished art knives, often with fully engraved handles and blades that tell a story. A jeweler by trade for 20 years before starting to make knives in 1993. First knife sold in 1994. **Mark:** On knives before 2010, Glenn Waters maker Japan or Glenn in Japanese. Knives since 2010 uses a new engraved logo that says Glenn in Japanese.

WATSON, BERT

9315 Meade St., Westminster, CO 80031, Phone: 303-587-3064, watsonbd21960@q.com

Specialties: Working/using straight knives of his design and to customer specs. **Patterns:** Hunters, utility/camp knives. **Technical:** Grinds O1, ATS-34, 440C, D2, A2 and others. **Prices:** $150 to $800. **Remarks:** Full-time maker. **Mark:** GTK and/or Bert.

WATSON, BILLY

440 Forge Rd, Deatsville, AL 36022, Phone: 334-365-1482, hilldweller44@att.net

Specialties: Working and using straight knives and folders of his design; period pieces. **Patterns:** Hunters, Bowies and utility/camp knives. **Technical:** Forges and grinds his own Damascus, 1095, 5160 and 52100. **Prices:** $40 to $1500. **Remarks:** Full-time maker; first knife sold in 1970. **Mark:** Last name.

WATSON, DANIEL

350 Jennifer Ln, Driftwood, TX 78619, Phone: 512-847-9679, info@angelsword.com; Web: http://www.angelsword.com

Specialties: One-of-a-kind knives and swords. **Patterns:** Hunters, daggers, swords. **Technical:** Hand-purify and carbonize his own high-carbon steel, pattern-welded Damascus, cable and carbon-induced crystalline Damascus. Teehno-Wootz™ Damascus steel, heat treats including cryogenic processing. European and Japanese tempering. **Prices:** $125 to $25,000. **Remarks:** Full-time maker; first knife sold in 1979. **Mark:** "Angel Sword" on forged pieces; "Bright Knight" for stock removal. Avatar on Techno-Wootz™ Damascus. Bumon on traditional Japanese blades.

WATSON, PETER

66 Kielblock St, La Hoff, NW, SOUTH AFRICA 2570, Phone: 018-84942

Specialties: Traditional working and using straight knives and folders of his design. **Patterns:** Hunters, locking folders and utility/camp knives. **Technical:** Sandvik and 440C. **Prices:** $120 to $250; some to $1500. **Remarks:** Part-time maker; first knife sold in 1989. **Mark:** Buffalo head with name.

WATSON, TOM

1103 Brenau Terrace, Panama City, FL 32405, Phone: 850-785-9209, tom@tomwatsonknives.com; Web: www.tomwatsonknives.com

Specialties: Utility/tactical LinerLocks and flipper folders. **Patterns:** Various patterns. **Technical:** Grinds D2 and CPM-154. **Prices:** $375 and up. **Remarks:** In business since 1978. **Mark:** Name and city.

WATTELET, MICHAEL A

PO Box 649, 125 Front, Minocqua, WI 54548, Phone: 715-356-3069, redtroll@frontier.com

Specialties: Working and using straight knives of his design and to customer specs; fantasy knives. **Patterns:** Daggers, fighters and swords. **Technical:** Grinds 440C and L6; forges and grinds O1. Silversmith. **Prices:** $75 to $1000; some to $5000. **Remarks:** Full-time maker; first knife sold in 1966. Doing business as M and N Arts Ltd. **Mark:** First initial, last name.

WATTS, JOHNATHAN

9440 S. Hwy. 36, Gatesville, TX 76528, Phone: 254-223-9669

Specialties: Traditional folders. **Patterns:** One and two blade folders in various blade shapes. **Technical:** Grinds ATS-34 and Damascus on request. **Prices:** $120 to $400. **Remarks:** Part-time maker; first knife sold in 1997. **Mark:** J Watts.

WATTS, RODNEY

Watts Custom Knives, 1100 Hwy. 71 S, Hot Springs, SD 57747, Phone: 605-890-0645, wattscustomknives@yahoo.com; www.wattscustomknives.com

Specialties: Fixed blades and some folders, most of maker's own designs, some Loveless and Johnson patterns. **Technical:** Stock remvoal method of blade making, using CPM 154 and ATS-34 steels. **Prices:** $450 to $1,100. **Remarks:** Part-time maker; first knife made in 2007. Won "Best New Maker" award at the 2011 BLADE Show. **Mark:** Watts over Custom Knives.

WEBSTER, BILL

58144 West Clear Lake Rd, Three Rivers, MI 49093, Phone: 269-244-2873, wswebster_5@msn.com Web: www.websterknifeworks.com

Specialties: Working and using straight knives, especially for hunters. His patterns are custom designed. **Patterns:** Hunters, skinners, camp knives, Bowies and daggers. **Technical:** Hand-filed blades made of D2 steel only, unless other steel is requested. Preferred handle material is stabilized and exotic wood and stag. Sheaths are hand-sewn by Bill Dehn in Three Rivers, MI. **Prices:** $75 to $500. **Remarks:** Part-time maker, first knife sold in 1978. **Mark:** Originally WEB stamped on blade, at present, Webster Knifeworks Three Rivers, MI laser etched on blade.

WEEKS, RYAN

PO Box 1101, Bountiful, UT 84001, Phone: 801-755-6789, ryan@ryanwknives.com; Web: www.ryanwknives.com

Specialties: Military and Law Enforcement applications as well as hunting and utility designs. **Patterns:** Fighters, bowies, hunters, and custom designs, I use man made as well as natural wood and exotic handle materials. **Technical:** Make via forge and stock removal methods, preferred steel includes high carbon, CPM154 CM and ATS34, Damascus and San Mai. **Prices:** $160 to $750. **Remarks:** Part-time maker; Business name is "Ryan W. Knives." First knife sold in 2009. **Mark:** Encircled "Ryan" beneath the crossed "W" UTAH, USA.

WEEVER, JOHN

150 Valley View St., Glen Rose, TX 76043, Phone: 254-898-9595, john.weever@gmail.com; Web: WeeverKnives.com

Specialties: Traditional hunters (fixed blade, slip joint, and lockback) and tactical

Patterns: See website. **Technical:** Types of steel: S30V, Damascus or customer choice. Handles in mammoth ivory, oosic, horn, sambar, stag, etc. Sheaths in exotic leathers. **Prices:** $400 to $1200. **Remarks:** Stock removal maker full-time; began making knives in 1985. Member of knifemakers guild. **Mark:** Tang stamp: head of charging elephant with ears extended and WEEVER curved over the top.

WEHNER, RUDY

297 William Warren Rd, Collins, MS 39428, Phone: 601-765-4997

Specialties: Reproduction antique Bowies and contemporary Bowies in full and miniature. **Patterns:** Skinners, camp knives, fighters, axes and Bowies. **Technical:** Grinds 440C, ATS-34, 154CM and Damascus. **Prices:** $100 to $500; some to $850. **Remarks:** Full-time maker; first knife sold in 1975. **Mark:** Last name on Bowies and antiques; full name, city and state on skinners.

WEILAND JR., J REESE

PO Box 2337, Riverview, FL 33568, Phone: 813-671-0661, RWPHIL413@verizon.net; Web: www.reeseweilandknives.com

Specialties: Hawk bills; tactical to fancy folders. **Patterns:** Hunters, tantos, Bowies, fantasy knives, spears and some swords. **Technical:** Grinds ATS-34, 154CM, 440C, D2, O1, A2, Damascus. Titanium hardware on locking liners and button locks. **Prices:** $150 to $4000. **Remarks:** Full-time maker, first knife sold in 1978. Knifemakers Guild member since 1988.

WEINAND, GEROME M

14440 Harpers Bridge Rd, Missoula, MT 59808, Phone: 406-543-0845

Specialties: Working straight knives. **Patterns:** Bowies, fishing and camp knives, large special hunters. **Technical:** Grinds O1, 440C, ATS-34, 1084, L6, also stainless Damascus, Aebl and 304; makes all-tool steel Damascus; Dendritic D2 from powdered steel. Heat-treats. **Prices:** $30 to $100; some to $500. **Remarks:** Full-time maker; first knife sold in 1982. **Mark:** Last name.

WEINSTOCK, ROBERT

PO Box 170028, San Francisco, CA 94117-0028, Phone: 415-731-5968, robertweinstock@att.net

Specialties: Folders, slip joins, lockbacks, autos. **Patterns:** Daggers, folders. **Technical:** Grinds A2, O1 and 440C. Chased and hand-carved blades and handles. Also using various Damascus steels from other makers. **Prices:** $3000 to 7000. **Remarks:** Full-time maker; first knife sold in 1994. **Mark:** Last name carved in steel.

WEISS, CHARLES L

PO BOX 1037, Waddell, AZ 85355, Phone: 623-935-0924, weissknife@live.com

Specialties: High-art straight knives and folders; deluxe period pieces. **Patterns:** Daggers, fighters, boots, push knives and miniatures. **Technical:** Grinds 440C, 154CM and ATS-34. **Prices:** $300 to $1200; some to $2000. **Remarks:** Full-time maker; first knife sold in 1975. **Mark:** Name and city.

WELLING, RONALD L

15446 Lake Ave, Grand Haven, MI 49417, Phone: 616-846-2274

Specialties: Scagel knives of his design or to customer specs. **Patterns:** Hunters, camp knives, miniatures, bird, trout, folders, double edged, hatchets, skinners and some art pieces. **Technical:** Forges Damascus 1084 and 1095. Antler, ivory and horn. **Prices:** $250 to $3000. **Remarks:** Full-time maker. ABS Journeyman maker. **Mark:** First initials and or name and last name. City and state. Various scagel kris (1or 2).

WELLING, WILLIAM

Up-armored Knives, 5437 Pinecliff Dr., West Valley, NY 14171, Phone: 716-942-6031, uparmored@frontier.net; Web: www.up-armored.com

Specialties: Innovative tactical fixed blades each uniquely coated in a variety of Up-armored designed patterns and color schemes.Convexed edged bushcraft knives for the weekend camper, backpacker, or survivalist. Knives developed specifically for tactical operators. Leather- and synthetic-suede-lined Kydex sheaths. **Patterns:** Modern samples of time tested designs as well as contemporary developed cutting tools. **Technical:** Stock removal specializing in tested 1095CV and 5160 steels. **Prices:** $200 to $500. **Remarks:** Part-time maker; first knife sold in 2010. **Mark:** Skull rounded up by Up-Armored USA.

WERTH, GEORGE W

5223 Woodstock Rd, Poplar Grove, IL 61065, Phone: 815-544-4408

Specialties: Period pieces, some fancy. **Patterns:** Straight fighters, daggers and Bowies. **Technical:** Forges and grinds O1, 1095 and his Damascus, including mosaic patterns. **Prices:** $200 to $650; some higher. **Remarks:** Full-time maker. Doing business as Fox Valley Forge. **Mark:** Name in logo or initials connected.

WESCOTT, CODY

5330 White Wing Rd, Las Cruces, NM 88012, Phone: 575-382-5008

Specialties: Fancy and presentation grade working knives. **Patterns:** Hunters, locking folders and Bowies. **Technical:** Hollow-grinds D2 and ATS-34; all knives file worked. Offers some engraving. Makes sheaths. **Prices:** $110 to $500; some to $1200. **Remarks:** Full-time maker; first knife sold in 1982. **Mark:** First initial, last name.

WEST, CHARLES A

1315 S Pine St, Centralia, IL 62801, Phone: 618-532-2777

Specialties: Classic, fancy, high tech, period pieces, traditional and working/using straight knives and folders. **Patterns:** Bowies, fighters and locking folders. **Technical:** Grinds ATS-34, O1 and Damascus. Prefers hot blued finishes. **Prices:** $100 to $1000; some to $2000. **Remarks:** Full-time maker; first knife sold in 1963. Doing business as West Custom Knives. **Mark:** Name or name, city and state.

WESTBERG, LARRY

305 S Western Hills Dr, Algona, IA 50511, Phone: 515-368-1974, westberg@netamumail.com

Specialties: Traditional and working straight knives of his design and in standard patterns. **Patterns:** Bowies, hunters, fillets and folders. **Technical:** Grinds 440C, D2 and 1095. Heat-treats. Uses natural handle materials. **Prices:** $85 to $600; some to $1000. **Remarks:** Part-time maker; first knife sold in 1987. **Mark:** Last name-town and state.

WETTEN, BOBBY

550 W. Caracas Ave., Hershey, PA 17033, Phone: 717-439-7686, bobwetten@gmail.com; Web: https://bobbywett.wordpress.com

Patterns: Forged hunters, camp knives, bowies, fighters and tomahawks. Likes to make pieces that blend into nature. **Technical:** Forges 10xx, 5160 and W2 steels, occasionally doing stock removal pieces. Father-in-law Paul Wittle makes sheaths. **Prices:** $300 to $1,500. **Remarks:** First knife completed in 2006; ABS journeyman smith. **Mark:** BobbyWett (one word, no spaces).

WHEELER, GARY

351 Old Hwy 48, Clarksville, TN 37040, Phone: 931-552-3092, LR22SHTR@charter.net

Specialties: Working to high end fixed blades. **Patterns:** Bowies, Hunters, combat knives, daggers and a few folders. **Technical:** Forges 5160, 1095, 52100 and his own Damascus. **Prices:** $125 to $2000. **Remarks:** Full-time maker since 2001, first knife sold in 1985 collaborates/works at B&W Blade Works. ABS Journeyman Smith 2008. **Mark:** Stamped last name.

WHEELER, NICK

140 Studebaker Rd., Castle Rock, WA 98611, Phone: 360-967-2357, merckman99@yahoo.com

Specialties: Bowies, integrals, fighters, hunters and daggers. **Technical:** Forges W2, W1, 1095, 52100 and 1084. Makes own damascus, from random pattern to complex mosaics. Also grinds stainless and other more modern alloys. Does own heat-treating and leather work. Also commissions leather work from Paul Long. **Prices:** Start at $250. **Remarks:** Full-time maker; ABS member since 2001. Journeyman bladesmith. **Mark:** Last name.

WHEELER, ROBERT

289 S Jefferson, Bradley, IL 60915, Phone: 815-932-5854, b2btaz@brmemc.net

WHIPPLE, WESLEY A

1002 Shoshoni St, Thermopolis, WY 82443, Phone: 307-921-2445, wildernessknife@yahoo.com

Specialties: Working straight knives, some fancy. **Patterns:** Hunters, Bowies, camp knives, fighters. **Technical:** Forges high-carbon steels, Damascus, offers relief carving and silver wire inlay and checkering. **Prices:** $300 to $1400; some higher. **Remarks:** Full-time maker; first knife sold in 1989. A.K.A. Wilderness Knife and Forge. **Mark:** Last name/JS.

WHITE, BRYCE

1415 W Col Glenn Rd, Little Rock, AR 72210, Phone: 501-821-2956

Specialties: Hunters, fighters, makes Damascus, file work, handmade only. **Technical:** L6, 1075, 1095, O1 steels used most. **Patterns:** Will do any pattern or use his own. **Prices:** $200 to $300. Sold first knife in 1995. **Mark:** White.

WHITE, CALEB A.

502 W. River Rd. #88, Hooksett, NH 03106, Phone: 603-340-4716, caleb@calebwhiteknives.com; www.calebwhiteknives.com

Specialties: Hunters, tacticals, dress knives, daggers and utilitarian pieces. **Patterns:** Multiple. **Technical:** Mostly stock removal, preferring high-carbon steels. **Prices:** $275 to $4,100. **Remarks:** Full-time maker. **Mark:** Derivation of maker's last name, replacing the "T" with a symbol loosely based on the Templars' cross and shield.

WHITE, DALE

525 CR 212, Sweetwater, TX 79556, Phone: 325-798-4178, dalew@taylortel.net

Specialties: Working and using knives. **Patterns:** Hunters, skinners, utilities and Bowies. **Technical:** Grinds 440C, offers file work, fancy pins and scrimshaw by Sherry Sellers. **Prices:** From $45 to $300. **Remarks:** Sold first knife in 1975. **Mark:** Full name, city and state.

WHITE, LOU

7385 Red Bud Rd NE, Ranger, GA 30734, Phone: 706-334-2273

WHITE, RICHARD T

359 Carver St, Grosse Pointe Farms, MI 48236, Phone: 313-881-4690

WHITE, RUSSELL D.

4 CR 8240, Rienzi, MS 38865, Phone: 662-416-3461, rwhite292@gmail.com; Facebook: Handmade Knives by Russell White

Patterns: Hunters, bowies and camp knives using natural handle materials and micarta. **Technical:** Forges 1084, 15N20, 52100, 5160, O1 and damascus. **Prices:** Start at $200. **Remarks:** Part-time maker; first knife sold in 2010. ABS journeyman smith, sole authorship knifemaker offering handmade leather sheaths if wanted. **Mark:** R. White, J.S. on ricasso.

WHITENECT, JODY

Halifax County, Elderbank, NS, CANADA B0N 1K0, Phone: 902-384-2511

Specialties: Fancy and embellished working/using straight knives of his design and to customer specs. **Patterns:** Bowies, fighters and hunters. **Technical:** Forges 1095 and O1; forges and grinds ATS-34. Various filework on blades and bolsters. **Prices:** $200 to $400; some to $800. **Remarks:** Part-time maker; first knife sold in 1996. **Mark:** Longhorn stamp or engraved.

WHITESELL, J. DALE

P.O. Box 455, Stover, MO 65078, Phone: 573-569-0753, dalesknives@yahoo.com;

Web: whitesell-knives.webs.com

Specialties: Fixed blade working knives,a nd some collector pieces. **Patterns:** Hunting and skinner knives, camp knives, and kitchen knives. **Technical:** Blades ground from O1, 1095, and 440C in hollow, flat and saber grinds. Wood, bone, deer antler, and G10 are basic handle materials. **Prices:** $100 to $450. **Remarks:** Part-time maker, first knife sold in 2003. Doing business as Dale's Knives. All knives have serial number to indicate steel (since June 2010).**Mark:** Whitesell on the left side of the blade.

WHITLEY, L WAYNE
1675 Carrow Rd, Chocowinity, NC 27817-9495, Phone: 252-946-5648

WHITLEY, WELDON G
4308 N Robin Ave, Odessa, TX 79764, Phone: 432-530-0448, Fax: 432-530-0048, wgwhitley@juno.com

Specialties: Working knives of his design or to customer specs. **Patterns:** Hunters, folders and various double-edged knives. **Technical:** Grinds 440C, 154CM and ATS-34. **Prices:** $150 to $1250. **Mark:** Name, address, road-runner logo.

WHITTAKER, ROBERT E
PO Box 204, Mill Creek, PA 17060

Specialties: Using straight knives. Has a line of knives for buckskinners. **Patterns:** Hunters, skinners and Bowies. **Technical:** Grinds O1, A2 and D2. Offers filework. **Prices:** $35 to $100. **Remarks:** Part-time maker; first knife sold in 1980. **Mark:** Last initial or full initials.

WHITTAKER, WAYNE
2900 Woodland Ct, Metamore, MI 48455, Phone: 810-797-5315, lindorwayne@yahoo.com

Specialties: Liner locks and autos.**Patterns:** Folders. **Technical:** Damascus, mammoth, ivory, and tooth. **Prices:** $500 to $1500. **Remarks:** Full-time maker. **Mark:** Inside of backbar.

WICK, JONATHAN P.
5541 E. Calle Narciso, Hereford, AZ 85615, Phone: 520-227-5228, vikingwick@aol.com

Specialties: Fixed blades, pocketknives, neck knives, hunters, bowies, fighters, Roman-style daggers with full tangs, stick tangs and some integrals, and leather-lined, textured copper sheaths. **Technical:** Forged blades and own damascus and mosaic damascus, along with shibuichi, mokume, lost wax casting. **Prices:** $250 - $1800 and up. **Remarks:** Full-time maker, ABS member, sold first knife in 2008. **Mark:** J P Wick, also on small blades a JP over a W.

WICKER, DONNIE R
2544 E 40th Ct, Panama City, FL 32405, Phone: 904-785-9158

Specialties: Traditional working and using straight knives of his design or to customer specs. **Patterns:** Hunters, fighters and slip-joint folders. **Technical:** Grinds 440C, ATS-34, D2 and 154CM. Heat-treats and does hardness testing. **Prices:** $90 to $200; some to $400. **Remarks:** Part-time maker; first knife sold in 1975. **Mark:** First and middle initials, last name.

WIGGINS, BILL
105 Kaolin Lane, Canton, NC 28716, Phone: 828-226-2551, wncbill@bellsouth.net Web: www.wigginsknives.com

Specialties: Forged working knives. **Patterns:** Hunters, Bowies, camp knives and utility knives of own design or will work with customer on design. **Technical:** Forges 1084 and 52100 as well as making own Damascus. **Prices:** $250 - $1500. **Remarks:** Part-time maker. First knife sold in 1989. ABS board member. **Mark:** Wiggins

WILBURN, AARON
2521 Hilltop Dr., #364, Redding, CA 96002, Phone: 530-227-2827, wilburnforge@yahoo.com; Web: www.wilburnforge.com

Patterns: Daggers, bowies, fighters, hunters and slip-joint folders. **Technical:** Forges own damascus and works with high-carbon steel. **Prices:** $500 to $5,000. **Remarks:** Full-time maker and ABS master smith. **Mark:** Wilburn Forge.

WILKINS, MITCHELL
15523 Rabon Chapel Rd, Montgomery, TX 77316, Phone: 936-588-2696, mwilkins@consolidated.net

WILLEY, WG
14210 Sugar Hill Rd, Greenwood, DE 19950, Phone: 302-349-4070, Web: www.willeyknives.com

Specialties: Fancy working straight knives. **Patterns:** Small game knives, Bowies and throwing knives. **Technical:** Grinds 440C and 154CM. **Prices:** $350 to $600; some to $1500. **Remarks:** Part-time maker; first knife sold in 1975. Owns retail store. **Mark:** Last name inside map logo.

WILLIAMS, JASON L
PO Box 67, Wyoming, RI 02898, Phone: 401-539-8353, Fax: 401-539-0252

Specialties: Fancy and high tech folders of his design, co-inventor of the Axis Lock. **Patterns:** Fighters, locking folders, automatics and fancy pocket knives. **Technical:** Forges Damascus and other steels by request. Uses exotic handle materials and precious metals. Offers inlaid spines and gemstone thumb knobs. **Prices:** $1000 and up. **Remarks:** Full-time maker; first knife sold in 1989. **Mark:** First and last initials on pivot.

WILLIAMS, MICHAEL
333 Cherrybark Tr., Broken Bow, OK 74728, Phone: 580-420-3051, hforge@pine-net.com; Web: www.williamscustomknives.com

Specialties: Functional, personalized, edged weaponry. Working and collectible art. **Patterns:** Bowies, hunters, camp knives, daggers, others. **Technical:** Forges high carbon

steel and own forged Damascus. **Prices:** $500 - $12000. **Remarks:** Full-time ABS Master Smith. **Mark:** Williams MS.

WILLIAMS, ROBERT
15962 State Rt. 267, East Liverpool, OH 43920, Phone: 203-979-0803, wurdmeister@gmail.com; Web: www.customstraightrazors.com

Specialties: Custom straight razors with a philosophy that form must follow function, so shaving performance drives designs and aesthetics. **Technical:** Stock removal and forging, working with 1095, O1 and damascus. Natural handle materials and synthetics, accommodating any and all design requests and can incorporate gold inlays, scrimshaw, hand engraving and jewel setting. All work done in maker's shop, sole-source maker shipping worldwide. **Remarks:** Full-time maker; first straight razor in 2005. **Mark:** Robert Williams - Handmade, USA with a hammer separating the two lines.

WILLIAMS JR., RICHARD
1440 Nancy Circle, Morristown, TN 37814, Phone: 615-581-0059

Specialties: Working and using straight knives of his design or to customer specs. **Patterns:** Hunters, dirks and utility/camp knives. **Technical:** Forges 5160 and uses file steel. Hand-finish is standard; offers filework. **Prices:** $80 to $180; some to $250. **Remarks:** Spare-time maker; first knife sold in 1985. **Mark:** Last initial or full initials.

WILLIAMSON, TONY
Rt 3 Box 503, Siler City, NC 27344, Phone: 919-663-3551

Specialties: Flint knapping: knives made of obsidian flakes and flint with wood, antler or bone for handles. **Patterns:** Skinners, daggers and flake knives. **Technical:** Blades have width/thickness ratio of at least 4 to 1. Hafts with methods available to prehistoric man. **Prices:** $58 to $160. **Remarks:** Student of Errett Callahan. **Mark:** Initials and number code to identify year and number of knives made.

WILLIS, BILL
RT 7 Box 7549, Ava, MO 65608, Phone: 417-683-4326

Specialties: Forged blades, Damascus and carbon steel. **Patterns:** Cable, random or ladder lamented. **Technical:** Professionally heat treated blades. **Prices:** $75 to $600. **Remarks:** Lifetime guarantee on all blades against breakage. All work done by maker; including leather work. **Mark:** WF.

WILLUMSEN, MIKKEL
Nyrnberggade 23, S Copenhagen, DENMARK 2300, Phone: 4531176333, mw@willumsen-cph.com Web: www.wix.com/willumsen/urbantactical

Specialties: Folding knives, fixed blades, and balisongs. Also kitchen knives. **Patterns:** Primarily influenced by design that is function and quality based. Tactical style knives inspired by classical designs mixed with modern tactics. **Technical:** Uses CPM 154, RW 134, S30V, and carbon fiber titanium G10 for handles.**Prices:** Starting at $600.

WILSON, CURTIS M
PO Box 383, Burleson, TX 76097, Phone: 817-295-3732, cwknifeman2026@att.net; Web: www.cwilsonknives.com

Specialties: Traditional working/using knives, fixed blade, folders, slip joint, LinerLock® and lock back knives. Art knives, presentation grade Bowies, folder repair, heat treating services. Sub-zero quench. **Patterns:** Hunters, camp knives, military combat, single and multi-blade folders. Dr's knives large or small or custom design knives. **Technical:** Grinds ATS-34, 440C 52100, D2, S30V, CPM 154, mokume gane, engraves, scrimshaw, sheaths leather of kykex heat treating and file work. **Prices:** $150-750. **Remarks:** Part-time maker since 1984. Sold first knife in 1993. **Mark:** Curtis Wilson in ribbon or Curtis Wilson with hand made in a half moon.

WILSON, JAMES G
PO Box 4024, Estes Park, CO 80517, Phone: 303-586-3944

Specialties: Bronze Age knives; Medieval and Scottish-styles; tomahawks. **Patterns:** Bronze knives, daggers, swords, spears and battle axes; 12-inch steel Misericorde daggers, sgian dubhs, "his and her" skinners, bird and fish knives, capers, boots and daggers. **Technical:** Casts bronze; grinds D2, 440C and ATS-34. **Prices:** $49 to $400; some to $1300. **Remarks:** Part-time maker; first knife sold in 1975. **Mark:** WilsonHawk.

WILSON, MIKE
1416 McDonald Rd, Hayesville, NC 28904, Phone: 828-389-8145

Specialties: Fancy working and using straight knives of his design or to customer specs, folders. **Patterns:** Hunters, Bowies, utility knives, gut hooks, skinners, fighters and miniatures. **Technical:** Hollow grinds 440C, 1095, D2, XHP and CPM-154. Mirror finishes are standard. Offers filework. **Prices:** $130 to $600. **Remarks:** Full-time maker; first knife sold in 1985. **Mark:** Last name.

WILSON, P.R. "REGAN"
805 Janvier Rd., Scott, LA 70583, Phone: 504-427-1293, pat71ss@cox.net; www.acadianawhitetailtaxidermy.com

Specialties: Traditional working knives. **Patterns:** Old-school working knives, trailing points, drop points, hunters, boots, etc. **Technical:** 440C, ATS-34 and 154CM steels, all hollow ground with mirror or satin finishes. **Prices:** Start at $175 with sheath. **Remarks:** Mentored by Jim Barbee; first knife sold in 1988; lessons and guidance offered in maker's shop. **Mark:** Name and location with "W" in center of football-shaped logo.

WILSON, RON
2639 Greenwood Ave, Morro Bay, CA 93442, Phone: 805-772-3381

Specialties: Classic and fantasy straight knives of his design. **Patterns:** Daggers, fighters, swords and axes, mostly all miniatures. **Technical:** Forges and grinds Damascus and various tool steels; grinds meteorite. Uses gold, precious stones and exotic wood. **Prices:** Vary. **Remarks:** Part-time maker; first knives sold in 1995. **Mark:** Stamped first and last initials.

WILSON, RW

PO Box 2012, Weirton, WV 26062, Phone: 304-723-2771, rwknives@comcast.net or rwknives@hotmail.com; Web: www.rwwilsonknives.com, Facebook: RW Wilson Knives

Specialties: Custom-made knives and tomahawks. **Patterns:** Bowies, drop-point hunters, skinners, tomahawks and more. **Technical:** Grinds. **Prices:** $7 to $5,000. **Remarks:** First knife sold in 1966. Made tomahawks for the movie "Jeremiah Johnson." **Mark:** "RW Wilson" above a tomahawk and "Weirton WV" under tomahawk.

WILSON, STAN

8931 Pritcher Rd, Lithia, FL 33547, Phone: 727-461-1992, swilson@stanwilsonknives.com; Web: www.stanwilsonknives.com

Specialties: Fancy folders and automatics of his own design. **Patterns:** Locking liner folders, single and dual action autos, daggers. **Technical:** Stock removal, uses Damascus, stainless and high carbon steels, prefers ivory and pearl, Damascus with blued finishes and filework. **Prices:** $400 and up. **Remarks:** Member of Knifemakers Guild and Florida Knifemakers Association. Full-time maker will do custom orders. **Mark:** Name in script.

WILSON, VIC

9130 Willow Branch Dr, Olive Branch, MS 38654, Phone: 901-591-6550, vdubjr55@earthlink.net; Web: www.knivesbyvic.com

Specialties: Classic working and using knives and folders. **Patterns:** Hunters, boning, utility, camp, my patterns or customers. **Technical:** Grinds O1 and D2. Also does own heat treating. Offer file work and decorative liners on folders. Fabricate custom leather sheaths for all knives. **Prices:** $150 to $400. **Remarks:** Part-time maker, first knife sold in 1989. **Mark:** Etched V over W with oval circle around it, name, Memphis, TN.

WINGO, GARY

240 Ogeechee, Ramona, OK 74061, Phone: 918-536-1067, wingg_2000@yahoo.com; Web: www.geocities.com/wingg_2000/gary.html

Specialties: Folder specialist. Steel 440C, D2, others on request. Handle bone-stag, others on request. **Patterns:** Trapper three-blade stockman, four-blade congress, single- and two-blade barlows. **Prices:** 150 to $400. **Mark:** First knife sold 1994. Steer head with Wingo Knives or Straight line Wingo Knives.

WINGO, PERRY

22 55th St, Gulfport, MS 39507, Phone: 228-863-3193

Specialties: Traditional working straight knives. **Patterns:** Hunters, skinners, Bowies and fishing knives. **Technical:** Grinds 440C. **Prices:** $75 to $1000. **Remarks:** Full-time maker; first knife sold in 1988. **Mark:** Last name.

WINKLER, DANIEL

PO Box 2166, Blowing Rock, NC 28605, Phone: 828-295-9156, danielwinkler@bellsouth.net; Web: www.winklerknives.com

Specialties: Forged cutlery styled in the tradition of an era past as well as producing a custom-made stock removal line. **Patterns:** Fixed blades, friction folders, lock back folders, and axes/tomahawks. **Technical:** Forges, grinds, and heat treats carbon steels, specialty steels, and his own Damascus steel. **Prices:** $350 to $4000+. **Remarks:** Full-time maker since 1988. Exclusively offers leatherwork by Karen Shook. ABS Master Smith; Knifemakers Guild voting member. **Mark:** Hand forged: Dwinkler; Stock removal: Winkler Knives

WINN, MARVIN

Maxcutter Custom Knives, 587 Winn Rd., Sunset, LA 70584, Phone: 214-471-7012, maxcutter03@yahoo.com Web: www.maxcutterknives.com

Patterns: Hunting knives, some tactical and some miniatures. **Technical:** 1095, 5160, 154 CM, 12C27, CPM S30V, CPM 154, CTS-XHP and CTS-40CP blade steels, damascus or to customer's specs. Stock removal. **Prices:** $200 to $2,000. **Remarks:** Part-time maker. First knife made in 2002. **Mark:** Name and state.

WINN, TRAVIS A.

558 E 3065 S, Salt Lake City, UT 84106, Phone: 801-467-5957

Specialties: Fancy working knives and knives to customer specs. **Patterns:** Hunters, fighters, boots, Bowies and fancy daggers, some miniatures, tantos and fantasy knives. **Technical:** Grinds D2 and 440C. Embellishes. **Prices:** $125 to $500; some higher. **Remarks:** Part-time maker; first knife sold in 1976. **Mark:** TRAV stylized.

WINSTON, DAVID

1671 Red Holly St, Starkville, MS 39759, Phone: 601-323-1028

Specialties: Fancy and traditional knives of his design and to customer specs. **Patterns:** Bowies, daggers, hunters, boot knives and folders. **Technical:** Grinds 440C, ATS-34 and D2. Offers filework; heat-treats. **Prices:** $40 to $750; some higher. **Remarks:** Part-time maker; first knife sold in 1984. Offers lifetime sharpening for original owner. **Mark:** Last name.

WIRTZ, ACHIM

Mittelstrasse 58, Wuerselen, GERMANY 52146, Phone: 0049-2405-462-486, wootz@web.de

Specialties: Medieval, Scandinavian and Middle East-style knives. **Technical:** Forged blades only, Damascus steel, Wootz, Mokume. **Prices:** Start at $200. **Remarks:** Part-time maker. First knife sold in 1997. **Mark:** Stylized initials.

WISE, DONALD

304 Bexhill Rd, St Leonardo-On-Sea, East Sussex, ENGLAND TN3 8AL

Specialties: Fancy and embellished working straight knives to customer specs. **Patterns:** Hunters, Bowies and daggers. **Technical:** Grinds Sandvik 12C27, D2 D3 and O1. Scrimshaws. **Prices:** $110 to $300; some to $500. **Remarks:** Full-time maker; first knife sold in 1983. **Mark:** KNIFECRAFT.

WITHERS, TIM

WITHERS KNIVES, 4625 N. Granada Ln., Linden, CA 95236, tim@withersknives.com; Web: www.withersknives.com

Specialties: Loveless and original designs. **Patterns:** Bowies, fighters, hunters, daggers and custom pieces. **Technical:** Stock removal method of blade making using ATS-34, 440C, 1095 and CPM 154 steels, and with hollow and flat grinds. Heat-treating includes sub-zero quenching done in-house. Every blade Rockwell Hardness tested. Uses Micarta, exotic wood, stag and mother-of-pearl handles, and each knife comes with a quality 8-9-ounce leather sheath, also made in-house. **Prices:** $350 to $1,100. **Remarks:** Part-time maker; first knife completed in 2011. **Mark:** TIM WITHERS over LINDEN, CA.

WOLF, BILL

4618 N 79th Ave, Phoenix, AZ 85033, Phone: 623-910-3147, bwcustomknives143@gmail.com Web: www.billwolfcustomknives.com

Specialties: Investment grade knives. **Patterns:** Own designs or customer's. **Technical:** Grinds stainless and all steels. **Prices:** $400 to ? **Remarks:** First knife made in 1988. **Mark:** WOLF

WOLF JR., WILLIAM LYNN

4006 Frank Rd, Lagrange, TX 78945, Phone: 409-247-4626

WOOD, ALAN

Greenfield Villa, Greenhead, Brampton, ENGLAND CA8 7HH, info@alanwoodknives.com; Web: www.alanwoodknives.com

Specialties: High-tech working straight knives of his design. **Patterns:** Hunters, utility/camp and bushcraft knives. **Technical:** Grinds 12C27, RWL-34, stainless Damascus and O1. Blades are cryogenic treated. **Prices:** $200 to $800; some to $1,200. **Remarks:** Full-time maker; first knife sold in 1979. Not currently taking orders. **Mark:** Full name with stag tree logo.

WOOD, OWEN DALE

6492 Garrison St, Arvada, CO 80004-3157, Phone: 303-456-2748, wood.owen@gmail.com; Web: www.owenwoodknives.net

Specialties: Folding knives and daggers. **Patterns:** Own Damascus, specialties in 456 composite blades. **Technical:** Materials: Damascus stainless steel, exotic metals, gold, rare handle materials. **Prices:** $1000 to $9000. **Remarks:** Folding knives in art deco and art noveau themes. Full-time maker from 1981. **Mark:** OWEN WOOD.

WOOD, WEBSTER

22041 Shelton Trail, Atlanta, MI 49709, Phone: 989-785-2996, mainganikan@src-milp.com

Specialties: Works mainly in stainless; art knives, Bowies, hunters and folders. **Remarks:** Full-time maker; first knife sold in 1980. Retired guild member. All engraving done by maker. **Mark:** Initials inside shield and name.

WORLEY, JOEL A., J.S.

PO BOX 64, Maplewood, OH 45340, Phone: 937-638-9518, jaworleyknives@gmail.com

Specialties: Bowies, hunters, fighters, utility/camp knives also period style friction folders. **Patterns:** Classic styles, recurves, his design or customer specified. **Technical:** Most knives are fileworked and include a custom made leather sheath. Forges 5160, W2, Cru forge V, files own Damascus of 1080 and 15N20. **Prices:** $250 and up. **Remarks:** Part-time maker. ABS journeyman smith. First knife sold in 2005. **Mark:** First name, middle initial and last name over a shark incorporating initials.

WRIGHT, KEVIN

671 Leland Valley Rd W, Quilcene, WA 98376-9517, Phone: 360-765-3589, kevinw@ptpc.com

Specialties: Fancy working or collector knives to customer specs. **Patterns:** Hunters, boots, buckskinners, miniatures. **Technical:** Forges and grinds L6, 1095, 440C and his own Damascus. **Prices:** $75 to $500; some to $2000. **Remarks:** Part-time maker; first knife sold in 1978. **Mark:** Last initial in anvil.

WRIGHT, L.T.

130b Warren Ln., Wintersville, OH 43953, Phone: 740-317-1404, lt@ltwrightknives.com; Web: www.ltwrightknives.com

Specialties: Hunting, bushcraft and tactical knives. **Patterns:** Drop-point hunters,spear-point bushcraft and tactical. **Technical:** Grinds A2, D2 and O1. **Remarks:** Full-time maker.

WRIGHT, RICHARD S

PO Box 201, 111 Hilltop Dr, Carolina, RI 02812, Phone: 401-364-3579, rswswitchblades@hotmail.com; Web: www.richardswright.com

Specialties: Bolster release switchblades, tactical automatics. **Patterns:** Folding fighters, gents pocket knives, one-of-a-kind high-grade automatics. **Technical:** Reforges and grinds various makers Damascus. Uses a variety of tool steels. Uses natural handle material such as ivory and pearl, extensive file-work on most knives. **Prices:** $850 and up. **Remarks:** Full-time knifemaker with background as a gunsmith. Made first folder in 1991. **Mark:** RSW on blade, all folders are serial numbered.

WRIGHT, ROBERT A

21 Wiley Bottom Rd, Savannah, GA 31411, Phone: 912-777-7864; Cell: 912-656-9085, maker@robwrightknives.com; Web: www.RobWrightKnives.com

Specialties: Hunting, skinning, fillet, fighting and tactical knives. **Patterns:** Custom designs by client and/or maker. **Technical:** All types of steel, including CPM-S30V, D2, 440C, O1 tool steel and damascus upon request, as well as exotic wood and other high-quality handle materials. **Prices:** $200 and up depending on cost of steel and other materials. **Remarks:** Full-time maker, member of The Knifemakers' Guild and Georgia Custom Knifemaker's Guild. **Mark:** Etched maple leaf with maker's name: R.A. Wright.

WRIGHT, TIMOTHY
PO Box 3746, Sedona, AZ 86340, Phone: 928-282-4180
   Specialties: High-tech folders and working knives. **Patterns:** Interframe locking folders, non-inlaid folders, straight hunters and kitchen knives. **Technical:** Grinds BG-42, AEB-L, K190 and Cowry X; works with new steels. All folders can disassemble and are furnished with tools. **Prices:** $150 to $1800; some to $3000. **Remarks:** Full-time maker; first knife sold in 1975. **Mark:** Last name and type of steel used.

WUERTZ, TRAVIS
2487 E Hwy 287, Casa Grande, AZ 85222, Phone: 520-723-4432

WULF, DERRICK
25 Sleepy Hollow Rd, Essex, VT 05452, Phone: 802-777-8766, dickwulf@yahoo.com
Web: www.dicksworkshop.com
   Specialties: Makes predominantly forged fixed blade knives using carbon steels and his own Damascus.**Mark:** "WULF".

WYATT, WILLIAM R
Box 237, Rainelle, WV 25962, Phone: 304-438-5494
   Specialties: Classic and working knives of all designs. **Patterns:** Hunters and utility knives. **Technical:** Forges and grinds saw blades, files and rasps. Prefers stag handles. **Prices:** $45 to $95; some to $350. **Remarks:** Part-time maker; first knife sold in 1990. **Mark:** Last name in star with knife logo.

WYLIE, TOM
Peak Knives, 2 Maun Close, Sutton-In-Ashfield, Notts, England NG17 5JG, tom@peakknives.com
   Specialties: Knives for adventure sports and hunting, mainly fixed blades. **Technical:** Damasteel or European stainless steel used predominantly, handle material to suit purpose, embellished as required. Work can either be all handmade or CNC machined. **Prices:** $450+. **Remarks:** Pro-Am maker. **Mark:** Ogram "tinne" in circle of life, sometimes with addition of maker's name.

Y

YASHINSKI, JOHN L
207 N Platt, PO Box 1284, Red Lodge, MT 59068, Phone: 406-446-3916
   Specialties: Indian knife sheaths, beaded, tacked, painted rawhide sheaths, antiqued to look old, old beads and other parts, copies of originals. Write with color copies to be made. **Prices:** $100 to $600. Call to discuss price variations.

YESKOO, RICHARD C
76 Beekman Rd, Summit, NJ 07901

YONEYAMA, CHICCHI K.
5-19-8 Nishikicho, Tachikawa-City, Tokyo, JAPAN 190-0022, Phone: 081-1-9047449370, chicchi.ky1007@gmail.com; Web: https://sites.google.com/site/chicchiyoneyama/
   Specialties: Folders, hollow ground, lockback and slip-joint folders with interframe handles. **Patterns:** Pocketknives, desk and daily-carry small folders. **Technical:** Stock-removal method on ATS-34, 440C, V10 and SG2/damascus blade steels. **Prices:** $300 to $1,000 and up. **Remarks:** Full-time maker; first knife sold in 1999. **Mark:** Saber tiger mark with logos/Chicchi K. Yoneyama.

YORK, DAVID C
PO Box 3166, Chino Valley, AZ 86323, Phone: 928-636-1709, dmatj@msn.com
   Specialties: Working straight knives and folders. **Patterns:** Prefers small hunters and skinners; locking folders. **Technical:** Grinds D2. **Prices:** $75 to $300; some to $600. **Remarks:** Part-time maker; first knife sold in 1975. **Mark:** Last name.

YOSHIHARA, YOSHINDO
8-17-11 Takasago Katsushi, Tokyo, JAPAN

YOSHIKAZU, KAMADA
540-3 Kaisaki Niuta-cho, Tokushima, JAPAN, Phone: 0886-44-2319

YOSHIO, MAEDA
3-12-11 Chuo-cho tamashima, Kurashiki-city, Okayama, JAPAN, Phone: 086-525-2375

YOUNG, BUD
Box 336, Port Hardy, BC, CANADA V0N 2P0, Phone: 250-949-6478
   Specialties: Fixed blade, working knives, some fancy. **Patterns:** Drop-points to skinners. **Technical:** Hollow or flat grind, 5160, 440C, mostly ATS-34, satin finish. Using supplied damascus at times. **Prices:** $150 to $2000 CDN. **Remarks:** Spare-time maker; making knives since 1962; first knife sold in 1985. Not taking orders at this time, sell as produced. **Mark:** Name.

YOUNG, CLIFF
Fuente De La Cibeles No 5, Atascadero, San Miguel De Allende, GJ, MEXICO 37700, Phone: 011-52-415-2-57-11
   Specialties: Working knives. **Patterns:** Hunters, fighters and fishing knives. **Technical:** Grinds all; offers D2, 440C and 154CM. **Prices:** Start at $250. **Remarks:** Part-time maker; first knife sold in 1980. **Mark:** Name.

YOUNG, GEORGE
713 Pinoak Dr, Kokomo, IN 46901, Phone: 765-457-8893
   Specialties: Fancy/embellished and traditional straight knives and folders of his design and to customer specs. **Patterns:** Hunters, fillet/camp knives and locking folders. **Technical:** Grinds 440C, CPM440V, and stellite 6K. Fancy ivory, black pearl and stag for handles. Filework: all stellite construction (6K and 25 alloys). Offers engraving. **Prices:** $350 to $750; some $1500 to $3000. **Remarks:** Full-time maker; first knife sold in 1954. Doing business as Young's Knives. **Mark:** Last name integral inside Bowie.

YOUNG, JOHN
483 E. 400 S, Ephraim, UT 84627, Phone: 435-340-1417 or 435-283-4555
   Patterns: Fighters, hunters and bowies. **Technical:** Stainless steel blades, including ATS-34, 440C and CTS-40CP. **Prices:** $800 to $5,000. **Remarks:** Full-time maker since 2006; first knife sold in 1997. **Mark:** Name, city and state.

YOUNG, RAYMOND L
CUTLER/BLADESMITH, 2922 Hwy 188E, Mt. Ida, AR 71957, Phone: 870-867-3947
   Specialties: Cutler-Bladesmith, sharpening service. **Patterns:** Hunter, skinners, fighters, no guard, no ricasso, chef tools. **Technical:** Edge tempered 1095, 516C, mosaic handles, water buffalo and exotic woods. **Prices:** $100 and up. **Remarks:** Federal contractor since 1995. Surgical steel sharpening. **Mark:** R.

YURCO, MICKEY
PO Box 712, Canfield, OH 44406, Phone: 330-533-4928, shorinki@aol.com
   Specialties: Working straight knives. **Patterns:** Hunters, utility knives, Bowies and fighters, push knives, claws and other hideouts. **Technical:** Grinds 440C, ATS-34 and 154CM; likes mirror and satin finishes. **Prices:** $20 to $500. **Remarks:** Part-time maker; first knife sold in 1983. **Mark:** Name, steel, serial number.

Z

ZAFEIRIADIS, KONSTANTINOS
Dionyson Street, Marathon Attiki, GREECE 19005, Phone: 011-30697724-5771 or 011-30697400-6245
   Specialties: Fixed blades, one-of-a-kind swords with bronze fittings made using the lost wax method. **Patterns:** Ancient Greek, central Asian, Viking, bowies, hunting knives, fighters, daggers. **Technical:** Forges 5160, O1 and maker's own damascus. **Prices:** $1,100 and up. **Remarks:** Full-time maker; first knife sold in 2010. **Mark:** (backward K)ZK.

ZAHM, KURT
488 Rio Casa, Indialantic, FL 32903, Phone: 407-777-4860
   Specialties: Working straight knives of his design or to customer specs. **Patterns:** Daggers, fancy fighters, Bowies, hunters and utility knives. **Technical:** Grinds D2, 440C; likes filework. **Prices:** $75 to $1000. **Remarks:** Part-time maker; first knife sold in 1985. **Mark:** Last name.

ZAKABI, CARL S
PO Box 893161, Mililani Town, HI 96789-0161, Phone: 808-626-2181
   Specialties: User-grade straight knives of his design, cord wrapped and bare steel handles exclusively. **Patterns:** Fighters, hunters and utility/camp knives. **Technical:** Grinds 440C and ATS-34. **Prices:** $90 to $400. **Remarks:** Spare-time maker; first knife sold in 1988. Doing business as Zakabi's Knifeworks LLC. **Mark:** Last name and state inside a Hawaiian sharktooth dagger.

ZAKHAROV, GLADISTON
Rua Pernambuca, 175-Rio Comprido (Long River), Jacaret-SP, BRAZIL 12302-070, Phone: 55 12 3958 4021, Fax: 55 12 3958 4103, arkhip@terra.com.br; Web: www.arkhip.com.br
   Specialties: Using straight knives of his design. **Patterns:** Hunters, kitchen, utility/camp and barbecue knives. **Technical:** Grinds his own "secret steel." **Prices:** $30 to $200. **Remarks:** Full-time maker. **Mark:** Arkhip Special Knives.

ZBORIL, TERRY
5320 CR 130, Caldwell, TX 77836, Phone: 979-535-4157, tzboril@tconline.net
   Specialties: ABS Journeyman Smith.

ZEMBKO III, JOHN
140 Wilks Pond Rd, Berlin, CT 06037, Phone: 860-828-3503, johnzembko@hotmail.com
   Specialties: Working knives of his design or to customer specs. **Patterns:** Likes to use stabilized high-figured woods. **Technical:** Grinds ATS-34, A2, D2; forges O1, 1095; grinds Damasteel. **Prices:** $50 to $400; some higher. **Remarks:** First knife sold in 1987. **Mark:** Name.

ZEMITIS, JOE
14 Currawong Rd, Cardiff Heights, NSW, AUSTRALIA 2285, Phone: +610249549907 or +614034599396, jjvzem@bigpond.com
   Specialties: Traditional working straight knives. **Patterns:** Hunters, Bowies, tantos, fighters and camp knives. **Technical:** Grinds O1, D2, W2 and 440C. Embellishes; offers engraving. **Prices:** $150 to $3000. **Remarks:** Full-time maker; first knife sold in 1983. **Mark:** First initial, last name and country, or last name.

ZERMENO, WILLIAM D.
9131 Glenshadow Dr, Houston, TX 77088, Phone: 281-726-2459, will@wdzknives.com Web: www.wdzknives.com
   Specialties: Tactical/utility folders and fixed blades. **Patterns:** Frame lock and liner lock folders the majority of which incorporate flippers and utility fixed blades. **Technical:** Grinds CPM 154, S30V, 3V and stainless Damascus. **Prices:** $250 - $600. **Remarks:** Part-time maker, first knife sold in 2008. Doing business as www.wdzknives.com. **Mark:** WDZ over logo.

ZIEBA, MICHAEL
95 Commercial St., #4, Brooklyn, NY 11222, Phone: 347-335-9944, ziebametal@gmail.com; Web: www.ziebaknives.com or www.brooklynknives.com
   Specialties: High-end kitchen knives under maker's last name, ZIEBA, also tactical knives under HUSSAR name. **Technical:** Uses stainless steels: CPM S30V, CPM S35VN, CPM S60V, CPM D2 and AEB-L, and high-carbon steels: 52100 and Aogami #2. Forges carbon steel in his shop. **Remarks:** Full-time maker. **Marks:** Feather logo (kitchen knives only with 24k gold as a standard), ZIEBA (kitchen knives and folders) and "H" Hussar (tactical).

custom knifemakers

ZIMA, MICHAEL F

732 State St, Ft. Morgan, CO 80701, Phone: 970-867-6078, Web: http://www.zimaknives.com

Specialties: Working and collector quality straight knives and folders. **Patterns:** Hunters, lock backs, LinerLock®, slip joint and automatic folders. **Technical:** Grinds Damascus, 440C, ATS-34 and 154CM. **Prices:** $200 and up. **Remarks:** Full-time maker; first knife sold in 1982. **Mark:** Last name.

ZIMMERMAN, NATHAN

416 S. Comanche Ln., Waukesha, WI 53188, Phone: 262-510-3563, zimknives@gmail.com; Web: www.zimknives.com

Specialties: Custom high-end chef's knives. Large, elaborate fantasy weapons. **Patterns:** Unique matching sets of kitchen knives, as well as various hunters, fighters and utility knives. **Technical:** Thin-ground AEB-L chef's knives, forged 1084 knives with hamons (temper lines). Uses burls, Micartas, bone and horn. Favorite handle materials include ebony, African blackwood, bog oak and ironwood. **Prices:** Start at $200. **Remarks:** Full-time maker and knife sharpener; first knife sold in 2012. **Mark:** Hand-chiseled Z with dash. Signature on forged blades.

ZINKER, BRAD

BZ KNIVES, 1591 NW 17 St, Homestead, FL 33030, Phone: 305-216-0404, bzinker@gmail.com

Specialties: Fillets, folders and hunters. **Technical:** Uses ATS-34 and stainless Damascus. **Prices:** $200 to $600. **Remarks:** Voting member of Knifemakers Guild and Florida Knifemakers Association. **Mark:** Offset connected initials BZ.

ZIRBES, RICHARD

Neustrasse 15, Niederkail, GERMANY 54526, Phone: 0049 6575 1371, r.zirbes@freenet.de Web: www.zirbes-knives.com www.zirbes-messer.de

Specialties: Fancy embellished knives with engraving and self-made scrimshaw (scrimshaw made by maker). High-tech working knives and high-tech hunters, boots, fighters and folders. All knives made by hand. **Patterns:** Boots, fighters, folders, hunters. **Technical:** Uses only the best steels for blade material like CPM-T 440V, CPM-T 420V, ATS-34, D2, C440, stainless Damascus or steel according to customer's desire. **Prices:** Working knives and hunters: $200 to $600. Fancy embellished knives with engraving and/or scrimshaw: $800 to $3000. **Remarks:** Part-time maker; first knife sold in 1991. Member of the German Knifemaker Guild. **Mark:** Zirbes or R. Zirbes.

ZOWADA, TIM

4509 E Bear River Rd, Boyne Falls, MI 49713, Phone: 231-838-4120, timzowada@gmail.com; Web: www.tzknives.com

Specialties: Working knives and straight razors. **Technical:** Forges O1, L6, his own Damascus and smelted steel "Michi-Gane". **Prices:** $200 to $2500; some to $5000. **Remarks:** Full-time maker; first knife sold in 1980. **Mark:** Gothic, lower case "TZ"

ZSCHERNY, MICHAEL

1840 Rock Island Dr, Ely, IA 52227, Phone: 319-321-5833, zscherny knives@aol.com

Specialties: Quality folders--slip joints and flipper folders. **Patterns:** Liner-lock and lock-back folders in titanium, working straight knives. **Technical:** Grinds ATS-34 and commercial damascus, prefers natural materials such as pearls and ivory. Uses Timascus, mokume, san mai and carbon fibers. **Prices:** Start at $600. **Remarks:** Full-time maker, first knife sold in 1978. **Mark:** Last name with image of a scorpion.

AK

Barlow, Jana Poirier	Anchorage
Brennan, Judson	Delta Junction
Breuer, Lonnie	Wasilla
Broome, Thomas A	Kenai
Chamberlin, John A	Anchorage
Cornwell, Jeffrey	Anchorage
Desrosiers, Adam	Petersburg
Desrosiers, Haley	Petersburg
Dufour, Arthur J	Anchorage
England, Virgil	Anchorage
Flint, Robert	Anchorage
Gouker, Gary B	Sitka
Harding, Jacob	Fairbanks
Harvey, Mel	Nenana
Hibben, Westley G	Anchorage
Hook, Bob	North Pole
Kelsey, Nate	Palmer
Knapp, Mark	Fairbanks
Lance, Bill	Palmer
Lance, Lucas	Wasilla
Malaby, Raymond J	Juneau
Mcfarlin, Eric E	Kodiak
Miller, Nate	Fairbanks
Miller, Terry	Healy
Mirabile, David	Juneau
Moore, Marve	Willow
Parrish Iii, Gordon A	North Pole
Stegall, Keith	Wasilla
Van Cleve, Steve	Sutton

AL

Alverson, Tim (R.V.)	Arab
Batson, James	Huntsville
Baxter, Dale	Trinity
Bell, Tony	Woodland
Brothers, Dennis L.	Oneonta
Coffman, Danny	Jacksonville
Conn Jr., C T	Attalla
Daniels, Alex	Town Creek
Dark, Robert	Oxford
Deibert, Michael	Trussville
Durham, Kenneth	Cherokee
Elrod, Roger R	Enterprise
Gilbreath, Randall	Dora
Golden, Randy	Montgomery
Grizzard, Jim	Oxford
Hammond, Jim	Birmingham
Heeter, Todd S.	Mobile
Howard, Durvyn M.	Hokes Bluff
Howell, Keith A.	Oxford
Howell, Len	Opelika
Howell, Ted	Wetumpka
Huckabee, Dale	Maylene
Hulsey, Hoyt	Attalla
Mccullough, Jerry	Georgiana
Mcnees, Jonathan	Northport
Militano, Tom	Jacksonville
Morris, C H	Frisco City
Pardue, Melvin M	Repton
Ploppert, Tom	Cullman
Russell, Tom	Jacksonville
Sinyard, Cleston S	Elberta
Smith, Lacy	Jacksonville
Thomas, David E	Lillian
Washburn Jr., Robert Lee	Tuscaloosa
Watson, Billy	Deatsville

AR

Anders, David	Center Ridge
Ardwin, Corey	Bryant
Barker, Reggie	Taylor
Barnes Jr., Cecil C.	Center Ridge
Brown, Jim	Little Rock
Browning, Steven W	Benton
Bullard, Benoni	Bradford
Bullard, Tom	Flippin
Chambers, Ronny	Beebe
Cook, James R	Nashville
Copeland, Thom	Nashville
Cox, Larry	Murfreesboro
Crawford, Pat And Wes	West Memphis
Crotts, Dan	Elm Springs
Crowell, James L	Mtn. View
Dozier, Bob	Springdale
Duvall, Fred	Benton
Echols, Rodger	Nashville
Edge, Tommy	Cash
Ferguson, Lee	Hindsville
Fisk, Jerry	Nashville
Fitch, John S	Clinton
Flournoy, Joe	El Dorado
Foster, Ronnie E	Morrilton
Foster, Timothy L	El Dorado
Frizzell, Ted	West Fork
Gadberry, Emmet	Hattieville
Greenaway, Don	Fayetteville
Herring, Morris	Dyer
Hutchinson, Alan	Conway
Kirkes, Bill	Little Rock
Koster, Daniel	Bentonville
Krein, Tom	Gentry
Lawrence, Alton	De Queen
Lemoine, David C	Mountain Home
Livesay, Newt	Siloam Springs
Lunn, Gail	Mountain Home
Lunn, Larry A	Mountain Home
Lynch, Tad	Beebe
Maringer, Tom	Springdale
Martin, Hal W	Morrilton
Massey, Roger	Texarkana
Newberry, Allen	Lowell
Newton, Ron	London
Nolte, Barbie	Lowell
Nolte, Steve	Lowell
Olive, Michael E	Leslie
Passmore, Jimmy D	Hoxie
Pearce, Logan	De Queen
Perry, Jim	Hope
Perry, John	Mayflower
Peterson, Lloyd (Pete) C	Clinton
Polk, Clifton	Van Buren
Polk, Rusty	Van Buren
Randow, Ralph	Greenbrier
Red, Vernon	Conway
Reeves, J.R.	Texarkana
Rhea, Lin	Prattsville
Richards, Ralph (Bud)	Bauxite
Roberts, T. C. (Terry)	Siloam Springs
Seward, Ben	Austin
Stanley, John	Crossett
Stout, Charles	Gillham
Sweaza, Dennis	Austin
Townsend, Allen Mark	Texarkana
Townsley, Russell	Floral
Upton, Tom	Rogers
Walker, Jim	Morrilton
Ward, Chuck	Benton
White, Bryce	Little Rock
Young, Raymond L	Mt. Ida

AZ

Allan, Todd	Glendale
Ammons, David C	Tucson
Bennett, Glen C	Tucson
Birdwell, Ira Lee	Congress
Boye, David	Dolan Springs
Cheatham, Bill	Laveen
Dawson, Barry	Prescott Valley
Dawson, Lynn	Prescott Valley
Deubel, Chester J.	Tucson
Dodd, Robert F	Camp Verde
Fuegen, Larry	Prescott
Genovese, Rick	Tonto Basin
Goo, Tai	Tucson
Hancock, Tim	Scottsdale
Harris, John	Quartzsite
Hoel, Steve	Pine
Holder, D'Alton	Wickenburg
Jackson, Laramie	Claysprings
Jensen, Eli	Prescott
Karp, Bob	Phoenix
Kiley, Mike And Jandy	Chino Valley
Kopp, Todd M	Apache Jct.
Lee, Randy	St. Johns
Mcfall, Ken	Lakeside
Mcfarlin, J W	Lake Havasu City
Miller, Michael	Kingman
Montell, Ty	Thatcher
Mooney, Mike	Queen Creek
Newhall, Tom	Tucson
Purvis, Bob And Ellen	Tucson
Robbins, Bill	Sierra Vista
Rybar Jr., Raymond B	Camp Verde
States, Joshua C	New River
Tamboli, Michael	Glendale
Tyre, Michael A	Wickenburg
Weiss, Charles L	Waddell
Wick, Jonathan P.	Hereford
Wolf, Bill	Phoenix
Wright, Timothy	Sedona
Wuertz, Travis	Casa Grande
York, David C	Chino Valley

CA

Abegg, Arnie	Huntington Beach
Adkins, Richard L	Mission Viejo
Andrade, Don Carlos	Los Osos
Athey, Steve	Riverside
Barnes, Gregory	Altadena
Barnes, Roger	Bay Point
Barnes, Roger	Bay Point
Barron, Brian	San Mateo
Begg, Todd M.	Petaluma
Benson, Don	Escalon
Berger, Max A.	Carmichael
Bolduc, Gary	Corona
Bost, Roger E	Palos Verdes
Boyd, Francis	Berkeley
Breshears, Clint	Manhattan Beach
Brooks, Buzz	Los Angles
Brous, Jason	Buellton
Browne, Rick	Upland
Bruce, Richard L.	Yankee Hill
Butler, Bart	Ramona
Cabrera, Sergio B	Wilmington
Cantrell, Kitty D	Ramona
Caston, Darriel	Folsom
Caswell, Joe	Newbury
Clinco, Marcus	Venice
Coffey, Bill	Clovis
Coleman, John A	Citrus Heights
Colwell, Kevin	Cheshire
Connolly, James	Oroville
Cucchiara, Matt	Fresno
Davis, Charlie	Lakeside
De Maria Jr., Angelo	Carmel Valley
Dion, Greg	Oxnard
Dobratz, Eric	Laguna Hills
Doolittle, Mike	Novato
Driscoll, Mark	La Mesa
Dwyer, Duane	Escondido
Ellis, William Dean	Sanger
Emerson, Ernest R	Harbor City
English, Jim	Jamul
Ernest, Phil (Pj)	Whittier
Essegian, Richard	Fresno
Felix, Alexander	Torrance
Ferguson, Jim	Lakewood
Finney, Garett	Loomis
Forrest, Brian	Descanso
Fraley, D B	Dixon
Fred, Reed Wyle	Sacramento
Freeman, Matt	Fresno
Freer, Ralph	Seal Beach
Fulton, Mickey	Willows
Girtner, Joe	Brea
Grayman, Mike	Lake Arrowhead
Guarnera, Anthony R	Quartzhill
Hall, Jeff	Paso Robles
Hardy, Scott	Placerville
Harris, Jay	Redwood City
Helton, Roy	San Diego
Herndon, Wm R "Bill"	Acton
Hink Iii, Les	Stockton
Hoy, Ken	North Fork

Humenick, Roy	Rescue
Jacks, Jim	Covina
Jackson, David	Lemoore
Jensen, John Lewis	Pasadena
Johnson, Randy	Turlock
Kazsuk, David	Menifee
Kelly, Dave	Los Angeles
Keyes, Dan	Chino
Kilpatrick, Christian A	Citrus Hieghts
Koster, Steven C	Huntington Beach
Larson, Richard	Turlock
Leland, Steve	Fairfax
Lin, Marcus	Mission Viejo
Lockett, Sterling	Burbank
Luchini, Bob	Palo Alto
Maccaughtry, Scott F.	Camarillo
Mackie, John	Whittier
Massey, Ron	Joshua Tree
Mata, Leonard	San Diego
Maxwell, Don	Clovis
Mcabee, William	Colfax
Mcclure, Michael	Menlo Park
Mcgrath, Patrick T	Westchester
Melin, Gordon C	La Mirada
Meloy, Sean	Lemon Grove
Montano, Gus A	San Diego
Morgan, Jeff	Santee
Moses, Steven	Santa Ana
Mutz, Jeff	Rancho Cucamonga
Naten, Greg	Bakersfield
Orton, Rich	Wilmington
Osborne, Donald H	Clovis
Palm, Rik	San Diego
Panchenko, Serge	Citrus Heights
Perry, Chris	Fresno
Pfanenstiel, Dan	Modesto
Pitt, David F	Anderson
Quesenberry, Mike	Blairsden
Randall, Patrick	Newbury Park
Rozas, Clark D	Wilmington
Schmitz, Raymond E	Valley Center
Schneider, Herman J.	Apple Valley
Schroen, Karl	Sebastopol
Sharp, David	Hesperia
Sibrian, Aaron	Ventura
Sjostrand, Kevin	Visalia
Slobodian, Scott	San Andreas
Smith, Shawn	Clouis
Sornberger, Jim	Volcano
Steinberg, Al	Laguna Woods
Stimps, Jason M	Orange
Strider, Mick	Escondido
Terrill, Stephen	Springville
Tingle, Dennis P	Jackson
Tobolak, Libor	San Marcos
Torres, Henry	Clovis
Vagnino, Michael	Visalia
Velick, Sammy	Los Angeles
Warren, Al	Roseville
Watanabe, Wayne	Montebello
Weinstock, Robert	San Francisco
Wilburn, Aaron	Redding
Wilson, Ron	Morro Bay
Withers, Tim	Linden

CO

Anderson, Mel	Hotchkiss
Booco, Gordon	Hayden
Brock, Kenneth L	Allenspark
Burrows, Chuck	Durango
Corich, Vance	Morrison
Davis, Don	Loveland
Dennehy, John D	Greeley
Dill, Robert	Loveland
Fairly, Daniel	Bayfield
Fredeen, Graham	Colorado Springs
Fronefield, Daniel	Peyton
Graham, Levi	Greeley
High, Tom	Alamosa
Hockensmith, Dan	Berthoud
Hughes, Ed	Grand Junction
Hughes, Tony	Littleton

Irie, Michael L	Colorado Springs
Kitsmiller, Jerry	Montrose
Leck, Dal	Hayden
Mcwilliams, Sean	Carbondale
Miller, Hanford J	Lakespur
Miller, M A	Northglenn
Nolen, Steve	Longmont
Ott, Fred	Durango
Owens, John	Buena Vista
Rexford, Todd	Florissant
Roberts, Chuck	Golden
Rollert, Steve	Keenesburg
Ronzio, N. Jack	Fruita
Sanders, Bill	Mancos
Thompson, Lloyd	Pagosa Springs
Urbach, Scott	Aurora
Waites, Richard L	Broomfield
Watson, Bert	Westminster
Wilson, James G	Estes Park
Wood, Owen Dale	Arvada
Zima, Michael F	Ft. Morgan
Redd, Bill	Broomfield

CT

Buebendorf, Robert E	Monroe
Chapo, William G	Wilton
Cross, Kevin	Portland
Framski, Walter P	Prospect
Jean, Gerry	Manchester
Loukides, David E	Cheshire
Meyer, Christopher J	Tolland
Parkinson, Matthew	Wolcott
Plunkett, Richard	West Cornwall
Rainville, Richard	Salem
Swarz-Burt, Peter T.	Wolcott
Turecek, Jim	Ansonia
Vitale, Mace	Guilford
Zembko Iii, John	Berlin

DE

Willey, Wg	Greenwood

FL

Adams, Les	Cape Coral
Alexander,, Oleg, And Cossack Blades	Wellington
Anders, Jerome	Miramar
Angell, Jon	Hawthorne
Atkinson, Dick	Wausau
Barnes, Gary L.	Defuniak Springs
Barry Iii, James J.	West Palm Beach
Beers, Ray	Lake Wales
Benjamin Jr., George	Kissimmee
Bosworth, Dean	Key Largo
Bradley, John	Pomona Park
Bray Jr., W Lowell	New Port Richey
Brown, Harold E	Arcadia
Butler, John	Havana
Clark, Jason	O'Brien
D'Andrea, John	Citrus Springs
Davis, John H.	Fruitland Park
Davis Jr., Jim	Zephyrhills
Dietzel, Bill	Middleburg
Dintruff, Chuck	Plant City
Dotson, Tracy	Baker
Ellerbe, W B	Geneva
Ellis, Willy B	Tarpon Springs
Enos Iii, Thomas M	Orlando
Fowler, Charles R	Ft McCoy
Franklin, Mike	Clermont
Gallagher, Scott	Santa Rosa Beach
Gamble, Roger	Newberry
Gardner, Robert	West Palm Beach
Ghio, Paolo	Pensacola
Goers, Bruce	Lakeland
Granger, Paul J	Largo
Greene, Steve	Intercession City
Griffin Jr., Howard A	Davie
Grospitch, Ernie	Orlando
Heaney, John D	Haines City
Heitler, Henry	Tampa
Hodge Iii, John	Palatka
Hostetler, Larry	Fort Pierce

Hostetter, Wally	San Mateo
Humphreys, Joel	Lake Placid
Hunter, Richard D	Alachua
Hytovick, Joe "Hy"	Dunnellon
Jernigan, Steve	Milton
Johanning Custom Knives, Tom	Sarasota
Johnson, John R	Plant City
King, Bill	Tampa
Krapp, Denny	Apopka
Levengood, Bill	Tampa
Long, Glenn A	Dunnellon
Lovestrand, Schuyler	Vero Beach
Lozier, Don	Ocklawaha
Lyle Iii, Ernest L	Chiefland
Mandt, Joe	St. Petersburg
Mason, Bill	Hobe Sound
Mcdonald, Robert J	Loxahatchee
Miller, Ronald T	Largo
Miller, Steve	Clearwater
Newton, Larry	Jacksonville
Ochs, Charles F	Largo
Overall, Jason	Sanford
Owens, Donald	Melbourne
Parker, Cliff	Zephyrhills
Partridge, Jerry D.	DeFuniak Springs
Pattay, Rudy	Citrus Springs
Pendray, Alfred H	Williston
Philippe, D A	The Villages
Piergallini, Daniel E	Plant City
Randall Made Knives,	Orlando
Raymond, Michael	Malabar
Renner, Terry	Palmetto
Robinson, Calvin	Pace
Robinson Iii, Rex R	Leesburg
Roddenberry, Charles	Live Oak
Rodkey, Dan	Hudson
Romeis, Gordon	Fort Myers
Russ, Ron	Williston
Schwarzer, Lora Sue	Crescent City
Schwarzer, Stephen	Crescent City
Smith, Michael J	Brandon
Stapleton, William E	Merritt Island
Steck, Van R	Orange City
Stephan, Daniel	Valrico
Stipes, Dwight	Palm City
Straight, Kenneth J	Largo
Tabor, Tim	Lutz
Turnbull, Ralph A	Spring Hill
Vogt, Donald J	Tampa
Watson, Tom	Panama City
Weiland Jr., J Reese	Riverview
Wicker, Donnie R	Panama City
Wilson, Stan	Lithia
Zahm, Kurt	Indialantic
Zinker, Brad	Homestead

GA

Arrowood, Dale	Sharpsburg
Ashworth, Boyd	Powder Springs
Barker, John	Cumming
Barker, Robert G.	Bishop
Beaver, Dirk	Ellijay
Bentley, C L	Albany
Bish, Hal	Jonesboro
Brach, Paul	Cumming
Bradley, Dennis	Blairsville
Buckner, Jimmie H	Putney
Busbie, Jeff	Bloomingdale
Cambron, Henry	Dallas
Chamblin, Joel	Concord
Crockford, Jack	Chamblee
Daniel, Travis E	Thomaston
Davidson, Scott	Alto
Davis, Steve	Powder Springs
Fowler, Stephan	Acworth
Frost, Dewayne	Barnesville
Gaines, Buddy	Commerce
Glover, Warren D	Cleveland
Greene, David	Covington
Hammond, Hank	Leesburg
Hammond, Ray	Buford
Hardy, Douglas E	Franklin

Hensley, Wayne	Conyers
Hewitt, Ronald "Cotton"	Adel
Hinson And Son, R	Columbus
Hoffman, Kevin L	Savannah
Hossom, Jerry	Duluth
Kimsey, Kevin	Cartersville
King, Fred	Cartersville
Knott, Steve	Guyton
Landers, John	Newnan
Lockett, Lowell C.	Canton
Lonewolf, J Aguirre	Demorest
Mathews, Charlie And Harry	Statesboro
Mcgill, John	Blairsville
Mitchell, James A	Columbus
Moncus, Michael Steven	Smithville
Parks, John	Jefferson
Poole, Marvin O	Commerce
Powell, Robert Clark	Smarr
Prater, Mike	Flintstone
Price, Timmy	Blairsville
Ragsdale, James D	Ellijay
Roghmans, Mark	LaGrange
Sangster, Joe	Vienna
Sculley, Peter E	Rising Fawn
Snow, Bill	Columbus
Sowell, Bill	Macon
Stafford, Richard	Warner Robins
Surls, W. Allen	Buford
Thompson, Kenneth	Duluth
Tomey, Kathleen	Macon
White, Lou	Ranger
Wright, Robert A	Savannah

HI

Evans, Vincent K And Grace	Keaau
Gibo, George	Hilo
Lui, Ronald M	Honolulu
Mann, Tim	Honokaa
Matsuoka, Scot	Mililani
Mayo Jr., Tom	Waialua
Mitsuyuki, Ross	Honolulu
Onion, Kenneth J	Kaneohe
Ouye, Keith	Honolulu
Salter, Gregg	Waikoloa
Watanabe, Melvin	Kailua
Zakabi, Carl S	Mililani Town

IA

Brooker, Dennis	Chariton
Brower, Max	Boone
Clark, Howard F	Runnells
Cockerham, Lloyd	Denham Springs
Helscher, John W	Washington
Lainson, Tony	Council Bluffs
Lewis, Bill	Riverside
Mckiernan, Stan	Lamoni
Miller, James P	Fairbank
Thie, Brian	Burlington
Trindle, Barry	Earlham
Westberg, Larry	Algona
Zscherny, Michael	Ely

ID

Alderman, Robert	Sagle
Bair, Mark	Firth
Bloodworth Custom Knives,	Meridian
Burke, Bill	Boise
Eddy, Hugh E	Caldwell
Farr, Dan	Post Falls
Hackney, Dana A.	Naples
Hawk, Grant And Gavin	Idaho City
Hogan, Thomas R	Boise
Horton, Scot	Buhl
Howe, Tori	Athol
Mann, Michael L	Spirit Lake
Metz, Greg T	Cascade
Patton, Dick And Rob	Nampa
Quarton, Barr	McCall
Rohn, Fred	Coeur d'Alene
Sawby, Scott	Sandpoint
Sparks, Bernard	Dingle
Steiger, Monte L	Genesee

Tippetts, Colten	Hidden Springs
Towell, Dwight L	Midvale
Trace Rinaldi Custom Blades,	Plummer

IL

Armour, Dave	Auburn
Bloomer, Alan T	Maquon
Camerer, Craig	Chesterfield
Cook, Louise	Ozark
Cook, Mike	Ozark
Detmer, Phillip	Breese
Dicristofano, Anthony P	Melrose Park
Eaker, Allen L	Paris
Hall, Scott M.	Geneseo
Hawes, Chuck	Weldon
Heath, William	Bondville
Hill, Rick	Maryville
Kovar, Eugene	Evergreen Park
Kulis, David S.	Chicago
Leone, Nick	Pontoon Beach
Markley, Ken	Sparta
Meers, Andrew	Carbondale
Meier, Daryl	Carbondale
Myers, Paul	Wood River
Myers, Steve	Carlinville
Nowland, Rick	Waltonville
Pellegrin, Mike	Troy
Pritchard, Ron	Dixon
Roosevelt, Russell	Albion
Rosenbaugh, Ron	Crystal Lake
Rossdeutscher, Robert N	Arlington Heights
Rzewnicki, Gerald	Elizabeth
Schneider, Craig M	Claremont
Smale, Charles J	Waukegan
Smith, John M	Centralia
Todd, Richard C	Chambersburg
Veit, Michael	LaSalle
Voss, Ben	Victoria
Werth, George W	Poplar Grove
West, Charles A	Centralia
Wheeler, Robert	Bradley

IN

Ball, Ken	Mooresville
Barkes, Terry	Edinburgh
Barrett, Rick L. (Toshi Hisa)	Goshen
Bose, Reese	Shelburn
Bose, Tony	Shelburn
Chaffee, Jeff L	Morris
Claiborne, Jeff	Franklin
Cramer, Brent	Wheatland
Crowl, Peter	Waterloo
Curtiss, David	Granger
Damlovac, Sava	Indianapolis
Darby, Jed	Greensburg
Fitzgerald, Dennis M	Fort Wayne
Fraps, John R	Indianapolis
Good, D.R.	Tipton
Harding, Chad	Solsberry
Imel, Billy Mace	New Castle
Johnson, C E Gene	Chesterton
Kain, Charles	Indianapolis
Keeslar, Steven C	Hamilton
Keeton, William L	Laconia
Kinker, Mike	Greensburg
Largin, Ken	Connersville
Mayville, Oscar L	Marengo
Miller, Levi	Howe
Minnick, Jim & Joyce	Middletown
Patton, Phillip	Yoder
Quakenbush, Thomas C	Ft Wayne
Robertson, Leo D	Indianapolis
Seib, Steve	Evansville
Shull, James	Rensselaer
Smock, Timothy E	Marion
Thayer, Danny O	Romney
Young, George	Kokomo

KS

Bradburn, Gary	Wichita
Burrows, Stephen R	Humboldt
Chard, Gordon R	Iola

Craig, Roger L	Topeka
Culver, Steve	Meriden
Darpinian, Dave	Olathe
Dawkins, Dudley L	Topeka
Dick, Dan	Hutchinson
Evans, Phil	Columbus
Finley, Jon M.	Leawood
Hegwald, J L	Humboldt
Herman, Tim	Olathe
Keranen, Paul	Tacumseh
King Jr., Harvey G	Alta Vista
Kraft, Steve	Abilene
Lamb, Curtis J	Ottawa
Magee, Jim	Salina
Petersen, Dan L	Auburn
Stice, Douglas W	Wichita

KY

Addison, Kyle A	Hazel
Baskett, Barbara	Eastview
Baskett, Lee Gene	Eastview
Bybee, Barry J	Cadiz
Carter, Mike	Louisville
Downing, Larry	Bremen
Dunn, Steve	Smiths Grove
Edwards, Mitch	Glasgow
Finch, Ricky D	West Liberty
Fister, Jim	Simpsonville
France, Dan	Cawood
Frederick, Aaron	West Liberty
Greco, John	Greensburg
Hibben, Daryl	LaGrange
Hibben, Gil	LaGrange
Hoke, Thomas M	LaGrange
Holbrook, H L	Sandy Hook
Jeffries, Mike	Louisville
Keeslar, Joseph F	Almo
Pease, W D	Ewing
Pierce, Harold L	Louisville
Rados, Jerry F	Columbia
Richerson, Ron	Greenburg
Rigney Jr., Willie	Bronston
Smith, Chris	Burgin
Smith, John W	West Liberty
Soaper, Max H.	Henderson
Steier, David	Louisville
Vance, David	West Liberty
Wallingford Jr., Charles W	Union

LA

Blaum, Roy	Covington
Caldwell, Bill	West Monroe
Calvert Jr., Robert W (Bob)	Rayville
Capdepon, Randy	Carencro
Capdepon, Robert	Carencro
Chauvin, John	Scott
Dake, C M	New Orleans
Dake, Mary H	New Orleans
Durio, Fred	Opelousas
Faucheaux, Howard J	Loreauville
Fontenot, Gerald J	Mamou
Gorenflo, James T (Jt)	Baton Rouge
Graves, Dan	Shreveport
Johnson, Gordon A.	Choudrant
Ki, Shiva	Baton Rouge
Laurent, Kermit	LaPlace
Lemaire, Ryan M.	Abbeville
Leonard, Randy Joe	Sarepta
Mitchell, Max Dean And Ben	Leesville
Phillips, Dennis	Independence
Potier, Timothy F	Oberlin
Primos, Terry	Shreveport
Provenzano, Joseph D	Ponchatoula
Randall Jr., James W	Keithville
Reggio Jr., Sidney J	Sun
Tilton, John	Iowa
Trisler, Kenneth W	Rayville
Wilson, P.R. "Regan"	Scott
Winn, Marvin	Sunset

MA

Banaitis, Romas	Medway

Cooper, Paul	Woburn
Dailey, G E	Seekonk
Dugdale, Daniel J.	Walpole
Gedraitis, Charles J	Holden
Grossman, Stewart	Clinton
Hinman, Theodore	Greenfield
Jarvis, Paul M	Cambridge
Johnson, Timothy A.	Worcester
Khalsa, Jot Singh	Millis
Klein, Kevin	Boston
Kubasek, John A	Easthampton
Lapen, Charles	W. Brookfield
Little, Larry	Spencer
Martin, Randall J	Bridgewater
Mcluin, Tom	Dracut
Moore, Michael Robert	Lowell
Rebello, Indian George	New Bedford
Rizzi, Russell J	Ashfield
Rua, Gary	Fall River
Saviano, James	Douglas
Siska, Jim	Westfield
Smith, J D	Melrose
Stuart, Mason	Mansfield
Vining, Bill	Methuen

MD

Aylor, Erin Lutzer	Myersville
Bagley, R. Keith	White Plains
Barnes, Aubrey G.	Hagerstown
Cohen, N J (Norm)	Baltimore
Dement, Larry	Prince Fredrick
Fuller, Jack A	New Market
Gossman, Scott	Whiteford
Hart, Bill	Pasadena
Heard, Tom	Waldorf
Hendrickson, E Jay	Frederick
Hendrickson, Shawn	Knoxville
Kreh, Lefty	"Cockeysville"
Mccarley, John	Taneytown
Mcgowan, Frank E	Sykesville
Merchant, Ted	White Hall
Nicholson, R. Kent	Monkton
Nuckels, Stephen J	Hagerstown
Presti, Matt	Union Bridge
Sentz, Mark C	Taneytown
Smit, Glenn	Aberdeen
Sontheimer, G Douglas	Gaithersburg
Spickler, Gregory Noble	Sharpsburg
St. Clair, Thomas K	Monrovia
Walker, Bill	Stevensville

ME

Bohrmann, Bruce	Yarmouth
Breda, Ben	Hope
Ceprano, Peter J.	Auburn
Coombs Jr., Lamont	Bucksport
Gray, Daniel	Brownville
Hillman, Charles	Friendship
Leavitt Jr., Earl F	E. Boothbay
Oyster, Lowell R	Corinth
Sharrigan, Mudd	Wiscasset
Steingass, T.K.	Bucksport

MI

Ackerson, Robin E	Buchanan
Alcorn, Douglas A.	Chesaning
Andrews, Eric	Grand Ledge
Arms, Eric	Tustin
Behnke, William	Kingsley
Booth, Philip W	Ithaca
Carr, Tim	Muskegon
Carroll, Chad	Grant
Cashen, Kevin R	Hubbardston
Cook, Mike A	Portland
Cousino, George	Onsted
Cowles, Don	Royal Oak
Doyle, John	Gladwin
Ealy, Delbert	Indian River
Erickson, Walter E.	Atlanta
Gordon, Larry B	Farmington Hills
Gottage, Dante	Clinton Twp.
Gottage, Judy	Clinton Twp.

Haas, Randy	Marlette
Harm, Paul W	Attica
Harrison, Brian	Cedarville
Hartman, Arlan (Lanny)	Baldwin
Hoffman, Jay	Munising
Hughes, Daryle	Nunica
Lankton, Scott	Ann Arbor
Lark, David	Kingsley
Logan, Iron John	Leslie
Marsh, Jeremy	Ada
Mills, Louis G	Ann Arbor
Morris, Michael S.	Yale
Nevling, Mark	Owosso
Noren, Douglas E	Springlake
Parker, Robert Nelson	Royal Oak
Repke, Mike	Bay City
Rose Ii, Doun T.	Fife Lake
Sakmar, Mike	Howell
Sandberg, Ronald B	Brownstown
Tally, Grant	Flat Rock
Van Eizenga, Jerry W	Nunica
Vasquez, Johnny David	Wyandotte
Viste, James	Hamtramck
Webster, Bill	Three Rivers
Welling, Ronald L	Grand Haven
White, Richard T	Grosse Pointe Farms
Whittaker, Wayne	Metamore
Wood, Webster	Atlanta
Zowada, Tim	Boyne Falls

MN

Andersen, Karl B.	Warba
Burns, Robert	Carver
Davis, Joel	Albert Lea
Hagen, Doc	Pelican Rapids
Hansen, Robert W	Cambridge
Hebeisen, Jeff	Hopkins
Johnson, Jerry L	Worthington
Johnson, Keith R.	Bemidji
Johnson, R B	Clearwater
Knipschield, Terry	Rochester
Leblanc, Gary E	Little Falls
Maines, Jay	Wyoming
Mesenbourg, Nick	Inver Grove Heights
Metsala, Anthony	Princeton
Mickley, Tracy	North Mankato
Ritchie, Adam	Bloomington
Rohde, Daniel S.	Winona
Rydbom, Jeff	Annandale
Shadley, Eugene W	Grand Rapids
Taber, David E.	Winona
Voorhies, Les	Faribault

MO

Abernathy, Lance	North Kansas City
Allred, Elvan	St. Charles
Andrews, Russ	Sugar Creek
Betancourt, Antonio L.	St. Louis
Braschler, Craig W.	Zalma
Buxton, Bill	Kaiser
Chinnock, Daniel T.	Union
Cover, Jeff	Potosi
Cover, Raymond A	Mineral Point
Dippold, Al	Perryville
Duncan, Ron	Cairo
Eaton, Frank L Jr	Farmington
Ehrenberger, Daniel Robert	Mexico
Engle, William	Boonville
Hanson, Kyle S.	Success
Hanson Iii, Don L.	Success
Harrison, Jim (Seamus)	St. Louis
Kinnikin, Todd	Pacific
Knickmeyer, Hank	Cedar Hill
Knickmeyer, Kurt	Cedar Hill
Krause, Jim	Farmington
Lee, Ethan	Sturgeon
Martin, Tony	Arcadia
Mccrackin, Kevin	House Spings
Mccrackin And Son, V J	House Spings
Miller, William (Bill)	Warsaw
Mosier, David	Independence
Mulkey, Gary	Branson

Muller, Jody	Goodson
Newcomb, Corbin	Moberly
Ramsey, Richard A	Neosho
Rardon, A D	Polo
Rardon, Archie F	Polo
Riepe, Richard A	Harrisonville
Robbins, Howard P	Flemington
Robbins, Landon	Crane
Royer, Kyle	Clever
Schow, Lyle	Harrisonville
Scroggs, James A	Warrensburg
Seaton, David D	Rolla
Smith, Jerry W.	Willow Springs
Sonntag, Douglas W	Nixa
Sonntag, Jacob D	St. Robert
Sonntag, Kristopher D	Nixa
Steketee, Craig A	Billings
Stormer, Bob	Dixon
Waide, Rusty	Buffalo
Warden, Roy A	Union
Whitesell, J. Dale	Stover
Willis, Bill	Ava

MS

Black, Scott	Picayune
Boleware, David	Carson
Cohea, John M	Nettleton
Davis, Jesse W	Coldwater
Davison, Todd A.	Kosciusko
Evans, Bruce A	Booneville
Flynt, Robert G	Gulfport
Jones, Jack P.	Ripley
Lamey, Robert M	Biloxi
Lebatard, Paul M	Vancleave
May, Charles	Aberdeen
Mayo Jr., Homer	Biloxi
Nichols, Chad	Blue Springs
Phillips, Donavon	Morton
Pickett, Terrell	Lumberton
Provost, J.C.	Laurel
Robinson, Chuck	Picayune
Shiffer, Steve	Leakesville
Smith, J.B.	Perkinston
Taylor, Billy	Petal
Tribble, Skylar	Leakesville
Vandeventer, Terry L	Byram
Vardaman, Robert	Hattiesburg
Wehner, Rudy	Collins
White, Russell D.	Rienzi
Wilson, Vic	Olive Branch
Wingo, Perry	Gulfport
Winston, David	Starkville

MT

Barnes, Jack	Whitefish
Barnes, Wendell	Clinton
Barth, J.D.	Alberton
Beam, John R.	Kalispell
Beaty, Robert B.	Missoula
Behring, James	Missoula
Bell, Don	Lincoln
Bizzell, Robert	Butte
Brooks, Steve R	Walkerville
Caffrey, Edward J	Great Falls
Campbell, Doug	McLeod
Carlisle, Jeff	Simms
Christensen, Jon P	Stevensville
Colter, Wade	Colstrip
Conklin, George L	Ft. Benton
Conti, Jeffrey D	Judith Gap
Crowder, Robert	Thompson Falls
Curtiss, Steve L	Eureka
Dunkerley, Rick	Lincoln
Eaton, Rick	Broadview
Ellefson, Joel	Manhattan
Fassio, Melvin G	Lolo
Forthofer, Pete	Whitefish
Fritz, Erik L	Forsyth
Gallagher, Barry	Lincoln
Harkins, J A	Conner
Hintz, Gerald M	Helena
Hulett, Steve	West Yellowstone

Kauffman, Dave	Clancy
Kelly, Steven	Bigfork
Mcguane Iv, Thomas F	Bozeman
Mckee, Neil	Stevensville
Moyer, Russ	Havre
Nedved, Dan	Kalispell
Olson, Joe	Great Falls
Parsons, Pete	Helena
Patrick, Willard C	Helena
Peele, Bryan	Thompson Falls
Pursley, Aaron	Big Sandy
Rodewald, Gary	Hamilton
Ruana Knife Works,	Bonner
Smith, Josh	Frenchtown
Taylor, Shane	Miles City
Thill, Jim	Missoula
Weinand, Gerome M	Missoula
Yashinski, John L	Red Lodge

NC

Baker, Herb	Eden
Barefoot, Joe W.	Wilmington
Best, Ron	Stokes
Bisher, William (Bill)	Denton
Brackett, Jamin	Fallston
Britton, Tim	Winston-Salem
Busfield, John	Roanoke Rapids
Craddock, Mike	Thomasville
Crist, Zoe	Flat Rock
Drew, Gerald	Mill Spring
Gaddy, Gary Lee	Washington
Gahagan, Kyle	Moravian Falls
Gingrich, Justin	Wade
Goode, Brian	Shelby
Greene, Chris	Shelby
Gross, W W	Archdale
Hall, Ken	Waynesville
Hege, John B.	Danbury
Hoffman, Liam	Newland
Johnson, Tommy	Troy
Livingston, Robert C	Murphy
Maynard, William N.	Fayetteville
Mcghee, E. Scott	Clarkton
Mclurkin, Andrew	Raleigh
Mcnabb, Tommy	Bethania
Mcrae, J Michael	Mint Hill
Neely, Jonathan	Greensboro
Nichols, Calvin	Raleigh
Parrish, Robert	Weaverville
Patrick, Chuck	Brasstown
Patrick, Peggy	Brasstown
Pica, Daniel	Pittsboro
Randall, Steve	Lincolnton
Rapp, Steven J	Marshall
Santini, Tom	Pikeville
Scholl, Tim	Angier
Simmons, H R	Aurora
Sirois, Darrin	Fayetteville
Sterling, Murray	Mount Airy
Summers, Arthur L	Concord
Sutton, S Russell	New Bern
Vail, Dave	Hampstead
Wacholz, Doc	Marble
Wagaman, John K	Selma
Walker, Don	Burnsville
Warren, Daniel	Canton
Whitley, L Wayne	Chocowinity
Wiggins, Bill	Canton
Williamson, Tony	Siler City
Wilson, Mike	Hayesville
Winkler, Daniel	Blowing Rock

ND

Kommer, Russ	Fargo
Pitman, David	Williston

NE

Archer, Ray And Terri	Omaha
Hielscher, Guy	Alliance
Jokerst, Charles	Omaha
Lyons, William R. (Bill)	Palisade
Marlowe, Charles	Omaha

Moore, Jon P	Aurora
Sloan, David	Diller
Suedmeier, Harlan	Nebraska City
Syslo, Chuck	Omaha
Tiensvold, Alan L	Rushville
Tiensvold, Jason	Rushville
Till, Calvin E And Ruth	Chadron

NH

Hudson, C Robbin	Rochester
Jonas, Zachary	Wilmot
Saindon, R Bill	Goshen
Ward, Tom	Wilmot
White, Caleb A.	Hooksett

NJ

Fisher, Lance	Pompton Lakes
Grussenmeyer, Paul G	Cherry Hill
Knowles, Shawn	Great Meadows
Lesswing, Kevin	Bayonne
Licata, Steven	Boonton
Mccallen Jr., Howard H	So Seaside Park
Nadeau, Brian	Stanhope
Pressburger, Ramon	Howell
Sheets, Steven William	Mendham
Slee, Fred	Morganville
Viele, H J	Westwood
Yeskoo, Richard C	Summit

NM

Black, Tom	Albuquerque
Burnley, Lucas	Albuquerque
Chavez, Ramon	Belen
Cherry, Frank J	Albuquerque
Cordova, Joey	Bernalillo
Cordova, Joseph G	Bosque Farms
Cumming, Bob	Cedar Crest
Digangi, Joseph M	Los Ojos
Duran, Jerry T	Albuquerque
Dyess, Eddie	Roswell
Fisher, Jay	Clovis
Garner, George	Albuquerque
Goode, Bear	Navajo Dam
Gunter, Brad	Tijeras
Hartman, Tim	Albuquerque
Hethcoat, Don	Clovis
Kimberley, Richard L.	Santa Fe
Leu, Pohan	Rio Rancho
Lewis, Tom R	Carlsbad
Lynn, Arthur	Galisteo
Macdonald, David	Los Lunas
Meshejian, Mardi	Santa Fe
Reid, Jim	Albuquerque
Rogers, Richard	Magdalena
Schaller, Anthony Brett	Albuquerque
Stalcup, Eddie	Gallup
Swearingen, Kurt	Cedar Crest
Terzuola, Robert	Albuquerque
Trujillo, Albert M B	Bosque Farms
Walker, Michael L	Pueblo Sur Taos
Wescott, Cody	Las Cruces

NV

Barnett, Van	Reno
Bingenheimer, Bruce	Spring Creek
Cameron, Ron G	Logandale
Dellana,	Reno
George, Tom	Henderson
Hrisoulas, Jim	Henderson
Kreibich, Donald L.	Reno
Nishiuchi, Melvin S	Las Vegas
Rougeau, Derick	Sparks
Thomas, Devin	Panaca
Washburn, Arthur D	Pioche

NY

Baker, Wild Bill	Boiceville
Castellucio, Rich	Amsterdam
Cimms, Greg	Pleasant Valley
Daly, Michael	Brooklyn
Davis, Barry L	Castleton
Gregory, Matthew M.	Glenwood
Hobart, Gene	Windsor

Johnson, Mike	Orient
Johnston, Dr. Robt	Rochester
Lamothe, Jordan	Granville
Lamothe, Jordan	Granville
Levin, Jack	Brooklyn
Loos, Henry C	New Hyde Park
Ludwig, Richard O	Maspeth
Lupole, Jamie G	Kirkwood
Manaro, Sal	Holbrook
Maragni, Dan	Georgetown
Mccornock, Craig	Willow
Meerdink, Kurt	Barryville
Merola, Jim	Brooklyn
Miller, Chelsea Grace	Brooklyn
Nazz, Theo "Rock"	New York
Page, Reginald	Groveland
Rachlin, Leslie S	Elmira
Rappazzo, Richard	Cohoes
Rotella, Richard A	Niagara Falls
Scheid, Maggie	Rochester
Schippnick, Jim	Sanborn
Serafen, Steven E	New Berlin
Skiff, Steven	Broadalbin
Smith, Lenard C	Valley Cottage
Smith, Raymond L	Erin
Summers, Dan	Whitney Pt.
Szilaski, Joseph	Pine Plains
Turner, Kevin	Montrose
Welling, William	West Valley
Zieba, Michael	Brooklyn

OH

Busse, Jerry	Wauseon
Coffee, Jim	Norton
Collins, Lynn M	Elyria
Coppins, Daniel	Cambridge
Cottrill, James I	Columbus
Crews, Randy	Patriot
Downing, Tom	Cuyahoga Falls
Downs, James F	Powell
Etzler, John	Grafton
Francis, John D	Ft. Loramie
Gittinger, Raymond	Tiffin
Glover, Ron	Cincinnati
Greiner, Richard	Green Springs
Hinderer, Rick	Shreve
Humphrey, Lon	Newark
Imboden Ii, Howard L.	Dayton
Johnson, Wm. C. "Bill"	Enon
Jones, Roger Mudbone	Waverly
Kiefer, Tony	Pataskala
Landis, David E. Sr.	Galion
Longworth, Dave	Felicity
Maienknecht, Stanley	Sardis
Marshall, Rex	Wilmington
Mcdonald, Rich	Hillboro
Mcgroder, Patrick J	Madison
Mercer, Mike	Lebanon
Morgan, Tom	Beloit
Munjas, Bob	Waterford
O'Machearley, Michael	Wilmington
Panak, Paul S	Andover
Potter, Billy	Dublin
Roddy, Roy "Tim"	Hubbard
Rose, Derek W	Gallipolis
Rowe, Fred	Amesville
Salley, John D	Tipp City
Schuchmann, Rick	New Richmond
Sheely, "Butch" Forest	Grand Rapids
Shinosky, Andy	Canfield
Shoemaker, Carroll	Northup
Shoemaker, Scott	Miamisburg
Spinale, Richard	Lorain
Strong, Scott	Beavercreek
Summers, Dennis K	Springfield
Thomas, Kim	Seville
Thourot, Michael W	Napoleon
Tindera, George	Brunswick
Trout, George H.	Wilmington
Votaw, David P	Pioneer
Williams, Robert	East Liverpool
Worley, Joel A., J.S.	Maplewood

Wright, L.T.	Wintersville
Yurco, Mickey	Canfield
Stidham, Daniel	Gallipolis

OK

Baker, Ray	Sapulpa
Cleveland, Mike	Mustang
Coye, Bill	Tulsa
Crenshaw, Al	Eufaula
Crowder, Gary L	Sallisaw
Damasteel Stainless Damascus,	Norman
Darby, David T	Cookson
Dill, Dave	Bethany
Duff, Bill	Poteau
Dunlap, Jim	Sallisaw
Gepner, Don	Norman
Haze, Jeff	Skiatook
Heimdale, J E	Tulsa
Kennedy Jr., Bill	Yukon
Kirk, Ray	Tahlequah
Lairson Sr., Jerry	Ringold
Martin, John Alexander	Okmulgee
Mcclure, Jerry	Norman
Menefee, Ricky Bob	Blanchard
Midgley, Ben	Wister
Miller, Michael E	Chandler
Parsons, Larry	Mustang
Pridgen Jr., Larry	Davis
Schreiner, Terry	Duncan
Shropshire, Shawn	Piedmont
Spivey, Jefferson	Yukon
Stanford, Perry	Broken Arrow
Tomberlin, Brion R	Norman
Williams, Michael	Broken Bow
Wingo, Gary	Ramona

OR

Allen, Jim	Bend
Bell, Gabriel	Coquille
Bell, Michael	Coquille
Berg, Lee	Roseburg
Bochman, Bruce	Grants Pass
Brandt, Martin W	Springfield
Buchanan, Thad	Powell Butte
Buchanan, Zac	Eugene
Buchner, Bill	Idleyld Park
Busch, Steve	Oakland
Carter, Murray M	Hillsboro
Coon, Raymond C	Damascus
Dixon Jr., Ira E	Cave Junction
Emmerling, John	Gearheart
Frank, Heinrich H	Newport
Goddard, Wayne	Eugene
Harsey, William H	Creswell
Horn, Jess	Eugene
House, Cameron	Salem
Kelley, Gary	Aloha
Lake, Ron	Eugene
Lewis, Mike	Coquille
Little, Gary M	Broadbent
Magruder, Jason	Medford
Martin, Gene	Williams
Ochs, Eric	Sherwood
Olson, Darrold E	McMinnville
Pruyn, Peter	Grants Pass
Richard, Raymond	Gresham
Richards, Chuck	Salem
Rider, David M	Eugene
Sarganis, Paul	Jacksonville
Scarrow, Wil	Gold Hill
Schoeningh, Mike	North Powder
Schrader, Robert	Bend
Sevey Custom Knife,	Gold Beach
Sheehy, Thomas J	Portland
Sibert, Shane	Gladstone
Smith, Rick	Rogue River
Spake, Jeremy	Portland
Squire, Jack	McMinnville
Stucky, Daniel	Springfield
Tendick, Ben	Eugene
Thompson, Leon	Forest Grove
Thompson, Tommy	Portland

Tuch, William	Portland
Turner, Mike	Williams
Vallotton, Butch And Arey	Oakland
Vallotton, Rainy D	Umpqua
Vallotton, Shawn	Oakland
Vallotton, Thomas	Oakland
Ward, Ken	Grants Pass
Warren, Alan And Carroll	Portland
Kurt, David	Molalla

PA

Anderson, Gary D	Spring Grove
Anderson, Tom	Manchester
Appleby, Robert	Shickshinny
Bennett, Brett C	Reinholds
Besedick, Frank E	Monongahela
Blystone, Ronald L.	Creekside
Candrella, Joe	Warminster
Clark, D E (Lucky)	Johnstown
Corkum, Steve	Littlestown
Darby, Rick	Levittown
Evans, Ronald B	Middleton
Frey Jr., W Frederick	Milton
Fry, Dean	Wellsboro
Godlesky, Bruce F.	Apollo
Goldberg, David	Ft Washington
Gottschalk, Gregory J	Carnegie
Harner Iii, "Butch" Lloyd R.	Littlestown
Heinz, John	Upper Black Eddy
Johnson, John R	New Buffalo
Kolenko, Vladimir	Huntingdon Valley
Krammes, Jeremy	Schuylkill Haven
Malloy, Joe	Freeland
Marlowe, Donald	Dover
Mensch, Larry C	Milton
Miller, Rick	Rockwood
Moore, Ted	Elizabethtown
Morett, Donald	Lancaster
Nealy, Bud	Stroudsburg
Neilson, J	Towanda
Nguyen, Mike	Pittsburgh
Ogden, Bill	Avis
Parker, J E	Clarion
Root, Gary	Erie
Rose, Bob	Wagontown
Rupert, Bob	Clinton
Sass, Gary N	Sharpsville
Scimio, Bill	Spruce Creek
Sinclair, J E	Pittsburgh
Steigerwalt, Ken	Orangeville
Stroyan, Eric	Dalton
Takach, Andrew	Elizabeth
Wetten, Bobby	Hershey
Whittaker, Robert E.	Mill Creek

RI

Dickison, Scott S	Portsmouth
Jacques, Alex	Warwick
Mchenry, William James	Wyoming
Olszewski, Stephen	Coventry
Williams, Jason L	Wyoming
Wright, Richard S	Carolina

SC

Beatty, Gordon H.	Seneca
Branton, Robert	Awendaw
Cox, Sam	Gaffney
Denning, Geno	Gaston
Estabrook, Robbie	Conway
Frazier, Jim	Wagener
Gainey, Hal	Greenwood
George, Harry	Aiken
Gregory, Michael	Belton
Hendrix, Jerry	Clinton
Hendrix, Wayne	Allendale
Hucks, Jerry	Moncks Corner
Kay, J Wallace	Liberty
Knight, Jason	Harleyville
Kreger, Thomas	Lugoff
Langley, Gene H	Florence
Lutz, Greg	Greenwood
Manley, David W	Central

Miles Jr., C R "Iron Doctor"	Lugoff
Odom Jr., Victor L.	North
O'Quinn, W. Lee	Elgin
Page, Larry	Aiken
Parler, Thomas O	Charleston
Peagler, Russ	Moncks Corner
Perry, Johnny	Inman
Smith, Ralph L	Taylors
Thomas, Rocky	Moncks Corner
Tyser, Ross	Spartanburg

SD

Boley, Jamie	Parker
Boysen, Raymond A	Rapid Ciy
Ferrier, Gregory K	Rapid City
Thomsen, Loyd W	Custer
Watts, Rodney	Hot Springs

TN

Accawi, Fuad	Oak Ridge
Adams, Jim	Cordova
Bailey, Joseph D.	Nashville
Bartlett, Mark	Lawrenceburg
Blanchard, G R (Gary)	Dandridge
Breed, Kim	Clarksville
Brend, Walter	Etowah
Burris, Patrick R	Athens
Byrd, Wesley L	Evensville
Canter, Ronald E	Jackson
Casteel, Dianna	Monteagle
Casteel, Douglas	Monteagle
Claiborne, Ron	Knox
Conley, Bob	Jonesboro
Coogan, Robert	Smithville
Corby, Harold	Johnson City
Elishewitz, Allen	Lenoir City
Ewing, John H	Clinton
Fitz, Andrew A. Sr. And Jr.	Milan
Hale, Lloyd	Pulaski
Harley, Larry W	Bristol
Hughes, Dan	Spencer
Hurst, Jeff	Rutledge
Hutcheson, John	Chattanooga
Johnson, David A	Pleasant Shade
Johnson, Ryan M	Signal Mountain
Kemp, Lawrence	Ooltewah
Kilroy, Kyle	Knoxville
Kistner, Dee	Crossville
Levine, Bob	Tullahoma
Mccarty, Harry	Blaine
Mcdonald, W.J. "Jerry"	Germantown
Moulton, Dusty	Loudon
Oates, Lee	Bethpage
Raley, R. Wayne	Collierville
Ridge, Tim	Crossville
Sampson, Lynn	Jonesborough
Smith, Newman L.	Gatlinburg
Soileau, Damon	Kingsport
Taylor, C. Gray	Fall Branch
Vanderford, Carl G	Columbia
Wall, Greg	Michie
Ward, W C	Clinton
Wheeler, Gary	Clarksville
Williams Jr., Richard	Morristown

TX

Alexander, Eugene	Ganado
Aplin, Spencer	Brazoria
Appleton, Ron	Bluff Dale
Ashby, Douglas	Dallas
Baker, Tony	Allen
Barnes, Marlen R.	Atlanta
Barr, Judson C.	Irving
Batts, Keith	Hooks
Blackwell, Zane	Eden
Blum, Kenneth	Brenham
Bradley, Gayle	Weatherford
Bratcher, Brett	Plantersville
Brewer, Craig	Killeen
Broadwell, David	Wichita Falls
Brooks, Michael	Lubbock
Brown, Douglas	Fort Worth

Budell, Michael	Brenham
Bullard, Randall	Canyon
Burden, James	Burkburnett
Buzek, Stanley	Waller
Callahan, F Terry	Boerne
Carey, Peter	Lago Vista
Carpenter, Ronald W	Jasper
Carter, Fred	Wichita Falls
Champion, Robert	Amarillo
Chase, John E	Aledo
Chew, Larry	Weatherford
Childers, David	Montgomery
Churchman, T W (Tim)	Bandera
Cole, James M	Bartonville
Connor, John W	Odessa
Connor, Michael	Winters
Cooke, Mark	Spring
Cornett, Brian	McKinney
Costa, Scott	Spicewood
Crain, Jack W	Granbury
Crouch, Bubba	Pleasanton
Crowner, Jeff	Plano
Darcey, Chester L	College Station
De Mesa, John	Lewisville
Dean, Harvey J	Rockdale
Debaud, Jake	Plano
Delong, Dick	Centerville
Dietz, Howard	New Braunfels
Dominy, Chuck	Colleyville
Dyer, David	Granbury
Eldridge, Allan	Ft. Worth
Epting, Richard	College Station
Eriksen, James Thorlief	Garland
Evans, Carlton	Fort Davis
Fant Jr., George	Atlanta
Ferguson, Jim	San Angelo
Fisher, Josh	Murchison
Foster, Al	Magnolia
Foster, Norvell C	Marion
Fritz, Jesse	Slaton
Fry, Jason	Hawley
Fuller, Bruce A	Blanco
Gann, Tommy	Canton
Garner, Larry W	Tyler
Gatlin, Steve	Schwartz
George, Les	Corpus Christi
Graham, Gordon	New Boston
Green, Bill	Sachse
Griffin, John	Hockley
Grimes, Mark	Bedford
Guinn, Terry	Eastland
Halfrich, Jerry	San Marcos
Hamlet Jr., Johnny	Clute
Hand, Bill	Spearman
Hawkins, Buddy	Texarkana
Hawkins Jr., Charles R.	San Angelo
Hawley, Troy G.	Ivanhoe
Haynes, Jerry	Gunter
Hays, Mark	Austin
Hemperley, Glen	Willis
Hicks, Gary	Tuscola
Hill, Steve E	Spring Branch
Horrigan, John	Burnet
Howell, Jason G	Lake Jackson
Hudson, Robert	Humble
Hughes, Lawrence	Plainview
Hunt, Raymon E.	Irving
Huse, James D. Ii	Buda
Jackson, Charlton R	San Antonio
Jaksik Jr., Michael	Fredericksburg
Jangtanong, Suchat	Dripping Springs
Keller, Bill	San Antonio
Lance, Dan	Weatherford
Laplante, Brett	McKinney
Lay, L J	Burkburnett
Lemcke, Jim L	Houston
Lennon, Dale	Alba
Lister Jr., Weldon E	Boerne
Love, Ed	San Antonio
Lovett, Michael	Mound
Luchak, Bob	Channelview
Lucie, James R	Austin

Luckett, Bill	Weatherford
Majors, Charlie	Montgomery
Martin, Michael W	Beckville
Mcconnell Jr., Loyd A	Marble Falls
Merz Iii, Robert L	Katy
Minchew, Ryan	Midland
Mitchell, Wm Dean	Warren
Moen, Jerry	Dallas
Moore, James B	Ft. Stockton
Neely, Greg	Bellaire
O'Brien, Mike J.	San Antonio
Ogletree Jr., Ben R	Livingston
Ott, Ted	Elgin
Overeynder, T R	Arlington
Ownby, John C	Murphy
Packard, Ronnie	Bonham
Pardue, Joe	Hillister
Patterson, Pat	Barksdale
Payne, Travis	Telephone
Peters, Daniel	El Paso
Pierce, Randall	Arlington
Pollock, Wallace J	Cedar Park
Polzien, Don	Lubbock
Powers, Walter R.	Lolita
Ralph, Darrel	Forney
Ray, Alan W	Lovelady
Richardson, Percy	Lufkin
Richardson Iii, Percy (Rich)	Lufkin
Richardson Jr., Percy	Lufkin
Roberts, Jack	Houston
Rucker, Thomas	Spring
Ruple, William H	Pleasanton
Ruth, Michael G	Texarkana
Ruth, Jr., Michael	Texarkana
Schorsch, Kendall	Jourdanton
Self, Ernie	Dripping Springs
Shipley, Steven A	Richardson
Sloan, Shane	Newcastle
Smart, Steve	McKinney
Snody, Mike	Aransas Pass
Stokes, Ed	Hockley
Stone, Jerry	Lytle
Stout, Johnny	New Braunfels
Swenson, Luke	Lakehills
Thuesen, Ed	Damon
Truncali, Pete	Nevada
Van Reenen, Ian	Amarillo
Vickers, David	Montgomery
Ware, Tommy	Onalaska
Watson, Daniel	Driftwood
Watts, Johnathan	Gatesville
Weever, John	Glen Rose
White, Dale	Sweetwater
Whitley, Weldon G	Odessa
Wilkins, Mitchell	Montgomery
Wilson, Curtis M	Burleson
Wolf Jr., William Lynn	Lagrange
Zboril, Terry	Caldwell
Zermeno, William D.	Houston

UT

Allred, Bruce F	Layton
Black, Earl	Salt Lake City
Carter, Shayne	Payson
Ence, Jim	Richfield
Ennis, Ray	Ogden
Erickson, L.M.	Ogden
Hunter, Hyrum	Aurora
Johnson, Steven R	Manti
Jorgensen, Carson	Mt Pleasant
Lang, David	Kearns
Maxfield, Lynn	Layton
Nell, Chad	St. George
Nielson, Jeff V	Monroe
Nunn, Gregory	Castle Valley
Palmer, Taylor	Blanding
Peterson, Chris	Salina
Ramos, Steven	West Jordan
Ricks, Kurt J.	Trenton
Strickland, Dale	Monroe
Szczerbiak, Maciej	St. George
Velarde, Ricardo	Park City

Weeks, Ryan	Bountiful
Winn, Travis A.	Salt Lake City
Young, John	Ephraim
Jenkins, Mitch	Manti
Johnson, Jerry	Spring City

VA

Apelt, Stacy E	Norfolk
Arbuckle, James M	Yorktown
Ball, Butch	Floyd
Ballew, Dale	Bowling Green
Barnhill, Wess	Spotsylvania
Batson, Richard G.	Rixeyville
Beverly Ii, Larry H	Spotsylvania
Catoe, David R	Norfolk
Davidson, Edmund	Goshen
Foster, Burt	Bristol
Goodpasture, Tom	Ashland
Harley, Richard	Bristol
Harris, Cass	Bluemont
Hedrick, Don	Newport News
Hendricks, Samuel J	Maurertown
Holloway, Paul	Norfolk
Jones, Barry M And Phillip G	Danville
Jones, Enoch	Warrenton
Kearney, Jarod	Swoope
Klein, Kieran	Check
Martin, Herb	Richmond
Mccoun, Mark	DeWitt
Metheny, H A "Whitey"	Spotsylvania
Mills, Michael	Colonial Beach
Murski, Ray	Reston
Norfleet, Ross W	Providence Forge
Parks, Blane C	Woodbridge
Pawlowski, John R	Barhamsville
Schlueter, David	Madison Heights
Schwartz, Aaron	Woodbridge
Vanhoy, Ed And Tanya	Abingdon
Vestal, Charles	Abingdon
Ward, Ron	Rose Hill

VT

Bensinger, J. W.	Marshfield
Haggerty, George S	Jacksonville
Kelso, Jim	Worcester
Wulf, Derrick	Essex

WA

Amoureux, A W	Northport
Ber, Dave	San Juan Island
Berglin, Bruce	Mount Vernon
Bromley, Peter	Spokane
Brothers, Robert L	Colville
Brunckhorst, Lyle	Bothell
Buckner, Tom	Olympia
Bump, Bruce D.	Walla Walla
Butler, John R	Shoreline
Campbell, Dick	Colville
Chamberlain, Jon A	E. Wenatchee
Conway, John	Kirkland
Crowthers, Mark F	Rolling Bay
D'Angelo, Laurence	Vancouver
Davis, John	Selah
De Wet, Kobus	Yakima
Diaz, Jose	Ellensburg
Diskin, Matt	Freeland
Erickson, Daniel	Snohomish
Ferry, Tom	Auburn
Gray, Bob	Spokane
Gray, Robb	Seattle
Greenfield, G O	Everett
Hansen, Lonnie	Spanaway
House, Gary	Ephrata
Keyes, Geoff P.	Duvall
Leeper, Dan	Olympia
Lisch, David K	Yelm
Norton, Don	Port Townsend
O'Malley, Daniel	Seattle
Padilla, Gary	Bellingham
Pedersen, Ole	Monroe
Podmajersky, Dietrich	Seattle
Rader, Michael	Bothell

Roeder, David	Kennewick
Rogers, Ray	Wauconda
Sanford, Dick	Chehalis
Schempp, Ed	Ephrata
Schempp, Martin	Ephrata
Shoger, Mark O	Kalama
Stegner, Wilbur G	Rochester
Sterling, Thomas J	Coupeville
Straub, Salem F.	Tonasket
Swyhart, Art	Klickitat
Thomas, Bob	Ferndale
Wheeler, Nick	Castle Rock
Wright, Kevin	Quilcene

WI

Boyes, Tom	West Bend
Brandsey, Edward P	Janesville
Bruner, Fred Jr.	Fall Creek
Carr, Joseph E.	Menomonee Falls
Coats, Ken	Stevens Point
Delarosa, Jim	Waterford
Deyong, Clarence	Sturtevant
Franklin, Larry	Stoughton
Haines, Jeff	Mayville
Hoffman, Jess	Shawano
Johnson, Richard	Germantown
Kanter, Michael	New Berlin
Kohls, Jerry	Princeton
Kolitz, Robert	Beaver Dam
Lary, Ed	Mosinee
Lerch, Matthew	Sussex
Maestri, Peter A	Spring Green
Martin, Cory	Racine
Martin, Peter	Waterford
Mikolajczyk, Glen	Caledonia
Millard, Fred G	Richland Center
Montgomery, Stephen R.	Madison
Nelson, Ken	Racine
Niemuth, Troy	Sheboygan
Ponzio, Doug	Beloit
Rabuck, Jason	Springbrook
Revishvili, Zaza	Madison
Ricke, Dave	West Bend
Rochford, Michael R	Dresser
Roush, Scott	Washburn
Schrap, Robert G	Wauwatosa
Steinbrecher, Mark W	Pleasant Prairie
Wattelet, Michael A	Minocqua
Zimmerman, Nathan	Waukesha

WV

Derr, Herbert	St. Albans
Drost, Jason D	French Creek
Drost, Michael B	French Creek
Elliott, Jerry	Charleston
Groves, Gary	Canvas
Jeffries, Robert W	Red House
Liegey, Kenneth R	Millwood
Maynard, Larry Joe	Crab Orchard
Morris, Eric	Beckley
Pickens, Selbert	Dunbar
Reynolds, Dave	Harrisville
Small, Ed	Keyser
Tokar, Daniel	Shepherdstown
Wilson, Rw	Weirton
Wyatt, William R	Rainelle

WY

Amos, Chris	Riverton
Ankrom, W.E.	Cody
Banks, David L.	Riverton
Barry, Scott	Laramie
Bartlow, John	Sheridan
Casey, Kevin	Lander
Deveraux, Butch	Riverton
Draper, Audra	Riverton
Draper, Mike	Riverton
Fowler, Ed A.	Riverton
Friedly, Dennis E	Cody
Kilby, Keith	Cody
Oliver, Todd D	Cheyenne
Rexroat, Kirk	Banner

Reynolds, John C	Gillette
Rodebaugh, James L	Carpenter
Ross, Stephen	Evanston
Spragg, Wayne E	Lovell
Whipple, Wesley A	Thermopolis

ARGENTINA

Ayarragaray, Cristian L.	Parana, Entre Rios
Bertolami, Juan Carlos	Neuquen
Gibert, Pedro	San Martin de los Andes, Neuquen
Kehiayan, Alfredo	Maschwitz, Buenos Aires
Montenegro, Facundo	Merlo (5881) San Luis
Rho, Nestor Lorenzo	Junin, Buenos Aires
Santiago, Abud	Buenos Aires

AUSTRALIA

Barnett, Bruce	Mundaring, WA
Bennett, Peter	Engadine, NSW
Brodziak, David	Albany, WA
Crawley, Bruce R	Croydon, VIC
Cross, Robert	Tamworth, NSW
Del Raso, Peter	Mt. Waverly, VIC
Fludder, Keith	Tahmoor, New South Wales
Gerner, Thomas	Walpole, WA
Giljevic, Branko	New South Wales
Green, William (Bill)	View Bank, VIC
Harvey, Max	Western Australia 6149
Hedges, Dee	Bedfordale, WA
Husiak, Myron	Altona, VIC
K B S, Knives	North Castlemaine, VIC
Maisey, Alan	Vincentia, NSW
Mcintyre, Shawn	Hawthornm, E VIC
Phillips, Alistair	Amaroo, ACT
Tasman, Kerley	Pt Kennedy, WA
Zemitis, Joe	Cardiff Heights, NSW

BELGIUM

Dox, Jan	Schoten
Laurent, Veronique	Brussels
Lurquin, Samuel	Binches
Monteiro, Victor	Maleves Ste Marie
Veronique, Laurent	Bruxelles

BRAZIL

Bodolay, Antal	Belo Horizonte, MG
Boeck, Sandro Eduardo	Cachoeira do Sul - RS
Bossaerts, Carl	Ribeirao Preto, SP
Campos, Ivan	Tatui, SP
Cecchini, Gustavo T.	Sao Jose Rio Preto SP
Dionatam, Franco	Ibitinga-SP
Dionatam, Franco	Jardim Filadelfia, Ibitinga-SP
Dorneles, Luciano Oliverira	Nova Petropolis, RS
Gaeta, Angelo	Centro Jau, SP-CEP: 14.201310
Garcia, Mario Eiras	Caxingui, SP
Glasser, Roger Cesar	679 - Sao Paulo - SP
Goncalves, Luiz Gustavo	124A -Sao Paulo - SP
Ikoma, Flavio	Presidente Prudente, SP
Lala, Paulo Ricardo P	
And Lala, Roberto P.	Presidente Prudente, SP
Neto Jr., Nelson And	
De Carvalho, Henrique M.	Braganca Paulista, SP
Paulo, Fernandes R	Lencois Paulista, SP
Petean, Francisco And Mauricio	Birigui, SP
Ricardo Romano, Bernardes	Itajuba MG
Sfreddo, Rodrigo Menezes	Nova Petropolis, RS
Vilar, Ricardo	Mairipora, SP
Vilar, Ricardo Augusto Ferreira	Mairipora, SP
Villa, Luiz	Itaim Bibi, SP
Zakharov, Gladiston	Jacaret-SP

CANADA

Arnold, Joe	London, ON
Beauchamp, Gaetan	Stoneham, QC
Beets, Marty	Williams Lake, BC
Bell, Donald	Bedford, NS
Berg, Lothar	Kitchener ON
Beshara, Brent (Besh)	NL
Boos, Ralph	Edmonton, AB
Bourbeau, Jean Yves	Ile Perrot, QC
Bradford, Garrick	Kitchener, ON
Bucharsky, Emil	Spruce Grove, Alberta
Daley, Mark	Waubaushene, Ontario
Dallyn, Kelly	Calgary, AB

De Braga, Jose C.	Trois Rivieres, QC
Debraga, Jovan	Quebec
Deringer, Christoph	Cookshire, QC
Desaulniers, Alain	Cookshire, QC
Diotte, Jeff	LaSalle, ON
Doiron, Donald	Messines, QC
Doucette, R	Brantford, ON
Doussot, Laurent	St. Bruno, QC
Downie, James T	Ontario
Friesen, Dave J	British Columbia
Frigault, Rick	Golden Lake, ON
Ganshorn, Cal	Regina, SK
Garvock, Mark W	Balderson, ON
Gilbert, Chantal	Quebec City, QC
Haslinger, Thomas	British Columbia V1B 3G7
Hayes, Wally	Essex, ON
Hindmarch, Garth	Carlyle, SK
Hofer, Louis	Rose Prairie, BC
Jobin, Jacques	Levis, QC
Kaczor, Tom	Upper London, ON
Lambert, Kirby	Regina, SK
Langley, Mick	Qualicum Beach, BC
Lay, R J (Bob)	Logan Lake, BC
Leber, Heinz	Hudson's Hope, BC
Lemelin, Stephanie	Brossard
Lightfoot, Greg	Kitscoty, AB
Linklater, Steve	Aurora, ON
Loerchner, Wolfgang	Bayfield, ON
Maneker, Kenneth	Galiano Island, BC
Marchand, Rick	Lunenburg, Nova Scotia
Marzitelli, Peter	Langley, BC
Massey, Al	Mount Uniacke, NS
Mckenzie, David Brian	Campbell River, BC
Miville-Deschenes, Alain	Quebec
Moeller, Harald	Parksville, BC
Moizis, Stan	Delta, British Columbia (BC)
Nease, William	LaSalle, ON
Niro, Frank	Kamloops, B.C.
O'Hare, Sean	Grand Manan, NB
Olson, Rod	Nanton, AB
Painter, Tony	Whitehorse, YT
Patrick, Bob	S. Surrey, BC
Pepiot, Stephan	Winnipeg, MB
Piesner, Dean	Conestogo, ON
Poirier, Rick	New Brunswick E4V 2W7
Rassenti, Peter	Quebec J7P 4C2
Ridley, Rob	Sundre, AB
Ross, Tim	Thunder Bay, ON
Schoenfeld, Matthew A	Galiano Island, BC
St. Amour, Murray	Beachburg, Ontario
Stancer, Chuck	Calgary, AB
Storch, Ed	Mannville, AB
Stuart, Steve	Gores Landing, ON
Sylvester, David	Compton, QC
Tedford, Steven J.	Colborne, ON
Tighe, Brian	St. Catharines, ON
Toner, Roger	Pickering, ON
Vanderkolff, Stephen	Mildmay, ON
Whitenect, Jody	Elderbank, NS
Young, Bud	Port Hardy, BC

CZECH REPUBLIC

Kislinger, Milos	Dobronin 314 58812
Rusnak, Josef	323 00 Plzen
Sevecek, Pavel	Brodek U Konice
Tesarik, Richard	614 00 Brno

DENMARK

Andersen, Henrik Lefolii	Fredensborg
Anso, Jens	Sporup
Rafn, Dan C.	7400 Herning
Strande, Poul	Dastrup
Vensild, Henrik	Auning
Willumsen, Mikkel	S Copenhagen

ENGLAND

Bailey, I.R.	Colkirk
Barker, Stuart	Wigston, Leicester
Boden, Harry	Derbyshire
Ducker, Brian	Colkirk
Farid, Mehr R	Kent
Harrington, Roger	East Sussex

Nowacki, Stephen R.   Southampton, Hampshire
Orford, Ben   Worcestershire
Price, Darrell Morris   Devon
Stainthorp, Guy   Stroke-on-Trent
Wardell, Mick   N Devon
Wise, Donald   East Sussex
Wood, Alan   Brampton
Wylie, Tom   Sutton-In-Ashfield, Notts

FINLAND
Hankala, Jukka   39580 Riitiala
Nylund, Erik   65320 Vaasa
Palikko, J-T   00190 Helsinki
Ruusuvuori, Anssi   Piikkio
Tuominen, Pekka   Tossavanlahti
Vilppola, Markku   Turku

FRANCE
Bennica, Charles   Moules et Baucels
Chomilier, Alain And Joris   Clermont-Ferrand
Doursin, Gerard   Pernes les Fontaines
Grangette, Alain   23210 Azat-Chatenet
Graveline,
  Pascal And Isabelle   Moelan-sur-Mer
Headrick, Gary   Juan Les Pins
Laroche, Jean-Marc   78160 Marly le Roi
Madrulli, Mme Joelle   Salon De Provence
Regel, Jean-Louis   Saint Leger de Fougeret
Reverdy, Nicole And Pierre   Romans
Thevenot, Jean-Paul   Dijon
Viallon, Henri   Thiers

GERMANY
Boehlke, Guenter   56412 Grobholbach
Borger, Wolf   Graben-Neudorf
Dell, Wolfgang   Owen-Teck
Drumm, Armin   Dornstadt
Faust, Joachim   Goldkronach
Fruhmann, Ludwig   Burghausen
Greiss, Jockl   Schenkenzell
Hehn, Richard Karl   Dorrebach
Herbst, Peter   Lauf a.d. Pegn.
Joehnk, Bernd   Kiel
Kressler, D F   D-28832 Achim
Rankl, Christian   Munchen
Rinkes, Siegfried   Markterlbach
Selzam, Frank   Bad Koenigshofen
Steinau, Jurgen   Berlin
Tritz, Jean-Jose   Hamburg
Wirtz, Achim   Wuerselen
Zirbes, Richard   Niederkail

GREECE
Ioannis-Minas, Filippou   Athens
Zafeiriadis, Konstantinos   Marathon Attiki

IRELAND
Moore, Davy   Quin, Co Clare

ISRAEL
Shadmot, Boaz   Arava

ITALY
Ameri, Mauro   Genova
Ballestra, Santino   Ventimiglia
Bertuzzi, Ettore   Bergamo
Bonassi, Franco   Pordenone
Esposito, Emmanuel   Buttigliera Alta TO
Fogarizzu, Boiteddu   Pattada
Frizzi, Leonardo   Firenze
Garau, Marcello   Oristano
Giagu, Salvatore
  And Deroma Maria Rosaria   Pattada (SS)
Mainolfi, Dr. Riccardo   Positano (SA)
Moro, Corrado   Torino
Mura, Denis   Cascina (Pi)
Puddu, Salvatore   (Cagliari) Sardinia
Ramondetti, Sergio   CHIUSA DI PESIO (CN)
Riboni, Claudio   Truccazzano (MI)
Scordia, Paolo   Roma
Simonella, Gianluigi   Maniago
Toich, Nevio   Vincenza
Tschager, Reinhard   Bolzano

JAPAN
Aida, Yoshihito   Tokyo
Ebisu, Hidesaku   Hiroshima
Fujikawa, Shun   Osaka
Fukuta, Tak   Gifu
Hara, Koji   Gifu
Hirayama, Harumi   Saitama
Hiroto, Fujihara   Hiroshima
Isao, Ohbuchi   Fukuoka
Ishihara, Hank   Chiba
Kagawa, Koichi   Kanagawa
Kanki, Iwao   Hyogo
Kansei, Matsuno   Gifu
Kato, Shinichi   Aichi
Katsumaro, Shishido   Hiroshima
Keisuke, Gotoh   Oita
Koyama, Captain Bunshichi   Aichi
Makoto, Kunitomo   Hiroshima
Matsuno, Kansei   Gifu-City
Matsusaki, Takeshi   Nagasaki
Michinaka, Toshiaki   Tottori
Narasada, Mamoru   NAGANO
Ryuichi, Kuki   Saitama
Shigeno, Mamoru   Saitama, 350-1320
Shinozaki, Akio   Fukuoka-ken
Sugihara, Keidoh   Osaka
Sugiyama, Eddy K   Oita
Tamatsu, Kunihiko   Kochi-ken
Toshifumi, Kuramoto   Fukuoka
Uchida, Chimata   Kumamoto
Wada, Yasutaka   Nara
Waters, Glenn   Hirosaki City
Yoneyama, Chicchi K.   Tokyo
Yoshihara, Yoshindo   Tokyo
Yoshikazu, Kamada   Tokushima
Yoshio, Maeda   Okayama

MEXICO
Scheurer, Alfredo E Faes   Distrito Federal
Sunderland, Richard   Puerto Escondido, OA
Ware, J.D.   Merida, Yucatan
Young, Cliff   San Miguel De Allende, GJ

NAMIBIA
Naude, Louis   Okahandja

NETHERLANDS
Brouwer, Jerry   Alkmaar
Sprokholt, Rob   Gatherwood
Van De Manakker, Thijs   Holland
Van Den Elsen, Gert   Tilburg
Van Eldik, Frans   Loenen
Van Ryswyk, Aad   Vlaardingen

NEW ZEALAND
Bassett, David J.   Auckland
Gunther, Eddie   Auckland
Jansen Van Vuuren, Ludwig   Dunedin
Knapton, Chris C.   Henderson, Aukland
Pennington, C A   Kainga Christchurch
Reddiex, Bill   Palmerston North
Sandow, Brent Edward   Auckland
Sands, Scott   Christchurch 9
Van Dijk, Richard   Harwood Dunedin

NICARAGUA
Morales, Ramon   Managua

NORWAY
Bache-Wiig, Tom   Eivindvik
Sellevold, Harald   Bergen
Vistnes, Tor   Svelgen

RUSSIA
Kharlamov, Yuri   Tula

SLOVAKIA
Albert, Stefan   Filakovo 98604
Bojtos, Arpad   98403 Lucenec
Kovacik, Robert   Tomasovce 98401
Mojzis, Julius   98511 Halic
Pulis, Vladimir   96701 Kremnica
Santa, Ladislav "Lasky"   97637 Hrochot

SOUTH AFRICA
Arm-Ko Knives,   Marble Ray , KZN
Baartman, George   Bela-Bela, LP
Bauchop, Robert   Munster, KN
Beukes, Tinus   Vereeniging, GT
Bezuidenhout, Buzz   Malvern, KZN
Boardman, Guy   New Germany, KZN
Brown, Rob E   Port Elizabeth, EC
Burger, Fred   Munster, KZN
Burger, Tiaan   Pretoria, GT
Culhane, Sean K.   Horizon, Roodepoort, 1740
Dickerson, Gavin   Petit, GT
Fellows, Mike   Riversdale 6670
Grey, Piet   Naboomspruit, LP
Harvey, Kevin   Belfast, LP
Herbst, Gawie   Akasia, GT
Herbst, Thinus   Akasia, GT
Horn, Des   Onrusrivier, WC
Klaasee, Tinus   George, WC
Kojetin, W   Germiston, GT
Lancaster, C G   Free State
Liebenberg, Andre   Randburg, GT
Mackrill, Stephen   Johannesburg, GT
Mahomedy, A R   Marble Ray, KZN
Mahomedy, Humayd A.R.   Marble Ray, KZN
Mitchell, Alan   Randburg, Gauteng
Oelofse, Tinus   Glenstantia, Pretoria
Owen, David J.A.   Johannesburg
Pienaar, Conrad   Free State
Prinsloo, Theuns   Free State
Rietveld, Bertie   Magaliesburg, GT
Russell, Mick   Port Elizabeth, EC
Schoeman, Corrie   Free State
Schutte, Neill   Bloemfontein
Smith, Stuart   Gauteng
Steyn, Peter   Freestate
Thorburn, Andre E.   Warmbaths, LP
Van Den Berg, Neels   Pretoria, Gauteng
Van Der Westhuizen, Peter   Mossel Bay, SC
Van Heerden, Andre   Pretoria, GT
Watson, Peter   La Hoff, NW

SOUTH AUSTRALIA
Edmonds, Warrick   Adelaide Hills

SPAIN
Goshovskyy, Vasyl   Castellon de la Plana

SWEDEN
Bergh, Roger   Bygdea
Eklund, Maihkel   Farila
Embretsen, Kaj   Edsbyn
Hedlund, Anders   Brastad
Henningsson, Michael   430 83 Vrango (Gothenburg)
Hogstrom, Anders T   37011 Backaryd
Johansson, Anders   Grangesberg
Lundstrom, Jan-Ake   Dals-Langed
Lundstrom, Torbjorn (Tobbe)   Are
Nilsson, Jonny Walker   93391 Arvidsjaur
Nordell, Ingemar   FSrila
Persson, Conny   Loos
Styrefors, Mattias   Boden
Vogt, Patrik   Halmstad

SWITZERLAND
Roulin, Charles   Geneva

UNITED KINGDOM
Hague, Geoff   Quarley, Hampshire
Horne, Grace   Sheffield
Maxen, Mick   Hatfield, Herts

URUGUAY
Gonzalez, Leonardo Williams   Maldonado
Symonds, Alberto E   Montevideo

ZIMBABWE
Burger, Pon   Bulawayo

Knifemakers listed here are in good standing with these organizations.

the knifemakers' guild
2017 membership

a Les Adams, Mike "Whiskers" Allen

b Robert K. Bagley, Tony Baker, Robert Ball, James J. Barry, III, John Bartlow, Barbara Baskett, Gene Baskett, Michael S. Blue, Arpad Bojtos, Tony Bose, Dennis Bradley, W. Lowell Bray, Jr., Fred Bruner, Jr., John Busfield

c Harold J. "Kit" Carson, Michael Carter, Dianna Casteel, Douglas Casteel, Daniel Chinnock, Richard Clow, Kenneth R. Coats, George Cousino, Pat Crawford, Kevin Cross, Daniel Cummings

d George Dailey, Alex K. Daniels, Edmund Davidson, Scott Davidson, John H. Davis, Steve Davis, David Dodds, Tom Downing, James Downs, Will Dutton

e Jim Elliott, William B. Ellis, James T. Eriksen, Carlton R. Evans

f Cliff Fendley, Lee Ferguson, Robert G. Flynt, John R. Fraps

g Steve Gatlin, Warren Glover, Gregory J. Gottschalk

h Philip (Doc) L. Hagen, Jim Hammond, Rade Hawkins, Earl Jay Hendrickson, Wayne G. Hensley, Gil Hibben, Wesley G. Hibben, Kevin Hoffman, Larry Hostetler, Rob Hudson, Roy Humenic

i Billy Mace Imel, Michael Irie

j Brad Johnson, Jerry L. Johnson, Ronald B. Johnson, Steven R. Johnson, William "Bill" C. Johnson, Lonnie L. Jones

k William L. Keeton, Bill Kennedy, Jr., Bill King, Harvey King, Jeff Knox

l Tim "Chops" Lambkin, Ed Lary, Paul M. LeBetard, Gary E. LeBlanc, David C. Lemoine, William S. Letcher, Jack Levin, Bob Levine, Ken Linton, Don Lozier, Bill Luckett, Gail Lunn, Ernest Lyle

m Stephen Mackrill, Riccardo Mainolfi, Joe Malloy, Herbert A. Martin, Charlie B. Mathews, Harry S. Mathews, Ken McFall, Ted Merchant, Robert L. Merz, III, Toshiaki Michinaka, James P. Miller, Stephen C. Miller, Jerry Moen, Kyle Moen, Jeff Morgan, Stephen D. Myers

n Bud Nealy, Larry Newton, Ross W Norfleet

o Clifford W. O'Dell, Charles F. Ochs, III, Ben R. Ogletree, Sean O'Hare, Jr., Warren Osborne, T. R. Overeynder, John E. Owens

p Larry Page, Cliff Parker, Jerry Partridge, John R. Pawlowski, W. D. Pease, Michael Pellegrin, Alfred Pendray, James J. Pengov, Jr., John W. PerMar, John Perry, Daniel Piergallini, Leon Pittman, Otakar Pok, Larry Pridgen, Jr., Joseph R. Prince

r James D. Ragsdale, Simone Raimondi, Steven Rapp, Carl E. Rechsteiner, Lin Rhea, Joseph Calvin Robinson, Michael Rochford, Gordon Romeis, A.G. Russell

s Michael A. Sakmar, Joseph A. Sangster, Kenneth Savage, Scott W. Sawby, Juergen Schanz, Mike Schirmer, Mark C. Sentz, Eugene W. Shadley, John I Shore, Jim Siska, Steven C. Skiff, Ralph Smith, James Rodney Sornberger, David Steier, Murray Sterling, Douglas W. Stice, Russ Sutton

t Leon Thompson, Bobby L. Toole, Reinhard Tschager, Ralph Turnbull

v Charles Vestal, Donald Vogt

w George A. Walker, Charles B. Ward, John S. Weever, Wayne Whittaker, Stan Wilson, Daniel Winkler, Marvin Winn

y George L. Young, Mike Yurco

z Brad Zinker

abs master smith listing

a David Anders, Gary D. Anderson, E. R. Russ Andrews II

b Gary Barnes, Aubrey G. Barnes Sr., James L. Batson, Jimmie H. Buckner, Bruce D. Bump, Bill Burke, Bill Buxton

c Ed Caffrey, Murray M. Carter, Kevin R. Cashen, Hsiang Lin (Jimmy) Chin, Jon Christensen, Howard F. Clark, Wade Colter, Michael Connor, James R. Cook, Joseph G. Cordova, Jim Crowell, Steve Culver

d Sava Damlovac, Harvey J. Dean, Christoph Deringer, Adam DesRosiers, Bill Dietzel, Audra L. Draper, Rick Dunkerley, Steve Dunn, Kenneth Durham

e Dave Ellis

f Robert Thomas Ferry III, Jerry Fisk, John S. Fitch, Joe Flournoy, Don Fogg—retired, Burt Foster, Ronnie E. Foster, Larry D. Fuegen, Bruce A. Fuller, Jack A. Fuller

g Tommy Gann, Bert Gaston, Thomas Gerner, Greg Gottschalk

h Tim Hancock, Don L. Hanson III, Heather Harvey, Kevin Harvey, Wally Hayes, E. Jay Hendrickson, Don Hethcoat, John Horrigan, Gary House, Rob Hudson

j Jim L. Jackson—retired

k Joseph F. Keeslar, Keith Kilby, Ray Kirk, Hank Knickmeyer, Jason Knight, Bob Kramer

l Jerry Lairson Sr.

m J. Chris Marks, John Alexander Martin, Roger D. Massey, Victor J. McCrackin, Shawn McIntyre, Hanford J. Miller, Wm Dean Mitchell

n Greg Neely, J. Neilson, Ron Newton, Douglas E. Noren

o Charles F. Ochs III

p Alfred Pendray, Dan Petersen Ph.D., Alex Dwight Phillips, Timothy Potier

q Mike Quesenberry

r Michael Rader, J. W. Randall, Kirk Rexroat, Linden W. Rhea, James L. Rodebaugh, Kyle Royer, Raymond B. Rybar Jr.

s James P. Saviano, Stephen C. Schwarzer, Mark C. Sentz, Rodrigo Menezes Sfreddo, J.D. Smith, Josh Smith, Raymond L. Smith, Bill Sowell, Charles Stout, Joseph Szilaski

t Shane Taylor, Jean-paul Thevenot, Jason Tiensvold, Brion Tomberlin, P. J. Tomes, Henry Torres

v Michael V. Vagnino Jr., Terry L. Vandeventer

w James L. Walker, Daniel Warren, Aaron Michael Wilburn, Michael L. Williams, Daniel Winkler

professional knifemaker's association

Mike Allen, Pat Ankrom, Shane Paul Atwood, Eddie J. Baca, D. Scott Barry, John Bartlow, Donald Bell, Tom Black, Justin Bridges, Kenneth L. Brock, Lucas Burnley, Craig Camerer, Tim S. Cameron, Ken Cardwell, David Clark, Vance Corich, Del Corsi, Culpepper & Co., John Easter, Ray W. Ennis, Lee Ferguson, Chuck Fraley, Graham Fredeen, Bob Glassman, Levi Graham, Bob Ham, Alford "Alf" Hanna, James Helm, Wayne Hensley, Gary Hicks, Guy E. Hielscher, Jay Higgins, Mike L. Irie, Mitch Jenkins, Harvey King, Todd Kopp, Jim Krause, Tom Krein, Scott Kuntz, Tim "Chops" Lambkin, James R. Largent, Ken Linton, Arthur Lynn, Jim Magee, Jerry & Sandy McClure, Mardi Meshejian, Clayton Miller, Michael Miller, Tyree L. Montell, Mike Mooney, Steve Myers, Robert Nash, Fred A. Ott, William Pleins, James L. Poplin, Bill Post, Calvin Powell, Steve Powers, Peter Pruyn, Bill Redd, Jim Reid, Steve Rollert, David Ruana, Dennis "Bud" Ruana, Don Ruana, Walter Scherar, Terry Schreiner, M.L. "Pepper" Seaman, Eugene Solomonik, Eddie F. Stalcup, Craig Steketee, Douglas Stice, Mark Strauss, Kurt Swearingen, James D. Thrash, Ed Thuesen, Albert Trujillo, Pete Truncali, Charles Turnage, Mike Tyre, Dick Waites, James Walton, Al Warren, Rodney Watts, Hans Weinmueller, Harold J. Wheeler, Jacob Wilson, R.W. Wilson, Michael C. Young, Monte Zavatta, Russ Zima, Daniel F. Zvonek

state/regional associations

arizona knife collectors association

Lee Beene, Larry Braasch, Bill Cheatam, Bob Dodd, Gary Fields, Tim Hancock, Bob Haskins, D'Alton Holder, Gerard Hurst, Todd M. Kopp, Mike Mooney, Jim Ort, Brian Quinn, Ray Rybar, Paul Vandine, Jim Yarbrough

australian knifemakers guild inc.

Peter Bald, Bruce Barnett, Alex Bean, Walter Bidgood, Matt Black, Scott Broad, David Brodziak, Matt Brook, Zac Cheong, Stephen Cooper, Peter Del Raso, Michael Fechner, Keith Fludder, John Foxwell, Alfred Frater, Adam Fromholtz, Thomas Gerner, Branko Giljevic, James Gladstone, Peter Gordon, Karim Haddad, Mal Hannan, Jamie Harrington, Rod Harris, Glenn Michael Henke, Robert Herbert, Joe Kiss, Michael Masion, Maurie, McCarthy, Shawn McIntyre, Will Morrison, Garry Odgers, Adam Parker, Terri Parker, Jeff Peck, Alistair Phillips, Fred Rowley, Wayne Saunders, Doug Timbs, Stewart Townsend, Rob Wakelin, Jason Weightman, Ross Yeats, Joe Zemitis

california knifemakers association

Paul Anderson, Stewart Anderson, Elmer Art, Kendell Banks, Harold Bishop, Gary Bolduc, Anton Bosch, Roger Bost, Sean P. Bourke, John Burens, Mike Butcher, Joe Caswell, Jon Chabot, Marcus Clinco, George Cummings, Mike Daly, Capt. J-C Demirdjian, Mike Desensi, Albert M. Dorado Sr., Frank Dunkin, Vern Edler III, Eddie Escobar, Chuck Faulkner, Alex Felix, Jim Ferguson, Marcus Flores, Lowell Ford, Brian Forrest, Randy Freer, Bill Fried, Joe Girtner, John Glueck, Corey Gray, Richard Grimm, Ron Gue, Eva Gulbrandsen, Rich Hale, Tim Harbert, John Harris, Roy Helton, Daniel Hernandez, Wm. R. 'Bill' Herndon, Neal A. Hodges, Jerid Johnson, Lawrence Johnson, David Kazsuk, Paul Kelso, Bernie Kerkvliet, Steve Koster, Tom Lewis, Robert Liguori, John Mackie, Bob McCready, Gordon Melin, Jim Merritt, David Moody, Russ Moody, Gerald Morgan, Jeff Morgan, Tim Musselman, Jeff Mutz, Helen Nauert, Aram Nigoghossian, Bruce Oakley, Rich Orton, John Powers, Robert Reid, E.J. Robison, Valente Rosas, Clark Rozas, H.J. Schneider, Laurence Segel, Mikhail Shindel, Sam Silva, Matt Steeneken, Alexander Strickland, Bill Stroman, Reinhardt Swanson, Tony Swatton, Billy Tinkley, Scott Tolman, William Tracy, Bill Traylor, Tru-grit, Mike Tyre, Wayne Watanabe, Martin Wells, Blaine Whitney, Tim Withers, Trent Wong

canadian knifemakers guild

Gaetan Beauchamp, Charles Bennica, Paul Bold, Paolo Brignone, Mark Daley, Jose deBraga, Christoph Deringer, Alain Desaulniers, Rob Douglas, Jason Duclos, James Emmons, Emmanuel Esposito, Paul-Aime Fortier, Rick Frigault, Aaron Gough, Sharla and Shawn Hansen, Wally Hayes, Gil Hibben, Des Horn, Suchat Jangtanong, Nathan Knowles, Kirby Lambert, Stephanie Lemelin, Matthew Lerch, Steve Linklater, Elizabeth Loerchner, Wolfgang Loerchner, David MacDonald, Mike Mossington, William Nease, Rod Olson, Warren Osborne, Simone Raimondi, Steven Rapp, David Riccardo, Murray St. Amour, Paul Savage, Eugene Shadley, John W. Smith, Ken Steigerwalt, Jurgen Steinau, Brian Tighe, Libor Tobolak, Stephen Vanderkolff, Craig Wheatley, Murray White

finnish knifemakers guild

Tõnu Arrak, Andrea Bertini, Ralph Etzold, Jukka Hankala, Pasi Jaakonaho, Arto Liukko, Jari Liukko, Ilari Mehtonen, Denis Mura, Erik Nylund, Jakob Nylund, Simon Nylund, J-T Pälikkö, J-P Peltonen, Anssi Ruusuvuori, Teuvo Sorvari, Tapio Syrjälä, Pekka Tuominen, Rauno Vainionpää, Kay Vikström, Markku Vilppola

florida knifemaker's association

James J. Barry III, Terry Betts, Dennis Blaine, Dennis Blankenhem, Dean Bosworth, W. Lowell Bray Jr., Michael Buell, Patrick Burris, Lowell Cobb, John H. Davis, Jim Elliott, Tom M. Enos, Ernie Grospitch, Larry Hostetler, Joe "Hy" Hytovick, Tom Ivey, Mark James, Richard Johnson, Paul S. Kent, George Lambert, William (Bill) Letcher, Ernie Lyle, Steve Miller, James Mustain, Larry Newton, Dan Piergallini, Marvin Powell, Jr., Carlo Raineri, Roland Robidoux, Ann Sheffield/Sheffield Knifemaker's Supply, Jimmie Smith, Martin Snailgrove, Dale Thomas, John Thorsby, Ralph Turnbull, Louis M. Vallet, Voodoo Daggers, Don Vogt, ned Whitner, Stan Wilson, Denny Young, Maggie Young, Brad Zinker

georgia custom knifemakers' guild

Don R. Adams, Doug Adams, Larry Akins, Adam Andreasen, Joel Atkinson, Paul Brach, Dennis Bradley, Bobby Bragg, Steve Brazeale, Aaron Brewer, Marsha Brewer, Jerry Brinegar, James Brooker, Brian Brown, Mike Brown, Robert Busbee, Jeff Busbie, G.H. Caldwell, Henry Cambron, Rob Carper, Paul Chastain, Frank Chikey, Jim Collins, Jerry Costin, Nola Costin, Scott Davidson, Carol W. Dutton, Dan Eastland, Kerrie Edwards, Emory Fennell, Jarrett Fleming, Dylan Fletcher, Stephan Fowler, Jack Frost, Grady Gentles, Warren Glover, Jim Hamer, George Hancox, Rade Hawkins, Rebecca Hensley, Wayne Hensley, Ronald Hewitt, Kevin Hoffman, Jimmy Kirkland, Christopher Linton, Damon Lusky, Charlie Mathews, Harry Mathews, Vince McDowell, Larry McEachern, Russell McNabb, David McNeal, James Mitchell, Ralph Mitchell, Sandy Morrisey, Daniel Moye, Dan Peters, James Poplin, Joan Poythress, Carey Quinn, Jim Ragsdale, Nathan Raptis, Eddie Ray, Carl Rechsteiner, Adam Reese, David Roberts, Andy Roy, Joe Sangster, Jamey Saunders, Craig Schneeberger, Randy Scott, Ken Simmons, Jim Small, Dave Smith, Johnny Smith, Bill Snow, Luke Snyder, Brian Sorensen, Richard Stafford, Derek Stepp, Allen Suris, Cliff Thrower, Don Tommey, Owen Welch, Alex Whetsel, David White, Gerald White, Michael Wiesner, Chris Wilkes, Mike Wilson, Robert A. Wright, Judy Yoon

kansas custom knifemakers association

Roger Ball, James W. "Jim" Bevan, William Bevan, Gary Bradburn, Claude Campbell, Clint Childers, Roger Craig, Jacob Culver, Steve Culver, Mike Curran, Dave Darpinian, Richard Davis, Dan Dick, Ed Day, Laural "Shorty" Ediger, Jacob Ellis, Phil Evans, Andy Garrett, Jim Glines, Ernie Grospitch, Jim Haller Jr., Jim Haller Sr., Steve Hansen, Billy Helton, Jon Finley, Ross Jagears, Chris Jones, Donald Judd, Carolyn Kaberline, Paul Keranen, Harvey King, Ray Kirk, Doug Klaus, Troy Klaus, Bob Kneisler, Kelly Kneisler, Knives N' Such (Tom and Susie Durham), Tom Lyles, Bill Lyons, Matt Manley, Gilbert Masters, Bruce Miller, Channing "Red" Morford, Joe O'Neill, Dan L. Peterson, Lister Potter, John Sandy, Robert Schornick, M.L. "Pepper" Seaman, Joe Skupa, David Sloane, Eric Showalter, Michael Sparta, Greg Steinert, Douglas Stice, Frank Weiss, Jeff Wells, Kevin Werth, Jim Wharton, Wesley Workman, Roy C. Young III, Tony Zanussi

knife group association of oklahoma

Mike "Whiskers" Allen, Howard Allman, David Anders, Rocky Anderson, Dale Atkerson, Richard Barchenger, Roy Brinsfield, Troy Brown, Tom Buchanan, F. L. Clowdus, Charles Conner, Bill Coye, Gary Crowder, Steve Culver, Marc Cullip, David Darby, Voyne Davis, Dan Dick, Lynn Drury, Bill Duff, Steve Elmenhorst, Beau Erwin, David Etchieson, Harry Fentress, Lee Ferguson, Linda Ferguson, Gary Gloden, Steve Hansen, Paul Happy, Calvin Harkins, Billy Helton, Ed Hites, Tim Johnston, Les Jones, Jim Keen, Bill Kennedy, Stew Killiam, Andy Kirk, Ray Kirk, Nicholas Knack, Jerry Lairson, Sr., Al Lawrence, Ken Linton, Newt Livesay, Ron Lucus, Matt Manley, John

Martin, Jerry McClure, Sandy McClure, Jim McGuinn, Gary McNeill, Rick Menefee, Ben Midgley, Michael E. Miller, Roy Miller, Ray Milligan, Gary Mulkey, Allen Newberry, Jerald Nickels, Jerry Parkhurst, Chris Parson, Larry Parsons, Jerry Paul, Paul Piccola, Cliff Polk, Ron Reeves, Lin Rhea, Gary Robertson, Mike Ruth, Dan Schneringer, Terry Schreiner, Allen Shafer, Shawn Shropshire, Randell Sinnett, Clifford Smith, Doug Sonntag, Michel Sparkman, Perry Stanford, Jeremy Steely, Douglas Stice, Mike Stott, Michael Tarango, Don Thompson, Brian Tomberlin, Tom Upton, Chuck Ward, Jesse Webb, Jesse Webb, Rob Weber, Joe Wheeler, Bill Wiggins, Joe Wilkie, Daniel Zvonek

knifemakers' guild of southern africa

Jeff Angelo, John Arnold, George Baartman, Francois Basson, Rob Bauchop, George Beechey, Arno Bernard, Buzz Bezuidenhout, Harucus Blomerus, Chris Booysen, Thinus Bothma, Ian Bottomley, Peet Bronkhorst, Rob Brown, Fred Burger, Sharon Burger, Trevor Burger, William Burger, Brian Coetzee, Rucus Coetzee, Jack Connan, Larry Connelly, Andre de Beer, André de Villiers, Melodie de Witt, Gavin Dickerson, Roy Dunseith, Johan Ellis, Bart Fanoy, Mike Fellows, Werner Fourie, Andrew Frankland, Brian Geyer, Ettoré Gianferrari, Dale Goldschmidt, Stan Gordon, Nick Grabe, John Grey, Piet Grey, Heather Harvey, Kevin Harvey, Dries Hattingh, Gawie Herbst, Thinus Herbst, Greg Hesslewood, Rupert Holtshausen, Des Horn, Oubaas Jordaan, Nkosilathi Jubane, Billy Kojetin, Mark Kretschmer, Andre Lesch, Steven Lewis, Garry Lombard, Steve Lombard, Ken Madden, Abdur-Rasheed Mahomedy, Peter Mason, Shelley Mason, Francois Massyn, Edward Mitchell, George Muller, Günther Muller, Deon Nel, Tom Nelson, Andries Olivier, Christo Oosthuizen, Johan Oosthuysen, Cedric Pannell, Willie Paulsen, Nico Pelzer, Conrad Pienaar, David Pienaar, Jan Potgieter, Lourens Prinsloo, Theuns Prinsloo, Hilton Purvis, Derek Rausch, Chris Reeve, Martin Reeves, Bertie Rietveld, Melinda Rietveld, Dean Riley, John Robertson, Neels Roos, Corrie Schoeman, Neill Schutte, Eddie Scott, Harvey Silk, Mike Skellern, Toi Skellern, Carel Smith, Stuart Smith, Ken Smythe, Graham Sparks, Kosie Steenkamp, Willem Steenkamp, Peter Steyn, Peter Szkolnik, André Thorburn, Hennie Van Brakel, Fanie Van Der Linde, Johan van der Merwe, Van van der Merwe, Lieben Van Der Sandt, Marius Van der Vyver, Louis Van der Walt, Johann Van Deventer, Cor Van Ellinckhuijzen, Andre van Heerden, Ben Venter, Willie Venter, Gert Vermaak, René Vermeulen, Erich Vosloo, Jan Wahl, Desmond, Waldeck, Albie Wantenaar, Henning Wilkinson, John Wilmot, Wollie Wolfaardt, Owen Wood

montana knifemaker's association

Peter C. Albert, Gordon Alcorn, Chet Allinson, Marvin Allinson, Tim & Sharyl Alverson, Bill Amoureux, Wendell Barnes, Jim & Kay Barth, Bob & Marian Beaty, Donald Bell, Brett Bennett, Raymond Bernier, Bruce Bingenheimer, Robert Bizzell, BladeGallery, Chuck Bragg, Frederick Branch, Peter Bromley, Emil Bucharksky, Thomas and Linda Buckner, Bruce & Kay Bump, Chuck and Brenda Bybee, Jim & Kate Carroll, Rocco Chicarilli & Linda McNeese, Clayton Christofferson, Seth Coughlin, Bob Crowder, John Davis, John Doyal, Rich & Jacque Duxbury, Kevin Easley, Arnold Erhardt, Daniel Erickson, Mel & Darlene Fassio, E.V. Ford, Stephen & Kathy Garger, Chris & Jolene Giarde, Robb & Brandis Gray, Dana & Sandy Hackney, Doc & Lil Hagen, Gary & Betsy Hannon, Tedd Harris, Roger & Diane Hatt, Cal Heinrich, Sam & Joy Hensen, Gerald & Pamela Hintz, Tori Howe, Kevin Hutchins, Karl Jermunson, Keith Johnson, Don Kaschmitter, Steven Kelly, Jay Kemble, Dan & Penny Kendrick, Monte Koppes, Sheridan Lee, David Lisch, James Luman, Robert Martin, Neil McKee, Larry McLaughlin, Mac & Nancy McLaughlin, Phillip Moen, Daniel O'Malley, Tim Olds, Joe Olson, Collin Paterson, James Petri, Tim & Becca Pierce, Riley Pitchford, James Poling, Richard Prusz, Greg Rabatin, Jim Raymond, Darren Reeves, Tom Rickard and Cathy Capps, Ryan Robison, Ruana Knifeworks, Dean Schroeder, Rachel Slade, Gordon St. Clair, Terry Steigers, George Stemple, Dan & Judy Stucky, Art & Linda Swyhart, Jim Thill, James & Sharon Thompson, Dennis & Dora VanDyke, Bill & Lori Waldrup, Jonathan & Doris Walther, Michael Wattelet, Gerome & Darlene Weinand, Walter Wengrzynek, Daniel & Donna Westlind, Richard Wheeler, Sheldon & Edna Wickersham, Dave Wilkes, Randy Williams, R.W. Wilson, Mike & Seana Young

new england bladesmiths guild

Rick Barrett, Kevin Cashen, Mike Davis, Don Fogg, Burt Foster, Ric Furrer, Brian Lyttle, Bill McGrath, W.D. Pease, Jake Powning, Jim Siska, Tim Zowada

north carolina custom knifemakers' guild

Joe Aker, Dr. James Batson, Wayne Bernauer, Tom Beverly, William "Bill" Bisher, Jamin Brackett, William P. Brixon, Jr., Mark Carey, Barry Clodfelter, Travis Daniel, David Diggs, Jeffrey W. Foster, Jimmy Freeman, Russell Gardner, Anthony Griffin, Ken Hall, Mark Hall, Ed Halligan, Koji Hara, John

B. Hege, Lian Hoffman, Terrill Hoffman, Jesse Houser, B.R. Hughes, Dan Johnson, Tommy Johnson, Barry and Phillip Jones, Frank Joyce, Jake Kirks, Michael Lamb, Dr. Jim Lucie, Robert Luck, Stuart Maynard, Scott McGhee, Arthur McNeil, Carl Mickey Jr., William Morris, Randy Nance, Ron Newton, Victor L. Odom Jr., J.D. Palmer Jr., Howard Peacock, Daniel Pica, James Poplin, Murphy Ragsdale, Steve Randall, Bruce Ryan, Joel Sandifer, Tim Scholl, Andy Sharpe, William Shoaf, Harland Simmons, Jeff Simmons, Darrin Sirois, Gene Smith, Charles E. Staples Jr., Murray Sterling, Arthur Summers, Russell Sutton, Jed Taylor, Bruce Turner, Ed & Tanya Van Hoy, Christopher M. Williams, Michael Wilson, Daniel Winkler.

ohio knifemakers association

Raymond Babcock, Van Barnett, Steve Bottorff, Harold A. Collins, Larry Detty, Tom Downing, Jim Downs, Patty Ferrier, Jeff Flannery, James Fray, Bob Foster, Raymond Guess, Scott Hamrie, Rick Hinderer, Curtis Hurley, Ed Kalfayan, Michael Koval, Judy Koval, Gene Loro, Larry Lunn, Stanley Maienknecht, Dave Marlott, Mike Mercer, David Morton, Patrick McGroder, Charles Pratt, Darrel Ralph, Roy Roddy, Michael Sheppard, Carroll Shoemaker, Clifton Smith, Jerry Smith, John Smith, Art Summers, Jan Summers, Donald Tess, Dale Warther, John Wallingford, Earl Witsaman, Joanne Yurco, Mike Yurco

saskatchewan knifemakers guild

Dennis Allenback, Vern Alton, David Beck, Marty Beets, Dan Bowers, Clarence Broeksma, Irv Brunas, Emil Bucharsky, Jim Clow, Murray Cook, Don Crane, Jonathan Crane, Bob Crowder, Jim Dahlin, Cole Dale, Kim Davis, Kevin Donald, Jordan Doucette, Brian Drayton, Ray Fehler, Cal Ganshorn, Kaila Garchinski, Brandon Gray, Gary Greer, Wayne Hamilton, Kent Hanmer, Diane and Roger Hatt, Robert Hazell, Garth Hindmarch, Rolf Holzkaemper, Chris Johnson, Rod Johnson, Cliff Kaufmann, Donald Kreuger, Nathan Kunkel, Paul Laronge, Bryan Lipp, Jared Longard, Pat Macnamara, Chris Mathie, Len Meeres, Brian Mercer, Cory Miller, Robert Minnes, Ralph Mitton, Ron Nelson, Morris Nesdole, Ben Parry, Blaine Parry, Greg Penner, John Perron, Gary D. Peterson, Barry Popick, Jim Quickfall, Rob Robson, Pat de la Sablonniere, Robert Sainsbury, Kim Senft, Bob Serban, Carter Smyth, Don Spasoff, Ed Storch, Jim Takenaka, Isaac Tamlin, Tim Vanderwekken, Jay West, Merle Williams

south carolina association of knifemakers

Douglas Bailey, Ken Black, Dick Brainard, Bobby Branton, Richard Bridwell, Dan Cannady, Rodger Casey, Robert L. Davis, Geno Denning, Charlie Douan, Eddy T. Elsmore, Robert D. Estabrook, Lewis A. Fowler, Jim Frazier, Wayne Hendrix, T.J. Hucks, Johnny Johnson, Lonnie Jones, John Keaton, Col. Thomas Kreger, Gene Langley, David Manley, C.R. Miles, Gene Miller, Barry L. Myers, Paul G. Nystrom, Lee O'Quinn, Victor Odom Jr., Larry Page, Johnny L. Perry, James Rabb, Ricky Rankin, Jerry Riddle, Rick Rockwood, John Sarratt, Ralph L. Smith, David Stroud, Rocky Thomas, Justin Walker, Mickey Walker, H. Syd Willis Jr.

texas knifemakers' guild

Earl Adair, Jose Aguirre, Spencer Alpin, Lisa Aplin, Jayson Bartley, Bryan Borton, David Bryson, Rusty Bryson, Robert Cabrera, Dennis Clark, Chad Cunningham, Kevin Currington, Andrew Dear, Jacob DeBaud, Gary Dick, Edwin Eppenauer, Rocky Fivecoat, Burt Flanagan, Travis Fleming, Jason Fry, Travis Fry, Vincent Garcetti, Matthew Gaskill, Andrew Griggs, Lee Haag, Jeff Harrigan, Mike Harrigan, Guy Harris, Robert Harvey, Charles Hawkins, Troy Hawley, Jamie Herring, Valerie Hibbard, James Hobbs, Nick Huff, Raymond Hunt, James Huse, James Ivy, Bob Jankowski, Merrit Kendall, David Killingsworth, Robbie Killingsworth, Tommy Killingsworth, Tim Lambkin, Gary Langley, Ken Linton, Jim Martin, Brian McFarland, Jim McGuinn, Joe McNeely, Robert Merz, Don Metcalf, Brett Noake, Brandt Noel, Larry Nye, Daniel O'Connor, Jerry Othala, Ronnie Packard, David Patterson, Travis Payne, Jeffrey, Petzke, Gary Powell, Rick Richardson, J.D. Roach, Don Shipman, John Shore, Clint Smith, Johnny Stout, Anthony Stovall, Robert Sweisthal, Crystal Taylor, Tim Tellander, Adam White, Dale White, Steve White, Jason Wilder, Dustin Williams, Byron Witty, Tommy Wright

western canada knife association

Shane Alexander, Dennis Allenback, Neil Ashworth, Ardvan Austin, Jesse Bartram, Chris Bayley, Nathan and Lucas Beaudin, Bob and Liana Bellavance, Clare Broeksma, Irv Brunas, Emil Bucharsky, Bob Campenot, Jim, Bev, Joelle and Danielle Clow, Joseph Richard Paul Comeau, Del Corsi, Bruce Culberson, Edmund and Cheryl Davidson, Alex De Gagne, David Dextraze, Tyson Duffett, John Dziadyk, Black Ellis, Darcy Ellis, Gary Fedick, Al Fodchuk, Brian Fleury, Dave and Betty Gibbs, Darby Grady, Ryan Grottolo,

Dana and Sandy Hackney, Glen Hamilton, Wayne Hamilton, Cecil and Vi Harder, Ken Harding, David E. Hardy, Roger and Diane Hatt, Cal Heinrich, Garth Hindmarch, Kirk, Cheryl, Tom and Bailey May Hobbs, Carson House, William (Bill) R. Housden, Kaj Jacobsen, Jay and Maureen Kemble, Gerry Kievit, Doug Kirkness, Chris Kluftinger, Edward Kuznetov, Elinor Layden, Shea Layden, Jason and Kim Leclair, Terry and Carol Lee, Andrey Levin, Knut and Kyle Lie, Greg Lightfoot, Mel Long, Vernon Roy and Susan Lynes, Terry Mah, Dan Malinowski, Jared Manchester, Murray S. Matthews, Dion Meadows, Bill Missen, Harald Moeller, Terry, Tyler and Eric Monteith, Allen and Susan Neal, Ron and Linda Nelson, Tor and Erik Nenzen, Morris and

Nancy Nesdole, Rod and Wes Nielsen, Frank and Peggy Niro, Rod Olson, Dennis Paish, Ray Philpott, Lee Pierobon, Mike and Evelyn Pisio, Elliott, Jessica, and Olivia Reiter, Randolph and Rhonda Reiter, Matt Rehman, Rob and Marilyn Ridley, George Roberts, Bob Sainsbury, Andrew Samek, Jim and Deb Sandin, Allan Sinclair, Mike Stafford, Chuck and Anne Stancer, Don Stevenson, Ed Storch, Larry and Susan Strandquist, Jim Takenaka, Russell Thornberry, Bob Turner, Ron Twa, Tim Vanderwekken, Scott Van Scheik, Alexander Vasylkiewicz, Roderick Wacker, Walter Wenzl, Jay and Darlene West, Bill and Rita Wiebe, Harry Wilnechenko, Roy Wirtanen, Ryan, Amber, Evan and Brycen Wood, Laurie Yeadell

photo index

The firms listed here are special in the sense that they make or market special kinds of knives made in facilities they own or control either in the U.S. or overseas. Or they are special because they make knives of unique design or function. The second phone number listed is the fax number.

sporting cutlers

A.G. RUSSELL KNIVES INC
2900 S. 26th St
Rogers, AR 72758-8571
800-255-9034
fax 479-631-8493
ag@agrussell.com; www.agrussell.com
The oldest knife mail-order company, highest quality. Free catalog available. In these catalogs you will find the newest and the best. If you like knives, this catalog is a must

AL MAR KNIVES
PO Box 2295
Tualatin, OR 97062-2295
503-670-9080; fax 503-639-4789
info@almarknives.com;
www.almarknives.com
Featuring our Ultralight™ series of knives. Sere 2000™ Shrike, Sere™, Operator™, Nomad™ and Ultralight series™

ATLANTA CUTLERY CORP.
2147 Gees Mill Rd., Box 839
Conyers, GA 30013
770-922-7500; fax 770-918-2026
custserv@atlantacutlery.com;
www.atlantacutlery.com
Outdoor sporting and hunting knives, mail order

BARK RIVER KNIVES
6911 County Road 426 M.5 Road
Escanaba, MI 49829
906-789-1801
jacquie@barkriverknives.com
www.barkriverknifetool.com
Family-owned business producing bushcraft, hunting, Canadian, deluxe game, professional guide, search & rescue and EDC knives

BEAR & SON CUTLERY, INC.
111 Bear Blvd. SW
Jacksonville, AL 36265
256-435-2227; fax 256-435-9348
www.bearandsoncutlery.com
Bear Jaws®, three sizes of multi-tools, cutlery, hunting and pocketknives in traditional and innovative patterns and designs

BECK'S CUTLERY & SPECIALTIES
51 Highland Trace Ln.
Benson, NC 27504
919-902-9416
beckscutlery@embarqmail.com;
www.beckscutlery.com

BENCHMADE KNIFE CO. INC.
300 Beavercreek Rd
Oregon City, OR 97045
800-800-7427
info@benchmade.com;
www.benchmade.com
Sports, utility, law enforcement, military, gift and semi custom

BERETTA U.S.A. CORP.
17601 Beretta Dr.
Accokeek, MD 20607
301-283-2191
www.berettausa.com
Full range of hunting & specialty knives

BLACKHAWK PRODUCTS GROUP
6160 Commander Pkwy.
Norfolk, VA 23502
757-436-3101; fax 757-436-3088
cs@blackhawk.com
www.blackhawk.com
Leading manufacturer of tactical sheaths and knives

BLADE-TECH INDUSTRIES
5530 184th St. E, Ste. A
Puyallup, WA 98375
253-655-8059; fax 253-655-8066
tim@blade-tech.com
www.blade-tech.com

BLUE GRASS CUTLERY, INC.
20 E Seventh St, PO Box 156
Manchester, OH 45144
937-549-2602; 937-549-2709 or 2603
sales@bluegrasscutlery.com;
www.bluegrasscutlery.com
Manufacturer of Winchester Knives, John Primble Knives and many contract lines

BOKER USA INC
1550 Balsam St.
Lakewood, CO 80214-5917
800-992-6537; 303-462-0668
sales@bokerusa.com; www.bokerusa.com
Wide range of fixed-blade and folding knives for hunting, military, tactical and general use

BROUS BLADES
POB 550
Buellton, CA 93427
805-717-7192
contact@brousblades.com
www.brousblades.com
Custom and semi-custom knives

BROWNING
One Browning Place
Morgan, UT 84050
800-333-3504; Customer Service:
801-876-2711 or 800-333-3288
www.browning.com
Outdoor hunting & shooting products

BUCK KNIVES INC.
660 S Lochsa St
Post Falls, ID 83854-5200
800-326-2825; Fax: 800-733-2825
www.buckknives.com
Sports cutlery

BULLDOG BRAND KNIVES
P.O. Box 23852
Chattanooga, TN 37422
423-894-5102; fax 423-892-9165
Fixed blade and folding knives for hunting and general use

BUSSE COMBAT KNIFE CO.
11651 Co Rd 12
Wauseon, OH 43567
419-923-6471; 419-923-2337
www.bussecombat.com
Simple & very strong straight knife designs for tactical & expedition use

CAMILLUS C/O ACME UNITED CORP.
60 Round Hill Rd.
Fairfield, CT 06824
800-835-2263
orders@shopatron.com
www.camillusknives.com

CANAL STREET CUTLERY
30 Canal St.
Ellenville, NY 12428
845-647-5900
info@canalstreetcutlery.com
www.canalstreetcutlery.com
Manufacturers of pocket and hunting knives finished to heirloom quality

CAS IBERIA
650 Industrial Blvd
Sale Creek, TN 37373
800-635-9366
www.casiberia.com
Extensive variety of fixed-blade and folding knives for hunting, diving, camping, military and general use. Japanese swords and European knives

CASE, W.R. & SONS CUTLERY CO.
50 Owens Way
Bradford, PA 16701
800-523-6350; Fax: 814-368-1736
consumer-relations@wrcase.com
www.wrcase.com
Folding pocket knives

CHRIS REEVE KNIVES
2949 S. Victory View Way
Boise, ID 83709-2946
208-375-0367; Fax: 208-375-0368
crkinfo@chrisreeve.com;
www.chrisreeve.com
Makers of the Sebenza, Umnumzaan and Mnandi folding knives, the legendary Green Beret knife and other military knives

COAST CUTLERY CO
8033 N.E. Holman
Portland, OR 97218
800-426-5858; Fax: 503-234-4422
www.coastportland.com
Variety of fixed-blade and folding knives and multi-tools for hunting, camping and general use

COLD STEEL INC
6060 Nicolle St.
Ventura, CA 93003
800-255-4716 or 805-642-9727
sales@coldsteel.com
www.coldsteel.com
Wide variety of folding lockbacks and fixed-blade hunting, fishing and neck knives, as well as bowies, kukris, tantos, throwing knives, kitchen knives and swords

COLONIAL KNIFE, A DIVISION OF COLONIAL CUTLERY INT.
61 Dewey Ave.
Warwick, RI 02886
401-421-6500; Fax: 401-737-0054
stevep@colonialknifecorp.com
www.colonialknifecorp.com
Collectors edition specialty knives. Special promotions.

Old cutler, barion, trappers, military knives. Industrial knives-electrician.

CONDOR™ TOOL & KNIFE
7557 W. Sand Lake Rd., #106
Orlando, FL 32819
407-354-3488; Fax: 407-354-3489
rtj2@att.net; www.condortk.com

COLTELLERIE MASERIN SNC
Via Dei Fabbri n.19
33085 MANIAGO (PN)– ITALY
tel. +39 0427 71335
fax +39 0427 700 690
info@maserin.com
www.maserin.com
Gentlemen's knives, and high-tech, hunting, classic, outdoor, military, rescue, kitchen and sommelier models

CRAWFORD KNIVES, LLC
205 N Center
West Memphis, AR 72301
870-732-2452
www.crawfordknives.com
Folding knives for tactical and general use

CRKT
18348 SW 126th Place
Tualatin, OR 97062
800-891-3100; fax 503-682-9680
info@crkt.com; www.crkt.com
Complete line of sport, work and tactical knives

CUTCO CORPORATION
1116 E. State St.
Olean, NY 14760
716-372-3111
www.cutco.com
Household cutlery / sport knives

DPX GEAR INC.
2321 Kettner Blvd.
San Diego, CA 92101
619-780-2600; fax: 619-780-2605
www.dpxgear.com
Hostile environment survival knives and tools

EMERSON KNIVES, INC.
1234 254th St.
Harbor City, CA 90710
310-539-5633; fax: 310-539-5609
www.emersonknives.com
Hard use tactical knives; folding & fixed blades

ESEE KNIVES
POB 99
Gallant, AL 35972
256-613-0372
www.eseeknives.com
Survival and tactical knives

EXTREMA RATIO
Mauro Chiostri/Maurizio Castrati
Via Tourcoing 40/p
Prato (PO) 59100
ITALY
0039 0576 584639; fax: 0039 0576 584312
info@extremaratio.com
Tactical/military knives and sheaths, blades and sheaths to customers specs

FALLKNIVEN
Granatvägen 8
S-961 43 Boden
SWEDEN
46-(0)-921 544 22; Fax: 46-(0)-921 544 33
info@fallkniven.se; www.fallkniven.com
High quality stainless knives

FAMARS USA
2091 Nooseneck Hill Rd., Ste. 200
Coventry, RI 02816
855-FAMARS1 (326-2771)
www.famarsusa.com
FAMARS has been building guns for over 50 years. Known for innovative design, quality and craftsmanship. New lines of gentleman's knives, tactical fixed blades and folders, hunters and utility pieces.

FOX KNIVES USA
9918 162nd St. Ct. E, Ste. 14
Puyallup, WA 98375
303-263-2468
www.foxknivesusa.com
Designer, manufacturer and distributor of high-quality cutlery

FROST CUTLERY CO
PO Box 22636
Chattanooga, TN 37422
800-251-7768
www.frostcutlery.com
Wide range of fixed-blade and folding knives with a multitude of handle materials

GATCO SHARPENERS/TIMBERLINE
PO Box 600
Getzville, NY 14068
716-646-5700; fax: 716-646-5775
gatco@gatcosharpeners.com;
www.gatcosharpeners.com
Manufacturer of the GATCO brand of knife sharpeners and Timberline brand of knives

GERBER LEGENDARY BLADES
14200 SW 72nd Ave
Portland, OR 97223
503-403-1143; fax: 307-857-4702
www.gerbergear.com
Knives, multi-tools, axes, saws, outdoor products

GINSU/DOUGLAS QUIKUT
118 E. Douglas Rd.
Walnut Ridge, AR 72476
800-982-5233; fax: 870-886-9162
www.douglasquikut.com
Household cutlery

GROHMANN KNIVES
PO Box 40
116 Water St
Pictou, Nova Scotia B0K 1H0
CANADA
888-7KNIVES; Fax: 902-485-5872
www.grohmannknives.com
Fixed-blade belt knives for hunting and fishing, folding pocketknives for hunting and general use. Household cutlery.

H&B FORGE CO.
235 Geisinger Rd
Shiloh, OH 44878
419-895-1856
www.hbforge.com
Special order throwing knives and tomahawks, camp stoves, muzzleloading accroutements

HALLMARK CUTLERY
POB 220
Kodak, TN 37764
866-583-3912; fax: 901-405-0948
www.hallmarkcutlery.com
Traditional folders, tactical folders and fixed blades, multi-tools, shotgun shell knives, Bad Blood, Robert Klaas and Chief brand knives, and Super Premium care products

HISTORIC EDGED WEAPONRY
1021 Saddlebrook Dr
Hendersonville, NC 28739
828-692-0323; fax: 828-692-0600
histwpn@bellsouth.net
Antique knives from around the world; importer of puukko and other knives from Norway, Sweden, Finland and Lapland; also edged weaponry book "Travels for Daggers" by Eiler R. Cook

JOY ENTERPRISES-FURY CUTLERY
Port Commerce Center III
1862 M.L. King Jr. Blvd
Riviera Beach, FL 33404
800-500-3879; fax: 561-863-3277
mail@joyenterprises.com;
www.joyenterprises.com;
www.furycutlery.com
Fury™ Mustang™ extensive variety of fixed-blade and folding knives for hunting, fishing, diving, camping, military and general use; novelty key-ring knives. Muela Sporting Knives. Fury Tactical, Muela of Spain, Mustang Outdoor Adventure

KA-BAR KNIVES INC
200 Homer St
Olean, NY 14760
800-282-0130; fax: 716-790-7188
info@ka-bar.com; www.ka-bar.com *Manufacturer of law enforcement, military, hunting and outdoor knives*

KAI USA LTD.
18600 S.W. Teton Ave.
Tualatin, OR 97062
800-325-2891; fax 503-682-7168
info@kai-usa.com
www.kershawknives.com
Manufacturer of high-quality, lifetime-guaranteed knives. Kai USA brands include Kershaw Knives for everyday carrying, hunting, fishing and other outdoor use; Zero Tolerance Knives for professional use; and Shun Cutlery, providing premium-quality kitchen knives

KATZ KNIVES, INC.
10924 Mukilteo Speedway #287
Mukilteo, WA 98275
480-786-9334; fax 460-786-9338
katzkn@aol.com; www.katzknives.com

KELLAM KNIVES WORLDWIDE
P.O. Box 3438
Lantana, FL 33465
800-390-6918
info@kellamknives.com;
www.kellamknives.com
Largest selection of Finnish knives, handmade and production

KLOTZLI (MESSER KLOTZLI)
Hohengasse 3 CH 3400
Burgdorf
SWITZERLAND
41-(34)-422-23 78
info@klotzli.com; www.klotzli.com
High-tech folding knives for tactical and general use

KNIGHTS EDGE LTD.
5696 N. Northwest Highway
Chicago, IL 60646-6136
773-775-3888; fax 773-775-3339
sales@knightsedge.com;
www.knightsedge.com
Medieval weaponry, swords, suits of armor, katanas, daggers

KNIVES OF ALASKA, INC.
Charles or Jody Allen
3100 Airport Dr
Denison, TX 75020
903-786-7366; fax 903-786-7371
info@knivesofalaska.com;
www.knivesofalaska.com
High quality hunting & outdoorsmen's knives

KNIVES PLUS
2467 Interstate 40 West
Amarillo, TX 79109
800-359-6202
www.knivesplus.com
Retail cutlery and cutlery accessories since 1987; free catalog available

LANSKY KNIFE, TOOL & SHARPENERS
POB 800
Buffalo, NY 14231
716-877-7511; fax 716-877-6955
cfire@lansky.com
www.lansky.com
Knives, multi-tools, survival axes, sharpeners

LEATHERMAN TOOL GROUP, INC.
12106 N.E. Ainsworth Cir.
Portland, OR 97220-0595
800-847-8665; fax 503-253-7830
info@leatherman.com;
www.leatherman.com
Multi-tools

LONE STAR WHOLESALE
2401 Interstate 40 W
Amarillo, TX 79109
806-836-9540; fax 806-359-1603
sales@lswtexas.com
www.lswtexas.com
Great prices, dealers only, most major brands

MANTIS KNIVES
520 Cameron St.
Placentia, CA 92870
714-996-9673
gwest@mantis.bz
www.mantisknives.com
Manufacturer of utility, karambit, fixed and folding blades, and Neccessikeys

MARBLE ARMS C/O BLUE RIDGE KNIVES
166 Adwolfe Rd.
Marion, VA 24354-6664
276-783-6143
onestop@blueridgeknives.com
www.blueridgeknives.com

MASTER CUTLERY INC
700 Penhorn Ave
Secaucus, NJ 07094
888-227-7229; fax 888-271-7228
www.mastercutlery.com
Largest variety in the knife industry

MEYERCO USA
4481 Exchange Service Dr.
Dallas, TX 75236
214-467-8949; fax 214-467-9241
www.meyercousa.com
Folding tactical,rescue and speed-assisted pocketknives; fixed-blade hunting and fishing designs; multi-function camping tools and machetes

MICROTECH KNIVES
300 Chestnut Street Ext.
Bradford, PA 16701
814-363-9260; Fax: 814-363-9030
info@microtechknives.com

www.microtechknives.com
Manufacturers of the highest quality production knives

MISSION KNIVES
13771 Newhope St.
Garden Grove, CA 92843
714-638-4692; fax 714-638-4621
info@missionknives.com
www.missionknives.com
Manufacturer of titanium and steel knives and tools with over 20 years in business. Tactical, combat, military, law enforcement, EOD units, survivalist, diving, recreational straight blades, folding blades and mine probes, and more.

MOKI KNIFE COMPANY LTD.
15 Higashisenbo
Seki City GIFU
Pref JAPAN
575-22-4185; fax 575-24-5306
information@moki.co.jp
www.moki.co.jp
Pocketknives, folders, fixed-blade knives and gent's knives

MUSEUM REPLICAS LTD.
P.O. Box 840, 2147 Gees Mill Rd
Conyers, GA 30012
800-883-8838; fax: 770-388-0246
www.museumreplicas.com
Historically accurate and battle-ready swords and daggers

NEMESIS KNIVES, LLC
179 Niblick Rd., #180
Paso Robles, CA 93446
562-594-4740
info@nemesis-knives.com
www.nemesis-knives.com
Semi-custom and production kinves

ONTARIO KNIFE CO.
26 Empire St.
Franklinville, NY 14737
800-222-5233; fax 716-676-5535
knifesales@ontarioknife.com
www.ontarioknife.com
Fixed blades, tactical folders, military and hunting knives, machetes

OUTDOOR EDGE CUTLERY CORP.
9500 W. 49th Ave., #A-100
Wheat Ridge, CO 80033
800-447-3343; 303-530-7667
moreinfo@outdooredge.com;
www.outdooredge.com

PACIFIC SOLUTION MARKETING, INC.
1220 E. Belmont St.
Ontario, CA 91761
Tel: 877-810-4643
Fax: 909-930-5843
sales@pacificsolution.com
www.pacificsolution.com
Wide range of folding pocket knives, hunting knives, tactical knives, novelty knives, medieval armor and weapons as well as hand forged samurai swords and tantos

PARAGON SPORTS
867 Broadway at 18th St.
New York, NY 10003
800-961-3030 or 212-255-8889
customerservice@paragonsports.com
www.paragonsports.com
Folders, fixed blades, hunters, multi-tools, tool knives, handmade fixed blades and folders from top makers

PRO-TECH KNIVES LLC
17115 Alburtis Ave.
Artesia, CA 90701-2616

562-860-0678
service@protechknives.com
www.protechknives.com
Manufacturer specializing in automatic knives for police, military and discriminating collectors

QUEEN CUTLERY COMPANY
507 Chestnut St.
Titusville, PA 16354
814-827-3673; fax: 814-827-9693
jmoore@queencutlery.com
www.queencutlery.com
Pocketknives, collectibles, Schatt & Morgan, Robeson, club knives

RANDALL MADE KNIVES
4857 South Orange Blossom Trail
Orlando, FL 32839
407-855-8075; fax 407-855-9054
grandall@randallknives.com;
www.randallknives.com
Handmade fixed-blade knives for hunting, fishing, diving, military and general use

REMINGTON ARMS CO., INC.
870 Remington Drive
Madison, NC 27025-0700
800-243-9700
www.remington.com

RUKO LLC.
PO Box 38
Buffalo, NY 14207-0038
800-611-4433; fax 905-826-1353
info@rukoproducts.com
www.rukoproducts.com

SANTA FE STONEWORKS
3790 Cerrillos Rd.
Santa Fe, NM 87507
800-257-7625
knives@rt66.com
www.santafestoneworks.com
Gemstone handles

SARCO KNIVES LLC
449 Lane Dr
Florence AL 35630
256-766-8099; fax 256-766-7246
www.TriEdgeKnife.com
Etching and engraving services, club knives, etc. New knives, antique-collectible knives

SARGE KNIVES
2720 E. Phillips Rd.
Greer, SC 29650
800-454-7448; fax 864-331-0752
cgaines@sargeknives.com
www.sargeknives.com
High-quality, affordable pocketknives, hunting, fishing, camping and tactical. Custom engraving for promotional knives or personalized gifts

SOG SPECIALTY KNIVES & TOOLS, INC.
6521 212th St SW
Lynnwood, WA 98036
425-771-6230; fax 425-771-7689
sogsales@sogknives.com
www.sogknives.com
SOG assisted technology, Arc-Lock, folding knives, specialized fixed blades, multi-tools

SPARTAN BLADES, LLC
625 S.E. Service Rd.
Southern Pines, NC 28387
910-757-0035
contact@spartanbladesusa.com
www.spartanbladesusa.com
Tactical, combat, fighter, survival and field knives

SPYDERCO, INC.
820 Spyderco Way
Golden, CO 80403
800-525-7770; fax 303-278-2229
sales@spyderco.com
www.spyderco.com
Knives, sharpeners and accessories

STONE RIVER GEAR
75 Manor Rd.
Red Hook, NY 12571
203-470-2526; fax 866-258-7202
info@stonerivergear.com
www.stonerivergear.com
Fighters, tactical, survival and military knives, household cutlery, hunting knives, pocketknives, folders and utility tools

SWISS ARMY BRANDS INC.
15 Corporate Dr.
Orangeburg, NY 10962
800-431-2994
customer.service@swissarmy.com
www.swissarmy.com
Folding multi-blade designs and multi-tools for hunting, fishing, camping, hiking, golfing and general use. One of the original brands (Victorinox) of Swiss Army Knives

TAYLOR BRANDS LLC
1043 Fordtown Road
Kingsport, TN 37663
800-251-0254; fax 423-247-5371
info@taylorbrandsllc.com
www.taylorbrandsllc.com
Smith & Wesson Knives, Old Timer, Uncle Henry and Schrade.

TIMBERLINE KNIVES
7223 Boston State Rd.
Boston, NY 14075
800-liv-sharp; fax 716-646-5775
www.timberlineknives.com
High technology production knives for professionals, sporting, tradesmen and kitchen use

TRU-BALANCE KNIFE CO. EAST
PO Box 807
Awendaw, SC 29429
843-928-3624
Manufacturing and sale of throwing knives

UNITED CUTLERY
475 U.S. Hwy. 319 S
Moultrie, GA 31768
800-548-0835; fax 229-551-0182
customerservice@unitedcutlery.com
www.unitedcutlery.com
Wholesale only; pocket, sportsman knives, licensed movie knives, swords, exclusive brands

WILLIAM HENRY STUDIO
3200 NE Rivergate St
McMinnville, OR 97128
503-434-9700; Fax: 503-434-9704
www.williamhenry.com
Semi-production, handmade knives

WUU JAU CO. INC
2600 S Kelly Ave
Edmond, OK 73013
405-359-5031; fax 405-340-5965
mail@wuujau.com; www.wuujau.com
Wide variety of imported fixed-blade and folding knives for hunting, fishing, camping and general use. Wholesale to knife dealers only

XIKAR INC
3305 Terrace, PO Box 025757
Kansas City MO 64111-3637
888-266-1193; fax 917-464-6398
info@xikar.com; www.xikar.com
Gentlemen's cutlery and accessories

importers

A.G. RUSSELL KNIVES INC
2900 S. 26th St.
Rogers, AR 72758-8571
800-255-9034
fax 479-631-8493
ag@agrussell.com; www.agrussell.com
The oldest knife mail-order company, highest quality. Free catalog available. In these catalogs you will find the newest and the best. If you like knives, this catalog is a must. Celebrating over 40 years in the industry

ADAMS INTERNATIONAL KNIFEWORKS
8710 Rosewood Hills
Edwardsville, IL 62025
Importers & foreign cutlers

ATLANTA CUTLERY CORP.
P.O.Box 839
Conyers, Ga 30012
770-922-7500; Fax: 770-918-2026
custserve@atlantacutlery.com;
www.atlantacutlery.com
Exotic knives from around the world

BAILEY'S
PO Box 550
Laytonville, CA 95454
800-322-4539; 707-984-8115
baileys@baileys-online.com;
www.baileys-online.com

BELTRAME, FRANCESCO
Fratelli Beltrame F&C snc Via dei Fabbri 15/B-33085 MANIAGO (PN)
ITALY
39 0427 701859
www.italianstiletto.com

BOKER USA, INC.
1550 Balsam St
Lakewood, CO 80214-5917
800-992-6537; 303-462-0668
sales@bokerusa.com; www.bokerusa.com
Ceramic blades

CAMPOS, IVAN DE ALMEIDA
R. Stelio M. Loureiro, 205
Centro, Tatui
BRAZIL
00-55-15-33056867
www.ivancampos.net

C.A.S. IBERIA
650 Industrial Blvd
Sale Creek, TN 37373
800-635-9366; fax 423-332-7248
mhillian@casiberia.com; www.casiberia.com

CATOCTIN CUTLERY
PO Box 188
Smithsburg, MD 21783

CLASSIC INDUSTRIES
1325 Howard Ave, Suite 408
Burlingame, CA 94010

COAST CUTLERY CO.
8033 N.E. Holman
Portland, OR 97218
800-426-5858
staff@coastcutlery.com;
www.coastcutlery.com

COLUMBIA PRODUCTS CO.
PO Box 1333
Sialkot 51310
PAKISTAN

COLUMBIA PRODUCTS INT'L
PO Box 8243
New York, NY 10116-8243
201-854-3054; Fax: 201-854-7058
nycolumbia@aol.com; http://www.
columbiaproducts.homestead.com/cat.html
Pocket, hunting knives and swords of all kinds

COMPASS INDUSTRIES, INC.
104 E. 25th St
New York, NY 10010
800-221-9904; Fax: 212-353-0826
jeff@compassindustries.com;
www.compassindustries.com
Imported pocket knives

CONAZ COLTELLERIE
American Office
4179 Cristal Lake Dr.
Deerfield Beach, FL 33064
561-809-9701 or 754-423-3356
Fax: 954-781-3693
susanna@consigliscarperia.com;
www.consigliscarperia.it
Handicraft workmanship of knives of the ancient Italian tradition. Historical and collection knives

CONSOLIDATED CUTLERY CO., INC.
696 NW Sharpe St
Port St. Lucie, FL 34983
772-878-6139

CRAZY CROW TRADING POST
PO Box 847
Pottsboro, TX 75076
800-786-6210; Fax: 903-786-9059
info@crazycrow.com; www.crazycrow.com
Solingen blades, knife making parts & supplies

DER FLEISSIGEN BEAVER
(The Busy Beaver)
Harvey Silk
PO Box 1166
64343 Griesheim
GERMANY
49 61552231; 49 6155 2433
Der.Biber@t-online.de
Retail custom knives. Knife shows in Germany & UK

EXTREMA RATIO
Mauro Chiostri; Mavrizio Castrati
Via Tourcoing 40/p
59100 Prato (PO)
ITALY
0039 0576 58 4639; fax 0039 0576 584312
info@extremaratio.com;

www.extremaratio.com
Tactical & military knives manufacturing

FALLKNIVEN
Granatvagen 8
S-961 43 Boden
SWEDEN
+46 (0) 921 544 22; fax +46 (0) 921 544 33
info@fallkniven.se
www.fallkniven.com
High quality knives

FREDIANI COLTELLI FINLANDESI
Via Lago Maggiore 41
I-21038 Leggiuno
ITALY

GIESSER MESSERFABRIK GMBH, JOHANNES
Raiffeisenstr 15
D-71349 Winnenden
GERMANY
49-7195-1808-29
info@giesser.de; www.giesser.de
Professional butchers and chef's knives

HIMALAYAN IMPORTS
3495 Lakeside Dr
Reno, NV 89509
775-825-2279
unclebill@himalayan-imports.com; www.
himilayan-imports.com

IVAN DE ALMEIDA CAMPOS-KNIFE DEALER
R. Xi De Agosto
107, Centro, Tatui, Sp 18270
BRAZIL
55-15-251-8092; 55-15-251-4896
campos@bitweb.com.br
Custom knives from all Brazilian knifemakers

JOY ENTERPRISES
1862 Martin Luther King Jr. Blvd.
Riviera Beach, FL 33404
561-863-3205; fax 561-863-3277
mail@joyenterprises.com;
www.joyenterprises.com
Fury™, Mustang™, Hawg Knives, Muela

KELLAM KNIVES WORLDWIDE
POB 3438
Lantana, FL 33465
561-588-3185 or 800-390-6918
info@kellamknives.com;
www.kellamknives.com
Knives from Finland; own line of knives

KNIFE IMPORTERS, INC.
11307 Conroy Ln
Manchaca, TX 78652
512-282-6860, Fax: 512-282-7504
Wholesale only

KNIGHTS EDGE LTD.
5696 N Northwest Hwy
Chicago, IL 60646
773-775-3888; fax 773-775-3339
www.knightsedge.com
Exclusive designers of our Rittersteel, Stagesteel and Valiant Arms and knightedge lines of weapon

LEISURE PRODUCTS CORP.
PO Box 1171
Sialkot-51310
PAKISTAN

L. C. RISTINEN
Suomi Shop
17533 Co Hwy 38
Frazee MN 56544
218-538-6633; 218-538-6633
icrist@wcta.net
Scandinavian cutlery custom antique, books and reindeer antler

LINDER, CARL NACHF.
Erholungstr. 10
D-42699 Solingen
GERMANY
212 33 0 856; Fax: 212 33 71 04
info@linder.de; www.linder.de

MARTTIINI KNIVES
PO Box 44 (Marttiinintie 3)
96101 Rovaniemi
FINLAND

MATTHEWS CUTLERY
POB 2768
Moultrie, GA 31776
800-251-0123; fax 877-428-3599
www.matthewscutlery.com
Wholesale of major brands

MESSER KLÖTZLI
PO Box 104
Hohengasse 3, 3400 Burgdorf
SWITZERLAND
0041 (0)34 422 23 78; fax 0041 (0)34 422 76 93; info@klotzli.com; www.klotzli.com

MUSEUM REPLICAS LIMITED
2147 Gees Mill Rd
Conyers, GA 30012
800-883-8838; fax 770-388-0246
mrw@museumreplicas.com
www.museumreplicas.com
Subsidiary of Atlanta Cutlery. Battle-ready swords and other historic edged weapons, as well as clothing, jewelry and accessories.

NICHOLS CO.
Pomfret Rd
South Pomfret, VT 05067
Import & distribute knives from EKA (Sweden), Helle (Norway), Brusletto (Norway), Roselli (Finland). Also market Zippo products, Snow, Nealley axes and hatchets and snow & Nealy axes

NORMARK CORP.
Craig Weber
10395 Yellow Circle Dr
Minnetonka, MN 55343

PIELCU
Parque Empresarial Campollano
Avenida 2a Numero 25 (esquina con C/E)
02007 Albacete
SPAIN
+34 967 523 568; fax +34 967 523 569
pielcu@pielcu.com; www.grupopielcu.com
Tactical, outdoor, fantasy and sporting knives

PRODUCTORS AITOR, S.A.
Izelaieta 17
48260 Ermua
SPAIN
943-170850; 943-170001
info@aitor.com
Sporting knives

PROFESSIONAL CUTLERY SERVICES
9712 Washburn Rd
Downey, CA 90241
562-803-8778; 562-803-4261

Wholesale only. Full service distributor of domestic & imported brand name cutlery. Exclusive U.S. importer for both Marto Swords and Battle Ready Valiant Armory edged weapons

SVORD KNIVES
Smith Rd., RD 2
Waiuku, South Auckland
NEW ZEALAND
64 9 2358846; fax 64 9 2356483
www.svord.com

SWISS ARMY BRANDS INC.
15 Corporate Dr.
Orangeburg, NY 10962
800-431-2994 or 914-425-4700
customer.service@swissarmy.com
www.swissarmy.com
Importer and distributor of Victorinox's Swiss Army brand

TAYLOR BRANDS, LLC
1043 Fordtown Road
Kingsport, TN 37663
800-251-0254; fax 423-247-5371
info@taylorbrandsllc.com;
www.taylorbrandsllc.com
Fixed-blade and folding knives for tactical, rescue, hunting and general use. Also provides etching, engraving, scrimshaw services.

UNITED CUTLERY
475 U.S. Hwy. 319 S
Moultrie, GA 31768
800-548-0835 or 229-890-6669; fax 229-551-0182
customerservice@unitedcutlery.com www.unitedcutlery.com
Harley-Davidson ® Colt ® , Stanley ®, U21 ®, Rigid Knives ®, Outdoor Life ®, Ford ®, hunting, camping, fishing, collectible & fantasy knives

U.S. GLADIUS
www.usgladius.com
Knives based on the design of the Roman gladius, the standard arm of the Roman Legions.

VICTORINOX SWISS ARMY, INC.
7 Victoria Dr.
Monroe, CT 06468
203-929-6391
renee.hourigan@swissarmy.com
www.swissarmy.com
Genuine Swiss Army Knives and Swiss Watches

WORLD CLASS EXHIBITION KNIVES
Cary Desmon
941-504-2279
www.withoutequal.com
Carries an extensive line of Pius Lang knives

ZWILLING J.A. HENCKELS LLC
171 Saw Mill River Rd
Hawthorne, NY 10532
914-747-0300; fax 914-747-1850
info@jahenckels.com;
www.jahenckels.com
Zwilling, Henckels International, Miyabi, Staub, Demeyere kitchen cutlery, scissors, shears, gadgets, cookware, flatware

knifemaking supplies

AFRICAN IMPORT CO.
Alan Zanotti
22 Goodwin Rd
Plymouth, MA 02360
508-746-8552; 508-746-0404
africanimport@aol.com
Ivory

ALABAMA DAMASCUS STEEL
PO Box 54
WELLINGTON, AL 36279
256-310-4619 or 256-282-7988
sales@alabamadamascussteel.com
www.alabamadamascussteel.com
We are a manufacturer of damascus steel billets & blades. We also offer knife supplies. We can custom make any blade design that the customer wants. We can also make custom damascus billets per customer specs.

ALASKAN FOSSIL IVORY
Jerry Kochheiser
1109 W. Hanley Rd.
Mansfield, Ohio 44904
419 564 8781
jkochheiser@neo.rr.com
Selling fossil walrus ivory, mammoth ivory, stag tapers, stag scales, oosik and steller sea cow bone

ALPHA KNIFE SUPPLY
425-868-5880; Fax: 425-898-7715
chuck@alphaknifesupply.com;
www.alphaknifesupply.com
Inventory of knife supplies

AMERICAN SIEPMANN CORP.
65 Pixley Industrial Parkway
Rochester, NY 14624
585-247-1640; Fax: 585-247-1883
www.siepmann.com
CNC blade grinding equipment, grinding wheels, production blade grinding services. Sharpening stones and sharpening equipment

ANKROM EXOTICS
Pat Ankrom
306 1/2 N. 12th
Centerville, IA 52544
641-436-0235
ankromexotics@hotmail.com
www.ankromexotics.com
Stabilized handle material; Exotic burls and hardwoods from around the world; Stabilizing services available

ATLANTA CUTLERY CORP.
P.O.Box 839
Conyers, Ga 30012
770-922-7500; Fax: 770-918-2026
custserve@atlantacutlery.com;
www.atlantacutlery.com

BLADEMAKER, THE
Gary Kelley
17485 SW Phesant Ln
Beaverton, OR 97006
503-649-7867
garykelley@theblademaker.com;
www.theblademaker.com
Period knife and hawk blades for hobbyists & re-enactors and in dendritic D2 steel. "Ferroulithic" steel-stone spear point, blades and arrowheads

BOONE TRADING CO., INC.
PO Box 669
562 Coyote Rd
Brinnon, WA 98320
800-423-1945; Fax: 360-796-4511
bella@boonetrading.com
www.boonetrading.com
Ivory of all types, bone, horns

BORGER, WOLF
Benzstrasse 8
76676 Graben-Neudorf
GERMANY
wolf@messerschmied.de;
www.messerschmied.de

BOYE KNIVES
PO Box 1238
Dolan Springs, AZ 86441-1238
800-853-1617 or 928-272-0903
boye@citlink.net
www.boyeknives.com
Dendritic steel and Dendritic cobalt

BRONK'S KNIFEWORKS
Lyle Brunckhorst
Country Village
23706 7th Ave SE, Suite B
Bothell, WA 98021
425-402-3484
bronks@bronksknifeworks.com;
www.bronksknifeworks.com
Damascus steel

CRAZY CROW TRADING POST
PO Box 847
Pottsboro, TX 75076
800-786-6210; Fax: 903-786-9059
info@crazycrow.com; www.crazycrow.com
Solingen blades, knife making parts & supplies

CULPEPPER & CO.
Joe Culpepper
P.O. Box 690
8285 Georgia Rd.
Otto, NC 28763
828-524-6842; Fax: 828-369-7809
info@culpepperco.com
www.knifehandles.com
www.stingrayproducts.com
www.oldschoolknifeworks.com
Mother of pearl, bone, abalone, stingray, dyed stag, blacklip, ram's horn, mammoth ivory, coral, scrimshaw

CUTLERY SPECIALTIES
6819 S.E. Sleepy Hollow Lane
Stuart, FL 34997-4757
772-219-0436 or 800-229-5530
Dennis13@aol.com
www.restorationproduct.com
Exclusive distributor for Renaissance Wax/Polish and other restoration products

DAMASCUS USA
149 Deans Farm Rd
Tyner, NC 27980-9718
252-333-0349
rob@damascususa.com;
www.damascususa.com
All types of damascus cutlery steel, including 100 percent finished damascus blade blanks

DAN'S WHETSTONE CO., INC.
418 Hilltop Rd
Pearcy, AR 71964
501-767-1616; fax 501-767-9598
questions@danswhetstone.com;
www.danswhetstone.com
Natural abrasive Arkansas stone products

DIAMOND MACHINING TECHNOLOGY, INC. (DMT)
85 Hayes Memorial Dr
Marlborough, MA 01752
800-666-4DMT
dmtcustomercare@dmtsharp.com;
www.dmtsharp.com
Knife and tool sharpener—diamond, ceramic and easy edge guided sharpening kits

DIGEM DIAMOND SUPPLIERS
7303 East Earll Drive
Scottsdale, Arizona 85251
602-620-3999
eglasser@cox.net
#1 international diamond tool provider. Every diamond tool you will ever need 1/16th of an inch to 11'x9'. BURRS, CORE DRILLS, SAW BLADES, MILLING SHAPES, AND WHEELS

DIXIE GUN WORKS, INC.
1412 West Reelfoot Ave.
Union City, TN 38281
731-885-0700; Fax: 731-885-0440
www.dixiegunworks.com
Knife and knifemaking supplies

EZE-LAP DIAMOND PRODUCTS
3572 Arrowhead Dr
Carson City, NV 89706
775-888-9500; Fax: 775-888-9555
sales@eze-lap.com; www.eze-lap.com
Diamond coated sharpening tools

FINE TURNAGE PRODUCTIONS
Charles Turnage
1210 Midnight Drive
San Antonio, TX 78260
210-352-5660
info@fineturnage.com
www.fineturnage.com
Specializing in stabilized mammoth tooth and bone, mammoth ivory, fossil brain coral, meteorite, etc.

FLITZ INTERNATIONAL, LTD.
821 Mohr Ave
Waterford, WI 53185
800-558-8611; Fax: 262-534-2991
info@flitz.com; www.flitz.com
Metal polish, buffing pads, wax

FORTUNE PRODUCTS, INC.
2010A Windy Terrace
Cedar Park, TX 78613
800-742-7797; Fax: 800-600-5373
www.accusharp.com
AccuSharp knife sharpeners

GALLERY HARDWOODS
Larry Davis, Eugene, OR
www.galleryhardwoods.com
Stabilized exotic burls and woods

GILMER WOOD CO.
2211 NW St Helens Rd
Portland, OR 97210
503-274-1271; Fax: 503-274-9839
www.gilmerwood.com

GIRAFFEBONE KNIFE SUPPLY
3052 Isim Rd.
Norman, OK 73026
888-804-0683
sandy@giraffebone.com;
www.giraffebone.com
Exotic handle materials

GLENDO CORPORATION/GRS TOOLS
D.J. Glaser
900 Overlander Rd.
Emporia, KS 66801
620-343-1084; Fax: 620-343-9640
glendo@glendo.com; www.grstools.com
Engraving, equipment, tool sharpener, books/videos

HALPERN TITANIUM INC.
Les and Marianne Halpern
PO Box 214
4 Springfield St
Three Rivers, MA 01080
888-283-8627; Fax: 413-289-2372
info@halperntitanium.com;
www.halperntitanium.com
Titanium, carbon fiber, G-10, fasteners; CNC milling

HAWKINS KNIFE MAKING SUPPLIES
110 Buckeye Rd
Fayetteville, GA 30214
770-964-1023
Sales@hawkinsknifemakingsupplies.com
www.HawkinsKnifeMakingSupplies.com
All styles

HILTARY INDUSTRIES
6060 East Thomas Road
Scottsdale, AZ 85251
Office: 480-945-0700
Fax: 480-945-3333
usgrc@usgrc.biz, eglasser@cox.net
OEM manufacturer, knife and sword importer, appraiser, metal supplier, diamond products, stag, meteorite, reconstituted gems, exotic wood, leather and bone

HOUSE OF TOOLS LTD.
#54-5329 72 Ave. S.E.
Calgary, Alberta
CANADA T2C 4X
403-640-4594; Fax: 403-451-7006
www.houseoftools.net

INDIAN JEWELERS SUPPLY CO.
Mail Order: 601 E Coal Ave
Gallup, NM 87301-6005
2105 San Mateo Blvd NE
Albuquerque, NM 87110-5148
800-545-6540; fax: 888-722-4172
orders@ijsinc.com; www.ijsinc.com
Handle materials, tools, metals

INTERAMCO INC.
5210 Exchange Dr
Flint, MI 48507
810-732-8181; 810-732-6116
solutions@interamco.com
Knife grinding and polishing

JANTZ SUPPLY / KOVAL KNIVES
PO Box 584
309 West Main
Davis, OK 73030
800-351-8900; 580-369-3082
jantz@jantzusa.com
www.knifemaking.com
Pre shaped blades, kit knives, complete knifemaking supply line

JMD INTERNATIONAL
2985 Gordy Pkwy., Unit 405
Marietta, GA 30066
678-969-9147; Fax: 770-640-9852
knifesupplies@gmail.com;
www.knifesupplies.com;
Serving the cutlery industry with the finest selection of India stag, buffalo horn, mother-of-pearl and smooth white bone

JOHNSON, R.B.
I.B.S. Int'l. Folder Supplies, Box 11
Clearwater, MN 55320
320-558-6128; 320-558-6128
www.foldingknifesupplies.com
Threaded pivot pins, screws, taps, etc.

JOHNSON WOOD PRODUCTS
34897 Crystal Rd
Strawberry Point, IA 52076
563-933-6504

K&G FINISHING SUPPLIES
1972 Forest Ave
Lakeside, AZ 85929
928-537-8877; fax: 928-537-8066
csinfo@knifeandgun.com;
www.knifeandgun.com
Full service supplies

KOWAK IVORY
Roland and Kathy Quimby
(May-Sept): PO Box 350
Ester, AK 99725
907-479-9335
(Oct-April)
Green Valley, AZ 85662
520-207-6620
sales@kowakivory.com;
www.kowakivory.com
Fossil ivories

LITTLE GIANT POWER HAMMER
Roger Rice
6414 King Rd.
Nebraska City, NE 68410
402-873-6603
www.littlegianthammer.com
Rebuilds hammers and supplies parts

LIVESAY, NEWT
3306 S Dogwood St
Siloam Springs, AR 72761
479-549-3356; 479-549-3357
Combat utility knives, titanium knives, sportsmen knives, custom made orders taken on knives and after market Kydex© sheaths for commercial or custom cutlery

M MILLER ORIGINALS
Michael Miller
3030 E. Calle Cedral
Kingman AZ 86401
928-757-1359
mike@mmilleroriginals.com;
www.mmilleroriginals.com
Supplies stabilized juniper burl blocks and scales, mosaic damascus, damascus

MARKING METHODS, INC.
Sales
301 S. Raymond Ave
Alhambra, CA 91803-1531
626-282-8823; Fax: 626-576-7564
sales@markingmethods.com;
www.markingmethods.com
Knife etching equipment & service

MASECRAFT SUPPLY CO.
254 Amity St
Meriden, CT 06450
800-682-5489; Fax: 203-238-2373
info@masecraftsupply.com;
www.masecraftsupply.com
Natural & specialty synthetic handle materials & more

MEIER STEEL
Daryl Meier
75 Forge Rd
Carbondale, IL 62903
618-549-3234; Fax: 618-549-6239
www.meiersteel.com

NICO, BERNARD
PO Box 5151
Nelspruit 1200
SOUTH AFRICA
011-2713-7440099; 011-2713-7440099
bernardn@iafrica.com

NORRIS, MIKE
Rt 2 Box 242A
Tollesboro, KY 41189
606-798-1217
Damascus steel

NORTHCOAST KNIVES
17407 Puritas Ave
Cleveland, Ohio 44135
www.NorthCoastKnives.com
Tutorials and step-by-step projects. Entry level knifemaking supplies.

OSO FAMOSO
PO Box 654
Ben Lomond, CA 95005
831-336-2343
oso@osofamoso.com;
www.osofamoso.com
Mammoth ivory bark

OZARK CUTLERY SUPPLY
5230 S. MAIN ST.
Joplin, MO 64804
417-782-4998
ozarkcutlery@gmail.com
28 years in the cutlery business, Missouri's oldest cutlery firm

PARAGON INDUSTRIES, L.P.
2011 South Town East Blvd
Mesquite, TX 75149-1122
800-876-4328 or 972-288-7557
info@paragonweb.com;
www.paragonweb.com
Heat treating furnaces for knifemakers

POPLIN, JAMES / POP'S KNIVES & SUPPLIES
1654 S. Smyrna Church Rd.
Washington, GA 30673
706-678-5408
www.popsknifesupplies.com

POUL STRANDE
Søster Svenstrup Byvej 16
4130 Viby Sjælland
Denmark
45 46 19 43 05; Fax: 45 46 19 53 19
www.poulstrande.com

PUGH, JIM
PO Box 711
917 Carpenter
Azle, TX 76020
817-444-2679; Fax: 817-444-5455
Rosewood and ebony Micarta blocks, rivets for Kydex sheaths, 0-80 screws for folders

RADOS, JERRY
134 Willie Nell Rd.
Columbia, KY 42728
606-303-3334
jerryr@ttlv.net
www.radosknives.com
Damascus steel

REACTIVE METALS STUDIO, INC.
PO Box 890
Clarksdale, AZ 86324
800-876-3434; 928-634-3434; Fax: 928-634-6734
info@reactivemetals.com; www.reactivemetals.com

R. FIELDS ANCIENT IVORY
Donald Fields
790 Tamerlane St
Deltona, FL 32725
386-532-9070
donaldbfields@earthlink.net
Selling ancient ivories; Mammoth, fossil & walrus

RICK FRIGAULT CUSTOM KNIVES
1189 Royal Pines Rd.
Golden Lake, Ontario
CANADA K0J 1X0
613-401-2869
jill@mouseworks.net
www.rfrigaultknives.ca
Selling padded zippered knife pouches with an option to personalize the outside with the marker, purveyor, stores-address, phone number, email web-site or any other information needed. Available in black cordura, mossy oak camo in sizes 4"x2" to 20"x4.5"

RIVERSIDE MACHINE
201 W Stillwell Ave.
DeQueen, AR 71832
870-642-7643; Fax: 870-642-4023
uncleal@riversidemachine.net
www.riversidemachine.net

ROCKY MOUNTAIN KNIVES
George L. Conklin
PO Box 902, 615 Franklin
Ft. Benton, MT 59442
406-622-3268; Fax: 406-622-3410
bbgrus@ttc-cmc.net
Working knives

SAKMAR, MIKE
903 S. Latson Rd. #257
Howell, MI 48843
517-546-6388; Fax: 517-546-6399
sakmarent@yahoo.com
www.sakmarenterprises.com
Mokume bar stock. Retail & wholesale

SANDPAPER, INC. OF ILLINOIS
P.O. Box 2579
Glen Ellyn, IL 60138
630-629-3320; Fax: 630-629-3324
sandinc@aol.com; www.sandpaperinc.com
Abrasive belts, rolls, sheets & discs

SCHMIEDEWERKSTATTE
Markus Balbach e.K.
Heinrich-Worner-Str. 1-3
35789 Weilmunster-Laubuseschbach,
Germany
06475-8911 Fax: 912986
Damascus steel

SCHNEIDER, CRAIG M.
5380 N. Amity Rd.
Claremont, IL 62421
217-377-5715
rafetownslame@gmail.com
www.grindhaus.org
Offering dyed giraffe, camel and cattle bone, various horn, antler and teeth

SENTRY SOLUTIONS LTD.
PO Box 214
Wilton, NH 03086
800-546-8049; Fax: 603-654-3003
info@sentrysolutions.com;
www.sentrysolutions.com
Knife care products

**SHEFFIELD KNIFEMAKERS
SUPPLY, INC.**
PO Box 741107
Orange City, FL 32774
386-775-6453; fax: 386-774-5754
email@sheffieldsupply.com;
www.sheffieldsupply.com

SHINING WAVE METALS
PO Box 563
Snohomish, WA 98291
425-334-5569
info@shiningwave.com;
www.shiningwave.com
A full line of mokume-gane in precious and non-precious metals for knifemakers, jewelers and other artists

SMITH'S
747 Mid-America Blvd.
Hot Springs, AR 71913-8414
501-321-2244; Fax: 501-321-9232
sales@smithsproducts.com
www.smithsproducts.com

STAMASCUS KNIFEWORKS INC.
Ed VanHoy
24255 N Fork River Rd
Abingdon, VA 24210
276-944-4885; Fax: 276-944-3187
stamascus@centurylink.net
www.stamascusknifeworks.com
Blade steels

STOVER, JEFF
PO Box 43
Torrance, CA 90507
310-486-0976
edgedealer@aol.com;
www.edgedealer.com
Fine custom knives, top makers

TEXAS KNIFEMAKERS SUPPLY
10649 Haddington Suite 180
Houston TX 77043
713-461-8632; Fax: 713-461-8221
sales@texasknife.com;
www.texasknife.com
Complete line of knifemaking supplies, equipment, and custom heat treating

TRU-GRIT, INC.
760 E Francis St., Unit N
Ontario, CA 91761
909-923-4116; Fax: 909-923-9932
www.trugrit.com
The latest in Norton and 3/M ceramic grinding belts. Also Super Flex, Trizact, Norax and Micron belts to 3000 grit. All of the popular belt grinders. Buffers and variable speed motors. ATS-34, 440C, BG-42, CPM S-30V, 416 and Damascus steel

TWO FINGER KNIFE, LLC
4574 N. Haroldsen Dr.
Idaho Falls, ID 83401
208-523-7436; Fax: 208-523-7436
twofingerknife@gmail.com www.
twofingerknife.com
USA-forged and hand-ground finished damascus blades, and blades in 5160, 1095, 52100, D2, 440C, ATS 34, ELMAX and other steels. Finishes sword blades, sword-cane blades, damascus bar stock and tomahawk heads. Offers folder kits, custom sheaths, in-house heat treating.

WASHITA MOUNTAIN WHETSTONE CO.
PO Box 20378
Hot Springs, AR 71903-0378
501-525-3914; Fax: 501-525-0816
wmw@hsnp

WEILAND, J. REESE
PO Box 2337
Riverview, FL 33568
813-671-0661
rwphil413@verizon.net
www.reeseweilandknives.com

Folders, straight knives, etc.

WILSON, R.W.
PO Box 2012
113 Kent Way
Weirton, WV 26062
304-723-2771
rwknives@hotmail.com

WOOD CARVERS SUPPLY, INC.
PO Box 7500
Englewood, FL 34295
800-284-6229
teamwcs@yahoo.com
www.woodcarverssupply.com
Over 2,000 unique wood carving tools

WOOD LAB
Michael Balaskovitz
2471 6th St.
Muskegon Hts., MI 49444
616-322-5846
woodlabgroup@gmail.com
www.woodlab.biz
Acrylic stabilizing services and materials

**WOOD STABILIZING SPECIALISTS INT'L,
LLC**
2940 Fayette Ave
Ionia, IA 50645
800-301-9774; 641-435-4746
mike@stabilizedwood.com;
www.stabilizedwood.com
Processor of acrylic impregnated materials

ZOWADA CUSTOM KNIVES
Tim Zowada
4509 E. Bear River Rd
Boyne Falls, MI 49713
231-881-5056
tim@tzknives.com; www.tzknives.com
Damascus, pocket knives, swords, Lower case gothic tz logo

mail order, sales, dealers and purveyors

A.G. RUSSELL KNIVES INC
2900 S. 26th St
Rogers, AR 72758-8571
800-255-9034 or 479-631-0130
fax 479-631-8493
ag@agrussell.com; www.agrussell.com
The oldest knife mail-order company, highest quality. Free catalog available. In these catalogs you will find the newest and the best. If you like knives, this catalog is a must

ARIZONA CUSTOM KNIVES
Julie Maguire
3670 U.S. 1 S, Suite 260-F
St. Augustine, FL 32086
904-826-4178
sharptalk@arizonacustomknives.com; www.
arizonacustomknives.com
Color catalog $5 U.S. / $7 Foreign

ARTKNIVES.COM
Fred Eisen Leather & Art Knives
129 S. Main St.
New Hope, PA 18938
215-862-5988
fredeisen@verizon.net
www.artknives.com
Handmade knives from over 75 makers/high-quality manufacturers, leather sheath maker

ATLANTA CUTLERY CORP.
P.O.Box 839
Conyers, Ga 30012
770-922-7500; Fax: 770-918-2026
custserv@atlantacutlery.com; www.
atlantacutlery.com

BECK'S CUTLERY SPECIALTIES
51 Highland Trace Ln.
Benson, NC 27504
919-902-9416
beckscutlery@embarqmail.com;
www.beckscutlery.com
Knives

BLADE HQ
400 S. 1000 E, Ste. E
Lehi, UT 84043
888-252-3347 or 801-768-0232
questions@bladehq.com
www.bladehq.com
Online destination for knives and gear, specializing in law enforcement and military, including folders, fixed blades, custom knives, asisted-opening folders, automatics, butterfly knives, hunters, machetes, multi-tools, axes, knife cases, paracord, sharpeners, sheaths, lubricants and supplies

BLADEART.COM
14216 S.W. 136 St.
Miami, FL 33186
305-255-9176
sales@bladeart.com
www.bladeart.com
Custom knives, swords and gear

BLADEGALLERY.COM
107 Central Way
Kirkland, WA 98033
425-889-5980 or 877-56BLADE
info@bladegallery.com;
www.bladegallery.com
Bladegallery.com specializes in handmade, one-of-a-kind knives from around the world. We have an emphasis on forged knives and high-end gentlemen's folders

BLADEOPS, LLC
1352 W. 7800 S
West Jordan, UT 84088
888-EZ BLAD (392-5233)
trevor@bladeops.com
www.bladeops.com
Online dealer of all major brands of automatic knives, butterfly knives, spring-assisted folders, throwing knives, manual folders, survival and self-defense knives, sharpeners and paracord

BLUE RIDGE KNIVES
166 Adwolfe Rd
Marion, VA 24354
276-783-6143; fax 276-783-9298
onestop@blueridgeknives.com;
www.blueridgeknives.com
Wholesale distributor of knives

BOB'S TRADING POST
308 N Main St
Hutchinson, KS 67501
620-669-9441
bobstradingpost@cox.net;
www.bobstradingpostinc.com
Tad custom knives with Reichert custom sheaths one at a time, one of a kind

BOONE TRADING CO., INC.
PO Box 669
562 Coyote Rd
Brinnon, WA 98320
800-423-1945; Fax: 360-796-4511
bella@boonetrading.com
www.boonetrading.com
Ivory of all types, bone, horns

CARMEL CUTLERY
Dolores & 6th
PO Box 1346
Carmel, CA 93921
831-624-6699; 831-624-6780
sanford@carmelcutlery.com;
www.carmelcutlery.com
Quality custom and a variety of production pocket knives, swords; kitchen cutlery; personal grooming items

CLASSIC CUTLERY
66 N. Adams St., Ste. 1
Manchester, NH 03104
classiccutlery@earthlink.net
www.classiccutleryusa.com
Private-label zip-up knife cases and all brands of production cutlery and outdoor gear

CUTLERY SHOPPE
3956 E Vantage Pointe Ln
Meridian, ID 83642-7268
800-231-1272; Fax: 208-884-4433
orders@cutleryshoppe.com;
www.cutleryshoppe.com
Discount pricing on top quality brands

CUTTING EDGE, THE
2900 South 26th St
Rogers, AR 72758-8571
800-255-9034; Fax: 479-631-8493
ce_info@cuttingedge.com;
www.cuttingedge.com
After-market knives since 1968. They offer about 1,000 individual knives for sale each month. Subscription by first class mail, in U.S. $20 per year, Canada or Mexico by air mail, $25 per year. All overseas by air mail, $40 per year. The oldest and the most experienced in the business of buying and selling knives. They buy collections of any size, take knives on consignment. Every month there are 4-8 pages in color featuring the work of top makers

DENTON, JOHN W.
703 Hiawassee Estates Dr.
Hiawassee, GA 30546
706-781-8479
jwdenton@windstream.net
www.bobloveless knives.com
Loveless knives

EDGEDEALER.COM
PO BOX 43
TORRANCE, CA 90507
310-532-2166
edgedealer1@yahoo.com
www.edgedealer.com
Antiques

EPICUREAN EDGE
107 Central Way
Kirkland, WA 98033
425-889-5980
info@epicedge.com
www.epicedge.com
Specializing in handmade and one-of-a-kind kitchen knives from around the world

EXQUISITEKNIVES.COM
770 Sycamore Ave., Ste. 122, Box 451
Vista, CA 92083
760-945-7177
mastersmith@cox.net
www.exquisiteknives.com and
www.robertloveless.com
Purveyor of high-end custom knives

**FAZALARE INTERNATIONAL
ENTERPRISES**
PO Box 7062
Thousand Oaks, CA 91359
805-496-2002
ourfaz@aol.com
Handmade multiblades; older Case; Fight'n Rooster; Bulldog brand & Cripple Creek

FROST CUTLERY CO.
PO Box 22636
Chattanooga, TN 37422
800-251-7768
www.frostcutlery.com

GODWIN, INC. G. GEDNEY
PO Box 100
Valley Forge, PA 19481
610-783-0670; Fax: 610-783-6083
sales@gggodwin.com;
www.gggodwin.com
18th century reproductions

GPKNIVES, LLC
2230 Liebler Rd.
Troy, IL 62294
866-667-5965
gpk@gpknives.com
www.gpknives.com
Serving law enforcement, hunters, sportsmen and collectors

**GRAZYNA SHAW/QUINTESSENTIAL
CUTLERY**
POB 11
Clearwater, MN 55320
320-217-9002
gshaw@quintcut.com
www.quintcut.com
Specializing in investment-grade custom knives and early makers

GUILD KNIVES
Donald Guild
320 Paani Place 1A
Paia, HI 96779
808-877-3109
don@guildknives.com;
www.guildknives.com
Purveyor of custom art knives

HOUSE OF BLADES
6451 N.W. Loop 820
Ft. Worth, TX 76135
817-237-7721
sales@houseofblades.com
www.houseofbladestexas.com
Handmades, pocketknives, hunting knives, antique and collector knives, swords, household cutlery and knife-related items.

JENCO SALES, INC. / KNIFE IMPORTERS, INC. / WHITE LIGHTNING
PO Box 1000
11307 Conroy Ln
Manchaca, TX 78652
800-531-5301; fax 800-266-2373
jencosales@sbcglobal.net
Wholesale distributor of domestic and imported cutlery and sharpeners

KELLAM KNIVES WORLDWIDE
POB 3438
Lantana, FL 33465
800-390-6918; 561-588-3185
info@kellamknives.com;
www.kellamknives.com
Largest selection of Finnish knives; own line of folders and fixed blades

KNIFEART.COM
13301 Pompano Dr
Little Rock AR 72211
501-221-1010
connelley@knifeart.com
www.knifeart.com
Large internet seller of custom knives & upscale production knives

KNIFECENTER
5201 Lad Land Dr.
Fredericksburg, VA 22407
800-338-6799 or 301-486-0901
info@knifecenter.com
www.knifecenter.com

KNIFEPURVEYOR.COM LLC
919-295-1283
mdonato@knifepurveyor.com
www.knifepurveyor.com
Owned and operated by Michael A. Donato (full-time knife purveyor since 2002). We buy, sell, trade, and consign fine custom knives. We also specialize in buying and selling valuable collections of fine custom knives. Our goal is to make every transaction a memorable one.

KNIVES PLUS
2467 I 40 West
Amarillo, TX 79109
806-359-6202
salessupport@knivesplus.com
www.knivesplus.com
Retail cutlery and cutlery accessories since 1987

KRIS CUTLERY
2314 Monte Verde Dr
Pinole, CA 94564
510-758-9912 Fax: 510-758-9912
kriscutlery@aol.com; www.kriscutlery.com
Japanese, medieval, Chinese & Philippine

LONE STAR WHOLESALE
2401 Interstate 40 W
Amarillo, TX 79109
806-836-9540; fax 806-359-1603
sales@lswtexas.com
www.lswtexas.com
Nationwide distributor of knives, knife accessories and knife-related tools

MATTHEWS CUTLERY
PO Box 2768
Moultrie, GA 31776
800-251-0123; fax 877-428-3599
www.matthewscutlery.com

MOORE CUTLERY
PO Box 633
Lockport, IL 60441
708-301-4201
www.moorecutlery.com
Owned & operated by Gary Moore since 1991 (a full-time dealer). Purveyor of high quality custom & production knives

MUSEUM REPLICAS LIMITED
2147 Gees Mill Rd
Conyers, GA 30012
800-883-8838
www.museumreplicas.com
Historically accurate and battle ready swords & daggers

NEW GRAHAM KNIVES
560 Virginia Ave.
Bluefield, VA 24605
276-326-1384
mdye@newgraham.com
www.newgraham.com
Wide selection of knives from over 75 manufacturers, knife sharpening and maintenance accessories

NORDIC KNIVES
436 1st St., Ste. 203A
Solvang, CA 93463
805-688-3612; fax 805-688-1635
info@nordicknives.com
www.nordicknives.com
Custom and Randall knives

PARKERS' KNIFE COLLECTOR SERVICE
6715 Heritage Business Court
Chattanooga, TN 37421
423-892-0448; fax 423-892-9165
www.bulldogknives.org
Online and mail order dealer specializing in collectible knives, including Bulldog Knives, Weidmannsheil and Parker Eagle Brand. Parkers' Greatest Knife Show On Earth

PLAZA CUTLERY, INC.
3333 S. Bristol St., Suite 2060
South Coast Plaza
Costa Mesa, CA 92626
866-827-5292; 714-549-3932
dan@plazacutlery.com;
www.plazacutlery.com
Largest selection of knives on the west coast. Custom makers from beginners to the best. All customs, William Henry, Strider, Reeves, Randalls & others available online, by phone

ROBERTSON'S CUSTOM CUTLERY
4960 Sussex Dr
Evans, GA 30809
706-650-0252; 706-860-1623
customknives@comcast.net
www.robertsoncustomcutlery.com
World class custom knives, custom knife entrepreneur

RUMMELL, HANK
10 Paradise Lane
Warwick, NY 10990
845-769-7273
hank@newyorkcustomknives.com;
www.newyorkcustomknives.com

SCHENK KNIVES
4574 N. Haroldsen Dr.
Idaho Falls, ID 83401
208-523-2026
schenkknives@gmail.com
www.schenkknives.com
High-performance factory custom knives. All models offered in the USA forged from damascus steel, forged 52100 bearting steel and ELMAX stainless steel.

SMOKY MOUNTAIN KNIFE WORKS, INC.
2320 Winfield Dunn Pkwy
PO Box 4430
Sevierville, TN 37864
800-564-8374; 865-453-5871
info@smkw.com; www.smkw.com
The world's largest knife showplace, catalog and website

TRUE NORTH KNIVES
82 Blair Park Rd. #955
Williston, VT 05495
866-748-9985
info@TNKUSA.com
www.TNKUSA.com
Custom and production knife purveyor

VOYLES, BRUCE
PO Box 22007
Chattanooga, TN 37422
423-238-6753
bruce@jbrucevoyles.com;
www.jbrucevoyles.com
Knives, knife auctions

knife services

appraisers

Levine, Bernard, P.O. Box 2404, Eugene, OR, 97402, 541-484-0294, brlevine@ix.netcom.com

Russell, A.G., Knives Inc, 2900 S. 26th St., Rogers, AR 72758-8571, phone 800-255-9034 or 479-631-0130, fax 479-631-8493, ag@agrussell.com, www.agrussell.com

Voyles, J. Bruce, PO Box 22007, Chattanooga, TN 37422, 423-238-6753, bruce@jbrucevoyles.com, www.jbrucevoyles.com

custom grinders

McGowan Manufacturing Company, 4720 N. La Cholla Blvd., #190, Tucson, AZ, 85705, 800-342-4810, 520-219-0884, info@mcgowanmfg.com, www.mcgowanmfg.com, Knife sharpeners, hunting axes

Peele, Bryan, The Elk Rack, 215 Ferry St. P.O. Box 1363, Thompson Falls, MT, 59873

Schlott, Harald, Zingster Str. 26, 13051 Berlin, GERMANY, 049 030 9293346, harald.schlott@T-online.de, Custom grinder, custom handle artisan, display case/box maker, etcher, scrimshander

Wilson, R.W., P.O. Box 2012, Weirton, WV, 26062, 304-723-2771 rwknives@comcast.net, www.rwwilsonknives.com

custom handles

Alaskan Fossil Ivory, Jerry Kochheiser, 1109 W. Hanley Rd., Mansfield, Ohio 44904, 419 564 8781, jkochheiser@neo.rr.com, Selling fossil walrus ivory, mammoth ivory, stag tapers, stag scales, oosik and steller sea cow bone

Cooper, Jim, 1221 Cook St, Ramona, CA, 92065-3214, 760-789-1097, (760) 788-7992, jamcooper@aol.com

Burrows, Chuck, dba Wild Rose Trading Co, 102 Timber Ln., Durango, CO, 81303, 970-317-5592, chuck@wrtcleather.com, www.wrtcleather.com

Fields, Donald, 790 Tamerlane St, Deltona, FL, 32725, 386-532-9070, donaldfields@earthlink.net, Selling ancient ivories; mammoth & fossil walrus

Grussenmeyer, Paul G., 310 Kresson Rd, Cherry Hill, NJ, 08034, 856-428-1088, 856-428-8997, pgrussentne@comcast.net, www.pgcarvings.com

Holland, Dennis K., 4908-17th Pl., Lubbock, TX, 79416

Imboden II, Howard L., Hi II Originals, 620 Deauville Dr., Dayton, OH, 45429, 513-439-1536

Kelso, Jim, 577 Collar Hill Rd, Worcester, VT, 05682, 802-229-4254, (802) 229-0595

Marlatt, David, 67622 Oldham Rd., Cambridge, OH, 43725, 740-432-7549

Mead, Dennis, 2250 E. Mercury St., Inverness, FL, 34453-0514

Myers, Ron, 6202 Marglenn Ave., Baltimore, MD, 21206, 410-866-6914

Schlott, Harald, Zingster Str. 26, 13051 Berlin, GERMANY, 049 030 9293346, harald.schlott@T-online.de, Custom grinder, custom handle artisan, display case/box maker, etcher, scrimshander

Snell, Barry A., 4801 96th St. N., St. Petersburg, FL, 33708-3740

Vallotton, A., 621 Fawn Ridge Dr., Oakland, OR, 97462, 541-459-2216

Watson, Silvia, 350 Jennifer Lane, Driftwood, TX, 78619

Wilderness Forge, 315 North 100 East, Kanab, UT, 84741, 435-644-3674, bhatting@xpressweb.com

Williams, Gary, (GARBO), PO Box 210, Glendale, KY, 42740-2010 270-369-6752, scrimbygarbo@gmail.com, www.scrimbygarbo.com

display cases and boxes

Bill's Custom Cases, P O Box 603, Montague, CA, 96064, 541-727-7223, billscustomcases@earthlink.net, www.billscustomcases.com

Culpepper & Company, 8285 Georgia Rd., Otto, NC, 28763 828-524-6842, info@culpepperco.com, www.knifehandles.com

McLean, Lawrence, 12344 Meritage Ct, Rancho Cucamonga, CA, 91739, 714-848-5779, lmclean@charter.net

Miller, Michael K., M&M Kustom Krafts, 28510 Santiam Highway, Sweet Home, OR, 97386

Miller, Robert, P.O. Box 2722, Ormond Beach, FL, 32176

Retichek, Joseph L., W9377 Co. TK. D, Beaver Dam, WI, 53916

Robbins, Wayne, 11520 Inverway, Belvidere, IL, 61008

S&D Enterprises, 20 East Seventh St, Manchester, OH, 45144, 855-876-9693, 937-549-2602, sales@s-denterprises.com, www.s-denterprises.com, Display case/ box maker. Manufacturer of aluminum display, chipboard type displays, wood displays. Silk screening or acid etching for logos on product

Schlott, Harald, Zingster Str. 26, 13051 Berlin, GERMANY, 049 030 9293346, harald.schlott@T-online.de, Custom grinder, custom handle artisan, display case/box maker, etcher, scrimshander

engravers

Adlam, Tim, 1705 Witzel Ave., Oshkosh, WI, 54902, 920-235-4589, www.adlamengraving.com

Alcorn, Gordon, 10573 Kelly Canyon Rd., Bozeman, MT 59715, 406-586-1350, alcorncustom@yahoo.com, www.alcornengraving.com

Alfano, Sam, 45 Catalpa Trace, Covington, LA, 70433, alfano@gmail.com, www.masterengraver.com

Baron, David, Baron Engraving, 62 Spring Hill Rd., Trumbull, CT, 06611, 203-452-0515, sales@baronengraving.com, www.baronengraving.com, Polishing, plating, inlays, artwork

Bates, Billy, 2302 Winthrop Dr. SW, Decatur, AL, 35603, bbrn@aol.com, www.angelfire.com/al/billybates

Blair, Jim, PO Box 64, 59 Mesa Verde, Glenrock, WY, 82637, 307-436-8115, jblairengrav@msn.com, www.jimblairengraving.com

Booysen, Chris, South Africa, +27-73-284-1493, chris@cbknives.com, www.cbknives.com

Christensen, Bruce, 3072 W. Millerama Ave., West Valley City, UT 84119, 801-966-0805, cengraver@gmail.com

Churchill, Winston G., RFD Box 29B, Proctorsville, VT 05153, www.wchurchill.com

Collins, Michael, 405-392-2273, info@michaelcollinsart.com, www.michaelcollinsart.com

Cover, Raymond A., 1206 N. Third St., Festus, MO 63010 314-808-2508 cover@sbcglobal.net, http://learningtoengrave.com

DeLorge, Ed, 6734 W Main St, Houma, LA, 70360, 985-223-0206, delorge@triparish.net, http://www.eddelorge.com/

Dickson, John W., PO Box 49914, Sarasota, FL, 34230, 941-952-1907

Dolbare, Elizabeth, PO Box 502, Dubois, WY, 82513-0502 edolbare@hotmail.com, http://www.scrimshaw-engraving.com/

Downing, Jim, PO Box 4224, Springfield, MO, 65803, 417-865-5953, handlebar@thegunengraver.com, www.thegunengraver.com, engraver and scrimshaw artist

Duarte, Carlos, 108 Church St., Rossville, CA, 95678, 916-782-2617 carlossilver@surewest.net, www.carlossilver.com

Dubber, Michael W., 11 S. Green River Rd., Evansville, IN, 47715, 812-454-0271, m.dubber@firearmsengraving.com, www.firearmsengraving.com

Eaton, Rick, 313 Dailey Rd., Broadview, MT 59015, 406-667-2405, rick@eatonknives.com, www.eatonknives.com

Eklund, Maihkel, Föne Stam V9, S-820 41 Färila, SWEDEN, info@art-knives.com, www.art-knives.com

Eldridge, Allan, 7731 Four Winds Dr., Ft. Worth, TX 76133, 817-370-7778

Ellis, Willy B, Willy B's Customs, 1025 Hamilton Ave., Tarpon Springs, FL, 34689, 727-942-6420, wbflashs@verizon.net, www.willyb.com

Flannery Gun Engraving, Jeff, 11034 Riddles Run Rd., Union, KY, 41091, 859-384-3127, engraving@fuse.net, www.flannerygunengraving.com

Gournet, Geoffroy, 820 Paxinosa Ave., Easton, PA, 18042, 610-559-0710, ggournet@yahoo.com, www.gournetusa.com

Halloran, Tim, 316 Fenceline Dr., Blue Grass, IA 52726 563-260-8464, vivtim@msn.com, http://halloranengraving.com

Hands, Barry Lee, 30608 Fernview Ln., Bigfork, MT 59911, 406-249-4334, barry_hands@yahoo.com, www.barryleehands.com

Holder, Pat, 18910 McNeil Ranch Rd., Wickenburg, AZ 85390, 928-684-2025 dholderknives@commspeed.net, www.dholder.com

Ingle, Ralph W., 151 Callan Dr., Rossville, GA, 30741, 706-858-0641, riengraver@aol.com

Johns, Bill, 1716 8th St, Cody, WY, 82414, 307-587-5090, http://billjohnsengraver.com

Kelso, Jim, 577 Collar Hill Rd Worcester, VT, 05682, 802-229-4254, jimkelsojournal@gmail.com, www.jimkelso.com

Koevenig, Eugene and Eve, Koevenig's Engraving Service, Rabbit Gulch, Box 55, Hill City, SD, 57745-0055

Kostelnik, Joe and Patty, RD #4, Box 323, Greensburg, PA, 15601

Kudlas, John M., 55280 Silverwolf Dr, Barnes, WI, 54873, 715-795-2031, jkudlas@cheqnet.net, Engraver, scrimshander

Lark, David, 6641 Schneider Rd., Kingsley, MI 49649, Phone: 231-342-1076 dblark58@yahoo.com

Larson, Doug, Dragon's Fire Studio, Percival, IA, Phone: 402-202-3703 (cell) dragonsfirestudio@hotmail.com

Limings Jr., Harry, 5793 Nichels Ln., Johnstown, OH, 43031-9576

Lindsay, Steve, 3714 West Cedar Hill, Kearney, NE, 68845, Phone: 308-236-7885

steve@lindsayengraving.com, www.lindsayengraving.com
Lurth, Mitchell, 1317 7th Ave., Marion, IA 52302, Phone: 319-377-1899 www.lurthengraving.com
Lyttle, Brian, Box 5697, High River AB CANADA, T1V 1M7, Phone: 403-558-3638, brian@lyttleknives.com, www.lyttleknives.com
Lytton, Simon M., 19 Pinewood Gardens, Hemel Hempstead, Hertfordshire HP1 1TN, ENGLAND, 01-442-255542, simonlyttonengraver@virginmedia.com
Markow, Paul, 130 Spinnaker Ridge Dr. SW, B206, Huntsville, AL 35824, 256-513-9790, paul.markow@gmail.com, sites.google.com/site/artistictouch2010/engraving
Mason, Joe, 146 Value Rd, Brandon, MS, 39042, 601-519-8850, masonjoe@bellsouth.net, www.joemasonengraving.com
McCombs, Leo, 1862 White Cemetery Rd., Patriot, OH, 45658
McDonald, Dennis, 8359 Brady St., Peosta, IA, 52068
McLean, Lawrence, 12344 Meritage Ct, Rancho Cucamonga, CA, 91739, 714-848-5779, lmclean@charter.net
Meyer, Chris, 39 Bergen Ave., Wantage, NJ, 07461, 973-875-6299
Minnick, Joyce, 144 N. 7th St., Middletown, IN, 47356, 765-354-4108
Morgan, Tandie, P.O. Box 693, 30700 Hwy. 97, Nucla, CO, 81424
Morton, David A., 1110 W. 21st St., Lorain, OH, 44052
Moulton, Dusty, 135 Hillview Ln, Loudon, TN, 37774, 865-408-9779, dusty@moultonknives.com, www.moultonknives.com
Muller, Jody & Pat, 3359 S. 225th Rd., Goodson, MO, 65663, 417-852-4306/417-752-3260, mullerforge2@hotmail.com, www.mullerforge.com
Nelida, Toniutti, via G. Pasconi 29/c, Maniago 33085 (PN), ITALY
Nilsson, Jonny Walker, Akkavare 16, 93391 Arvidsjaur, SWEDEN, +(46) 702-144207, 0960.13048@telia.com, www.jwnknives.com
Parke, Jeff, 1365 Fort Pierce Dr. #3, St. George, UT 84790, Phone: 435-421-1692 jeffrey_parke@hotmail.com, https://www.facebook.com/jeff.parke1
Patterson, W.H., P.O. Drawer DK, College Station, TX, 77841
Peri, Valerio, Via Meucci 12, Gardone V.T. 25063, ITALY
Pilkington Jr., Scott, P.O. Box 97, Monteagle, TN, 37356, 931-924-3400, scott@pilkguns.com, www.pilkguns.com
Pulisova, Andrea, CSA 230-95, 96701 Kremnica, Slovakia, Phone: 00421 903-340076 vpulis@gmail.com
Rabeno, Martin, Spook Hollow Trading Co, 530 Eagle Pass, Durango, CO, 81301
Raftis, Andrew, 2743 N. Sheffield, Chicago, IL, 60614
Riccardo, David, Riccardo Fine Hand Engraving, Buckley, MI, Phone: 231-269-3028, riccardoengraving@acegroup.cc, www.riccardoengraving.com
Roberts, J.J., 7808 Lake Dr., Manassas, VA, 20111, 703-330-0448, jjrengraver@aol.com
Robidoux, Roland J., DMR Fine Engraving, 25 N. Federal Hwy. Studio 5, Dania, FL, 33004
Rosser, Bob, Hand Engraving, 2809 Crescent Ave Ste 20, Birmingham, AL, 35209, 205-870-4422, brengraver1@gmail.com, www.hand-engravers.com
Rudolph, Gil, 20922 Oak Pass Ave, Tehachapi, CA, 93561, 661-822-4949
Rundell, Joe, 6198 W. Frances Rd., Clio, MI, 48420
Schönert, Elke, 18 Lansdowne Pl., Central, Port Elizabeth, SOUTH AFRICA
Shaw, Bruce, P.O. Box 545, Pacific Grove, CA, 93950, 831-646-1937, 831-644-0941, shawdogs@aol.com
Simmons, Rick W., 3323 Creek Manor Dr., Kingwood, TX, 77339, 504-261-8450, exhibitiongrade@gmail.com www.bespokeengraving.com
Slobodian, Barbara, 4101 River Ridge Dr., PO Box 1498, San Andreas, CA 95249, 209-286-1980, fax 209-286-1982, barbara@dancethetide.com. Specializes in Japanese-style engraving.
Small, Jim, 2860 Athens Hwy., Madison, GA 30650, 706-818-1245, smallengrave@aol.com
Smith, Ron, 5869 Straley, Ft. Worth, TX, 76114
Smitty's Engraving, 21320 Pioneer Circle, Harrah, OK, 73045, 405-454-6968, mail@smittys-engraving.us, www.smittys-engraving.us
Soileau, Damon, P.O. Box 7292, Kingsport, TN 37664 423-297-4665, oiseaumetalarts@gmail.com, www.oiseaumetalarts.etsy.com
Spode, Peter, Tresaith Newland, Malvern, Worcestershire WR13 5AY, ENGLAND
Swartley, Robert D., 2800 Pine St., Napa, CA, 94558
Takeuchi, Shigetoshi, 21-14-1-Chome kamimuneoka Shiki shi, 353 Saitama, JAPAN
Theis, Terry, 21452 FM 2093, Harper, TX, 78631, 830-864-4438
Valade, Robert B., 931 3rd Ave., Seaside, OR, 97138, 503-738-7672, (503) 738-7672
Waldrop, Mark, 14562 SE 1st Ave. Rd., Summerfield, FL, 34491
Warenski-Erickson, Julie, 590 East 500 N., Richfield, UT, 84701, 435-627-2504, julie@warenskiknives.com, www.warenskiknives.com
Warren, Kenneth W., P.O. Box 2842, Wenatchee, WA, 98807-2842, 509-663-6123, (509) 663-6123
Whitmore, Jerry, 1740 Churchill Dr., Oakland, OR, 97462
Winn, Travis A., 558 E. 3065 S., Salt Lake City, UT, 84106, 801-467-5957

Zima, Russ, 7291 Ruth Way, Denver, CO, 80221, 303-657-9378, rzima@rzengraving.com, www.rzengraving.com

etchers

Baron Engraving, David Baron, 62 Spring Hill Rd., Trumbull, CT, 06611, 203-452-0515 sales@baronengraving.com, www.baronengraving.com
Fountain Products, 492 Prospect Ave., West Springfield, MA, 01089, 413-781-4651
Hayes, Dolores, P.O. Box 41405, Los Angeles, CA, 90041
Holland, Dennis, 4908 17th Pl., Lubbock, TX, 79416
Kelso, Jim, 577 Collar Hill Rd, Worcester, VT, 05682, 802-229-4254, jimkelsojournal@gmail.com, www.jimkelso.com
Larstein, Francine, Francine Etched Knives, 368 White Rd, Watsonville, CA, 95076, 800-557-1525/831-426-6046, francine@francinetchedknives.com, www.francinetchedknives.com
Lefaucheux, Jean-Victor, Saint-Denis-Le-Ferment, 27140 Gisors, FRANCE
Myers, Ron, 6202 Marglenn Ave., Baltimore, MD, 21206, (acid) etcher
Nilsson, Jonny Walker, Akkavare 16, 93391 Arvidsjaur, SWEDEN, +(46) 702-144207, 0960.13048@telia.com, www.jwnknives.com
Schlott, Harald, Zingster Str. 26, 13051 Berlin, GERMANY, 049 030 9293346, harald.schlott@T-online.de, Custom grinder, custom handle artisan, display case/box maker, etcher, scrimshander
Vallotton, A., Northwest Knife Supply, 621 Fawn Ridge Dr., Oakland, OR, 97462
Watson, Silvia, 350 Jennifer Lane, Driftwood, TX, 78619

heat treaters

Bodycote Inc., 443 E. High St., London, OH 43140 740-852-5000, chris.gattie@bodycote.com, www.bodycote.com
Kazou, Okaysu, 12-2 1 Chome Higashi, Ueno, Taito-Ku, Tokyo, JAPAN, 81-33834-2323, 81-33831-3012
O&W Heat Treat Inc., One Bidwell Rd., South Windsor, CT, 06074, 860-528-9239, (860) 291-9939, owht1@aol.com
Pacific Heat Treating, attn: B.R. Holt, 1238 Birchwood Drive, Sunnyvale, CA, 94089, 408-736-8500, www.pacificheattreating.com
Paul Bos Heat Treating c/o Paul Farner, Buck Knives: 660 S. Lochsa St., Post Falls, ID 83854, 208-262-0500, Ext. 211 / fax 800-733-2825, pfarner@buckknives.com, or contact Paul Bos direct: 928-232-1656, paulbos@buckknives.com
Progressive Heat Treating Co., 2802 Charles City Rd, Richmond, VA, 23231, 804-717-5353, 800-868-5457, sales@pecgears.com
Texas Heat Treating Inc., 155 Texas Ave., Round Rock, TX, 78680, 512-255-5884, buster@texasheattreating.com, www.texasheattreating.com
Texas Knifemakers Supply, 10649 Haddington, Suite 180, Houston, TX, 77043, 713-461-8632, sales@texasknife.com, www.texasknife.com
Tinker Shop, The, 1120 Helen, Deer Park, TX, 77536, 713-479-7286
Valley Metal Treating Inc., 355 S. East End Ave., Pomona, CA, 91766, 909-623-6316, ray@valleymt.net
Wilson, R.W., P.O. Box 2012, Weirton, WV, 26062, 304-723-2771 rwknives@comcast.net, rwwilsonknives.com

leather workers

Abramson, David, 116 Baker Ave, Wharton, NJ, 07885, 973-713-9776, lifter4him1@aol.com, www.liftersleather.com
Burrows, Chuck, dba Wild Rose Trading Co, 102 Timber Ln., Durango, CO 81303, 970-317-5592, wrtc@wrtleather.com, www.wrtcleather.com
Clements' Custom Leathercraft, Chas, 1741 Dallas St., Aurora, CO 80010, Phone: 303-364-0403, chasclements@comcast.net
Cole, Dave, 620 Poinsetta Dr., Satellite Beach, FL 32937, 321-773-1687, www.dcknivesandleather.blademakers.com. Custom sheath services.
CowCatcher Leatherworks, 2045 Progress Ct., Raleigh, NC 27608, Phone: 919-833-8262 cowcatcher1@ymail.com, www.cowcatcher.us
Cubic, George, GC Custom Leather Co., 10561 E. Deerfield Pl., Tucson, AZ, 85749, 520-760-0695, gcubic@aol.com
Dawkins, Dudley, 221 N. Broadmoor Ave, Topeka, KS, 66606-1254, 785-817-9343, dawkind@reagan.com, ABS member/knifemaker forges straight knives
Evans, Scott V, Edge Works Mfg, 1171 Halltown Rd, Jacksonville, NC, 28546, 910-455-9834, fax 910-346-5660, support@tacticalholsters.com, www.tacticalholsters.com
Genske, Jay, 283 Doty St, Fond du Lac, WI, 54935, 920-921-8019/Cell Phone 920-579-0144, jaygenske@hotmail.com, http: //genskeknives.weebly.com, Custom Grinder, Custom Handle Artisan
Green River Leather, 1098 Legion Park Road, PO BOX 190, Greensburg, KY, 42743, Phone: 270-932-2212 fax: 270-299-2471 email: info@greenriverleather.com
John's Custom Leather, John R. Stumpf, 523 S. Liberty St, Blairsville, PA, 15717, 724-459-6802, 724-459-5996, www.jclleather.com

Kravitt, Chris, Treestump Leather, 443 Cave Hill Rd., Waltham, ME, 04605-8706, 207-584-3000, sheathmkr@aol.com, www.treestumpleather.com, Reference: Tree Stump Leather

Layton, Jim, 2710 Gilbert Avenue, Portsmouth, OH, 45662, 740-353-6179

Lee, Sonja and Randy, P.O. Box 1873, 270 N 9th West, St. Johns, AZ, 85936, 928-337-2594, 928-337-5002, randylee.knives@yahoo.com, info@randyleeknives.com, Custom knifemaker; www.randyleeknives.com

Long, Paul, Paul Long Custom Leather, 108 Briarwood Ln. W, Kerrville, TX, 78028, 830-367-5536, PFL@cebridge.net

Lott, Sherry, 1098 Legion Park Road, PO BOX 190, Greensburg, KY, 42743, Phone: 270-932-2212 fax: 270-299-2471 email: info@greenriverleather.com, sherrylott@alltel.net

Mason, Arne, 258 Wimer St., Ashland, OR, 97520, 541-482-2260, (541) 482-7785, am@arnemason.com, www.arnemason.com

Metheny, H.A. "Whitey", 7750 Waterford Dr., Spotsylvania, VA 22551, 540-582-3228 Cell 540-842-1440, fax 540-582-3095, hametheny@aol.com, http://whitey.methenyknives.com

Morrissey, Martin, 4578 Stephens Rd., Blairsville, GA, 30512

Niedenthal, John Andre, Beadwork & Buckskin, Studio 3955 NW 103 Dr., Coral Springs, FL, 33065-1551, 954-345-0447, a_niedenthal@hotmail.com

Neilson, Tess, 187 Cistern Ln., Towanda, PA 18848, 570-721-0470, mountainhollow@epix.net, www.mountainhollow.net, Doing business as Neilson's Mountain Hollow

Parsons, Larry, 539 S. Pleasant View Dr., Mustang, OK 73064 405-376-9408 l.j.parsons@sbcglobal.net, www.parsonssaddleshop.com

Red's Custom Leather, Ed Todd, 9 Woodlawn Rd., Putnam Valley, NY 10579, 845-528-3783, redscustomleather@redscustomleather.com, www.redscustomleather.com

Rowe, Kenny, Rowe's Leather, 3219 Hwy 29 South, Hope, AR, 71801, 870-777-8216, fax 870-777-0935, rowesleather@yahoo.com, www.rowesleather.com

Schrap, Robert G., Custom Leather Knife Sheaths, 7024 W. Wells St., Wauwatosa, WI, 53213, 414-771-6472, fax 414-479-9765, rschrap@aol.com, www.customsheaths.com

Strahin, Robert, 401 Center St., Elkins, WV, 26241, 304-636-0128, rstrahin@copper.net, *Custom Knife Sheaths

Walker, John, 17 Laber Circle, Little Rock, AR, 72210, 501-455-0239, john.walker@afbic.com

miscellaneous

Robertson, Kathy, Impress by Design, PO Box 1367, Evans, GA, 30809-1367, 706-650-0982, (706) 860-1623, impressbydesign@comcast.net, Advertising/graphic designer

Strahin, Robert, 401 Center St., Elkins, WV, 26241, 304-636-0128, rstrahin@copper.net, *Custom Knife Sheaths

photographers

Alfano, Sam, 36180 Henery Gaines Rd., Pearl River, LA, 70452

Allen, John, Studio One, 3823 Pleasant Valley Blvd., Rockford, IL, 61114

Bilal, Mustafa, Turk's Head Productions, 908 NW 50th St., Seattle, WA, 98107-3634, 206-782-4164, (206) 783-5677, info@turkshead.com, www.turkshead.com, Graphic design, marketing & advertising

Bogaerts, Jan, Regenweg 14, 5757 Pl., Liessel, HOLLAND

Box Photography, Doug, 1804 W Main St, Brenham, TX, 77833-3420

Brown, Tom, 6048 Grants Ferry Rd., Brandon, MS, 39042-8136

Butman, Steve, P.O. Box 5106, Abilene, TX, 79608

Calidonna, Greg, 205 Helmwood Dr., Elizabethtown, KY, 42701

Campbell, Jim, 7935 Ranch Rd., Port Richey, FL, 34668

Cooper, Jim, Sharpbycoop.com Photography, 9 Mathew Court, Norwalk, CT 06851, jcooper@sharpbycoop.com, www.sharpbycoop.com

Courtice, Bill, P.O. Box 1776, Duarte, CA, 91010-4776

Crosby, Doug, RFD 1, Box 1111, Stockton Springs, ME, 04981

Danko, Michael, 3030 Jane Street, Pittsburgh, PA, 15203

Davis, Marshall B., P.O. Box 3048, Austin, TX, 78764

Earley, Don, 1241 Ft. Bragg Rd., Fayetteville, NC, 28305

Ehrlich, Linn M., 1850 N Clark St #1008, Chicago, IL, 60614, 312-209-2107

Etzler, John, 11200 N. Island Rd., Grafton, OH, 44044

Fahrner, Dave, 1623 Arnold St., Pittsburgh, PA, 15205

Faul, Jan W., 903 Girard St. NE, Rr. Washington, DC, 20017

Fedorak, Allan, 28 W. Nicola St., Amloops BC CANADA, V2C 1J6

Fox, Daniel, Lumina Studios, 6773 Industrial Parkway, Cleveland, OH, 44070, 440-734-2118, (440) 734-3542, lumina@en.com, www.lumina-studios.com

Francesco Pachi, Loc. Pometta 1, 17046 Sassello (SV) ITALY Tel-fax: 0039 019 724581, info@pachi-photo.com, www.pachi-photo.com

Freiberg, Charley, PO Box 42, Elkins, NH, 03233, 603-526-2767, charleyfreiberg@tds.net, charleyfreibergphotography.com

Gardner, Chuck, 116 Quincy Ave., Oak Ridge, TN, 37830

Gawryla, Don, 1105 Greenlawn Dr., Pittsburgh, PA, 15220

Goffe Photographic Associates, 3108 Monte Vista Blvd., NE, Albuquerque, NM, 87106

Hanusin, John, Reames-Hanusin Studio, PO Box 931, Northbrook, IL, 60065 0931, 847-564-2706

Hodge, Tom, 7175 S US Hwy 1 Lot 36, Titusville, FL, 32780-8172, 321-267-7989, egdoht@hotmail.com

Holter, Wayne V., 125 Lakin Ave., Boonsboro, MD, 21713, 301-416-2855, mackwayne@hotmail.com

Hopkins, David W, Hopkins Photography inc, 201 S Jefferson, Iola, KS, 66749, 620-365-7443, nhoppy@netks.net

LaFleur, Gordon, 111 Hirst, Box 1209, Parksville BC CANADA, V0R 270

Lear, Dale, 6544 Cora Mill Rd, Gallipolis, OH, 45631, 740-245-5482, dalelear@yahoo.com, Ebay Sales

LeBlanc, Paul, No. 3 Meadowbrook Cir., Melissa, TX, 75454

Lester, Dean, 2801 Junipero Ave Suite 212, Long Beach, CA, 90806-2140

Leviton, David A., A Studio on the Move, P.O. Box 2871, Silverdale, WA, 98383, 360-697-3452

Long, Gary W., 3556 Miller's Crossroad Rd., Hillsboro, TN, 37342, 931-596-2275

Martin, Cory, 4249 Taylor Harbor #7, Racine, WI 53403, 262-352-5392, info@corymartinimaging.com, www.corymartinimaging.com

McCollum, Tom, P.O. Box 933, Lilburn, GA, 30226

Mitch Lum Website and Photography, 22115 NW Imbrie Dr. #298, Hillsboro, OR 97124, mitch@mitchlum.com, www.mitchlum.com, 206-356-6813

Moake, Jim, 18 Council Ave., Aurora, IL, 60504

Moya Inc., 4212 S. Dixie Hwy., West Palm Beach, FL, 33405

Norman's Studio, 322 S. 2nd St., Vivian, LA, 71082

Owens, William T., Box 99, Williamsburg, WV, 24991

Pachi, Francesco, Loc. Pometta 1, 17046 Sassello (SV) ITALY Tel-fax: 0039 019 724581, info@pachi-photo.com, www.pachi-photo.com

Palmer Studio, 2008 Airport Blvd., Mobile, AL, 36606

Payne, Robert G., P.O. Box 141471, Austin, TX, 78714

Pigott, John, 9095 Woodprint LN, Mason, OH, 45040

Professional Medica Concepts, Patricia Mitchell, P.O. Box 0002, Warren, TX, 77664, 409-547-2213, pm0909@wt.net

Rasmussen, Eric L., 1121 Eliason, Brigham City, UT, 84302

Rhoades, Cynthia J., Box 195, Clearmont, WY, 82835

Rice, Tim, PO Box 663, Whitefish, MT, 59937

Richardson, Kerry, 2520 Mimosa St., Santa Rosa, CA, 95405, 707-575-1875, kerry@sonic.net, www.sonic.net/~kerry

Rob Andrew Photography, Rob Szajkowski, 7960 Silverton Ave., Ste. 125, San Diego, CA 92126, 760-920-6380, robandrewphoto@gmail.com, www.robandrewphoto.com

Ross, Bill, 28364 S. Western Ave. Suite 464, Rancho Palos Verdes, CA, 90275

Rubicam, Stephen, 14 Atlantic Ave., Boothbay Harbor, ME, 04538-1202

Rush, John D., 2313 Maysel St., Bloomington, IL, 61701

Schreiber, Roger, 429 Boren Ave. N., Seattle, WA, 98109

Semmer, Charles, 7885 Cyd Dr., Denver, CO, 80221

Silver Images Photography, 2412 N Keystone, Flagstaff, AZ, 86004

Slobodian, Scott, 4101 River Ridge Dr., P.O. Box 1498, San Andreas, CA, 95249, 209-286-1980, (209) 286-1982, www.slobodianswords.com

Smith, Earl W., 5121 Southminster Rd., Columbus, OH, 43221

Smith, Randall, 1720 Oneco Ave., Winter Park, FL, 32789

Storm Photo, 334 Wall St., Kingston, NY, 12401

Surles, Mark, P.O. Box 147, Falcon, NC, 28342

Third Eye Photos, 140 E. Sixth Ave., Helena, MT, 59601

Thurber, David, P.O. Box 1006, Visalia, CA, 93279

Tighe, Brian, 12-111 Fourth Ave., Ste. 376 Ridley Square, St. Catharines ON CANADA, L2S 3P5, 905-892-2734, www.tigheknives.com

Towell, Steven L., 3720 N.W. 32nd Ave., Camas, WA, 98607, 360-834-9049, sltowell@netscape.net

Verno Studio, Jay, 3030 Jane Street, Pittsburgh, PA, 15203

Ward, Chuck, 1010 E North St, PO Box 2272, Benton, AR, 72018, 501-778-4329, chuckbop@aol.com

Wise, Harriet, 242 Dill Ave., Frederick, MD, 21701

Worley, Holly, Worley Photography, 6360 W David Dr, Littleton, CO, 80128-5708, 303-257-8091, 720-981-2800, hsworley@aol.com, Products, Digital & Film

scrimshanders

Adlam, Tim, 1705 Witzel Ave., Oshkosh, WI, 54902, 920-235-4589, ctimadlam@new.rr.com, www.adlamengraving.com

Alpen, Ralph, 7 Bentley Rd., West Grove, PA, 19390, 610-869-7141

Anderson, Terry Jack, 10076 Birnamwoods Way, Riverton, UT, 84065-9073

Ashworth, Boyd, 1510 Bullard Pl., Powder Springs, GA 30127, 404-583-5652, boydashworthknives@comcast.net, www.boydashworthknives.com

Bailey, Mary W., 3213 Jonesboro Dr., Nashville, TN, 37214, Phone: 615-889-3172 mbscrim@aol.com

Baker, Duane, 2145 Alum Creek Dr., Cambridge Park Apt. #10, Columbus, OH, 43207

Barrows, Miles, 524 Parsons Ave., Chillicothe, OH, 45601

Brady, Sandra, Scrimshaw by Sandra Brady, 9608 Monclova Rd., Monclova, OH 43542, 419-866-0435, 419-261-1582 sandy@sandrabradyart.com, www.sandrabradyart.com

Beauchamp, Gaetan, 125 de la Riviere, Stoneham, QC, G3C 0P6, CANADA, 418-848-1914, fax 418-848-6859, knives@gbeauchamp.ca, www.gbeauchamp.ca

Bellet, Connie, PO Box 151, Palermo, ME, 04354 0151, 207-993-2327, phwhitehawk@gwl.net

Benade, Lynn, 2610 Buckhurst Dr, Beachwood, OH, 44122, 216-464-0777, llbnc17@aol.com

Bonshire, Benita, 1121 Burlington Dr., Muncie, IN, 47302

Boone Trading Co. Inc., P.O. Box 669, Brinnon, WA, 98320, 800-423-1945, bella@boonetrading.com, www.boonetrading.com

Bryan, Bob, 1120 Oak Hill Rd., Carthage, MO, 64836

Burger, Sharon, Glenwood, Durban KZN, South Africa, cell: +27 83 7891675, scribble@iafrica.com, www.sharonburger-scrimshaw.co.za/

Byrne, Mary Gregg, 1018 15th St., Bellingham, WA, 98225-6604

Cable, Jerry, 332 Main St., Mt. Pleasant, PA, 15666

Caudill, Lyle, 7626 Lyons Rd., Georgetown, OH, 45121

Cole, Gary, PO Box 668, Naalehu, HI, 96772, 808-929-9775, 808-929-7371

Collins, Michael, Rt. 3075, Batesville Rd., Woodstock, GA, 30188

Conover, Juanita Rae, P.O. Box 70442, Eugene, OR, 97401, 541-747-1726 or 543-4851, juanitaraeconover@yahoo.com

Courtnage, Elaine, Box 473, Big Sandy, MT, 59520

Cover Jr., Raymond A., 1206 N. 3rd St., Festus, MO, 63010, Phone: 314-808-2508 cover@sbcglobal.net, learningtoengravecom

Cox, J. Andy, 116 Robin Hood Lane, Gaffney, SC, 29340

Dietrich, Roni, Wild Horse Studio, 1257 Cottage Dr, Harrisburg, PA, 17112, 717-469-0587, ronimd@aol

Dolbare, Elizabeth, PO Box 502, Dubois, WY, 82513-0502

Eklund, Maihkel, Föne Stam V9, S-82041 Färila, SWEDEN, +46 6512 4192, info@art-knives.com, www.art-knives.com

Eldridge, Allan, 1424 Kansas Lane, Gallatin, TN, 37066

Ellis, Willy B., Willy B's Customs by William B Ellis, Tarpon Springs, FL, 34689, 727-942-6420, wbflashs@verizon.net, www.willyb.com

Fisk, Dale, Box 252, Council, ID, 83612, dafisk@ctcweb.net

Foster Enterprises, Norvell Foster, P.O. Box 200343, San Antonio, TX, 78220

Fountain Products, 492 Prospect Ave., West Springfield, MA, 01089

Gill, Scott, 925 N. Armstrong St., Kokomo, IN, 46901

Hands, Barry Lee, 30608 Fernview Ln., Bigfork, MT, 59911, 406-249-4334, barry_hands@yahoo.com, www.barryleehands.com

Hargraves Sr., Charles, RR 3 Bancroft, Ontario CANADA, K0L 1C0

Harless, Star, c/o Arrow Forge, P.O. Box 845, Stoneville, NC, 27048-0845

Harrington, Fred A., Summer: 2107 W Frances Rd, Mt Morris MI 48458 8215, Winter: 3725 Citrus, St. James City, FL, 33956, Winter 239-283-0721, Summer 810-686-3008

Hergert, Bob, 12 Geer Circle, Port Orford, OR, 97465, 541-332-3010, hergert@harborside.com, www.scrimshander.com

Hielscher, Vickie, 6550 Otoe Rd, P.O. Box 992, Alliance, NE, 69301, 308-762-4318, g-hielsc@bbcwb.net

High, Tom, 5474 S. 112.8 Rd., Alamosa, CO, 81101, 719-589-2108, rmscrimshaw@gmail.com, www.rockymountainscrimshaw.com, Wildlife Artist

Himmelheber, David R., 11289 40th St. N., Royal Palm Beach, FL, 33411

Holland, Dennis K., 4908-17th Place, Lubbock, TX, 79416

Hutchings, Rick "Hutch", 3007 Coffe Tree Ct, Crestwood, KY, 40014, 502-241-2871, baron1@bellsouth.net

Imboden II, Howard L., 620 Deauville Dr., Dayton, OH, 45429, 937-439-1536, Guards by the "Last Wax Technic"

Johnson, Corinne, W3565 Lockington, Mindora, WI, 54644

Johnston, Kathy, W. 1134 Providence, Spokane, WA, 99205

Karst Stone, Linda, 903 Tanglewood Ln, Kerrville, TX, 78028-2945, 830-896-4678, 830-257-6117, linda@karstone.com, www.karstone.com

Kelso, Jim, 577 Collar Hill Rd, Worcester, VT 05682, 802-229-4254 kelsomaker@gmail.com, www.jimkelso.com

Koevenig, Eugene and Eve, Koevenig's Engraving Service, Rabbit Gulch, Box 55, Hill City, SD, 57745-0055

Kostelnik, Joe and Patty, RD #4, Box 323, Greensburg, PA 15601

Lemen, Pam, 3434 N. Iroquois Ave., Tucson, AZ, 85705

Martin, Diane, 28220 N. Lake Dr., Waterford, WI, 53185

McDonald, René Cosimini-, 14730 61 Court N., Loxahatchee, FL, 33470

McFadden, Berni, 2547 E Dalton Ave, Dalton Gardens, ID, 83815-9631

McGowan, Frank, 12629 Howard Lodge Dr., Winter Add-2023 Robin Ct Sebring FL 33870, Sykesville, MD, 21784, 863-385-1296

McGrath, Gayle, PMB 232 15201 N Cleveland Ave, N Ft Myers, FL, 33903

McLaran, Lou, 603 Powers St., Waco, TX, 76705

McWilliams, Carole, P.O. Box 693, Bayfield, CO, 81122

Mitchell, James, 1026 7th Ave., Columbus, GA, 31901

Moore, James B., 1707 N. Gillis, Stockton, TX, 79735

Ochonicky, Michelle "Mike", Stone Hollow Studio, 31 High Trail, Eureka, MO, 63025, 636-938-9570, www.stonehollowstudio.com

Ochs, Belle, 124 Emerald Lane, Largo, FL, 33771, 727-536-3827, contact@oxforge.com, www.oxforge.com

Pachi, Mirella, Localita Pometta 1, 17046 Sassello (SV), ITALY, +39 019 72 00 86, www.pachi-photo.com

Parish, Vaughn, 103 Cross St., Monaca, PA, 15061

Peterson, Lou, 514 S. Jackson St., Gardner, IL, 60424

Pienaar, Conrad, 19A Milner Rd., Bloemfontein 9300, SOUTH AFRICA, Phone: 027 514364180 fax: 027 514364180

Poag, James H., RR #1 Box 212A, Grayville, IL, 62844

Polk, Trena, 4625 Webber Creek Rd., Van Buren, AR, 72956

Pulisova, Andrea, CSA 230-95, 96701 Kremnica, Slovakia, Phone: 00421 903-340076 vpulis@gmail.com, www.vpulis.host.sk

Purvis, Hilton, P.O. Box 371, Noordhoek, 7979, SOUTH AFRICA, 27 21 789 1114, hiltonp@telkomsa.net, http://capeknifemakersguild.com/?page_id=416

Ramsey, Richard, 8525 Trout Farm Rd, Neosho, MO, 64850

Ristinen, Lori, 14256 County Hwy 45, Menahga, MN, 56464, 218-538-6608, lori@loriristinen.com, www.loriristinen.com

Roberts, J.J., 7808 Lake Dr., Manassas, VA, 22111, 703-330-0448, jjrengraver@aol.com, www.angelfire.com/va2/engraver

Rudolph, Gil, 20922 Oak Pass Ave, Tehachapi, CA, 93561, 661-822-4949

Rundell, Joe, 6198 W. Frances Rd., Clio, MI, 48420

Satre, Robert, 518 3rd Ave. NW, Weyburn SK CANADA, S4H 1R1

Schlott, Harald, Zingster Str. 26, 13051 Berlin, +49 030 929 33 46, GERMANY, harald.schlott@web.de, www.gravur-kunst-atelier.de

Schulenburg, E.W., 25 North Hill St., Carrollton, GA, 30117

Schwallie, Patricia, 4614 Old Spartanburg Rd. Apt. 47, Taylors, SC, 29687

Selent, Chuck, P.O. Box 1207, Bonners Ferry, ID, 83805

Semich, Alice, 10037 Roanoke Dr., Murfreesboro, TN, 37129

Shostle, Ben, 1121 Burlington, Muncie, IN, 47302

Smith, Peggy, 676 Glades Rd., #3, Gatlinburg, TN, 37738

Smith, Ron, 5869 Straley, Ft. Worth, TX, 76114

Steigerwalt, Jim, RD#3, Sunbury, PA, 17801

Stuart, Stephen, 15815 Acorn Circle, Tavares, FL, 32778, 352-343-8423, (352) 343-8916, inkscratch@aol.com

Talley, Mary Austin, 2499 Countrywood Parkway, Memphis, TN, 38016, matalley@midsouth.rr.com

Thompson, Larry D., 23040 Ave. 197, Strathmore, CA, 93267

Toniutti, Nelida, Via G. Pascoli, 33085 Maniago-PN, ITALY

Trout, Lauria Lovestrand, 1136 19th St. SW, Vero Beach, FL 32962, 772-778-0282, lovestranded@aol.com

Tucker, Steve, 3518 W. Linwood, Turlock, CA, 95380

Tyser, Ross, 1015 Hardee Court, Spartanburg, SC, 29303

Velasquez, Gil, Art of Scrimshaw, 7120 Madera Dr., Goleta, CA, 93117

Williams, Gary, PO Box 210, Glendale, KY, 42740, 270-369-6752, scrimbygarbo@gmail.com, scrimbygarbo.com

Winn, Travis A., 558 E. 3065 S., Salt Lake City, UT 84106, 801-467-5957

Young, Mary, 4826 Storeyland Dr., Alton, IL, 62002

organizations

AMERICAN BLADESMITH SOCIETY
c/o Office Manager, Cindy Sheely; P. O. Box 160, Grand Rapids, Ohio 43522; cindy@americanbladesmith. com; (419) 832-0400; Web: www. americanbladesmith.com

AMERICAN KNIFE & TOOL INSTITUTE
Jan Billeb, Comm. Coordinator, AKTI, 22 Vista View Ln., Cody, WY 82414; 307-587-8296, akti@akti.org; www. akti.org

AMERICAN KNIFE THROWERS ALLIANCE
c/o Bobby Branton; POB 807; Awendaw, SC 29429; akta@akta-usa.com, www. AKTA-USA.com

ARIZONA KNIFE COLLECTOR'S ASSOCIATION
c/o Mike Mooney, President, 19432 E. Cloud Rd., Quen Creek, AZ 85142; Phone: 480-244-7768, mike@ moonblades.com, Web: www. arizonaknifecollectors.org

ART KNIFE COLLECTOR'S ASSOCIATION
c/o Mitch Weiss, Pres.; 2211 Lee Road, Suite 104; Winter Park, FL 32789

ARKANSAS KNIFEMAKERS ASSOCIATION
David Etchieson, 60 Wendy Cove, Conway, AR 72032; Phone: 501-554-2582, arknifeassn@yahoo.com, Web: www.arkansasknifemakers.com

AUSTRALASIAN KNIFE COLLECTORS
PO BOX 149 CHIDLOW 6556 WESTERN AUSTRALIA TEL: (08) 9572 7255; FAX: (08) 9572 7266. International Inquiries: TEL: + 61 8 9572 7255; FAX: + 61 8 9572 7266; akc@knivesaustralia.com.au, www. knivesaustralia.com.au

BAY AREA KNIFE COLLECTOR'S ASSOCIATION
c/o Larry Hirsch, 5339 Prospect Rd. #129, San Jose, CA 95129, bladeplay@ earthlink.net, Web: www.bakcainc.org

CALIFORNIA KNIFEMAKERS ASSOCIATION
c/o Clint Breshears, Membership Chairman; 1261 Keats St; Manhattan Beach CA 90266; 310-372-0739; breshears1@verizon.net
Dedicated to teaching and improving knifemaking

CANADIAN KNIFEMAKERS GUILD
c/o Wolfgang Loerchner; PO Box 255, Bayfield, Ont., CANADA N0M 1G0; 519-565-2196; info@ canadianknifemakersguild.com, www. canadianknifemakersguild.com

CUSTOM KNIFE COLLECTORS ASSOCIATION
c/o Kevin Jones, PO Box 5893, Glen Allen, VA 23058-5893; E-mail: customknifecollectorsassociation@ yahoo.com; Web: www.

customknifecollectorsassociation.com
The purpose of the CKCA is to recognize and promote the artistic significance of handmade knives, to advnace their collection and conservation, and to support the creative expression of those who make them. Open to collectors, makers purveyors, and other collectors. Has members from eight countries. Produced a calednar which features custom knives either owned or made by CKCA members.

CUTTING EDGE, THE
2900 S. 26th St., Rogers, AR 72758; 479-631-0130; 800-255-9034; ce_info@ cuttingedge.com, www.cuttingedge.com
After-market knives since 1968. We offer about 1,000 individual knives each month. The oldest and the most experienced in the business of buying and selling knives. We buy collections of any size, take knives on consignment or we will trade. Web: www.cuttingedge. com

FLORIDA KNIFEMAKERS ASSOCIATION
c/o President John H. Davis, (209) 740-7125; johndavis@custom-knifemaker. com, floridaknifemakers@gmail.com, Web: www.floridaknifemakers.org

JAPANESE SWORD SOCIETY OF THE U.S.
PO Box 712; Breckenridge, TX 76424, barry@hennick.ca, www.jssus.org

KNIFE COLLECTORS CLUB INC, THE
2900 S. 26th St, Rogers, AR 72758; 479-631-0130; 800-255-9034; ag@ agrussell.com; Web: www.agrussell. com/kcc-one-year-membership-usa-/p/ KCC/
The oldest and largest association of knife collectors. Issues limited edition knives, both handmade and highest quality production, in very limited numbers. The very earliest was the CM-1, Kentucky Rifle

KNIFEMAKERS' GUILD, THE
c/o Gene Baskett, Knifemakers Guild, 427 Sutzer Creek Rd., La Grange, KY 42732; 270-862-5019; Web: www. knifemakersguild.com

KNIFEMAKERS GUILD OF SOUTHERN AFRICA, THE
c/o Andre Thorburn; PO Box 1748; Bela Bela, Warmbaths, LP, SOUTH AFRICA 0480; +27 82 650 1441 andrethorburn@ gmail.com; Web: www.kgsa.co.za

MONTANA KNIFEMAKERS' ASSOCIATION, THE
1439 S. 5th W, Missoula, MT 59801; 406-728-2861; macnancymclaughlin@ yahoo.com, Web: www. montanaknifemakers.com
Annual book of custom knife makers' works and directory of knife making supplies; $19.99

NATIONAL KNIFE COLLECTORS ASSOCIATION
PO Box 21070; Chattanooga, TN 37424, 423-667-8199; nkcalisa@hotmail.com; Web: www.nkcalisa.wix.com/nkca-website-2

NEO-TRIBAL METALSMITHS
5920 W. Windy Lou Ln., Tucson, AZ 85742; Phone: 520-744-9777, taigoo@msn.com, Web: www.neo-tribalmetalsmiths.com

NEW ENGLAND CUSTOM KNIFE ASSOCIATION
Vickie Gray, Treasurer, 686 Main Rd, Brownville, ME 04414; Phone: 207-965-2191, Web: www.necka.net

NORTH CAROLINA CUSTOM KNIFEMAKERS GUILD
c/o Tim Scholl, President, 1389 Langdon Rd., Angier, NC 27501, 910-897-2051, tschollknives@live.com, Web: www. ncknifeguild.org

NORTH STAR BLADE COLLECTORS
PO Box 20523, Bloomington, MN 55420; info@nsbc.us, Web: www.nsbc.us

OHIO KNIFEMAKERS ASSOCIATION
c/o Jerry Smith, Anvils and Ink Studios, P.O. Box 151, Barnesville, Ohio 43713; jerry_smith@anvilsandinkstudios.com, Web: www.oocities.org/ohioknives/

OREGON KNIFE COLLECTORS ASSOCIATION
Web: www.oregonknifeclub.org

ROCKY MOUNTAIN BLADE COLLECTORS ASSOCIATION
Mike Moss. Pres., P.O. Box 324, Westminster, CO 80036; rmbladecollectors@gmail.com, Web: www.rmbladecollectors.org

SOUTH CAROLINA ASSOCIATION OF KNIFEMAKERS
c/o Col. Tom Kreger, President, (803) 438-4221; tdkreger@ bellsouth.net, Web: www. southcarolinaassociationofknifemakers. org

SOUTHERN CALIFORNIA BLADES KNIFE COLLECTORS CLUB
SC Blades, PO Box 231112, Encinitas, CA 92023-1112; Phone: 619-417-4329, scblades@att.net, Web: www.scblades. org

THE WILLIAM F. MORAN JR. MUSEUM & FOUNDATION
4204 Ballenger Creek Pike, Frederick, MD 21703, info@billmoranmuseum.com, www.williammoranmuseum.com

publications

AUTOMATIC KNIFE RESOURCE
c/o Lantama Cutlery, POB 721, Montauk, NY 11954; 631-668-5995; info@latama. net, Web: www.thenewsletter.com,
Unique compilation and archive for the switchblade/automatic knife fan. Sheldon Levy's Newsletter was first published in 1992, and was a labor of love from its inception and has remained informative and insightful.

BLADE AND BLADE'S COMPLETE KNIFE GUIDE
700 E. State St., Iola, WI 54990-0001; 715-445-4612; Web: www.blademag. com, www.KnifeForums.com, www. ShopBlade.com, facebook.com/ blademag

The world's No. 1 knife magazine. The most indepth knife magazine on the market, covering all aspects of the industry, from knifemaking to production knives and handmade pieces. With 13 issues per year, BLADE® boasts twice the distribution of its closest competitor.

CUTLERY NEWS JOURNAL (BLOG)
http://cutlerynewsjournal.wordpress.com
Covers significant happenings from the world of knife collecting, in addition to editorials, trends, events, auctions, shows, cutlery history, and reviews

KNIFE MAGAZINE
PO Box 3395, Knoxville, TN 37927; Phone: 865-397-1955, knifepub@ knifeworld.com, www.knifeworld.com
Since 1977, a monthly knife publication covering all types of knives

KNIVES ILLUSTRATED
22840 Savi Ranch Pkwy. #200, Yorba Linda, CA 92887; Phone: 714-200-1963; bmiller@engagedmediainc.com; Web: www.knivesillustrated.com
All encompassing publication focusing on factory knives, new handmades, shows and industry news

THE LEATHER CRAFTERS & SADDLERS JOURNAL
222 Blackburn St., Rhinelander, WI 54501; Phone: 715-362-5393; info@ leathercraftersjournal.com, Web: www. leathercraftersjournal.com
Bi-monthly how-to leathercraft magazine